Lecture Notes in Computer Science   12509

More information about this subseries at http://www.springer.com/series/7412

George Bebis · Zhaozheng Yin ·
Edward Kim · Jan Bender ·
Kartic Subr · Bum Chul Kwon ·
Jian Zhao · Denis Kalkofen ·
George Baciu (Eds.)

Advances in Visual Computing

15th International Symposium, ISVC 2020
San Diego, CA, USA, October 5–7, 2020
Proceedings, Part I

 Springer

Editors
George Bebis
University of Nevada Reno
Reno, NV, USA

Zhaozheng Yin
Stony Brook University
Stony Brook, NY, USA

Edward Kim
Drexel University
Philadelphia, PA, USA

Jan Bender
RWTH Aachen University
Aachen, Germany

Kartic Subr
University of Edinburgh
Edinburgh, UK

Bum Chul Kwon
IBM Research – Cambridge
Cambridge, MA, USA

Jian Zhao
University of Waterloo
Waterloo, ON, Canada

Denis Kalkofen
Graz University of Technology
Graz, Austria

George Baciu
The Hong Kong Polytechnic University
Hong Kong, Hong Kong

ISSN 0302-9743   ISSN 1611-3349   (electronic)
Lecture Notes in Computer Science
ISBN 978-3-030-64555-7   ISBN 978-3-030-64556-4   (eBook)
https://doi.org/10.1007/978-3-030-64556-4

LNCS Sublibrary: SL6 – Image Processing, Computer Vision, Pattern Recognition, and Graphics

This Springer imprint is published by the registered company Springer Nature Switzerland AG
The registered company address is: Gewerbestrasse 11, 6330 Cham, Switzerland

Preface

It is with great pleasure that we welcome you to the proceedings of the 15th International Symposium on Visual Computing (ISVC 2020), which was held virtually during October 5–7, 2020. ISVC provides a common umbrella for the four main areas of visual computing including vision, graphics, visualization, and virtual reality. The goal is to provide a forum for researchers, scientists, engineers, and practitioners throughout the world to present their latest research findings, ideas, developments, and applications in the broader area of visual computing.

This year, the program consisted of 6 keynote presentations, 16 oral sessions, 2 poster sessions, 2 special tracks, and 1 tutorial. We received 175 submissions for the main symposium from which we accepted 65 papers for oral presentation and 41 papers for poster presentation. Special track papers were solicited separately through the Organizing and Program Committees of each track. A total of 12 papers were accepted for oral presentation from 18 submissions.

All papers were reviewed with an emphasis on the potential to contribute to the state of the art in the field. Selection criteria included accuracy and originality of ideas, clarity and significance of results, and presentation quality. The review process was quite rigorous, involving three independent blind reviews followed by several days of discussion. During the discussion period we tried to correct anomalies and errors that might have existed in the initial reviews. Despite our efforts, we recognize that some papers worthy of inclusion may not have been included in the program. We offer our sincere apologies to authors whose contributions might have been overlooked.

We wish to thank everybody who submitted their work to ISVC 2020 for review. It was because of their contributions that we succeeded in having a technical program of high scientific quality. In particular, we would like to thank the keynote speakers, the program chairs, the Steering Committee, the International Program Committee, the special track organizers, the tutorial organizers, the reviewers, the sponsors, and especially the authors who contributed their work to the symposium. In particular, we would like to express our appreciation to Springer for sponsoring the Best Paper Award this year.

Despite all the difficulties due to the pandemic, we sincerely hope that ISVC 2020 offered participants opportunities for professional growth.

October 2020

George Bebis
Zhaozheng Yin
Edward Kim
Jan Bender
Kartic Subr
Bum Chul Kwon
Jian Zhao
Denis Kalkofen
George Baciu

Organization

Steering Committee

George Bebis	University of Nevada, Reno, USA
Sabine Coquillart	Inria, France
James Klosowski	AT&T Labs Research, USA
Yoshinori Kuno	Saitama University, Japan
Steve Lin	Microsoft, USA
Peter Lindstrom	Lawrence Livermore National Laboratory, USA
Kenneth Moreland	Sandia National Laboratories, USA
Ara Nefian	NASA Ames Research Center, USA
Ahmad P. Tafti	Mayo Clinic, USA

Computer Vision Chairs

Zhaozheng Yin	Stony Brook University, USA
Edward Kim	Drexel University, USA

Computer Graphics Chairs

Jan Bender	RWTH Aachen University, Germany
Kartic Subr	The University of Edinburgh, UK

Virtual Reality Chairs

Denis Kalkofen	Graz University of Technology, Austria
George Baciu	The Hong Kong Polytechnic University, Hong Kong

Visualization Chairs

Jian Zhao	University of Waterloo, Canada
Bum Chul Kwon	IBM Research, USA

Publicity

Ali Erol	Eksperta Software, Turkey

Tutorials and Special Tracks

Emily Hand	University of Nevada, Reno, USA
Alireza Tavakkoli	University of Nevada, Reno, USA

Awards

Zehang Sun   Apple, USA
Gholamreza Amayeh   Aurora, USA

Web Master

Isayas Berhe Adhanom   University of Nevada, Reno, USA

Program Committee

Nabil Adam   Rutgers University, USA
Emmanuel Agu   Worcester Polytechnic Institute, USA
Touqeer Ahmad   University of Colorado Colorado Springs, USA
Alfonso Alba   Universidad Autónoma de San Luis Potosí, Mexico
Kostas Alexis   University of Nevada, Reno, USA
Usman Alim   University of Calgary, Canada
Amol Ambardekar   Microsoft, USA
Mehdi Ammi   University Paris 8, France
Mark Apperley   University of Waikato, New Zealand
Antonis Argyros   Foundation for Research and Technology - Hellas,
                                 Greece
Vijayan K. Asari   University of Dayton, USA
Aishwarya Asesh   Adobe, USA
Vassilis Athitsos   The University of Texas at Arlington, USA
Melinos Averkiou   University of Cyprus, Cyprus
George Baciu   The Hong Kong Polytechnic University, Hong Kong
Chris Holmberg Bahnsen   Aalborg University, Denmark
Abdul Bais   University of Regina, Canada
Abhishek Bajpayee   Massachusetts Institute of Technology, USA
Peter Balazs   University of Szeged, Hungary
Selim Balcisoy   Sabanci University, Turkey
Reneta Barneva   State University of New York at Fredonia, USA
Ronen Barzel   Independent
Fereshteh S Bashiri   University of Wisconsin-Madison, USA
Aryabrata Basu   Emory University, USA
Anil Ufuk Batmaz   Simon Fraser University, Canada
George Bebis   University of Nevada, Reno, USA
Jan Bender   RWTH Aachen University, Germany
Ayush Bhargava   Key Lime Interactive, USA
Harsh Bhatia   Lawrence Livermore National Laboratory, USA
Sanjiv Bhatia   University of Missouri-St. Louis, USA
Mark Billinghurst   University of Canterbury, New Zealand
Ankur Bist   G. B. Pant University of Agriculture and Technology,
                                 India
Ayan Biswas   Los Alamos National Laboratory, USA

Dibio Borges	Universidade de Brasília, Brazil
David Borland	RENCI, The University of North Carolina at Chapel Hill, USA
Nizar Bouguila	Concordia University, Canada
Alexandra Branzan Albu	University of Victoria, Canada
Jose Braz Pereira	EST Setúbal, IPS, Portugal
Wolfgang Broll	Ilmenau University of Technology, Germany
Gerd Bruder	University of Central Florida, USA
Tolga Capin	TED University, Turkey
Bruno Carvalho	Federal University of Rio Grande do Norte, Brazil
Sek Chai	SRI International, USA
Jian Chang	Bournemouth University, UK
Sotirios Chatzis	Cyprus University of Technology, Cyprus
Rama Chellappa	University of Maryland, USA
Cunjian Chen	Michigan State University, USA
Yang Chen	HRL Laboratories, LLC, USA
Zhonggui Chen	Xiamen University, China
Yi-Jen Chiang	New York University, USA
Isaac Cho	North Carolina A&T State University, USA
Amit Chourasia	University of California, San Diego, USA
Kichung Chung	Oracle Corporation, USA
Sabine Coquillart	Inria, France
Andrew Cunningham	University of South Australia, Australia
Tommy Dang	Texas Tech University, USA
Aritra Dasgupta	New York University, USA
Jeremie Dequidt	University of Lille, France
Sotirios Diamantas	Tarleton State University, USA
Alexandra Diehl	University of Konstanz, Germany
John Dingliana	Trinity College Dublin, Ireland
Cosimo Distante	CNR, Italy
Ralf Doerner	RheinMain University of Applied Sciences, Germany
Anastasios Doulamis	Technical University of Crete, Greece
Shengzhi Du	Tshwane University of Technology, South Africa
Ye Duan	University of Missouri, USA
Soumya Dutta	Los Alamos National Laboratory, USA
Achim Ebert	University of Kaiserslautern, Germany
Christian Eckhardt	California Polytechnic State University, USA
Mohamed El Ansari	Ibn Zohr University, Morocco
El-Sayed M. El-Alfy	King Fahd University of Petroleum and Minerals, Saudi Arabia
Barrett Ens	Monash University, Australia
Alireza Entezari	University of Florida, USA
Ali Erol	Sigun Information Technologies, UK
Thomas Ertl	University of Stuttgart, Germany
Mohammad Eslami	Technical University of Munich, Germany
Guoliang Fan	Oklahoma State University, USA

Stefan Jeschke	NVIDIA, USA
Ming Jiang	Lawrence Livermore National Laboratory, USA
Sungchul Jung	HIT Lab NZ, New Zealand
Stefan Jänicke	Leipzig University, Germany
Denis Kalkofen	Graz University of Technology, Austria
Ho Chuen Kam	The Chinese University of Hong Kong, Hong Kong
George Kamberov	University of Alaska Anchorage, USA
Gerda Kamberova	Hofstra University, USA
Martin Kampel	Vienna University of Technology, Austria
Takashi Kanai	The University of Tokyo, Japan
Kenichi Kanatani	Okayama University, Japan
David Kao	NASA Ames Research Center, USA
Hirokatsu Kataoka	National Institute of Advanced Industrial Science and Technology (AIST), Japan
Rajiv Khadka	Idaho National Laboratory, USA
Waqar Khan	Wellington Institute of Technology, New Zealand
Deepak Khosla	HRL Laboratories, USA
Edward Kim	Drexel University, USA
Hyungseok Kim	Konkuk University, South Korea
Kangsoo Kim	University of Central Florida, USA
Min H. Kim	Korea Advanced Institute of Science and Technology, South Korea
James Klosowski	AT&T Labs Research, USA
Steffen Koch	University of Stuttgart, Germany
Stefanos Kollias	National Technical University of Athens, Greece
Takashi Komuro	Saitama University, Japan
Dimitris Kosmopoulos	University of Patras, Greece
Jens Krueger	COVIDAG, SCI Institute, USA
Arjan Kuijper	TU Darmstadt, Germany
Yoshinori Kuno	Saitama University, Japan
Tsz Ho Kwok	Concordia University, Canada
Bum Chul Kwon	IBM Research, USA
Hung La	University of Nevada, Reno, USA
Robert Laganière	University of Ottawa, Canada
Yu-Kun Lai	Cardiff University, UK
Robert S Laramee	Swansea University, UK
Manfred Lau	City University of Hong Kong, Hong Kong
D. J. Lee	Brigham Young University, UK
Gun Lee	University of South Australia, Australia
Robert R. Lewis	Washington State University, USA
Frederick Li	Durham University, UK
Xin Li	Louisiana State University, USA
Kuo-Chin Lien	XMotors.ai, USA
Chun-Cheng Lin	National Chiao Tung University, Taiwan
Stephen Lin	Microsoft, China

Peter Lindstrom	Lawrence Livermore National Laboratory, USA
Shiguang Liu	Tianjin University, China
Zhanping Liu	Old Dominion University, USA
Manuel Loaiza	Universidad Católica de San Pablo, Peru
Benjamin Lok	University of Florida, USA
Leandro Loss	QuantaVerse, ITU, USA, and ESSCA, France
Joern Loviscach	University of Applied Sciences, Germany
Aidong Lu	University of North Carolina at Charlotte, USA
Xun Luo	Tianjin University of Technology, China
Brendan Macdonald	National Institute for Occupational Safety and Health, USA
Sokratis Makrogiannis	Delaware State University, USA
Luigi Malomo	ISTI-CNR, Italy
Steve Mann	University of Toronto, Canada
Kulsoom Mansoor	University of Washington Bothell, USA
Rafael M. Martins	Linnaeus University, Sweden
Yoshitaka Masutani	Hiroshima City University, Japan
Sherin Mathews	McAfee, USA
Kresimir Matkovic	VRVis Research Center, Austria
Stephen Maybank	Birkbeck, University of London, UK
Tim Mcgraw	Purdue University, USA
Tim McInerney	Ryerson University, Canada
Henry Medeiros	Marquette University, USA
Qurban Memon	United Arab Emirates University, UAE
Daniel Mestre	Aix-Marseille University, France
Jean Meunier	University of Montreal, Canada
Xikui Miao	Brigham Young University, UK
Gabriel Mistelbauer	Otto-von-Guericke University, Germany
Kenneth Moreland	Sandia National Laboratories, USA
Shigeo Morishima	Waseda University, Japan
Brendan Morris	University of Nevada, Las Vegas, USA
Michela Mortara	CNR-IMATI, Italy
Chouaib Moujahdi	Mohammed V University in Rabat, Morocco
Christos Mousas	Purdue University, USA
Chris Muelder	University of California, Davis, USA
Soraia Musse	Pontificia Universidade Catolica do Roi Grande do Sul, Brazil
Kawa Nazemi	Darmstadt University of Applied Sciences, Germany
Ara Nefian	NASA, USA
Quang Vinh Nguyen	Western Sydney University, Australia
Mircea Nicolescu	University of Nevada, Reno, USA
Christophoros Nikou	University of Ioannina, Greece
Mark Nixon	University of Southampton, UK
Junyong Noh	Korea Advanced Institute of Science and Technology, South Korea
Klimis Ntalianis	University of West Attica, Greece

Scott Nykl	Air Force Institute of Technology, USA
Yoshihiro Okada	Kyushu University, Japan
Gustavo Olague	CICESE, Mexico
Francisco Ortega	Florida International University, USA
Francisco Ortega	Colorado State University, USA
Masaki Oshita	Kyushu Institute of Technology, Japan
Volker Paelke	Hochschule Bremen, Germany
Kalman Palagyi	University of Szeged, Hungary
Alex Pang	University of California, Santa Cruz, USA
George Papagiannakis	University of Crete, Greece
George Papakostas	EMT Institute of Technology, Greece
Michael Papka	Argonne National Laboratory and Northern Illinois University, USA
Giuseppe Patanè	CNR-IMATI, Italy
Maurizio Patrignani	Roma Tre University, Italy
Shahram Payandeh	Simon Fraser University, Canada
Helio Pedrini	University of Campinas, Brazil
Jaako Peltonen	Tampere University, Finland
Euripides Petrakis	Technical University of Crete, Greece
Bill Pike	Pacific Northwest National Laboratory, USA
Claudio Pinhanez	IBM Research, Brazil
Giuseppe Placidi	University of L'Aquila, Italy
Vijayakumar Ponnusamy	SRM Institute of Science and Technology, India
Kevin Ponto	University of Wisconsin-Madison, USA
Jiju Poovvancheri	University of Victoria, Canada
Nicolas Pronost	Université Claude Bernard Lyon 1, France
Helen Purchase	The University of Glasgow, UK
Hong Qin	Stony Brook University, USA
Christopher Rasmussen	University of Delaware, USA
Emma Regentova	University of Nevada, Las Vegas, USA
Guido Reina	University of Stuttgart, Germany
Erik Reinhard	InterDigital, USA
Banafsheh Rekabdar	Southern Illinois University Carbondale, USA
Paolo Remagnino	Kingston University, UK
Hongliang Ren	National University of Singapore, Singapore
Benjamin Renoust	Osaka University, Japan
Theresa-Marie Rhyne	Consultant
Eraldo Ribeiro	Florida Institute of Technology, USA
Peter Rodgers	University of Kent, UK
Paul Rosen	University of South Florida, USA
Isaac Rudomin	BSC, Spain
Amela Sadagic	Naval Postgraduate School, USA
Filip Sadlo	Heidelberg University, Germany
Punam Saha	University of Iowa, USA
Naohisa Sakamoto	Kobe University, Japan
Kristian Sandberg	Computational Solutions, Inc., USA

Stefano Tubaro	Politecnico di Milano, Italy
Georg Umlauf	HTWG Konstanz, Germany
Georg Umlauf	University of Applied Science Constance, Germany
Daniela Ushizima	Lawrence Berkeley National Laboratory, USA
Dimitar Valkov	University of Münster, Germany
Krishna Venkatasubramanian	University of Rhode Island, USA
Jonathan Ventura	California Polytechnic State University San Luis Obispo, USA
Athanasios Voulodimos	University of West Attica, Greece
Chaoli Wang	University of Notre Dame, USA
Cuilan Wang	Georgia Gwinnett College, USA
Benjamin Weyers	University of Trier, Germany
Thomas Wischgoll	Wright State University, USA
Kin Hong Wong	The Chinese University of Hong Kong, Hong Kong
Panpan Xu	Bosch Research North America, USA
Wei Xu	Brookhaven National Lab, USA
Yasuyuki Yanagida	Meijo University, Japan
Fumeng Yang	Brown University, USA
Xiaosong Yang	Bournemouth University, UK
Hsu-Chun Yen	National Taiwan University, Taiwan
Lijun Yin	State University of New York at Binghamton, USA
Zhaozheng Yin	Stony Brook University, USA
Zeyun Yu	University of Wisconsin-Milwaukee, USA
Chunrong Yuan	Technische Hochschule Köln, Germany
Xiaoru Yuan	Peking University, China
Xenophon Zabulis	FORTH-ICS, Greece
Jiri Zara	Czech Technical University in Prague, Czech Republic
Wei Zeng	Florida International University, USA
Zhao Zhang	Hefei University of Technology, China
Jian Zhao	University of Waterloo, Canada
Ye Zhao	Kent State University, USA
Ying Zhu	Georgia State University, USA
Changqing Zou	University of Maryland, USA
Ignacio Zuleta	University of California, San Francisco, USA

Special Tracks

Computational Bioimaging

Organizers

Tavares João Manuel R. S.	Universidade do Porto, Portugal
Jorge Renato Natal	Universidade do Porto, Portugal

Computer Vision Advances in Geo-Spatial Applications and Remote Sensing

Organizers

Nefian Ara	NASA Ames Research Center, USA
Nestares Oscar	Intel Research, USA
Edwards Laurence	NASA Ames Research Center, USA
Zuleta Ignacio	Planet Labs, USA
Coltin Brian	NASA Ames Research Center, USA
Fong Terry	NASA Ames Research Center, USA

Tutorial

Evolutionary Computer Vision

Organizers

Olague Gustavo	CICESE Research Center, Mexico

Abstracts of Keynote Talks

Can Computers Create Art?

Aaron Hertzmann

Adobe Research, USA

Abstract. In this talk, I will discuss whether computers, using Artificial Intelligence (AI), could create art. I cover the history of automation in art, examining the hype and reality of AI tools for art together with predictions about how they will be used. I will also discuss different scenarios for how an algorithm could be considered the author of an artwork, which, I argue, comes down to questions of why we create and appreciate artwork.

Spatial Perception and Presence in Virtual Architectural Environments

Victoria Interrante

University of Minnesota, USA

Abstract. Immersive Virtual Reality (VR) technology has tremendous potential applications in architecture and design. In this talk I will review some of the work being done in my lab to enhance the utility of VR for architecture and design applications, focusing primarily on the investigation of factors influencing spatial perception accuracy in immersive architectural environments, but also including the use of VR technology to investigate questions of interest to architectural and interior designers such as how wallpaper patterns and window features affect people's subjective experience in architectural interiors.

The Shape of Art History in the Eyes of the Machine

Ahmed Elgammal

Rutgers University, USA

Abstract. In this talk, I will present results of research activities at the Art and Artificial Intelligence Laboratory at Rutgers University. We investigate perceptual and cognitive tasks related to human creativity in visual art. In particular, we study problems related to art styles, influence, and the quantification of creativity. We develop computational models that aim at providing answers to questions about what characterizes the sequence and evolution of changes in style over time. The talk will cover advances in automated prediction of style, how that relates to art history methodology, and what that tells us about how the machine sees art history. The talk will also delve into our recent research on quantifying creativity in art in regards to its novelty and influence, as well as computational models that simulate the art-producing system.

Object-Oriented Image Stitching

Ramin Zabih

Cornell University's New York City and Google, USA

Abstract. Image stitching is one of the most widely used applications of computer vision, appearing in well-known applications like Google Street View and panorama mode in commercial cell phones. However, despite the prevalence of artifacts and errors, there has been little to no progress in stitching research over the last ten years. There is no generally accepted evaluation metric and relatively few attempts to directly deal with large view point changes or object movement. We describe a reframing of stitching that exploits the importance of objects, and the algorithmic and evaluation techniques that naturally result. We will also present a technique that directly addresses the most visually disruptive stitching errors and can act as an alarm bell for these errors in stitching results. These ideas can be naturally extended to the panorama algorithms widely used in smartphones. Joint work with Charles Herrmann, Chen Wang, Richard Bowen, and Emil Keyder, from Cornell Tech and Google Research.

Fun with Visualization in the Data Deluge

Ross Maciejewski

Arizona State University, USA

Abstract. From smart phones to fitness trackers to sensor enabled buildings, data is currently being collected at an unprecedented rate. Now, more than ever, data exists that can be used to gain insight into questions that run the gamut from nonsensical to essential. One key technology for gaining insight into data is visualization. In this talk, we will explore how visualization can be leveraged to help us entertain fun and unique questions in the data deluge. We will investigate how social media can help us predict the next blockbuster film, how much information does your name carry, how Google Street View can open a world of questions for urban planners, and more. By thinking about fun questions for datasets, we will demonstrate how visual computing can help build cross-domain collaborations, paving the way to discover new insights and challenges.

Understanding Visual Appearance from Micron to Global Scale

Kavita Bala

Cornell University, USA

Abstract. Augmented reality/mixed reality (AR/MR) technologies are poised to create compelling and immersive user experiences by combining computer vision and computer graphics. Imagine users interacting with the world around them through their AR device. Visual search tells them what they are seeing, while computer graphics augments reality by overlaying real objects with virtual objects. AR/VR can have a far-ranging impact across many applications, such as retail, virtual prototyping, and entertainment.

In this talk, I will describe my group's research on these complementary areas: graphics models for realistic visual appearance, and visual search and fine-grained recognition for scene understanding. We will also see how these technologies can go beyond AR/VR applications to enable visual discovery – using recognition as a core building block, we can mine social media images at a global scale to discover visual patterns and trends across geography and time.

Contents – Part I

Video Analysis and Event Recognition

ST: Computational Bioimaging

Applications

Biometrics

Motion and Tracking

ST: Computer Vision Advances in Geo-Spatial Applications and Remote Sensing

Contents – Part II

Posters

Deep Learning

Regularization and Sparsity for Adversarial Robustness and Stable Attribution

Daniel Schwartz$^{(\boxtimes)}$, Yigit Alparslan, and Edward Kim

Drexel University, Philadelphia, PA 19104, USA
{des338,ya332,ek826}@drexel.edu

Abstract. In recent years, deep neural networks (DNNs) have had great success in machine learning and pattern recognition. It has been shown that these networks can match or exceed human-level performance in difficult image recognition tasks. However, recent research has raised a number of critical questions about the robustness and stability of these deep learning architectures. Specifically, it has been shown that they are prone to adversarial attacks, i.e. perturbations added to input images to fool the classifier, and furthermore, trained models can be highly unstable to hyperparameter changes. In this work, we craft a series of experiments with multiple deep learning architectures, varying adversarial attacks, and different class attribution methods on the CIFAR-10 dataset in order to study the effect of sparse regularization to the robustness (accuracy and stability), in deep neural networks. Our results both qualitatively show and empirically quantify the amount of protection and stability sparse representations lend to machine learning robustness in the context of adversarial examples and class attribution.

Keywords: Robust machine learning · Regularization · Sparsity · Attribution · Artificial intelligence safety · Adversarial attacks · Image perturbation · Black-box approach

1 Introduction

In recent decades, advances in deep neural networks (DNN) have allowed computers to achieve or even exceed human-level performance on difficult image recognition tasks. DNNs are widely used today in several critical fields, such as bio-authentication systems, facial recognition, autonomous vehicles, malware detection, and spam filtering. These DNNs, and other machine learning models, typically maximize or minimize some objective function while enforcing some regularization in the training process.

Regularization in machine learning (ML) offers many benefits when optimizing an algorithm. Regularization induces sparsity on the activations and parameters of the system, improving generalizability and interpretability [7]. Mathematically, the form of regularization we investigate constrains the coefficients of the system, driving the estimates towards zero. This technique is known to

© Springer Nature Switzerland AG 2020
G. Bebis et al. (Eds.): ISVC 2020, LNCS 12509, pp. 3–14, 2020.
https://doi.org/10.1007/978-3-030-64556-4_1

discourage the learning of complex models, reduce the flexibility of the model, increase sparsity, and avoid overfitting to the training data.

However, in the context of robust machine learning, the impact of regularization has not been thoroughly explored. We hypothesize that regularization increases robustness in non-traditional ways. If we define robust ML as the ability of an algorithm to be consistent across training and testing, the overfitting properties of regularization are important. If we further define robust ML as the ability of the algorithm to maintain a stable performance after the addition of noise to the dataset, the generalizability of regularization will help. In this work, we explore robustness with respect towards two major unsolved research questions in deep learning, i.e. robustness of deep learning to adversarial examples, and to interpretation via classification attribution. Specifically, we ask the question, does sparse regularization improve the robustness against different adversarial examples? Does the introduction of sparse regularization maintain deep neural network models' attribution consistent across parameterizations?

2   Background

We will mathematically define a regularization term (or regularizer) $R(f)$ as the following term added to a loss function,

$$\min_f \sum_{i=1}^{N} V(f(x_i), y_i) + \lambda R(f) \tag{1}$$

where V is a loss function that quantifies the cost of predicting $f(x)$ when the label or ground truth is y, and where N is the size of the training set and i refers to a single sample. The λ term is a hyperparameter that controls the weight of the regularizer. A more flexible model would be allowed to increase the magnitude of its coefficients, while a more constrained model would have a larger value of λ and thus have smaller valued coefficients.

If we define $f(x) = x \cdot w$, i.e. the approximation of y as characterized by an unknown vector of parameters (weights), w, we can then define $R(f)$ as $||w||_2^2$ for the case of L2 regularization e.g. Ridge regression, $||w||_1$ in the case of L1 regularization e.g.. Lasso, and $(\alpha||w||_1 + (1-\alpha)||w||_2^2), \alpha \in [0,1]$ for Elastic Net. The L2 penalizes large values of w, while the L1 norm drives some of the coefficients exactly to zero, enforcing sparsity.

2.1   Related Work in Adversarial Attacks

Although state-of-the-art deep neural networks have achieved high recognition for various image classification tasks, the architectures used for these tasks have been shown to be unstable to small, well-sought, perturbations of images. Szegedy et al. [16] showed that adversarial examples on ImageNet were so minute and fine-grained that they were indistinguishable to the human eye and could generalize across many different architectures on different folds of the dataset.

Thus, the architectures can be seen more as "memorizing" a mapping from the images to a text classification as opposed to understanding the underlying meaning and generalizing concepts across different images. Furthermore, deep learning classification has a tendency to learn surface regularities in the data, and not truly learn the abstract concepts of classes and objects [8].

Current attacks that have been studied in the field, such as those of [2,12] have been studied as proof-of-concepts, where adversarial attackers are assumed to have full knowledge of the classifier (e.g. model, architecture, model weights, parameters, training and testing datasets). The strongest attack in the literature at the time of writing this article is Carlini's attack based on the L2 norm, and it is a white-box attack requiring full knowledge of the model. Much of this research has been interested in developing the most effective attacks possible, to be used as standards against which to test the robustness of image classifier DNNs. With less knowledge of the classifier model, the effectiveness of the attack decreases.

2.2   Related Work in Image Attribution

Image attribution is the concept of determining what parts of the image contribute to the classification, and how important are these parts of the image to the end result. Most attribution methods work by either perturbing the input signal in some way and observing the change in the output, or by backtracking the influence of the input via a modification of backpropagation. The use of backpropogation only requires a single forward and backwards pass through the model, and are thus efficient to compute [3]. The perturbation-based methods do not require access to the model, and thus can be leveraged on black-box models.

We can visualize the attribution which provide insight into the classifier decision. These visualizations have been used to characterize which parts of an input are most responsible for the output. This lends some interpretability to the model, and can be used to explain the prediction result. We propose the robustness of the attribution methods can be measured by quantifying the change in attribution when choosing different hyperparameters for the model, or altering the type and scale of perturbation to the input image [1].

3   Methodology

In this section, we describe the different deep learning architectures, the adversarial attacks, and attribution techniques used to evaluate our hypothesis on regularization and sparsity on robust machine learning.

3.1   Image Classification Architectures

ResNet [5] - It is becoming more popular and common in the machine learning community to increase the depth of deep learning architectures to improve accuracy and generalizability. However, as the network increases in depth, the performance may begin to drop due to the vanishing gradient problem. Moreover, accuracy gets saturated and degrades rapidly resulting in the problem of degradation when the depth of a network increases. ResNet introduces a solution by construction to the deeper model and adding layers of identity shortcuts. The concept of an identity shortcut connection is that it can skip one or more layers performing identity mappings. They show it is easier to optimize the residual mapping than to optimize the original, unreferenced mapping. The intuition for this architecture is that the deep residual learning framework of a few stacked layers fitting an underlying mapping can be explicitly fit by a residual mapping.

MobileNet [6] - There have been various computer vision models proposed with a convolutional neural network (CNN) architecture for the task of image classification. In the field of utilizing computer vision models in mobile and embedded vision applications results in either the compression of pre-trained networks or to train small networks. On the other hand, MobileNet is Google's "mobile-first" computer vision model for TensorFlow that maximizes accuracy while utilizing limited resources. One of the novel contributions in MobileNet is leveraging a Depthwise Separable Convolution within its architecture, a depthwise convolution followed by a pointwise convolution where a depthwise convolution is the channel-wise $D_k \times D_k$ spatial convolution and a pointwise convolution is the 1×1 convolution to change the dimension. This unique convolution reduces the amount of operations to be computed significantly while only losing 1% in accuracy.

VGG16 [15] - VGG-16 is a deep convolutional neural network that was adapted from AlexNet [9] in which it replaces the large kernels with multiple, smaller 3×3 kernel filters. The introduction of this model showed the advantages of adding depth complexity to convolutional neural networks in order to improve its accuracy and resulted in significant improvements to prior deep learning models. VGG is broken up into 5 groups, each with a convolutional layer followed by a max-pooling layer, with the last part of the architecture consisting of fully-connected layers. AlexNet has been found to capture more unrelated background information in its final convolutional layer that confuses the prediction, whereas VGG-16 helps cover the full receptive field with larger feature maps and thus, outperforms AlexNet.

3.2   Adversarial Attacks

Deep Fool [11] - Deep Fool is an untargeted white box attack that misclassifies an image with the minimal amount of perturbation possible. For intuition, in a binary classification problem, there exists a hyperplane separating two classes; DeepFool takes an input x and projects it onto the hyperplane while pushing it a little beyond, misclassifying it. As a result, in the multi-class extension of the problem of image classification, DeepFool projects the input, x, to the closest hyperplane and misclassifies it. Equation 2 represents the function to compute the closest hyperplane given an input x_0 where f are class labels and w are the gradients.

$$\hat{l}(\mathbf{x_0}) = \arg\min_{k \neq \hat{k}(\mathbf{x_0})} \frac{\left| f_k(\mathbf{x_0}) - f_{\hat{k}(\mathbf{x_0})}(\mathbf{x_0}) \right|}{\left\| \mathbf{w}_k - \mathbf{w}_{\hat{k}(\mathbf{x_0})} \right\|_2} \tag{2}$$

Fast Gradient Sign Method (FGSM) [4] - Most image classification archi-tectures are neural networks, which learn by updating weights via a backpropa-gation algorithm that computes gradients. Fast Gradient Sign Method uses the gradients of the neural network to generate an adversarial example by using the gradients of the loss with respect to the input image x to create a new image which maximizes this loss. Furthermore, the input image x is manipulated by adding or subtracting a small error ϵ to each pixel depending upon the sign of the gradient for a pixel. Eq. 3 represents the simple, cheap cost function to obtain the optimal max-norm constrained perturbation of an input image x, with parameters of the model θ, the cost to train the model $J(\theta, \mathbf{x}, y)$ and a small multiplier ϵ to guarantee small perturbations. The addition of errors in the direction of the gradient results in misclassification.

$$\eta = \epsilon \operatorname{sign}(\nabla_{\mathbf{x}} J(\theta, \mathbf{x}, y)) \tag{3}$$

Projected Gradient Descent (PGD) [10] - This targeted white box attack is an extension of FGSM and is often referred to as Iterative-Fast Gradient Sign Method (I-FGSM), where FGSM is applied to an image iteratively. Since this is a targeted class, the objective is not to simply just misclassify the image but to classify the image to a specific desired class. In FGSM, the loss is calculated with respect to the true class and added the gradients computed with respect to the true class increasing loss for the true class and misclassifying it. However, in this case, the loss is calculated with respect to the target class to minimize the loss for the target class moving in the direction of the target class. This process can be described as projecting onto a l_p ball with a defined radius and clipping the values of the adversarial sample so that it lies within the set data range. This multi-step variant of FGSM is shown in Eq. 4 where $\mathcal{S}$ is :

$$x^{t+1} = \prod_{x+\mathcal{S}} \left(x^t + \alpha \operatorname{sign}(\nabla_x L(\theta, x, y)) \right) \epsilon \tag{4}$$

3.3   Attribution Methods

Sliding Patch Method [17] - In this input perturbation attribution method, one can systematically occlude different portions of the input and monitor the output of the classifier. We slide an occlusion patch of different sizes across the input image. By investigating the changes that occur in prediction, one can create a heat attribution map. However, given different size occlusion patches, a robust machine learning method should generate a consistent attribution map. Our experiments look at the consistency of maps as a function of patch size.

Grad-CAM [14] - Gradient-weighted Class Activation Mapping (Grad-CAM) is a backtracking method that uses the gradients of a target in the final convolutional layer to produce a coarse localization map highlighting important regions in the image for the final prediction. Grad-CAM is able to localize class-discriminative regions while being orders of magnitude cheaper to compute than occlusion methods. These types of attribution visualizations are critical to provide interpretability to a model and build trust with the end user. For machine learning robustness, we postulate that slight transformations to the input image should not significantly alter the attribution maps.

4   Experiments and Results

For our experiments, we first validate that sparse regularization is able to maintain a high level of accuracy over a range of sparse penalty parameterizations. We then experiment with adversarial examples and empirically validate the effects of adding regularization to the attacked model. Lastly, we validate that sparse regularization has a consistency effect when exploring parameterizations and input perturbations for class attribution.

4.1   Sparse Regularization Effect on Average Density

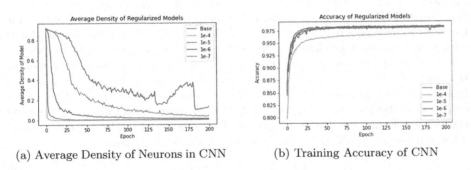

(a) Average Density of Neurons in CNN   (b) Training Accuracy of CNN

Fig. 1. A comparison of the average density of a single layer CNN and its regularized variants. This experiment shows the intuition that sparse CNNs (models with low average density) perform just as well if not better as dense CNNs.

While we are researching different regularization methods, we note that there is a clear connection between regularization and sparsity in the weights of the model and output of representation. Sparsity is induced by forms of regularization (L1, Elastic Net, Dropout, etc.), which provide us with the many benefits of regularized models. A common metric to measure sparsity is the Average Activity Ratio (AVR) or the average density of neurons activated per stimulus. Representationally the activation of a neuron denotes the use of an additional dimension used to encode the data. Thus, the least amount of neurons activated per projection into the output space, the sparser the representation of the data.

Our first experiment is to empirically show that sparse regularization performs on par with a non-regularized counterpart. The distinguishing feature of sparse coding compared to local or dense code is that its activity ratio lies in the range of $[0, 0.5]$. For intuition, we train a single layer CNN and impose a sparsity constraint on a cross entropy loss in Eq. 5,

$$L = -\frac{1}{m} \sum_{i=1}^{m} (y_i \cdot \log(\hat{y}_i) + (1 - y_i) \cdot \log(1 - \hat{y}_i)) + \lambda \sum_j |a_j| \qquad (5)$$

where m indicates the number of examples and i indicates the specific example being trained. Additionally, y_i refers to the ground truth target and $\hat{y}_i$ is the predicted output from the single layer CNN. Lastly, the last term of the loss function represents the regularization on the network, where $|a_{i,j}|$ is the absolute value of the activation for the hidden neuron j in the CNN layer and for each example the sum of activations for all hidden neurons is regularized by λ, a hyperparameter that affects the sparsity constraint. The closer λ is to 1, the more sparsity encouraged and the closer λ is to 0, the less sparsity is encouraged. We set λ to 0 for the base model and scale λ from $1e - 4$ (0.0001) down to $1e - 7$ (0.0000001) to examine the different effects sparsity has on training accuracy.

In Fig. 1, we achieve sparse code without losing much in terms of accuracy. There are 39, 200 trainable neurons in the network and the graph of the Average Density denotes the decimal equivalent of the quotient of number of neurons activated divided by the total number of trainable neurons. It is clear that the regularization encourages the Average Density to decrease, but the accuracy of the less dense models are just as accurate, if not better.

4.2 Robustness Against Adversarial Attacks

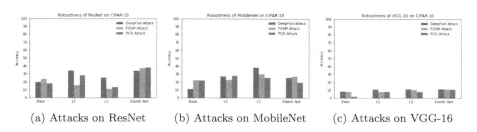

| (a) Attacks on ResNet | (b) Attacks on MobileNet | (c) Attacks on VGG-16 |

Fig. 2. A comparison of the accuracy achieved on different architectures when attacked by an adversarial algorithm (DeepFool, FGSM, and PGD). In nearly all cases, regularization helps improve the robustness of the model. Elastic net regularization is most consistent with robustness against adversarial attack.

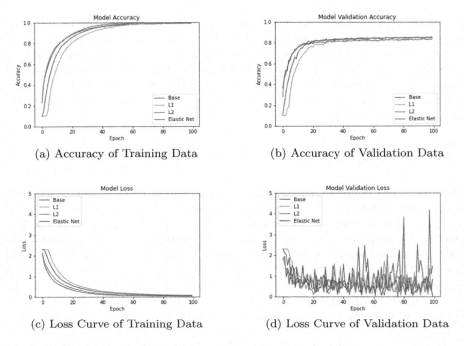

(a) Accuracy of Training Data   (b) Accuracy of Validation Data

(c) Loss Curve of Training Data   (d) Loss Curve of Validation Data

Fig. 3. VGG-16 training and validation accuracy and loss on CIFAR-10. In (d) the base model validation loss is beginning to show signs of overfitting as the loss starts to demonstrate high variance.

Next, we run experimentation on how regularization can improve robustness against adversarial attacks on the architectures: ResNet, MobileNet, and VGG-16. We train each architecture: ResNet-50, MobileNet, and VGG-16 on the CIFAR-10 dataset, then generate adversarial images using the various attacks: DeepFool, Fast Gradient Sign Method (FGSM), and Projected Gradient Descent from [13]. Next, we retrain the networks on the training set augmented with the adversarial images i.e. adversarial training, and evaluate the classifier on the test set and record the accuracy of the network on the adversarial images. To regularize each of the tested network, we impose layer weight regularizers on all 2D convolutional layers as well as all fully-connected layers. We do this by applying a regularizer penalty on the layer's kernel. We implement three different versions of each architecture with a distinct regularizer. We compute the penalty for the layer's kernel by the l_1 norm in which the loss is equivalent to $\mathcal{L}(x) = l_1 \times \|x\|$ where l_1 is the regularization factor set to 0.01. We also run a series of experiments where the models are regularized by the l_2 norm such that the loss is computed as $\mathcal{L}(x) = l_2 \times x^2$ where l_2 is the regularization factor set to 0.01. Lastly, we run a series of experiments where the models are regularized by both the l_1 and l_2 norms, e.g.. elastic net. As we can see in Fig. 2 and in Table 1, imposing sparse regularization on these deep learning architectures ensures

Table 1. Accuracy on testing samples that have been attacked by different adversarial algorithms (DeepFool, FGSM, and PGD) on CV Models Trained on CIFAR-10 (ResNet, MobileNet, VGG-16). Quantitatively, we see gains in robustness for regularization techniques across all architectures, and all attacks.

Model	Regularization	DeepFool[11]	FGSM[4]	PGD[10]
ResNet	Base	19.60	23.80	18.00
	L1	**34.20**	16.00	28.40
	L2	25.20	11.40	13.20
	Elastic Net	33.80	**37.40**	**38.20**
MobileNet	Base	11.40	22.20	22.00
	L1	27.20	22.60	**28.00**
	L2	**38.40**	**30.20**	25.40
	Elastic Net	25.40	27.00	19.40
VGG16	Base	8.40	7.60	1.60
	L1	10.80	8.00	8.00
	L2	11.30	10.20	8.00
	Elastic Net	**11.40**	**11.40**	**10.80**

a more robust generalized model. We believe the restriction on the number of nodes activated encourages only the most important features to be represented when encoding into an embedding. Indeed, it appears that in every account, the regularized models demonstrate some effectiveness towards mitigating adversarial attacks.

The training process, e.g.. model accuracy and loss, can be seen in Fig. 3. We can see that the regularized models take slightly longer to converge, but all models are able to achieve the same accuracy and loss on the training and validation sets. However, in the case of no regularization, the validation loss begins to vary wildly, Fig. 3(d). This is likely due to the fact that the model is beginning to overfit to the training data.

4.3 Stability in Class Attribution

For our final experiment, we investigate how regularization can improve robustness in the attribution task. Namely, we propose that for a model to be robust, it should maintain a level of consistency in the explanation e.g.. class attribution maps, as the hyperparameters of the system are perturbed. If the attribution maps drastically vary from small changes in the input size, or patch size, then the model would not be considered robust. We can quantitatively measure the level of consistency between attribution maps by a pixel-wise sum of squared distances (SSD) between examples. For the attribution task, we use two distinct methods - Grad-CAM a gradient based attribution method, and an occlusion method using Sliding Patches.

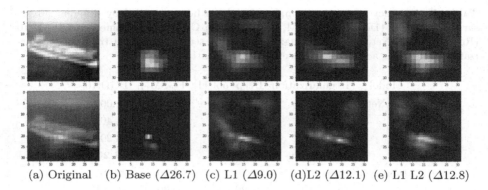

(a) Original   (b) Base (Δ26.7)   (c) L1 (Δ9.0)   (d)L2 (Δ12.1)   (e) L1 L2 (Δ12.8)

Fig. 4. Attribution heat maps generated by the Sliding Patch method. The first row shows the original image (a) and the heat map generated for the resulting class using a patch size of 4 and a jump size of 2. The second row shows an overlay of the heat map on the original image (a) and the heat map generated using a patch size of 2 and a jump size of 2. The sum of squared differences between row 1 and row 2 are shown as Δ for each of the methods.

We are able to visualize the attribution maps given example CIFAR images for the occlusion Sliding Patch method, Fig. 4. In this method, we first slide a gray patch of size 4×4 across the image with a stride (jump parameter) of 2. We observe the output of the model and can quantify how much the occluded patch effects the classification output. The attribution heat maps for the 4×4 patch can be seen in first row of Fig. 4. We then change the parameters of the system by sliding a 2×2 patch across the image with a stride of 2. We can see that this parameter change does have an effect on the end result as seen in row 2 of Fig. 4. We compute the SSD from row 1 and row 2 to compute the difference between maps. A more consistent map would have lower SSD. As shown numerically over 1,000 random CIFAR-10 images, see Table 2, L1 regularization has the best and lowest overall attribution change for the Sliding Patch method.

Next, we evaluate the Grad-CAM method, which can be seen in Fig. 5. Similar to the occlusion method, we can compare the SSD between row 1 and row 2 attribution maps. However, in this case there is no internal parameterization of the Grad-CAM method. Thus, in order to evaluate stability of the method, we slightly transform the input image. For our experiment, we chose to blur the original image via a Gaussian kernel of size $\sigma = 0.5$. The intuition is that a slightly blurred version of an image should not change the attribution map drastically. And in fact, we show that the regularized models do improve the stability of attribution as quantitatively shown in Table 2.

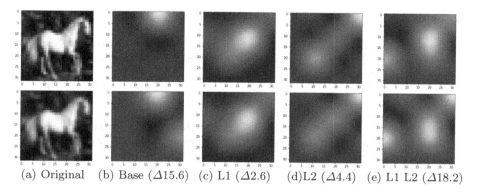

(a) Original   (b) Base (Δ15.6)   (c) L1 (Δ2.6)   (d)L2 (Δ4.4)   (e) L1 L2 (Δ18.2)

Fig. 5. Attribution heat maps generated by the Grad-CAM method. The first row shows the original image (a) and the heat map generated for the resulting class. The second row shows the original image blurred by a Gaussian kernel with $\sigma = 0.5$ (a) and the heat map generated on the blurred image. The sum of squared differences between row 1 and row 2 are shown as Δ for each of the methods.

Table 2. Sum of Squared Differences (SSD) of Attribution heat maps when altering a hyperparameter of the system. For Sliding Patches, we change the patch size from 4 pixels to 2 pixels. For Grad-CAM, we transform the input image by a Gaussian blur kernel with $\sigma = 0.5$.

Attribution	Base	L1	L2	Elastic Net
Sliding Patch[17]	26.31 ± 27.19	**18.51 ± 15.28**	18.62 ± 13.48	20.92 ± 17.83
Grad-CAM[14]	24.53 ± 34.19	15.13 ± 24.95	15.12 ± 20.92	**13.96 ± 22.51**

5   Conclusion

In this paper, we have analyzed the performance of image classification architectures and the effect that robustness and sparsity has on their robustness against adversarial attacks and the stability when performing image attribution. We have shown that enforcing sparsity, especially in the form of regularization upon the convolutional and fully-connected layers within these deep neural architectures has helped the robustness of the model and outperform the base model without regularization in correctly classifying images despite various adversarial attacks against the dataset. We looked at different attacks exploiting vulnerabilities in the architectures themselves as well as some attacks whose only objective was to misclassify the image. Our results as indicated in Table 1 and visualized in Fig. 2, show the benefits of imposing regularization to combat adversarial attacks to computer vision models. Furthermore, we show that sparse regularization creates stability within image attribution frameworks. Specifically, Elastic Net seemed to produce the most robust results across all attacks and all attribution methods.

References

1. Bansal, N., Agarwal, C., Nguyen, A.: Sam: the sensitivity of attribution methods to hyperparameters. In: Proceedings of the IEEE/CVF Conference on Computer Vision and Pattern Recognition, pp. 8673–8683 (2020)
2. Carlini, N., Wagner, D.: Towards evaluating the robustness of neural networks. In: 2017 IEEE Symposium on Security and Privacy (SP), pp. 39–57. IEEE. (2017). https://arxiv.org/pdf/1608.04644.pdf
3. Fong, R., Patrick, M., Vedaldi, A.: Understanding deep networks via extremal perturbations and smooth masks. In: Proceedings of the IEEE International Conference on Computer Vision, pp. 2950–2958 (2019)
4. Goodfellow, I.J., Shlens, J., Szegedy, C.: Explaining and harnessing adversarial examples. arXiv preprint arXiv:1412.6572 (2014)
5. He, K., Zhang, X., Ren, S., Sun, J.: Deep residual learning for image recognition. In: Proceedings of the IEEE Conference on Computer Vision and Pattern Recognition, pp. 770–778 (2015). http://arxiv.org/abs/1512.03385
6. Howard, A.G., et al.: Mobilenets: efficient convolutional neural networks for mobile vision applications. arXiv preprint arXiv:1704.04861 (2017)
7. Kim, E., Hannan, D., Kenyon, G.: Deep sparse coding for invariant multimodal halle berry neurons. In: Proceedings of the IEEE Conference on Computer Vision and Pattern Recognition, pp. 1111–1120 (2018)
8. Kim, E., Rego, J., Watkins, Y., Kenyon, G.T.: Modeling biological immunity to adversarial examples. In: Proceedings of the IEEE/CVF Conference on Computer Vision and Pattern Recognition, pp. 4666–4675 (2020)
9. Krizhevsky, A., Sutskever, I., Hinton, G.E.: Imagenet classification with deep convolutional neural networks. Commun. ACM 60(6), 84–90 (2017). https://doi.org/10.1145/3065386
10. Madry, A., Makelov, A., Schmidt, L., Tsipras, D., Vladu, A.: Towards deep learning models resistant to adversarial attacks. arXiv preprint arXiv:1706.06083 (2017)
11. Moosavi-Dezfooli, S., Fawzi, A., Frossard, P.: Deepfool: a simple and accurate method to fool deep neural networks. In: Proceedings of the IEEE Conference on Computer Vision and Pattern Recognition, pp. 2574–2582 (2015). http://arxiv.org/abs/1511.04599
12. Papernot, N., McDaniel, P., Wu, X., Jha, S., Swami, A.: Distillation as a defense to adversarial perturbations against deep neural networks. In: 2016 IEEE Symposium on Security and Privacy (SP), (pp. 582–597. IEEE (2016). https://arxiv.org/pdf/1511.04508.pdf
13. Nicolae, M., et al.: Adversarial robustness toolbox v0.2.2. CoRR abs/1807.01069 (2018), http://arxiv.org/abs/1807.01069
14. Selvaraju, R.R., Cogswell, M., Das, A., Vedantam, R., Parikh, D., Batra, D.: Grad-cam: visual explanations from deep networks via gradient-based localization. In: Proceedings of the IEEE International Conference on Computer Vision, pp. 618–626 (2017)
15. Simonyan, K., Zisserman, A.: Very deep convolutional networks for large-scale image recognition. arXiv preprint arXiv:1409.1556 (2014)
16. Szegedy, C., et al.: Intriguing properties of neural networks. arXiv preprint arXiv:1312.6199 (2013)
17. Zeiler, M.D., Fergus, R.: Visualizing and understanding convolutional networks. In: Fleet, D., Pajdla, T., Schiele, B., Tuytelaars, T. (eds.) ECCV 2014. LNCS, vol. 8689, pp. 818–833. Springer, Cham (2014). https://doi.org/10.1007/978-3-319-10590-1_53

Self-Competitive Neural Networks

Iman Saberi and Fathiyeh Faghih[(⊠)]

College of Engineering Department of Electrical and Computer Engineering,
University of Tehran, Tehran, Iran
{iman.saberi,f.faghih}@ut.ac.ir

Abstract. Deep Neural Networks (DNNs) have improved the accuracy
of classification problems in lots of applications. One of the challenges in
training a DNN is its need to be fed by an enriched dataset to increase its
accuracy and avoid it suffering from overfitting. One way to improve the
generalization of DNNs is to augment the training data with new synthesized adversarial samples. Recently, researchers have worked extensively
to propose methods for data augmentation. In this paper, we generate
adversarial samples to refine the Decision boundaries of each class. In
this approach, at each stage, we use the model learned by the primary
and generated adversarial data (up to that stage) to manipulate the primary data in a way that look complicated to the DNN. The DNN is
then retrained using the augmented data and then it again generates
adversarial data that are hard to predict for itself. As the DNN tries to
improve its accuracy by competing with itself (generating hard samples
and then learning them), the technique is called Self-Competitive Neural Network (SCNN). To generate such samples, we pose the problem
as an optimization task, where the network weights are fixed and use
a gradient descent based method to synthesize adversarial samples that
are on the boundary of their true labels and the nearest wrong labels.
Our experimental results show that data augmentation using SCNNs can
significantly increase the accuracy of the original network. As an example, we can mention improving the accuracy of a CNN trained with 1000
limited training data of MNIST dataset from 94.26% to 98.25%.

Keywords: Deep Neural Networks · Data augmentation · Computer
vision

1 Introduction

Deep learning models have performed remarkably well on many classification
problems. With the advent of Convolutional Neural Networks (CNNs) [9], significant improvements have been reported in computer vision tasks. One of the
main challenges in training a deep neural model is providing a big dataset in
order to prevent model from overfitting. The challenge is more significant in
small datasets, such as medical image analysis. Data augmentation is a known
solution in the literature to improve model generalization.

© Springer Nature Switzerland AG 2020
G. Bebis et al. (Eds.): ISVC 2020, LNCS 12509, pp. 15–26, 2020.
https://doi.org/10.1007/978-3-030-64556-4_2

One of the well-known techniques for data augmentation are Generative Adversarial Networks (GANs) [6]. They are used to generate new data in order to inflate the training dataset [1, 3, 6, 10]. There are, however, challenges in data generation using these networks. First, the aim of GANs is to find a Nash equilibrium of a non-convex game with continuous and high-dimensional parameters, while they are typically trained based on a gradient descent based technique designed to minimize a cost function (instead of finding a Nash equilibrium of a game). Therefore, these algorithms may fail to converge [7], and hence, synthesis of high resolution data may be very difficult using this technique. Another limitation of GANs is their need to substantial amount of primary data in order to train the discriminator well, and hence, they are not practical in small datasets [13].

In this paper, we propose a novel approach in this field that concentrates on the weaknesses of the functional structure of DNNs in order to improve their accuracy. The non-polynomial architecture of DNNs consists of deep linear and nonlinear operations, and hence, the Decision boundary of each class cannot be easily determined. We present a method to refine the DoAs of the network by synthesizing harder samples from the primary input dataset. The synthesizer network modifies each sample in a way that it is located on the boundary of its true label and its nearest wrong label in the trained embedded network. The synthesizer tries to generate more complicated samples from the primary data, and then the embedded network tries to learn them correctly. This cycle is repeated as many times as the accuracy of the embedded network increases. Similar to GANs, our approach consists of two networks, a synthesizer and an embedded network. However, unlike GANs that try to play a minimax game and converge to a Nash equilibrium, in our approach, the two networks separately try to minimize their loss function based on a gradient descent method in order to improve the accuracy and robustness of the embedded network.

Our experimental results demonstrate that our proposed technique can improve the accuracy of networks, especially in small datasets. We selected a limited set of 1000 training data from the MNIST dataset, and fed them to an SCNN. We observed that the accuracy of the baseline well-trained embedded network was increased from 94.26% to 98.25% using our technique. We also did experiments on Fashion MNIST and Cifar10 datasets as harder datasets. The results show 1.35% increase in the accuracy of the Fashion MNIST dataset and 4.85% increase in the accuracy of the Cifar10 dataset, compared to the baseline Resnet18 Model.

2   Related Work

Mining hard examples was previously studied in the literature [14, 15]. The idea is to select or generate optimal and informative samples in order to enrich the dataset. Data augmentation techniques in the literature can be categorized into data wrapping and oversampling methods. Data wrapping augmentations transform the existing samples, such that their labels are preserved. Geometric and color transformations, random erasing, adversarial training, and style transfer networks are examples of data wrapping techniques. Oversampling augmentation methods generate new instances and add them to the training set. Oversampling encompasses augmentations, such as mixing images, feature space augmentation, and GANs. These two categories do not form a mutually exclusive dichotomy [13]. Our approach is a data wrapping augmentation technique that tries to manipulate each sample, such that it is located on the boundary of its true label and its nearest wrong label.

In [5], the authors propose a method to seek small transformations that yield maximal classification loss on the transformed sample based on a trust region strategy. This work is similar to our idea in the criterion of generating informative augmented data. However, our strategy in synthesizing augmented samples is totally different. The proposed algorithm in [5] selects a set of possible transformations, where each one has a specific degree of freedom. The algorithm applies a set of transformations that make the cost function have the most value. Our technique is different in that a gradient descent method tries to move each sample in a direction to be located on the decision boundary for that sample.

The closest work to this paper is [12], where the authors designed an augmentation network that competes against a target network by generating hard examples (using GAN structure). The algorithm selects a set of augmentations that have the maximal loss against random augmentation samples. The idea is to apply a reward/penalty strategy and formalize the problem as a minimax game for effective generation of hard samples. Our paper is different in that we do not make the generator network to select the best strategy from a set of predefined strategies. Instead, a gradient descent method decides what is the best transformation parameters in order to manipulate each sample. Also, we pose the problem as minimizing two cost functions separately, instead of playing a minimax game.

3   Self-Competitive Neural Network

3.1   SCNN Architecture

The architecture of a Self-Competitive Neural Network (SCNN) contains two main parts:

1. An embedded neural network: The goal of SCNN is to improve the accuracy of this network. The internal design of this network is crucial in order to have a powerful model. The embedded neural network can be of any type, such as Convolutional Neural Network (CNN).
2. An Adversarial Data Synthesizer (ADS) network: This network is constructed by concatenation of a number of differentiable components and the embedded network. The aim of this network is synthesizing difficult data for the embedded network. The differentiable components take the input data and try to learn their parameters in a way that the synthesized data is predicted as the nearest wrong label by the embedded network. The details of the internal structure of this component will be discussed in Sect. 4.

The training life cycle of an SCNN has three main phases (Fig. 1):

1. Training with primary data: In this phase, the embedded network is trained by the main input dataset.
2. Adversarial data synthesis: After training the embedded network by the primary data, the weights of the embedded network are set as immutable, and the primary input data is manipulated in a way that the embedded network predicts the synthesized data by a wrong label. In other words, the ADS network manipulates the input data in a way that they are more difficult for the embedded network to predict correctly.
3. Training with adversarial data: In this phase, the SCNN uses the synthesized data from the previous phase, sets the weights of the embedded network as mutable, and the embedded network is trained by the synthesized adversarial data.

You can see the embedded network in the both the training phases and the data generation phase. The difference is that in the training phases, the weights of the embedded network are mutable and learned during these steps. However, in the data generation phase, the weights are an immutable part of the ADS network, and hence, they are not changed.

The three phases are repeated in a cycle as many times as the accuracy of the embedded network improves. In each cycle, the weights of the embedded network are tuned by the primary data (phase 1), the ADS synthesizes new data from the primary input data that seem harder for the embedded network to predict correctly (phase 2), and the embedded network is trained by the synthesized harder boundary data (phase 3). This procedure can be considered as *online* strategy, where the underlying embedded network is improved gradually by harder data. Another approach is *offline*, where the model is trained from scratch by the primary and harder data generated in the training life cycle of an SCNN. It is obvious that the offline approach is more expensive, but as we will show in Sect. 5, the resulting accuracy of this approach is better than the online strategy.

4   Details of SCNN

The main idea of SCNN can be thought of as a competition between the embedded neural network and the adversarial data synthesizer, where during the training phases (both training with primary data and adversarial data), the embedded network tries to correctly predict the labels of the primary and adversarial data. On the other hand, during the adversarial data synthesis, the SCNN tries to manipulate the input data in a way that the embedded network predicts the manipulated data with wrong labels.

For simplicity in explanation and without loss of generality, consider a MultiLayer Perceptron (MLP) as an embedded network. A loss function is defined in a way that explains how much the outputs of the network are different from the correct labels. The optimizer uses gradient descent to minimize this function.

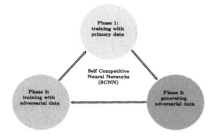

Fig. 1. The life cycle of training a SCNN

The main idea of SCNN is to fix the weights of the embedded neural network, and use the gradient descent technique in order to manipulate the input data and generate a set of adversarial data. As an example, the architecture of the ADS network with MLP as the embedded network is presented in Fig. 2. In this structure, the input vector $X = [x_1, x_2, ..., x_n]$ is fed to a (a set of) differentiable component(s) that try to manipulate the input data to a vector $X' = [x'_1, x'_2, ..., x'_n]$, which is fed to the embedded network. To do that, we define an optimization problem, where the parameters of the differentiable components are trained based on a cost function that is defined in a way that the manipulated data is predicted as the nearest wrong label by the embedded neural network.

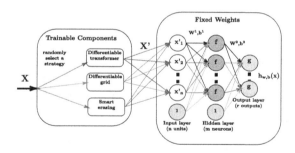

Fig. 2. Adversarial data synthesizer network

The trainable components are designed based on the type of the input dataset. In this paper, we consider three main trainable components for the *image* samples:

- **Differentiable transformer:** We use Spatial Transformer Network (STN) layer introduced in [8] for this transformation. It takes a vector of size 6 per image to perform an affine transformation (such as rotation, zoom, shearing) on the input image. For example, if we have an input image and the coordinate of each pixel is identified by (x_i^s, y_i^s), and (x_i^t, y_i^t) represents the coordinate of the pixel after the affine transformation, we have:

$$G_t = \tau_\theta(G_i) = \begin{pmatrix} x_i^t \\ y_i^t \end{pmatrix} = \begin{bmatrix} \theta_{11} & \theta_{12} & \theta_{13} \\ \theta_{21} & \theta_{22} & \theta_{23} \end{bmatrix} \begin{pmatrix} x_i^s \\ y_i^s \\ 1 \end{pmatrix} \qquad (1)$$

where G_i is the initial grid of the input feature map, and G_t is the final grid of the feature map after applying the transformation τ_θ on G_i. The most important feature of this component is that it is differentiable with respect to its transformation parameters, which means the gradient descent can learn them based on a defined cost function.

- **Differentiable grid:** We design this component to be more flexible to perform grid manipulation in the input feature map. It is a differentiable component that manipulates the grid of the input image in three main steps:
  1. Convolution on a null input space: For each input image, we generate a null input space (δ) based on sampling from uniform distribution $U(-1,+1)$ with the same size as the input image size, denoted by (W,H). This space is the starting point for grid manipulation, and will be trained during the adversarial data synthesis phase. After that, we define a Gaussian kernel window, which is convolved with this null space, and as a result, we will have a smoothed null input space, as depicted in Fig. 3a. The convolved null space (μ) can be computed as follows:

$$\delta_{ij} \sim U(-1,+1) : \; i \in [1...W] \; j \in [1...H]$$

$$\mu_{ij} = \delta_{ij} \circledast Kernel_{ij} = \sum_{m=1}^{w_K} \sum_{n=1}^{h_k} Kernel_{m,n}(\Phi_\mu, \Phi_\sigma)\delta_{i-m,j-n} : \qquad (2)$$

$$\forall i \in [1...W] \; \forall j \in [1...H]$$

   where $Kernel$ is a predefined 2D Gaussian kernel with size (w_K, h_K), and mean and standard deviation equal to Φ_μ and Φ_σ, respectively. Note that this kernel is immutable during the training phase of the input null space.
  2. Generating the manipulated grid: In this step, the convolved null space (μ) is added to the initial grid (G_i) of the input image, and as a result, the manipulated grid (G_t) is generated, as shown in Fig. 3b.

$$G_t = G_i + \mu \qquad (3)$$

  3. Image sampling: The main operation of this step is an image interpolation based on the manipulated grid generated in the previous step. As depicted in Fig. 3c, the image sampler takes an image and a manipulated grid as input, and computes the interpolated output image based on the manipulated grid. The Final output image can be computed as follows:

$$O_i^c = \sum_{n=1}^{H} \sum_{m=1}^{W} I_{nm}^c k(x_i^t - m; \Phi_x)k(y_i^t - n; \Phi_y)$$

$$\forall i \in [1...HW] \; \forall c \in [1...C] \qquad (4)$$

$$(x^t, y^t) \in G_t$$

where k is a generic sampling kernel function that performs the image interpolation. It can be any image interpolation function (e.g.. bilinear), and Φ_x and Φ_y are the parameters of this kernel function. I^c_{nm} is the input value at location (n, m) in channel c of the input image, and O^c_i is the output value for pixel i at location (x^t_i, y^t_i).

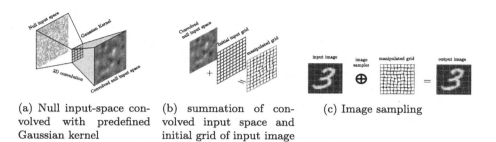

(a) Null input-space convolved with predefined Gaussian kernel

(b) summation of convolved input space and initial grid of input image

(c) Image sampling

Fig. 3. Three main steps of the differentiable grid component

- **Smart erasing:** Random erasing is one of the most effective data augmentation techniques which is mostly used in DNNs [11]. This component exploits erasing technique in order to smartly erase some parts of the input data in a way that the erased samples maximize the loss function. This component has four main steps:
  1. Defining an NxN trainable mask (M): this mask covers the input data and responsible for distinguishing which parts of the input have the most significant effect on classifying the input data. Parameter N could be varied based on input size(for example, for a 32×32 input size, N could be 4 or 8).
  2. A 3D-Upsampling operation: this operation fits the size of the grid to the size of the input image. for instance, for a 4×4 grid, we use an $8 \times 8 \times 3$ Upsampling operation in order to make a $32 \times 32 \times 3$ grid(same size as the input data). The elements of the upsampled grid are multiplied to input data.
  3. Finding attention area: From the previous step, we prepare a trainable grid that covers the input data. Now, we train this grid in order to distinguish which parts of the input data have the most significant effect on classifying tasks (Fig. 4.b).
  4. Erasing the most effective grids: after finding attention areas, grids with the most impact on the classifying task are deleted or replaced with noisy data.(Fig. 4d and e). There are two possibilities, if the removed area is a part of the background, it will help classifying task that decreases the importance of this part. If the removed area is an essential part of the input, the algorithm tries to identify the input without considering this part.

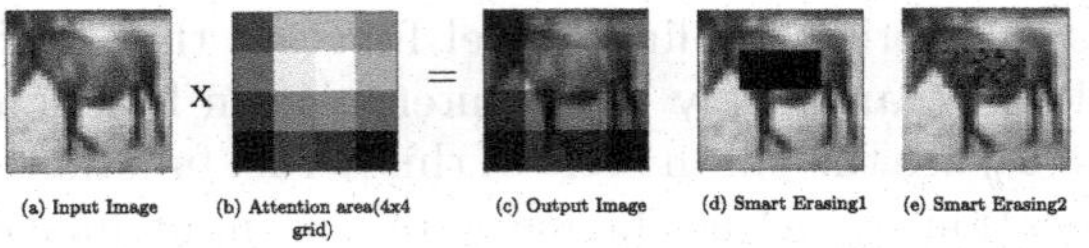

(a) Input Image   (b) Attention area(4x4 grid)   (c) Output Image   (d) Smart Erasing1   (e) Smart Erasing2

Fig. 4. Applying smart erasing on a specific image of cifar10 database

We defined three components, the transformer component which is differentiable with respect to its transformation parameters θ, and the grid manipulation component, which is differentiable with respect to its null input space δ and the smart erasing component which is differentiable with respect to its defined mask (M). Let's denote the output of the transformer component with $V_{(X_j|\theta)}$ and the output of the grid manipulation component with $O_{(X_j|\delta)}$ and the output of the random erasing component with $E_{(X_j|M)}$ for input sample X_j. X' (the generated adversarial data to be fed to the embedded network) can be computed as follows (Fig. 2):

$$X' = \begin{cases} V_{(X|\theta)} & or \\ O_{(X|\delta)} & or \\ E_{(X|M)} \end{cases} \tag{5}$$

The corresponding function of the adversarial data synthesizer network is as follows:

$$h^{ADS}(X|\theta,\delta) = h^{MLP}(X') \tag{6}$$

where h^{ADS} is the corresponding function of the ADS network, and h^{MLP} is the corresponding function of the embedded network (MLP in this example). The goal is to optimize parameters θ, δ and M in a way that the output of the ADS becomes the nearest wrong label for each input data. For defining an appropriate loss function, we need to define the following variables:

$$\begin{aligned} \hat{y}_j &= \arg\max_i h_i(X_j|\theta,\delta)^{ADS} \\ \check{y}_j &= \arg\max_i h_i(X_j|\theta,\delta)^{ADS} : i \neq \hat{y}_j \\ \bar{y}_j &= \begin{cases} (y_j + \alpha\check{y}_j) & if \ \hat{y}_j = y_j \\ (y_j + \alpha\hat{y}_j) & if \ \hat{y}_j \neq y_j \end{cases} \end{aligned} \tag{7}$$

where $\hat{y}_j$ is the index of the largest output of the ADS network, $\check{y}_j$ is the index of the second largest output of the ADS network, and $\bar{y}_j$ is the desired output of the ADS network for generating harder samples. Note that $\bar{y}_j$ is constructed by a linear combination of the correct label y_j, and the nearest wrong label for the input data X_j. Also, α is the strength rate of moving the input data to the boundary of its true label and the nearest wrong label. Now, we can define the loss function of the ADS, as follows:

$$loss^{ADS} = -\sum_{i=1}^{n}\sum_{k=1}^{K} \bar{y}_{ik} log(\hat{y}_{ik}) \tag{8}$$

The goal is to optimize parameters (θ, δ, M), such that the manipulated input data is predicted with a wrong label, or becomes closer to the boundary of its true label and its nearest wrong label.

5   Experimental Results

We implemented SCNN on three datasets; MNIST, Fashion MNIST, and Cifar10. The underlying embedded network is a CNN for MNIST and Fashion MNIST datasets, consisting of a convolutional, a BatchNormalization, and a pooling layer, repeated three times in a stack. Size of all filters is (3×3) and number of filters in convolution layers are 64, 128 and 256 respectively. We also add a fully-connected hidden layer(with 512 neurons) to the end of last convolution layer. All activation functions are ReLu to have less intensive computation overhead in the training phase. For Cifar10 dataset we choose Resnet18 structure as our underlying embedded network. Number of filters in resnet18 start with 64 and we use a dropout layer(mask ratio:0.2) after the fully connected layer of Resnet18.

5.1   Limited MNIST

We randomly selected 1000 samples of the MNIST handwritten dataset to have a more challenging problem. SCNN generated 1,000,000 adversarial hard samples in 50 cycles. For comparison with random augmentation, we use the Augmentor tool [2] that applies random augmentation operations, such as rotation, scaling, shearing, flipping, random erasing, and elastic transformations. The results based on the online strategy for baseline model, Augmentor tool, and SCNN are shown in Fig. 8a. It can be observed that the SCNN approach experiences less overfitting compared to other approaches. The final accuracy results are depicted in Table 1. In Fig. 5, we illustrate the process of synthesizing a hard sample by applying gradient descent on the trainable parameters of the transformer, where a sample with true label 2 is transformed, such that its label is predicted as 8.

Fig. 5. Data manipulation based on differentiable transformer on MNIST sample data

5.2   Fashion MNIST

We use the entire 60,000 samples in the training dataset of Fashion MNIST, and generated 600,000 adversarial hard samples in 10 cycles. Once the baseline model was trained by the primary data, and another time, it is trained by the adversarial and primary data. The results are shown in Fig. 8b, and the final accuracy after 100 epochs is shown in Table 2. It can be observed that SCNN experiences less overfitting compared to the baseline model. Figure 6 illustrates the synthesis of a hard sample by applying gradient descent on the trainable parameters of the differentiable grid, where the goal is to manipulate a sample with true label 0 (T-shirt), such that it is predicted as label 3 (Dress).

Fig. 6. Data manipulation based on differentiable grid on Fashion-MNIST sample data

5.3   Cifar10

This dataset is more complicated, consisting of 50,000 training data. We generated 100,000 adversarial data in 5 cycles. The baseline model was trained by 1.the primary data, 2.the primary data with random augmentation, 3.the primary data with AutoAugment approach which is introduced in [4] and 4.the primary data with the SCNN. The results are shown in Fig. 8c, after epoch 150 we retrain our network with generated adversarial data and primary data, as a result we firstly observed a decrease in the accuracy after epoch 150. The final accuracy of these approaches is shown in Table 3. Figure 6 illustrates synthesizing a hard sample by applying gradient descent on the trainable parameters of the differentiable grid, where the generated sample is finally predicted correctly, but with less confidence. So we can see that after multiple cycles, the label of the adversarial data may still be predicted correctly.

Fig. 7. Data manipulation based on differentiable grid on Cifar10 sample data

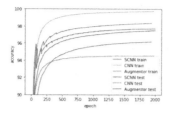

(a) Online Strategy for limited
MNIST dataset

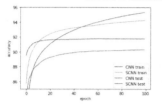 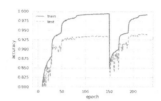

(b) Offline Strategy for (c) Online Strategy for Cifar10
Fashion-MNIST dataset dataset

Fig. 8. Performance of SCNN for different datasets

Table 1. Test accuracy of different approaches on the Limited MINST(1000 train data)

Network Type	Test accuracy(online strategy)	Test accuracy(offline strategy)
Baseline	94.26	94.26
Baseline + Augmentor	96.20	96.64
Baseline + SCNN	97.63	**98.25**

Table 2. Test accuracy of CNN baseline model and SCNN on the Fashion MNIST dataset

Network Type	Test accuracy(online strategy)	Test accuracy(offline strategy)
Baseline CNN	90.11	90.11
Baseline + Augmentor	90.54	90.74
SCNN	91.03	**91.45**

Table 3. Test accuracy of different approaches on the Cifar10 dataset

Network Type	Test accuracy
Resnet18	89.2
Resnet18 + Random Augmentation	93.3
Resnet18 + AutoAugment	93.83
Resnet18 + SCNN	**94.11**

6 Conclusion and Future Work

We introduced a new approach for generating harder samples for DNNs. An SCNN contains two sub-networks, an embedded network, and a synthesizer network. We also proposed three differentiable image manipulator components which parameters can be learned in a way that can transfer a sample to the boundary of its true label and its nearest wrong label. We observed that the accuracy and the robustness of SCNNs are improved in comparison with their baseline models. As a future work, this approach can be extended by designing differentiable manipulator components for other types of input data, such as texts, graphs, and voice.

References

1. Antoniou, A., Storkey, A., Edwards, H.: Data augmentation generative adversarial networks. arXiv preprint arXiv:1711.04340 (2017)
2. Bloice, M.D., Stocker, C., Holzinger, A.: Augmentor: an image augmentation library for machine learning. arXiv preprint arXiv:1708.04680 (2017)
3. Bowles, C., et al.: Gan augmentation: augmenting training data using generative adversarial networks. arXiv preprint arXiv:1810.10863 (2018)
4. Cubuk, E.D., Zoph, B., Mané, D., Vasudevan, V., Le, Q.V.: Autoaugment: learning augmentation strategies from data. In: IEEE/CVF Conference on Computer Vision and Pattern Recognition (CVPR), pp. 113–123 (2019)
5. Fawzi, A., Samulowitz, H., Turaga, D., Frossard, P.: Adaptive data augmentation for image classification. In: IEEE International Conference on Image Processing (ICIP), pp. 3688–3692. IEEE (2016)
6. Goodfellow, I., et al.: Generative adversarial nets. In: Advances in neural information processing systems, pp. 2672–2680 (2014)
7. Goodfellow, T.S., Zaremba, W., Ian, V.C.: Improved techniques for training gans. arXiv preprint arXiv:1606.03498 (2016)
8. Jaderberg, M., et al.: Spatial transformer networks. In: Advances in Neural Information Processing Systems, pp. 2017–2025 (2015)
9. LeCun, Y., Bottou, L., Bengio, Y., Haffner, P.: Gradient-based learning applied to document recognition. Proc. IEEE **86**(11), 2278–2324 (1998)
10. Nielsen, C., Okoniewski, M.: Gan data augmentation through active learning inspired sample acquisition. In: Proceedings of the IEEE Conference on Computer Vision and Pattern Recognition Workshops, pp. 109–112 (2019)
11. O'Gara, S., McGuinness, K.: Comparing data augmentation strategies for deep image classification. IMVIP 2019: Irish Machine Vision & Image Processing (2019)
12. Peng, X., Tang, Z., Yang, F., Feris, R.S., Metaxas, D.: Jointly optimize data augmentation and network training: adversarial data augmentation in human pose estimation. In: Proceedings of the IEEE Conference on Computer Vision and Pattern Recognition, pp. 2226–2234 (2018)
13. Shorten, C., Khoshgoftaar, T.M.: A survey on image data augmentation for deep learning. J. Big Data **6**(1), 60 (2019)
14. Shrivastava, A., Gupta, A., Girshick, R.: Training region-based object detectors with online hard example mining. In: Proceedings of the IEEE Conference on Computer Vision and Pattern Recognition, pp. 761–769 (2016)
15. Uijlings, J.R., Van De Sande, K.E., Gevers, T., Smeulders, A.W.: Selective search for object recognition. Int. J. Comput. Vis. **104**(2), 154–171 (2013)

A Novel Contractive GAN Model for a Unified Approach Towards Blind Quality Assessment of Images from Heterogeneous Sources

Tan Lu$^{(\boxtimes)}$ (ID) and Ann Dooms (ID)

Department of Mathematics and Data Science,
Vrije Universiteit Brussel, Brussels, Belgium
{tan.lu,ann.dooms}@vub.be

Abstract. The heterogeneous distributions of pixel intensities between natural scene and document images casts challenges for generalizing quality assessment models across these two types of images, where human perceptual scores and optical character recognition accuracy are the respective quality metrics. In this paper we propose a novel contractive generative adversarial model to learn a unified quality-aware representation of images from heterogeneous sources in a latent domain. We then build a unified image quality assessment framework by applying a regressor in the unveiled latent domain, where the regressor operates as if it is assessing the quality of a single type of images. Test results on blur distortion across three benchmarking datasets show that the proposed model achieves promising performance competitive to the state-of-the-art simultaneously for natural scene and document images.

Keywords: Contractive generative adversarial learning ·
Heterogeneous sources · Unified blind image quality assessment

1 Introduction

The rapid development in digital and mobile technologies led to massive creation, processing and communication of digital images, where the majority of them are either natural scene images (NSIs), mostly published on the Internet using mobile applications such as Instagram, Facebook or Wechat [3], or document images (DIs) that are mainly produced in digitization projects for preservation of legacy books or manuscripts [1]. During image capturing and processing [15], the content of a digital image can easily get distorted in the aforementioned scenarios. Therefore image quality assessment (IQA), which studies the objective evaluation of the quality of a given image, has attracted much attention.

This research is supported by the Auditing Digitisation Outputs in the Cultural Heritage Sector (ADOCHS) project (Contract No. BR/154/A6/ADOCHS), financed by the Belgian Science Policy (Belspo) within the scope of the BRAIN programme and by funding from the Flemish Government under the "Onderzoeksprogramma Artificiële Intelligentie (AI) Vlaanderen" programme.

© Springer Nature Switzerland AG 2020
G. Bebis et al. (Eds.): ISVC 2020, LNCS 12509, pp. 27–38, 2020.
https://doi.org/10.1007/978-3-030-64556-4_3

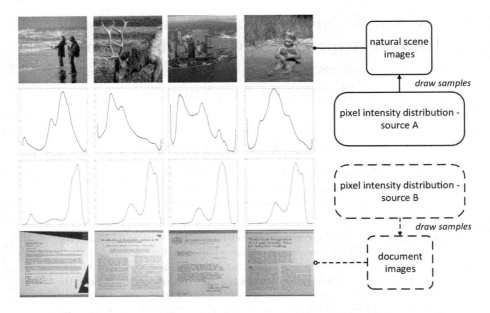

Fig. 1. NSIs and DIs drawn from two heterogeneous sources.

In particular, human perceptual scores (e.g. differential mean opinion score or DMOS) and optical character recognition (OCR) accuracy are widely used as the quality metrics for NSIs and DIs respectively.

Recent advances have seen encouraging performance from deep convolutional neural network (DCNN) based no-reference (NR) IQA models for NSIs [2,5,7,13]. Kim *et al.* [7] proposed to extract quality-aware feature maps using an 8-layered CNN module. By regressing the extracted features onto an objective error map, the volume of the training space is increased to exploit the vast learning capacity of deep models. Bosse *et al.* [2] developed a DCNN based IQA model which can operate in both an full-reference (FR) and NR manner. Their network comprises of mainly 12 weight layers organized in a feature extraction and a regression module. A survey on DCNN based IQA models for NSIs is provided in [8]. Similar performances are also reported for document IQA (DIQA) [6,11,19]. Li *et al.* [11] proposed an attention based approach where CNN and RNN (recurrent neural network) are integrated to form an interactive glimpse-action mechanism. Attention of the model is automatically directed to text regions where a series of glimpse patches are extracted for quality evaluation. Transfer learning has also been applied for DIQA [16], where we exploited the knowledge learned on NSI classification towards document quality assessment.

A unified NR IQA (UIQA) model is necessary whenever a mix of different types of images or images with mixed content are presented for quality assessment. One such example concerns large-scale digitization of mixed files (such as photos, newspapers, pages containing both texts and photos, etc.). A quality check is required to monitor these digitization processes, where existing

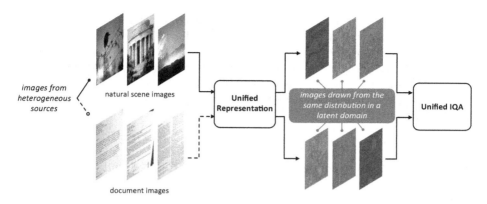

Fig. 2. Generalization of images from heterogeneous sources towards a unified representation.

content-specific (e.g. NSI) IQA models fall short to present reliable assessment when exposed to images with unknown content (e.g. documents). Another example is given by new mobile applications which extract information-of-interest from images with mixed content (e.g. for bookkeeping). These will also greatly benefit from a unified model for quality assessment before their processing.

As depicted in Fig. 1, NSIs and DIs come with different distributions, which can be seen as samples drawn from two heterogeneous sources. This hampers the straight-forward development of content-independent IQA models which can operate on different types of images in a unified manner. We recently proposed a UIQA model using a DCNN network [17], where NSIs and DIs are regressed to their quality scores simultaneously. However, a proper generalization across different types of images is currently still missing.

In this paper we propose a novel contractive generative adversarial model to generalize NSIs and DIs in a latent domain. This allows us to learn a common quality-aware representation of these two types of images, where the generalized images can be viewed as samples drawn from the same distribution, as demonstrated in Fig. 2. Unified quality assessment is then performed in the latent domain, where the IQA model operates as if it is processing a single type of images.

2 Contractive Generative Adversarial Learning for Unified Quality Assessment

2.1 Formulation

Consider a compact space $\mathcal{X}$ in $\mathbb{R}^n$. Let $\mathbb{F}$ be a set of bounded measurable functions defined on $\mathcal{X}$ such that $f \in \mathbb{F} : \mathcal{X} \to \mathcal{X}$. Let $\mathbb{P}$ be a set of measurable probability distributions on $\mathcal{X}$. We define a domain $\mathcal{X}_D$ as a subspace of $\mathcal{X}$ which can be characterized using $p_D \in \mathbb{P}$. That is, the points $x_D \in \mathcal{X}_D$ can be seen as samples drawn from the distribution p_D.

Given two domains $\mathcal{X}_A$ and $\mathcal{X}_B$ with heterogeneous distributions p_A and p_B, we wish to find $\mathcal{X}_l$ with distribution p_l such that for all $x_a \in \mathcal{X}_A$ and $x_b \in \mathcal{X}_B$, $f_l(x_a), f_l(x_b) \in \mathcal{X}_l$, where $f_l \in \mathbb{F}$. The latent domain $\mathcal{X}_l$ therefore serves as a unified representation of $\mathcal{X}_A$ and $\mathcal{X}_B$, where samples $f_l(x_a), f_l(x_b)$ representing original heterogeneous sources are now drawn from the same distribution p_l.

To solve for the function f_l to unveil the latent domain $\mathcal{X}_l$, we consider a distance measure d:

$$d_{p,q\in\mathbb{P}}(f) = \max_{k\in 1,2,\dots} \left| \mathbb{E}_{x\sim p} f^k(x) - \mathbb{E}_{x\sim q} f^k(x) \right|, \tag{1}$$

where $p, q \in \mathbb{P}$ characterize two known domains in $\mathcal{X}$, $f \in \mathbb{F}$ and k is a positive integer to specify the order of the moment to be matched in the latent domain. Given a set of samples $\{x_a^i\}$ and $\{x_b^j\}$ from domains $\mathcal{X}_A$ and $\mathcal{X}_B$, where $i = 1, 2, \dots, M$ and $j = 1, 2, \dots, N$, we can learn the function f_l by minimizing an empirical evaluation of $d(f)$:

$$\min_{f} d_{p_A,p_B\in\mathbb{P}}(f)$$

$$= \min_{f} \max_{k\in 1,2,\dots} \left| \frac{1}{M} \sum_{i=1}^{M} f^k(x_a^i) - \frac{1}{N} \sum_{j=1}^{N} f^k(x_b^j) \right|. \tag{2}$$

Given a measurable function f, (2) can be applied to learn f_l using standard techniques such as back-propagation. Specifically, f is updated such that the two distributions, where samples $\{f(x_a^i)\}$ and $\{f(x_b^j)\}$ are drawn, are pulled towards each other through moment matching (at some arbitrarily high order). Note that a direct solution to (2) is intractable, and one may therefore put a constraint on k to obtain an approximated f_l such that the distributions of samples mapped from different sources are matched to a certain order. Alternatively, we propose contractive generative adversarial learning to derive a non-degenerated solution to (2). In particular, we solve the following optimization problem:

$$f_l = \arg\min_{f} \max_{D} \Big\{ \mathbb{E}_{x\sim p_B} \{\log[D(f(x))]\} +$$

$$\mathbb{E}_{x\sim p_A} \{\log[1 - D(f(x))]\} \Big\}, \tag{3}$$

where $D : \mathcal{X} \to [0,1]$ is a real-valued function. (3) is an extension to the original GAN, where functions D and f can be seen as the discriminator and generator [4]. Note that given a bounded space $\mathcal{X}$, we can always impose weights decay on the network to ensure that f is bounded. We now show that solving the optimization in (3) gives a non-degenerated solution f_l to (2).

Let p'_A, p'_B be the generator's distributions over domains $\mathcal{X}_A$ and $\mathcal{X}_B$ respectively, the optimal discriminator D_{opt} can be obtained by the max-game of (3):

$$\max_{D} \Big\{ \mathbb{E}_{x\sim p'_B} \{\log[D(x)]\} + \mathbb{E}_{x\sim p'_A} \{\log[1 - D(x)]\} \Big\}$$

$$= \max_{D} \int [p'_B log(D(x)) + p'_A log(1 - D(x))] dx$$

from which it is straightforward to show that:

$$D_{\mathrm{opt}}(x) = \frac{p'_B}{p'_A + p'_B}. \tag{4}$$

With the optimal discriminator D_{opt}, we solve the min-game for f_l:

$$\min_{f} \left\{ \mathop{\mathbb{E}}_{x \sim p'_B} \{\log[D_{\mathrm{opt}}(x)]\} + \mathop{\mathbb{E}}_{x \sim p'_A} \{\log[1 - D_{\mathrm{opt}}(x)]\} \right\}$$

$$= \min_{f} \left\{ \mathop{\mathbb{E}}_{x \sim p'_B} \{\log[\frac{p'_B}{p'_A + p'_B}]\} + \mathop{\mathbb{E}}_{x \sim p'_A} \{\log[\frac{p'_A}{p'_A + p'_B}]\} \right\},$$

where the minimum is achieved only when

$$p'_A = p'_B. \tag{5}$$

When an optimal generator f_l is achieved, the distributions of the variables $f_l(x)$ and $f_l(x)$ completely match each other, which gives a minimum $d(f)$:
$$\scriptstyle x \in \mathcal{X}_A \qquad x \in \mathcal{X}_B$$

$$\mathop{d}_{p_A, p_B}(f)|_{f=f_l} = \mathop{max}_{k \in 1,2,\dots} \left| \mathop{\mathbb{E}}_{x \sim p_A} f^k(x) - \mathop{\mathbb{E}}_{x \sim p_B} f^k(x) \right|,$$

$$= \mathop{max}_{k \in 1,2,\dots} \left| \int [x^k p'_A - x^k p'_B] dx \right|$$

$$= 0$$

A major difference between (3) and GAN is that, the generator tries to fool the discriminator both on 'true' and 'false' samples in the min-max game. Hence the model not only pulls the distribution of domain $\mathcal{X}_A$ towards that of domain $\mathcal{X}_B$, but also pulls the distribution of domain $\mathcal{X}_B$ towards that of domain $\mathcal{X}_A$. That is, we are learning a contractive mapping in the probability space $\mathbb{P}$:

$$d(f(p_A,)f(p_B)) \le \alpha d(p_A, p_B), \tag{6}$$

where d is a measure of the distance between p_A and p_B. The function f is optimized in the training process in such a way that its Lipschitz constant α is progressively reduced towards zero, while the model converges to f_l. As such, we refer to (3) as a contractive GAN (C-GAN).

2.2 A Unified Blind Image Quality Assessment Model Using C-GAN

We apply C-GAN to learn a quality-aware unified representation of NSIs and DIs, where the generalized image samples corresponding to NSIs and DIs in the latent domain are regressed towards their respective quality scores. Hence the model always presents a reliable quality prediction, which represents either perceptual score (if the input is NSI) or OCR error rate (if the input is DI). The main structure of the model is depicted in Fig. 3 and the objective is:

$$\min_{R,f} \max_{D} \left\{ \mathbb{E}_{x \sim p_B} \{\log[D(f(x))]\} + \mathbb{E}_{x \sim p_A} \{\log[1 - D(f(x))]\} \right.$$
$$\left. + \mathbb{E}_{x \sim p_A} \{|R(f(x)) - t_A|\} + \mathbb{E}_{x \sim p_B} \{|R(f(x)) - t_B|\} \right\}, \tag{7}$$

where t_A and t_B are the ground-truth quality scores for NSIs and DIs respectively and R denotes the regressor which assumes a standard structure as presented in Fig. 3. For the generator and the discriminators, we adopt the structure proposed in [23]. Furthermore, we introduce quality discriminators with the following objective [14]:

$$\max_{D_A} \left\{ \mathbb{E}_{x \sim p_A} \{\log[1 - |D_A(f(x)) - \sigma(x)|]\} \right\} +$$
$$\max_{D_B} \left\{ \mathbb{E}_{x \sim p_B} \{\log[1 - |D_B(f(x)) - \sigma(x)|]\} \right\}, \tag{8}$$

where

$$\sigma(x) = \begin{cases} 1, & \text{if } |R(x) - t| \le \epsilon \\ 0, & \text{otherwise} \end{cases} \tag{9}$$

serves as quality reinforcement in the latent domain.

3   Experiments

We conduct tests using benchmark NSI and DI IQA datasets, namely CSIQ [10], LIVE [21], and the SOC [9] datasets.

(1) *CSIQ dataset:* this dataset contains 866 quality impaired images generated from 30 reference images using six types of distortions at four to five different levels. Specifically, JPEG compression, JPEG-2000 compression, global contrast decrements, additive pink Gaussian noise (APGN), additive white Gaussian noise and Gaussian blurring are simulated in the dataset.

(2) *LIVE dataset:* 982 images are generated from 29 high-resolution pristine images, where five different types of distortions, namely JPEG compression, JPEG-2000 compression, additive white Gaussian noise (AWGN), Gaussian blurring and transmission error simulated using a fast-fading (FF) Rayleigh channel, each with different levels of severity, are simulated.

(3) *SOC dataset:* there are 175 document images with high resolution of 1840 × 3264. These images are grouped into 25 sets, where each set contains 6 to 8 pictures taken from the same document. By adjusting the focal distance during the digitization process, different levels of focal-blur were introduced when creating the images. Three different types of OCR engines (namely ABBYY FineReader, Tesseract and Omnipage) were used during the OCR accuracy evaluation process, where ABBYY FineReader demonstrated the best performance [9].

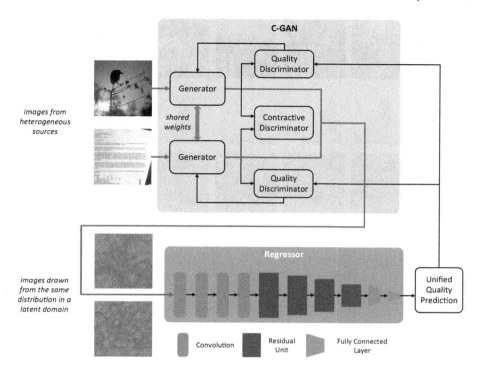

Fig. 3. Structure of the proposed UIQA model using contractive GAN (C-GAN). In our implementation, only one generator is used to simultaneously map NSIs and DIs into a latent domain, where the distributions of these two types of images are contracted towards each other. The image samples in the latent domain are then fed into a quality regressor, which operates as if image samples drawn from a same distribution are being processed. Note that the proposed UIQA model preserves the correct quality information for different types of images. That is, the output quality prediction represents a perceptual score (DMOS) when a NSI is presented to the model. On the other hand, when a DI is fed into the model, the output quality score represents a OCR error rate prediction.

For natural scene images from CSIQ and LIVE datasets, the default DMOS scores are used as quality labels. For document images, we use the OCR error rate $\beta_{doc_i} = 1 - \alpha_{doc_i}$ as the quality label for image i, where α_{doc_i} is the OCR accuracy (obtained based on the ABBYY FineReader OCR output) of the image. When preparing training and testing samples from the images, overlapping patches of 256×256 are extracted, where stride is set to 128×128.

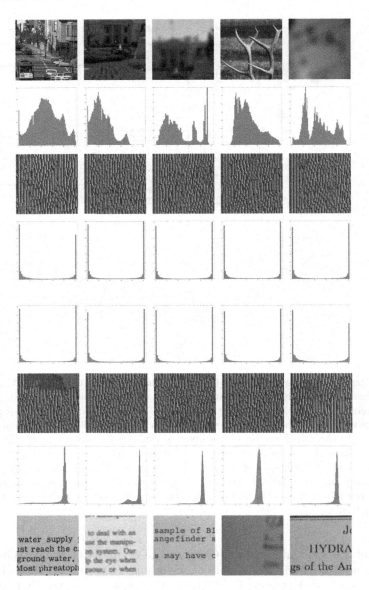

Fig. 4. A visual evaluation of the proposed UIQA model using C-GAN. The top and bottom rows represent NSI and DI patches which are fed into the UIQA model. The distributions of the gray-scale intensity of these patches are depicted immediately in the rows below/above. It can be seen that the distributions from NSIs and DIs are distinctively different. The corresponding contracted samples in the latent domain are depicted (in the rows below/above the distributions of the NSI and DI image patches), together with their respective distributions (in the middle two rows). The C-GAN operates to contract the distributions of these two types of images such that the samples in the latent domain appear to have similar characteristics and distributions, as if they were drawn from a same source.

Table 1. Performance of the proposed UIQA model.

IQA Models	CSIQ		SOC	
	PLCC	SRCC	PLCC	SRCC
BLIINDS2 [20]	-	0.880	N.A.	
DIQA [7]	-	0.870		
CORNIA [22]	-	0.854		
NRSL [12]	-	**0.896**		
CNN [6]	N.A.		0.950	0.898
CNN [11]			0.926	0.857
RNN [11]			**0.956**	0.916
LDA [18]			-	0.913
Sparse Model [19]			0.935	**0.928**
Proposed method	0.92	0.89	0.932	0.916

Note that document images from the SOC dataset only contains blur distortions, hence we only consider Gaussian blur on CSIQ and LIVE datasets in our experiments (such that the emphasis is put on generalizing across images from heterogeneous sources, and that the evaluation is not affected by unbalanced noise types). Meanwhile, the proposed UIQA model preserves the correct image quality information in a unified framework. That is, the model processes NSIs and DIs blindly and uniformly without having to distinguish these two types of images from each other. Nevertheless, the outputs of the model is content-aware with respect to the inputs. Specifically, when a NSI is presented to the UIQA model, the output number is a perceptual score (i.e. DMOS). On the other hand, OCR error rate is predicted when a DI is fed into the model.

We first test the performance of the UIQA model under a CSIQ+SOC configuration, where the proposed UIQA model is trained using an Adam optimizer for 20 epochs, before being tested simultaneously on NSIs and DIs. We adopt the commonly used Pearson's linear correlation coefficient (PLCC) and Spearman's rank correlation coefficient (SRCC) as performance metrics. The random split is repeated 10 times and median PLCC and SRCC are reported in Table 1, while a visual evaluation of the model is presented Fig. 4.

It can be seen that the proposed UIQA model achieves promising results, where the performance is competitive to the state-of-the-art simultaneously on natural scene and document images. Meanwhile, within the UIQA model itself, balanced performances on the two types of images are observed. This suggests a good generalization in the latent domain, where the contracted samples exhibit similar characteristics and distributions. Indeed, as shown in Fig. 4, the unified representation learned in the latent domain presents homogeneous samples for the IQA model, which then operates as if it is evaluating quality from the same type of images.

Table 2. Cross-dataset test of the proposed UIQA model.

IQA Models	LIVE	
	PLCC	SRCC
BLIINDS2 [20]	-	0.915
DIQA [7]	-	**0.962**
CORNIA [22]	-	0.957
NRSL [12]	-	0.808
Proposed method	0.91	0.952

We further conduct a cross-dataset evaluation, where the UIQA model trained under CSIQ + SOC configuration is tested on the LIVE [21] dataset. Compared to state-of-the-art results reported on LIVE, the proposed model also performs competitively as shown in Table 2. This further demonstrates the generalization capacity of the proposed model, where the quality information learned on CSIQ + SOC configuration can be effectively cross-applied on the LIVE dataset.

4 Conclusion

The heterogeneous distributions of different types of images cast challenges for the development of UIQA models which are required when mixed images are to be processed in a blind and unified manner. In this paper we formulate a novel contractive GAN model, which operates to contract two different types of distributions towards each other in a latent domain. This helps to learn a unified representation of images from heterogeneous sources, where the generalized images can be seen as samples drawn from a single distribution in the latent domain.

We further develop a UIQA framework based on the proposed C-GAN model, where NSIs and DIs are first processed by the C-GAN model to derive a unified representation. The generalized image samples are then fed into a quality regressor, which operates as if it is processing images of a same type. In the meanwhile, the outputs of the UIQA framework are content-aware with respect to the inputs, where perceptual scores and OCR error rates are predicted for NSIs and DIs respectively. The performance of the proposed UIQA model is first tested with respect to Gaussian blur under a CSIQ+SOC configuration, where promising results are obtained simultaneously on NSIs and DIs. Meanwhile, a balanced performance is observed within the UIQA framework on these two types of images. This indicates that a good generalization across these two types of images is achieved in the latent domain. We further conducted a cross-dataset evaluation, where the UIQA model trained under the CSIQ+SOC configuration is applied on images from the LIVE dataset. Test results show that the UIQA framework performs consistently when cross-applied on the LIVE dataset.

We conclude that the proposed model performs competitively to the state-of-the-art simultaneously on NSIs and DIs, and that a proper generalization across these two types of images is achieved using the proposed C-GAN model. This encourages future work on contractive generative adversarial learning.

References

1. Antonacopoulos, A., Downton, A.C.: Special issue on the analysis of historical documents. Int. J. Doc. Anal. Recogn. **9**, 75–77 (2007)
2. Bosse, S., Maniry, D., Müller, K.R., Wiegand, T., Samek, W.: Deep neural networks for no-reference and full-reference image quality assessment. IEEE Trans. Image Process. **27**, 206–219 (2018)
3. Cai, H., Li, L., Yi, Z., Gang, M.: Towards a blind image quality evaluator using multi-scale second-order statistics. Signal Process. Image Commun. **71**, 88–99 (2019)
4. Goodfellow, I.J., et al.: Generative adversarial nets. In: Proceedings 27th International Conference on Neural Information Processing Systems, pp. 2672–2680 (2014)
5. Kang, L., Ye, P., Li, Y., Doermann, D.: Convolutional neural networks for no-reference image quality assessment. In: Proceedings 27th IEEE Conference on Computer Vision and Pattern Recognition, pp. 1733–1740 (2014)
6. Kang, L., Ye, P., Li, Y., Doermann, D.: A deep learning approach to document image quality assessment. In: Proceedings 2014 IEEE International Conference on Image Processing (ICIP), pp. 2570–2574 (2014)
7. Kim, J., Nguyen, A.D., Lee, S.: Deep cnn-based blind image quality predictor. IEEE Trans. Neural Netw. Learn. Syst. **30**, 11–24 (2019)
8. Kim, J., Zeng, H., Ghadiyaram, D., Lee, S., Zhang, L., Bovik, A.C.: Deep convolutional neural models for picture-quality prediction challenges and solutions to data-driven image quality assessment. IEEE Signal Process. Mag. **34**, 130–141 (2017)
9. Kumar, J., Ye, P., Doermann, D.: A dataset for quality assessment of camera captured document images. In: Iwamura, M., Shafait, F. (eds.) CBDAR 2013. LNCS, vol. 8357, pp. 113–125. Springer, Cham (2014). https://doi.org/10.1007/978-3-319-05167-3_9
10. Larson, E.C., Chandler, D.M.: Most apparent distortion: full-reference image quality assessment and the role of strategy. J. Electron. Imaging **19**, 011006-1–011006-21 (2010)
11. Li, P., Peng, L., Cai, J., Ding, X., Ge, S.: Attention based rnn model for document image quality assessment. In: Proceedings 2017 14th IAPR International Conference on Document Analysis and Recognition (ICDAR), pp. 819–825 (2017)
12. Li, Q., Lin, W., Xu, J., Fang, Y.: Blind image quality assessment using statistical structural and luminance features. IEEE Trans. Multimedia **21**, 3339–3352 (2013)
13. Li, Y., Po, L.M., Feng, L., Yuan, F.: No-reference image quality assessment with deep convolutional neural networks. In: Proceedings IEEE International Conference on Digital Signal Processing, pp. 685–689 (2016)
14. Lin, K.Y., Wang, G.: Hallucinated-iqa: no-reference image quality assessment via adversarial learning. In: Proceedings IEEE/CVF Conference on Computer Vision and Pattern Recognition, pp. 732–741 (2018)

15. Liu, L., Liu, B., Huang, H., Bovik, A.C.: No-reference image quality assessment based on spatial and spectral entropies. Signal Process. Image Commun. **29**, 856–863 (2014)
16. Lu, T., Dooms, A.: A deep transfer learning approach to document image quality assessment. In: Proceedings International Conference on Document Analysis and Recognition (ICDAR), pp. 1372–1377 (2019)
17. Lu, T., Dooms, A.: Towards content independent no-reference image quality assessment using deep learning. In: Proceedings IEEE 4th International Conference on Image, Vision and Computing (ICIVC), pp. 276–280 (2019)
18. Peng, X., Cao, H., Natarajan, P.: Document image ocr accuracy prediction via latent dirichlet allocation. In: Proceedings 13th International Conference on Document Analysis and Recognition (ICDAR), pp. 771–775 (2015)
19. Peng, X., Cao, H., Natarajan, P.: Document image quality assessment using discriminative sparse representation. In: Proceedings 12th IAPR Workshop on Document Analysis Systems (DAS), pp. 227–232 (2016)
20. Saad, M.A., Bovik, A.C., Charrier, C.: Blind image quality assessment - a natural scene statistics approach in the dct domain. IEEE Trans. Image Process. **21**, 3339–3352 (2013)
21. Sheikh, H.R., Wang, Z., Cormack, L., Bovik, A.C.: Live image quality assessment database release 2, http://live.ece.utexas.edu/research/quality
22. Ye, P., Kumar, J., Kang, L., Doermann, D.: Unsupervised feature learning framework for no-reference image quality assessment. In: Proceedings IEEE Conference on Computer Vision and Pattern Recognition, pp. 1098–1105 (2012)
23. Zhu, J.Y., Park, T., Isola, P., Efros, A.A.: Unpaired image-to-image translation using cycle-consistent adversarial networks. In: Proceedings IEEE International Conference on Computer Vision (ICCV), pp. 2242–2251 (2017)

Nonconvex Regularization for Network Slimming: Compressing CNNs Even More

Kevin Bui[1], Fredrick Park[2], Shuai Zhang[1], Yingyong Qi[1], and Jack Xin[1(✉)]

[1] Department of Mathematics, University of California, Irvine,
Irvine, CA 92697, USA
{kevinb3,szhang3,yqi,jack.xin}@uci.edu
[2] Department of Mathematics and Computer Science,
Whittier College, Whittier 90602, CA, USA
fpark@whittier.edu

Abstract. In the last decade, convolutional neural networks (CNNs) have evolved to become the dominant models for various computer vision tasks, but they cannot be deployed in low-memory devices due to its high memory requirement and computational cost. One popular, straightforward approach to compressing CNNs is network slimming, which imposes an ℓ_1 penalty on the channel-associated scaling factors in the batch normalization layers during training. In this way, channels with low scaling factors are identified to be insignificant and are pruned in the models. In this paper, we propose replacing the ℓ_1 penalty with the ℓ_p and transformed ℓ_1 (Tℓ_1) penalties since these nonconvex penalties outperformed ℓ_1 in yielding sparser satisfactory solutions in various compressed sensing problems. In our numerical experiments, we demonstrate network slimming with ℓ_p and Tℓ_1 penalties on VGGNet and Densenet trained on CIFAR 10/100. The results demonstrate that the nonconvex penalties compress CNNs better than ℓ_1. In addition, Tℓ_1 preserves the model accuracy after channel pruning, and $\ell_{1/2,3/4}$ yield compressed models with similar accuracies as ℓ_1 after retraining.

Keywords: Convolutional neural networks · Sparse optimization · ℓ_1 regularization · ℓ_p regularization · Batch normalization · Channel pruning · Nonconvex optimization

1 Introduction

In the past years, convolutional neural networks (CNNs) evolved into superior models for various computer vision tasks, such as image classification [18,26,41] and image segmentation [10,32,38]. Unfortunately, training a highly accurate CNN is computationally demanding. State-of-the-art CNNs such as Resnet [18] can have up to at least a hundred layers and thus require millions of parameters to train and billions of floating-point-operations to execute. Consequently, deploying CNNs in low-memory devices, such as mobile smartphones, is difficult, making their real-world applications limited.

To make CNNs more practical, many works proposed several different directions to compress large CNNs or to learn smaller, more efficient models from scratch. These directions include low-rank approximation [13,23,45–47], weight quantization [11,12,27,53,59], and weight pruning [1,16,19,28]. One popular direction is to

ⓒ Springer Nature Switzerland AG 2020
G. Bebis et al. (Eds.): ISVC 2020, LNCS 12509, pp. 39–53, 2020.
https://doi.org/10.1007/978-3-030-64556-4_4

sparsify the CNN while training it [2,6,39,44]. Sparsity can be imposed on various types of structures existing in CNNs, such as filters and channels [44].

One interesting yet straightforward approach in sparsifying CNNs was *network slimming* [31]. This method imposes ℓ_1 regularization on the scaling factors in the batch normalization layers. Due to ℓ_1 regularization, scaling factors corresponding to insignificant channels are pushed towards zeroes, narrowing down the important channels to retain, while the CNN model is being trained. Once the insignificant channels are pruned, the compressed model may need to be retrained since pruning can degrade its original accuracy. Overall, network slimming yields a compressed model with low run-time memory and number of computing operations.

In this paper, we propose replacing ℓ_1 regularization in network slimming with an alternative nonconvex regularization that promotes better sparsity. Because the ℓ_1 norm is a convex relaxation of the ℓ_0 norm, a better penalty would be nonconvex and it would interpolate ℓ_0 and ℓ_1. Considering these properties, we examine ℓ_p [7,9,48] and transformed ℓ_1 ($T\ell_1$) [56,57] because of their superior performances in recovering satisfactory sparse solutions in various compressed sensing problems. Furthermore, both regularizers have explicit formulas for their subgradients, which allow us to directly perform subgradient descent [40].

2   Related Works

2.1   Compression Techniques for CNNs

Low-rank Decomposition. Denton *et al.* [13] compressed the weight tensors of convolutional layers using singular value decomposition to approximate them. Jaderberg *et al.* [23] exploited the redundancy between different feature channels and filters to approximate a full-rank filter bank in CNNs by combinations of a rank-one filter basis. These methods focus on decomposing pre-trained weight tensors. Wen *et al.* [45] proposed *force regularization* to train a CNN towards having a low-rank representation. Xu *et al.* [46,47] proposed trained rank pruning, an optimization scheme that incorporates low-rank decomposition into the training process. Trained rank pruning is further strengthened by nuclear norm regularization.

Weight Quantization. Quantization aims to represent weights with low-precision (≤ 8 bits arithmetic). The simplest form of quantization is binarization, constraining weights to only two values. Courbariaux *et al.* [12] proposed BinaryConnect, a method that trains deep neural networks (DNNs) with strictly binary weights. Neural networks with ternary weights have also been developed and investigated. Li *et al.* [27] proposed ternary weight networks, where the weights are only $-1, 0$, or $+1$. Zhu *et al.* [59] proposed Trained Ternary Quantization that constrains the weights to more general values $-W^n, 0$, and W^p, where W^n and W^p are parameters learned through the training process. For more general quantization, Yin *et al.* [53] proposed BinaryRelax, which relaxes the quantization constraint into a continuous regularizer for the optimization problem needed to be solved in CNNs.

Pruning. Han *et al.* [16] proposed a three-step framework to first train a CNN, prune weights if below a fixed threshold, and retrain the compressed CNN. Aghasi *et al.* [1]

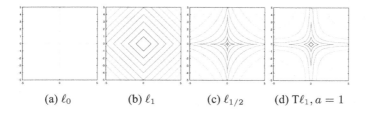

(a) ℓ_0 (b) ℓ_1 (c) $\ell_{1/2}$ (d) $T\ell_1, a = 1$

Fig. 1. Contour plots of sparse regularizers.

proposed using convex optimization to determine which weights to prune while preserving model accuracy. For CNNs, channel or filter pruning are preferred over individual weight pruning since the former significantly eliminates more unnecessary weights. Li *et al.* [28] calculated the sum of absolute weights for each filter of the CNN and pruned the filters with the lowest sums. On the other hand, Hu *et al.* [19] proposed a metric that measures the redundancies in channels to determine which to prune. Network slimming [31] is also another method of channel pruning since it prunes channels with the lowest associated scaling factors.

Sparse Optimization. Sparse optimization methods aim to train DNNs towards a compressed structure from scratch by introducing a sparse regularization term to the objective function being minimized. BinaryRelax [53] and network slimming [31] are examples of sparse optimization methods for CNNs. Alvarez and Salzmann [2] and Scardapane *et al.* [39] applied group lasso [55] and sparse group lasso [39] to CNNs to obtain group-sparse networks. Non-convex regularizers have also been examined recently. Xue and Xin [51] applied ℓ_0 and transformed ℓ_1 to three-layer CNNs that classify shaky vs. normal handwriting. Ma *et al.* [36] proposed integrated $T\ell_1$, which combines group sparsity and $T\ell_1$, and applied it to CNNs for image classification.

2.2 Regularization Penalty

Let $x = (x_1, \ldots, x_n) \in \mathbb{R}^n$. The ℓ_1 penalty is described by

$$\|x\|_1 = \sum_{i=1}^{n} |x_i|, \tag{1}$$

while the ℓ_0 penalty is described by

$$\|x\|_0 = \sum_{i=1}^{n} \mathbb{1}_{\{x_i \neq 0\}}, \quad \text{where} \quad \mathbb{1}_{\{z \neq 0\}} = \begin{cases} 1 & \text{if } z \neq 0 \\ 0 & \text{if } z = 0. \end{cases} \tag{2}$$

Although ℓ_1 regularization is popular in sparse optimization in various applications such as compressed sensing [3,4,54] and compressive imaging [24,35], it may not actually yield the sparsest solution [7,33,34,48,57]. Moreover, it is sensitive to outliers and it may yield biased solutions [15].

A nonconvex alternative to the ℓ_1 penalty is the ℓ_p penalty

$$\|x\|_p = \left(\sum_{i=1}^n |x_i|^p \right)^{1/p} \tag{3}$$

for $p \in (0,1)$. The ℓ_p penalty interpolates ℓ_0 and ℓ_1 because as $p \to 0^+$, we have $\ell_p \to \ell_0$, and as $p \to 1^-$, we have $\ell_p \to \ell_1$. It was shown to recover sparser solution than did ℓ_1 for certain compressed sensing problems [8,9]. Empirical studies [9,49] demonstrated that for $p \in [1/2, 1)$, as p decreases, the solution becomes sparser by ℓ_p minimization, but for $p \in (0, 1/2)$, the performance becomes no longer significant. In [50], $\ell_{1/2}$ was verified to be an unbiased estimator. Moreover, it demonstrated success in image deconvolution [5,25], hyperspectral unmixing [37], and image segmentation [29]. Numerically, in compressed sensing, a small value ϵ is added to x_i to avoid blowup in the subgradient when $x_i = 0$. In this work, we will examine across different values of p since ℓ_p regularization may work differently in deep learning than in other areas.

Lastly, the $T\ell_1$ penalty is formulated as

$$P_a(x) = \sum_{i=1}^n \frac{(a+1)|x_i|}{a + |x_i|} \tag{4}$$

for $a > 0$. $T\ell_1$ interpolates ℓ_0 and ℓ_1 because as $a \to 0^+$, we have $T\ell_1 \to \ell_0$, and as $a \to +\infty$, we have $T\ell_1 \to \ell_1$. This penalty enjoys three properties – unbiasedness, sparsity, and continuity – that a sparse regularizer should have [15]. The $T\ell_1$ penalty was demonstrated to be robust by outperforming ℓ_1 and ℓ_p in compressed sensing problems with both coherent and incoherent sensing matrices [56,57]. Additionally, the $T\ell_1$ penalty yields satisfactory, sparse solutions in matrix completion [58] and deep learning [36].

Figure 1 displays the contour plots of the aforementioned regularizers. With ℓ_1 regularization, the solution tends to coincide with one of the corners of the rotated squares, making it sparse. For $\ell_{1/2}$ and $T\ell_1$, the level lines are more curved compared to ℓ_1, which encourages the solutions to coincide with one of the corners. Hence, solutions tend to be sparser with $\ell_{1/2}$ and $T\ell_1$ regularization than with ℓ_1 regularization.

3   Proposed Method

3.1   Batch Normalization Layer

Batch normalization [22] has been instrumental in speeding the convergence and improving generalization of many deep learning models, especially CNNs [18,43]. In most state-of-the-arts CNNs, a convolutional layer is always followed by a batch normalization layer. Within a batch normalization layer, features generated by the preceding convolutional layer are normalized by their mean and variance within the same

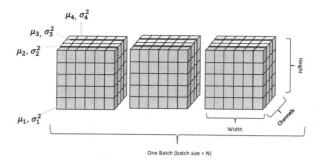

Fig. 2. Visualization of batch normalization on a feature map. The mean and variance of the values of the pixels of the same colors corresponding to the channels are computed and are used to normalize these pixels.

channel. Afterward, a linear transformation is applied to compensate for the loss of their representative abilities.

We mathematically describe the process of the batch normalization layer. First we suppose that we are working with 2D images. Let x be a feature computed by a convolutional layer. Its entry x_i is indexed by We define the index set $S_i = \{k : k_C = i_C\}$, where k_C and i_C are the respective subindices of k and i along the C axis. The mean μ_i and variance σ_i^2 are computed as follows:

$$\mu_i = \frac{1}{|S_i|} \sum_{k \in S_i} x_k, \quad \sigma_i^2 = \frac{1}{|S_i|} \sum_{k \in S_i} (x_k - \mu_i)^2 + \epsilon \tag{5}$$

for some small value $\epsilon > 0$, where $|\mathcal{A}|$ denotes the cardinality of the set $\mathcal{A}$. Then x is normalized as $\hat{x}_i = \frac{x_i - \mu_i}{\sigma_i}$ for each index i. In short, the mean and variance are computed from pixels of the same channel index, and these values are used to normalize these pixels. Visualization is provided in Fig. 2. Lastly, the output of the batch normalization layer is computed as a linear transformation of the normalized features:

$$y_i = \gamma_{i_C} \hat{x}_i + \beta_{i_C}, \tag{6}$$

where $\gamma_{i_C}, \beta_{i_C} \in \mathbb{R}$ are trainable parameters.

3.2 Network Slimming with Nonconvex Sparse Regularization

Since the scaling factors γ_{i_C}'s in (6) are associated with the channels of a convolutional layer, we aim to penalize them with a sparse regularizer in order to determine which channels are irrelevant to the compressed CNN model. Suppose we have a training dataset that consists of N input-output pairs $\{(x_i, y_i)\}_{i=1}^N$ and a CNN with L convolutional layers, where each is followed by a batch normalization layer. Then we have a set of vectors $\{(\gamma_l, \beta_l)\}_{l=1}^L$ for each layer l, where $\gamma_l = (\gamma_{l,1}, \ldots, \gamma_{l,C_l})$ and $\beta_l = (\beta_{l,1}, \ldots, \beta_{l,C_l})$ with C_l being the number of channels in the lth convolutional layer. Let W be the set of weight parameters such that $\{(\gamma_l, \beta_l)\}_{l=1}^L \subset W$. Hence, the

Table 1. Sparse regularizers and their subgradients.

Name	$\mathcal{R}(x)$	$\partial R(x)$
ℓ_1	$\|x\|_1 = \sum_{i=1}^{n} \|x_i\|$	$\partial\|x\|_1 = \left\{ z \in \mathbb{R}^n : z_i = \begin{cases} \operatorname{sgn}(x_i) & \text{if } x_i \neq 0 \\ z_i \in [-1,1] & \text{if } x_i = 0 \end{cases} \right\}$
ℓ_p	$\|x\|_p^p = \sum_{i=1}^{n} \|x_i\|^p$	$\partial\|x\|_p^p = \left\{ z \in \mathbb{R}^n : z_i = \begin{cases} \dfrac{p \cdot \operatorname{sgn}(x_i)}{\|x_i\|^{1-p}} & \text{if } x_i \neq 0 \\ z_i \in \mathbf{R} & \text{if } x_i = 0 \end{cases} \right\}$
$\mathrm{T}\ell_1$	$P_a(x) = \sum_{i=1}^{n} \dfrac{(a+1)\|x_i\|}{a + \|x_i\|}$	$\partial P_a(x) = \left\{ z \in \mathbb{R}^n : z_i = \begin{cases} \dfrac{a(a+1)\operatorname{sgn}(x_i)}{(a + \|x_i\|)^2} & \text{if } x_i \neq 0 \\ 0 & \text{if } x_i = 0 \end{cases} \right\}$

trainable parameters W of the CNN are learned by minimizing the following objective function:

$$\frac{1}{N}\sum_{i=1}^{N}\mathcal{L}(h(x_i,W),y_i) + \lambda\sum_{l=1}^{L}\mathcal{R}(\gamma_l), \tag{7}$$

where $h(\cdot,\cdot)$ is the output of the CNN used for prediction, $\mathcal{L}(\cdot,\cdot)$ is a loss function, $\mathcal{R}(\cdot)$ is a sparse regularizer, and $\lambda > 0$ is a regularization parameter for $\mathcal{R}(\cdot)$. When $\mathcal{R}(\cdot) = \|\cdot\|_1$, we have the original network slimming method. As mentioned earlier, since ℓ_1 regularization may not yield the sparsest solution, we investigate the method with a nonconvex regularizer, where $\mathcal{R}(\cdot)$ is $\|\cdot\|_p^p$ or $P_a(\cdot)$. To minimize (7) in general, stochastic gradient descent is applied to the first term while subgradient descent is applied to the second term [40]. Subgradients of the regularizers are presented in Table 1. After the CNN is trained, channels with low scaling factors are pruned, leaving us with a compressed model.

4   Experiments

We apply the proposed nonconvex network slimming with ℓ_p and $\mathrm{T}\ell_1$ regularization on CIFAR 10/100 datasets on VGGNet [41] and Densenet [20]. Code for the experiments is given at https://github.com/kbui1993/NonconvexNetworkSlimming.

Both sets of CIFAR 10/100 consist of 32×32 natural images. CIFAR 10 has 10 classes; CIFAR 100 has 100 classes. CIFAR 10/100 is split between a training set of 50,000 images and a test set of 10,000 images. Standard augmentation [18,21,30] is applied to the CIFAR 10/100 images.

For our experiments, we train VGGNet with 19 layers and Densenet with 40 layers for five runs with and without scaling-factor regularization as done in [31]. (We refer "regularized models" as the models with scaling-factor regularization.) On CIFAR 10/100, the models are trained for 160 epochs with a training batch size of 64. They are optimized using stochastic gradient descent with learning rate 0.1. The learning rate decreases by a factor of 10 after 80 and 120 epochs. We use weight decay of 10^{-4} and Nesterov momentum [42] of 0.9 without dampening. Weight initialization is based on [17] and scaling factor initialization is set to all be 0.5 as done in [31].

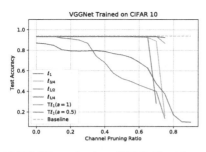
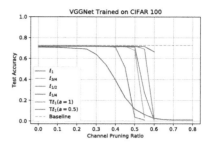

(a) VGGNet trained on CIFAR 10 with
$\lambda = 10^{-4}$

(b) VGGNet trained on CIFAR 100 with
$\lambda = 10^{-4}$

Fig. 3. Effect of channel pruning ratio on the mean test accuracy of five runs of VGGNet on CIFAR 10/100. Baseline refers to the mean test accuracy of the unregularized model that is not pruned.

Table 2. Effect of channel pruning ratio on the mean pruned ratio of parameters of five runs of VGGNet trained on CIFAR 10/100 for each regularization.

Pruning Ratio	CIFAR 10						CIFAR 100					
	ℓ_1	$\ell_{3/4}$	$\ell_{1/2}$	$\ell_{1/4}$	$T\ell_1\ (a=1)$	$T\ell_1\ (a=0.5)$	ℓ_1	$\ell_{3/4}$	$\ell_{1/2}$	$\ell_{1/4}$	$T\ell_1\ (a=1)$	$T\ell_1\ (a=0.5)$
0.10	0.2110	0.2114	0.2112	0.1995	**0.2116**	0.2094	0.2191	0.2198	**0.2202**	0.2200	0.2187	0.2167
0.20	0.3934	0.3955	**0.3962**	0.3766	0.3935	0.3929	0.4036	0.4064	**0.4085**	0.4071	0.4047	0.4033
0.30	0.5488	0.5513	**0.5529**	0.5299	0.5494	0.5492	0.5583	0.5604	**0.5629**	0.5621	0.5599	0.5597
0.40	0.6756	0.6796	**0.6809**	0.6620	0.6788	0.6783	0.6745	0.6801	0.6841	**0.6853**	0.6822	0.6849
0.50	0.7753	0.7799	0.7810	0.7707	0.7806	**0.7822**	0.7535	0.7654	0.7719	**0.7816**	0.7718	**0.7799**
0.60	0.8471	0.8524	0.8543	0.8576	0.8555	**0.8592**	N/A	N/A	0.8307	**0.8571**	0.8290	0.8409
0.70	0.8881	0.8969	0.9001	**0.9214**	0.9034	0.9088	N/A	N/A	N/A	**0.9148**	N/A	N/A
0.80	N/A	N/A	N/A	**0.9654**	N/A	N/A	N/A	N/A	N/A	**0.9654**	N/A	N/A
0.90	N/A	N/A	N/A	**0.9905**	N/A	N/A	N/A	N/A	N/A	N/A	N/A	N/A

With regularization parameter $\lambda = 10^{-4}$, we train the regularized models with ℓ_1, $\ell_p(p = 0.25, 0.5, 0.75)$, and $T\ell_1(a = 0.5, 1)$ penalties on the scaling factors.

4.1 Channel Pruning

After training, we prune the regularized models globally. In particular, we specify a ratio such as 0.35 or a percentage such as 35%, determine the 35th percentile among all scaling factors of the network and set it as a threshold, and prune away channels whose scaling factors are below that threshold. After pruning, we compute the compressed networks' mean test accuracies. Mean test accuracies are compared against the baseline test accuracy computed from the unregularized models. We evaluate the mean test accuracies as we increase the channel pruning ratios in increment of 0.05 to the point where a layer has no more channels.

For VGGNet, the mean test accuracies across the channel pruning ratios are shown in Fig. 3. The mean pruned ratios of parameters (the number of parameters pruned to the total number of parameters) are shown in Table 2. For CIFAR 10, according to Fig. 3a, the mean test accuracies for $\ell_{1/2}$ and $\ell_{1/4}$ are not robust against pruning

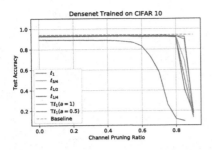
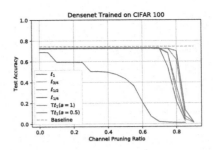

(a) Densenet-40 trained on CIFAR 10 with $\lambda = 10^{-4}$

(b) Densenet-40 trained on CIFAR 100 with $\lambda = 10^{-4}$

Fig. 4. Effect of channel pruning ratio on the mean test accuracy of five runs of Densenet on CIFAR 10/100. Baseline refers to the mean test accuracy of the unregularized model that is not pruned.

Table 3. Effect of channel pruning ratio on the mean pruned ratio of parameters of five runs of Densenet-40 trained on CIFAR 10/100 for each regularization.

Pruning Ratio	CIFAR 10						CIFAR 100					
	ℓ_1	$\ell_{3/4}$	$\ell_{1/2}$	$\ell_{1/4}$	$T\ell_1 (a = 1)$	$T\ell_1 (a = 0.5)$	ℓ_1	$\ell_{3/4}$	$\ell_{1/2}$	$\ell_{1/4}$	$T\ell_1 (a = 1)$	$T\ell_1 (a = 0.5)$
0.10	0.0922	0.0932	0.0933	**0.0935**	**0.0935**	**0.0935**	0.0918	0.0919	0.0920	**0.0926**	**0.0926**	0.0925
0.20	0.1835	0.1864	0.1859	0.1871	0.1863	**0.1872**	0.1834	0.1839	0.1841	**0.1853**	0.1846	0.1849
0.30	0.2757	0.2787	0.2797	**0.2813**	0.2785	0.2808	0.2753	0.2757	0.2762	**0.2785**	0.2772	0.2775
0.40	0.3673	0.3714	0.3726	**0.3752**	0.3717	0.3739	0.3669	0.3676	0.3685	**0.3717**	0.3691	0.3698
0.50	0.4595	0.4642	0.4662	**0.4705**	0.4641	0.4673	0.4584	0.4595	0.4606	**0.4651**	0.4615	0.4624
0.60	0.5515	0.5562	0.5588	**0.5669**	0.5573	0.5616	0.5498	0.5513	0.5526	**0.5594**	0.5535	0.5546
0.70	0.6438	0.6490	0.6512	**0.6656**	0.6514	0.6549	0.6412	0.6433	0.6444	**0.6573**	0.6455	0.6471
0.80	0.7375	0.7425	0.7447	**0.7702**	0.7446	0.7488	0.7339	0.7356	0.7367	**0.7628**	0.7378	0.7392
0.90	0.8376	0.8402	0.8436	N/A	0.8423	**0.8445**	N/A	0.8334	N/A	N/A	0.8348	**0.8360**

since they gradually decrease as the channel pruning ratio increases. On the other hand, $\ell_{3/4}$ and $T\ell_1$ are more robust than ℓ_1 to channel pruning since their accuracies drop at higher pruning ratios. So far, we see $T\ell_1(a = 0.5)$ to be the most robust with its mean test accuracy to be close to its pre-pruned mean test accuracy. For CIFAR 100, in Fig. 3b, ℓ_1 is less robust than $\ell_{3/4}$, $\ell_{1/2}$ and $T\ell_1$. Like for CIFAR 10, $T\ell_1(a = 0.5)$ is the most robust since its accuracy does not drop off until after 55% of channels are pruned while the accuracies of the other regularizers drop by when 50% of channels are pruned. According to Table 2, the pruned ratio of parameters are comparable among the regularizers for each channel pruning percentage, but always a nonconvex regularizer prunes more weight parameters than does ℓ_1.

For Densenet-40, the mean test accuracies across the channel pruning ratios are depicted in Fig. 4. The mean pruned ratios of parameters are shown in Table 3. For both CIFAR 10/100, $\ell_{1/4}$ is the least robust among the regularizers and following it is ℓ_1. $T\ell_1(a = 0.5)$ is the most robust because its test accuracy drops at a higher pruning ratio than do other regularizers. According to Table 3, ℓ_1 compresses the models the least while generally $\ell_{1/4}$ prunes the most number of parameters for both CIFAR 10/100.

Overall, we see that as $p \to 0^+$, ℓ_p regularization tends to prune more weight parameters, but its mean test accuracy decreases and it becomes less robust against pruning. Because smaller value of p strongly encourages sparsity, many of the scaling factors are close to zeroes, causing their respective subgradients to become larger and thus affecting the model accuracy. For $T\ell_1$, $a = 0.5$ manages to prune more weight parameters than does $a = 1.0$ and it improves the robustness of the model against pruning.

Table 4. Results from retrained VGGNet on CIFAR 10/100 after pruning. Baseline refers to the VGGNet model trained without regularization on the scaling factors.

	Number of Parameters	Pruning Percentage (%)	Average Test Accuracy before Retraining (%)	Average Test Accuracy after Retraining (%)
Baseline	20.04M	0.00	93.83	N/A
ℓ_1 (0% Pruned)	20.04M	0.00	93.63	N/A
ℓ_1 (70% Pruned)	2.24M	88.81	28.28	93.91
$\ell_{3/4}$ (0% Pruned)	20.04M	0.00	93.53	N/A
$\ell_{3/4}$ (70% Pruned)	2.07M	89.69	88.87	93.90
$\ell_{3/4}$ (75% Pruned)	1.79M	91.06	16.18	93.79
$\ell_{1/2}$ (0% Pruned)	20.04M	0.00	93.57	N/A
$\ell_{1/2}$ (70% Pruned)	2.00M	90.01	40.07	93.77
$\ell_{1/2}$ (75% Pruned)	1.66M	91.70	13.65	93.82
$\ell_{1/4}$ (0% Pruned)	20.04M	0.00	86.97	N/A
$\ell_{1/4}$ (70% Pruned)	1.58M	92.14	47.59	92.15
$\ell_{1/4}$ (90% Pruned)	0.19M	99.05	10.00	81.57
$T\ell_1 (a = 1)$ (0% Pruned)	20.04M	0.00	93.55	N/A
$T\ell_1 (a = 1)$ (70% Pruned)	1.93M	90.35	93.54	93.86
$T\ell_1 (a = 1)$ (75% Pruned)	1.66M	91.71	86.83	93.82
$T\ell_1 (a = 0.5)$ (0% Pruned)	20.04M	0.00	93.15	N/A
$T\ell_1 (a = 0.5)$ (70% Pruned)	1.83M	90.88	93.14	93.75
$T\ell_1 (a = 0.5)$ (75% Pruned)	1.53M	92.38	92.38	93.77

(a) CIFAR 10

	Number of Parameters	Pruning Percentage (%)	Average Test Accuracy before Retraining (%)	Average Test Accuracy after Retraining (%)
Baseline	20.08M	0.00	72.73	N/A
ℓ_1 (0% Pruned)	20.08M	0.00	72.57	N/A
ℓ_1 (55% Pruned)	4.31M	78.53	1.00	72.98
$\ell_{3/4}$ (0% Pruned)	20.08M	0.00	72.14	N/A
$\ell_{3/4}$ (55% Pruned)	4.10M	79.59	3.40	73.26
$\ell_{1/2}$ (0% Pruned)	20.08M	0.00	72.06	N/A
$\ell_{1/2}$ (55% Pruned)	3.95M	80.35	27.32	73.25
$\ell_{1/2}$ (60% Pruned)	3.40M	91.70	1.08	71.45
$\ell_{1/4}$ (0% Pruned)	20.08M	0.00	70.95	N/A
$\ell_{1/4}$ (55% Pruned)	3.58M	82.19	6.30	72.20
$\ell_{1/4}$ (80% Pruned)	0.69M	99.05	1.00	15.43
$T\ell_1 (a = 1)$ (0% Pruned)	20.08M	0.00	72.07	N/A
$T\ell_1 (a = 1)$ (55% Pruned)	3.94M	80.37	69.13	73.08
$T\ell_1 (a = 1)$ (60% Pruned)	3.43M	91.71	1.84	72.93
$T\ell_1 (a = 0.5)$ (0% Pruned)	20.08M	0.00	71.63	N/A
$T\ell_1 (a = 0.5)$ (55% Pruned)	3.72M	81.46	71.57	72.69
$T\ell_1 (a = 0.5)$ (60% Pruned)	3.20M	92.38	66.50	72.61

(b) CIFAR 100

4.2   Retraining After Pruning

After a model is pruned, we retrain it without regularization on the scaling factors with the same optimization setting as the first time training it. The purpose of retraining is to at least recover the model's original accuracy prior to pruning. For VGGNet, the results are shown in Table 4; for Densenet-40, the results are shown in Table 5.

Table 5. Results from retrained Densenet-40 on CIFAR 10/100 after pruning. Baseline refers to the Densenet-40 model trained without regularization on the scaling factors.

	Number of Parameters	Pruning Percentage (%)	Average Test Accuracy before Retraining (%)	Average Test Accuracy after Retraining (%)
Baseline	1.02M	0.00	94.25	N/A
ℓ_1 (0 % Pruned)	1.02M	0.00	93.46	N/A
ℓ_1 (82.5% Pruned)	0.25M	76.21	78.27	93.46
ℓ_1 (90% Pruned)	0.17M	83.76	17.47	91.42
$\ell_{3/4}$ (0% Pruned)	1.02M	0.00	93.19	N/A
$\ell_{3/4}$ (82.5% Pruned)	0.25M	76.57	90.17	93.33
$\ell_{3/4}$ (90% Pruned)	0.16M	84.02	15.06	91.54
$\ell_{1/2}$ (0% Pruned)	1.02M	0.00	93.28	N/A
$\ell_{1/2}$ (82.5% Pruned)	0.25M	76.84	83.17	93.43
$\ell_{1/2}$ (90% Pruned)	0.16M	84.36	13.76	91.31
$\ell_{1/4}$ (0% Pruned)	1.02M	0.00	89.48	N/A
$\ell_{1/4}$ (82.5% Pruned)	0.22M	79.81	11.29	91.68
$\ell_{1/4}$ (85% Pruned)	0.18M	82.57	10.05	91.44
$T\ell_1 (a = 1)$ (0% Pruned)	1.02M	0.00	93.16	N/A
$T\ell_1 (a = 1)$ (82.5% Pruned)	0.25M	76.80	93.17	93.26
$T\ell_1 (a = 1)$ (90% Pruned)	0.16M	84.23	18.91	91.70
$T\ell_1 (a = 0.5)$ (0% Pruned)	1.02M	0.00	92.78	N/A
$T\ell_1 (a = 0.5)$ (82.5% Pruned)	0.24M	77.21	92.74	93.05
$T\ell_1 (a = 0.5)$ (90% Pruned)	0.16M	84.45	18.12	91.69

(a) CIFAR 10

	Number of Parameters	Pruning Percentage (%)	Average Test Accuracy before Retraining (%)	Average Test Accuracy after Retraining (%)
Baseline	1.06M	0.00	74.58	N/A
ℓ_1 (0% Pruned)	1.06M	0.00	73.24	N/A
ℓ_1 (75% Pruned)	0.35M	68.74	54.68	73.73
ℓ_1 (85% Pruned)	0.23M	78.08	2.94	72.40
$\ell_{3/4}$ (0% Pruned)	1.06M	0.00	72.97	N/A
$\ell_{3/4}$ (75% Pruned)	0.34M	68.93	68.60	73.75
$\ell_{3/4}$ (85% Pruned)	0.23M	78.26	4.44	72.63
$\ell_{3/4}$ (90% Pruned)	0.18M	83.34	1.23	69.33
$\ell_{1/2}$ (0% Pruned)	1.06M	0.00	72.98	N/A
$\ell_{1/2}$ (75% Pruned)	0.34M	69.13	66.59	73.39
$\ell_{1/2}$ (85% Pruned)	0.23M	78.42	5.05	72.52
$\ell_{1/4}$ (0% Pruned)	1.06M	0.00	69.02	N/A
$\ell_{1/4}$ (75% Pruned)	0.32M	70.81	7.25	71.62
$\ell_{1/4}$ (85% Pruned)	0.19M	82.28	1.00	67.76
$T\ell_1 (a = 1)$ (0% Pruned	1.06M	0.00	72.63	N/A
$T\ell_1 (a = 1)$ (75% Pruned)	0.34M	69.13	72.34	73.42
$T\ell_1 (a = 1)$ (85% Pruned)	0.23M	78.47	7.5	72.52
$T\ell_1 (a = 1)$ (90% Pruned)	0.18M	83.49	1.24	69.98
$T\ell_1 (a = 0.5)$ (0% Pruned)	1.06M	0.00	72.57	N/A
$T\ell_1 (a = 0.5)$ (75% Pruned)	0.34M	69.33	72.59	73.23
$T\ell_1 (a = 0.5)$ (85% Pruned)	0.23M	78.58	13.41	72.56
$T\ell_1 (a = 0.5)$ (90% Pruned)	0.17M	83.60	1.37	70.16

(b) CIFAR 100

For VGGNet on CIFAR 10, we examine models pruned at 70%, the highest percentage that ℓ_1-regularized models can be pruned at. According to Table 4a, the nonconvex regularized models, except for $\ell_{1/4}$, attain similar mean test accuracy after retraining as the ℓ_1-regularized models. However, test accuracies of only ℓ_1, $\ell_{3/4}$, and $T\ell_1(a = 1.0)$ exceed the baseline mean test accuracy. Although ℓ_1 has higher test accuracy than other nonconvex regularized models, it is less compressed than the other regularized models. We also examine higher percentages for other nonconvex regularized models. Mean test accuracies improve for $\ell_{1/2}$ and $T\ell_1(a = 0.5)$, but they drop slightly for most other models. $\ell_{1/4}$ experiences the worst decrease, but it is due to having 90% of its channel pruned, resulting in significantly more weight parameters pruned compared to other nonconvex regularized models.

For VGGNet on CIFAR 100, we examine the mean test accuracy at 55%, the highest percentage that the ℓ_1-regularized models can be pruned at. By Table 4b, only $\ell_{3/4}$, $\ell_{1/2}$, and $T\ell_1(a = 1.0)$ outperform ℓ_1 in terms of compression and mean test accuracy. Increasing the pruning percentages higher for some other models, we observe slight decrease in test accuracies for $\ell_{1/2}$ and $T\ell_1(a = 0.5, 1)$. The $\ell_{1/4}$-regularized models are unable to recover its original test accuracy as evident by their mean test accuracy of 15.43% with 80% of channels pruned.

For Densenet-40 on CIFAR 10, from Table 5a, when 82.5% channels are pruned, ℓ_1 has the least number of weight parameters pruned. In addition, with better compression, the other nonconvex regularized models have slightly lower mean test accuracies after retraining. Models regularized with $\ell_{1/4}$ have the worst mean test accuracy of 91.68%. Increasing the channel pruning percentages, we observe that the mean test accuracies decrease from at least 93% to 91–92% for all models, except $\ell_{1/4}$. Models regularized with $\ell_{3/4}$ and $T\ell_1(a = 0.5, 1)$ have higher mean test accuracy and less weight parameters than models regularized with ℓ_1. For this set of models, the trade off between accuracy and compression is apparent.

In Table 5b, all regularized models, except for $\ell_{1/4}$ have at least 73% as their mean test accuracies after pruning 75% of their total channels and retraining them. The ℓ_1 regularized models are the least compressed compared to the nonconvex regularized models. Pruning at least 85% of the total channels decreases the mean test accuaracies after retraining. Again, accuracy is sacrificed by compressing the models even further.

5 Conclusion

We suggest a novel improvement to the network slimming method by replacing the ℓ_1 penalty with either the ℓ_p or $T\ell_1$ penalties on the scaling factors in the batch normalization layer. We demonstrate the effectiveness of the nonconvex regularizers with VGGNet and Densenet-40 trained on CIFAR 10/100 in our experiments. We observe that nonconvex regularizers compress the models more than ℓ_1 at the same channel pruning ratios. In addition, $T\ell_1$ preserves the model accuracy against channel pruning, while $\ell_{3/4}$ and $\ell_{1/2}$ result in more compressed models than does ℓ_1 with similar or higher model accuracy after retraining the pruned models. Hence, if deep learning practitioners do not have the option to retrain a compressed model, they should select $T\ell_1$ penalty for network slimming. Otherwise, they should choose $\ell_p, p \geq 0.5$ for a model with better accuracy attained after retraining. For future direction, we plan to apply relaxed variable splitting method [14] to regularization of the scaling factors in order to apply other nonconvex regularizers such as $\ell_1 - \ell_2$ [34,52].

Acknowledgments. The work was partially supported by NSF grants IIS-1632935, DMS-1854434, DMS-1952644, and a Qualcomm Faculty Award. The authors thank Mingjie Sun for having the code for [31] available on GitHub.

References

1. Aghasi, A., Abdi, A., Romberg, J.: Fast convex pruning of deep neural networks. SIAM J. Math. Data Sci. **2**(1), 158–188 (2020)
2. Alvarez, J.M., Salzmann, M.: Learning the number of neurons in deep networks. In: Advances in Neural Information Processing Systems. pp. 2270–2278 (2016)
3. Candès, E.J., Romberg, J., Tao, T.: Robust uncertainty principles: Exact signal reconstruction from highly incomplete frequency information. IEEE Trans. Inf. Theory **52**(2), 489–509 (2006)
4. Candès, E.J., Romberg, J.K., Tao, T.: Stable signal recovery from incomplete and inaccurate measurements. Commun. Pure Appl. Math. **59**(8), 1207–1223 (2006)
5. Cao, W., Sun, J., Xu, Z.: Fast image deconvolution using closed-form thresholding formulas of $L_q(q = 1/2, 2/3)$ regularization. J. Vis. Commun. Image Represent. **24**(1), 31–41 (2013)
6. Changpinyo, S., Sandler, M., Zhmoginov, A.: The power of sparsity in convolutional neural networks. arXiv preprint arXiv:1702.06257 (2017)
7. Chartrand, R.: Exact reconstruction of sparse signals via nonconvex minimization. IEEE Signal Process. Lett. **14**(10), 707–710 (2007)
8. Chartrand, R., Staneva, V.: Restricted isometry properties and nonconvex compressive sensing. Inverse Prob. **24**(3), 035020 (2008)
9. Chartrand, R., Yin, W.: Iteratively reweighted algorithms for compressive sensing. In: 2008 IEEE International Conference on Acoustics, Speech and Signal Processing. pp. 3869–3872. IEEE (2008)
10. Chen, L.C., Papandreou, G., Kokkinos, I., Murphy, K., Yuille, A.L.: Deeplab: semantic image segmentation with deep convolutional nets, atrous convolution, and fully connected crfs. IEEE Trans. Pattern Anal. Mach. Intell. **40**(4), 834–848 (2017)
11. Chen, W., Wilson, J., Tyree, S., Weinberger, K., Chen, Y.: Compressing neural networks with the hashing trick. In: International conference on machine learning. pp. 2285–2294 (2015)
12. Courbariaux, M., Bengio, Y., David, J.P.: Binaryconnect: Training deep neural networks with binary weights during propagations. In: Advances in neural information processing systems. pp. 3123–3131 (2015)
13. Denton, E.L., Zaremba, W., Bruna, J., LeCun, Y., Fergus, R.: Exploiting linear structure within convolutional networks for efficient evaluation. In: Advances in neural information processing systems. pp. 1269–1277 (2014)
14. Dinh, T., Xin, J.: Convergence of a relaxed variable splitting method for learning sparse neural networks via ℓ_1, ℓ_0, and transformed-ℓ_1 penalties. In: Proceedings of SAI Intelligent Systems Conference. pp. 360–374. Springer (2020)
15. Fan, J., Li, R.: Variable selection via nonconcave penalized likelihood and its oracle properties. J. Am. Stat. Assoc. **96**(456), 1348–1360 (2001)
16. Han, S., Pool, J., Tran, J., Dally, W.: Learning both weights and connections for efficient neural network. In: Advances in Neural Information Processing Systems. pp. 1135–1143 (2015)

17. He, K., Zhang, X., Ren, S., Sun, J.: Delving deep into rectifiers: surpassing human-level performance on imagenet classification. In: Proceedings of the IEEE International Conference on Computer Vision. pp. 1026–1034 (2015)
18. He, K., Zhang, X., Ren, S., Sun, J.: Deep residual learning for image recognition. In: Proceedings of the IEEE Conference on Computer Vision and Pattern Recognition. pp. 770–778 (2016)
19. Hu, H., Peng, R., Tai, Y.W., Tang, C.K.: Network trimming: a data-driven neuron pruning approach towards efficient deep architectures. arXiv preprint arXiv:1607.03250 (2016)
20. Huang, G., Liu, Z., Van Der Maaten, L., Weinberger, K.Q.: Densely connected convolutional networks. In: Proceedings of the IEEE Conference on Computer Vision and Pattern Recognition. pp. 4700–4708 (2017)
21. Huang, G., Sun, Yu., Liu, Z., Sedra, D., Weinberger, K.Q.: Deep networks with stochastic depth. In: Leibe, B., Matas, J., Sebe, N., Welling, M. (eds.) ECCV 2016. LNCS, vol. 9908, pp. 646–661. Springer, Cham (2016). https://doi.org/10.1007/978-3-319-46493-0_39
22. Ioffe, S., Szegedy, C.: Batch normalization: Accelerating deep network training by reducing internal covariate shift. In: International Conference on Machine Learning. pp. 448–456 (2015)
23. Jaderberg, M., Vedaldi, A., Zisserman, A.: Speeding up convolutional neural networks with low rank expansions. arXiv preprint arXiv:1405.3866 (2014)
24. Jung, H., Ye, J.C., Kim, E.Y.: Improved k-t blast and k-t sense using focuss. Phys. Med. Biol. **52**(11), 3201 (2007)
25. Krishnan, D., Fergus, R.: Fast image deconvolution using hyper-laplacian priors. In: Advances in Neural Information Processing Systems. pp. 1033–1041 (2009)
26. Krizhevsky, A., Sutskever, I., Hinton, G.E.: Imagenet classification with deep convolutional neural networks. In: Advances in Neural Information Processing Systems. pp. 1097–1105 (2012)
27. Li, F., Zhang, B., Liu, B.: Ternary weight networks. arXiv preprint arXiv:1605.04711 (2016)
28. Li, H., Kadav, A., Durdanovic, I., Samet, H., Graf, H.P.: Pruning filters for efficient convnets. arXiv preprint arXiv:1608.08710 (2016)
29. Li, Y., Wu, C., Duan, Y.: The TVp regularized mumford-shah model for image labeling and segmentation. IEEE Trans. Image Process. **29**, 7061–7075 (2020)
30. Lin, M., Chen, Q., Yan, S.: Network in network. arXiv preprint arXiv:1312.4400 (2013)
31. Liu, Z., Li, J., Shen, Z., Huang, G., Yan, S., Zhang, C.: Learning efficient convolutional networks through network slimming. In: Proceedings of the IEEE International Conference on Computer Vision. pp. 2736–2744 (2017)
32. Long, J., Shelhamer, E., Darrell, T.: Fully convolutional networks for semantic segmentation. In: Proceedings of the IEEE Conference on Computer Vision and Pattern Recognition. pp. 3431–3440 (2015)
33. Lou, Y., Osher, S., Xin, J.: Computational aspects of constrained $L_1 - L_2$ minimization for compressive sensing. In: Le Thi, H.A., Pham Dinh, T., Nguyen, N.T. (eds.) Modelling, Computation and Optimization in Information Systems and Management Sciences. AISC, vol. 359, pp. 169–180. Springer, Cham (2015). https://doi.org/10.1007/978-3-319-18161-5_15
34. Lou, Y., Yin, P., He, Q., Xin, J.: Computing sparse representation in a highly coherent dictionary based on difference of L_1 and L_2. J. Sci. Comput. **64**(1), 178–196 (2015)
35. Lustig, M., Donoho, D., Pauly, J.M.: Sparse mri: the application of compressed sensing for rapid mr imaging. Magn. Res. Med. An Off. J. Int. Soc. Magn. Res. Med. **58**(6), 1182–1195 (2007)
36. Ma, R., Miao, J., Niu, L., Zhang, P.: Transformed ℓ_1 regularization for learning sparse deep neural networks. Neural Networks **119**, 286–298 (2019)

37. Qian, Y., Jia, S., Zhou, J., Robles-Kelly, A.: Hyperspectral unmixing via $L_{1/2}$ sparsity-constrained nonnegative matrix factorization. IEEE Trans. Geosci. Remote Sens. **49**(11), 4282–4297 (2011)

38. Ronneberger, O., Fischer, P., Brox, T.: U-net: convolutional networks for biomedical image segmentation. In: Navab, N., Hornegger, J., Wells, W.M., Frangi, A.F. (eds.) MICCAI 2015. LNCS, vol. 9351, pp. 234–241. Springer, Cham (2015). https://doi.org/10.1007/978-3-319-24574-4_28

39. Scardapane, S., Comminiello, D., Hussain, A., Uncini, A.: Group sparse regularization for deep neural networks. Neurocomputing **241**, 81–89 (2017)

40. Shor, N.Z.: Minimization methods for non-differentiable functions, vol. 3. Springer Science & Business Media (2012)

41. Simonyan, K., Zisserman, A.: Very deep convolutional networks for large-scale image recognition. arXiv preprint arXiv:1409.1556 (2014)

42. Sutskever, I., Martens, J., Dahl, G., Hinton, G.: On the importance of initialization and momentum in deep learning. In: International Conference on Machine Learning. pp. 1139–1147 (2013)

43. Szegedy, C., Vanhoucke, V., Ioffe, S., Shlens, J., Wojna, Z.: Rethinking the inception architecture for computer vision. In: Proceedings of the IEEE Conference on Computer Vision and Pattern Recognition. pp. 2818–2826 (2016)

44. Wen, W., Wu, C., Wang, Y., Chen, Y., Li, H.: Learning structured sparsity in deep neural networks. In: Advances in Neural Information Processing Systems. pp. 2074–2082 (2016)

45. Wen, W., Xu, C., Wu, C., Wang, Y., Chen, Y., Li, H.: Coordinating filters for faster deep neural networks. In: Proceedings of the IEEE International Conference on Computer Vision. pp. 658–666 (2017)

46. Xu, Y., et al.: Trained rank pruning for efficient deep neural networks. arXiv preprint arXiv:1812.02402 (2018)

47. Xu, Y., et al.: Trp: Trained rank pruning for efficient deep neural networks. arXiv preprint arXiv:2004.14566 (2020)

48. Xu, Z., Chang, X., Xu, F., Zhang, H.: $\ell_{1/2}$ regularization: a thresholding representation theory and a fast solver. IEEE Trans. Neural Netw. Learn. Syst. **23**(7), 1013–1027 (2012)

49. Xu, Z., Guo, H., Wang, Y., Hai, Z.: Representative of $L_{1/2}$ regularization among $L_q(0 \leq q \leq 1)$ regularizations: an experimental study based on phase diagram. Acta Automatica Sinica **38**(7), 1225–1228 (2012)

50. Xu, Z., Zhang, H., Wang, Y., Chang, X., Liang, Y.: $L_{1/2}$ regularization. Sci. China Inf. Sci. **53**(6), 1159–1169 (2010)

51. Xue, F., Xin, J.: Learning sparse neural networks via ℓ_0 and $t\ell_1$ by a relaxed variable splitting method with application to multi-scale curve classification. In: Le Thi, H.A., Le, H.M., Pham Dinh, T. (eds.) WCGO 2019. AISC, vol. 991, pp. 800–809. Springer, Cham (2020). https://doi.org/10.1007/978-3-030-21803-4_80

52. Yin, P., Lou, Y., He, Q., Xin, J.: Minimization of ℓ_{1-2} for compressed sensing. SIAM J. Sci. Comput. **37**(1), A536–A563 (2015)

53. Yin, P., Zhang, S., Lyu, J., Osher, S., Qi, Y., Xin, J.: Binaryrelax: a relaxation approach for training deep neural networks with quantized weights. SIAM J. Imag. Sci. **11**(4), 2205–2223 (2018)

54. Yin, W., Osher, S., Goldfarb, D., Darbon, J.: Bregman iterative algorithms for ℓ_1-minimization with applications to compressed sensing. SIAM J. Imag. Sci. **1**(1), 143–168 (2008)

55. Yuan, M., Lin, Y.: Model selection and estimation in regression with grouped variables. J. Royal Stat. Soc.: Series B (Stat. Methodol.) **68**(1), 49–67 (2006)

56. Zhang, S., Xin, J.: Minimization of transformed l_1 penalty: closed form representation and iterative thresholding algorithms. Commun. Math. Sci. **15**(2), 511–537 (2017)

57. Zhang, S., Xin, J.: Minimization of transformed l_1 penalty: theory, difference of convex function algorithm, and robust application in compressed sensing. Math. Program. **169**(1), 307–336 (2018)
58. Zhang, S., Yin, P., Xin, J.: Transformed Schatten-1 iterative thresholding algorithms for low rank matrix completion. Commun. Math. Sci. **15**(3), 839–862 (2017)
59. Zhu, C., Han, S., Mao, H., Dally, W.J.: Trained ternary quantization. arXiv preprint arXiv:1612.01064 (2016)

Biologically Inspired Sleep Algorithm
for Variational Auto-Encoders

Sameerah Talafha[1], Banafsheh Rekabdar[1], Christos Mousas[2(✉)],
and Chinwe Ekenna[3]

[1] Southern Illinois University Carbondale, Carbondale, IL, USA
sameerah.talafha@siu.edu, brekabdar@cs.siu.edu
[2] Purdue University, Indiana, USA
cmousas@purdue.edu
[3] University at Albany, New York, USA
cekenna@albany.edu

Abstract. Variational auto-encoders (VAEs) are a class of likelihood-based generative models that operate by providing an approximation to the problem of inference by introducing a latent variable and encoder/decoder components. However, the latent codes usually have no structure, are not informative, and are not interpretable. This problem is amplified if these models need to be used for auxiliary tasks or when different aspects of the generated samples need to be controlled or interpreted by humans. We address these issues by proposing a biologically realistic sleep algorithm for VAEs (VAE-sleep). The algorithm augments the normal training phase of the VAE with an unsupervised learning phase in the equivalent spiking VAE modeled after how the human brain learns, using the Mirrored Spike Timing Dependent Plasticity learning rule. We hypothesize the proposed unsupervised VAE-sleep phase creates more realistic feature representations, which in turn lead to increase a VAE's robustness to reconstruct the input. We conduct quantitative and qualitative experiments, including comparisons with the state-of-the-art on three datasets: CelebA, MNIST, and Fashion-MNIST. We show that our model performs better than the standard VAE and varitional sparse coding (VSC) on benchmark classification task by demonstrating improved classification accuracy and significantly increased robustness to the number of latent dimensions. As a result of experiments suggest, the proposed method shows improved performance in comparison with other widely used methods and performs favorably under the metrics PSNR, SSIM, LPIPS. The quantitative evaluations also suggest that our model can generate more realistic images compared to the state of arts when tested on disturbed or noisy inputs.

Keywords: Variational auto encoder · Spiking neural network · Sleep algorithm.

1 Introduction

Deep neural networks (DNNs) perform well at solving problems that would be prohibitive for human or statistical standards to data classification. Recently, realistic image generation using generative DNNs has been at the forefront of research in machine learning and computer vision. Variational auto-encoder (VAE) [1] is a generative model

© Springer Nature Switzerland AG 2020
G. Bebis et al. (Eds.): ISVC 2020, LNCS 12509, pp. 54–67, 2020.
https://doi.org/10.1007/978-3-030-64556-4_5

used to reconstruct training inputs and create random samples from its learned representations. VAEs offer an efficient way of performing approximate posterior inference with otherwise intractable generative models and yield probabilistic encoding functions that can map complex high-dimensional data to lower-dimensional representations [2]. However, traditional VAEs usually produce latent codes that are not interpretable. This makes the results unsuitable for auxiliary tasks (for example, clustering, segmentation, and classification) and human interpretation. This is contrary to a good generative model as it should not only be able to draw samples from the distribution of data being modeled but also be useful for inference [3]. Moreover, the performance of the VAEs is significantly worsened when the inputs are noisy, rendering them ineffective for the auxiliary tasks [4]. Spiking neural networks (SNNs) are the third generation of neural networks, in which neurons communicate through binary signals known as spikes [5–7]. SNNs are energy-efficient than DNNs making them suitable for hardware implementation because spikes bring the opportunity of using event-based hardware as well as simple energy-efficient accumulators instead of complex energy-hungry multiply-accumulators that are usually employed in DNNs hardware [8]. SNNs have been proven to be less prone to performance deterioration to noisy inputs than their DNNs counterparts [9]. The spatio-temporal capacity of SNNs makes them potentially stronger than DNNs; however, harnessing their ultimate power is not straightforward [7]. Recently, mimicking biologically inspired learning in VAE has been demonstrated using the Variational Sparse Coding (VSC) model [10], which modeled sparsity in the latent space of VAE with a Spike and Slab prior distribution resulting in latent codes with improved sparsity and interpretability. However, the approach mentioned above falls short in mimicking biologically realistic learning compared to approaches like spike-timing-dependent plasticity (STDP). Sleep mechanism is essential to several brain functions of humans and animals, including how neurons communicate with each other. During the sleep phase, there is the reactivation of neurons involved in a previously learned activity and this reactivation is likely to invoke the same spatio-temporal pattern as the pattern observed during training in the awake stage [11]. In neuroscience, it is hypothesized that sleep can improve memory, learning, increase attention, and robustness against noise in both humans and animals. In this work, we employ the notion of sleep from biology and apply an off-line unsupervised "sleep" stage to modify the parameters of a fully connected VAE. Our model combines ideas from VAE [1] and the sleep mechanism [12] leveraging the advantages of deep and spiking neural networks (DNN–SNN). During the sleep stage, sleep functions' choice of Mirrored STDP rules [13] increases a subject's ability to form logical connections between memories and to generalize knowledge learned during the awake stage. We hypothesize that sleep could aid in reducing an auto-encoder loss function hence improving VAE output interpretability and producing latent codes that are less dispersed. To the best of our knowledge, this work provides a step towards mimicking the biological sleep stage in the context of learning in generative models like variational auto-encoder. Our contributions are summarized below:

1. We report positive results for image reconstruction datasets (MNIST, CelebA, and Fashion-MNIST) where following sleep the generation produces examples that are more distinct than the original input than before VAE-sleep.

2. We illustrate that our VAE-sleep algorithm creates latent codes which hold a high level of information about our input (image) compared to the standard VAE [1] and VSC [10].
3. We illustrate that our model has a more robust architecture whereby performance on noisy inputs is higher compared to the standard VAE [1] and VSC [10].

The rest of the paper is organized as follows: in Sect. 2 we review related work, Sect. 3 describes our proposed model, 4 details the evaluation, experimental design, and results. Section 5 concludes the paper with remarks on the obtained results.

2   Background and Related Work

2.1   Varitional Auto-Encoder (VAE)

VAE is an unsupervised model with efficient coding with goals to maximize the marginal likelihood $\prod p(x_i)$ with respect to the decoding parameter θ of the likelihood function $p_\theta(z|x)$ and the encoding parameter ϕ of the recognition model $q_\phi(z|x)$. The input $x_i \in \mathcal{R}^{M \times 1}$ is passed to the encoder network, producing an approximate posterior $q_\phi(z|x)$ over latent variables z. The sample $z_i \in \mathcal{R}^{J \times 1}$ is drawn from a prior $p(z)$ which can be chosen to take different parametric forms. In most types of VAEs, the prior takes the form of a multivariate Gaussian with identity covariance $\mathcal{N}(z; 0, I)$. For example, if q were Gaussian, it would be the mean and variance of z for each data point $\phi_{x_i} = (\mu_{x_i}, \sigma^2_{x_i})$. Then, z_i is passed through the feedforward decoder network to compute the probability of the input $p_\theta(x|z)$ given the sample. The $p_\theta(x|z)$ is chosen to fit the expected nature of variation in the observations. The key step in the derivation of VAE's loss function is the definition of a lower bound on the log-likelihood $\log p_\theta(x)$, referred as the **E**vidence **L**ower **BO**und (ELBO) that depends on $q_\phi(z|x)$ [10]. Based on Jensen's inequality, the ELBO can be formulated as

$$\log p_\theta(x_i) = \int p_\theta(x_i|z)p(z)\frac{q_\phi(z|x)}{q_\phi(z|x)}dz \geqslant \mathcal{L}_{\theta,\phi;x_i}, \tag{1}$$

$$\mathcal{L}_{\theta,\phi;x_i} = \mathbb{E}_{q_\phi(z|x_i)}\left[\log p_\theta(x_i|z)\right] - \mathcal{D}_{KL}(q_\phi(z|x_i)\|p_\theta(z)). \tag{2}$$

ELBO is divided into two terms; the first term is the reconstruction likelihood that maximizes the expectation of the data likelihood under the recognition function. The second term is the Kullback-Leibler (KL) that ensures the learned distribution q is similar to the true prior distribution p, as shown in the following. The value of ELBO is tight when the difference between approximate and true posterior is zero, $q_\phi(z|x) = p_\theta(z|x)$, and the tightness of the bound depends on the KL divergence of $q_\phi(z|x)$ and $p_\theta(z|x)$. The images generated by VAEs are usually not realistic and blurry [3]. Using Convolutional Neural Networks (CNN) improves the performance of VAE by capturing important perceptual features such as spatial correlation [14], but the fidelity and naturalness of reconstruction are still unsatisfactory [10].

2.2 Varitional Sparse Coding (VSC)

VSC approach comprises of increasing sparsity in the latent space of VAE, representing it as a binary spike and Slab probability density function (PDF) [10]. It employs the non-linear features that constitute variability in data and exemplifies them as few non-zero elements in sparse vectors. Let s_j denote a binary spike and z_j a continuous slab variable. s_j value is either one or zero with defined probabilities α and $(1 - \alpha)$ respectively and z_j distribution is either a Gaussian or a Delta function centered at zero, conditioned on whether s_j is one or zero respectively. As VAE, $p_\theta(x|z)$ denote a probabilistic decoder with a neural network to generate observed data x from sparse vectors in the latent space. The prior probability density $p(z_s)$ over the latent variable z_i is defined below:

$$p_s(z) = \prod_{j=1}^{J} \left(\alpha \mathcal{N}(z_j; 0, 1) + (1 - \alpha)\delta(z_j) \right), \tag{3}$$

Where $\delta(\cdot)$ indicates the Dirac delta function centered at zero. The distribution of representation corresponding to the x approximated by the variational posterior $q_\phi(z|x)$, which is produced by an encoder with a neural network of the form

$$q_\phi(z|x_i) = \prod_{j=1}^{J} \left(\gamma_{i,j} \mathcal{N}(z_{i,j}\mu_{z,i,j}\sigma_{z,i,j}^2) + (1 - \gamma_{i,j})\delta(z_{j,j}) \right), \tag{4}$$

Where $\mu_{z,i,j}$ is the mean, $\sigma_{z,i,j}^2$ is the variance, and $\gamma_{i,j}$ is a Spike probabilities vector constrained between 0 and 1. They are the outputs of the recognition function $p(z|x_i)$ composed of a neural network which takes as input an observation x_i. The $p(z|x_i)$ allows for the posterior to match the prior and allows the freedom to control the Gaussian moments and the Spike probabilities independently enable the model to encode information in the latent space. In contrast to Eq. 3, which represents standard Slab and Spike distribution, Eq. 4 describes distribution of Slab variables having Gaussian distributions $\mathcal{N}(z_{i,j}; \mu_{z,i,j}, \sigma_{z,i,j}^2)$ and Spike variables having probabilities of being one $\gamma_{i,j}$. VSC's loss function introduces a sparsity KL divergence penalty term with the two terms of ELBO, hence modifying Eq. 2 as:

$$\mathcal{L}_{\theta,\phi;x_i} = \mathbb{E}_{q_\phi(z|x_i)}\left[\log p_\theta(x_i|z)\right] + \underset{\theta,\phi,w,x_u}{\arg\max} \sum -\mathcal{D}_{KL}(q_\phi(z|x_i)\|p(z))$$
$$-J \cdot \mathcal{D}_{KL}(\bar{\gamma}_{u*}\|\alpha), \tag{5}$$

where $\bar{\gamma}_{u*}$ is the average Spike probability of each pseudo input recognition model that matches with the prior sparsity α in the latent space. Despite its utility to improve the performance of VAE model, the implementation is not biologically realistic [10].

3 Proposed Model

3.1 Spiking Varitional Auto-Encoder (SVAE)

While DNNs' cell is designed to simulate highly simplified brain dynamics, SNNs' cell aims to closely model temporal brain dynamics. SNNs are combining digital-analog

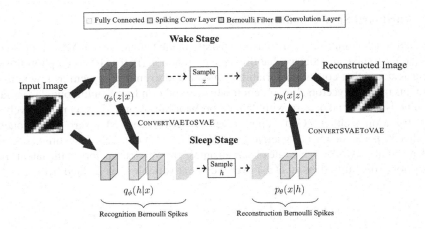

Fig. 1. The block diagram of our proposed model.

machines that use the temporal dimension, not just as a neutral substrate for computing, but as a means to encode and process information. Training for probabilistic models of SNNs has recently been investigated in variational inference principles based on the unsupervised mechanism of STDP which updates synaptic weights based on local input and output spikes [12]. In this section, we present the details of our spiking varitional auto-encoder (SVAE). We propose to use mirrored spike-timing-dependent plasticity (Mirrored STDP) [13] instead of STDP [15], since Mirrored STDP follows a learning rule that approximately minimizes auto-encoder loss function compared to STDP. STDP changes in feedforward synaptic strength, but it does not cause the correct changes for the feedback synapses. On the other hand, under Mirrored STDP the plasticity due to any pair of visible and hidden spikes will be the same for the feedforward connections as for the feedback connections, up to a scaling factor. The Mirrored STDP learning rule is given by:

$$\Delta w_{ji} = \begin{cases} a_{LTP} \times (w_{ji} - w_{LB}) \times (w_{UP} - w_{ji}) & t_i - t_j \leq 0, \\ a_{LTD} \times (w_{ji} - w_{LB}) \times (w_{UP} - w_{ji}) & t_i - t_j > 0, \end{cases} \qquad (6)$$

where j and i refer to the hidden- and visible-synaptic neurons, respectively, Δw_{ji} is the amount of weight change for the synapse connecting the two neurons, and a_{LTP}, and a_{LTD} scale the magnitude of weight change. Besides, $(w_{ji} - w_{LB}) \times (w_{UP} - w_{ji})$ is a stabilizer term which slows down the weight change when the synaptic weight is close to the weight's lower w_{LB} and upper w_{UB} bounds. We use simulated networks of leaky integrate-and-fire (LIF) neurons in the experiments, which is the most popular one for building SNNs. LIF neurons are characterized by the internal state called the membrane potential. The membrane potential integrates the inputs over time and generates an output spike when the neuronal firing threshold. The objective of SVAE learning is to find weights such that the reconstruction closely matches the original stimulus input, thus ensuring that the hidden unit representation is a good one; intuitively, reconstructions can only be accurate when the hidden layer retains sufficient information about the visible layer. Each observation (in our case, an image), $x^m \in \{n_v \times T\}$ with $m = [1, ..., M]$ in the training set is a collection of n_v pixels of T binary samples with value "1" representing a spike. Parameter n_v is hence the number of observed, or visible spike trains. All M examples in the training set $\mathcal{X} = \{x^m\}_{m=1}^{M}$ are convention-ally assumed to be independent and identically distributed (i.i.d.) according to the given true data distribution. SVAE's decoder is a generative probabilistic SNN whose behav-ior is defined by a parameterized joint distribution $p_\theta(x, h)$ over visible spiking signals $x = [x_1, ..., x_{n_v}]$ and hidden spiking signals $h = [h_1, ..., h_{n_h}]$. The joint distribution of x and h is modeled as:

$$p_\theta(x, h) = p_\theta(h)p_\theta(x|h) = \prod_{j=1}^{n_h} p_{\theta_j}(h_j) \prod_{i=1}^{n_v} p_{\theta_i}(x_i|h), \qquad (7)$$

where parameter n_h is hence the number of hidden spike trains, and θ is the vector of parameters that define the prior distribution $p_\theta(h)$ of the latent spikes and the condi-tional distribution $p_\theta(x|h)$. Each the hidden spiking signal (latent spike) has Bernoulli samples distributed as:

$$p_{\theta_j}(h_j) = \prod_{t=1}^{T} F\left((2h_{j,t} - 1)\,\theta_j\right), \qquad (8)$$

where θ_j is the prior log-likelihood ratio for every sample $h_{j,t} \in 0, 1$, and $F(x)$ is the ReLU function. Since x is conditionally independent to h, the conditional distribu-tion is as shown in Eq. 9:

$$p_{\theta_i}(x_i|h) = \prod_{t=1}^{T} F\left((2x_{i,t} - 1)\,u_{i,t}\right), \qquad (9)$$

where $u_{i,t}$ is the membrane potential of the i-th visible neuron at time t. The $u_{i,t}$ evolves over time as a dynamic system that depends on the past spiking behaviour of the hidden and visible neuron i, as explained next. Assuming a feedforward synaptic memory of τ_α samples and a feedback memory of τ_β samples, the membrane potential is as shown in Eq. 10:

$$u_{i,t} = \sum_{j=1}^{n_h} \alpha_{j,i}^T h_{j,t-\tau_\alpha}^{-1} + \beta_i^T x_{i,t-\tau_\beta}^{t-1} + \gamma_i, \qquad (10)$$

where $\alpha_{j,i} \in \mathcal{R}^{\tau_\alpha \times 1}$ is the kernel for the synapse between hidden neuron j and visible neuron i, and $\beta_{j,i} \in \mathcal{R}^{\tau_\beta \times 1}$ is the feedback filter for dynamic spikes of neuron i. We model the feedforward and feedback filters as the linear combination of $K_\alpha \leqslant \tau_\alpha$ and $K_\beta \leqslant \tau_\beta$ basis functions, respectively:

$$\alpha_{j,i} = Aw_{j,i} = \sum_{k=1}^{K_\alpha} w_{j,i,k} a_k, \qquad (11)$$

$$\beta_{j,i} = Bv_{j,i} = \sum_{k=1}^{K_\beta} v_{j,i,k} b_k, \tag{12}$$

where $A = [a_1, ..., a_{K_\alpha}]$ and $B = [b_1, ..., b_{K_\beta}]$ are the basis vectors, $w_{j,i} = [w_{j,i,1}, ..., w_{j,i,K_\alpha}]^T$ and $v_{j,i} = [v_{j,i,1}, ..., v_{j,i,K_\beta}]^T$ are learnable weights. SVAE's encoder creates output spiking signals h according to the variational distribution $q_\phi(h|x)$ given the visible spiking signals x as.

$$q_\phi(h|x) = \prod_{j=1}^{n_h} \prod_{t=1}^{T} F\left((2h_{j,t} - 1)\, \tilde{u}_{j,t}\right), \tag{13}$$

where $\tilde{u}_{j,t}$ is the varitional membrane potential given as:

$$\tilde{u}_{i,t} = \sum_{i=1}^{n_v} \tilde{w}_{j,i}^T A^T x_{i,t+1}^{t+\tau_\alpha} + \tilde{v}_{j,i}^T B^T h_{j,t+1}^{t+\tau_\beta} + \tilde{\gamma}_i. \tag{14}$$

The gradient of the ELBO for x with respect to the model parameters θ and ϕ can be calculated as:

$$\nabla_\theta \mathcal{L}_{\theta,\phi}(x) = \mathbb{E}_{q_\phi(h|x)} \left[\nabla_\theta \log p_\theta(x, h) \right], \tag{15}$$

$$\nabla_\phi \mathcal{L}_{\theta,\phi}(x) = \mathbb{E}_{q_\phi(h|x)} \left[l_\phi(x, h) \nabla_\phi, \log q_\phi(h|x) \right], \tag{16}$$

where,

$$l_\phi(x, h) = \log p_\theta(x, h) - \log q_\phi(x|h). \tag{17}$$

3.2   VAE-Sleep

Algorithm 1 shows the pseudo-code for our VAE-sleep algorithm. In the wake stage, We train the VAE using stochastic gradient descent to optimize the loss with respect to the encoder's parameters and decoder θ and ϕ with backpropagation by applying re-parameterization trick [1]. In CONVERTVAETOSVAE function, we assume the VAE utilizes ReLU neurons with no bias in each layer. This assumption is made so that the output neuron's activation can be treated as a firing rate, either zero or positive, and the thresholds of all LIF neurons in SVAE in a given layer are of the same scale. Therefore, the weights from the VAE are directly mapped to the SVAE as in [17]. After training, the network structure is converted into SVAE. Next, we run a sleep stage in which inputs to each neuron of the visible layer must be presented as Bernoulli spike-trains to propagate activity from the visible layer to the hidden layers of the network. For that, we convert inputs (real-valued pixel intensities or features) to Bernoulli spike-trains using the Berniolli Filter [18]. At each iteration, we feed the SVAE architecture (the encoder followed by the decoder) with input data. The neurons in SVAE only fire termed as 'spikes', when the neurons reach a certain *threshold* membrane potential.

Algorithm 1. VAE-Sleep

---

   procedure CONVERTVAETOSVAE(*vae*)

      Map the weights from (*vae*) with ReLU units to network integrate-fire units

      Apply weight normalization [16] and return scales for each layer in encoder and decoder

   return *svae*, *scales*

   end procedure

   procedure CONVERTSVAETOVAE(*svae*)

      Directly map the weights from LIF neurons in SNN layer (*svae*) to ReLU neuron (*vae*) in DNN layer **return** (*vae*)

   end procedure

   procedure SLEEP(*save*, I, *scales*)   ▷ I is input

      Initialize u (voltage) = 0 vectors for all neurons

      for $t \leftarrow 1, Ts$ **do**   ▷ Ts – sleep duration

         $S(1) \leftarrow$ Convert input I to Bernoulli-distributed spike train

         for $l \leftarrow 2, n$ **do**   ▷ n – number of layers

            $u(l, t) \leftarrow u(l, t-1) + (scales(l-1)\mathbf{W}(1, l-1)S(l-1))$ ▷ $W_{l,l-1}$ – weights

            $S(l, t) \leftarrow u(l, t) > threshold(l)$

$$\mathbf{W}(1, l-1) \leftarrow \begin{cases} \mathbf{W}(1, l-1) + \Delta\mathbf{W} \text{ if } S(l) = 1 \ \& \ S(l-1) = 1 \\ \mathbf{W}(1, l-1) - \Delta\mathbf{W} \text{ if } S(l) = 1 \ \& \ S(l-1) = 0 \end{cases} \quad \text{▷ *mSTDP}$$

         end for

      end for

   end procedure

   procedure MAIN

      Initialize neural netowrk (*vae*) with ReLU neurons and bias = 0.

      Train *vae* using backpropgation with respect θ and ϕ by applying re-parameterization trick

      $svae, scales = $ CONVERTVAETOSVAE(*vae*)

      $svae = $ SLEEP(*svae*, Training data X, *scales*)

      $vae = $ CONVERTSVAETOVAE(*svae*)

   end procedure

   *mSTDP: Mirrored Spike Timing Dependent Plasticity

We compare the encoded-decoded output with the input data and gradient of the ELBO with respect θ and ϕ, the error through the architecture and the Mirrored STDP rule is applied to update weights. After the sleep stage, the SVAE network is converted back into the VAE (CONVERTSVAETOVAE), and testing is performed. The block diagram of our proposed model is shown in Fig. 1.

4 Experiment Results and Dataset

We benchmark our model using the following datasets commonly used for evaluating VAEs' performance: (a.) MNIST [19], (b.) Fashion-MNIST [20], and (c.) CelebA [21].We compared the performance of our SVAE model with the performance of VAE and VSC implemented in [10]. The VAE model is a Convolutional Variational auto-encoder (CVAE). The detailed architecture of CVAE is as described in Table 1. To establish a valid benchmark, we implemented the VSC architecture in the same way as the VAE model. Table 2 summarizes the parameters used for training the VAE and the VSC models. Our proposed model (Fig. 1) consists of two stages: wake and sleep. For the wake stage, a CVAE model is used. The architecture of the CVAEs' encoder consisted of 2 convolutional layers for MNIST and Fashion-MNIST datasets and 4 layers for the CelebA, each with 32 channels, 4 × 4 kernels, and a stride of 2. This was followed by 2 fully connected layers, each of 256 units. The latent distribution consisted of one fully connected layer of the mean and log standard deviation of Gaussian random variables. The decoder architecture is simply the transpose of the encoder, but with the output parametrizing the Bernoulli distributions over the pixels. The sleep stage (Sect. 3.2), is implemented as the SVAE model explained in Sect. (3.1). SVAE constitutes spiking convolution layers with LIF neurons to replicate convolution layers in the VAE model used during the wake stage. The parameters used for training the SVAE are shown in Table 4. To evaluate the robustness of our method on noisy inputs, we create a noisy test set. In this test set, we distort the inputs by adding noise vectors sampled from a standard normal distribution (Gaussian noise) to the test image encodings.

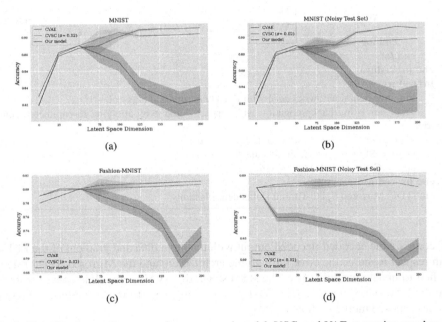

Fig. 2. Classification performance of our proposed model, VSC, and VAE at varying number of latent space dimensions for MNIST and Fashion-MNIST datasets vs noisy MNIST and noisy Fashion-MNIST datasets (distorted with gaussian noise).

4.1 Quantitative Evaluation

We used the following metrics – Peak Signal to Noise Ratio (PSNR) [22], Structural Similarity Index (SSIM) [23], and Learned Perceptual Image Patch Similarity (LPIPS) [24] to evaluate the quality of the generated images and learning in the latent space

Table 1. CVAEs' Encoder and Decoder architecture details.

Dataset	Encoder	Decoder
CelebA	Input 64 × 64 × 3 RGB image	Input: the latent variable z
	4 × 4 conv. 32 ReLU. stride 2	FC. 256 ReLU
	4 × 4 conv. 32 ReLU. stride 2	FC.4 × 4 × 64 ReLU
	4 × 4 conv. 64 ReLU. stride 2	4 × 4 deconv. 64 ReLU. stride 2
	4 × 4 conv. 64 ReLU. stride 2	4 × 4 deconv. 32 ReLU. stride 2
	FC. 256	4 × 4 deconv. 32 ReLU. stride 2
	FC latent-sz (Mean)‖FC latent-sz, Sigmoid (Std. dev.)	4 × 4 deconv. 3. stride 2
MNIST/Fashion-MNIST	Input 28 × 28 × 1 grey-scale image	Input : the latent variable z
	4 × 4 conv. 32 ReLU. stride 2	FC. 256 ReLU
	4 × 4 conv. 32 ReLU. stride 2	FC.4 × 4 × 32 ReLU
	FC. 256	deconv. 32 ReLU. stride 2
	FC latent-sz (Mean) ‖FC latent-sz, Sigmoid (Std. dev.)	4 × 4 deconv. 1. stride 2

Table 2. Parameters used for training VAE and VSC; hidden-sz: number of hidden neurons, latent-sz: number of latent dimensions, Epochs: number of training epochs, lr: learning rate, log-interval: number of batches before logging training status, β: adjustable hyperparameter to balance latent channel capacity and independence constraints with reconstruction accuracy, c: stability of the gradient ascent.

Dataset	hidden-sz	latent-sz	Epochs	lr	log-interval	normalize	β	$\Delta\beta$	α	c	Δ c	iterations
CelebA	256	400	500	$3e-4$	500	False	4	0	$1e-2$	50	$1e-3$	20,000
MNIST/Fashion-MNIST	256	200	100	$1e-4$	500	False	2	0	$1e-2$	50	$1e-3$	20,000

[10] as well as to evaluate the quality of the latent codes which affect the performance of auxiliary tasks like classification. PSNR is a standard error metric used to compare image compression quality defined as in Eq. 18:

$$\text{PSNR} = -10 \log \left(\frac{(2^n - 1)^2}{\text{MSE}} \right), \tag{18}$$

where MSE is the Mean Square Error between the ground truth image X and the generated image Y as in Eq. 19:

$$\text{MSE} = \frac{1}{\text{HW}} \sum_{i=1}^{H} \sum_{j=1}^{W} |X_{i,j} - Y_{i,j}|, \tag{19}$$

Table 3. Parameters used for training SVAE. Input rate: maximum firing rate of the input neurons, Sleep duration: length of sleep (number of images presented during sleep stage), Thresholds: neuronal firing thresholds for each layer of neurons, Synaptic AMPA current: scale factor of weights during sleep stage, upper-bound: weights' upper bound range, lower-bound: weights' lower bound range, ρ: target activation rate.

Dataset	Input rate	Sleep duration	Thresholds	Synaptic AMPA current	upper-bound	lower-bound	ρ
CelebA	500Hz	200600	15,40,23,0.9	2.19	0.013	0.019	0.02
MNIST/Fashion-MNIST	40 Hz	48000	36.18, 23.36	2.19	0.0063	0.0069	0.02

SSIM is used to evaluate differences of brightness, contrast, and image structure (it's range: $[0, 1]$) defined as Eq. 20:

$$SSIM(X, Y) = \frac{(2\mu_{X,Y}\mu_Y + C_1)(2\sigma_{XY} + C_2)}{(\mu_X^2 + \mu_Y^2 + C_1)(\sigma_X^2 + \sigma_Y^2 + C_2)}, \tag{20}$$

where μ_X and μ_Y denote the mean values of images X and Y, σ_X and σ_Y denote the variances of X and Y, σ_{XY} is the covariance between X and Y, and C is a constant.

In contrast to SSIM and PSNR which lean towards preference of blurry predictions over sharper but imperfect generations, LPIPS has a better correlation to human judgment. Given two images [25] LPIPS returns a weighted L_2 distance (image differences) in the space of hidden unit when run through the convolutional part of an image classification network such as Visual Geometry Group (VGG). Table 4 (left hand side) shows the quantitative evaluation of the generation results for the metrics mentioned above. Generally, VAE generates distorted images when tested with noisy test sets [4], so, in order to evaluate the effect of the noise, we test VAE, VSC, and our model with noisy test sets. Table 4 (right hand side) presents the quantitative evaluation of the generation results for the noisy test sets. We report the average PSNR, SSIM, and LPIPS of the closet samples to the ground truth for each test image. Our model outperforms the VAE and VSC on all metrics by a significant margin. Learning in the latent space measures the ability of a model to recover latent codes that hold a high level of information about the input by performing a standard classification experiment using the latent variables as input features. Figure 2 shows the classification performance obtained on the test sets MNIST and Fashion-MNIST, noisy MNIST, and noisy Fashion-MNIST. As Fig. 2 presents, VAE reaches its peak performance for the optimal choice of latent space dimensions, but yields inefficient codes if the latent space is too large. However, the performance of our model and VSC is independent of latent space dimensions, making them able to reliably recover efficient codes without the need to specify an optimal latent space size. Additionally, our model outperforms VSC for noisy test images.

Table 4. Quantitative evaluation for test set with and without noise.

Dataset	Model	test set without noise			noisy test set		
		PSNR ($\uparrow$)	SSIM ($\uparrow$)	LPIPS-VGG ($\downarrow$)	PSNR ($\uparrow$)	SSIM ($\uparrow$)	LPIPS-VGG ($\downarrow$)
CelebA	CVAE	20.9 dB	0.620	0.021	16.70 dB	0.430	0.034
	CVSC	28.9 dB	0.789	0.014	24.10 dB	0.700	0.023
	Our Model	**29.6 dB**	**0.800**	**0.013**	**27.20 dB**	**0.750**	**0.019**
MNIST	CVAE	33.00dB	0.833	0.017	29.00dB	0.659	0.025
	CVSC	34.40dB	0.960	**0.012**	30.40dB	0.870	0.021
	Our Model	**34.57dB**	**0.965**	**0.012**	**32.57dB**	**0.910**	**0.014**
Fashion-MNIST	CVAE	30.30dB	0.590	0.019	21.65dB	0.430	0.027
	CVSC	30.55dB	0.760	0.014	26.97dB	0.680	0.022
	Our Model	**31.07dB**	**0.800**	**0.015**	**28.97dB**	**0.710**	**0.018**

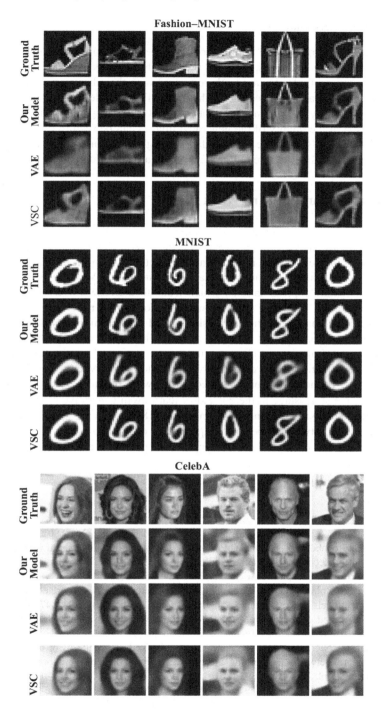

Fig. 3. Examples of image reconstruction for the CelebA, MNIST, and Fashion-MNIST datasets.

4.2   Qualitative Evaluation

Figure 3 shows the qualitative comparisons between our proposed model, VAE and VSC for three different datasets. As Fig. 3 presents the samples generated by our model more closely resemble the ground truth compared with the other models, hence proving our hypothesis that using sleep algorithm on VAE (VAE–sleep algorithm) improves output interpretability and producing latent code that is less dispersed. The most noticeable distinction in the quality of the generated images can be seen in the output of our model vs VSC and VAE for the CelebA dataset (Fig. 3), not only the images are more clear, but also, our model is able to retain and replicate facial features in more details.

5   Conclusion and Future Work

In this work, we propose a biologically realistic sleep algorithm for VAEs. The algorithm augments the normal training phase of the VAE with an unsupervised learning phase in the equivalent SVAE modeled after how the human brain learns, using the Mirrored STDP rules. We hypothesize that the unsupervised VAE-sleep phase creates more natural feature representations, which leads to increase a VAE's robustness to reconstruct the input. We show that our model performs better than the standard VAE and VSC on benchmark classification task (MNIST and Fashion-MNIST) by demonstrating improved classification accuracy and significantly increased robustness to the number of latent dimensions. The quantitative evaluations show that our model can generate more realistic images compared to the state of arts when tested on disturbed or noisy inputs. To the best of our knowledge, this work provides a step towards mimicking biological sleep stage in the context of learning in generative models like VAE. Future work includes: improving spike encoding [18] used in the spiking convolution layer, scaling the network to perform experiments on images with a larger size than we currently experiment with, and applying the sleep stage to a generative model for a spatio-temproal dataset like video.

References

1. Kim, H., Mnih, A.: Disentangling by factorising. arXiv preprint arXiv:1802.05983 (2018)
2. Talafha, S., Rekabdar, B., Ekenna, C.P., Mousas, C.: Attentional adversarial variational video generation via decomposing motion and content. In: 2020 IEEE 14th International Conference on Semantic Computing (ICSC). IEEE, pp. 45–52 (2020)
3. Brown, P.E., Roberts, G.O., Kåresen, K.F., Tonellato, S.: Blur-generated non-separable space-time models. J. Royal Stat. Soc. Series B (Stat. Methodol.) 62(4), 847–860 (2000)
4. Roy, S.S., Ahmed, M., Akhand, M.A.H.: Noisy image classification using hybrid deep learning methods. J. Inf. Commun. Technol. 17(2), 233–269 (2018)
5. Rekabdar, B., Nicolescu, M., Nicolescu, M., Louis, S.: Using patterns of firing neurons in spiking neural networks for learning and early recognition of spatio-temporal patterns. Neural Comput. Appl. 28(5), 881–897 (2016). https://doi.org/10.1007/s00521-016-2283-y
6. Rekabdar, B., Fraser, L., Nicolescu, M., Nicolescu, M.: A real-time spike-timing classifier of spatio-temporal patterns. Neurocomputing 311, 183–196 (2018)

7. Rekabdar, B., Nicolescu, M., Kelley, R., Nicolescu, M.: An unsupervised approach to learning and early detection of spatio-temporal patterns using spiking neural networks. J. Intell. Robotic Syst. **80**(1), 83–97 (2015)
8. Ankit, A., Sengupta, A., Panda, P., Roy, K.: Resparc: a reconfigurable and energy-efficient architecture with memristive crossbars for deep spiking neural networks. In: Proceedings of the 54th Annual Design Automation Conference 2017, pp. 1–6 (2017)
9. Iakymchuk, T., Rosado-Muñoz, A., Guerrero-Martínez, J.F., Bataller-Mompeán, M., Francés-Víllora, J.V.: Simplified spiking neural network architecture and stdp learning algorithm applied to image classification. EURASIP J. Image Video Process. **2015**(1), 4 (2015)
10. Tonolini, F., Jensen, B.S., Murray-Smith, R.: Variational sparse coding. In: PMLR Uncertainty in Artificial Intelligence. pp. 690–700 (2020)
11. Wilson, M.A., McNaughton, B.L.: Reactivation of hippocampal ensemble memories during sleep. Science **265**(5172), 676–679 (1994)
12. Tadros, T., Krishnan, G., Ramyaa, R., Bazhenov, M.: Biologically inspired sleep algorithm for increased generalization and adversarial robustness in deep neural networks. In: International Conference on Learning Representations (2019)
13. Burbank, K.S.: Mirrored stdp implements autoencoder learning in a network of spiking neurons. PLoS Comput. Biol. **11**(12), e1004566 (2015)
14. Pu, Y., et al.: Variational autoencoder for deep learning of images, labels and caption. In: Advances in Neural Information Processing Systems, pp. 2352–2360 (2016)
15. Mozafari, M., Ganjtabesh, M., Nowzari-Dalini, A., Thorpe, S.J., Masquelier, T.: Bio-inspired digit recognition using reward-modulated spike-timing-dependent plasticity in deep convolutional networks. Pattern Recogn. **94**, 87–95 (2019)
16. Salimans, T., Kingma, D.P.: Weight normalization: A simple reparameterization to accelerate training of deep neural networks. In: Advances in Neural Information Processing Systems, pp. 901–909 (2016)
17. Rueckauer, B., Liu, S.-C.: Conversion of analog to spiking neural networks using sparse temporal coding. In: IEEE International Symposium on Circuits and Systems (ISCAS). pp. 1–5, IEEE (2018)
18. Hazan, H., Saunders, D.J., Khan, H., Patel, D., Sanghavi, D.T., Siegelmann, H.T., Kozma, R.: Bindsnet: a machine learning-oriented spiking neural networks library in python. Front. Neuroinf. **12**, 89 (2018)
19. LeCun, Y.: The mnist database of handwritten digits (1998)
20. Xiao, H., Rasul, K., Vollgraf, R.: Fashion-mnist: a novel image dataset for benchmarking machine learning algorithms. arXiv preprint arXiv:1708.07747 (2017)
21. Liu, Z., Luo, P., Wang, X., Tang, X.: Large-scale celebfaces attributes (celeba) dataset. vol. 15(2018)
22. Huynh-Thu, Q., Ghanbari, M.: Scope of validity of psnr in image/video quality assessment. Electron. Lett. **44**(13), 800–801 (2008)
23. Wang, Z., Bovik, A.C., Sheikh, H.R., Simoncelli, E.P., et al.: Image quality assessment: from error visibility to structural similarity. IEEE Trans. Image Process. **13**(4), 600–612 (2004)
24. Zhang, R., Isola, P., Efros, A.A., Shechtman, E., Wang, O.: The unreasonable effectiveness of deep features as a perceptual metric. In: Proceedings of the IEEE Conference on Computer Vision and Pattern Recognition. pp. 586–595 (2018)
25. Zhang, X., Zou, J., He, K., Sun, J.: Accelerating very deep convolutional networks for classification and detection. IEEE Trans. Pattern Anal. Mach. Intell. **38**(10), 1943–1955 (2015)

A Deep Genetic Programming Based Methodology for Art Media Classification Robust to Adversarial Perturbations

Gustavo Olague[1]([⊠]), Gerardo Ibarra-Vázquez[2], Mariana Chan-Ley[1],
Cesar Puente[2], Carlos Soubervielle-Montalvo[2], and Axel Martinez[1]

[1] EvoVisión Laboratory, CICESE Research Center, Carretera Ensenada-Tijuana
3918, Zona Playitas 22860, Ensenada, B.C., Mexico
[2] Universidad Autónoma de San Luis Potosí, Facultad de Ingeniería. Dr. Manuel
Nava 8, Col. Zona Universitaria Poniente, San Luis Potosí, S.L.P. 78290, Mexico

Abstract. Art Media Classification problem is a current research area
that has attracted attention due to the complex extraction and analysis of features of high-value art pieces. The perception of the attributes
can not be subjective, as humans sometimes follow a biased interpretation of artworks while ensuring automated observation's trustworthiness.
Machine Learning has outperformed many areas through its learning
process of artificial feature extraction from images instead of designing handcrafted feature detectors. However, a major concern related to
its reliability has brought attention because, with small perturbations
made intentionally in the input image (adversarial attack), its prediction can be completely changed. In this manner, we foresee two ways of
approaching the situation: (1) solve the problem of adversarial attacks
in current neural networks methodologies, or (2) propose a different approach that can challenge deep learning without the effects of adversarial
attacks. The first one has not been solved yet, and adversarial attacks
have become even more complex to defend. Therefore, this work presents
a Deep Genetic Programming method, called Brain Programming, that
competes with deep learning and studies the transferability of adversarial
attacks using two artworks databases made by art experts. The results
show that the Brain Programming method preserves its performance in
comparison with AlexNet, making it robust to these perturbations and
competing to the performance of Deep Learning.

Keywords: Brain Programming · Deep learning · Symbolic learning ·
Art media classification · Adversarial attacks

1 Introduction

Art media refers to the materials and techniques used by an artist to create
an artwork. The categorization problem of visual art media is an open research
area with challenging tasks, such as the classification of fine art pieces, which is

© Springer Nature Switzerland AG 2020
G. Bebis et al. (Eds.): ISVC 2020, LNCS 12509, pp. 68–79, 2020.
https://doi.org/10.1007/978-3-030-64556-4_6

extremely difficult due to the selection of features that distinguish each medium. For example, an art expert analyzes the style, genre, and media from artworks to classify them.

The artwork style is associated with the author's school and is usually described by its distinctive visual elements, techniques, and methods. Recognition of the form is related to the localization of features at different levels. The classical hierarchy of genres ranks history-painting and portrait as high, while landscapes and still-life are low because they did not contain persons. Therefore, handling these many aspects of an automated classification system is a big challenge.

The recent progress of Machine Learning (ML) in Computer Vision (CV) tasks has made methodologies such as Deep Learning (DL) adaptable to many research areas like the categorization problem of art media. Commonly, these methodologies learn from the visual content and contextual information of the image to assign the class or category to which it belongs. DL is known to achieve exemplary performance in many areas. However, recent studies have demonstrated that Adversarial Attacks (AA) pose a predicting threat to DL's success because with small perturbations intentionally created, they could lead to incorrect outputs to a model.

In this matter, AA is a popular research topic covering all aspects of the attack architectures and defense mechanisms to diminish the attack damage. Nevertheless, despite significant efforts to solve this problem, attacks have become more complex and challenging to defend. Today, researchers study AA from different viewpoints. On the one hand, white-box attacks refer to when the targeted model is known, including its parameter values, architecture, and training method. On the other hand, black-box attacks are when AA generates adversarial examples or perturbed images with no information on the targeted architecture model during learning [1]. Another feature of the attacks is that it can be specifically designed to predict a desirable class (targeted attack) or produce an incorrect output no matter the class (untargeted attack). Furthermore, it has been reported that AA can be transferable from an ML model to others. Hence, we foresee two ways to approach the situation: (1) solve the problem of adversarial attacks in current neural networks methodologies, or (2) propose a different approach that can challenge deep learning by being immune to adversarial attacks.

This article presents a study of the transferability and the effects of adversarial attacks made for deep learning to an approach that solves the problem of image classification through a genetic programming based (GP-like) methodology called "Brain Programming" (BP) (explained in Sect. 4). Extend the study of the effects of *adversarial attacks* on a different approach for image classification would highlight the differences between performance and robustness to these perturbations.

2   Related Research

The categorization problem of art media in CV has arisen from the need to have automatic systems for identifying valuable artwork pieces to have a trustworthy analysis that can not be subjective as humans are prone to be. Firstly, hand-crafted feature extraction approaches were used to solve the problem. One of the first approaches [8] proposed a Discrete Cosine Transform (DCT) coefficients scheme for feature extraction for painter identification by classifying the artist's style. They were able to find five painters among 30 artworks with encouraging but not perfect results.

Later, wavelets were used to analyze several features from artworks like texture, geometry, style, brush strokes, and contours. In [13], artist classification was made using wavelets of brush strokes drawn on ancient paintings. In [7], wavelets were used with several classification algorithms such as support vector machines (SVM), hidden Markov models, among others for artist identification of 101 high-resolution grayscale paintings. In [2], it is presented a comparative study of different classification methodologies based handcrafted features such as semantic-level features with an SVM, color SIFT (Scale-Invariant Feature Transform) and opponent SIFT with bag-of-words and latent Dirichlet allocation with a generative bag-of-words topic model for fine-art genre classification.

Recently, ML approaches benefit from the learning process to acquire features from the images' visual content. For example, in [9], they proposed a GP method that uses transform-based evolvable features to evolve features that are evaluated through a standard classifier. In [4,15], authors reported using a GP-like methodology that aims to emulate the behavior of the brain based on neuroscience knowledge for art media categorization having competitive results with a DL model. Nevertheless, approaches based on convolutional neural network (CNN) became famous because of their outstanding performances in many areas. Bar et al. [3] proposed a compact binary representation combined with the PiCoDes descriptors from a deep neural network to identify artistic styles in paintings showing exceptional results on a large-scale collection of paintings. In [17], they employ a deep CNN to recognize artistic media from artworks and classify them into several categories such as oil-paint brush, pastel, pencil, and watercolor. They compare their results with that of trained humans having comparable results.

Thus, even CNN architectures have classified large-scale sets of images with multiple classes with similar results that trained humans, the security concerns about these architectures make them unreliable. The brittleness is because, with small perturbations produced on the image, DL can be intentionally fooled. For example, there are critical areas in museums and galleries such as artist identification and forgery detection, where the confidence of the prediction must not depend on a system that can be manipulated by an imperceptible perturbation. This catastrophic scenario could lead to forgeries to circulate on the market or be misattributed to a specific artist.

3   Problem Statement

In this section, we detail the serious problem in the DL structure to the adversarial attacks. First, given an input image $\mathbf{x}$ and its corresponding label y, DL establish a relationship within the data by the following equation:

$$y = f(\mathbf{x}) = \mathbf{w}^\mathsf{T}\mathbf{x} \quad , \tag{1}$$

where function $f()$ is the DL model, whose associated weights parameters are $\mathbf{w}$. However, an erroneous behavior is notable when the input image suffers a small change in its pixels $\mathbf{x}_\rho = \mathbf{x} + \rho$ such that:

$$f(\mathbf{x}) \neq f(\mathbf{x}_\rho) \tag{2}$$

$$||\mathbf{x} - \mathbf{x}_\rho||_p < \alpha \tag{3}$$

where $p \in N, p \geq 1, \alpha \in R, \alpha \geq 0$. So, it can be defined an Adversarial Example as an intentional modified input $\mathbf{x}_\rho$ that is classified differently than $\mathbf{x}$ by the DCNN model, with a limited level of change in the pixels of $||\mathbf{x} - \mathbf{x}_\rho||_p < \alpha$, so that it may be imperceptible to a human eye.

The simplest explanation of how adversarial examples works to attack DL models is that most digital images use 8-bit per channel per pixel. So, each step of $1/255$ limits the data representation; the information in between is not used. Therefore, if every element of a perturbation ρ is smaller than the data resolution, it is coherent for the linear model to predict distinct given an input $\mathbf{x}$ than to an adversarial input $\mathbf{x}_\rho = \mathbf{x} + \rho$. We assume that forasmuch as $||\rho||_\infty < \alpha$, where α is too small to be discarded, the classifiers should predict the same class to $\mathbf{x}$ and $\mathbf{x}_\rho$.

Nonetheless, after applying the weight matrix $\mathbf{w} \in \mathbf{R}^{M \times N}$ to the adversarial example, we obtain the dot product defined by $\mathbf{w}^\mathsf{T}\mathbf{x}_\rho = \mathbf{w}^\mathsf{T}\mathbf{x} + \mathbf{w}^\mathsf{T}\rho$. Hence, the adversarial example will grow the activation by $\mathbf{w}^\mathsf{T}\rho$. Note that the dimensionality of the problem does not grow with $||\rho||_\infty$; thus, the activation change caused by perturbation ρ can grow linearly with n. As a result, the perturbation can make many imperceptible changes to the input to obtain big output changes.

DL's behavior is hugely linear to be immune to adversarial examples, and nonlinear models such as sigmoid networks are set up to be in the non-saturating most of the time, becoming them more like a linear model. Hence, every perturbation as accessible or challenging to compute should also affect deep neural networks. Therefore, when a model is affected by an adversarial example, this image often affects another model, no matter if the two models have different architectures or were trained with different databases. They just have to be set up for the same task to change the result [5].

4   Methodology

The experiment consists of studying the transferability of an AA from CNN to BP. This problem's methodology considers unconventional training, validation, and test databases since we apply two different image databases compiled by art experts. Training and validation databases are constructed from the Kaggle database, while testing uses a standard database WikiArt (See Table 1). The aim is to emulate a real-world scenario where the trained models are tested with an unseen standard benchmark compiled by a different group of experts.

Validation and test databases are used to compute adversarial examples using the fast gradient signed method (FGSM) and AlexNet architecture using standard values for scale $\epsilon = 2, 4, 8, 16, 32$ to build the perturbations. The implementation of the FGSM was made on Pytorch v1.1. AlexNet was trained using transfer learning with the pre-trained model from Pytorch, and BP utilizes the models reported in [4, 15].

We formulate the art media classification problem in terms of a binary classification, whose main goal is to find the class elements. Also, we employ classification accuracy as a measure of performance for the classifiers, which is simply the rate of correct classifications given by the following formula:

$$Accuracy = \frac{1}{N} \sum_{n=1}^{N} d(y\prime_n, y_n)$$

where N is the total of test images, $y\prime_n$ is the predicted label for the image n, y_n is the original label for the image n, and $d(x, y) = 1$ if $x = y$ and 0 otherwise. In the following sections, the methods used for the experiment are briefly explained.

4.1 Brain Programming

BP is an evolutionary paradigm for solving CV problems that is reported in [6, 14, 16]. This methodology extracts characteristics from images through a hierarchical structure inspired by the brain's functioning. BP proposes a GP-like method, using a multi-tree representation for individuals. The main goal is to obtain a set of evolutionary visual operators ($EVOs$), also called visual operators (VOs), which are embedded within a hierarchical structure called the artificial visual cortex (AVC).

BP can be summarized in two steps: first, the evolutionary process whose primary purpose is to discover functions to optimize complex models by adjusting the operations within them. Second, the AVC, a hierarchical structure inspired by the human visual cortex, uses the concept of composition of functions to extract features from images. The model can be adapted depending on the task, whether it is trying to solve the focus of attention for saliency problems or the complete AVC for categorization/classification problems. In this section, we briefly described the BP workflow (see Fig. 1), but further details are explained in [4].

Initialization. First, we set the parameters of the evolutionary process of BP and establish the image databases. Next, a random initial population is created to evolve the population. In BP, an individual is a computer program represented by syntactic trees embedded into a hierarchical structure.

Individuals within the population contain a variable number of syntactic trees, ranging from 4 to 12, one for each evolutionary visual operator (VO_O,

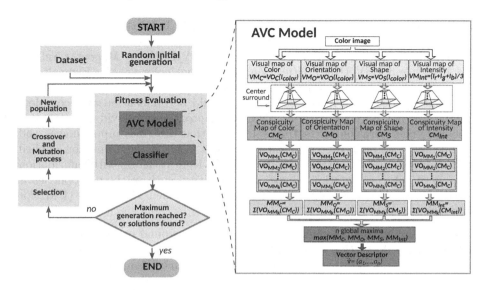

Fig. 1. Brain Programming workflow

VO_C, VO_S, VO_I) regarding orientation, color, shape, and intensity; and at least one tree to merge the visual maps produced and generate the Mental Maps (MM). Details about the usage of these visual operators are explained in detail in [4, 6, 14].

Functions within each VO are defined with expert knowledge to attend characteristics related to the dimension they represent and updated through genetic operations. After creating the first generation, the AVC model is used to evaluate the population's fitness, as shown in Fig. 1.

Fitness function: Artificial Virtual Cortex (AVC). The evolutionary loop starts evaluating each individual by using the VOs generated in the previous step to extract features from input images through the AVC structure depicted in Fig. 1. The result of this procedure is a descriptor vector that encodes the object. Then, BP uses an SVM to calculate the classification rate for a given training image database. We explain the detailed steps below. The entrance to the system is an RGB image that belongs to a predefined class. This system follows a function-based instead of data-based paradigm; hence, we define an image I as the graph-of-a-function.

Definition 1. Image as the graph of a function. *Let f be a function $f : U \subset \mathbb{R}^2 \to \mathbb{R}$. The graph or image I of f is the subset of $\mathbb{R}^3$ that consist of the points $(x, y, f(x, y))$, in which the ordered pair (x, y) is a point in U and $f(x, y)$ is the value at that point. Symbolically, the image $I = \{(x, y, f(x, y)) \in \mathbb{R}^3 | (x, y) \in U\}$.*

This definition is based on the fact that the images result from the impression of variations in light intensity along the two-dimensional plane.

Visual Maps. Each input image is transformed to build the set $I_{color} = \{I_r,$ $I_g, I_b, I_c, I_m, I_y, I_k, I_h, I_s, I_v\}$, where each element corresponds to the color components of the RGB (red, green, blue), CMYK (Cyan, Magenta, Yellow, and black) and HSV (Hue, Saturation, and Value) color spaces. Elements on I_{color} are the inputs to four VOs defined by each individual. It is important to note that each solution in the population should be understood as a complete system and not only as a list of three-based programs. Individuals represent a possible configuration for feature extraction that describes input images and are optimized through the evolutionary process. Each VO is a function applied to the input image to extract specific features from it, along with information streams of color, orientation, shape, and intensity; each of these properties is called a dimension. The output to VO is an image called Visual Map (VM) for each dimension.

Conspicuity Maps. The next step is the center-surround process; it efficiently combines the information from the VMs and is useful for detecting scale invariance in each of the dimensions. This process is performed by applying a Gaussian smoothing over the VM at nine scales; this processing reduces the visual map's size by half on each level forming a pyramid. Subsequently, the six levels of the pyramid are extracted and combined. Since the levels have different sizes, each level is normalized and scaled to the visual map's dimension using polynomial interpolation. This technique simulates the center-surround process of the biological system. After extracting features, the brain receives stimuli from the vision center and compares it with the receptive field's surrounding information. The goal is to process the images so that the results are independent of scale changes. The entire process ensures that the image regions are responding to the indicated area. This process is carried out for each characteristic dimension; the results are called Conspicuity Maps (CM), focusing only on the searched object by highlighting the most salient features.

Mental Maps. Following the AVC flowchart, all information obtained is synthesized to build maps that discriminate against the unwanted information previously computed by the CMs. These new maps are called Mental Maps (MMs).

The AVC model uses a set-of-functions to extract the images' discriminant characteristics; it uses a functional approach. Thus, a set of k VOs is applied to the CMs for the construction of the MMs. These VOs correspond to the remaining part of the individual that has not been used. Unlike the operators used for the VMs, the operators' whole set is the same for all the dimensions. These operators filter the visual information and extract the information that characterizes the object of interest. Then, using Eq. (4), where d is the dimension, and k represents the cardinality of the set of VO_{MM_k}, we apply the MMs for each dimension.

$$MM_d = \sum_{i=1}^{k} VO_{MM_i}(CM_d) \tag{4}$$

Descriptor Vector and Classification. The following stage in the model is the construction of the image descriptor vector (DV). The system concatenates the four MMs and uses a max operation to extract the n highest values; these values are used to construct the DV. Once we get the descriptor vectors of all the images in the database, the system trains an SVM. The classification score obtained by the SVM indicates the fitness of the individual.

Selection and Reproduction. A set of individuals is selected from the population with a probability based on fitness to participate in the genetic recombination, and the best individual is retained for further processing. The new individual of the population is created from the selected individual by applying genetic operators. Like genetic algorithms, BP executes the crossover between two selected parents at the chromosome level using a "cut-and-splice" crossover. Thus, all data beyond the selected crossover point is swapped between both parents A and B. The result of applying a crossover at the gene level is performed by randomly selecting two subtree crossover points between both parents. The selected genes are swapped with the corresponding subtree in the other parent. The chromosome level mutation leads to selecting a random gene of a given parent to replace such substructure with a new randomly mutated gene. The mutation at the gene level is calculated by applying a subtree mutation to a probabilistically selected gene; the subtree after that point is removed and replaced with a new subtree.

Stop Criteria. The evolutionary loop is terminated until one of these two conditions is reached: (1) an acceptable classification rate, or (2) the total number of generations.

4.2 Convolutional Neural Networks

The ML community introduced the idea of designing DL models that build features from images. LeCun et al. [12] presented the modern framework of CNN, but the first time that CNN starts attracting attention was with the development of the AlexNet model [10]. The authors participated in the ImageNet Large-Scale Visual Recognition Challenge 2012, where they reduced by half the error rate on the image classification task.

AlexNet layer-architecture consists of 5 convolutional, three max-pooling, two normalization, and three fully connected layers (the last with 1000 softmax outputs), 60 Million parameters in 500,000 neurons. Additionally, Alex et al. [10] introduced the use of ReLU (Rectified Linear Unit) as an activation function with the benefits of much faster training than using tanh or sigmoid functions. To prevent overfitting, they also introduced the dropout and data augmentation methods.

4.3 Adversarial Attack

The FGSM [5] is the most popular, easy, and widely used method for computing adversarial examples from an input image, see Fig. 2. It increases the loss of the classifier by solving the following equation: $\rho = \epsilon \ \text{sign}(\nabla J(\theta, \mathbf{x}, y_l))$, where

$\nabla J()$ computes the gradient of the cost function around the current value of the model parameters θ with the respect to the image $\mathbf{x}$ and the target label y_l. sign() denotes the sign function which ensures that the magnitude of the loss is maximized and ϵ is a small scalar value that restricts the norm L_∞ of the perturbation.

The perturbations generated by FGSM take advantage of the linearity of the deep learning models in the higher dimensional space to make the model misclassify the image. The implication of the linearity of deep learning models discovered by FSGM is that it exists transferability between models. Kurakin et al. in [11] reported that after using the ImageNet database, the top-1 error rate using the perturbations generated by FGSM is around 63–69% for $\epsilon \in [2, 32]$.

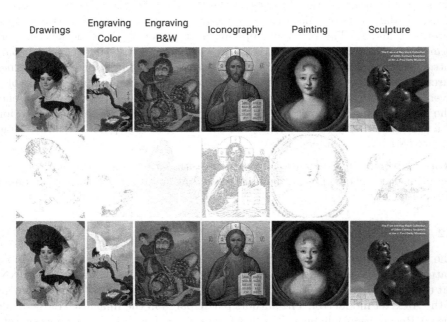

Fig. 2. Illustrations of adversarial examples from each class generated using FGSM. The first row shows an image from each class. In the second row, the perturbations computed by the FGSM are presented. The third row shows the resulting adversarial example at $\epsilon = 32$, the strongest perturbation.

4.4   Database Collection

We follow the protocol and databases from the experiment of the art media categorization problem reported in [4]. The training and validation set of images are obtained from the digitized artwork database downloaded from the Kaggle website. This database comprises five categories of art media: drawing, painting, iconography, engraving, and sculpture. For class engraving, there were two different kinds of engravings. Most of them were engravings with only one color defining the art piece. The other style was Japanese engravings, which introduce color to the images. Therefore, the engraving class was split into engraving grayscale and color. For testing, a standard database WikiArt is used from which it was selected images of the same categories. Since the Wikiart engraving class is grayscale, the ukiyo-e class (Japanese engravings) from Wikiart was used as the engraving color class. Also, the set of images of the category landscapes, which are paintings from renowned artists, is added to test the painting class. Table 1 provides the number of images for each database.

Table 1. Total number of images per class obtained from Kaggle and Wikiart Databases

	Drawings	Engraving gray scale	Engraving color	Painting	Iconography	Sculpture	Caltech Background
Train	553	426	30	1021	1038	868	233
Validation	553	284	19	1021	1038	868	233
Wikiart	204	695	1167	2089	251	116	233
Wikiart Landscapes				136			

5   Results

In this section, we present and discuss the experimental results summarized in Tables 2 and 3. Table 2 provides results for the five classes of the Kaggle database. Each method presents its performance for training, validation, and the adversarial examples from the FGSM computed with the validation database using $\epsilon = 2, 4, 8, 16, 32$. Table 3 shows the result for the Wikiart images where both methods were tested. It is shown the outcome of the model for the clean images as well as the adversarial examples.

We observe in Table 2 that AlexNet surpassed BP in almost every class when considering the validation database except for the painting class. However, as we add perturbations to the validation images, the effect of AA becomes more notable. It is shown how the performance of AlexNet deteriorates in proportion to the AA. In the worst-case–Engraving color images–there is a drop in performance from 94.72% to 17.22% of classification accuracy. On the other hand, BP preserves its performance on all experiments even when we added the most substantial perturbation of $\epsilon = 32$. Hence, if we look at each of the comparisons (bold numbers), BP outperforms AlexNet.

For the testing part (see Table 3), we have that BP obtained notable better results for painting, painting landscapes, and drawings. In contrast, AlexNet obtained superior performance on engraving grayscale, engraving color, and iconography. We should mention that in any case, the results of both methods are very good. For the sculpture class, BP matches the performance of AlexNet with a difference of around 0.6%. Then again, the susceptibility of AlexNet to the AA is a significant problem. Its accounts fall abruptly on all classes; meanwhile, the BP output remains steady.

Table 2. Results obtained after applying BP and AlexNet on the Kaggle database. Each method presents its classification accuracy for training, validation, and the adversarial examples using FGSM computed from the validation database at $\epsilon = 2, 4, 8, 16, 32$

	Brain Programming (BP)							AlexNet						
	train	val	$\epsilon2$	$\epsilon4$	$\epsilon8$	$\epsilon16$	$\epsilon32$	train	val	$\epsilon2$	$\epsilon4$	$\epsilon8$	$\epsilon16$	$\epsilon32$
Sculpture	93.26	92.79	**92.79**	**92.79**	**92.79**	**92.79**	**92.79**	99.36	**95.78**	90.93	90.93	63.24	27.5	14.57
Painting	99.68	**99.04**	**98.25**	**98.25**	**98.48**	**98.41**	**98.48**	98.96	97.69	93.46	93.46	83.01	66.99	69.30
Engraving gray scale	89.76	92.05	92.23	92.23	**92.23**	91.70	91.87	99.76	**99.29**	**96.11**	**96.11**	78.62	56.71	47.88
Engraving color	98.33	97.37	**97.37**	**97.37**	**97.37**	**97.37**	**97.37**	100	100	73.68	73.68	23.68	13.16	15.79
Iconography	92.84	91.42	91.42	91.42	**91.42**	**91.42**	**91.42**	99.61	**98.66**	**96.30**	**96.30**	83.24	52.26	38.39
Drawings	96.56	90.59	**90.59**	**90.59**	**90.59**	**90.59**	**90.59**	96.44	**91.35**	85.75	85.75	66.79	44.91	35.62

Table 3. Results obtained after applying BP and AlexNet on the Wikiart database. Each method presents its classification accuracy for testing, and the adversarial examples using FGSM computed from the test database at $\epsilon = 2, 4, 8, 16, 32$

	Brain Programming (BP)						AlexNet					
	test	$\epsilon2$	$\epsilon4$	$\epsilon8$	$\epsilon16$	$\epsilon32$	test	$\epsilon2$	$\epsilon4$	$\epsilon8$	$\epsilon16$	$\epsilon32$
Sculpture	90.54	**90.83**	**90.83**	**90.83**	**90.83**	**90.83**	91.15	87.61	87.61	65.49	44.25	36.87
Painting	100	**95.65**	**95.65**	**95.65**	**95.65**	**95.65**	94.06	90.57	90.57	64.64	41.04	41.00
Painting Landscapes	100	100	100	100	100	100	93.77	86.99	86.99	61.25	41.46	35.77
Engraving gray scale	91.55	92.64	92.64	**91.97**	**91.72**	**91.63**	**98.58**	**94.06**	**94.06**	75.06	57.32	54.64
Engraving color	89.92	**89.68**	**89.68**	**89.74**	**89.86**	**89.80**	94.72	73.55	73.55	25.49	12.30	17.22
Iconography	91.74	91.66	91.66	**91.82**	**91.74**	**91.74**	96.07	93.39	93.39	70.04	37.40	28.72
Drawings	**94.05**	**94.28**	**94.28**	93.59	93.81	94.50	86.73	77.8	77.8	57.21	41.19	32.72

6   Conclusions and Future Work

In conclusion, AA are a severe threat to the security of DL models. Their performance can be extremely weakened with such small perturbations. With traditional CV approaches, it is not easy to obtain results comparable to DL models. However, we propose a GP-like methodology inspired by the brain's behavior to solve art media classification. This work innovates compared with a DL model by considering performance and robustness against adversarial attacks. Also, we want to extend the robustness to adversarial attacks using CV mainstream approaches from image classification for future work. Furthermore, we will increase the number of adversarial attacks to assess the classifiers' performance under various conditions.

References

1. Akhtar, N., Mian, A.: Threat of adversarial attacks on deep learning in computer vision: a survey. IEEE Access **6**, 14410–14430 (2018)
2. Arora, R.S., Elgammal, A.: Towards automated classification of fine-art painting style: a comparative study. In: Proceedings of the 21st International Conference on Pattern Recognition (ICPR2012), pp. 3541–3544. IEEE (2012)

3. Bar, Y., Levy, N., Wolf, L.: Classification of artistic styles using binarized features derived from a deep neural network. In: Agapito, L., Bronstein, M.M., Rother, C. (eds.) ECCV 2014. LNCS, vol. 8925, pp. 71–84. Springer, Cham (2015). https:// doi.org/10.1007/978-3-319-16178-5_5
4. Chan-Ley, M., Olague, G.: Categorization of digitized artworks by media with brain programming. Appl. Opt. **59**(14), 4437–4447 (2020)
5. Goodfellow, I.J., Shlens, J., Szegedy, C.: Explaining and harnessing adversarial examples. In: 3rd International Conference on Learning Representations, ICLR 2015, Conference Track Proceedings p. 11 (2015)
6. Hernández, D.E., Clemente, E., Olague, G., Briseño, J.L.: Evolutionary multiobjective visual cortex for object classification in natural images. J. Comput. Sci. **17**, 216–233 (2016). https://doi.org/10.1016/j.jocs.2015.10.011
7. Johnson, C.R., et al.: Image processing for artist identification. IEEE Signal Process. Mag. **25**(4), 37–48 (2008)
8. Keren, D.: Painter identification using local features and naive bayes. In: Object Recognition Supported by User Interaction for Service Robots, vol. 2, pp. 474–477. IEEE (2002)
9. Kowaliw, T., McCormack, J., Dorin, A.: Evolutionary automated recognition and characterization of an individual's artistic style. In: IEEE Congress on Evolutionary Computation, pp. 1–8. IEEE (2010)
10. Krizhevsky, A., Sutskever, I., Hinton, G.E.: Imagenet classification with deep convolutional neural networks. In: Pereira, F., Burges, C.J.C., Bottou, L., Weinberger, K.Q. (eds.) Advances in Neural Information Processing Systems 25, pp. 1097–1105. Curran Associates, Inc. (2012). http://papers.nips.cc/paper/4824-imagenet-classification-with-deep-convolutional-neural-networks.pdf
11. Kurakin, A., Goodfellow, I.J., Bengio, S.: Adversarial machine learning at scale. In: ICLR 2017 Conference Track Proceedings 5th International Conference on Learning Representations, p. 17 (2017)
12. LeCun, Y., et al.: Backpropagation applied to handwritten zip code recognition. Neural Comput. **1**(4), 541–551 (1989)
13. Li, J., Wang, J.Z.: Studying digital imagery of ancient paintings by mixtures of stochastic models. IEEE Trans. Image Process. **13**(3), 340–353 (2004)
14. Olague, G., Clemente, E., Hernández, D.E., Barrera, A., Chan-Ley, M., Bakshi, S.: Artificial visual cortex and random search for object categorization. IEEE Access **7**, 54054–54072 (2019)
15. Olague, G., Chan-Ley, M.: Hands-on artificial evolution through brain programming. In: Banzhaf, W., Goodman, E., Sheneman, L., Trujillo, L., Worzel, B. (eds.) Genetic Programming Theory and Practice XVII. GEC, pp. 227–253. Springer, Cham (2020). https://doi.org/10.1007/978-3-030-39958-0_12
16. Olague, G., Hernández, D.E., Llamas, P., Clemente, E., Briseño, J.L.: Brain programming as a new strategy to create visual routines for object tracking. Multimed. Tools Appl. **78**(5), 5881–5918 (2018). https://doi.org/10.1007/s11042-018-6634-9
17. Yang, H., Min, K.: Classification of basic artistic media based on a deep convolutional approach. Visual Comput. **36**(3), 559–578 (2019). https://doi.org/10.1007/s00371-019-01641-6

rcGAN: Learning a Generative Model for Arbitrary Size Image Generation

Renato B. Arantes$^{(\boxtimes)}$, George Vogiatzis, and Diego R. Faria

Aston University, Aston St, Birmingham B4 7ET, England
{180178991,g.vogiatzis,d.faria}@aston.ac.uk
https://www2.aston.ac.uk/

Abstract. We introduce rcGAN, a new generative method that is capable of synthesising arbitrary sized, high-resolution images derived from a single reference image used to train our model. Our two-steps method uses a randomly conditioned convolutional generative adversarial network (rcGAN) trained on patches obtained from a reference image. It can capture the reference image internal patches distribution and then produce high-quality samples that share with this image the same visual attributes. After training, the rcGAN generates recursively an arbitrary number of samples which are then stitched together to produce an image whose size is determined by the number of samples that are used to synthesise it. Our proposed method can provide a practically infinite number of variations of a single input image that offers enough variability while preserving the essential large scale constraints. We experiment with our two-steps method on many types of models, including textures, building facades and natural landscapes, comparing very positively against others methods.

Keywords: GAN · Conditional GAN · Texture generation.

1 Introduction

When rendering photo-realistic images using computer graphics, real objects and their properties such as geometry, materials or light must be explicitly modelled, normally a time consuming and expensive process. In recent years, data-driven photo-realistic image synthesis has emerged as a viable alternative for certain classes of a scene. Available methods can be grouped into parametric and non-parametric. Non-parametric methods have a long history and are typically based on compositing from pre-existing exemplar images [1,4,6,10]. While they often succeed in generating very realistic images, they suffer from a lack of variability in the generated content. On the other hand, parametric methods based on deep neural architectures, have delivered promising results in the last few years. Parametric approaches are trained to reproduce the realism of real image datasets while maintaining a level of randomness and variety that is not achieved by non-parametric models [3,14]. However, with a few exceptions (e.g. [13,20]),

Electronic supplementary material The online version of this chapter (https://doi.org/10.1007/978-3-030-64556-4_7) contains supplementary material, which is available to authorized users.

© Springer Nature Switzerland AG 2020
G. Bebis et al. (Eds.): ISVC 2020, LNCS 12509, pp. 80–94, 2020.
https://doi.org/10.1007/978-3-030-64556-4_7

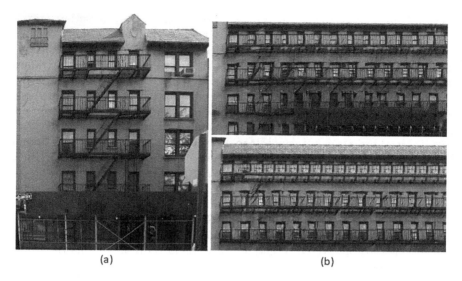

(a) (b)

Fig. 1. Our rcGAN in action. The task is to learn a model that can generate image patches that are sewed to build a bigger image. (a) Original image of size 405 × 512 pixels. (b) Synthetic images of size 640 × 320 pixels each.

parametric models are rarely able to scale up to full-resolution images. In this paper, we investigate whether GANs [8], one of the most successful parametric models, might be employed to generate new, high-resolution images, based on an individual reference image. With our two-steps method, we aim to create images that are similar to the reference one and also shares its main characteristics, see Fig. 1 for an example. The proposed method, which we denote as randomly conditioned GAN (or rcGAN for short), is tested on many types of scene, including textures, natural landscapes and building facades, comparing very positively against other single image GAN based approaches. This paper makes the following contributions:

- We present a novel GAN architecture that is randomly conditioned by a subset of pixels in the input image.
- We show how such an architecture can be used to progressively *grow* a realistic high-resolution image.
- We show how the synthesising process can be guided by carefully selecting the input seed, as outlined in Sect. 4.

Our code is available at https://github.com/renaaran/rcGAN.

2 Related Work

The generative adversarial networks (GANs), introduced by Goodfellow *et al.* [8], implements a new strategy for image synthesis in computer vision. Compared with traditional supervised machine learning methods, generative adversarial networks employ the concept of adversarial training, where two models are simultaneously trained: a generative model G that captures the data distribution, and a discriminator model D that estimates the probability that a sample came from the training data rather than G. The generator learns the data distribution p_g, over the data x, by creating a mapping function from a prior noise distribution $p_z(z)$ to data space as $G(z; \theta_g)$. Further, the discriminator, $D(x; \theta_d)$, outputs a single scalar representing the probability that x came from the training data instead of p_g.

In [18] Radford *et al.* introduced the deep convolutional generative adversarial networks (DCGANs) that creates a link among the achievements of CNNs for supervised learning and unsupervised learning. As stated by Goodfellow [9] the majority of GANs today are generally based on the DCGAN architecture, including the two-steps approach that is presented in this paper, where we combine the DCGAN architecture and the conditional GAN (cGAN) approach. Introduced by Mirza and Osindero in [15], a conditional GAN (cGAN) is a model where both the generator and the discriminator are conditioned on any information **y**. This information could be an image, as in our two-steps method, or any other additional information, such as a class label. In [15] the conditioning is done by supplying the condition **y** into both the generator and discriminator. In our method, on the other hand, we are using an alternate approach where we are conditioning only the generator as in [16].

In [11] Iizuka *et al.* introduce a triple network architecture for inpainting. A completion network that is fully convolutional, used to complete the image, a global context discriminator and a local context discriminator. Both are secondary networks used only during the training process. These discriminators are used to discover if an image is coherent or not. The global discriminator gets the whole picture as input and evaluates the global coherence of the scene. In opposition, the local discriminator tries to estimate the quality of a more specific region by looking only at a small part around a painted area. Our procedure can also be considered as an inpainting method as we use a conditional GAN to generate image blocks that match a given patch extracted from the source image, used to train our model. In the opposite direction of most works presented here, we propose to create a new image entirely from scratch, which is based on the given reference image. This approach is the originality of our proposed method: instead of generating a patch that fills a hole in an image, our proposed two-steps method uses that image as a model to synthesise randomly conditioned patches that later on are stitched together to create an arbitrary sized image. The number of patches stitched together is what determines the size of the generated image.

Since its introduction, the GAN architecture has been used in the area of texture synthesis and transfer. We presented some of these efforts above. However, there are more two parametric works that worth to be mentioned. They are the work of [7,17]. In [17] Portilla *et al.* proposed a method to generate random images parameterised by a collection of statistics constraints that are related to scale, orientation and spatial positions. On the other hand, using a CNN

[7] Gatys *et al.* proposed a parametric texture model that represent textures as a correlation among features maps in different layers of the convolutional neural network. Similar to both [7,17], the work presented in this paper can also be regarded as a texture generator. One advantage of our method is that we work with a patch-based strategy that enables our model to encode both high-frequency textures as well as large scale interactions. We can, consequently, generate arbitrary sized images with consistent characteristics like the aligned windows in the building facades.

Single Image GANs. In Spatial-GAN (SGAN), Jetchev *et al.* [12] extended the input noise distribution space from a single vector to a spatial tensor and recently, Bergmann *et al.* further developed this approach by proposing the Periodic Spatial-GAN (PSGAN) [2], which extends the structure of the input noise distribution by constructing tensors with different configurations and dimensions.

SinGAN [20] introduced by Shaham *et al.* is also a single image model for texture generation, as PSGAN and our proposed models. SinGAN is designed to deal with natural images, and it is built as a pyramid of fully convolutional GANs, each in charge of learning the patch distribution at a different scale of the image. SinGAN can produce realistic image samples that consist of complex textures and non-repetitive global structures.

Achieving impressive results, InGAN was developed by Shocker *et al.* [21] and intended to capture the unique image-specific patch-distribution and map them to new images with different size and shapes that share with the source one the same patch distribution, which they loosely call "same DNA". They also proposed a new Encoder-Encoder architecture, called "Internal GAN", that encodes an image-specific internal statistics, which they claim provides a single unified framework for a variety of tasks.

3 Randomly Conditioned GANs

Using just one image for training our rcGAN, we would like to get as a result a synthesised image that is different from the reference image used to train the rcGAN, but at the same time shares its main features. As an example, we used the facade [19] in Fig. 2a to train our rcGAN and we would like, at the end of our two-steps pipeline, to get an image like the one in the Fig. 2b. The Fig. 2b was synthesised by our two-steps process, as outlined in Sect. 3.2.

3.1 Conditioning by Randomly Selecting (CRS)

To synthesise arbitrary sized, high-resolution images, we developed a method built on deep convolutional generative adversarial networks (DCGAN) [18] and conditional GAN (cGAN) [15]. To train our rcGAN model, we extract patches from the source image I and use these patches for training and for conditioning our generator G. To condition our generator G we developed a new algorithm that *Conditions by Randomly Selecting (CRS)* pieces of a given image patch. These are presented as a condition to the generator G, which then generates a

Source image (272 × 512 pixels).

Synthesised image (1280 × 1280 pixels).

Fig. 2. Large-scale image generation. Reference image utilised to train our rcGAN method and a 1.6 Mpx synthetic output.

plausible *completion* of these patches. The *(CRS)* algorithm works as described in Algorithm 1.

On every iteration of the training process a batch is processed by the *(CRS)* algorithm to generate several different condition sub-patches that will be presented to the rcGAN generator. Figure 3 is an example of our *(CRS)* algorithm in action.

3.2 Training a rcGAN

Our proposed rcGAN architecture consists of a non-conditioned discriminator D and a conditioned generator G. The generator takes as input a noise vector z sampled from a normal distribution concatenated with a $N \times N$ image patch S, previously processed by the Algorithm 1, and then outputs another $N \times N$ image patch S^*.

Instead of conditioning all layers, we are only conditioning the first and last layers of the generator G. Empirical tests demonstrated that this approach speeds up the training process and doesn't compromise the quality of the generated patch S^*. For the first layer of the generator G, we concatenate the reshaped input image patch S with the provided noise vector before we feed it to this layer. For the last layer, we also concatenate the output of the penultimate layer with the reshaped input image patch S, and supplies this concatenation as input for this layer. See Fig. 4 for the proposed generator network architecture.

Algorithm 1. Conditioning by Randomly Selecting (CRS)

Input:

– An image patch S of size $N \times N$ and a random number r, generated between $[w \dots N - w]$, where $w = \lfloor N/6 \rfloor$.
– An integer number p, which is uniformly sampled from P, the set of possible ways of selecting parts of S as a condition sub-patch C_p.

The set P is composed of the following possible ways of sampling from S:

1. **Full patch**. The image patch is fully selected. The patch S is presented to our rcGAN without any extraction.
2. **Horizontal up**. All S pixels with coordinate (x, y) that has $y > r$ are selected as a condition.
3. **Horizontal down**. All S pixels with coordinate (x, y) that has $y < r$ are selected as a condition.
4. **Vertical left**. All S pixels with coordinate (x, y) that has $x < r$ are selected as a condition.
5. **Vertical right**. All S pixels with coordinate (x, y) that has $x > r$ are selected as a condition.
6. **Vertical and horizontal**. A combination of horizontal and vertical erasing, where the resulting selection is a corner condition.

Output: Condition C_p sub-patch extracted from S.

Fig. 3. Conditioning by Randomly Selecting (CRS). Examples of the six ways of generating conditions to our rcGAN, before and after merging the condition S with S^*. The green line on the right is there only to make it easier to visualise the inpainted area.

That generated output image patch S^* is then merged with S, as in Fig. 5, to create a resulting image. The discriminator network D, see Fig. 6, seeks to distinguish between the real and the generated image patches, while the generator network G strives to mislead it into misclassifying. Observe that our approach

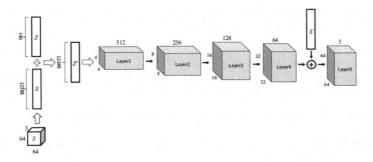

Fig. 4. Generator architecture. Initially, the 64 × 64 input patch is reshaped and then concatenated with the input noise vector z. Finally, before being processed by the last layer, the output of the penultimate layer is concatenated with the condition vector S.

diverges from [15] as we are conditioning only the generator G, letting the discriminator D as proposed by [18], without any constraint.

Following Shrivastava *et al.* in [22], instead of only outputting a probability of a patch S^* being real or fake, our discriminator D outputs a grid where each grid position corresponds to a local part of S^*, and represents the estimated probability that a local part of S^* is real or is being generated by G. This approach helps to improve the synthetic image quality and preserve the level of detail.

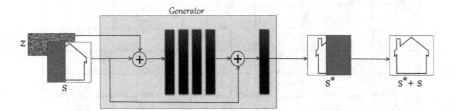

Fig. 5. Generator flow. An input $N \times N$ image, processed by the Algorithm 1, is used to condition the generator. The $N \times N$ output of the generator S^* is merged with S before it's given as input for the discriminator.

4   Patch Compositing

The second step of our rcGAN method is the generation of arbitrarily sized synthetic images. After training, our rcGAN recursively generates a sequence of samples which are then stitched together to synthesise a larger image. To stitch the GAN generated patches, we propose a compositing algorithm, inspired by the *image quilting* algorithm proposed by Efros *et al.* [5], that works as follows:

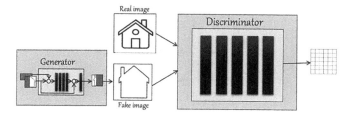

Fig. 6. Discriminator flow. The discriminator receives as input a set of $N \times N$ patches and seeks to distinguish among those obtained from actual images and those resulted from merging S and S^*.

To generate a synthetic image, with $M \times M$ blocks, each of them of size $N \times N$, we start by randomly selecting a patch S, or a *"seed"*, from the source image I, the same used to train our GAN, with size $N \times N/2$. This patch S is them passed to the generator G as a condition C_1. The right half part of the generator output S^* is extracted, also with size $N \times N/2$, and then stitched together with S, forming the first block B_1 of size $N \times N$. To generate the left half part of block B_2, we take B_1 right half part as a condition C_2, and again give this patch as a condition to the generator G. The right half part of the generator output S^* is extracted and then stitched together with B_1. We repeat this process until we have the first row, with M blocks of size $N \times N$ each. See Fig. 7.

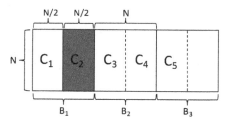

Fig. 7. Column conditioning. The previous generated patch C_{i-1} is used as a condition to generate the current patch C_i, in grey, and so on.

To generate the subsequent rows the process is the same, but how the generator G is conditioned is different. For the first block $(i,1)$ of a row $i > 1$, the half bottom part of the block $(i-1,1)$ is selected as a condition, Fig. 8 shows an example.

For the subsequent blocks (i,j) in this row i, a corner condition is selected from the blocks $(i,j-1)$, $(i-1,j-1)$ and $(i-1,j)$. See Fig. 9 for an example. With this strategy is possible to synthesise images of any size.

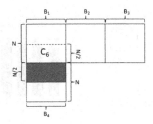

Fig. 8. Inner row conditioning. How the condition of the first block of an inner row $i > 1$ is selected. The condition C_6 is used to generate the top half part, in grey, of block B_4 in this example.

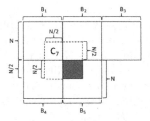

Fig. 9. Inner block in an inner row conditioning. How the condition of the inner blocks in a inner row $i > 1$ is selected. To generate the top left part of block B_5, in grey, a corner condition is selected from the blocks B_1, B_2 and B_4.

5   Experimental Results

For all experiments executed with our rcGAN model, the block size N was 64 pixels, the size of the rcGAN input and synthesised patches. The results of our proposed two-steps method for a wide variety of input images are presented in Fig. 11. Column two was created using SinGAN [20]; column three is InGAN [21] generated, column four was generated with *Spatial GAN* [12] and column five was created using our two-steps method as outlined in Sect. 3.2. The facades used to train the models were obtained from the *CMP Facade Database* [19].

We notice that SinGAN can only properly handle natural images like the one in Fig. 11 row two. For the other types of images, SinGAN generated samples that lost the overall structure presented in the source image, e.g. the apple in row one. The facades also lost the alignment of the windows and balcony railings. Spatial-GAN unsuccessfully handles most images presented to it and cannot preserve the existing spatial information in the facades; except for the input in row ten, where it was capable of generating aligned windows. Regarding texture generation, Spatial-GAN was effective in creating high-quality textures like the ones in rows two and four. InGAN delivered impressive results and can handle all types of pictures shown, and as our method can synthesise images of any size but suffer from lack of flexibility. Examples can be seen in row seven, where we could get rid of the tree in the middle and also the light pole at the top. At row ten, we could also generate an image that does not have the tree and the light pole presented in the input image on its right. In row eleven, he could produce a new shadow pattern, and in row twelve and thirteen, by carefully selecting the seed during the generation process, we could get rid of the grey areas. To visualise how this can be done, see Fig. 10 for an example of how seed selection can be used to avoid undesired features in the synthesised image.

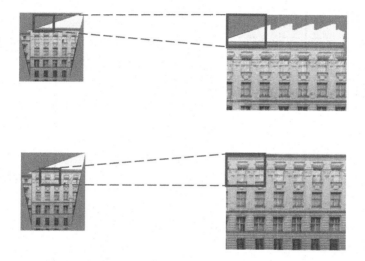

Fig. 10. rcGAN seed selection. Above, the seed was selected randomly, and the synthetic image has the non desired grey area on top. Bellow, the seed was chosen carefully intending to avoid the grey area to be synthesised in the output image.

One case of failure of our method results in a sort of *degenerated* condition. If our rcGAN generated patch S^* has some errors, *i.e.* some non-realistic appearance, then the next patch generated which is conditioned on it, is extra deteriorated. This results in a succession of progressively worse image patches driving to a resulting unrealistic image. See Fig. 13 for examples. This is resultant from the recursive application of the rcGAN patches that follows a linear path through the image .

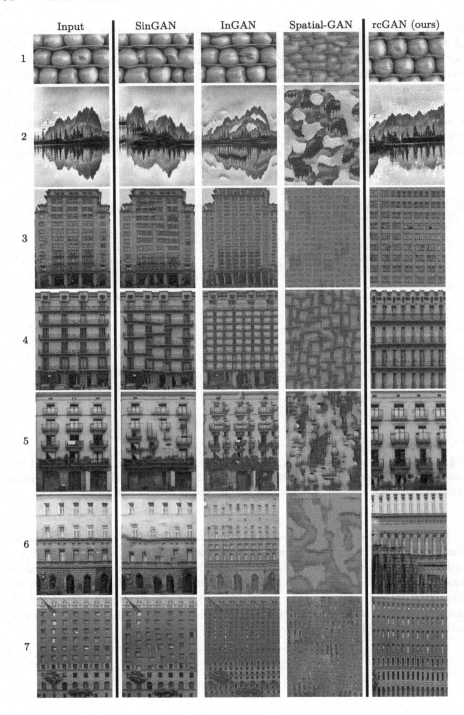

Fig. 11. Image Synthesis: The images size varies according to model output.

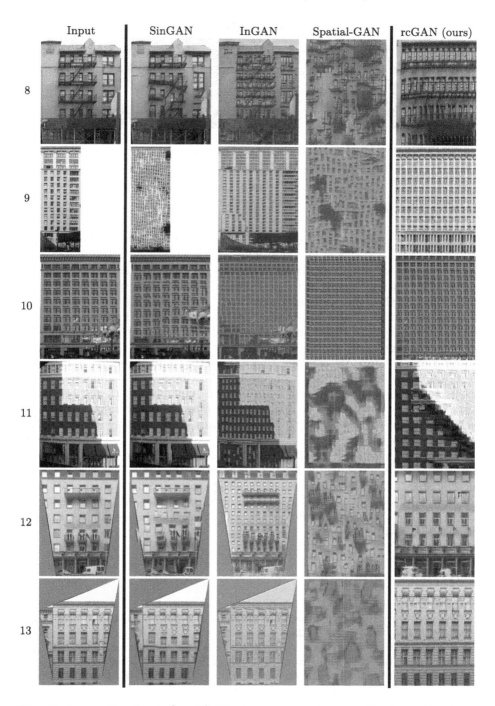

Fig. 12. Image Synthesis (cont.): The images size varies according to model output.

Fig. 13. A mode collapse case. The rcGAN is employed recursively and linearly to synthesise the image, sometimes letting errors to accumulate.

6   Conclusion

In this paper, we proposed a two-steps process to generate images, which is built on a randomly conditioned DCGAN. Our process uses only a single reference image to train our rcGAN to create image patches that will be later on stitched together to synthesise an arbitrary sized image. The size of the resultant image is constrained by the number of generated image patches that are stitched together to create it. Our rcGAN is conditioned on randomly selected adjacent parts of the image and learn how to complete it by producing a *matching* image area. We compare the results of our two-steps methods with *SinGAN* [20], *InGAN* [21] and *Spatial-GAN* [12]. We conclude that despite the simplicity of our framework, as we use just a single DCGAN, our proposed technique can handle any input image: textures, natural landscapes and facades. Our framework also compares very favourably against the comparing techniques, plus additionally provides more control over the synthesised image features, a capability which the other methods do not offer.

As a subsequent work, we aim to improve our model by replacing its architecture based on a simple DCGAN with state of the art recent architectures such as *StyleGAN* [14] seeking to enhance the synthetic image quality. We also intend to improve the synthesising process by allowing the selection of multiples seeds that can be placed on different parts of the output image, aiming to have a fine control over the synthesising process.

References

1. Barnes, C., Shechtman, E., Finkelstein, A., Goldman, D.B.: PatchMatch: a randomized correspondence algorithm for structural image editing. ACM Trans. Graph. (Proc. SIGGRAPH) **28**(3), 24 (2009)
2. Bergmann, U., Jetchev, N., Vollgraf, R.: Learning texture manifolds with the periodic spatial GAN. In: Precup, D., Teh, Y.W. (eds.) Proceedings of the 34th International Conference on Machine Learning. Proceedings of Machine Learning Research, vol. 70, pp. 469–477. PMLR, International Convention Centre, Sydney, Australia (06–11 Aug 2017)

3. Brock, A., Donahue, J., Simonyan, K.: Large scale GAN training for high fidelity natural image synthesis. In: International Conference on Learning Representations (2019)
4. Chen, T., Cheng, M.M., Tan, P., Shamir, A., Hu, S.M.: Sketch2photo: internet image montage. In: ACM SIGGRAPH Asia 2009 Papers. pp. 124:1–124:10. SIG-GRAPH Asia 2009, ACM, New York, NY, USA (2009)
5. Efros, A.A., Freeman, W.T.: Image quilting for texture synthesis and transfer. In: Proceedings of the 28th Annual Conference on Computer Graphics and Interactive Techniques. pp. 341–346. SIGGRAPH 2001, ACM, New York, NY, USA (2001)
6. Efros, A.A., Leung, T.K.: Texture synthesis by non-parametric sampling. In: Proceedings of the International Conference on Computer Vision. vol. 2, p. 1033. ICCV 1999, IEEE Computer Society, Washington, DC, USA (1999)
7. Gatys, L.A., Ecker, A.S., Bethge, M.: Texture synthesis using convolutional neural networks. In: Proceedings of the 28th International Conference on Neural Information Processing Systems. vol. 1, pp. 262–270. NIPS 2015, MIT Press, Cambridge, MA, USA (2015)
8. Goodfellow, I., et al.: Generative adversarial nets. In: Ghahramani, Z., Welling, M., Cortes, C., Lawrence, N.D., Weinberger, K.Q. (eds.) Advances in Neural Information Processing Systems 27, pp. 2672–2680. Curran Associates, Inc. (2014)
9. Goodfellow, I.J.: NIPS 2016 tutorial: Generative adversarial networks (2017), http://arxiv.org/abs/1701.00160
10. Hays, J., Efros, A.A.: Scene completion using millions of photographs. In: ACM SIGGRAPH 2007 Papers. SIGGRAPH 2007, ACM, New York, NY, USA (2007)
11. Iizuka, S., Simo-Serra, E., Ishikawa, H.: Globally and locally consistent image completion. ACM Trans. Graph. **36**(4), 11–14 (2017)
12. Jetchev, N., Bergmann, U., Vollgraf, R.: Texture synthesis with spatial generative adversarial networks (2016), http://arxiv.org/abs/1611.08207
13. Karras, T., Aila, T., Laine, S., Lehtinen, J.: Progressive growing of GANs for improved quality, stability, and variation. In: International Conference on Learning Representations (2018)
14. Karras, T., Laine, S., Aila, T.: A style-based generator architecture for generative adversarial networks (2018), http://arxiv.org/abs/1812.04948
15. Mirza, M., Osindero, S.: Conditional generative adversarial nets (2014), http://arxiv.org/abs/1411.1784
16. Pathak, D., Krähenbühl, P., Donahue, J., Darrell, T., Efros, A.: Context encoders: feature learning by inpainting. In: Computer Vision and Pattern Recognition (CVPR) (2016)
17. Portilla, J., Simoncelli, E.P.: A parametric texture model based on joint statistics of complex wavelet coefficients. Int. J. Comput. Vis. **40**(1), 49–70 (2000)
18. Radford, A., Metz, L., Chintala, S.: Unsupervised representation learning with deep convolutional generative adversarial networks (2016), http://arxiv.org/abs/1511.06434
19. Radim Tyleček, R.Š.: Spatial pattern templates for recognition of objects with regular structure. In: Proceedings of GCPR. Saarbrucken, Germany (2013)
20. Rott Shaham, T., Dekel, T., Michaeli, T.: Singan: learning a generative model from a single natural image. In: IEEE International Conference on Computer Vision (ICCV) (2019)

21. Shocher, A., Bagon, S., Isola, P., Irani, M.: Ingan: capturing and retargeting the "DNA" of a natural image. In: The IEEE International Conference on Computer Vision (ICCV) (2019)
22. Shrivastava, A., Pfister, T., Tuzel, O., Susskind, J., Wang, W., Webb, R.: Learning from simulated and unsupervised images through adversarial training (2016), http://arxiv.org/abs/1612.07828

Sketch-Inspector: A Deep Mixture Model for High-Quality Sketch Generation of Cats

Yunkui Pang[1](✉), Zhiqing Pan[2], Ruiyang Sun[3], and Shuchong Wang[4]

[1] University of Southern California, Los Angeles, CA, USA
yunkuipa@usc.edu
[2] Sun Yat-sen University, Guangzhou, China
panzhq@mail2.sysu.edu.cn
[3] University of Waterloo, Waterloo, Canada
sunruiyang@live.cn
[4] Michigan State University, East Lansing, MI, USA
wangsh91@msu.edu

Abstract. With the involvement of artificial intelligence (AI), sketches can be automatically generated under certain topics. Even though breakthroughs have been made in previous studies in this area, a relatively high proportion of the generated figures are too abstract to recognize, which illustrates that AIs fail to learn the general pattern of the target object when drawing. This paper posits that supervising the process of stroke generation can lead to a more accurate sketch interpretation. Based on that, a sketch generating system with an assistant convolutional neural network (CNN) predictor to suggest the shape of the next stroke is presented in this paper. In addition, a CNN-based discriminator is introduced to judge the recognizability of the end product. Since the base-line model is ineffective at generating multi-class sketches, we restrict the model to produce one category. Because the image of a cat is easy to identify, we consider cat sketches selected from the *QuickDraw* data set. This paper compares the proposed model with the original Sketch-RNN on 75K human-drawn cat sketches. The result indicates that our model produces sketches with higher quality than human's sketches.

Keywords: Sketch generation · VAE · CNN · RNN

1 Introduction

Sketches are images drawn by humans with symbols, lines, strokes or shapes. Unlike real-life image, they do not always present the entire appearance of things, but can indicate not only the idea of artists but also the theme [1]. Therefore, with the popularity of image generation, sketches, as a unique form of an image, receives people's attention for its abstractness.

Traditional generative models such as generative adversarial network [7], variational inference [11], and auto regressive models [12] produce an image from the pixel level. Indeed, these models are capable of generating sketch-like images.

© Springer Nature Switzerland AG 2020
G. Bebis et al. (Eds.): ISVC 2020, LNCS 12509, pp. 95–106, 2020.
https://doi.org/10.1007/978-3-030-64556-4_8

However, they lose the essence of sketch by depicting objects by ordered strokes [8]. Therefore, models based on sequential vectors instead of pixel image were developed for AI sketching.

Several breakthroughs have been made in AI sketching. Sketch-RNN [8] was firstly proposed in 2017 to draw sketches like humans. Sketch-pix2seq [3] in late 2017 added CNN layers to enhance model's generation ability over multiple categories. Jaques et al. [10] used facial expression feedback to improve the model's accuracy in 2018. In the same year, Sketch-aae introduced Reinforcement Learning into sketch generation and trained a GAN model to sketch. Inspired by their insights, we have focused on one aspect that was ignored in previous research: let AI 'see' and evaluate what it has drawn and then adjust its previous behavior based on evaluation might improve the quality of generated sketches.

Our paradigm is based on the observation of the process of human sketching. We noticed that humans use erasers to erase what they have drawn and change the trail of stroke based on their general evaluation of the current drawing. This strategy gives human more opportunities to revise the painting, which gives them a greater likelihood to produce high-quality paintings. We want to examine the effectiveness of this strategy on AI sketching. Therefore, we proposed a CNN-based decoder to assist the variational autoencoder (VAE) based on recurrent neural network (RNN).

This paper makes the following contributions:

1. Proposed CNN network to enhance the quality of sketches produced by Sketch-RNN. The process adjusts the position of each stroke in the generated sketch.
2. Validated the performance of our system through multiple methods, including Discriminator model and t-SNE. Our model successfully misleads the discriminator to view generated sketches as the original one drawn by a human, and the rate is 46% more than the original Sketch-RNN. The t-SNE result suggests that features of sketches produced by our model are more stable than those produced by Sketch-RNN.

According to the original paper of the base-line model [8], one main drawback of the model is its low productivity to generate identifiable multi-class sketches. To guarantee accuracy, we use a pre-trained model that concentrates on one category. Considering that cats are relatively easier to recognize compared with complicated figures such as mermaids or lobsters [8], we choose cat sketches selected from *QuickDraw* data set.

2   Related Works

Ha et al. [8] investigated Sketch-RNN to generate sketches similar to human-drawn sketches in 2017. The model is a sequence-to-sequence variational autoencoder. A novel representation of sketches, sequence of pixel coordinates of strokes, was proposed to satisfy the input format of the model. After that, several works managed to improve the method. Chen et al. [3] substituted the bi-directional

RNN encoder with a CNN encoder to predict mean and standard deviation of the Normal-distributed position of strokes in 2017. This helped the model to remember more sketches of different models while producing less recognizable sketches as a compromise. Wu et al. [15] used Sketchsegenet to instruct RNN to sketch more like human, which can assist AI to understand the order of strokes and the meaning of each stroke. In 2018, Diaz Aviles and his lab [5] developed a CNN-based GAN that generates sheep sketches. Cao et al. [2] introduced a CNN-based method into the original Sketch-RNN, which applied a CNN model to help RNN-based encoder extract latent features from original sketches. The added CNN helped the model to remember more skethes from different categories and generate more recognizable sketches.

Other researchers tried different training processes to improve the model. Jaques et al. [10] used facial expression from volunteers when they saw a sketch as a feedback to improve the model. They labeled the facial expressions into positive and negative ones. The model was designed to achieve positive feedback as much as possible. Another work [13] used Reinforcement Learning accompanied with a GAN model to draw sketches. They proposed VASkeGAN based on Sketch-RNN. The model added a GRU based recurrent neural network as a discriminator. Policy gradient was used in training model and stroke proposal.

All these works explored the potential improvement directions with different models and achieved some amount of success. However, we found that no one considered an external feedback when the model is sketching. In order to achieve this goal, we added a CNN on the decoder part. Our work differs from the previous research by a simultaneous adjustment of strokes on generation from the aspect of reducing disordered strokes produced by the model.

3 Methodology

3.1 Data Set

We used the data set of cat sketches provided by *QuickDraw* from Google. It contains 100,000 of human drawn cat sketches. The format of the data set is $[\Delta x, \Delta y, p_1, p_2, p_3]$. Δx and Δy denotes the distance from the previous point in the x-y coordinate. p_1, p_2 and p_3 represents the state of drawing process. p_1 means the current stroke continues to this point. p_2 means the end of the current stroke. p_3 means the end of the whole sketch.

The data set was divided into three parts: 70,000 training set, 2,500 test set and 2,500 validation set. 15,000 sketches from the training set were further randomly selected to train our model.

3.2 Model

Sketch-RNN. Sketch-RNN is based on the variational autoencoder. The encoder of the model is a bidirectional RNN. It accepts a sequence of strokes in a format of $[\Delta x, \Delta y, p_1, p_2, p_3]$ as mentioned above. The output is also a sequence with the same format. Both of the sequences are organized in a time order.

To generate a sketch, the encoder first produces a hidden vector given sequences of strokes. The vector is the last output node in the encoder. Since the VAE model assumes that data follows normal distribution, the vector is further compressed into mean and standard deviation of the distribution. Then random sampling under this normal distribution is used to produce the input of the decoder. The decoder is composed of LSTM cells, using the output of the encoder and the last stroke it produces to generate the next stroke. The initial stroke is fixed as (0, 0, 1, 0, 0), indicating that it is a base point and the current stroke should be continued. The output format of the decoder is $(\omega, \mu_x, \mu_y, \sigma_x, \sigma_y, corr_{xy}, \rho)$. The Gaussian mixture model is involved to generate the next point of the stroke by sampling.

For the training part, Sketch-RNN uses two loss functions. The first is Reconstruction Loss L_R, and the other is Kull-Leibler Divergence Loss L_{KL} According to [15], The Loss function can be written as:

$$L(S) = E_A(z|S)[\log B(S'|z)] - D_{KL}(A(z|S)\|B(z)) \tag{1}$$

The input S is the sequence of strokes. The first part $E_A(\cdot)$ is the Reconstruction Loss L_R, which measures the similarity between the generated sketches and the original sketches in the training set. The second part $D_{KL}(\cdot)$ is the Kull-Leibler Divergence Loss L_{KL}, which compares the distribution of the generated strokes and those in training set. $A(\cdot)$ and $B(\cdot)$ correspondingly represent the output of the encoder and the decoder.

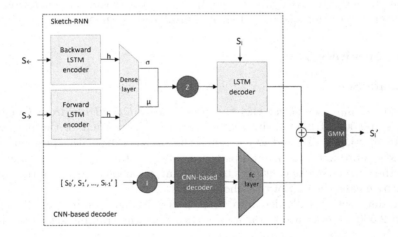

Fig. 1. VAE model we proposed

Our Model. As is shown in Fig. 1, our model extends the original model. To enhance the quality of sketches produced by Sketch-RNN, we added an extra CNN-based decoder. This CNN-based decoder is parallel to the original decoder. Instead of producing any new strokes, the CNN decoder only adjusts the position of the strokes generated by Sketch-RNN. We first applied weight on both the CNN decoder output and the RNN output. Then we added them together and used a Gaussian mixture model to sample the predicted next point of the stroke.

The structure of the CNN model is shown in Fig. 2, with 6 convolutional layers, 1 flatten layer, and 3 dense layers. The input is an image, which gathers all previous generated strokes $[S_0, S_1, \ldots, S_{t-1}]$ and transforms them into a sketch-like image. The size of the image is $[128, 128]$, which is a trade-off between the efficiency of computing and the clearness of the features in the image. The output is a sequence in the format of $(\omega, \mu_1, \mu_2, \sigma_1, \sigma_2, corr_{xy}, \rho)$, which is the same as that of the original decoder.

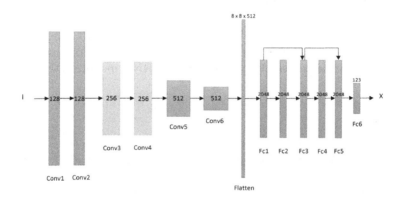

Fig. 2. CNN-based decoder

For the detail of the CNN implementation, we adjusted our model by trial and error. The depth for each kernel on each convolutional layer is (3, 128, 128, 256, 256, 512), with strides (1, 2, 1, 2, 2, 2) on each layer. We then flattened the last output of the convolutional layer and used the structure of residual network [9] to extract features in the image and generate the latent distribution for the next stroke point. In the convolutional layers we used ReLU (Rectified Linear Unit) [6] as the activation function. ELU (Exponential Linear Unit) [4] was applied in dense connected layers.

3.3 Loss Function

The loss function is the sum of two separated parts. The first part is the point offset Loss L_S. This loss function minimizes the offset of the predicted point (Δ_x, Δ_y) :

$$L_S = -\frac{1}{S_{max}} \sum_{i=1}^{S_{stop}} log(\sum^{M}_{j=1} \prod_{j,i} \mathcal{N}(\Delta_{x_i}, \Delta_{y_i} | \mu_{x,j,i}, \mu_{y,j,i}, \sigma_{x,j,i}, \sigma_{y,j,i}, Corr_{xy,j,i}))$$

$$(2)$$

The generated offset (Δ_x, Δ_y) is discarded if the length of the generated sequence is longer than S_{stop}. S_{stop} is controlled by the output (p_1, p_2, p_3) of the decoder where $\sum_{i=1}^{3} p_i = 1$. The other loss function L_P minimizes the difference between the generated pen states (p_1, p_2, p_3) and these of labels:

$$L_P = -\frac{1}{S_{max}} \sum_{i=1}^{S_{max}} \sum_{k=1}^{3} P_{k,i} log(q_{k,i}) \qquad (3)$$

Unlike L_S, L_P is calculated through all the output (p_1, p_2, p_3) of the decoder until it reaches the max sequence length. $q_{k,i}$ here means the categorical distribution of the ground truth (p_1, p_2, p_3), where $\sum_{k=1}^{3} \sum_{i=1}^{S_{max}} q_{k,i} = 1$. The total loss function is:

$$L = L_S + L_P \qquad (4)$$

This loss function is applied to train CNN-based decoder. To ensure stability and quality of generated strokes, we use Sketch-RNN model pretrained on cat sketch data set.

3.4   Training

We used cat sketches to train the CNN model. The data set is divided into 10,000 training samples, 2,500 test samples and 2,500 validation samples. For each sketch, we randomly cropped the sequence of strokes into two parts. We used the first part as the input to the CNN-based decoder and the second part as labels.

Normalization was used to pre-process the images. The normalization process is defined as:

$$(r', g', b') = 1 - (r, g, b)/255.0 \qquad (5)$$

By normalization, dark strokes are mapped to 1's while background is mapped to 0's, which is easier for convolutional layers to extract features from the images.

To ensure the training process is stable, we have adjusted the learning rate to 10^{-6}. Loss value fluctuation is shown in Fig. 3 as train iterations.

3.5   Evaluation

To examine whether our model could make better adjustments to the generated sketch, we designed two different approaches to evaluate the performance of our model.

Discriminator Model. Inspired by the Discriminator in GAN [7], we used a CNN-based model to judge whether a generated sketch is closer to human-drawn sketches or not. The goal for this CNN-based model is to accurately distinguish among three classes: sketches from Sketch-RNN, sketches from our model, and human-drawn sketches. Our model succeeds when it misleads the CNN-based model and the sketches generated by it are classified as human-drawn sketches. Additionally, if the discriminator fails to precisely discern sketches generated

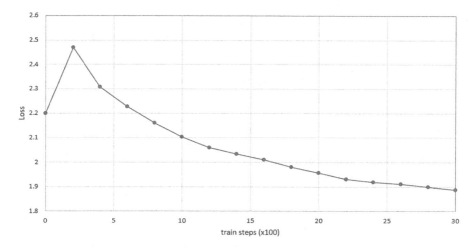

Fig. 3. Loss value on train steps

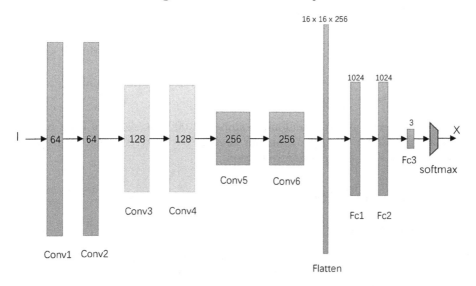

Fig. 4. CNN-based Discriminator

between Sketch-RNN and our model, it indicates that the features of sketches produced by our model have no significant difference compared to those produced by Sketch-RNN.

As is shown in Fig. 4, the input I denotes image input to the model. The output X the output, is a three-dimensional vector, representing three categories: sketches generated by Sketch-RNN, sketches generated by our model, and sketches drawn by humans. The model uses six layers, with (64, 64, 128, 128,

256, 256) kernels for each layer. The size of kernels on each layer is $[3 \times 3]$. The stride for each layer is (1, 2, 1, 2, 1, 2). Activation function used in convolution layers is ReLU while that used in fully connected layers is ELU.

We trained the Discriminator Model on a total of 30,000 cat sketches, including 10,000 sketches generated by Sketch-RNN, 10,000 produced by our model, and 10,000 drawn by human. The validation set contains 3,000 cat sketches, including 1,000 Sketch-RNN generated sketches, 1,000 our model generated sketches, and 1,000 human-drawn sketches. We achieved 95.2% accuracy on recognizing human-drawn sketches, 70.3% accuracy on recognizing sketches from Sketch-RNN, 63.2% accuracy on recognizing sketches from our model. The result analysis will be discussed in Sect. 4.2.1.

t-SNE. T-distributed Stochastic Neighbor Embedding (t-SNE) [14] is applied to measure the similarity of features in the sketches. This method maps a high-dimensional data set into a low-dimensional space, which is convenient for visualization. Similar objects will be placed close to each other while dissimilar objects will be distantly located.

We used t-SNE to analyze our model to answer two questions (compared with Sketch-RNN):

1) Whether our model exerted significant change to the distribution of strokes; and
2) Whether our model reduces disordered strokes. Or, which model is able to create sketches with more creativity.

In our experiment, We randomly sampled 1,000 cat sketches from Sketch-RNN and 1,000 cat sketches from our model. We plotted a scatter graph to visualize the result of dimension reduction.

4   Experimental Results

4.1   Image Results

When comparing images generated by our model with those produced by Sketch-RNN, we found out an interesting feature in our model: it tended to add 'eyes' on the face of cat sketches. Figure 5 displays some images that illustrate this character, where the images labeled 'Sketch-RNN' were produced by Sketch-RNN, while images labeled 'Proposed' were produced by our model.

The cartoon-like eyes generated by our model indicated that our model has the ability to understand what the network is drawing. More importantly, our model can recognize what features the original sketches have while Sketch-RNN forgets to present.

To further illustrate the quality of sketches our model generated, we present 50 sketches generated by each model randomly picked from a total of 2,000 sketches. Sketches generated by Sketch-RNN (Fig. 6(a)) and our model (Fig. 6(b)) are shown.

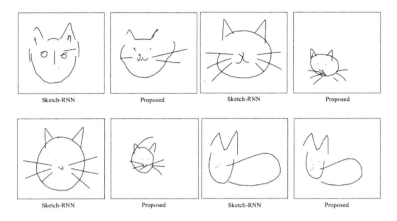

Fig. 5. Comparison of sketches generated by Sketch-RNN and our model

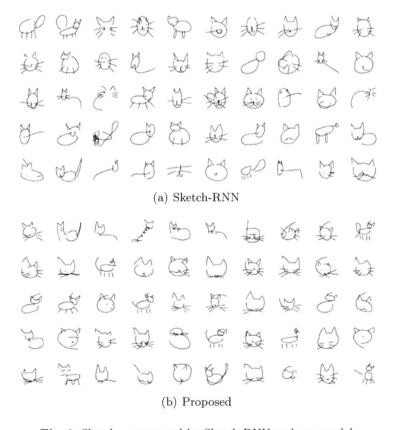

(a) Sketch-RNN

(b) Proposed

Fig. 6. Sketches generated by Sketch-RNN and our model

4.2   Evaluation Results

Discriminator. Firstly, we used the Discriminator as described in Sect. 3.5.1. We randomly sampled 1,000 Sketch-RNN generated sketches, 1,000 our model generated sketches, and 1,000 human-drawn sketches as validation set. Table 1 shows the percentage of classification results by Discriminator. The first column represents the actual class sketches belong to. The first row denotes the predicted class of sketches made by the Discriminator.

Table 1. Classification results by discriminator

Label	Predict		
	Sketch-RNN	Our model	uman-drawn
Sketch-RNN	70.6%	22.0%	7.4%
Our model	23.2%	63.2%	13.6%
Human-drawn	0.9%	3.9%	95.2%

Classification accuracy for each of the three classes: 'Sketh-RNN', 'Our model' and 'Human-drawn' sketches is 70.6%, 63.2% and 95.2% correspondingly. The model could not distinguish between sketches from Sketch-RNN and our model very well. This indicates that the features of sketches generated by our model are similar to those generated by Sketch-RNN.

Table 1 also illustrates the ability of a model to mislead the discriminator to view the sketch as the original one drawn by humans. Our model has a 13.6% of probability to successfully mislead the discriminator. Sketch-RNN has a 7.4% of probability to confuse the discriminator. Therefore, our model produces sketches with more features that the original sketches possess.

t-SNE. As is shown in Fig. 7, the red dots are sketches generated by our model. The orange dots are sketches generated by Sketch-RNN. The scatter graph shows that sketches produced by our model are more concentrated than those produced by Sketch-RNN. This indicates that the features in the cat sketches from our model is more unified. Hence our model generates sketches with more stable features while Sketch-RNN is more creative, which is able to generate sketches with more feature diversity.

Compared with the results in Sect. 4.2.1, Our model has learned some features from human-drawn sketches. Therefore, our model is able to confuse the discriminator to judge its sketches as human-drawn with higher probability. Our t-SNE analysis suggests that our model applies the features it learned from human-drawn sketches more often. Combining these two results together, we can conclude that our model reduces the number of disordered strokes and produces sketches that are more similar to human-drawn sketches.

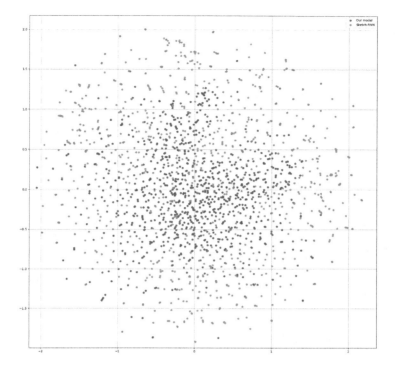

Fig. 7. t-SNE result

5   Conclusion

In this paper, we introduce a CNN-based decoder, a model that improves the quality of sketches drawn by Sketch-RNN. The decoder learns from incomplete human-drawn sketches and predicts the next stroke. Both the Discriminator model and t-SNE were used for evaluation. We compared the evaluation results between our model and Sketch-RNN, and found that our model produces sketches with higher quality. However, since the CNN-based decoder has to produce predictions on each iteration of generation, our model is four times slower than Sketch-RNN. We have only tested our model on a data set of cat sketches. More experiments on different sketch data sets need to be conducted.

Acknowledgments. We would like to express our great appreciation to Professor Gregory Kesden, Carnegie Mellon University, for his constructive suggestions and patient guidance. We would also like to thank Kexin Feng, Ph.D. student at Texas A&M University, and Naijing Zhang, student at UC Berkeley, for their encouragement and critiques for this project.

References

1. Bleiweiss, C.S.: The Sketchbook Challenge. Potter Craft (2012)
2. Cao, N., Yan, X., Shi, Y., Chen, C.: Ai-sketcher : A deep generative model for producing high-quality sketches. In: AAAI (2019)
3. Chen, Y., Tu, S., Yi, Y., Xu, L.: Sketch-pix2seq: a model to generate sketches of multiple categories (2017)
4. Clevert, D.A., Unterthiner, T., Hochreiter, S.: Fast and accurate deep network learning by exponential linear units (elus) (2016)
5. Diaz-Aviles, E.: Dreaming of electric sheep. https://medium.com/libreai/dreaming-of-electric-sheep-d1aca32545dc
6. Glorot, X., Bordes, A., Bengio, Y.: Deep sparse rectifier neural networks. J. Mach. Learn. Res. **15**, 315–323 (2011)
7. Goodfellow, I.J., et al.: Generative adversarial networks (2014)
8. Ha, D., Eck, D.: A neural representation of sketch drawings (2017)
9. He, K., Zhang, X., Ren, S., Sun, J.: Deep residual learning for image recognition. In: 2016 IEEE Conference on Computer Vision and Pattern Recognition (CVPR). pp. 770–778 (2016)
10. Jaques, N., Engel, J., Ha, D., Bertsch, F., Picard, R., Eck, D.: Learning via social awareness: improving sketch representations with facial feedback (2018). https://openreview.net/forum?id=Bkyn3dJPG
11. Kingma, D.P., Welling, M.: Auto-encoding variational bayes (2013)
12. Reed, S., et al.: Parallel multiscale autoregressive density estimation (2017)
13. Balasubramanian, S., Balasubramanian, V.N.: Teaching gans to sketch in vector format (2019)
14. van der Maaten, L., Hinton, G.: Visualizing high-dimensional data using t-sne. J. Mach. Learn. Res. **9**, 2579–2605 (2008)
15. Wu, X., Qi, Y., Liu, J., Yang, J.: Sketchsegnet: a rnn model for labeling sketch strokes. In: 2018 IEEE 28th International Workshop on Machine Learning for Signal Processing (MLSP), pp. 1–6 (2018)

Depthwise Separable Convolutions and Variational Dropout within the context of YOLOv3

Joseph Chakar, Rayan Al Sobbahi, and Joe Tekli$^{(\boxtimes)}$

Lebanese American University, 36 Byblos, Mount Lebanon, Lebanon
{joseph.elchakar,rayan.alsobbahi}@lau.edu, joe.tekli@lau.edu.lb

Abstract. Deep learning algorithms have demonstrated remarkable performance in many sectors and have become one of the main foundations of modern computer-vision solutions. However, these algorithms often impose prohibitive levels of memory and computational overhead, especially in resource-constrained environments. In this study, we combine the state-of-the-art object-detection model YOLOv3 with depthwise separable convolutions and variational dropout in an attempt to bridge the gap between the superior accuracy of convolutional neural networks and the limited access to computational resources. We propose three lightweight variants of YOLOv3 by replacing the original network's standard convolutions with depthwise separable convolutions at different strategic locations within the network, and we evaluate their impacts on YOLOv3's size, speed, and accuracy. We also explore variational dropout: a technique that finds individual and unbounded dropout rates for each neural network weight. Experiments on the PASCAL VOC benchmark dataset show promising results where variational dropout combined with the most efficient YOLOv3 variant lead to an extremely sparse solution that reduces 95% of the baseline network's parameters at a relatively small drop of 3% in accuracy.

Keywords: Computer Vision · Object Detection · Convolutional Neural Network · Depthwise Separable Convolution · Network Sparsification · Variational Dropout

1 Introduction

Convolutional Neural Networks (CNNs) have witnessed tremendous growth following the release of AlexNet [1] at the ImageNet Large Scale Visual Recognition Challenge 2012 (ILSVRC2012) competition [2]. Due to their accuracy and generalizability compared with traditional techniques, CNNs have become the dominant approach for a variety of real-life applications, particularly in the field of computer vision.

Perhaps one of the most fundamental problems in this area is the task of object detection, which is characterized by two main categories of deep learning based solutions: i) two-stage and ii) single-stage detectors. In two-stage detectors like R-CNN (Regions with CNN features) [3], Fast R-CNN [4], and Faster R-CNN [5], region proposal networks generate regions of interest that are sent down a detection pipeline. In contrast,

© Springer Nature Switzerland AG 2020
G. Bebis et al. (Eds.): ISVC 2020, LNCS 12509, pp. 107–120, 2020.
https://doi.org/10.1007/978-3-030-64556-4_9

the single-stage framework treats object detection as a regression problem by learning the bounding box coordinates and class probabilities in one forward pass over a dense sampling of possible locations. State-of-the-art one-stage detectors include SSD (Singe Shot MultiBox Detector) [6] and YOLO (You Only Look Once) [7–9]. While two-stage detectors reach higher accuracy levels, single-stage ones usually achieve higher inference speeds. In this context, the trade-off between accuracy and speed continues to be a major challenge for modern convolutional object detectors.

Among the one-stage models, YOLOv3 [9] is one of the most recent and popular when it comes to balancing these two key performance criteria for practical applications. Despite its efficient architecture, YOLOv3 still has millions of parameters that come with a heavy computational cost and a large run-time memory footprint. The computational resources required to train such a large neural network on large benchmark datasets like PASCAL VOC (Pattern Analysis, Statistical Modelling and Computational Learning Visual Object Classes) [10] and MS COCO (Microsoft Common Objects in Context) [11] can often be prohibitive, and this issue of high computation overhead and power consumption often hinders its deployment on resource-constrained devices.

In this study, we reduce YOLOv3's size and induce a high state of sparsity within its network in order to produce an efficient object-detection model fit for resource-limited environments. To do so, we propose three lightweight variants of YOLOv3 by replacing its standard convolutions with depthwise separable convolutions at different strategic locations, and we evaluate their impacts on the original network's size, speed, and accuracy using the PASCAL VOC benchmark dataset. We then apply variational dropout [12] to the most efficient YOLOv3 variant, which leads to an extremely sparse solution that effectively compresses the baseline model by a factor of 20, thus reducing 95% of the latter's parameters at a relatively small decrease of 3% in its accuracy, depending on the batch size.

The remainder of the paper is organized as follows. Section 2 provides preliminary notions regarding depthwise separable convolutions and variational dropout. Section 3 briefly reviews the background and related works. Section 4 presents our proposal. Section 5 describes our experimental evaluation and results, before concluding in Section 6 with future directions.

2 Preliminaries

2.1 YOLOv3 Model

The concept of the YOLO object-detection algorithm [7–9] is built on a unique set of characteristics that stands out from traditional systems in order to reduce computational complexity and achieve real-time inference speeds while maintaining high accuracy. It reasons globally about the full image by handling the task of object detection as an integrated regression problem to predict bounding boxes and their associated class probabilities in one single evaluation. First, the input image is divided into an $S \times S$ grid, where each grid cell is responsible for detecting the object that falls into it. Furthermore, the classification network architecture relies on 1×1 reduction layers followed by 3×3 convolutional layers. Lastly, a multi-part loss function that combines: i) a confidence loss, ii) a bounding box loss whenever the prediction box contains objects, and iii) a classification loss, is used to optimize the neural network's parameters. The original version of YOLO [7] has many shortcomings, e.g.: i) it imposes strong spatial constraints on bounding box predictions, ii) it struggles with detecting and localizing small objects, and iii) it is not able to properly generalize to objects with new or unusual aspect ratios. The second version, YOLOv2 [8], comes with several improvements and has established itself on standard detection tasks like PASCAL VOC. It introduces predefined anchor boxes that assist the prediction boxes, as well as a multi-scale training method, which offers a tradeoff between speed and accuracy by allowing the model to run at varying input image sizes. In the third and most powerful installment in this series, YOLOv3 [9], the backbone network has been upgraded to the state-of-the-art Darknet-53 feature extractor, on top of which several convolutional layers are stacked for the task of detection. YOLOv3 is capable of accurately detecting large, medium, and small objects by making predictions at three consecutive scales located at three different stages within the network. At each scale, a 3D tensor encodes: i) the four bounding box offsets, ii) the level of confidence of having an object, and iii) the corresponding class predictions.

Despite being cited as one of the fastest deep learning based object detectors, YOLOv3 has a large runtime memory footprint. In an attempt to resolve this issue, the YOLO series comes with a lightweight version called tiny YOLO, which decreases the number of floating point operations per second (FLOPS) by over 85%. However, this reduction in model size and inference time comes with a sharp drop of around 20% in the MS COCO detection accuracy. In this regard, striking a good balance between accuracy and speed remains a major computer-vision challenge to date. Various approaches to produce efficient machine learning models have been proposed in the literature e.g., [13–16], but for the sake of this study, we mainly focus on deep learning based object-detection solutions that use i) depthwise separable convolutions or ii) network sparsification as their underlying foundations.

2.2 Depthwise Separable Convolutions

A depthwise separable convolution is a form of factorized convolution. It separates the latter's spatial and channel components into two layers: i) a depthwise convolutional layer, which applies a single filter to each input channel, and ii) a pointwise or 1×1 convolutional layer, which multiplies the depthwise layer's outputs to generate the same output of the original convolution.

Compared with the standard convolution, which filters the input channels and combines them into a new set of outputs in a single step, the depthwise separable convolution substantially reduces a convolutional neural network's size and computational cost. In fact, a standard convolutional layer takes a $D_F \times D_F \times M$ feature map as input and outputs a $D_G \times D_G \times N$ feature map, where D_F and D_G are the respective spatial width and height of the square input and output feature maps, and M and N respectively designate the number of input channels and number of output channels. This standard network unit is thus parameterized by a convolutional kernel K of size $D_K \times D_K \times M \times N$. Similarly, D_K here represents the spatial dimension of the kernel, which is taken to be square. For the average convolution with a stride of one and padding where the input and output feature maps have the same spatial dimensions, the computational cost depends multiplicatively on the input depth N, the output depth M, the kernel size $D_K \times D_K$, and the feature map size $D_F \times D_F$, and comes down to:

$$D_K^2 \times M \times N \times D_F^2 \tag{1}$$

Using the alternative separable representation, the standard convolution is first broken into a depthwise convolution that filters the input channels and comes at the computational cost of $D_K^2 \times M \times D_F^2$. An additional 1×1 pointwise layer is then needed to generate new features across the N output channels, at the computational cost of $M \times N \times D_F^2$. Consequently, the total computational cost of the depthwise separable convolution is equal to the sum of the two previous terms:

$$D_K^2 \times M \times D_F^2 + M \times N \times D_F^2 \tag{2}$$

As can be seen, this approach is significantly more efficient than the traditional one, and this translates into a drastic reduction in computation of:

$$\frac{D_K^2 \times M \times D_F^2 + M \times N \times D_F^2}{D_K^2 \times M \times N \times D_F^2} = \frac{1}{N} + \frac{1}{D_K^2} \tag{3}$$

Similar to MobileNets [17], YOLOv3 relies heavily on 3×3 convolutional filters. This conversion thus lowers the computation of each convolution by up to 9 times. Even though these calculations do not take the effect of having strides and valid padding into consideration, these results safely generalize to input and output feature maps of different sizes. Nonetheless, this drop in the number of parameters is associated with a minor drop in performance. In Section 4, we describe three experimental setups that produce different reductions in size and accuracy based on which YOLOv3 standard convolutions are changed to depthwise separable convolutions.

2.3   Network Sparsification Using Variational Dropout

Sparsification is another leading approach to address the speed-versus-accuracy challenge of object-detection models. Sparsity is achieved when a proportion of a model is comprised of zero values. With most of the elements set to zero, sparse matrix formats can be used to store and perform efficient mathematical operations on the resulting weight matrices. Dropout [18] is a popular and empirically effective way of sparsifying a neural network and controlling over-fitting by randomly dropping out or ignoring a certain pre-defined percentage of neural network units during training. Variational dropout (VD) [19] is a more recent neural network regularization technique originally proposed as a Bayesian reinterpretation of Gaussian dropout [20], which is a more efficient approximation of the standard (binary) dropout. Simply put, variational dropout is a generalization of Gaussian dropout with learnable dropout rates. It has been later extended in [12] to include more specific dropout rates, where individual weight parameters with high dropout values can be removed post-training to get highly sparse models with a virtually identical performance.

For a training set D of N samples $(x_i, y_i)_{i=1}^N$ and a classification problem where the goal is to learn the weight parameters w of the conditional probability $p(y|x, w)$, Bayesian inference is used to update an initial belief over w in the form of a prior distribution $p(w)$ with observed data D into a belief in the form of a posterior distribution $p(w|D)$:

$$p(w|D) = p(D|w)/p(D) \tag{4}$$

Since computing the true posterior distribution $p(w|D)$ is computationally intractable, an approximation is used instead [12]. In variational inference, the parameters ϕ of some model $q_\phi(w)$ are optimized such that the approximated parameterized model is as close as possible to the true posterior distribution, as evaluated by the Kullback-Leibler (KL) divergence between the two distributions. In practice, this divergence is minimized by maximizing the variational lower-bound equation, which is the difference between the expected log-likelihood $L_D(\phi)$ and the KL-divergence regularization of $q_\phi(w)$ with respect to $p(w)$, as shown below:

$$L(\phi) = L_D(\phi) - D_{KL}(q_\phi(w)||p(w)) \tag{5}$$

where:

$$L_D(\phi) = \sum_{(x,y)\in D} E_{q_\phi}[log(p(y|x,w))] \tag{6}$$

Using the Stochastic Gradient Variational Bayes (SGVB) algorithm [19], the log-likelihood is reduced to the standard cross-entropy loss, which is typically used to minimize the divergence of the predicted label from the true one, while the KL divergence term serves as a regularization term. Note that in the standard formulation of VD, the weights of neural network are assumed to be drawn from a fully-factorized Gaussian approximate posterior:

$$w_{ij} \sim q_\phi(w_{ij}) = \mathcal{N}\left(\theta_{ij}, \sigma_{ij}^2\right) \tag{7}$$

where θ_{ij} and $\sigma_{ij}^2 = \alpha_{ij}\theta_{ij}^2$ are the mean and variance of this Gaussian distribution, with α_{ij} being a parameter that defines the dropout rate p_{ij} of the weight w_{ij} as follows:

$$p_{ij} = \frac{\alpha_{ij}}{1 + \alpha_{ij}} \tag{8}$$

If $\alpha_{ij} = 0$, then w_{ij} is fully preserved with no dropout rate. In contrast, when $\alpha_{ij} \to +\infty$, $p_{ij} \to 1$, w_{ij} can be completely removed to sparsify the model. For each training step, the weights are sampled from the normal distribution $\mathcal{N}$, and the so-called re-parameterization trick [21, 22] is used to differentiate the loss with respect to the parameters through this sampling operation:

$$w_{ij} = \theta_{ij}\left(1 + \sqrt{\alpha_{ij}}\,\epsilon_{ij}\right) \sim \mathcal{N}(w_{ij}|\theta_{ij}, \alpha_{ij}\theta_{ij}^2) \tag{9}$$

where $\epsilon_{ij} \sim \mathcal{N}(0, 1)$. Via this parameterization, the mean and variance of the neural network parameters can be directly optimized. For a log-uniform prior on the weights $p(w)$, the KL divergence component of the $D_{KL}(q_\phi(\omega_{ij})||p(\omega_{ij}))$ objective function can be accurately approximated using the following equation [12]:

$$D_{KL} \approx \frac{k_1}{1 + e^{-(k_2 + k_3 log \alpha_{ij})}} - 0.5 log\left(1 + \frac{1}{\alpha_{ij}}\right) + C \tag{10}$$

where $k_1 = 0.63576$, $k_2 = 1.87320$, $k_3 = 1.48695$, and $C = -k_1$.

The authors in [12] highlight some difficulties in training certain models with a learnable sparse architecture from a random initialization, as large portions of the model tend to adopt high dropout rates before a useful representation is learned from the data. To address this issue, they propose to start from a pre-trained network or use warm-up, i.e., re-scale the KL divergence term during the training by adding a regularizer coefficient, and then gradually increase it from 0 to 1. We adopt a similar approach in our study, but we instead apply variational dropout to an efficient and lightweight YOLOv3 variant based on depthwise separable convolutions.

3 Related Works

3.1 Depthwise Separable Convolution Approaches

Recently, several deep learning models have been built on depthwise separable convolutions. MobileNets [17] are a family of fast and small-sized deep neural networks which are based on depthwise separable convolutions and include two global hyperparameters to tune their latency and accuracy. The first parameter is a width multiplier, which can scale down the input and output channels of a given layer to thin the latter uniformly. The second is a resolution multiplier, which can be applied to the input image to reduce the internal representation of every layer. After varying these two hyperparameters, different trade-offs for reducing the network size and accuracy are achieved, and the authors compare their results with those of popular models in various applications. Instead of building new models from scratch, many researchers have focused on redesigning YOLO's architecture in order to create lighter versions that increase inference speed while maintaining high detection accuracy. One example of a small-sized YOLOv3 variant that relies on depthwise separable convolutions is Mini-YOLOv3 [23], which consists of a new backbone network with a parameter size of only 16% that of Darknet-53. In the residual layers of Mini-YOLOv3, the authors use a 1×1 convolution to increase the input dimension and then decrease it, leaving the 3×3 layer in an inverted bottleneck with larger input/output dimensions. To compensate for the large calculations associated with these operations, the authors group the convolutions and add a channel shuffle to enable cross-group information flow. Furthermore, they introduce a Multi-Scale Feature Pyramid Network (MSFPN) based on a U-shaped structure to improve the performance of the multi-scale object detection task. In this MSFPN, a Concat model first fuses the backbone's three feature maps to generate the base feature. An Encoder-Decoder then generates a group of multi-scale features, and a Feature Fusion model finally aggregates the three feature maps and group of multi-scale features into a feature pyramid. The Mini-YOLOv3 model achieves accuracy levels comparable to those of YOLOv3 on the MS COCO dataset, but at double the inference speed. Another example of a lightweight model is YOLOv3-Lite [24]. The feature extraction backbone of this network is 13-layers deep and is built entirely on depthwise separable convolutions. Similarly to YOLOv3, each convolution layer is followed by batch normalization and ReLU non-linearity layers. The authors also adopt the idea of a feature pyramid network that combines low- and high-resolution information at three different scales to detect large, medium, and small scale objects. Their lightweight detection network uses the YOLOv3 bounding box regression strategy, and it reaches a detection accuracy comparable to that of YOLOv3 on a custom dataset for cracks in aircraft structures.

3.2 Network Sparsification Approaches

Some of the recent solutions that have been proposed to sparsify the YOLOv3 neural network are presented in [25, 28]. In the first study [25], the authors impose channel-level sparsity on YOLOv3's convolutional layers by applying L1 regularization to the γ regularizer of the batch normalization layers. L1 regularization is a technique used to penalize a neural network's loss function in proportion to the sum of the absolute values of the weights. It helps drive the weights of irrelevant features to zero, thus sparsifying the model. The authors also integrate a spatial pyramid pooling (SPP) module, which consists of multiple parallel maxpool layers with different kernel sizes, in order to extract additional multi-scale features and further improve the detection accuracy. They then apply L1 regularization to their YOLOv3-SPP3 model and use a penalty factor to optimize the resulting L1 loss term. After the sparsity training, the authors introduce a global threshold to control the pruning ratio and carefully prune each feature channel to maintain the integrity of the network connections. Finally, they follow a fine-tuning operation and incremental pruning strategy to compensate for any performance degradation and prevent over-pruning. Their proposed SlimYOLOv3 model is evaluated on the VisDrone2018-Det benchmark dataset [26] for Unmanned Aerial Vehicles (UAV) applications [27], and experimental results using different pruning ratios show a decrease in parameter size of down to 92% with a detection accuracy comparable to that of YOLOv3. In [28], the authors use variational dropout to sparsify YOLOv3 on a self-collected dataset about road traffic in Vietnam. Both YOLOv3 and YOLOv3-VD are initialized from the pre-trained weights obtained on the COCO dataset, but during the training of YOLOv3-VD, a scaling factor is used to balance the variational dropout loss term with the network loss function. The authors successfully eliminate up to 91% of the original network weight parameters with only a 3% drop in accuracy, and their experimental results show that the sparsity level gradually increases such that the final layers can be completely pruned.

4 Proposal: Separable YOLOv3 with Variational Dropout

After careful examination of the YOLOv3 architecture, we set out to study the size-accuracy trade-off associated with substituting standard convolutions with depthwise separable ones and adding variational dropout. Our approach's overall process is depicted in Fig. 1, and consists of three main components: i) integrating depthwise separable convolutions in YOLOv3 to produce three lightweight variants, ii) training these three separable models on the PASCAL VOC dataset, and then iii) applying variational dropout to the best performing model. We rely on a TensorFlow implementation of YOLOv3[1], which is an overall faithful reproduction of the original model [9] but with several tweaks such as: i) replacing the original loss with a GIoU (General Intersection of Union) loss,

---

[1] https://github.com/YunYang1994/tensorflow-yolov3.

ii) using cosine scheduling for the learning rate, and iii) implementing different data augmentation techniques. Even though they drastically affect the network's performance, these modifications have no impact on this study, since all the experiments are done under the same settings.

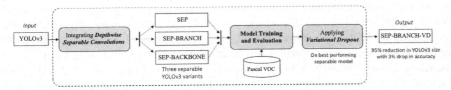

Fig. 1. Simplified activity diagram describing our approach

4.1 Separable YOLOv3 Configurations

We produce three separable models by replacing YOLOv3's standard convolutions with depthwise separable ones at different locations within the network:

- **SEP:** All standard convolutions are replaced with depthwise separable convolutions, except those with a 1×1 filter, since reducing and then restoring the dimensions of the multiple 1×1 convolutions spread throughout the network would greatly weaken the feature learning and expression ability of the model. Note that this exception is extended to the two remaining models.
- **SEP-BRANCH:** All standard convolutions are replaced with depthwise separable convolutions, except for the detection layers, which are marked by the last two convolutions of each of YOLOv3's three detection scales.
- **SEP-BACKBONE:** Only the standard convolutions of the Darknet-53 backbone are replaced with depthwise separable convolutions.

Note that each convolution in YOLOv3 is followed by a batch normalization layer and a leaky ReLU activation function. Similarly, batch normalization and the leaky ReLU nonlinearity are applied after each of the depthwise and pointwise 1×1 convolutions.

4.2 Separable YOLOv3 Model

We conduct the variational dropout tests on the best performing model, which turns out to be SEP-BRANCH based on our empirical results reported in Section 5. We follow Gale et al.'s [29] TensorFlow implementation of variational dropout, which is publicly available online[2].

Given that the depthwise separable factorization splits the standard convolution into a depthwise convolution and a pointwise convolution, with $w_{d_{ij}}$ and $w_{p_{ij}}$ as their respective

---

[2] https://github.com/google-research/googleresearch/tree/master/state_of_sparsity/layers/variational_dropout.

weights, we apply a variational distribution with learnable parameters θ, σ^2, and α to each weight. We then appropriately sum the two resulting KL-divergence terms and add them to the global network loss, along with the divergence term of the standard convolutions. The multi-part loss function becomes as follows:

$$L_{total} = L_{GIoU} + L_{Conf} + L_{Prob} + \lambda D_{KL} \tag{11}$$

Knowing that training the model with VD from the start is not recommended [12], we use a regularizer coefficient λ to balance YOLOv3's loss and the KL-divergence term. Similarly to the study in [28], we gradually ramp the regularizer coefficient to induce sparsity. We train the model without any VD loss ($\lambda = 0$) from the obtained VOC weights until we reach convergence after 35 epochs. We then set the divergence coefficient to $\lambda = 10^{-6}$ for 10 epochs, and raise it to $\lambda = 10^{-5}$ for an additional 10 epochs. Afterwards, we notice that additional training starts to increase the network's sparsity level at the expense of its accuracy. As a result, we lower the learning rate to 10^{-6} to fine-tune the model sparsity over 10 epochs.

5   Experimental Results

5.1   Separable YOLOv3 Models

We train YOLOv3 and its three depthwise separable variants (SEP, SEP-BRANCH, and SEP-BACKBONE) from scratch and under the same configuration settings on the PASCAL VOC dataset (VOC2007+2012 trainval for the train set, and VOC2007 test for the test set): i) a total number of 100 epochs (including 5 warm-up epochs), ii) a learning rate starting at 10^{-4} and gradually decreasing to 10^{-6} following a cosine scheduling, and iii) a batch size of 8. The training was conducted on Google Colab[3] using a Tesla P100 GPU. The performance of each separable model is compared to that of the original network in terms of i) mean average precision (mAP), ii) model size, and iii) inference speed. Our goal is to find the drop in accuracy associated with the convolutional factorization and to identify the most efficient model. Results are provided in Table 1 and visualized in Fig. 2.

Results show that the conversion to depthwise separable convolutions seems to be associated with a slight drop in accuracy, compared with a sharp decrease in the number of trainable parameters and model size. Even though only the Darknet-53 backbone is subject to this conversion in the SEP-BACKBONE architecture, the latter's accuracy is comparable to that of its counterparts and fails to justify its significant increase in model size. This is probably due to the fact that two types of convolutions do not mix well together, especially when they show large differences in their number of parameters and feature extraction capabilities. While all the separable models seem to be on a par with YOLOv3 in terms of accuracy, the SEP-BRANCH model reduces 70% of YOLOv3's size with only a 3% drop in accuracy, and thus offers the best trade-off between accuracy and speed.

---

[3] https://colab.research.google.com/.

Table 1. Results for YOLOv3 and its separable variants for a 416 × 416 input

Model	mAP (IoU = 0.5)	# of trainable parameters	Model size (MB[1])	Inference time (milliseconds)
YOLOv3	71.48%	61,626,049	951	32.88
SEP	68.09%	12,211,426	201	26.55
SEP-BRANCH	68.45%	17,706,594	284	27.07
SEP-BACKBONE	68.89%	28,696,930	451	28.22

[1]The model size represents the size of the checkpoint files obtained during the training, which are significantly larger than the compressed files used for inference.

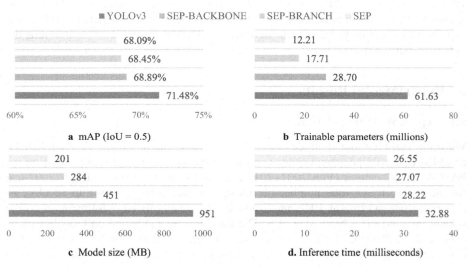

Fig. 2. Results for YOLOv3 and its separable variants for a 416 × 416 input

5.2 YOLOv3 Model

In the second stage of this work, we apply variational dropout to the SEP-BRANCH model in order to produce a sparse and compact model suitable for real-time applications. Even though adding variational dropout doubles the total number of trainable parameters, the SEP-BRANCH model with variational dropout – noted SEP-BRANCH-VD – still amounts to less than 60% of YOLOv3's trainable parameters. We train both the SEP-BRANCH and SEP-BRANCH-VD models using the same settings adopted in the previous experiment, to the exception of batch size, which we set to 2 (instead of 8). We use a smaller batch size to cater for the large computation overhead associated with the variational dropout terms. Results obtained on the PASCAL VOC dataset are shown in Table 2. They demonstrate the effectiveness of variational dropout when applied to the depthwise separable convolutions of a deep and complex network like YOLOv3 and trained on a large benchmark dataset. They also show that this technique can drop most of the model's weights without damaging its performance. In fact, for a batch size of 2, SEP-BRANCH-VD reaches a mAP equal to that of SEP-BRANCH with only 18% of the latter's parameters, and just 5% of YOLOv3's baseline parameters. However, adding variational dropout has two major drawbacks: i) it requires more than double the training time, and ii) it requires significantly larger computational resources to run on a larger batch size of 8 and preserve the original mAP levels. Nonetheless, for a batch size of 8, we expect the SEP-BRANCH-VD model to sustain a mAP of at least 68% and thus, relatively to YOLOv3, limit the drop in accuracy to 3%.

Table 2. Results of SEP-BRANCH trained with variational dropout

Model	mAP (IoU = 0.5)	# of weight parameters	# of zero weight parameters	Sparsity level
YOLOv3 (batch size of 8)	71.48%	61,626,049	–	–
SEP-BRANCH (batch size of 8)	68.45%	17,706,594	–	–
SEP-BRANCH (batch size of 2)	65.35%	17,706,594	–	–
SEP-BRANCH-VD (batch size of 2)	65.42%	17,706,594	14,584,999	82.37%

During inference, we set to zero all weight parameters with a $log\alpha$ value greater than 3, as they correspond to weights with a dropout rate larger than 95% [12]. Accuracy can be traded for more sparsity by decreasing the $log\alpha$ threshold. For example, with a threshold of 1, the SEP-BRANCH-VD model achieves 84.3% global sparsity with 64% test set accuracy. We provide in Table 3 the test set accuracy and global sparsity level under different thresholds, and our results show that the drop in accuracy does not justify the minor increase in sparsity.

Table 3. SEP-BRANCH-VD results under different $log\alpha$ thresholds

$log\alpha$ threshold	mAP	Sparsity level
3	65.42%	82.37%
2	64.85%	83.20%
1	64.04%	84.30%
0	60.41%	85.50%

Considering that variational dropout distributes sparsity non-uniformly across the neural network layers, we can make several observations regarding sparsity ratio distribution across the convolutional weights:

- First, the overall sparsity level seems to be gradually increasing throughout the network, which is consistent with the findings in [28]. The first convolutions are almost fully condensed (sparsity levels go from 0% to 30%), whereas the last ones are almost entirely sparse (sparsity levels between 60% and 97%).
- Second, the average sparsity level for the depthwise convolutions is 11%, in contrast with 58% for the pointwise convolutions. This can be due to the fact that depthwise convolutions extract features from the input channels, while pointwise convolutions combine the filtered inputs into a new set of output channels.
- Third, higher sparsity ratios are achieved in standard convolutions (average sparsity level of 70%) compared with depthwise separable convolutions. In particular, the highest sparsity levels are seen at the detection layers, where they reach values greater than 90%.
- Fourth, by examining the sparsity distribution across the different convolutional layers, we notice that the zero values are spread rather randomly across the weight matrices, and do not follow any recognizable pattern.

Lastly, given that a new YOLOv4 model [30] has just been released, we hope that the redundancy seen within the convolutional weights leads to a better understanding of the workings and generalization properties of YOLOv3, and in the future helps the design of more efficient models that focus on parameter and layer quality rather than quantity.

6   Conclusion

6.1   YOLOv3 Model

This study introduces a lightweight and sparse YOLOv3-based model by combining depthwise separable convolutions with VD. We first propose three different YOLOv3 variants by integrating depthwise separable convolutions at different strategic locations within the original network. Results for all three models are satisfactory, with the most efficient model reducing YOLOv3's size by a factor of 3.5 at only a 3% drop in accuracy. We then apply VD to this compact model and further eliminate more than 82% of its weight values, thus effectively removing 95% of YOLOv3's total parameters without any additional drop in accuracy – given that the same batch size is used. The obtained results i) validate the effectiveness of depthwise separable convolutions, ii) demonstrate that a deep and complex neural network based on YOLOv3 and depthwise separable convolutions can undergo extensive sparsification on a large benchmark dataset, and iii) give insights into the relevance of the different YOLOv3 layers.

6.2   Discussion and Future Works

The scope of our present work includes evaluating certain properties related to depthwise separable convolutions and VD within the context of YOLOv3, rather than reaching a global optimum and maximizing the mAP. Therefore, the training hyperparameters need to be reviewed and carefully fine-tuned if higher accuracy levels are to be achieved for all the models evaluated in this study. Moreover, YOLOv3 is typically trained on the MS COCO dataset, and the resulting weights are usually used to initialize the training on PASCAL VOC or any custom dataset. It would be therefore interesting to replicate our experiments on the significantly larger and more varied COCO dataset and check whether depthwise separable convolutions can leverage the transfer learning property on the VOC dataset as well as standard convolutions do. It would be also interesting to learn whether the sparse topology learned on the COCO dataset using VD can be used to initialize the training on the VOC dataset, since performing the training phase in a fully sparse manner would greatly accelerate the time-to-solution and might even allow the training to be conducted on resource-constrained embedded devices. Finally, knowing that sparsification is an intermediate but crucial step to network compression, our approach can be combined with data compression techniques like quantization and Huffman coding [31] and then integrated with light-weight deep learning frameworks such as TensorFlow Lite in order to reach real-time processing for on-device inference.

References

1. Krizhevsky, A., Sutskever, I., Hinton, G.: ImageNet classification with deep convolutional neural networks. Commun. ACM **60**(6), 84–90 (2017)
2. Russakovsky, O., et al.: ImageNet large scale visual recognition challenge. Int. J. Comput Vision **115**(3), 211–252 (2015). https://doi.org/10.1007/s11263-015-0816-y
3. Girshick, R., Donahue, J., Darrell, T., Malik, J.: Rich feature hierarchies for accurate object detection and semantic segmentation. In: IEEE Conference on Computer Vision & Pattern Recognition, (CVPR 2014), pp. 580–587 (2014)
4. Girshick, R.: Fast R-CNN. In: 2015 IEEE International Conference on Computer Vision (ICCV 2015), pp. 1440–1448 (2015)
5. Ren, S., He, K., Girshick, R., Sun, J.: Faster R-CNN: Towards real-time object detection with region proposal networks. IEEE Trans. Pattern Anal. Mach. Intell. **39**(6), 1137–1149 (2017)
6. Liu, W., et al: Ssd: single shot multibox detector. Comput. Res. Repository, CoRR abs/1512.02325 (2016)
7. Redmon, J., Divvala, S., Girshick, R., Farhadi, A.: You only look once: unified, real-time object detection. In: 2016 IEEE Conference on Computer Vision and Pattern Recognition (CVPR 2016), pp. 779–788 (2016)
8. Redmon, J., Farhadi, A.: Yolo9000: Better, faster, stronger. Comput. Res. Repository, CoRR abs/1612.08242 (2016)
9. Redmon, J., Farhadi, A.: Yolov3: An incremental improvement. Comput. Res. Repository, CoRR abs/1804.02767 (2018)
10. Everingham, M., Van Gool, L., Williams, C.K.I., Winn, J., Zisserman, A.: The pascal visual object classes (Voc) challenge. Inter. J. Comput. Vis. **88**(2), 303–338 (2010). https://doi.org/10.1007/s11263-009-0275-4
11. Lin, Tsung-Yi., et al.: Microsoft COCO: common objects in context. In: Fleet, D., Pajdla, T., Schiele, B., Tuytelaars, T. (eds.) ECCV 2014. LNCS, vol. 8693, pp. 740–755. Springer, Cham (2014). https://doi.org/10.1007/978-3-319-10602-1_48
12. Molchanov, D., Ashukha, A., Vetrov, D.: Variational dropout sparsifies deep neural networks. Comput. Res. Repository, CoRR abs/1701.05369 (2017)
13. Salem, C., Azar, D., Tokajian, S.: An image processing and genetic algorithm-based approach for the detection of Melanoma in patients. Meth. Inf. Med. (2018). https://doi.org/10.3412/ME17-01-0061

14. Abu-Khzam, F.N., Li, S., Markarian, C., der auf Heide, F.M., Podlipyan, P.: Efficient parallel algorithms for parameterized problems. Theor. Comput. Sci. **786**, 2–12 (2019)
15. Abu-Khzam, F.N., Markarian, C., auf der Heide, F.M., Schubert, M.: Approximation and heuristic algorithms for computing backbones in asymmetric Ad-hoc networks. Theor. Comput. Syst. **62**(8), 1673–1689 (2018). https://doi.org/10.1007/s00224-017-9836-z
16. Abu-Khzam, F.N., Daudjee, K., Mouawad, A.E., Nishimura, N.: On scalable parallel recursive backtracking. J. Parallel Distrib. Computing **84**, 65–75 (2015)
17. Howard, A.G., et al.: Mobilenets: efficient convolutional neural networks for mobile vision applications. Comput. Res. Repository, CoRR abs/1704.04861 (2017)
18. Hinton, G.E., Srivastava, N., Krizhevsky, A., Sutskever, I., Salakhutdinov, R.R.: Improving neural networks by preventing co-adaptation of feature detectors. Comput. Res. Repository, CoRR abs/1207.0580 (2012)
19. Kingma, D.P., Salimans, T., Welling, M.: Variational dropout and the local reparameterization trick. Comput. Res. Repository, CoRR abs/1506.02557 (2015)
20. Wang S., Manning C.: Fast dropout training. In: International Conference on Machine Learning (ICML 2013), pp. 118–126 (2013)
21. Kingma, D.P., Welling, M.: Auto-encoding variational bayes. Comput. Res. Repository, CoRR abs/1312.6114 (2014)
22. Rezende, D., Mohamed, S., Wierstra, D.: Stochastic Backpropagation and approximate inference in deep generative models. In: International Conference on Machine Learning, vol. 32, pp. II-1278–II-1286 (2014)
23. Mao, Q., Sun, H., Liu, Y., Jia, R.: Mini-YOLOv3: real-time object detector for embedded applications. IEEE Access **7**, 133529–133538 (2019)
24. Li, Y., Han, Z., Xu, H., Liu, L., Li, X., Zhang, K.: YOLOv3-lite: a lightweight crack detection network for aircraft structure based on depthwise separable convolutions. Appl. Sci. **9**(18), 3781 (2019)
25. Zhang, P., Zhong, Y., and Li, X.: SlimYolov3: narrower, faster and better for real-time UAV applications. In: 2019 IEEE/CVF International Conference on Computer Vision Workshop (ICCVW 2019), pp. 37–45 (2019)
26. Zhu, P., et al.: VisDrone-VDT2018: the vision meets drone video detection and tracking challenge results. In: Leal-Taixé, L., Roth, S. (eds.) ECCV 2018. LNCS, vol. 11133, pp. 496–518. Springer, Cham (2019). https://doi.org/10.1007/978-3-030-11021-5_29
27. Ebrahimi, D., Sharafeddine, S., Ho, P., Assi, C.: Autonomous UAV trajectory for localizing ground Objects: a Reinforcement Learning approach. IEEE Trans. on Mobile Computing (2020). https://doi.org/10.1109/TMC.2020.2966989
28. Sang, D.V., Hung, D.V.: YOLOv3-VD: a sparse network for vehicle detection using variational dropout. In: International Symposium on Information and Communication Technology (SoICT 2019), pp. 280–284 (2019)
29. Gale, T., Elsen, E., Hooker, S.: The State of sparsity in deep neural networks. Comput. Res. Repository, CoRR abs/1902.09574 (2019)
30. Bochkovskiy, A., Wang, C. Y., Liao, H.Y.: YOLOv4: optimal speed and accuracy of object detection. Comput. Res. Repository, CoRR abs/2004.10934 (2020)
31. Han, S., Mao, H., Dally, W.J.: Deep compression: compressing deep neural networks with pruning, trained quantization and Huffman coding. Comput. Res. Repository, CoRR abs/1510.00149 (2015)

Uncertainty Estimates in Deep Generative Models Using Gaussian Processes

Kai Katsumata[1]([✉])[ID] and Ryoga Kobayashi[2][ID]

[1] Graduate School of Information Science and Technology, The University of Tokyo,
Tokyo, Japan
`katsumata@nlab.ci.i.u-tokyo.ac.jp`
[2] Graduate School of Media and Governance, Keio University, Tokyo, Japan
`ryoga@sfc.keio.ac.jp`

Abstract. We propose a new framework to estimate the uncertainty of deep generative models. In real-world applications, uncertainty allows us to evaluate the reliability of the outcome of machine learning systems. Gaussian processes are widely known as a method in machine learning which provides estimates of uncertainty. Moreover, Gaussian processes have been shown to be equivalent to deep neural networks with infinitely wide layers. This equivalence suggests that Gaussian process regression can be used to perform Bayesian prediction with deep neural networks. However, existing Bayesian treatments of neural networks via Gaussian processes have only been applied so far to supervised learning; we are not aware of any work using neural networks and Gaussian processes for unsupervised learning. We extend the Bayesian Gaussian process latent variable model, an unsupervised learning method using Gaussian processes, and propose a Bayesian deep generative model by approximating the expectations of complex kernels. With a series of experiments, we validate that our method provides estimates of uncertainty from the relevance between variance and the output quality.

Keywords: Gaussian process · Neural network · Deep learning · Gaussian process latent variable model · Bayesian learning

1 Introduction

In this paper, we propose a Bayesian deep generative model using Gaussian process latent variable models (GPLVMs), which calculate predictive distributions to treat the uncertainty. There has been great discussion about the reliability of deep learning models. Especially, a lack of reliability is a big issue with deep neural networks [12]. This weakness is due to the fact that fitting performance is the primary focus of deep models, and reliability is often overlooked [22]. We tackle the issue by using Gaussian processes, which offer reliable posterior predictive distributions from a Bayesian perspective [21]. Some studies [9,23] claim

© Springer Nature Switzerland AG 2020
G. Bebis et al. (Eds.): ISVC 2020, LNCS 12509, pp. 121–132, 2020.
https://doi.org/10.1007/978-3-030-64556-4_10

that many existing deep learning models that only predict the expected value of outputs sometimes provide unreliable outcomes. This behavior is hypothesized to be caused by the use of a deterministic inference process and focusing on model fitting [6]. Then, the current deep neural networks cannot be fully trusted because they work well only in unrealistically idealized environments, and provide unreliable outputs for unforeseen inputs in the real-world.

Lee et al. [16] approach the reliability issue of deep neural networks by constructing Bayesian neural networks from Gaussian processes in the context of supervised learning. Gaussian processes that correspond to a deep neural network achieve high performance and provide estimates of uncertainty. Bayesian GPLVMs [24], which use Gaussian processes for unsupervised learning, can only be used with a few kernels as the model requires analytic formulas involving the kernel function for optimization.

In this paper, we combine Bayesian GPLVMs and deep kernels for reliable deep generative models. We cannot straightforwardly combine these methods, because a close form solution for the ψ statistics cannot be derived. Employing Monte-Carlo approximation allows us to combine Bayesian GPLVMs and deep kernels because it provides differentiable methods for calculating the ψ statistics. The model can exploit state-of-the-art DNN architectures using deep kernels corresponding to these architectures and suit various datasets. Our work differs from many existing deep generative models [9,14] in that our method can control the quality of output because it can treat the uncertainty. In the experiments, we remove unconfident data points to reduce the gap between the actual data distribution and the generated data distribution. Our contributions are as follows:

– We propose a GPLVM based deep generative model by incorporating deep kernels into Bayesian GPLVMs.
– We demonstrate that our method provides a useful estimate of uncertainty through experiments that investigate the relevance between the variance and the quality of the expectations in the vein of Lee et al. [16].

2   Related Work

The majority of the research into uncertainty of deep learning focuses on supervised learning. Neal [18] has shown that infinitely wide neural networks are equivalent to Gaussian processes. Moreover, Lee et al. [16] have constructed infinitely wide neural networks using Gaussian processes and have achieved higher prediction accuracy than neural networks trained via gradient methods. Recent work extends the framework introduced by Lee et al. [16] for fully-connected neural networks to other deep neural network architectures. Novak et al. [19] proved the correspondence between deep convolutional neural networks and Gaussian processes, and Garriga-Alonso et al. [7] have shown the correspondence between deep convolutional neural networks with residual blocks and Gaussian processes. Yang [25] unified these results by introducing a notation for expressing various neural network layers and revealed relationships between Gaussian processes and various architectures of neural networks.

An area that is less related is that of Deep Gaussian Processes [2,5]. They are concerned with stacking Gaussian processes to construct rich models. Our study differs from these in that our model corresponds to a deep neural network. They also employ the reparametrization trick to propagate gradients between Gaussian process components rather than for Monte-Carlo integration.

On the other hand, little attention has been given to the relationship between Gaussian processes and deep generative models for unsupervised learning. We find clues in GPLVMs [15,24] to answer this question. Lawrence [15] converted Gaussian process regression to latent variable model called GPLVMs, which models potentially nonlinear relationships between observed data and latent variables using a Gaussian process. GPLVMs require complex computation for optimization, unlike regular Gaussian process regression.

3   Bayesian GPLVM

In this section, we introduce Bayesian GPLVMs. Let $Y \in \mathbb{R}^{N \times D}$ be observed data where N is the number of observations, and D is the dimension of a data point. Latent variables $X \in \mathbb{R}^{N \times Q}$ are not observed where Q is the dimension of a latent point. We can express the likelihood function for a data point under a Gaussian process as

$$p(Y|X) = \prod_{d=1}^{D} \mathcal{N}(y_d|\mathbf{0}_N, K_{XX} + \beta^{-1}I_N).$$

where y_d is the d-th column of Y, the kernel matrix K_{XX} is an $N \times N$ covariance matrix defined by a kernel function $k(x, x')$ such as linear kernels, and β is a hyperparameter corresponding to the precision of the additive Gaussian noise. The mapping from latent variable space to observed data space is performed via Gaussian process regression. It is possible to interpret the generation process of Bayesian GPLVMs as deep neural networks that map unobserved latent variables to observed data. By using this variational distribution q with variational parameters $\{\mu_n, \sigma_n^2\}_{n=1}^{N}$, Jensen's lower bound on log marginal likelihood $\log p(Y)$ can be expressed as:

$$F(q) = \int q(X) \log p(Y|X) dX - \int q(X) \log \frac{q(X)}{p(X)} dX$$

$$= \sum_{d=1}^{D} \tilde{F}_d(q) - \mathrm{KL}(q\|p).$$

Titsias and Lawrence [24] have given $\tilde{F}_d(q)$ for optimization of Bayesian GPLVMs. Using the set of inducing points $Z \in \mathbb{R}^{M \times Q}$ and Ψ statistics:

$\psi_0 = \mathrm{tr}\left(\langle \boldsymbol{K_{XX}} \rangle_{q(\boldsymbol{X})}\right)$, $\boldsymbol{\Psi}_1 = \langle \boldsymbol{K_{XZ}} \rangle_{q(\boldsymbol{X})}$, and $\boldsymbol{\Psi}_2 = \langle \boldsymbol{K_{ZX}K_{XZ}} \rangle_{q(\boldsymbol{X})}$, the closed-form evidence lower bound is

$$\tilde{F}_d(q) \geq \log\left[\frac{\beta^{\frac{N}{2}}|\boldsymbol{K_{ZZ}}|^{\frac{1}{2}}}{(2\pi)^{\frac{N}{2}}|\beta\boldsymbol{\Psi}_2 + \boldsymbol{K_{ZZ}}|^{\frac{1}{2}}}\exp(-\frac{1}{2}\boldsymbol{y}_d^T W \boldsymbol{y}_d)\right] - \frac{\beta\psi_0}{2} + \frac{\beta}{2}\mathrm{tr}(\boldsymbol{K_{ZZ}^{-1}\boldsymbol{\Psi}_2}),$$

where $W = \beta\boldsymbol{I}_N - \beta^2\boldsymbol{\Psi}_1(\beta\boldsymbol{\Psi}_2 + \boldsymbol{K_{ZZ}})^{-1}\boldsymbol{\Psi}_1^T$ and, we define expectations under the distribution $q(\boldsymbol{X})$ as $\langle \cdot \rangle_{q(\boldsymbol{X})}$. The rest of $F(q)$ consists of the Kullback Leibler divergence between two Gaussian distributions and can be analytically derived. As a result of this approximation, we can avoid calculating the $N \times N$ covariance matrix in the optimization process. We optimize the variational parameters $\{\boldsymbol{\mu}_n, \boldsymbol{\sigma}_n^2\}_{n=1}^N$ and $\boldsymbol{Z}$ with gradient-based methods such as Adam [13]. Using integral notation, ψ_0 is written as

$$\psi_0 = \sum_{n=1}^N \int k(\boldsymbol{x}_n, \boldsymbol{x}_n)\mathcal{N}(\boldsymbol{x}_n|\boldsymbol{\mu}_n, \boldsymbol{\sigma}_n^2)d\boldsymbol{x}_n.$$

$\boldsymbol{\Psi}_1$ is the $N \times M$ matrix such that

$$(\boldsymbol{\Psi}_1)_{nm} = \int k(\boldsymbol{x}_n, \boldsymbol{z}_m)\mathcal{N}(\boldsymbol{x}_n|\boldsymbol{\mu}_n, \boldsymbol{\sigma}_n^2)d\boldsymbol{x}_n.$$

Here, $\boldsymbol{z}_m$ is the m-th row of $\boldsymbol{Z}$. $\boldsymbol{\Psi}_2$ is the $M \times M$ matrix such that

$$(\boldsymbol{\Psi}_2)_{mm} = \sum_{n=1}^N \int k(\boldsymbol{x}_n, \boldsymbol{z}_m)k(\boldsymbol{z}_m', \boldsymbol{x}_n)\mathcal{N}(\boldsymbol{x}_n|\boldsymbol{\mu}_n, \boldsymbol{\sigma}_n^2)d\boldsymbol{x}_n.$$

However, we only obtain analytic forms of the $\boldsymbol{\Psi}$ statistics for a few simple kernels. We construct Bayesian deep generative models by applying deep kernels [4] to Bayesian GPLVMs in the manner of Lee et al. [16]. In Bayesian GPLVMs, the distribution of observed data follows Gaussian processes. Since this distribution corresponds to the distribution in a Gaussian process, the Gaussian process followed by $\boldsymbol{y}_d$ given the latent variable $\boldsymbol{X}$ in GPLVMs is equivalent to neural networks. The decoder of Bayesian GPLVMs fixed latent variables is equivalent to Gaussian process regression.

4   Approximate $\boldsymbol{\Psi}$ Statistics

In this section, we aim to integrate deep kernels into Bayesian GPLVMs. We introduce an approximation of $\boldsymbol{\Psi}$ statistics by employing Monte-Carlo integration to intractable deep kernels. Titsias and Lawrence [24] have only shown the analytic solution for simple kernel functions such as RBF kernels and linear kernels. However, their analytical solution is not applicable to other types of kernels, including deep kernels. Deep kernels have high capacity as these are recursive and especially complex. In fact, previous studies achieve high performance on image classification tasks by using Gaussian process regression involving these kernels. As the integral is intractable, we perform a differentiable approximate integration to derive the required Ψ statistics. The expected value of $f(\boldsymbol{x})$ following a distribution $p(\boldsymbol{x})$ can be approximated by $\hat{f} = \frac{1}{\tau}\sum_{i=1}^{\tau} f(\boldsymbol{x}_i)$ where $\boldsymbol{x}_1, \boldsymbol{x}_2, \ldots, \boldsymbol{x}_\tau$ are i.i.d samples drawn from $p(\boldsymbol{x})$, and τ is the total number of samples. This is an unbiased estimator since $\mathbb{E}[\hat{f}] = \mathbb{E}[f]$. The approximation has the variance $\mathrm{Var}[\hat{f}] = \frac{1}{\tau}\mathbb{E}\left[(f - \mathbb{E}[f])^2\right]$. The accuracy of the estimator depends only on the number of sampling points and not on the dimensionality of $\boldsymbol{x}$. We can safely apply this to high dimensional latent variables.

Assume that $\boldsymbol{x}$ follows a Gaussian distribution with mean $\boldsymbol{\mu}$ and variance $\boldsymbol{\sigma}^2$. We want to sample data from the distribution $p(\boldsymbol{x})$, but sampling is generally non-differentiable. We use the reparameterization trick

$$\boldsymbol{\epsilon} \sim \mathcal{N}(\mathbf{0}_D, \boldsymbol{I}_D), \quad \boldsymbol{\mu} + \boldsymbol{\sigma} \cdot \boldsymbol{\epsilon} \sim \mathcal{N}(\boldsymbol{\mu}, \boldsymbol{\sigma}^2), \tag{1}$$

as used in variational autoencders (VAEs) for differentiable sampling [14] from Gaussian distributions. Using Monte-Carlo approximation and Eq. (1), we can calculate the Ψ statistics as

$$\psi_0 \approx \frac{1}{\tau}\sum_{n=1}^{N}\sum_{i=1}^{\tau} k(\boldsymbol{x}_{ni}, \boldsymbol{x}_{ni}), \tag{2}$$

$$(\boldsymbol{\Psi}_1)_{nm} \approx \frac{1}{\tau}\sum_{i=1}^{\tau} k(\boldsymbol{x}_{ni}, \boldsymbol{z}_m), \tag{3}$$

$$(\boldsymbol{\Psi}_2)_{mm'} \approx \frac{1}{\tau}\sum_{n=1}^{N}\sum_{i=1}^{\tau} k(\boldsymbol{x}_{ni}, \boldsymbol{z}_m)k(\boldsymbol{z}'_m, \boldsymbol{x}_{ni}), \tag{4}$$

respectively, where $\boldsymbol{x}_{ni} = \boldsymbol{\mu}_n + \boldsymbol{\sigma}_n \cdot \boldsymbol{\epsilon}_i$. The inducing point $\boldsymbol{z}_m$ is a variational parameter but is treated as a constant in the calculations of expected values due to the integration of $\boldsymbol{x}_n$. The lower bound can be jointly maximized over the variational parameters $\{(\boldsymbol{\mu}_n, \boldsymbol{\sigma}_n^2)\}_{n=1}^{N}$ and $\boldsymbol{Z}$ given Eqs. (2) to (4) for deep kernels using gradient methods.

Using optimized variational parameters consisting of $\boldsymbol{\mu}$, $\boldsymbol{\sigma}^2$, and $\boldsymbol{Z}$, we can obtain the mean and variance given new latent points, which based on the results of Quiñonero-Candela et al. [20], take the form:

$$\mathbb{E}\left[\boldsymbol{y}^*|\boldsymbol{x}^*, \mathcal{D}\right] = B^T \boldsymbol{\Psi}_1^*, \tag{5}$$

$$\mathrm{Var}\left[\boldsymbol{y}^*|\boldsymbol{x}^*, \mathcal{D}\right] = B^T(\boldsymbol{\Psi}_2^* - \boldsymbol{\Psi}_1^*(\boldsymbol{\Psi}_1^*)^T)B - \mathrm{tr}\left(\left[\boldsymbol{K}_{MM}^{-1} - (\boldsymbol{K}_{MM} + \beta\boldsymbol{\Psi}_2)^{-1}\right]\boldsymbol{\Psi}_2^*\right)\boldsymbol{I}_D$$
$$+ \psi_0^* \boldsymbol{I}_D + \beta^{-1}\boldsymbol{I}_D. \tag{6}$$

Here, $B = \beta(\boldsymbol{K}_{MM} + \beta\boldsymbol{\Psi}_2)^{-1}\boldsymbol{\Psi}_1^T \boldsymbol{Y}$, $\psi_0^* = \mathrm{tr}\left(\langle \boldsymbol{K}_{\boldsymbol{x}^*\boldsymbol{x}^*}\rangle_{q(\boldsymbol{x}^*)}\right)$, $\boldsymbol{\Psi}_1^* = \langle \boldsymbol{K}_{\boldsymbol{Z}\boldsymbol{x}^*}\rangle_{q(\boldsymbol{x}^*)}$, and $\boldsymbol{\Psi}_2^* = \langle \boldsymbol{K}_{\boldsymbol{Z}\boldsymbol{x}^*}\boldsymbol{K}_{\boldsymbol{x}^*\boldsymbol{Z}}\rangle_{q(\boldsymbol{x}^*)}$. $\boldsymbol{x}^*$ consists of $\{\boldsymbol{\mu}^*, \boldsymbol{\sigma}^{2*}\}$, and $\mathcal{D}$ consists of training data $\boldsymbol{Y}$ and optimized variational parameters $\boldsymbol{\mu}$, $\boldsymbol{\sigma}^2$, and $\boldsymbol{Z}$.

We obtain the fixed latent variables after the optimization. We also earn the expected value and variance for new latent space points employing Eq. (5) and Eq. (6) on the optimized latent variables just like the Bayesian GPLVM. Those results can be applied to reliable classification on the latent space and reliable data generation.

Table 1. The average of the classification accuracy of the nearest neighbor classification in latent space constructed by each model. We report the averaged accuracy on the test dataset over five trials. For each trial, we use 80% of the dataset as the training set and the rest as the test set. Our method achieves superior performance over other methods in the USPS dataset.

	Oil flow	USPS
VAE [14]	89.0	87.1
Bayesian GPLVM (Linear) [24]	89.0	79.8
Bayesian GPLVM (RBF) [24]	**96.0**	90.4
Our method	95.0	**93.9**

5   Experiments

To evaluate the proposed method, we now conduct experiments with some standard machine learning datasets and image datasets. Some experiments report the classification accuracy on learned latent representations and the quality of reconstructed data. The last two experiments in Sect. 5.3 aim to validate the usefulness of predicted uncertainty, the principal purpose of this study. In Sect. 5.3, we verify the usefulness of the variance on the latent space and demonstrate the usefulness of the variance of the generated data space.

Our models are composed of four layers for all experiments in this section. The number of samples used to approximate Ψ statistics is set to 10. In our model and the Bayesian GPLVM, the means in the variational distribution are initialized based on PCA, the variances of the variational distribution are initialized to 0.1, and 20 inducing points are used. We use Adam [13] as an optimization method for all models used in our experiments.

5.1   Classification Experiments

We apply the method to multi-phase oil flow data [1] and compare classification accuracy with related work, just like experiments in Titsias and Lawrence [24]. The dataset consists of 1000 observations distributed equally among the three classes. Each 12-dimensional data point belongs to one of three different geometrical configurations. The first experiment aims to show that our model learns better latent representations than existing methods. We take the latent variables to be ten-dimensional. For comparison, Table 1 shows the average and of the accuracy of k-nearest neighbor method ($k = 5$) trained on the latent space

Our model   Bayesian GPLVM [24]   GAN [9]   Ground truth

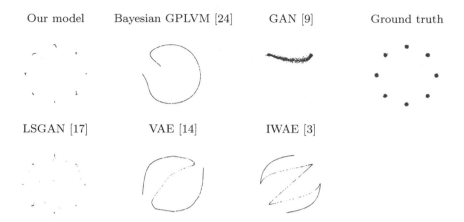

LSGAN [17]   VAE [14]   IWAE [3]

Fig. 1. Generated data mapped from latent space sampled randomly. The first row shows results from the proposed method, Bayesian GPLVM, GAN and the ground truth data points. The second row shows results from the LSGAN, VAE, and IWAE. Our method produces the closest distribution to the ground truth distribution.

over five runs for our model, the Bayesian GPLVM, and the VAE. We apply a linear kernel and an RBF kernel to the Bayesian GPLVM for the experiments. First, we mapped all 1000 of the data points to latent space using each model. Second, we considered the nearest neighbor classifier in the latent space to quantify the quality of latent representations optimized by each model. The encoder and decoder of VAE are composed of four layers for a fair comparison with our model. The dimension of the hidden layer in the VAE is hand-tuned between 32 and 512 to achieve the best accuracy. The accuracy of our model was five points higher than the Bayesian GPLVM with linear kernels and the VAE and was slightly worse than the Bayesian GPLVM with RBF kernels.

We also illustrate the method in handwritten digit recognition datasets as with an above experiment. We conduct the nearest neighbor classification in the latent space for the subset of 7291 of the digits 0–9 from the USPS dataset [10]. Each image of size 16×16 pixels was transformed into the vector row of dimension 256, representing handwritten digits as inputs to a fully connected layer. Table 1 shows results by our model, the Bayesian GPLVM with linear kernels, the Bayesian GPLVM with RBF kernels, and the VAE. For all models, we use ten latent dimensions. We use those models with the same setting as the experiments for Oil Flow data. We report the averaged accuracy over five independent runs for each model. Our model achieves the highest accuracy in the four models, including deterministic deep generative models and classical generative models.

5.2   Gaussian Mixture Distribution Data

Figure 1 shows the results of the data generation experiment on the toy dataset consisting of samples from Gaussian mixture distribution. The distribution has

Table 2. The negative log likelihood between the generated data and the ground truth data for experiments on grayscale and RGB images datasets and the classification accuracy. Our method outperforms other methods on almost datasets in both classification accuracy and negative log likelihood.

Method	MNIST		Fashion-MNIST		CIFAR-10		CIFAR-100	
	NLL ↓	Acc ↑	NLL ↓	Acc ↑	NLL ↓	Acc ↑	NLL ↓	Acc ↑
VAE [14]	125.32	76.7	247.65	61.6	1941.77	24.4	1899.36	4.5
IWAE [3]	126.23	87.6	**241.77**	69.2	1927.23	21.6	1927.23	4.6
Bayesian GPLVM [24]	122.01	87.7	246.98	74.1	1887.05	25.7	1829.82	5.4
Our method	**121.80**	**87.8**	244.87	**78.1**	**1860.27**	**27.4**	**1809.17**	**6.3**

eight modes, which are arranged in a circle. The dataset consists of 100 data points drawn with equal probability from the eight Gaussian distributions with different means. This experiment aims to show whether the model can reproduce this distribution from the training data. We compare the proposed method with the Bayesian GPLVM, Generative Adversarial Network (GAN) [8], LSGAN [17], VAE, and imporatance weighted autoencders (IWAE) [3]. The LSGAN and IWAE are improved models of the GAN and VAE, respectively. The generated data is computed by $\mathbb{E}\left[\boldsymbol{y}^*|\boldsymbol{x}^*, \mathcal{D}\right]$, where $\mathcal{D}$ is the training data following the two-dimensional Gaussian mixture distribution and the variational parameters, and $\boldsymbol{x}^*$ is the test data points sampled from a uniform distribution in all models. All the models without Bayesian GPLVM are composed of four layers. We take the latent variables for all models to be one-dimensional as the dataset consists of two-dimensional data. Our model requires the latent dimension less than the data dimension, and we need the same condition for both models.

Figure 1 illustrates the results of this experiment. In Fig. 1, the rightmost panel shows a scatter plot of the ground truth data, which is the mixture of eight Gaussian distributions. The GAN only generates two out of the eight modes of Gaussian mixture distribution. The phenomenon is referred to as the mode collapse and lack of diversity these are some of the most common issues with vanilla GANs [11]. In contrast, our model successfully generates all eight modes of the Gaussian mixture distribution. We conduct a quantitative evaluation using Maximum Mean Discrepancy (MMD). The MMD scores of our model, Bayesian GPLVM, GAN, LSGAN, VAE, and IWAE are 0.0335, 0.1814, 1.0975, 0.0571, 0.3228, and 0.1644, respectively. The generated distribution by our model is closest to the ground truth distribution in all models.

Furthermore, we conduct experiments for additional image datasets, MNIST, Fashion-MNIST, CIFAR-10, and CIFAR-100. We pick 20 or 200 samples per class for each dataset. MNIST and Fashion-MNIST contain 28×28 grayscale images, and CIFAR-10 and CIFAR-100 contain 32×32 RGB images. We compare the proposed method with the VAE, IWAE, and Bayesian GPLVM. Table 2 shows the classification accuracy in the manner described above and the negative log likelihood of reconstructed data from latent points. The whole dataset size is 2000 for all datasets. The proposed method outperforms other methods, without the negative log likelihood on Fashion-MNIST.

5.3   Variance Analysis

The remaining experiments demonstrate the usefulness of uncertainty of outputs obtained by our model. First, we show that the model allocates low variance to confident outputs and allocates high variance to unconfident outputs. Second, we disregard generated samples with a large variance to reduce the gap between the true data distribution and the generated data distribution by our models.

Table 3. Comparative study of the averaged variance of correct and incorrect predictions. The left column shows Eq. (7) and the right column shows Eq. (8). Our method allocates the low variance to high confidence outputs and the high variance to low confidence outputs, unlike the VAE.

	Correct	Incorrect
VAE	14.911	14.357
Our model	4.277	16.859

We compare the variance of outputs between our method and VAE following the variance analysis in Lee et al. [16]. The purpose of this experiment is to show whether the variance of the latent variables obtained through the optimization of the model is useful for solving classification problems in the latent variable space. We compare the variance of correct and incorrect classification results for test data by performing nearest neighbors over expectations μ in the latent space constructed by each model. We agree that μ^* and μ' denote a set of size N of latent variables randomly sampled from μ and its complement set $\mu \setminus \mu^*$. The predicted label corresponding to μ_n with nearest neighbors with μ' is defined by $knn_{\mu'}(\mu_n)$. Let the average variance of correct data be defined as

$$\frac{\sum_{n=1}^{N} \sum_{i=1}^{Q} \sigma_{n,i}^2 \mathbf{1}\left(knn_{\mu'}(\mu_n^*) = y_n\right)}{\sum_{n=1}^{N} \mathbf{1}\left(knn_{\mu'}(\mu_n^*) = y_n\}\right)}, \tag{7}$$

and let the average variance of incorrect data be defined as

$$\frac{\sum_{n=1}^{N} \sum_{i=1}^{Q} \sigma_{n,i}^2 \mathbf{1}\left(knn_{\mu'}(\mu_n^*) \neq y_n\right)}{\sum_{n=1}^{N} \mathbf{1}\left(knn_{\mu'}(\mu_n^*) \neq y_n\}\right)}, \tag{8}$$

where μ_n^* is a test point in μ^*, σ_n^2 is the variance of latent variables and corresponds to μ_n^*, and y_n is a given label corresponding to μ_n.

Table 3 shows the averaged variance on correct and incorrect predictions for the VAE and our model. For the VAE, the averaged variance on incorrect predictions is approximately equal to that on correct predictions. However, the averaged variance on incorrect predictions in our model is four times larger than that on correct predictions. In other words, our model allocates large variance for untrust outputs corresponding to unpredictable inputs. In our model, a large variance implies a high uncertainty of prediction and a small variance implies a low degree of uncertainty.

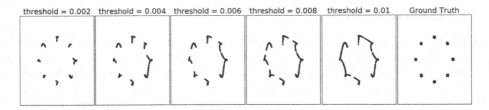

Fig. 2. Comparative study of distributions generated for each threshold by our model. Each column shows a scatter plot of generated samples with the variance less than the threshold. The rightmost column shows a scatter plot of the training data. Our method controls the quality of generated samples using the variance of predictions.

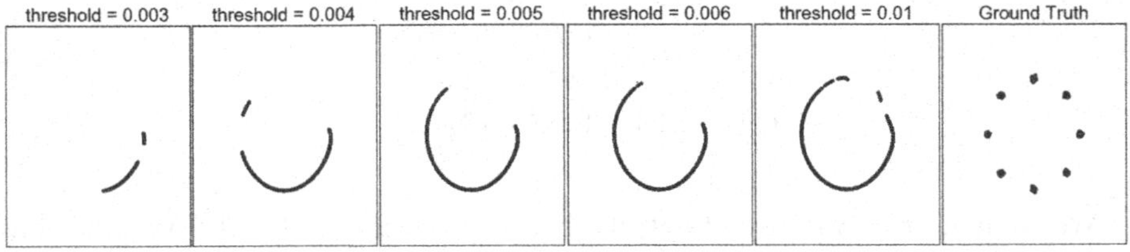

Fig. 3. Comparative study of distributions generated for each threshold of the Bayesian GPLVM with an RBF kernel.

Figures 2 and 3 illustrate the relationship between the variance of outputs and the quality of the generated data. Figure 2 shows the generated data reconstructed from the latent variables independently sampled from a uniform distribution over $[-3, 3]$ with our model, and Fig. 3 also shows the generated data with the Bayesian GPLVM model. The purpose of this experiment is to show the relevance between the variance and quality of the generated data by the optimized model. We exclude data points with variance greater than or equal to the threshold in each panel. We plot the set of points:

$$\left\{ \boldsymbol{m}_n \mid \max(\boldsymbol{s}_n^2) < t \right\}, \quad n = 1, 2, \ldots, N, \tag{9}$$

where $\boldsymbol{m}_n$ is $\mathbb{E}\left[\boldsymbol{y}_n^* | \boldsymbol{x}_n^*, \mathcal{D}\right]$, $\boldsymbol{s}_n^2$ is $\mathrm{Var}\left[\boldsymbol{y}_n^* | \boldsymbol{x}_n^*, \mathcal{D}\right]$, N is the size of test points, and t is a threshold. The variational parameters $\boldsymbol{\mu}$, $\boldsymbol{\sigma}^2$, and $\boldsymbol{Z}$ of $\mathcal{D}$ are learned latent variables from the training dataset by each model. We note that these thresholds depend on the dataset and network architecture.

In Figs. 2 and 3, we show five plots with different thresholds and the ground truth plot. In Fig. 2, the plot most similar to the ground truth plot is the leftmost plot with the smallest threshold. Conversely, when we assign a large threshold, the model generates a different distribution from the ground truth data distribution. Our model produces a closer distribution to the ground truth distribution with smaller thresholds, unlike Bayesian GPLVM. From the above results, our model control the quality of generated data using the confidence of predictions.

6   Conclusion

In this paper, we develop a Bayesian deep generative model that produces an estimate of uncertainty for generated data by applying deep kernels to Bayesian GPLVMs. For this purpose, we employ an approximate intractable integration to evaluate expectations of deep kernel functions. We present a series of experiments showing that the proposed method offers uncertainty of model outputs, which can then be used for decision-making at higher levels and post-processes. Our model has an advantage compared to the deep generative model and the classical Bayesian generative model. Moreover, we show that our models can provide a useful estimate of uncertainty based on the comparison of the variance of credible predictions and incredible predictions.

Acknowledgments. The authors have benefited from many suggestions and English editing from Mayayuki Takeda and Ryo Kamoi.

References

1. Bishop, C.: Analysis of multiphase flows using dual-energy gamma densitometry and neural networks. Nucl. Instrum. Meth. Phys. Res. **A327**, 580–593 (1993). https://doi.org/10.1016/0168-9002(93)90728-Z
2. Bui, T.D., Hernández-Lobato, J.M., Hernández-Lobato, D., Li, Y., Turner, R.E.: Deep Gaussian processes for regression using approximate expectation propagation. In: Proceedings of the 33rd International Conference on International Conference on Machine Learning, ICML 2016, vol. 48, pp. 1472–1481 (2016)
3. Burda, Y., Grosse, R.B., Salakhutdinov, R.: Importance weighted autoencoders. In: Bengio, Y., LeCun, Y. (eds.) 4th International Conference on Learning Representations, ICLR (2016)
4. Cho, Y., Saul, L.K.: Kernel methods for deep learning. In: Conference on Neural Information Processing Systems (NIPS) (2009)
5. Damianou, A., Lawrence, N.: Deep Gaussian processes. In: Proceedings of the Sixteenth International Workshop on Artificial Intelligence and Statistics (AISTATS), pp. 207–215, AISTATS 2013 (2013)
6. Gal, Y.: Uncertainty in Deep Learning. Ph.D. thesis, University of Cambridge (2016)
7. Garriga-Alonso, A., Rasmussen, C.E., Aitchison, L.: Deep convolutional networks as shallow Gaussian processes. In: International Conference on Learning Representations (ICLR) (2019)
8. Goodfellow, I., et al.: Generative adversarial nets. In: Conference on Neural Information Processing Systems (NIPS) (2014)
9. Goodfellow, I., Shlens, J., Szegedy, C.: Explaining and harnessing adversarial examples. In: International Conference on Learning Representations (ICLR) (2015)
10. Hull, J.J.: A database for handwritten text recognition research. IEEE Trans. Pattern Analy. Mach. Intell. **16**(5), 550–554 (1994). https://doi.org/10.1109/34.291440
11. Im, D.J., Ma, A.H., Taylor, G.W., Branson, K.: Quantitatively evaluating GANs with divergences proposed for training. In: International Conference on Learning Representations (ICLR) (2018)

12. Kendall, A., Gal, Y.: What uncertainties do we need in Bayesian deep learning for computer vision? In: Conference on Neural Information Processing Systems (NIPS) (2017)
13. Kingma, D.P., Ba, J.: Adam: a method for stochastic optimization. In: International Conference on Learning Representations (ICLR) (2015)
14. Kingma, D.P., Welling, M.: Auto-encoding variational bayes. In: International Conference on Learning Representations (ICLR) (2014)
15. Lawrence, N.D.: Gaussian process latent variable models for visualisation of high dimensional data. In: Conference on Neural Information Processing Systems (NIPS) (2003)
16. Lee, J., Sohl-dickstein, J., Pennington, J., Novak, R., Schoenholz, S., Bahri, Y.: Deep neural networks as Gaussian processes. In: International Conference on Learning Representations (ICLR) (2018)
17. Mao, X., Li, Q., Xie, H., Lau, R.Y.K., Wang, Z.: Multi-class generative adversarial networks with the L2 loss function. CoRR abs/1611.04076 (2016)
18. Neal, R.M.: Bayesian Learning for Neural Networks. Ph.D. thesis, University of Toronto (1995)
19. Novak, R., et al.: Bayesian deep convolutional networks with many channels are Gaussian processes. In: International Conference on Learning Representations (ICLR) (2019)
20. Quiñonero-Candela, J., Girard, A., Rasmussen, C.E.: Prediction at an uncertain input for Gaussian processes and relevance vector machines - application to multiple-step ahead time-series forecasting. Tech. Rep. IMM-2003-18 (2003)
21. Rasmussen, C.E., Williams, C.K.: Gaussian Processes for Machine Learning. MIT Press, Adaptive Computation and Machine Learning (2006)
22. Serre, T.: Deep learning: the good, the bad, and the ugly. Ann. Rev. Vis. Sci. 5(1), 399–426 (2019). https://doi.org/10.1146/annurev-vision-091718-014951
23. Tabacof, P., Tavares, J., Valle, E.: Adversarial images for variational autoencoders abs/1612.00155 (2016)
24. Titsias, M., Lawrence, N.D.: Bayesian gaussian process latent variable model. In: International Conference on Artificial Intelligence and Statistics (AISTATS) (2010)
25. Yang, G.: Tensor programs I: wide feedforward or recurrent neural networks of any architecture are gaussian processes. In: Conference on Neural Information Processing Systems (NeurIPS) (2019)

Segmentation

Towards Optimal Ship Navigation Using Image Processing

Bekir Sahin[1]([✉]), Zia Uddin[2], and Ahmet Soylu[1]

[1] Norwegian University of Science and Technology, Gjøvik, Norway
{bekir.sahin,ahmet.soylu}@ntnu.no
[2] SINTEF AS, Oslo, Norway
zia.uddin@sintef.no

Abstract. Shipping transportation developed over years with the technological advancements. Modern ship navigation is conducted with the help of Automatic Radar Plotting Aid (ARPA) and Electronic Chart Display and Information System (ECDIS). Location map, marine traffic, geographical conditions, and obstacles in a region can be monitored by these technologies. The obstacles may vary from icebergs and ice blocks to islands, debris, rocks, or other vessels in a given vicinity. In this study, we propose an approach for route optimization using two-dimensional radar images and image segmentation in an environment with obstacles. The navigation algorithm takes image segmentation results as an input and finds the optimal route (i.e. safest and shortest). One of the advantages of this study is that the obstacles are not solely polygonal, but they may be in any shape, size, and color. The proposed approach has some practical and computational limitations; however, the future unmanned vessels could benefit from the improved applications of this route optimization approach in terms of energy consumption, time, and workforce.

Keywords: Navigation · Imaging · Route planning · Path optimization · Safety

1 Introduction

Maritime transportation is of significance in terms of global merchandise, since %90 of cargoes is carried by commercial ships. According to United Nations Conference on Trade and Development (UNCTAD, 2016), the number of total ships navigating through the world is 90917 with 1.8 billion deadweight tons. Maritime transportation will maintain its crucial position in the future due to new shipping routes (i.e. Arctic region), active global economy (i.e. One Belt One Road), technological advancements, such as unmanned vessels, and new energy sources. The global demand pushes the shipping industry to be cheaper, involve less risks, and be eco-friendly. In this study, the ship navigation problem is investigated with the aim of finding an optimal route (shortest and safest simultaneously) in a given maritime environment with obstacles using image processing. The idea is to see whether an optimal path could be found from the radar images collected from Automatic Radar Plotting Aid (ARPA), an electronic navigation equipment, after determining the obstacles such as other vessels, islands, and icebergs.

© Springer Nature Switzerland AG 2020
G. Bebis et al. (Eds.): ISVC 2020, LNCS 12509, pp. 135–147, 2020.
https://doi.org/10.1007/978-3-030-64556-4_11

Since we are using static radar snapshots, the obstacles in this study are static, but in any shape or size rather than polygonal. The shortest path algorithm is not deterministic; therefore, we do not directly include distance, size etc. Moreover, information regarding the weather and atmospheric conditions, such as wind, current, waves, and rain are not considered. One of the novelties of this study is that the safety distance to the obstacles can be predefined. We set it proportional to the size of obstacles to be more realistic.

In the literature, route optimization problem is studied by considerable number of scholars. In a study, the optimal path on a given graph is computed by considering the ship turn angles and safety zone [1]. However, the special coordinates of graph are pre-defined, which makes the approach semi-automatic and input dependent. In this study, we overcome this shortcoming by utilizing object segmentation regardless of spatial and temporal information. In other words, we do not need to have coordinates of obstacles as priori data. There are applications in various other domains, such as medical, robotics, security, etc. using image processing [2–10]. The segmentation of objects on medical images has been a central task for some time, which requires abstracting semantically significant information from the background [11]. In robotics, real-time tool/device navigation is performed by image-guided platforms, where an object can be traced through a set of sequential frames by state-of-the-art image processing algorithms. Security applications, such as anomaly detection also extensively studied in the previous decades, which are dedicated to detecting suspicious activity by analyzing the optical flow between the sequential image frames. To the best of our knowledge, this is the first study for optimizing ship navigation combining image processing and computational geometry. We processed simulated radar images as input and obtained the safest/shortest path using Dijsktra algorithm.

The rest of the paper is organized as follows. Section 2 provides the methodology in a stepwise manner. Section 3 demonstrates the application on an empirical study. Finally, Sect. 4 concludes the paper by discussing the limitations of this study and gives the future research perspective.

2 Methodology

The steps of the methodology are provided in a stepwise manner in the followings.

2.1 Radar Images

Due to the complex structure of radar images, we adopted a formal image segmentation method. This complexity stems from ice melting, which is represented as gradually changing intensity patches on an image. This requires us to employ robust image segmentation methods that tackle intensity inhomogeneity.

Active Contour Models (ACM) have been one of the most popular methods in image segmentation [12]. There are two classes of active contour models: region-based and edge-based. Edge-based models use image gradients to stop the contour evolution when the contour reaches to object boundary. Classical edge-based ACM have an edge-stopping and balloon force terms to adjust the motion of initial contour. The edge-based stopping term is used for stopping the contour on the object boundary, whereas balloon force term is used for shrinking or expanding the active contour to provide flexibility for placing the initial curve far from the target object on image. Notably, the choice of balloon force is a challenging task such that if it is too large, evolving contour may leak through the weak boundaries. If the balloon force is not large enough, evolving contour may not snap bay-like parts of the irregularly shaped images [12]. Region-based active contours are preferable in image segmentation applications with weak object boundaries. The reason is that region-based models do not use image gradients. Additionally, the location of initial contour does not affect the segmentation results significantly. One of the most common region-based ACM is Chan-Vese method which has been successful for segmenting images with two regions that have distinct pixel intensity mean. Vese and Chan [13, 14] adopt a multi-phase level set formulation to discriminate multiple regions on an image. Due to the assumption that an image consists of statistically homogeneous segments, these models are called piecewise constant (PC) models [15]. However, the regions on images do not appear statistically homogeneous, and therefore PC models do not output desired segments on those types of images. To overcome these limitations, a piecewise smooth model is proposed [14]. A method to segment images with intensity inhomogeneity is also developed; however, both methods are computationally expensive [16].

Considering the structure of radar images on which melting ice is represented in a gradually decreasing intensity, we adopt the method proposed by Li et al. [12] so that our segmentation core can handle inhomogeneity. The approach is to utilize a kernel function to embed a local binary fitting energy into a region-based contour model [12]. Here, the energy functional is minimized via variational level sets without re-initialization [17].

Mumford Shah Functional. Mumford-Shah is one of the earliest segmentation models using variational calculus to minimize the energy in a formal way. Mumford Shah model aims to find an optimal contour C that separates the sub-regions from each other, and a u function that is smooth approximation of the image I. The energy functional proposed [18] is given as follows:

$$F^{MS}(u, C) = \int_{\Omega} (I - u)^2 dxdy + v \int_{\Omega \setminus C} |\nabla u|^2 dxdy + v|C| \tag{1}$$

where|C| represents the length of contour C.

Nevertheless, non-convexity of the functional and unknown set C and u make energy minimizing difficult in Eq. (1). To address these limitations, some alternative works have been proposed, i.e. Chan-Vese piecewise constant (PC), and Chan-Vese piecewise smooth (PS) methods.

Piecewise Constant Model. Chan-Vese modified Mumford-Shah functional based on an assumption that the image u consists of two sub-regions, which are piecewise constant. In other words, pixel intensities of these regions are represented by two constants. The energy functional that Chan-Vese aims to minimize for an image $I(x)$ is given as follows:

$$E^{CV}(C, c_1, c_2) = \lambda_1 \int_{C_{in}} |I(x) - c_1|^2 dx + \lambda_2 \int_{C_{out}} |I(x) - c_2|^2 dx + v|C| \tag{2}$$

where C_{out} and C_{in} represent the region outside and inside, c_1 and c_2 are two constants to approximate the pixel intensity inside and outside of the contour C. First two terms in Eq. (2) are called global binary fitting energy. This energy can be minimized by the steepest descent method representing the contour C by zero level set. Notably, in Eq. (2), c_1 and c_2 are related to global image properties, interior and exterior of the contour respectively. However, such image properties do not suffice if the image displays intensity and inhomogeneity inside and outside the contour.

Piecewise Smooth Model and its Difficulties. The PS model is proposed to address the limitations of PC model regarding image inhomogeneity [14, 16]. Rather than approximating an image I by a piecewise constant function, the PS model utilizes two smooth functions $u + (x)$ and $u-(x)$ in the sub-regions of interior and exterior of the contour C, which can be expressed mathematically as in the following: $\Omega^+ = \{x \in \Omega : \phi(x) < 0\}$ and $\Omega^- = \{x \in \Omega : \phi(x) < 0\}$, respectively. Function $u + (x)$ and $u - (x)$ are defined on mutually exclusive sub-regions respectively. However, the level set function is defined on the full domain. Additionally, smoothing the terms of $u + (x)$ and $u - (x)$, which are represented as $\mu \int |\nabla u^+|^2 dx$ and $\mu \int |\nabla u^-|^2 dx$ complicates the minimization of the energy functional in such a way that these terms enforce the solution of two partial differential equations (PDEs) with the two unknown $u +$ and $u -$ in each iteration throughout level set solution. Moreover, practical domain re-initialization of the level set function to a signed distance function is required. Obviously, the need for extension of $u +$ and $u -$ and the re-initialization of PDEs for $u +$ and $u -$ increase the computational cost of PS model.

Local Binary Fitting (LBF). Li et al. developed the LBF model incorporating the local image information in segmentation problem [12]. LBF can handle intensity inhomogeneities and is computationally more efficient than PS model. The main idea is to introduce a kernel function to set a LBF energy functional as in the following:

$$
\begin{aligned}
E^{LBF}(\phi, f_1, f_2) &= \int_\Omega E_x^{LBF} dx \\
&= \lambda_1 \int \left[\int K_\sigma(x - y)|I(y) - f_1(x)|^2 H(\phi(y))dy \right] dx \\
&+ \lambda_2 \int \left[\int K_\sigma(x - y)|I(y) - f_2(x)|^2 (1 - H(\phi(y))dy \right] dx \quad (3)
\end{aligned}
$$

where fixed parameters of λ_1 and λ_2 are positive constants, $I : \Omega \rightarrow R$ is a given vector valued image, K_σ is a Gaussian kernel of which standard deviation is represented by σ, and f_1 and f_2 are the smoothing functions that approximate the image intensity in the vicinity of every x point, which is the center point of integral in Eq. (3). In this kernel, localization property results in larger values at the points y near point x, whereas leads to smaller values as y departs from x. Therefore, the image intensities at the points where y is close to the point x weighs in the values of f_1 and f_2 which are to minimize the Eq. (3).

Functional E^{LBF} can be minimized with respect to level set ϕ, and the gradient descent is expressed as follows:

$$
\frac{\partial \phi}{\partial t} = -\delta_\varepsilon(\phi)(\lambda_1 e_1 - \lambda_2 e_2) \quad (4)
$$

In order to secure stability, a distance regularization term is added to Eq. (4). Final form of functional is as follows:

$$\frac{\partial \phi}{\partial t} = \mu(\nabla^2 \phi - div(\frac{\phi}{|\nabla \phi|})) + v\delta_\varepsilon(\phi)div(\frac{\nabla \phi}{|\nabla \phi|}) - \delta_\varepsilon(\phi)(\lambda_1 e_1 - \lambda_2 e_2) \qquad (5)$$

Interested readers are referred to Li et al. [12] for further details about the solution for minimization of Eq. (3). Parameters λ_1 and λ_2 control the weight of integrals over interior and exterior regions of the contour C. e_1 and e_2 are given in the Eq. (6) as follows:

$$e_1(x) = \int_\Omega K_\sigma(y - x)|I(x) - f_1(y)|^2 dy$$

$$e_2(x) = \int_\Omega K_\sigma(y - x)|I(x) - f_2(y)|^2 dy \qquad (6)$$

Notably, the standard deviation σ has a significant role in scaling the region from initial neighborhood to the entire image and must be chosen optimally to avoid undesirable outputs and high computational cost.

Local Fitted Image. Zhang et al. improved the idea of Li et al. in terms of decreasing the computational cost by eliminating the convolution terms from being computed in each iteration [17]. Their local fitted image (LFI) is formulated as follows:

$$I^{LFI} = m_1 H_\varepsilon(\phi) + m_2(1 - H_\varepsilon(\phi)) \qquad (7)$$

where constant of m_1 and m_2 are expressed as follows:

$$m_1 = mean(I \in (x \in (\phi(x) < 0) \cap W_k(x)))$$

$$m_2 = mean(I \in (x \in (\phi(x) > 0) \cap W_k(x))) \qquad (8)$$

where $w_k(x)$ is a rectangular window function which is to be convolved with a standard deviation σ and size of $4k + 1$ by $4k + 1$, where k can be selected as the greatest integer less than σ. They proposed to minimize the difference between the original image and the fitted image by solving an energy functional in the frame LFI. Formal representation of this energy is as follows:

$$E^{LIF}(\phi) = \frac{1}{2}\int_\Omega (I_x - I^{LFI}(x))^2 dx \qquad (9)$$

Energy in Eq. (9) can be minimized by the steepest descent method for which the flow is expressed as follows:

$$\frac{\partial \phi}{\partial t} = (I - I^{LFI})(m_1 - m_2)\delta(\phi)) \qquad (10)$$

where δ_ε the regularized Dirac function. Hence, the total level set formulation is defined as in the following:

$$\frac{\partial \phi}{\partial t} = \mu(\nabla^2 \phi - div(\frac{\phi}{|\nabla \phi|})) + v\delta_\varepsilon(\phi)div(\frac{\nabla \phi}{|\nabla \phi|}) + (I - I^{LFI})(m_1 - m_2)\delta_\varepsilon(\phi)) \quad (11)$$

Notably, Eq. (11) avoids the need for re-initialization of level set which decreases the computational cost as well. Due to massive numbers of obstacles on radar images, we reduced the input size of path planning task by zooming predefined location on a radar image.

2.2 Simulated Images

Border Detection. Border detection consists of two steps. First, we separate the black pixels from foreground and then delineate the contour that circumscribe the objects. Obtaining spatial information of the border contour is a significant step to create obstacles for path planning phase.

Thresholding. Thresholding is one of the basic approaches of image segmentation which generates binary images from gray scale images [19]. Basic image thresholding is adopted to isolate object pixels from the background of original image. The philosophy of the image thresholding is to partition the image based on the intensity value of the pixels with respect to pre-determined threshold (T) such that if a pixel's intensity is less than T, thresholding substitutes the pixel with a black pixel.

Boundary Tracing. We use a Matlab function, *bwboundary* that implements Moore-Neighbour tracing algorithm [20]. This algorithm is initiated at a black pixel toward any direction. Each time it hits a black pixel, it backtracks the white pixel that it previously departed from. This case repeats, if it meets a black pixel. The algorithm terminates when it revisits the starting pixel.

Border Expansion. Border expansion consists of two steps. First one is dedicated to find outermost points on the object border. This can be achieved by finding the convex hull points of the border. We stretch the convex points in the desired amount. Significantly, we must note that border inflation is proportional to object size. In the last step, we need to have a continuous curve to circumscribe the objects so that safe path computations will be accurate. To this end, we fit a contour using *imresize* routine provided by Matlab. Notably, obstacle borders are expanded proportionally to their areas. We computed areas of obstacles, which are 2D contours, using *polyarea* routine provided by Matlab.

Determining Outermost Points of Objects' Borders. Border expansion is completed by computing the convex hull which is the smallest convex set that contains the points [21]. The algorithm is as follows [22]:

```
Algorithm QUICKHULL
QuickHull(a,b,S)
if isEmpty(S) then return()
else
   c ← indexOf(maxDistance from ab)
   A ← rightPoints(a,c)
   B ← rightPoints(c,b)
   return QuickHull(a,c,A)+(c)+QuickHull(c,b,B)
```

Interpolation for Encapsulating New Object Borders. Bilinear interpolation is one of the basic resampling techniques and used for producing a reasonably realistic image. Image scaling is performed by moving the pixels in a certain direction based on the given scale parameter. However, some pixels may not be assigned to appropriate values during scale-up process if the scale factor is a non-integral. To handle this case, appropriate intensity or color values are assigned to these gaps so that output image does not have holes (non-valued pixels).

Bilinear interpolation takes average of the adjacent 2×2 window of known pixel values, which gives the interpolated value. The weight of each 4-pixel values is based on the Euclidean distance of pixels to the each of the known points. The algorithm development is given below.

Let us assume, we are after finding the value of a function f at the (x, y) point. Consider the value of f at the four points, $W_{11} = (x_1, y_1)$, $W_{12} = (x_1, y_2)$, $W_{21} = (x_2, y_1)$, $W_{22} = (x_2, y_2)$,

$$f(x_1) = \frac{x_2 - x}{x_2 - x_1} f(W_{11}) + \frac{x - x_1}{x_2 - x_1} f(W_{21}) \tag{12}$$

$$f(x, y_2) = \frac{x_2 - x}{x_2 - x_1} f(W_{12}) + \frac{x - x_1}{x_2 - x_1} f(W_{22}) \tag{13}$$

$$f(x, y) = \frac{y_2 - y}{y_2 - y_1} f(x, y_1) + \frac{y - y_1}{y_2 - y_1} f(x, y_2) \tag{14}$$

$$\approx \frac{y_2 - y}{y_2 - y_1} \left(\frac{x_2 - x}{x_2 - x_1} f(W_{11}) + \frac{x - x_1}{x_2 - x_1} f(W_{21}) \right) + \frac{y - y_1}{y_2 - y_1} \left(\frac{x_2 - x}{x_2 - x_1} f(W_{12}) + \frac{x - x_1}{x_2 - x_1} f(W_{22}) \right) \tag{15}$$

$$= \frac{1}{(x_2 - x_1)(y_2 - y_1)} \left[x_2 - x \quad x - x_1 \right] \begin{bmatrix} f(W_{11}) & f(W_{12}) \\ f(W_{21}) & f(W_{22}) \end{bmatrix} \begin{bmatrix} y_2 - y \\ y - y_2 \end{bmatrix} \tag{16}$$

Shortest Path Algorithm. In this study, Dijkstra algorithm is employed for shortest path between two predefined points. The algorithm is given as follows [23, 24]:

```
Algorithm DIJKSTRA (G,w,s)
d[s] = 0
for each v∈V-{s}
  do d[v] = ∞
S = Ø
Q = V
while Q ≠ Ø
  do u = extractMin(Q)
  S = S ∪ {u}
  for each v ∈ adj{u}
    do if d[v] > d[u] + w(u, v)
      then d[v] = d[u] + w(u, v)
```

Smoothing Process. Having characteristic maneuvers, the path we found is not realistic in terms of ship navigation. After obtaining the shortest and safest path, smoothing is conducted by using the conventional smooth routine in MATLAB.

3 Empirical Study

In this section, an empirical evaluation of the proposed approach is presented based on the radar images.

3.1 Radar Images

The input of the proposed system is a snapshot of a radar image where the ship is at the center as a dot. Generally, radar images (see Fig. 1 (a)) have annotations, and mark-ups on it which must be cleaned. We impainted the images manually; therefore, the input will be the image shown in Fig. 1 (b).

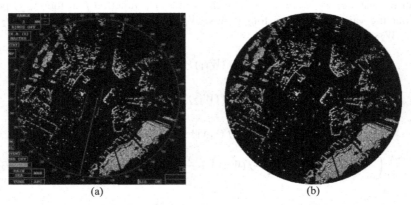

(a)   (b)

Fig. 1. (a) Radar Screen (Courtesy of Buffalo Computer Graphics) and (b) manually impainted real radar image.

To perform the segmentation, an initial contour must be placed. This initial contour evolves the around the boundary of foreground objects as the result of image segmentation process as shown in Fig. 2 (a). Initial contour localization is not automatically done due to the 'region' related sensitivity of segmentation algorithm. In Fig. 2 (a), a region that has similar intensity with the desired output is selected as the initial contour. In Fig. 2 (b), output mask of the segmentation is shown.

Note that, shortest path algorithm takes a binary matrix as an input, where ones represent the obstacles and zeros represent the background. Hence, the image shown in Fig. 2 (b), which is stored as a binary matrix in computer, can be passed to shortest path algorithm Fig. 3.

However, the vast number of segmented objects (see Fig. 2 (b) and Fig. 3(a)) severely increase the computational time to compute the shortest path yet may lead ship to penetrate through the group of objects. To avoid this case, we propose to merge the obstacles which are in high proximity to each other (see Fig. 3 (b)). Merging process is done using a MATLAB routine called *bwconvhull*. Here, the merged obstacles are shown, and the image is the input of shortest path algorithm.

Figure 4 (a) represents the shortest path from the center of the image to the desired destination. In order to show the applicability and generality, we use whole image as a

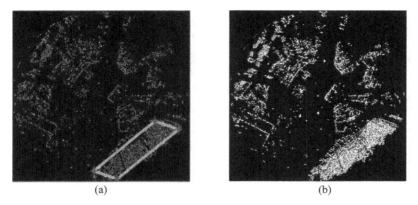

Fig. 2. (a) Initial contour is manually placed, and (b) segmented radar image.

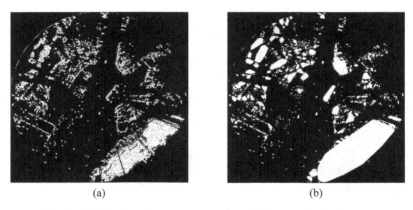

Fig. 3. (a) All obstacles are segmented, and (b) merged radar image.

region with obstacles as shown in Fig. 4 (b). It is assumed that the ship starts to navigate intended region from the top left point through the bottom right corner. The shortest and safest path is successfully found as in Fig. 4 (b).

Nevertheless, the shortest path we found passes nearby obstacles as seen in Fig. 5 (a) and Fig. 5 (b), which is still not a desired case. To address this constraint, we propose to establish a 'safe zone' circumscribing each obstacle. This safe zone can be delineated by expanding the obstacle border. We tested that object boundary can expand from the outermost points (convex hull points) of the obstacle borders. We set the expansion amount directly proportional to obstacle area. Note that both for convex hull and polygon area calculation, we used MATLAB routines. After border expansion from convex points, we interpolated the new boundary using *imresize* to recapture the original shape of obstacles. Considering the large size of radar images and extensive computational cost for processing them, we reduced the number of obstacles by zooming a particular area of the radar image.

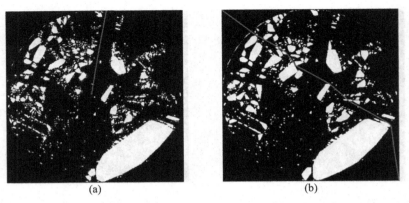

Fig. 4. (a) The shortest path where the ship's position is at the center of the image, and (b) the shortest path starting from top left to bottom right.

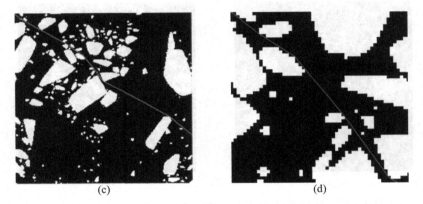

Fig. 5. (a) Screenshots of the zoomed region, and (b) closer look to the zoomed region.

3.2   Simulated Images

In the empirical study, the ship approaches a two-dimensional region with obstacles. The obstacles might be icebergs, islands, and also other ships. As it is seen in the Fig. 6 (a), the static obstacles are not polygonal and instead they might appear in any shape and size. The particulars of the ship are omitted and only the pivot point of the ship is considered as a navigating object. The ships must not touch the obstacles so as to navigate safely. Similarly, underwater of the icebergs are not observed visually, and it is mostly voluminous than the seen part. Therefore, the distance to the obstacles should be adjusted. In the Fig. 6 (b), the borders of the obstacles are detected. Besides any numerical assignments can be set for the safety distance of obstacles, we consider their sizes for the intended problem.

The shortest and safest path is found as given in Fig. 7 (a). To make it more realistic, the optimal route is smoothened (see Fig. 7 (b)).

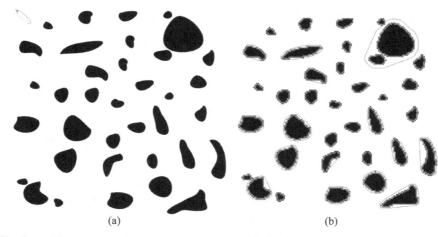

Fig. 6. (a) The region that the vessel encounters, and (b) borders of obstacles are detected for safe navigation.

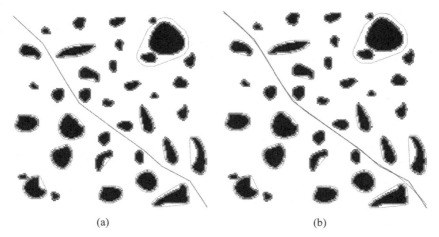

Fig. 7. (a) The shortest path that the vessel navigates safely, and (b) the shortest path with smoothing

4   Conclusions

Autonomous on-board management systems, including self-navigation, are highly important as they increase the speed and safety of the shipping operations. In this study, image processing approaches are implemented for determining the shortest and safest path based on static radar images. After processing images, Dijsktra algorithm is employed for two types of images (i) manually impainted real radar images and (ii) simulated images. Following conclusions are reached: any obstacles (ships, ice blocks, islands, etc.) observed on the radar screen can be processed; the obstacles in any shape, size and color are easily segmented; safe zones are calculated and tested for simulated images successfully; safe zones can also be considered for manually impainted real radar images; and, safe zones are determined based on the obstacles' volume.

Yet the proposed approach currently has certain limitations hindering its practical applicability, such as the high computation time required to process the images and run the algorithm and the facts that the obstacles are static and iceberg volume of underwater and weather and atmospheric conditions are not taken into account. Particularly, the environment, targets, and obstacles of the sea change continuously and the proposed approach needs to take this dynamism into account. Nevertheless, the work presented demonstrates that processing of radar images has potential to aid ship navigation and should be explored as a research direction.

Future work includes processing image sequences to mimic real time video analysis. Our goal is to plug the computational core we designed here to the on-board ships to conduct real time surveillance. Secondly, we argue that parallelization of the shortest path algorithm will decrease the computational time considering the large size of radar images, i.e. 619×619. Real radar images rather than manually impainted real radar images should also be extracted for processing. Lastly, instead of using convex points of the contours around obstacles for offsetting the border outward, constant velocity level set propagation can be used as a more formal mathematical approach [25]. Embedding the proposed algorithm to the ship's radar systems should be studied. Shortest path should be found in a dynamic manner; therefore, new shortest path algorithms (i.e. deterministic, heuristic approaches) can be deployed.

References

1. Ari, I., Aksakalli, V., Aydogdu, V., Kum, S.: Optimal ship navigation with safety distance and realistic turn constraints. Euro. J. Oper. Res. **229**(3), 707–717 (2013)
2. Austin, G.L., Bellon, A., Riley, M., Ballantyne, E.: Navigation by computer processing of marine radar images. J. Navig. **38**(03), 375–383 (1985)
3. Austin, G.L., Bellon, A., Ballantyne, E.: Sea trials of a navigation system based on computer processing of marine radar images. J. Navig. **40**(01), 73–80 (1987)
4. Kaya, S., et al.: Abrupt skin lesion border cutoff measurement for malignancy detection in dermoscopy images. BMC Bioinf. **17**(13), 367 (2016)
5. Bayraktar, M., Yeniaras, E., Kaya, S., Lawhorn, S., Iqbal, K., Tsekos, N.V.: Noise Sensitive Trajectory Planning for MR Guided TAVI. In: Pop, M., Wright, G.A. (eds.) FIMH 2017. LNCS, vol. 10263, pp. 195–203. Springer, Cham (2017). https://doi.org/10.1007/978-3-319-59448-4_19
6. Bayraktar, M., Sahin, B., Yeniaras, E., Iqbal, K.: Applying an active contour model for pre-operative planning of transapical aortic valve replacement. In: Linguraru, M.G., et al. (eds.) CLIP 2014. LNCS, vol. 8680, pp. 151–158. Springer, Cham (2014). https://doi.org/10.1007/978-3-319-13909-8_19
7. Bayraktar, M., Kaya, S., Yeniaras, E., Iqbal, K.: Trajectory smoothing for guiding aortic valve delivery with transapical access. In: Shekhar, R., et al. (eds.) CLIP 2016. LNCS, vol. 9958, pp. 44–51. Springer, Cham (2016). https://doi.org/10.1007/978-3-319-46472-5_6
8. Bayraktar, M.: Image detection and compression for memory efficient system analysis. In: Seventh International Conference on Machine Vision). International Society for Optics and Photonics (2015)

9. Bayraktar, M.: Image guided preoperative planning for aortic valve replacement (Doctoral dissertation, University of Houston (2011)
10. Li, S., Lu, R., Zhang, L., Peng, Y.: Image processing algorithms for deep-space autonomous optical navigation. J. Navig. **66**(04), 605–623 (2013)
11. Cremers, D., Rousson, M., Deriche, R.: A review of statistical approaches to level set segmentation: integrating color, texture, motion and shape. Int. J. Comput. Vis. **72**(2), 195–215 (2007)
12. Li, C., Kao, C.-Y., Gore, J.C., Ding, Z.: Implicit active contours driven by local binary fitting energy. In: IEEE Computer Society Conference on Computer Vision and Pattern Recognition, pp. 1–7 (2007)
13. Chan, T., Vese, L.: An active contour model without edges. International Conference on Scale-Space Theories in Computer Vision, pp. 141–151. Springer, Berlin Heidelberg (1999)
14. Vese, L.A., Chan, T.F.: A multiphase level set framework for image segmentation using the Mumford and Shah model. Int. J. Comput. Vis. **50**(3), 271–293 (2002)
15. Duan, Y., Huang, W., Zhou, J., Chang, H. and Zeng, T.: A Two-stage image segmentation method using Euler's elastica regularized Mumford-Shah model. In: 2014 22nd International Conference on IEEE Pattern Recognition (ICPR), pp. 118–123 (2014)
16. Tsai, A., Yezzi, A., Willsky, A.S.: Curve evolution implementation of the Mumford-Shah functional for image segmentation, denoising, interpolation, and magnification. IEEE Trans. Image Process. **10**(8), 1169–1186 (2001)
17. Zhang, K., Zhang, L., Song, H., Zhang, D.: Reinitialization-free level set evolution via reaction diffusion. IEEE Trans. Image Process. **22**(1), 258–271 (2013)
18. Mumford, D., Shah, J.: Optimal approximations by piecewise smooth functions and associated variational problems. Commun. Pure Appl. Math. **42**(5), 577–685 (1989)
19. Sezgin, M., Sankur, B.: Survey over image thresholding techniques and quantitative performance evaluation. J. Electron. Imaging **13**(1), 146–165 (2004)
20. Gonzalez, R.C., Woods, R.E., Eddins, S.L.: Digital Image Processing Using MATLAB®. McGraw Hill Education, New York (2010)
21. Barber, C.B., Dobkin, D.P., Huhdanpaa, H.: The quickhull algorithm for convex hulls. ACM Trans. Math. Softw. (TOMS) **22**(4), 469–483 (1996)
22. o'Rourke, J.: Computational Geometry in C. Cambridge University Press, Cambridge (1998)
23. Hart, C.: Graph Theory Topics in Computer Networking. University of Houston-Downtown, Department Computer and Mathematical Sciences, Senior Project (2013)
24. Dijkstra, E.W.: A note on two problems in connexion with graphs. Numer. Math. **1**, 269–271 (1959). https://doi.org/10.1007/BF01386390
25. Kimmel, R., Bruckstein, A.M.: Shape offsets via level sets. Comput. Aid. Des. **25**(3), 154–162 (1993)

Overscan Detection in Digitized Analog Films by Precise Sprocket Hole Segmentation

Daniel Helm[(⊠)] [iD] and Martin Kampel [iD]

Institute of Visual Computing and Human-Centered Technology,
Computer Vision Lab, TU Wien, Vienna, Austria
{daniel.helm,martin.kampel}@tuwien.ac.at

Abstract. Automatic video analysis is explored in order to understand and interpret real-world scenes automatically. For digitized historical analog films, this process is influenced by the video quality, video composition or scan artifacts called overscanning. The main aim of this paper is to find the Sprocket Holes (SH) in digitized analog film frames in order to drop unwanted overscan areas and extract the correct scaled final frame content which includes the most significant frame information. The outcome of this investigation proposes a precise overscan detection pipeline which combines the advantages of supervised segmentation networks such as DeepLabV3 with an unsupervised Gaussian Mixture Model for fine-grained segmentation based on histogram features. Furthermore, this exploration demonstrates the strength of using low-level backbone features in combination with low-cost CNN architectures like SqueezeNet in terms of inference runtime and segmentation performance. Moreover, a pipeline for creating photo-realistic frame samples to build a self-generated dataset is introduced and used in the training and validation phase. This dataset consists of 15000 image-mask pairs including synthetically created and deformed SHs with respect to the exact film reel layout geometry. Finally, the approach is evaluated by using real-world historical film frames including original SHs and deformations such as scratches, cracks or wet splices. The proposed approach reaches a Mean Intersection over Union (mIoU) score of 0.9509 (@threshold: 0.5) as well as a Dice Coefficient of 0.974 (@threshold: 0.5) and outperforms state-of-the-art solutions. Finally, we provide full access to our source code as well as the self-generated dataset in order to promote further research on digitized analog film analysis and fine-grained object segmentation.

Keywords: Deep learning · Segmentation · Video analysis · Overscan detection · Film preservation

1 Introduction

The available modern digitization infrastructure such as smart storage clusters allows archives, libraries or film museums to digitize their analog historical film

© Springer Nature Switzerland AG 2020
G. Bebis et al. (Eds.): ISVC 2020, LNCS 12509, pp. 148–159, 2020.
https://doi.org/10.1007/978-3-030-64556-4_12

collections. The digitization process of analog films involves various stages [7,18]. One fundamental stage is to scan the original film strips by using modern scanners such as the *Scanity HDR* or the *ScanStation 5K* [6]. During this process the frame content projected on different film reel types (e.g. 35 mm, 16 mm or 9.5 mm) is scanned and converted into a specific standard video format. However, the scan window used can include additional information such as black or white borders, Sprocket-Holes (SH) or parts of the next and previous frames. This effect is called *overscanning* [6] (see Fig. 1a, b). Film scanners can be configured to scan the strips including the overscan areas or not. In order to get all information projected on the original reels, historian film experts are interested to get digitized versions including also the overscan areas. However, for automatic film analysis tools such as classification of cinematographic settings [9], object detection [8] or scene understanding[15] it is of significance to get input frames including as much information as possible without showing additional overscan artifacts. The geometric layout of the SHs is a significant indicator for each individual film reel type (see Fig. 1c, d). Furthermore, it defines the geometric borders for the core frame window which includes the most significant information of an analog film. The scope of this work is on detecting SHs in digitized analog films [4] including overscan areas in order to crop only the original frame window. Historical films raise further challenges which make an automatic detection process not trivial. They can include different damages, such as cracks, scratches, dust or over- and underexposures [10,25]. Some examples are demonstrated in Fig. 2. These characteristics also affect the behavior of the SHs and make it challenging for traditional computer vision approaches [11].

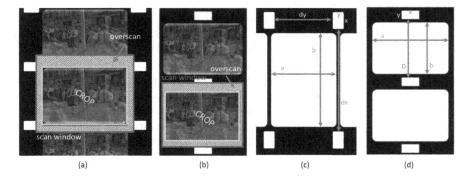

Fig. 1. Demonstration of the overscan effect during the scan process of analog films. a) 16 mm and b) 9.5 mm film reel with scan window (red) and final frame content (crop - yellow). b) 9.5 mm film reel c) 16 mm and b) 9.5 mm film reel geometry and sprocket hole layout. (Color figure online)

One similar exploration is focused on detecting the SHs in historical footage by using a fully unsupervised approach based on traditional image thresholding in combination with Connected Component Labeling and illustrates first

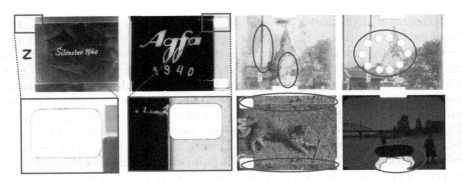

Fig. 2. Demonstration of original historical frames of digitized 9.5 mm and 16 mm film reel types. The reels visualizes different kinds of damages like scratches, cracks or dust (Efilms project [4]).

baseline results. However, for our best knowledge there are no further comparable investigations on automatically detecting overscan information in already scanned analog films by using segmentation algorithms [11].

This paper proposes a method in order to detect overscan information in digitized analog films by finding SHs. The approach is able to classify film reel types by exploring the geometry and layout of detected SHs (see Fig. 1c,d). The introduced approach is based on an adapted and optimized segmentation network in combination with an unsupervised Gaussian Mixture Model (GMM) for fine-grained segmentation results in order to calculate the exact frame crop window. Therefore, a dataset including 15000 extracted images of the benchmark database MS COCO [16] is created and used as base for our exploration. All image samples are enriched by synthetically generated SHs and are finally deformed to get photo-realistic samples representing the film reel types 16 mm and 9.5 mm. The final tests are done with a separate dataset including real-world and original 16 mm and 9.5 mm historical film frames related to the time of the National-Socialism [4]. Finally, this exploration points out the effectiveness of using low-level features in terms of inference runtime and segmentation performance. This investigation is evaluated by using state-of-the-art metrics such as mean Intersection over Union (mIoU) and dice coefficient. The **contribution of this paper** is summarized as follows:

- We provide a *novel Overscan Detection Pipeline* in order to precisely detect and remove overscan areas in digitized analog films.
- We create and provide a *self-generated dataset* based on MS COCO including synthetically generated sprocket-hole types of two different film reels (16 mm and 9.5 mm).
- We provide a fundamental base for further research on innovative digitization and fine-grained segmentation methods. Therefore we give full access to our sourcecode and self-generated dataset [GitHub-Repository: https://github.com/dahe-cvl/isvc2020_paper].

In Sect. 1, the motivation, the problem description as well as the main contributions of this work are introduced. Similar and alternative approaches are discussed in Sect. 2. A detailed insight of the methodological background of the explored pipeline is given in Sect. 3. Section 4 describes the results and points out the benefits of our proposed approach. We summarize our investigation with the conclusion in Sect. 5.

2 State-of-the-Art

Digitization and Video Restoration: Exploring automatic digitization mechanisms for historical analog film strips raise significant attention in the last decade [1,25]. The fundamental step is to scan these film reels with smart techniques which are based on sensible light sources in combination with an optical system demonstrated by Flueckiger et al. [6]. Few scanner systems such as the Scanity HDR are able to recognize overscan areas semi-automatically by registering SHs with dedicated camera systems and the corresponding frame lines (indicates the split between two consecutive frames). Furthermore, the multispectral characteristics are analyzed to achieve high-quality scans (e.g. color correction) [6]. However, there is no overall scanner technique which is able to handle each film reel type and detect the exact overscan areas automatically. Deeper automatic video analysis is based on detecting filmographic techniques such as shot detection [25] or shot type interpretation [20,21] and can be significantly influenced by these areas. Different explorations focus on the restoration of historical films [24,25]. Yeh et al. [23] and Iizuka and Simo-Serra [12] have published an approach in order to remove and clean-up film frames including small cracks or damage artifacts. The results are obtained by using Generative Adversarial Networks (GAN) or cycle GANs in order to generate synthetically frame realistic datasets for training their models.

Semantic Image Segmentation: There are several traditional computer vision techniques for segmentation such as *active contour, watershed* or *mean shift and mode finding* which can be used for finding geometries such as sprocket holes in images [22]. Semantic Image Segmentation is used in different computer vision domains such as object detection, scene understanding or medical imaging [26]. Since 2015 different technologies and mechanisms are explored in order to detect correlated areas in an image and classify these areas into various categories such as cars, persons or cats [2,3,8]. The Fully Convolutional Network (FCN) forms the major base and plays a significant role in this research area up to now with over 14000 citations [17]. Further investigations such as DeepLabV3 [2], DeepLabV3+ [3] or Mask-RCNN [8] are published and provide novel standard techniques in this domain. However, we are able to see significant performance improvements related to run-time [19] and pixel-based segmentation [14,26] since the last 5 years. Benchmark datasets such as PASCAL VOC [5] or MS COCO [16] are used to evaluate segmentation algorithms. Traditional segmentation techniques such as image thresholding demonstrates promising results by using Gaussian Mixture Models (GMM) as introduced by Zhao et al. [27] and

Karim and Mohamed [13]. However, there are only few investigations on detecting SHs to remove overscan areas by using unsupervised image histogram-based solutions [11]. To our best knowledge there is no investigation on detecting SHs in digitized analog films by using semantic image segmentation approaches.

3 Methodology

Dataset Preparation: Since there is no public dataset available which includes different types of SH, we created a dataset based on the benchmark dataset MS COCO [16]. Therefore, images from the categories person, cat and car are downloaded for the training set. However, the category does not have any significant effect for the further process. In order to get meaningful image samples including SH and the corresponding ground truth masks a two-step process is defined (see Fig. 3a). In the *first step* the ground truth masks (binary maps) for the reel type 16 mm and 9.5 mm are generated. The exact geometry and position layout of the SHs are used to create and position the holes (see Fig. 1c, d). Moreover, the position and scaling of the holes varies randomly in order to get diversity ground truth masks (see Fig. 3b). In the *second step* the masks are merged and overlapped with the image samples gathered from the MS COCO dataset. Finally, our self-generated dataset consists of 15000 samples including the ground truth masks and the images with synthetically generated SHs demonstrated in Fig. 3b. Compared with real original scanned films the first version of our dataset displays significant differences corresponding to the quality. Historical films include scratches and cracks as well as show enormous variances in the exposure. In a second version deformation strategies e.g., image blurring and changing the global contrast and brightness are used to get more reliable and challenging training samples compared to the final test set (see Fig. 3c). The final test set includes 200 extracted frames with manual pixel-based annotated masks showing 16 mm as well as 9.5 mm reel types. The frames are randomly extracted of 10 different digitized analog films from the project Ephemeral Films [4] (see Fig. 3c).

Overscan Segmentation Network: The proposed pipeline consists of three steps: Pre-Processing Module (PrePM), Segmentation Net (SegNet) and Post-Processing Module (Post PM). In the PrePM the input frame is pre-processed by applying standard functions such as grayscale conversion, resizing, zero centering and standardization. The first core part of the pipeline is SegNet which includes a pre-trained backbone CNN model in combination with a segmentation network head. The modules Connected Component Labeling Analysis (CCL), Gaussian Mixture Model (GMM), Reel Type Classifier (RTC) and Crop Window Calculator (CWC) form together the PostPM which is the second core part of our pipeline. Figure 4 illustrates a schematic overview of the pipeline used in this investigation during inference phase.

The SegNet module generates a binary mask which represents the predicted SH areas. These masks are post-processed in the next stage. The CCL process creates labeled connected components. Furthermore, a filtering process is applied in order to remove outliers like small false predicted areas which depends on the

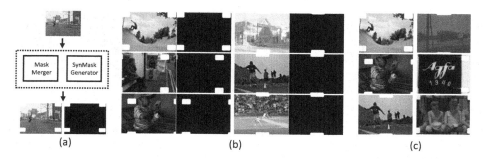

Fig. 3. Demonstration of the dataset used in this exploration. a) Schematic pipeline for generating synthetic samples b) Randomly selected examples of our self-generated dataset c) Comparison of synthetically generated samples (training/validation set) with real original film frames (test set).

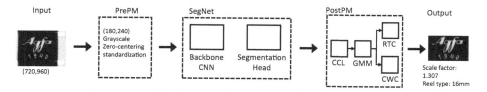

Fig. 4. Schematic overview of the Overscan Detection and Segmentation Pipeline used in this exploration.

frame composition. Since precise segmentation masks are needed to calculate the final crop window (CWC) the GMM module is introduced in this pipeline. This module is based on the corresponding histogram features of each predicted hole sub-area. These features can be used to predict the optimal threshold Th between background as well as hole pixels. The output is a precise thresholded SH in the input frame. Figure 5a illustrates the GMM thresholding process and the effect of using the combination of SegNet and GMM. In order to calculate the final crop window (CWC) the inner points of the holes are extracted (see Fig. 5b). By using these points (e.g. SH-16: 4 inner points, SH-9.5: 2 inner points) the center point related to the positions of the SHs can be calculated. Finally, the frame crop window is generated by specifying a scale-factor (e.g. SH-16 mm: 1.37 and SH-9.5 mm: 1.3) and maximizing it to the borders given through the inner points (see Fig. 5b). RTC is based on the fine-grained results of the GMM module as well as the calculated hole positions in the frame by using a $3x3$ helper grid (see Fig. 5c). This information is used to get a precise final classification result. For example, the fields 1, 3, 7 and 9 are related to SH-16 whereas field 2 and 8 corresponds to SH-9.5.

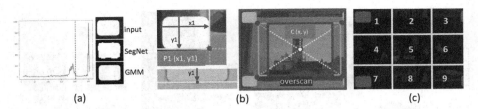

Fig. 5. Demonstration of a) effect of using unsupervised GMM process in PostPM b) inner point $P1(x1, y1)$ creation for SH-16 (top-left), SH-9.5 (bottom-left) and center point $C(x, y)$ calculation (right) as well as c) $3x3$ helper grid for hole position detection and RTC.

4   Experimental Results

The evaluation focus of this investigation is on precise segmentation of detected holes as well as runtime performance during inference phase. Therefore, two different experiments are defined, and evaluation metrics used are described as follows:

Metrics: The final segmentation results are evaluated by calculating metrics such as Mean Intersection over Union (mIoU - Jaccard Index) and Dice Coefficient (F1 Score). The model performance is assessed by interpreting training and validation loss curves over a training period of maximal 50 epochs. The exploration of the runtime performance is done by analyzing the inference time (seconds per processed frame) and using GPU as well as CPU. Finally, all generated results are compared with state-of-the-art solutions. **Experiment 1:** The first experiment focuses on evaluating the segmentation performance of the backbone networks MobileNetV2, SqueezeNet, VGG and Resnet101 in combination with the heads FCN and DeepLab. Since the objective is to mask SHs which are represented by significant edges and perceptual shapes in given frames we train the SegNet models with two different variants. In the first variant low-level features (LF) of the networks are used as input for the segmentation heads whereas the second variant is using the last feature layers (high-level features = HF) of each individual backbone network. The expectation is that the outputs of low-level layers include more significant features for detecting the holes as the feature vectors of deeper layers which are representing more abstract characteristics of an image. Furthermore, this exploration involves different training strategies such as learning rate reduction, early stopping and custom generated data augmentation (e.g. random horizontal and vertical flips).

The HF features represent the last layer of the feature extractor part of all backbone networks used in this evaluation. For example, the features of $layer30 - MaxPool2d$ in VGG16 or the $layer7 - bottleneck2$ in Resnet101. The output of $layer4 - InvertedResidual$ in MobileNetV2, $layer5 - MaxPool2d$ in SqueezeNet, $layer4 - bottleneck2$ in ResNet and $layer4 - MaxPool2d$ in VGG16 are used as LF (referred to pytorch implementations). The results of this experiment demonstrate that using LF in all model variants display significant better

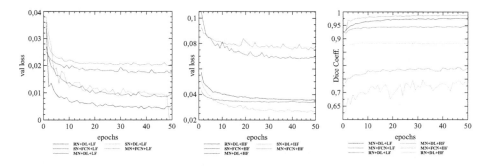

Fig. 6. Demonstration of the segmentation model performances by using different backbone networks over 50 training iterations. Validation loss - low-level features (left), validation loss - high-level features (middle) and validation dice coefficient (right).

segmentation results instead of using the last feature layers of the evaluated model architectures. Resnet101 (LF) in combination with the FCN segmentation head achieves the best results of a mIoU of 0.9407 at a threshold of 0.50 and a Dice score of 0.9684 (@0.5). Furthermore, the VGG16 (LF) in combination with the DeepLab head illustrate a mIoU of 0.9371 (@0.5) and a Dice score of 0.9660 (@0.5). The runtime optimized and compressed model MobileNetV2+DeepLab reaches scores of $mIoU$@0.5 $= 0.9096$ and a $Dice$@0.5 $= 0.9504$. All explored combinations demonstrate an averaged significant performance increase of a $\Delta mIoU$@0.8 $= 0.23(23\%)$. A further evaluation compares the state-of-the-art (SOTA) solutions DeepLabV3 and FCN with the SegNet models trained on our self-generated synthetically dataset. The SOTA models are pre-trained on Pascal VOC (21 classes) and adapted to distinguish only between SH and background pixels by adapting and retraining the last convolutional layer in the networks. The results of the new trained model variants with our introduced dataset outperforms the SOTA solutions. The effectiveness of the networks trained with our dataset is also demonstrated by the comparison to the histogram-based fully unsupervised solution [11]. The combination Resnet101+FCN+LF displays a performance increase of a $\Delta mIoU$@0.5 $= 0.12(12\%)$. An overview of all segmentation results is summarized in Table 1. The validation loss history of the experiments using LF as well as HF are visualized in Fig. 6 (left and middle). The right plot in Fig. 6 demonstrates the validation dice coefficients over the full training time of 50 epochs. **Experiment 2:** Since digitized analog films varies in terms of resolution and film length significantly we focus in this experiment on the runtime performance of our pipeline by analyzing compressed architectures such as MobilenetV2 or Squeezenet compared to very deep and large networks like VGG16 and Resnet101. For this experiment the model variants ResNet101+FCN+LF, VGG16+DL+LF, SqueezeNet+FCN+LF and MobileNetV2+DeepLab+LF are selected since they are showing the best mIoU and Dice coefficient scores with respect to the segmentation head used (see Table 1). In order to extract the exact frame window and remove only

Table 1. This table illustrates the segmentation result of experiment 1 on the final test set including real-world historical film frames. Mean Intersection over Union (mIoU@0.5 and 0.8) as well as the dice coefficient Dice@0.5.

Name	Low-level			High-level		
	mIoU@0.80	mIoU@0.50	Dice@0.50	mIoU@0.80	mIoU@0.50	Dice@0.50
DeepLabV3 [2]	–	–	–	0.4903	0.4988	0.5125
FCN [17]	–	–	–	0.6528	0.6418	0.7251
Histogram-based[11]	–	0.8233	0.8940	–	–	–
MobileNetV2 + FCN	0.8278	0.8751	0.9290	0.6142	0.6142	0,6951
MobileNetV2 + DeepLab	0.8547	**0.9096**	**0.9504**	0,5830	0,6271	0,7130
ResNet101 + FCN	0.9355	**0.9407**	**0.9684**	0.6552	0.6747	0,7640
ResNet101 + DeepLab	0.9122	0.9158	0.9527	0.6385	0.7082	0,7987
VGG16 + FCN	0.8738	0.6391	0.7231	0.6281	0.6788	0,7686
VGG16 + DeepLab	0.9325	**0.9371**	**0.9660**	0.6156	0.6888	0,7785
SqueezeNet + FCN	0.8169	**0.9051**	**0.9477**	0.6989	0.7570	0,8411
SqueezeNet + DeepLab	0.8226	0.8648	0.9222	0.6460	0.6999	0,7916

overscan information precise segmentation of the holes is needed. Therefore, this experiment also explores the effect of using the additional introduced GMM module in the PostPM stage. The performance evaluation of this experiment demonstrates that MobileNetV2+Deeplab+LF and Squeezenet+FCN+LF outperforms the other model combinations with respect to CPU runtime during inference time. One frame needs a process time of about 100 ms (CPU) and both models are able to process about 10 frames per second. However, the Resnet101+FCN+GMM+LF combination reaches similar scores as well as the best segmentation results. Table 2 summarizes the results of the performance experiments. The second part of experiment 2 explores segmentation results by using the additional GMM module in the PostPM stage. Table 3 gives an overview of the reached results and demonstrates the effect of using the GMM module. The variant MobileNetV2+Deeplab+LF displays an increase of the mIoU score (@0.5) of 2.5%. Table 3 points out that the holes are segmented significantly better by using the additional GMM module. However, in terms of runtime performance as well as segmentation results the combination Resnet101+FCN+GMM+LF demonstrates the overall best results in this exploration and outperforms state-of-the-art solutions [11] by a $\Delta mIoU$@0.5 = 12.76% and a $\Delta Dice$@0.5 = 8%. Figure 7 shows the influence of using this module on two example frames. The first image of both examples demonstrates two example SHs crops of the original image. In the next column the predicted masks without the GMM module are visualized and display that the holes are not segmented precisely. The final post-processed mask can be seen in the last column. Since GMM is based on histogram features the pipeline is able to generate an accurate mask which is used for calculating the final crop window in the last stage of our approach.

Table 2. Comparison of runtime performance metrics during inference time. The values displays the execution time in seconds per frame as well as the numbers of corresponding model parameters by using low-features (LF) and high-features (HF).

	nParams		Inference-GPU [sec/frm]		Inference-CPU [sec/frm]	
	LF	HF	LF	HF	LF	HF
SqueezeNet+FCN+GMM	62659	1312963	0,0377	0,0318	0,0982	0,1684
VGG16+DL+GMM	1435715	19437635	0,0346	0,0355	0,1659	0,1310
ResNet+FCN+GMM	373123	51939907	0,0291	0,0493	**0,1061**	**0,6142**
MobilenetV2+DL+GMM	28139	5911875	0,0288	0,0402	0,1003	0,0929
Squeezenet+FCN	62659	1312963	0,0325	0,0253	0,0929	0,1629
VGG16+Deeplab	1435715	19437635	0,0321	0,0253	0,1634	0,1260
Resnet+FCN	373123	51939907	0,0269	0,0380	0,1037	0,6094
MobilenetV2+Deeplab	28139	5911875	0,0260	0,0345	0,0975	0,0871

Table 3. Comparison of final test results with and without using additional GMM module.

	LF				HF			
Experiment	without GMM(@0.5)		GMM(@0.5)		without GMM(@0.5)		GMM(@0.5)	
	mIoU	Dice	mIoU	Dice	mIoU	Dice	mIoU	Dice
MobileNetV2+Deeplab	0.9040	0.9455	0.9295	0.9604	0.5960	0.6621	0.6847	0.7461
ResNet101+FCN	0.9349	0.9650	**0.9509**	**0.9740**	0.6088	0.6609	0.6633	0.7060
SqueezeNet+FCN	0.8953	0.9398	0.9216	0.9554	0.7172	0.7878	0.7885	0.8408
VGG16+DeepLab	0.9368	0.9621	0.9378	0.9624	0.6150	0.6639	0.6734	0.7093

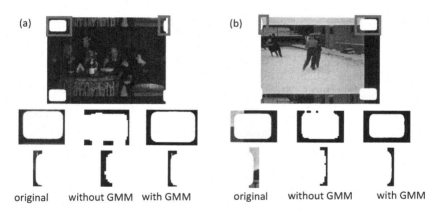

(a)   (b)

original   without GMM   with GMM   original   without GMM   with GMM

Fig. 7. This figure demonstrates two examples for fine-grained segmentation in (a) and (b) and compares the effect with and without using the additional GMM module.

5 Conclusion

This investigation proposes a novel Overscan Detection pipeline in order to get fine-grained masks showing SHs in real-world historical footage. The approach is based on a supervised segmentation network for pre-masking the holes which is trained on a self-generated dataset including synthetically created SHs as well as an unsupervised GMM module which is based on histogram-features. We conclude that using low-level features of the backbone networks outperform the evaluated combinations by an averaged $\Delta mIoU$@0.8 = 23%. Furthermore, this investigation visualizes the effectiveness of using a GMM in combination with a segmentation network and demonstrates a performance increase of $\Delta mIoU$@0.5 = 1.72% and $\Delta Dice$@0.5 = 1%). Moreover, the best model combination Resnet101+FCN+LF+GMM indicates a segmentation performance increase of $\Delta mIoU$@0.5 = 12.7% and $\Delta Dice$@0.5 = 8%). Finally, we propose a fundamental base for further research by providing full access to our sources as well as the generated dataset.

Acknowledgment. Visual History of the Holocaust: Rethinking Curation in the Digital Age (https://www.vhh-project.eu - last visited: 2020/09/30). This project has received funding from the European Union's Horizon 2020 research and innovation program under the Grant Agreement 822670.

References

1. Bhargav, S., Van Noord, N., Kamps, J.: Deep learning as a tool for early cinema analysis. In: SUMAC 2019 - Proceedings of the 1st Workshop on Structuring and Understanding of Multimedia heritAge Contents, co-located with MM 2019, pp. 61–68 (2019). https://doi.org/10.1145/3347317.3357240
2. Chen, L.C., Papandreou, G., Schroff, F., Adam, H.: Rethinking Atrous Convolution for Semantic Image Segmentation. arXiv e-prints arXiv:1706.05587, June 2017
3. Chen, L.-C., Zhu, Y., Papandreou, G., Schroff, F., Adam, H.: Encoder-decoder with atrous separable convolution for semantic image segmentation. In: Ferrari, V., Hebert, M., Sminchisescu, C., Weiss, Y. (eds.) ECCV 2018. LNCS, vol. 11211, pp. 833–851. Springer, Cham (2018). https://doi.org/10.1007/978-3-030-01234-2_49
4. Ephemeral films project (2015). http://efilms.ushmm.org. Accessed 20 Apr 2020
5. Everingham, M., Eslami, S.M.A., Van Gool, L., Williams, C.K.I., Winn, J., Zisserman, A.: The PASCAL visual object classes challenge: a retrospective. Int. J. Comput. Vision **111**(1), 98–136 (2014). https://doi.org/10.1007/s11263-014-0733-5
6. Flückiger, B., Pfluger, D., Trumpy, G., Aydin, T., Smolic, A.: Film material-scanner interaction. Technical report, University of Zurich, Zurich, February 2018. https://doi.org/10.5167/uzh-151114
7. Fossati, G., van den Oever, A.: Exposing the Film Apparatus. Amsterdam University Press (2016)
8. He, K., Gkioxari, G., Dollar, P., Girshick, R.: Mask R-CNN. In: Proceedings of the IEEE International Conference on Computer Vision 2017-October, pp. 2980–2988 (2017). https://doi.org/10.1109/ICCV.2017.322
9. Helm, D., Kampel, M.: Shot boundary detection for automatic video analysis of historical films. In: Cristani, M., Prati, A., Lanz, O., Messelodi, S., Sebe, N. (eds.) ICIAP 2019. LNCS, vol. 11808, pp. 137–147. Springer, Cham (2019). https://doi.org/10.1007/978-3-030-30754-7_14
10. Helm, D., Kampel, M.: Video shot analysis for digital curation and preservation of historical films. In: Rizvic, S., Rodriguez Echavarria, K. (eds.) Eurographics Workshop on Graphics and Cultural Heritage. The Eurographics Association (2019). https://doi.org/10.2312/gch.20191344

11. Helm, D., Pointner, B., Kampel, M.: Frame border detection for digitized historical footage. In: Roth, P.M., Steinbauer, G., Fraundorfer, F., Brandstötter, M., Perko, R. (eds.) Proceedings of the Joint Austrian Computer Vision and Robotics Workshop 2020, pp. 114–115. Verlag der Technischen Universität Graz (2020). https://doi.org/10.3217/978-3-85125-752-6-26

12. Iizuka, S., Simo-Serra, E.: DeepRemaster: temporal source-reference attention networks for comprehensive video enhancement. ACM Trans. Graph. (Proc. SIGGRAPH Asia 2019) **38**(6), 1–13 (2019)

13. Kalti, K., Mahjoub, M.: Image segmentation by gaussian mixture models and modified FCM algorithm. Int. Arab J. Inf. Technol. **11**(1), 11–18 (2014)

14. Laradji, I.H., Vazquez, D., Schmidt, M.: Where are the Masks: Instance Segmentation with Image-level Supervision. arXiv preprint arXiv:1907.01430 (2019)

15. Liang, Z., Guan, Y.S., Rojas, J.: Visual-semantic graph attention network for human-object interaction detection. arXiv abs/2001.02302 (2020)

16. Lin, T.-Y., et al.: Microsoft COCO: common objects in context. In: Fleet, D., Pajdla, T., Schiele, B., Tuytelaars, T. (eds.) ECCV 2014. LNCS, vol. 8693, pp. 740–755. Springer, Cham (2014). https://doi.org/10.1007/978-3-319-10602-1_48

17. Long, J., Shelhamer, E., Darrell, T.: Fully convolutional networks for semantic segmentation. In: IEEE Conference on Computer Vision and Pattern Recognition (CVPR), pp. 3431–3440 (2015). https://doi.org/10.1109/CVPR.2015.7298965

18. Pisters, P.: Filming for the Future: The Work of Louis van Gasteren. Amsterdam University Press (2017)

19. Poudel, R.P.K., Liwicki, S., Cipolla, R.: Fast-SCNN: Fast Semantic Segmentation Network. arXiv e-prints arXiv:1902.04502 (2019)

20. Savardi, M., Signoroni, A., Migliorati, P., Benini, S.: Shot scale analysis in movies by convolutional neural networks. In: Proceedings - International Conference on Image Processing, ICIP, pp. 2620–2624 (2018). https://doi.org/10.1109/ICIP.2018.8451474

21. Svanera, M., Savardi, M., Signoroni, A., Kovács, A.B., Benini, S.: Who is the director of this movie? Automatic style recognition based on shot features. CoRR abs/1807.0, pp. 1–13 (2018). http://arxiv.org/abs/1807.09560

22. Szeliski, R.: Segmentation. In: Szeliski, R. (ed.) Computer Vision, pp. 235–271. Springer, London (2011). https://doi.org/10.1007/978-1-84882-935-0_5

23. Yeh, R.A., Lim, T.Y., Chen, C., Schwing, A.G., Hasegawa-Johnson, M., Do, M.N.: Image restoration with deep generative models. In: 2018 IEEE International Conference on Acoustics, Speech and Signal Processing (ICASSP), pp. 6772–6776 (2018)

24. Zaharieva, M., Mitrović, D., Zeppelzauer, M., Breiteneder, C.: Film analysis of archived documentaries. IEEE Multimedia **18**(2), 38–47 (2011). https://doi.org/10.1109/MMUL.2010.67

25. Zeppelzauer, M., Mitrović, D., Breiteneder, C.: Archive film material - a novel challenge for automated film analysis. Frames Cinema J. **1**(1) (2012). https://www.ims.tuwien.ac.at/publications/tuw-216640

26. Zhang, L., Li, X., Arnab, A., Yang, K., Tong, Y., Torr, P.H.S.: Dual graph convolutional network for semantic segmentation. In: BMVC (2019)

27. Zhao, L., Zheng, S., Yang, W., Wei, H., Huang, X.: An image thresholding approach based on gaussian mixture model. Pattern Anal. Appl. **22**(1), 75–88 (2019). https://doi.org/10.1007/s10044-018-00769-w

Pixel-Level Corrosion Detection on Metal Constructions by Fusion of Deep Learning Semantic and Contour Segmentation

Iason Katsamenis[1] , Eftychios Protopapadakis[1(✉)] ,
Anastasios Doulamis[1] , Nikolaos Doulamis[1] , and Athanasios Voulodimos[2]

[1] National Technical University of Athens,
Heroon Polytechniou 9, Zografou Campus, 15780 Athens, Greece
{iasonkatsamenis,eftprot}@mail.ntua.gr
{adoulam,ndoulam}@cs.ntua.gr
[2] University of West Attica,
Agiou Spyridonos 28, Egaleo, 12243 Athens, Greece
avoulod@uniwa.gr

Abstract. Corrosion detection on metal constructions is a major challenge in civil engineering for quick, safe and effective inspection. Existing image analysis approaches tend to place bounding boxes around the defected region which is not adequate both for structural analysis and prefabrication, an innovative construction concept which reduces maintenance cost, time and improves safety. In this paper, we apply three semantic segmentation-oriented deep learning models (FCN, U-Net and Mask R-CNN) for corrosion detection, which perform better in terms of accuracy and time and require a smaller number of annotated samples compared to other deep models, e.g. CNN. However, the final images derived are still not sufficiently accurate for structural analysis and prefabrication. Thus, we adopt a novel data projection scheme that fuses the results of color segmentation, yielding accurate but over-segmented contours of a region, with a processed area of the deep masks, resulting in high-confidence corroded pixels.

Keywords: Semantic segmentation · Deep learning · Corrosion detection · Boundary refinement

1 Introduction

Metal constructions are widely used in transportation infrastructures, including bridges, highways and tunnels. Rust and corrosion may result in severe problems in safety. Hence, metal defect detection is a major challenge in civil engineering

This paper is supported by the H2020 PANOPTIS project "Development of a Decision Support System for Increasing the Resilience of Transportation Infrastructure based on combined use of terrestrial and airborne sensors and advanced modelling tools," under grant agreement 769129.

G. Bebis et al. (Eds.): ISVC 2020, LNCS 12509, pp. 160–169, 2020.
https://doi.org/10.1007/978-3-030-64556-4_13

to achieve quick, effective but also safe inspection, assessment and maintenance of the infrastructure [9] and deal with materials' deterioration phenomena that derive from several factors, such as climate change, weather events and ageing.

Current approaches in image analysis for detecting defects are through bounding boxes placed around defected areas to assist engineers to rapidly focus on damages [2,13,14,18]. Such approaches, however, are not adequate for a structural analysis since several metrics (e.g. area, aspect ratio, maximum distance) are required to assess the defect status. Thus, we need a more precise pixel-level classification which can also trigger the novel ideas in construction of *prefabrication* [5]. Prefabrication allows components to be built outside the infrastructure, decreasing maintenance cost and time, and improving traffic flows and working risks. Additionally, real-time classification response is necessary to achieve fast inspection of the critical infrastructure, especially on large-scale structures. Finally, a small number of training samples is available, due to the fact that specific traffic arrangements, specialized equipment and extra manpower are required, increasing the cost dramatically.

1.1 Related Work

Recently, deep learning algorithms [20] have been proposed for defect detection. Since the data received as 2D image inputs, convolutional neural networks (CNNs) have been applied to identify regions of interest [14]. Other approaches exploit the CNN structure to detect cracks in concrete and steel infrastructures [2,6], road damages [15,23] and railroad defects on metal surfaces [18]. Finally, the work of [3] combines a CNN and a Naïve Bayes data fusion scheme to detect crack patches on nuclear power plants.

The main problem of all the above-mentioned approaches is that they employ conventional deep models, such as CNNs, which require a large number of annotated data [11,12]. In our case, such a collection is an arduous task since the annotation should be carried out at pixel level by experts. For this reason, most of existing methods estimate the defected regions through boundary boxes. In addition, the computational complexity of the above methods is high, a crucial factor when inspecting large-scale infrastructures.

To address these constraints, we exploit alternative approaches in deep learning proposed for semantic segmentation but for applications different than defect detection in transportation networks such as Fully Convolutional Networks (FCN) [10], U-Nets [16] and Mask R-CNN [7]. The efficiency of the specific methods has been already verified in medical imaging (e.g. brain tumour and COVID-19 symptoms detection) [4,21,22].

1.2 Paper Contribution

In this paper, we apply three semantic segmentation-oriented deep models (FCN, U-Net and Mask R-CNN) to detect corrosion in metal structures since they perform more efficiently than traditional deep models. However, the masks derived are still inadequate for structural analysis and prefabrication because salient

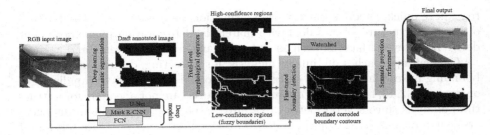

Fig. 1. An overview of the proposed methodology flowchart.

parts of a defected region, especially at the contours, are misclassified. Thus, a detailed, pixel-based mask should be extracted so that civil engineers can take precise measurements on it.

To overcome this problem, we combine through projection the results of color segmentation, which yields accurate contours but oversegments regions, with a processed area of the deep masks (through morphological operators), which indicate only high confident pixels of a defected area. The projection merges color segments belonging to a damaged area improving pixel-based classification accuracy. Experimental results on real-life corroded images, captured in European H2020 Panoptis project, prove the outperformance of the proposed scheme than using segmentation-oriented deep networks or traditional deep models.

2   The Proposed Overall Architecture

Let $I \in \mathbb{R}^{w \times h \times 3}$ an RGB image of size $w \times h$. Our problem involves a traditional binary classification: areas with intense corrosion grades (rust grade categories B, C and D) and areas of no or minor corrosion (category A). The rust grade categories stems from the standard ISO 8501-1 of civil engineering and are described in Sect. 5.1 and depicted in Fig. 3.

Figure 1 depicts the overall architecture of our approach. The RGB images are fed as inputs to the FCN, U-Net and Mask R-CNN deep models to carry out the semantic segmentation. Despite the effectiveness of these networks, inaccuracies still appear on the contours of the detected objects. Although these errors are small, when one measures them as a percentage of the total corroded region, they are very important for structural analysis and prefabrication.

To increase pixel-level accuracy of the derived masks, we combine color segmentation with the regions of the deep models. Color segmentation precisely localizes the contours of an object, but it over-segments it into multiple color areas. Instead, the masks of the deep networks correctly localize the defects, but fail to accurately segment the boundaries. Therefore, we shrink the masks of the deep models to find out the most confident regions, i.e., pixels indicating a defect with high probability. This is done through an erosion morphological operator applied on the initial detections. We also morphologically dilate the deep model regions to localize vague areas which we need to decide in what region they belong to. On that *extended mask*, we apply the watershed segmentation to generate color segments. Finally, we project the results of the color segmentation onto the high confident regions to merge together different color clusters of the same corrosion.

3   Deep Semantic Segmentation Models

Three types of deep networks are applied to obtain the semantic segments. The first is a Fully Convolutional Network (FCN) [10] which does not have any fully-connected layers, reducing the loss of spatial information and allowing faster computation. The second is a U-Net built for medical imaging segmentation [16]. The architecture is heavily based on FCN, though they have some key differences: U-Net (i) is symmetrical by having multiple upsampling layers and (ii) uses skip connections that apply a concatenation operator instead of adding up. Finally, the third model is the Mask R-CNN [7], which extends the Faster R-CNN by using a FCN. This model is able to define bounding boxes around the corroded areas and then segments the rust inside the predicted boxes.

To detect the defects, the models receive as input RGB data and generate, as outputs, binary masks, providing a pixel-level corrosion detection. However, the models fail to generate high fidelity annotations on a boundary level; contours over the detected regions fail to fully encapsulate the rusted regions of the object. As such, a region-growing approach, over these low confidence boundary regions, is applied to improve outcome's robustness and provide refined masks. For training the models, we use an annotated dataset which have been built by civil engineers under the framework of EU project H2020 PANOPTIS.

4   Refined Detection by Projection - Fusion with a Color Segmentation

The presence of inaccuracies in the contours of outputs of the aforementioned deep models is due to the multiple down/up-scaling processes within the convolutional layers of models. To refine the initially detected masks, the following steps are adopted: (i) Localizing a region of high-confident pixels to belong to a defect as a subset of the deep masked outputs. (ii) Localizing fuzzy regions which we cannot decide with confidence if they belong to a corroded area or not, through an extension of the deep output masks. (iii) Applying a color segmentation algorithm in the extended masks which contains both the fuzzy and the high-confident regions. (iv) Finally projecting the results of the color segmentation onto the high-confident area. The projection retains the accuracy in the contours (stemming from color segmentation) while merging different color segments of the same defect together.

Let us assume that, in an RGB image $I \in \mathbb{R}^{w \times h \times 3}$, we have a set of N corroded regions $R = \{R_1, ..., R_N\}$, generated using a deep learning approach. Each partition is a set of pixels $R_j = \{(x_i, y_i)\}_{i=1}^{m_j}, j = 1, ..., N$, where m_j is the

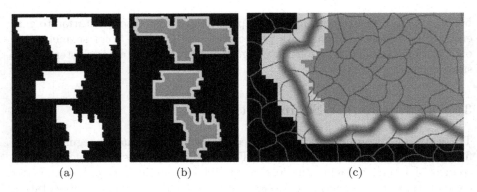

(a)   (b)   (c)

Fig. 2. Illustrating proposed projection method. (a) Detected regions of interest R_j (white). (b),(c) High confidence R_j^T (green) and fuzzy regions R_j^{F+} (yellow). (c) Color segments R_j^w (red) and the final refined contour $R_j^{(a)}$ (blue). (Color figure online)

number of pixels in each set. The remaining pixels represent the no-detection or background areas, denoted by R^B, so that $R \cup R^B = I$ (see Fig. 2a). Subsequently, for each R_j, $j = 1, ..., N$, we consider two subsets R_j^T and R_j^F, so that $R_j^T \cup R_j^F = R_j$. The first set R_j^T, corresponds to inner pixels of the region R_j, which are considered as true foreground and indicate high-confidence corroded areas. They can be obtained using an erosion morphological operator on R_j. The second set R_j^F, contains the remaining pixels $(x_i, y_i) \in R_j$ and their status is considered fuzzy.

We now define a new region $R_j^{F+} \supset R_j^F$, which is a slightly extended area of pixels of R_j^F, obtained using the dilation morphological operator. The implementation is carried out so that R_j^T and R_j^{F+} are adjacent, but non-overlapping. That is, $R_j^T \cap R_j^{F+} = \varnothing$. Summarizing, we have three sets of areas (see Fig. 2b): (i) True foreground or corroded areas $R^T = \{R_1^T, ..., R_N^T\}$ (green region in Fig. 2b), (ii) fuzzy areas $R^{F+} = \{R_1^{F+}, ..., R_N^{F+}\}$ (yellow region of Fig. 2b) and (iii) the remaining image areas R^B, denoting the background or no-detection areas (black region of Fig. 2b).

In the extended fuzzy region R^{F+}, we apply the watershed color segmentation algorithm [1]. Let us assume that the color segmentation algorithm produces M_j segments $s_{i,j}$, with $i = 1, ..., M_j$ for the j-th defected region (see the red region in Fig. 2c), all of which form a set $R_j^w = \bigcup_{i=1}^{M_j} s_{i,j}$. Then, we project segments R_j^w onto R_j^T in a way that:

$$R_j^{(a)} = \{s_{i,j} \in R_j^w : s_{i,j} \cap R_j^T \neq \varnothing\}, j = 1, ..., N \qquad (1)$$

Ultimately, the final detected region (see the blue region in Fig. 2c) is defined as the union of all sets R_j^T and $R_j^{(a)}$ over all corroded regions $j = 1, ..., N$.

5   Experimental Evaluation

5.1   Dataset Description

The dataset is obtained from heterogeneous sources (DSLR cameras, UAVs, cellphones) and contains 116 images of various resolutions, ranging from 194×259 to 4248×2852. All data have been collected under the framework of H2020 Panoptis project. For the dataset, 80% is used for training and validation, while the remaining 20% is for testing. Among the training data, 75% of them is used for training and the remaining 25% for validation. The images vary in terms of corrosion type, illumination conditions (e.g. overexposure, underexposure) and environmental landscapes (e.g. highways, rivers, structures). Furthermore, some images contain various types of occlusions, making detection more difficult.

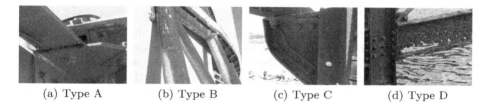

(a) Type A   (b) Type B   (c) Type C   (d) Type D

Fig. 3. Representative image examples of rust grades.

All images of the dataset were manually annotated by engineers within Panoptis project. Particularly, corrosion has been classified according to the ISO 8501-1 standard (see Fig. 3): (i) Type A: Steel surface largely covered with adhering mill scale but little, if any, rust. (ii) Type B: Steel surface which has begun to rust and from which the mill scale has begun to flake. (iii) Type C: Steel surface on which the mill scale has rusted away or from which it can be scraped, but with slight pitting visible under normal vision. (iv) Type D: Steel surface on which the mill scale has rusted away and on which general pitting is visible under normal vision.

5.2   Models Setup

A common case is the use of pretrained networks of specified topology. Generally, transfer learning techniques serve as starting points, allowing for fast initialization and minimal topological interventions. The FCN-8s variant [10,17], served as the main detector for the FCN model. Additionally, the Mask R-CNN detector was based on Inception V2 [19], pretrained over COCO [8] dataset. On the other hand, U-Net was designed from scratch. The contracting part, of the adopted variation, had the following setup: Input $\rightarrow$ 2@Conv $\rightarrow$ Pool $\rightarrow$ 2@Conv $\rightarrow$ Pool $\rightarrow$ 2@Conv $\rightarrow$ Drop $\rightarrow$ Pool, where 2@Conv denotes that two consecutive convolutions, of size 3×3, took place. Finally, for the decoder three corresponding upsampling layers were used.

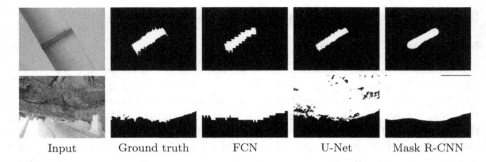

Input   Ground truth   FCN   U-Net   Mask R-CNN

Fig. 4. Visual comparison of the deep models' outputs, without applying boundary refinement.

5.3 Experimental Results

Figure 4 demonstrates two corroded images along with the respective ground truth annotation for all of the three deep models, without applying boundary refinement. In general, the results depict the semantic segmentation capabilities of the core models. Nevertheless, boundary regions are rather coarse. To refine these areas, we implement the color projection methodology as described in Sect. 4 and visualized in Fig. 5. In particular, it shows the defected regions before and after the boundary refinement (see the last two columns of Fig. 5). The corroded regions are illustrated in green for better clarification.

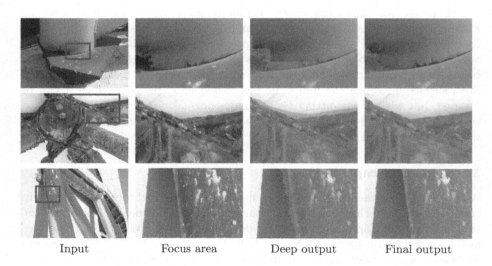

Input   Focus area   Deep output   Final output

Fig. 5. Boundary refinement outputs for specific areas.

Objective results are depicted in Fig. 6 using precision and F1-score. The proposed fusion method improves precision and slightly the F1-score.

U-Net performs slightly better in terms of precision than the rest ones, while for F1-score all deep models yield almost the same performance. Investigating the time complexity, U-Net is the fastest approach, followed by FCN (1.79 times slower) and last is Mask R-CNN (18.25 times slower). Thus, even if Mask R-CNN followed by boundary refinement performs better than the rest in terms of F1-score, it may not be used as the main detection mechanism due to the high execution times.

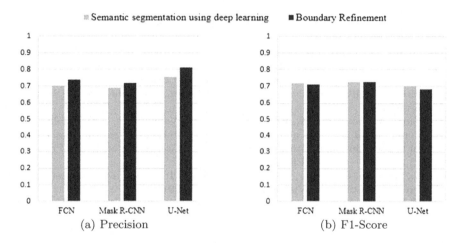

(a) Precision   (b) F1-Score

Fig. 6. Comparative performance metrics for the different deep models, before and after the boundary refinement.

6   Conclusions

In this paper, we propose a novel data projection scheme to yield accurate pixel-based detection of corrosion regions on metal constructions. This projection/fusion exploits the results of deep models, which correctly identify the semantic area of a defect but fail on the boundaries, and a color segmentation algorithm which over-segments the defect into multiple color areas but retains contour accuracy. The deep models were FCN, U-Net and Mask R-CNN. Experimental results and comparisons on real datasets verify the out-performance of the proposed scheme, even for very tough image content of multiple types of defects. The performance is evaluated on a dataset annotated by engineer experts. Though the increase in accuracy is relatively small, the new defected areas can significantly improve structural analysis and prefabrication than other traditional methods.

References

1. Beucher, S., et al.: The watershed transformation applied to image segmentation. In: Scanning Microscopy-Supplement, pp. 299–299 (1992)
2. Cha, Y.J., Choi, W., Büyüköztürk, O.: Deep learning-based crack damage detection using convolutional neural networks. Comput.-Aided Civil Infrastruct. Eng. **32**(5), 361–378 (2017)
3. Chen, F.C., Jahanshahi, M.R.: NB-CNN: deep learning-based crack detection using convolutional neural network and Naïve Bayes data fusion. IEEE Trans. Industr. Electron. **65**(5), 4392–4400 (2017)
4. Dong, H., Yang, G., Liu, F., Mo, Y., Guo, Y.: Automatic brain tumor detection and segmentation using U-net based fully convolutional networks. In: Valdés Hernández, M., González-Castro, V. (eds.) MIUA 2017. CCIS, vol. 723, pp. 506–517. Springer, Cham (2017). https://doi.org/10.1007/978-3-319-60964-5_44
5. Dong, Y., Hou, Y., Cao, D., Zhang, Y., Zhang, Y.: Study on road performance of prefabricated rollable asphalt mixture. Road Mater. Pavement Des. **18**(Suppl. 3), 65–75 (2017)
6. Doulamis, A., Doulamis, N., Protopapadakis, E., Voulodimos, A.: Combined convolutional neural networks and fuzzy spectral clustering for real time crack detection in tunnels. In: 2018 25th IEEE International Conference on Image Processing (ICIP), pp. 4153–4157. IEEE (2018)
7. He, K., Gkioxari, G., Dollár, P., Girshick, R.: Mask R-CNN. In: IEEE International Conference on Computer Vision, pp. 2961–2969 (2017)
8. Lin, T.Y., et al.: Microsoft coco: common objects in context. In: Fleet, D., Pajdla, T., Schiele, B., Tuytelaars, T. (eds.) European Conference on Computer Vision, pp. 740–755. Springer, Cham (2014). https://doi.org/10.1007/978-3-319-10602-1_48
9. Liu, Z., Lu, G., Liu, X., Jiang, X., Lodewijks, G.: Image processing algorithms for crack detection in welded structures via pulsed eddy current thermal imaging. IEEE Instrum. Meas. Mag. **20**(4), 34–44 (2017)
10. Long, J., Shelhamer, E., Darrell, T.: Fully convolutional networks for semantic segmentation. In: IEEE Conference on Computer Vision and Pattern Recognition, pp. 3431–3440 (2015)
11. Makantasis, K., Doulamis, A., Doulamis, N., Nikitakis, A., Voulodimos, A.: Tensor-based nonlinear classifier for high-order data analysis. In: 2018 IEEE International Conference on Acoustics, Speech and Signal Processing (ICASSP), pp. 2221–2225, April 2018. https://doi.org/10.1109/ICASSP.2018.8461418
12. Makantasis, K., Doulamis, A.D., Doulamis, N.D., Nikitakis, A.: Tensor-based classification models for hyperspectral data analysis. IEEE Trans. Geosci. Remote Sens. **56**(12), 6884–6898 (2018)
13. Protopapadakis, E., Voulodimos, A., Doulamis, A.: Data sampling for semi-supervised learning in vision-based concrete defect recognition. In: 2017 8th International Conference on Information, Intelligence, Systems Applications (IISA), pp. 1–6, August 2017. https://doi.org/10.1109/IISA.2017.8316454
14. Protopapadakis, E., Voulodimos, A., Doulamis, A., Doulamis, N., Stathaki, T.: Automatic crack detection for tunnel inspection using deep learning and heuristic image post-processing. Appl. Intell. **49**(7), 2793–2806 (2019). https://doi.org/10.1007/s10489-018-01396-y
15. Protopapadakis, E., Katsamenis, I., Doulamis, A.: Multi-label deep learning models for continuous monitoring of road infrastructures. In: Proceedings of the 13th ACM International Conference on PErvasive Technologies Related to Assistive Environments, pp. 1–7 (2020)

16. Ronneberger, O., Fischer, P., Brox, T.: U-net: convolutional networks for biomedical image segmentation. In: Navab, N., Hornegger, J., Wells, W.M., Frangi, A.F. (eds.) MICCAI 2015. LNCS, vol. 9351, pp. 234–241. Springer, Cham (2015). https://doi.org/10.1007/978-3-319-24574-4_28
17. Shuai, B., Liu, T., Wang, G.: Improving fully convolution network for semantic segmentation. arXiv preprint arXiv:1611.08986 (2016)
18. Soukup, D., Huber-Mörk, R.: Convolutional neural networks for steel surface defect detection from photometric stereo images. In: Bebis, G., et al. (eds.) ISVC 2014. LNCS, vol. 8887, pp. 668–677. Springer, Cham (2014). https://doi.org/10.1007/978-3-319-14249-4_64
19. Szegedy, C., Vanhoucke, V., Ioffe, S., Shlens, J., Wojna, Z.: Rethinking the inception architecture for computer vision. In: IEEE Conference on Computer Vision and Pattern Recognition, pp. 2818–2826 (2016)
20. Voulodimos, A., Doulamis, N., Doulamis, A., Protopapadakis, E.: Deep learning for computer vision: a brief review. Comput. Intell. Neurosci. **2018** (2018)
21. Voulodimos, A., Protopapadakis, E., Katsamenis, I., Doulamis, A., Doulamis, N.: Deep learning models for COVID-19 infected area segmentation in CT images. medRxiv (2020)
22. Vuola, A.O., Akram, S.U., Kannala, J.: Mask-RCNN and U-net ensembled for nuclei segmentation. In: 2019 IEEE 16th International Symposium on Biomedical Imaging (ISBI 2019), pp. 208–212. IEEE (2019)
23. Zhang, L., Yang, F., Zhang, Y., Zhu, Y.J.: Road crack detection using deep convolutional neural network. In: 2016 IEEE International Conference on Image Processing (ICIP), pp. 3708–3712. IEEE (2016)

CSC-GAN: Cycle and Semantic Consistency for Dataset Augmentation

Renato B. Arantes$^{(\boxtimes)}$, George Vogiatzis, and Diego R. Faria

Aston University, Aston Street, Birmingham B4 7ET, UK
{180178991,g.vogiatzis,d.faria}@aston.ac.uk
https://www2.aston.ac.uk/

Abstract. Image-to-image translation is a computer vision problem where a task learns a mapping from a source domain A to a target domain B using a training set. However, this translation is not always accurate, and during the translation process, relevant semantic information can deteriorate. To handle this problem, we propose a new cycle-consistent, adversarially trained image-to-image translation with a loss function that is constrained by semantic segmentation. This formulation encourages the model to preserve semantic information during the translation process. For this purpose, our loss function evaluates the accuracy of the synthetically generated image against a semantic segmentation model, previously trained. Reported results show that our proposed method can significantly increase the level of details in the synthetic images. We further demonstrate our method's effectiveness by applying it as a dataset augmentation technique, for a minimal dataset, showing that it can improve the semantic segmentation accuracy.

Keywords: GAN · Dataset augmentation · Semantic segmentation

1 Introduction

The sparsity of training data can hinder the performance of supervised machine learning algorithms which often require large amounts of data to train and avoid overfitting. Typical deep neural networks have hundreds of millions of parameters to learn, which requires many passes over the training data. On small datasets, running a large number of iterations can result in overfitting, which is usually remedied by one or more of the following: acquiring more data, applying regularisation and performing data augmentation. The latter approach is mostly limited to simple randomised manipulation of an existing dataset (*e.g.* affine warping, rotation or other small perturbations) [27]. In this paper, we leverage the recent success of adversarial image-to-image translation to propose a much more sophisticated approach for data augmentation that applies to semantic segmentation tasks. Under our scheme, an arbitrary number of new images is generated by 'translating' each ground truth label image in our training dataset, and the resulting image/labelling pairs are used to augment that dataset, leading

© Springer Nature Switzerland AG 2020
G. Bebis et al. (Eds.): ISVC 2020, LNCS 12509, pp. 170–181, 2020.
https://doi.org/10.1007/978-3-030-64556-4_14

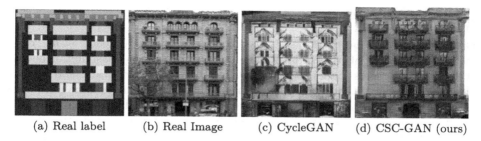

| (a) Real label | (b) Real Image | (c) CycleGAN | (d) CSC-GAN (ours) |

Fig. 1. Translation of facade label to a facade image. The task is to translate from label to image. (a) and (b) are the real label and the real image, (b) is CycleGAN generated, that incorrectly translates the facade behind the tree and the balcony railings. (c) Using our CSC-GAN, that implements semantic consistency in the translation process, the result is a more realistic image.

to improved accuracy. This is achieved by a new cycle-consistent, adversarially trained image-to-image translation model (CSC-GAN) that strengthens local and global structural consistency through pixel cycle-consistency and a semantic loss.

Synthesising realistic and high-resolution images is one of the most challenging tasks in computer vision and machine learning investigation areas [16]. The recent CycleGAN [30] introduced the concept of Cycle-consistency in the context of an image-to-image translation GAN model producing impressive results. In particular, it appears to be able to *translate* semantic labelling to the corresponding image, which seems perfect for data augmentation in semantic segmentation tasks. Unfortunately, CycleGAN fails to capture the relevant semantic constraints accurately (see Fig. 1(c)) and therefore, cannot be used for data augmentation.

The question we pose in this paper is: How can one maintain the semantic correspondence during the image-to-image translation process? Our answer is an additional objective that enforces semantic consistency while the cycle-consistency loss of CycleGAN helps the cross-domain transformation to retain local structural information. Our CSC-GAN also proved to be simpler than other methods [13], while generating realistic images with a significant increase on its level of details to such an extent that they can improve the performance of a state of the art semantic segmentation models like DeeplabV3 [5] and Fully-Convolutional Network (FCN) [20]. This is a significant achievement if we consider that (a) there is no new data or prior information that was fed to the model and (b) DeeplabV3 and FCN are already extremely good at extracting generalisable knowledge from any given dataset. Figure 1(d) is an example of our method's potential. We apply our CSC-GAN to an extremely sparse building facade dataset [24] that consists of only 606 images and labels. Our experiments verify that image-to-image translation methods strengthened by semantic consistency can be used to improve pixel-level semantic segmentation models.

2   Related Work

Generative adversarial networks (GANs), introduced by Goodfellow *et al.* [10], employ the concept of adversarial training, where two models are simultaneously trained: a generative model G that captures the data distribution, and a discriminator model D that estimates the probability that a sample came from the training data rather than G. The generator learns the data distribution p_g, over the data x, by creating a mapping function from a prior noise distribution $p_z(z)$ to data space as $G(z; \theta_g)$. Further, the discriminator, $D(x; \theta_d)$, outputs a single scalar representing the probability that x came from the training data instead of p_g. It has shown extraordinary results in many computer vision tasks such as style transfer [17,28], image generation [4,8,21], image translation [7,14,30], multi-domain image translation [7] and super-resolution [19].

The GAN framework was first introduced to generate visually realistic images and, since then, many applications have been proposed, including data augmentation [27], a technique widely used to increase the volume of data available for training.

One of the areas where GANs have been employed for data augmentation is Medical Imaging. Yi *et al.* in [29], surveyed 150 published articles in the medical image synthesis area and found that GANs are employed for image reconstruction, segmentation, detection, classification and cross-modality synthesis. The main reason for this widespread use seems to be the relative sparsity of labelled datasets in the highly specialized medical image domains.

The same conclusion is reached in Bowles *et al.* [3], where the use of GANs for augmenting CT scan data is investigated. They use a Progressive Growing of GANs (PGGAN) network [16] to generate the synthetic data in the joint image-label space. Their results show that GAN augmentation works better, the more sparse the dataset. Unfortunately the PGGAN framework is more suitable for spatially registered datasets (e.g. faces, or medical imaging). Using an extensive image dataset, Sandfort *et al.* [25] trained a CycleGAN model [30] to transform contrast Computed Tomography (CT) images into non-contrast images, for data augmentation in CT segmentation tasks. According to the authors, the publicly available datasets consists universally of contrast-enhanced CT images, while real-world data contains a certain percentage of non-contrast CT images. This domain shift affects the performance of real-world applications negatively. Using CycleGAN to alleviate this issue, the authors report significant improvement in CT segmentation tasks performance.

When the available data is not uniformly distributed between the distinct classes, the accuracy of an image classification model can degenerate. In [22], Mariani *et al.* propose a balancing generative adversarial network (BAGAN), an augmentation method that can generate new minority-class images and then restore the dataset balance. Likewise, in [1], Antoniou *et al.* proposed a Data Augmentation Generative Adversarial Network (DAGAN) architecture based on a conditional GAN, conditioned on images from a given class c, where the generator network also uses an encoder to project the condition down to a lower-dimensional manifold. Their adversarial training leads their system to generate new images from a given sample, one that appears to be within the same class but look different enough to be a diverse sample.

An impressive dataset augmentation method using GAN for semantic segmentation is introduced by Richter *et al.* in [2]. In their paper, they present an approach for creating a semantic label for images extracted from modern computer games. Using game engines to generate endless quantities of labelled data is a longstanding theme in Computer Vision research. Their experiments show that using the acquired data, to supplement real-world images, significantly increases accuracy, showing that a network trained on unrealistic data can generalise very well to existing datasets.

CyCADA, proposed by Hoffman *et al.* in [13], also explores ways of enforcing semantic consistency on image synthesis. This adversarial unsupervised adaptation algorithm aims to learn a model that correctly predicts a label for a target data. Their input is the source data X_S, the source label Y_S and the target data X_T. Their aim is to learn a model that can correctly predict the label Y_T for the target data X_T. In contrast, our work doesn't seek to predict but to increase the translated image quality with the help of a pre-defined classifier. We are provided with the source data X_S and the source label Y_S. Our purpose is to learn a model that do the translation $Y_S \rightarrow X_S$ more accurately.

3   Proposed Method

In this section, we present our *Cycle and Semantic Consistent GAN* (CSC-GAN) framework. We consider the problem of image-to-image translation with cycle and semantic consistency, where we are provided with the source data X and source labels Y. The aim is to learn a stochastic model f that translates a labelling into the corresponding image (*i.e.* $Y \rightarrow X$) in such a way that the resultant images are so realistic they can improve the results of a deep semantic segmentation model [5,20], when used as a dataset augmentation technique. To do so, we extend the CycleGAN framework by adding a new loss function $\mathcal{L}_{sem}$ that evaluates how accurate is the synthetic generated image against a previously trained semantic segmentation model g. To establish the background, we first review in the following sections, the GAN/Cycle-GAN models on which our method is based.

3.1   CycleGAN Loss Functions

The CycleGAN full objective is composed of an adversarial loss and a cycle consistency loss, as follows.

Adversarial Loss. The adversarial loss is given by

$$
\begin{aligned}
\mathcal{L}_{GAN}(G, D_Y) = \ &\mathbb{E}_{y \sim p_{data}(y)}[\log D_Y(y)] \\
&+ \mathbb{E}_{x \sim p_{data}(x)}[\log(1 - D_Y(G(x)))],
\end{aligned}
\tag{1}
$$

where G tries to generate images that look similar to images from domain Y and D_Y aims to distinguish between the translated samples $G(x)$ and real samples y.

G aims to minimise this objective against an adversary D that tries to maximise it.

Cycle Consistency Loss. Adversarial losses individually cannot guarantee that the learned function can map a single input x to a desired output y. To additionally decrease the space of possible mapping functions, CycleGAN authors argue that the learned mapping functions should be cycle-consistent, intending to encourage the source content to be preserved during the conversion process. For each image x from domain X, a different map F should be able to bring x back to the original image, *i.e.*, $x \to G(x) \to F(G(x)) \approx x$. This is called the *forward cycle consistency*. Similarly, for each image y from domain Y, G and F should also satisfy *backward cycle consistency*: $y \to F(y) \to G(F(y)) \approx y$. This behaviour is encouraged using a cycle consistency loss:

$$\mathcal{L}_{cyc}(G, F) = \mathbb{E}_{x \sim p_{data}(x)} \parallel F(G(x)) - x \parallel_1 \\ + \mathbb{E}_{y \sim p_{data}(y)} \parallel G(F(y)) - y \parallel_1 . \tag{2}$$

Full Objective. The CycleGAN full objective is

$$\mathcal{L}(G, F, D_X, D_Y) = \mathcal{L}_{GAN}(G, D_Y) \\ + \mathcal{L}_{GAN}(F, D_X) \\ + \lambda \mathcal{L}_{cyc}(G, F), \tag{3}$$

where λ controls the relative importance of the two objectives.

3.2   Semantic Consistency Objective

As we have access to the source labelled data, we aim to encourage high semantic consistency after image translation explicitly. For this purpose, we pre-train a semantic segmentation model g, on the same *training* set used to train our CSC-GAN model, and use this model g to evaluate the synthetic images during the CSC-GAN training. By fixing the model g weights during the CSC-GAN training, we guarantee that a good segmentation result, obtained from a synthetic image, is due to an improvement in the synthetic image quality, as the model g was trained on real images. Using the segmenter model g we propose our semantic consistency objective as

$$\mathcal{L}_{sem}(g, F) = \mathbb{E}_{y \sim p_{data}(y)} \mathcal{L}_{cs}[g(F(y)), y], \tag{4}$$

where $\mathcal{L}_{cs}[.,.]$ is the cross-entropy loss [13] comparing two segmentation masks $g(F(y))$ and y. This equation means that given a label $y \in Y$, the model g predicts the labels for $F(y)$, *i.e.*, the synthetic image generated using the real label y. The loss $\mathcal{L}_{sem}$ evaluates this prediction, and its result is added to the CycleGAN objective function, intending to help improve the overall synthetic image quality. It is interesting to note the superficial similarity between the semantic consistency loss $\mathcal{L}_{sem}$ and the third term of the cycle consistency loss

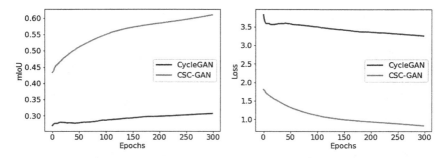

Fig. 2. Impact of the proposed semantic consistency loss over the synthetic images, during model training.

(Eq. 3). Both G and g map from images to labels but (a) g is producing 1-hot encoding per label while G produces an RGB image as in [30], hence the different choice of image distance metric and (b) g is a pre-trained network (we use the DeepLabV3 architecture) while G is a network we train adversarially. We experimented with removing the trainable G network but were unable to achieve a converged solution, possibly because G introduces a convex relaxation to the optimisation problem. The full objective is then

$$\mathcal{L}(G, F, D_X, D_Y) = \mathcal{L}_{GAN}(G, D_Y) \\ + \mathcal{L}_{GAN}(F, D_X) \\ + \lambda\mathcal{L}_{cyc}(G, F) \\ + \mu\mathcal{L}_{sem}(g, F). \tag{5}$$

where λ and μ are relative important weights. To show the impact of the new semantic consistency loss, Fig. 2 presents the evaluation comparison of the synthetic images, during model training, with and without our proposed loss. It shows a dramatic improvement in the mIoU score and the cross-entropy loss when the objective described in the Eq. 5 is used, instead of the regular Cycle-GAN loss defined in Eq. 3.

4   Experimental Results

In this section we present the attained results of our approach CSC-GAN compared against the Facade dataset [24] augmented with the regular CycleGAN model [30], SPADE model [23], which is a state-of-art label to image translation and two style transfer models [9, 15], being that [15] was designed explicitly for dataset augmentation. The datasets used on the experiments are listed in Table 1.

In order to compare these augmented datasets, for each one we trained two semantic segmentation models, DeeplabV3 [5] and Fully-Convolutional Network (FCN) [20], both with a ResNet101 [11] backbone. Each model is trained for

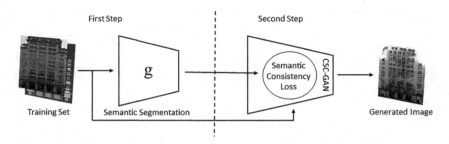

Fig. 3. CSC-GAN two steps. First we train a semantic segmentation model g on the *training* set, then we use it to evaluate the synthetic images quality during our model training.

Table 1. Datasets. Lists of all datasets used in the semantic consistency experiment.

Training set name	Size	Description
facade	484	Regular training set without any augmentation [24]
facade+CycleGAN	968	Regular plus images from regular CycleGAN model [30]
facade+SPADE	968	Regular plus images from SPADE model [23]
facade+Styleaug	968	Regular plus images from style augmentation model [15]
facade+Arbitrary	968	Regular plus images from arbitrary artistic stylization model [9]
facade+CSC-GAN	968	Regular plus images from our CSC-GAN model

50 epochs with a learning rate set to 0.0002 and the Adam optimiser [18]. The performance of each model is reported using the mean intersection-over-union (mIoU) score [26] evaluated over the *test* set.

The facade dataset [24] has been split into a *training* X_S, with 80% or 484 images and a *test* X_T set, with 20% or 122 images. As shown in Table 1, there are six variations of the *training* set, but the *test* set remains the same across all experiments.

The augmentation is done as follows: For each label $y \in X_S$ a synthetic image $x = F(y)$ is generated and the pair (y, x) is added to the dataset. By the end a new *training* set X'_S is created with size twice as X_S. This is done because one synthetic image per each label $y \in X_S$ is added to the new *training* set X'_S.

The CSC-GAN model is trained in two steps: First, we train the semantic segmentation model g on the regular facade dataset, which is used as a labeller during the CSC-GAN training, then we train the CSC-GAN model, as described above. Figure 3 illustrates these two stages.

Table 2 presents the results. Each experiment was executed 5 times and the results reported are the mean and the standard deviation for these 5 executions. The presented results show that the dataset augmented with images from our CSC-GAN model can outperform the regular facade dataset by approximately 4% when the DeeplabV3 [6] model is trained on it and by roughly 3% with the FCN [20] model, as shown in the last row on Table 2. SPADE also provided

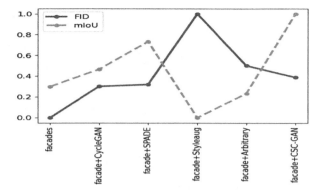

Fig. 4. FID x MioU. The graph suggests an inverse relationship between the two metrics. Data were normalised to fit in the same plot. The *Frechet Inception Distance* (FID) is a metric that compares statistics of real and generated images and summarises how similar the two groups of images are. A lower FID score indicates that the two groups of images are more similar.

Table 2. Experimental results. Accu. is the pixel accuracy; the FID [12] metric is calculated against the dataset without augmentation. Each experiment was executed 5 times, the mIoU and the pixel accuracy results reported are the mean and the standard deviation for these 5 executions.

Dataset name	FID	DeeplabV3 [6]		FCN [20]	
		mIoU	Accu.	mIou	Accu.
facades [24]		0.552 (0.016)	0.706 (0.013)	0.558 (0.003)	0.711 (0.002)
facade+CycleGAN [30]	**22.742**	0.557 (0.008)	0.710 (0.007)	0.562 (0.002)	0.714 (0.002)
facade+SPADE [23]	24.107	0.565 (0.009)	0.716 (0.008)	0.572 (0.004)	0.723 (0.003)
facade+Styleaug [15]	75.307	0.543 (0.005)	0.698 (0.005)	0.561 (0.005)	0.714 (0.004)
facade+Arbitrary [9]	37.804	0.550 (0.005)	0.703 (0.004)	0.562 (0.003)	0.714 (0.002)
facade+CSC-GAN (ours)	29.268	**0.573 (0.005)**	**0.723 (0.004)**	**0.574 (0.003)**	**0.724 (0.002)**

promising results, but it was also outperformed by our method. The datasets augmented by [15] and [23] got a decrease in performance concerning the regular Facade dataset, showing that style transfer is not a good technique for dataset augmentation on a per-pixel classification scenario as semantic segmentation. Also, the FID [12] metric in the first column suggests an inverse relation with the mIoU metric, as shown in Fig. 4. This inverse relationship is because the synthetic images must be within the original distribution, but it also has to look different enough to be regarded by the semantic segmentation model as a diverse sample. A low FID means that the synthetic images are too close to the original dataset distribution; therefore, they cannot be viewed as new samples. Conversely, a high FID means that the synthetic data are too diverse from the original data; hence they cannot be considered as samples from the same distribution.

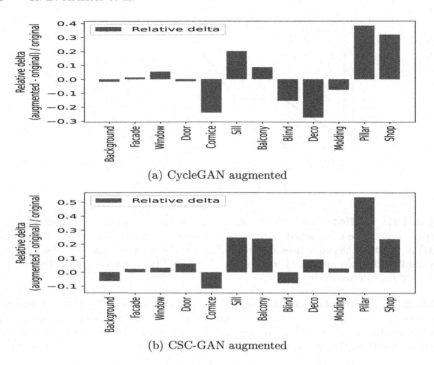

(a) CycleGAN augmented

(b) CSC-GAN augmented

Fig. 5. Figures (a) and (b) compare the correctly predicted segmentation pixels between the regular facade and the augmented datasets. Figure (b) shows that for the majority classes, our CSC-GAN model can produce more accurate images for data augmentation.

To better understand the improvement brought by our CSC-GAN, in Fig. 5 we compare the correctly predicted pixels of the models trained with CycleGAN and CSC-GAN augmented datasets with the model trained with the regular facade dataset. The comparisons are made over the test set segmentation results.

Figure 5(a) presents the comparison of the regular facade with CycleGAN; the graph shows that for six out of twelve labels, there is a drop in the correctly predicted pixels, being *cornice* and *deco* labels the ones that have the most significant difference. Conversely, in Fig. 5(b), except for *background*, *window* and *shop* the model trained with our CSC-GAN augmented dataset attained a substantial improvement in the correctly predicted pixels. Special attention must be taken to the *decoration* and *balcony* labels, two very challenging categories where our method presented a significant improvement over the facade dataset. The reason is the increase in level-of-detail obtained by the CSC-GAN model to the generated images, as we can see in Fig. 6.

In Fig. 6, column (c), note that our model is capable of learning the appearance of balcony railings and in the second row the extended model begins to show the pillar as a 3D structure, instead of just a flat shape as shown in column (b).

(a)   (b)   (c)

Fig. 6. Comparing images. Real image (a), regular CycleGAN model (b) and CSC-GAN model (c). The labels were omitted.

The third row, column (c), shows that the extended model can also learn the decoration, which the regular CycleGAN model represents as a flat shape.

5 Conclusion

In this paper, we propose a cycle consistent image generation framework that combines with semantic constraints to deliver increased level-of-detail in the generated images. This improvement enables the use of the method for data augmentation in the domain of semantic segmentation. As future work we intend to apply our model to photorealistic images of general scenes. We are also planning to investigate more challenging datasets, such as geospatial images. Another promising direction to explore is the domain-transfer effect that arises from cross-training the semantic segmentation model on different datasets.

References

1. Antoniou, A., Storkey, A., Edwards, H.: Data augmentation generative adversarial networks. arXiv preprint arXiv:1711.04340 (2017)
2. Antoniou, A., Storkey, A., Edwards, H.: Data augmentation generative adverdarial networks. Stat **1050**, 8 (2018)
3. Bowles, C., et al.: GAN augmentation: augmenting training data using generative adversarial networks (2018)
4. Brock, A., Donahue, J., Simonyan, K.: Large scale GAN training for high fidelity natural image synthesis (2018)
5. Chen, L., Papandreou, G., Schroff, F., Adam, H.: Rethinking atrous convolution for semantic image segmentation (2017)
6. Chen, L.C., Zhu, Y., Papandreou, G., Schroff, F., Adam, H.: Encoder-decoder with atrous separable convolution for semantic image segmentation. In: ECCV (2018)
7. Choi, Y., Choi, M., Kim, M., Ha, J.W., Kim, S., Choo, J.: Stargan: unified generative adversarial networks for multi-domain image-to-image translation. In: Proceedings of the IEEE Conference on Computer Vision and Pattern Recognition (2018)
8. Donahue, J., Simonyan, K.: Large scale adversarial representation learning (2019)
9. Ghiasi, G., Lee, H., Kudlur, M., Dumoulin, V., Shlens, J.: Exploring the structure of a real-time, arbitrary neural artistic stylization network. arXiv preprint arXiv:1705.06830 (2017)
10. Goodfellow, I., et al.: Generative adversarial nets. In: Ghahramani, Z., Welling, M., Cortes, C., Lawrence, N.D., Weinberger, K.Q. (eds.) Advances in Neural Information Processing Systems 27, pp. 2672–2680. Curran Associates, Inc. (2014)
11. He, K., Zhang, X., Ren, S., Sun, J.: Deep residual learning for image recognition. In: 2016 IEEE Conference on Computer Vision and Pattern Recognition, CVPR 2016, Las Vegas, NV, USA, 27–30 June 2016, pp. 770–778 (2016)
12. Heusel, M., Ramsauer, H., Unterthiner, T., Nessler, B., Hochreiter, S.: GANs trained by a two time-scale update rule converge to a local nash equilibrium. In: Advances in Neural Information Processing Systems, pp. 6626–6637 (2017)
13. Hoffman, J., et al.: Cycada: cycle-consistent adversarial domain adaptation. In: International Conference on Machine Learning, pp. 1989–1998 (2018)
14. Isola, P., Zhu, J.Y., Zhou, T., Efros, A.A.: Image-to-image translation with conditional adversarial networks. In: 2017 IEEE Conference on Computer Vision and Pattern Recognition (CVPR), pp. 5967–5976 (2017)
15. Jackson, P.T., Abarghouei, A.A., Bonner, S., Breckon, T.P., Obara, B.: Style augmentation: data augmentation via style randomization. In: CVPR Workshops, pp. 83–92 (2019)
16. Karras, T., Aila, T., Laine, S., Lehtinen, J.: Progressive growing of GANs for improved quality, stability, and variation. In: International Conference on Learning Representations (2018)
17. Karras, T., Laine, S., Aila, T.: A style-based generator architecture for generative adversarial networks (2018)
18. Kingma, D.P., Ba, J.: Adam: a method for stochastic optimization. arXiv preprint arXiv:1412.6980 (2014)

19. Ledig, C., et al.: Photo-realistic single image super-resolution using a generative adversarial network. In: 2017 IEEE Conference on Computer Vision and Pattern Recognition (CVPR), pp. 105–114 (2017)
20. Long, J., Shelhamer, E., Darrell, T.: Fully convolutional networks for semantic segmentation. In: Proceedings of the IEEE Conference on Computer Vision and Pattern Recognition, pp. 3431–3440 (2015)
21. Lučić, M., Ritter, M., Tschannen, M., Zhai, X., Bachem, O.F., Gelly, S.: High-fidelity image generation with fewer labels. In: International Conference on Machine Learning (2019)
22. Mariani, G., Scheidegger, F., Istrate, R., Bekas, C., Malossi, A.C.I.: BAGAN: data augmentation with balancing GAN. CoRR abs/1803.09655 (2018)
23. Park, T., Liu, M.Y., Wang, T.C., Zhu, J.Y.: Semantic image synthesis with spatially-adaptive normalization. In: Proceedings of the IEEE Conference on Computer Vision and Pattern Recognition (2019)
24. Radim Tyleček, R.Š.: Spatial pattern templates for recognition of objects with regular structure. In: Proceedings of GCPR, Saarbrucken, Germany (2013)
25. Sandfort, V., Yan, K., Pickhardt, P.J., Summers, R.M.: Data augmentation using generative adversarial networks (CycleGAN) to improve generalizability in CT segmentation tasks. Sci. Rep. 9(1), 1–9 (2019)
26. Shelhamer, E., Long, J., Darrell, T.: Fully convolutional networks for semantic segmentation. IEEE Trans. Pattern Anal. Mach. Intell. 39(4), 640–651 (2017)
27. Shorten, C., Khoshgoftaar, T.M.: A survey on image data augmentation for deep learning. J. Big Data 6(1), 60 (2019)
28. Wang, X., Gupta, A.: Generative image modeling using style and structure adversarial networks. CoRR abs/1603.05631 (2016)
29. Yi, X., Walia, E., Babyn, P.: Generative adversarial network in medical imaging: a review. Med. Image Anal. 58, 101552 (2019)
30. Zhu, J.Y., Park, T., Isola, P., Efros, A.A.: Unpaired image-to-image translation using cycle-consistent adversarial networks. In: 2017 IEEE International Conference on Computer Vision (ICCV) (2017)

Improvements on the Superpixel Hierarchy Algorithm with Applications to Image Segmentation and Saliency Detection

Marcos J. C. E. Azevedo$^{(\boxtimes)}$ and Carlos A. B. Mello

Centro de Informética, Universidade Federal de Pernambuco, Recife, Brazil
{mjcea,cabm}@cin.ufpe.br

Abstract. Superpixel techniques aim to divide an image into predefined number of regions or groups of pixels, to facilitate operations such as segmentation. However, finding the optimal number of regions for each image becomes a difficult task due to the large difference of features observed in images. However, with the help of edge and color information, we can target an ideal number of regions for each image. This work presents two modifications to the known Superpixel hierarchy algorithm. These changes aim to define the number of superpixels automatically through edge information with different orientations and the Hue channel of the HSV color model. The results are presented quantitatively and qualitatively for edge detection and saliency estimation problems. The experiments were conducted on the BSDS500 and ECSSD datasets.

Keywords: Superpixel · Image segmentation · Saliency map

1 Introduction

Superpixel techniques aim to group pixels under a unique label, creating a so called superpixel, which can be used for different types of applications [8,21,25]. Its concept was first introduced in [20] when they were used for segmentation based on Gestalt laws. After that, superpixels were more widely used through the well-known Simple Linear Iterative Clustering (SLIC) algorithm [1]. The input for SLIC is the k number of equally-sized superpixels in the final image. This number is essential for a good segmentation.

Image segmentation plays a key role in computer vision. Its main goal is to divide an image into small parts for further object detection and recognition. It is the first and fundamental step of several applications. The segmentation of an image can be done in many ways, without the use of superpixels (as in [5,16–18]), or with them (as [27]).

The result of a superpixel processing can be seen as an intermediate representation of an image. In Fig. 1, we can see different ways of representing an

G. Bebis et al. (Eds.): ISVC 2020, LNCS 12509, pp. 182–193, 2020.
https://doi.org/10.1007/978-3-030-64556-4_15

image through different number of superpixels. It is easy to identify the relationship between this number and the image visualization. For example, for four superpixels (Fig. 1.b), the aircraft is represented in a very simple way with few details. For 256 superpixels (Fig. 1.d), some details are perceptible, just as for the intermediary value of 128 superpixels (Fig. 1.c). Despite the loss of details, the shape of the aircraft has been almost completely preserved in all cases. Thus, for example, in an application that aims to detect the position of the aircraft, the reduction of details would help to simplify the task.

Fig. 1. (a) Original image and its segmented version for (b) 4, (c) 128 and (d) 256 superpixels.

Among several characteristics found in an image, we can mention color (which can be related to similarity information) and edge (which can be related to discontinuity information). Both color and edge can compose an important knowledge to guide the process of superpixel segmentation. The Superpixel Hierarchy algorithm (SH) [22] makes use of color and edge information to perform the segmentation through the region merging in which the pixels are weighted and, from their similarities, grouped together. The work also shows that edge information is very useful in the process of merging regions. However, just as SLIC, they do not define the number of superpixels in an image automatically; it must be set by the user according to the image.

This paper proposes modifications to the original version of SH algorithm to make its execution automatic for each image. The first modification is related to how the number of superpixels can be defined from the number of distinct tones present in the image. The second modification is by improving the edge information used.

In the following section, some related works are described. In Sect. 3, the proposed modifications are explained. Section 4 presents the experiments and quantitative and qualitative results which are described and compared. Section 5 concludes the paper with possible future works.

2   Related Works

To evaluate the performance of our proposal, the superpixel images are submitted to different edge detection algorithms. Among them, Structured Forest Edges (SFE) [6] (which is used in [22] to feed the edge information), Holistically-Nested Edge Detection (HED) [23] (with its Deep Learning approach), and the well-known Globalized Probability of Boundary (gPb) [13]. For this reason, these algorithms are summarized in this section.

The Structured Forest Edge Detection (SFE) is used in the original version of SH due to its low processing time. The authors also evaluate the running time for superpixel generation (which is out of our scope). SFE detects edges using a previously trained Random Forests (RF) to label each pixel of the input image as edge or not in 16x16 masks.

The Holistically-Nested Edge Detection (HED) is part of a category of edge detection algorithms that make use of Deep Learning techniques, in particular Convolutional Neural Networks (CNN) [10]. Its architecture is exclusively formed by convolution layers to learn the hierarchical representation of the edges (size, shape, etc.).

Finally, the Globalized Probability of Boundary (gPb) edge detector is an extension of Pb [15], but with edges definition based on global information from eight different orientations. Local information of color, texture, and brightness, is also used. The great advantage of gPb over other algorithms is exactly in collecting information from various orientations, having success where several algorithms fail.

3   Proposed Modifications on Superpixel Hierarchy Algorithm

Superpixel Hierarchy [22] has two parameters that guide the pixels grouping process: the number of superpixels and the edge information. The number of superpixels represents the number of regions present in the final image. Figure 2 exemplifies a result for five and three superpixels. As we can see, the segmented image for 3 superpixels does not have the region of the bear. Thus, it is easy to conclude that the number of superpixels has major impact on the final result.

Fig. 2. Example of (a) an original image, its SH segmented version for (b) 5 superpixels and (c) 3 superpixels, where the bear was suppressed.

The second parameter (edge information) has also a big impact on the final result. In the original work [22], the authors show the difference between the algorithm with and without edge information. Thus, by adding more information to the process, they achieved better results. However, still according to the authors, the use of different edge detection algorithms does not result in a big difference, although it exists in a small form.

The first objective of our method is to try to identify a suitable value for the number of superpixels for each image, automatically. Regardless how many different colors can be represented in an image in RGB color model, usually, just few distinct "tones" can be clustered. In this sense, "tone" is an informal way to define the hue which is the attribute of the pixel to be clustered. For example, the blue hue can be clustered in many different colors (as a dark blue or a light blue) [19]. Thus, the first step is to identify the number of distinct "tones" present in the image and define it as the number of superpixels to be used.

As a first improvement, the input image is converted into the HSV color model, which is inspired by the human visual system. As explained before, it is important to group pixels with similar hue, this is why the image is converted into HSV (in fact, just the hue channel is needed). The hue component is used for grouping. Any clustering algorithm could be used in order to group similar pixels. We propose the application of the Mean Shift (MS) [9] clustering algorithm to the hue channel. One of the reasons to choose MS is that there is no need for a training step in proper datasets, in contrast to supervised machine learning techniques. The MS presents as disadvantage its high computational cost, but the kernel bandwidth value is its unique parameter which has several automation proposals for different applications [7,28]. We have decided to perform the tests for a single bandwidth value for all images; this value was chosen from empirical tests, observing the metrics used in the experiments. Thus, for this work, the bandwidth value is equal to 0.75. MS automatically returns the number of groups present in the hue channel of the input image; a value close to the number of colors observed by the human eye. This is considered as the number of superpixels. Figure 3 shows examples of images with their number of superpixels defined using MS.

Fig. 3. Examples of SH result with number of superpixels defined automatically by Mean Shift over the hue version of the images. Original images are presented in the left column and their respective superpixel versions are in the right column.

As mentioned previously, the second parameter of the method is the edge information that helps the SH algorithm during the fusion process between the different regions. In [22], the authors show that the use of this information is crucial to achieve good quality results, but different edge detection methods did not caused significant differences. Thus, as a second improvement, instead of providing only a single edge image to the algorithm, we propose the use of the gPb edge images created for each of the eight different orientations, as shown in Fig. 4. For these gPb images, superpixel images are created. Thus, at the end of the process, we have eight superpixel images for the input image. The resulting SH images for each gPb orientations are shown in Fig. 5 for the bear image example; in this figure, we can see how the edge information impacts the generation of superpixel images. For the edge image in Fig. 4a, which has a limited quantity of edge information, the superpixel image created (Fig. 5a) shows no similarity to the original image.

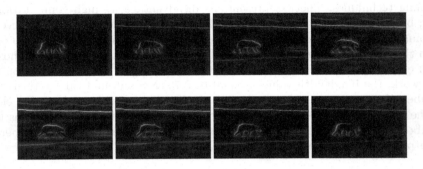

Fig. 4. gPb images for eight different orientations for the bear image of Fig. 2a.

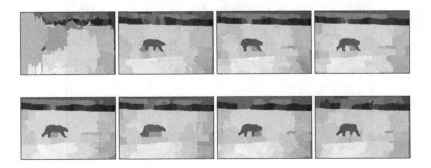

Fig. 5. Superpixel images created for the eight gPb edge images.

4 Experiments and Results

Unlike the original method, which has only one superpixel image as the final result, we have eight superpixel images for each input image. Therefore, the amount of edge information added to the method is much higher than the original method. Thus, to evaluate the performance of this addition together with the use of mean shift, we evaluated the result with a benchmark on edge detection problem. We also did a qualitative analysis for saliency detection application. Both experiments were performed on the 200 test images of the BSDS500 database [2]; saliency is also analyzed in the Extended Complex Scene Saliency Dataset (ECSSD) [24].

4.1 Edge Detection Experiments

The first step is to generate the intermediate edge images. For each superpixel image, an edge image is generated by Structured Forest Edge Detection (SFE), as shown in Fig. 6. Just as in [22], we have also used SFE due to its low running time. These intermediate edge images are grouped into a single image, as shown in Fig. 7, and submitted to the benchmark. This final image was created by a sequence of sum and normalization of the intermediate edge images. Following the methodology of [2], they were evaluated for a fixed threshold for all images (the Optimal Dataset Scale - ODS), the best threshold for each image (the Optimal Image Scale - OIS), and the average precision (AP) for 30 thresholds.

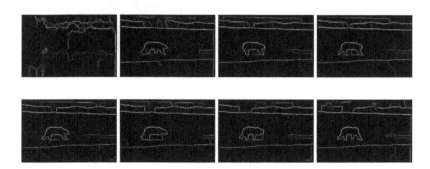

Fig. 6. Eight intermediate edge images generated by SFE for each edge orientation of gPb.

We have also investigated the number of superpixels defined by MS on our proposal and observed that, for 10 images (from the 200 images dataset), Mean Shift returned the value of 1; this happened in images with few different tones. Thus, we conducted two experiments to verify the impact of this issue. In the first, the results of the algorithm without any interference on the number of superpixels defined by MS (called SHm) were analyzed. In the second, we defined a minimum value of five superpixels (called SHm5) - it is important to remember

Fig. 7. Image resulting from the combination of the intermediate edge images.

that this should be a low value due to the small number of different tones in the images. Figure 8 illustrates this problem with two sample images and the results for the fixed minimum number of superpixels. The benchmark results for these experiments for the complete training dataset are provided in Table 1.

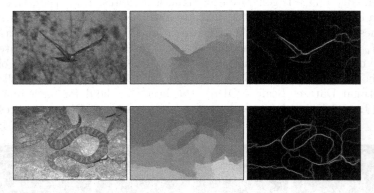

Fig. 8. Examples of images that MS had difficulty to identify the distinct number of colors: (a and d) original images, (b and e) their versions with number of superpixels fixed at 5 and (c and f) their edge images by SFE.

Observing the results on Table 1, we can notice that the performance of SFE, HED, and gPb algorithms are very close, as already shown in [22]. For the modified version of SH, we can see that the main difference is in the AP value to the version with the minimum number of superpixels fixed at five, achieving 0.63 whereas other methods obtained around 0.60. For ODS and OIS values, all methods provided very close results.

We have also made a comparison with the original version of SH, as shown in Table 2. In this table, it is shown the results for 100 to 500 superpixels as well as 1,000 and the total number of pixels in the images (called NP). This was done to compare the performance of our proposal with the version of the algorithm with no automatic definition of the number of superpixels. Because of the previous results, we are always using the fixed minimum number of 5 superpixels.

Table 1. Results of the proposed method compared to HED, SFE and gPb, considering the minimum number of superpixels.

	SFE	HED	GPB	SHm	SHm5
ODS	0.677	0.677	0.677	0.666	0.675
OIS	0.689	0.690	0.690	0.684	**0.694**
AP	0.605	0.605	0.605	0.615	**0.638**

Table 2. Benchmark results from the original version of SH for different numbers of superpixel for the BSDS500 database.

	100	200	300	400	500	1000	NP
ODS	0.669	0.682	0.692	0.696	0.700	0.709	0.719
OIS	0.681	0.694	0.705	0.708	0.711	0.722	0.740
AP	0.584	0.610	0.626	0.634	0.636	0.643	0.624

Table 2 shows that SH achieves stable results around 500 superpixels. We can see that the difference for the values 500 and 1000 is not very high, despite the number of superpixels has doubled, especially when the threshold is the same for all images. About AP, SH improved the edge identification even when compared to the NP version, since the boundaries between the regions are redefined, leading to the removal of irrelevant edges. It is important to observe that superpixels make the images more simple; this can lead to a faster application of a segmentation algorithm with the image divided into a proper number of superpixels (as it was shown in Fig. 1b). Comparing Tables 1 and 2, one can see that we have achieved results quantitatively very satisfactory automatically, without a brute force search for the best number of superpixels.

4.2 Saliency Detection

A saliency estimator aims to create a saliency map which is a gray level image, where dark tones mean not important areas, while light tones mean more important areas. For saliency detection, the eight superpixel images (as the ones in Fig. 5) are grouped into a single image in a similar way to what was done to combine the intermediate edge images. This grouping of the superpixel images is exemplified in Fig. 9. This image is then submitted to the *Minimum Barrier Salient Object Detection* (MBS+) [26], *Visual Saliency by Extended Quantum Cuts* (EQCUT) [3,4], *Inner and Inter Label Propagation: Salient Object Detection in the Wild* (LPS) [11,12] and *Saliency Optimization from Robust Background Detection* (RBD) [29] algorithms. Figure 10 and Fig. 11 present the saliency maps applied to the original SH with 100, 300 and 500 predefined superpixels, the original image and SH after our proposal for the MBS+ algorithm.

In Fig. 10e, we can see that areas around the owl have less light gray tones, when compared to the other results in the same figure. In this sense, the owl is more salient than the other elements of the scene as would be expected. The differences between the results in Fig. 11 is even more clear. Although it is a very challenging image, the two runners are better detected after our proposal (Fig. 11e), especially in relation to the amount of detected background in the other results.

Fig. 9. (left column) Original images and (right column) the results after grouping the eight superpixel images.

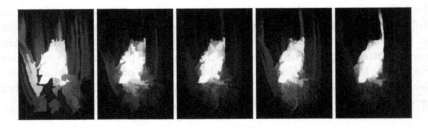

Fig. 10. Saliency map generated by MBS+ for the superpixel images from SH with (a) 100, (b) 300 and (c) 500 superpixels; then (d) the map for the original image (number of superpixels equals to the number of pixels of the original image) and (e) our proposal. The original image is shown in Fig. 5 top-left.

We also conducted quantitative experiments on the Extended Complex Scene Saliency Dataset (ECSSD) [24] database (with 1,000 images) for the weighted-F_β [14] and Precision-Recall (PR) Curve metrics. As we can see in Table 3 and Fig. 12, both metrics show that our proposal achieved similar results for the problem of saliency detection, improving the results for LPS, EQCUT and RBD algorithms. Similar to the BSDS500, the Mean Shift clustering algorithm also had problems in defining the number of colors for a small set of images.

Fig. 11. Another example of saliency map generated by MBS+ for the superpixel images from SH with (a) 100, (b) 300 and (c) 500 superpixels; (d) the map for the original image (number of superpixels equals to the number of pixels of the original image) and (e) our proposal. The original image is shown in Fig. 5 bottom-left.

Table 3. Weighted-F_β results for problem of saliency detection in the ECSSD database, analyzing the Sh algorithm with 100, 300 and 500 superpixels, the original image and after our proposal with minimum number of superpixels.

	100	300	500	NP	SHm5
MBS+	0.564	0.566	0.563	0.561	0.561
LPS	0.457	0.461	0.460	0.456	0.473
EQCUT	0.495	0.496	0.496	0.492	0.523
RBD	0.534	0.517	0.517	0.513	0.547

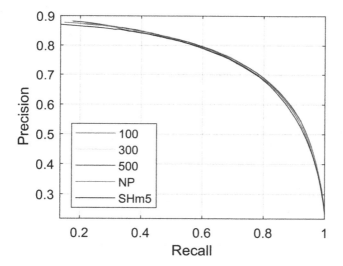

Fig. 12. Precision-recall curves of the tested methods.

5   Conclusions and Future Work

Superpixel segmentation techniques are widely used in several areas. Generally, their result is a superpixel image containing regions regarding the number of superpixels previously defined. This is the proposal of Superpixel Hierarchy algorithm [22]. In our proposal, two modifications to SH are presented. The first is the automatic definition of the number of superpixels for an image based on the number of similar colors; the second is the addition of edge information for different orientations to improve the results.

To evaluate the performance of our modifications, the superpixel images were submitted to edge and saliency detection problems. The method achieved very satisfactory results overall and, in some cases, improvements for saliency maps. Our proposal presented good results in a completely automatic way, without the need to set manually the number of superpixels. The drawback is its running time, since no training is conducted.

For future work, other ways to automate the choice of superpixel numbers will be evaluated. The MS has a high execution time, so analyzing other cost-effective proposals will also be considered. As the proposed method results in eight superpixel images for each input image, performing traditional area evaluation is not an easy task. Therefore, we will also perform an analysis in ways to group the images into a single image.

References

1. Achanta, R., Shaji, A., Smith, K., Lucchi, A., Fua, P., Süsstrunk, S.: SLIC superpixels compared to state-of-the-art superpixel methods. IEEE Trans. Pattern Anal. Mach. Intell. **34**(11), 2274–2282 (2012)
2. Arbelaez, P., Maire, M., Fowlkes, C., Malik, J.: Contour detection and hierarchical image segmentation. IEEE Trans. Pattern Anal. Mach. Intell. **33**(5), 898–916 (2011). https://doi.org/10.1109/TPAMI.2010.161
3. Aytekin, C., Kiranyaz, S., Gabbouj, M.: Automatic object segmentation by quantum cuts. In: 2014 22nd International Conference on Pattern Recognition, pp. 112–117 (2014)
4. Aytekin, C., Ozan, E.C., Kiranyaz, S., Gabbouj, M.: Visual saliency by extended quantum cuts. In: 2015 IEEE International Conference on Image Processing (ICIP), pp. 1692–1696 (2015)
5. Chen, L.C., Papandreou, G., Schroff, F., Adam, H.: Rethinking atrous convolution for semantic image segmentation (2017)
6. Dollár, P., Zitnick, C.L.: Structured forests for fast edge detection. In: 2013 IEEE International Conference on Computer Vision, pp. 1841–1848 (2013)
7. Fang, B., Zhang, X., Ma, Y., Han, Y.: DTI images segmentation based on adaptive bandwidth mean shift algorithm. In: 2016 13th International Computer Conference on Wavelet Active Media Technology and Information Processing (ICCWAMTIP), pp. 248–251 (2016)
8. Fang, F., Wang, T., Zeng, T., Zhang, G.: A superpixel-based variational model for image colorization. IEEE Trans. Visualization Comput. Graph. 1 (2019)
9. Fukunaga, K., Hostetler, L.: The estimation of the gradient of a density function, with applications in pattern recognition. IEEE Trans. Inf. Theory **21**(1), 32–40 (1975)
10. Goodfellow, I., Bengio, Y., Courville, A.: Deep Learning. MIT Press, Cambridge (2016). http://www.deeplearningbook.org
11. Li, H., Lu, H., Lin, Z., Shen, X., Price, B.: Inner and inter label propagation: salient object detection in the wild. IEEE Trans. Image Process. **24**(10), 3176–3186 (2015)
12. Li, H., Lu, H., Lin, Z., Shen, X., Price, B.: Inner and inter label propagation: salient object detection in the wild (2015)

13. Maire, M., Arbelaez, P., Fowlkes, C., Malik, J.: Using contours to detect and localize junctions in natural images. In: 2008 IEEE Conference on Computer Vision and Pattern Recognition, pp. 1–8 (2008)
14. Margolin, R., Zelnik-Manor, L., Tal, A.: How to evaluate foreground maps. In: 2014 IEEE Conference on Computer Vision and Pattern Recognition, pp. 248–255 (2014)
15. Martin, D.R., Fowlkes, C.C., Malik, J.: Learning to detect natural image boundaries using local brightness, color, and texture cues. IEEE Trans. Pattern Anal. Mach. Intell. **26**(5), 530–549 (2004)
16. Nameirakpam, D., Singh, K., Chanu, Y.: Image segmentation using k -means clustering algorithm and subtractive clustering algorithm. Procedia Comput. Sci. **54**, 764–771 (2015). https://doi.org/10.1016/j.procs.2015.06.090
17. Nock, R., Nielsen, F.: Statistical region merging. IEEE Trans. Pattern Anal. Mach. Intell. **26**(11), 1452–1458 (2004)
18. Otsu, N.: A threshold selection method from gray-level histograms. IEEE Trans. Syst. Man Cybern. **9**(1), 62–66 (1979)
19. Reinhard, E., Khan, E.A., Akyz, A.O., Johnson, G.M.: Color Imaging: Fundamentals and Applications. A. K. Peters, Ltd., Wellesley (2008)
20. Ren, X., Malik, J.: Learning a classification model for segmentation. In: Proceedings Ninth IEEE International Conference on Computer Vision, vol. 1, pp. 10–17 (2003)
21. Wang, Y., Ding, W., Zhang, B., Li, H., Liu, S.: Superpixel labeling priors and MRF for aerial video segmentation. IEEE Trans. Circ. Syst. Video Technol. 1 (2019)
22. Wei, X., Yang, Q., Gong, Y., Ahuja, N., Yang, M.: Superpixel hierarchy. IEEE Trans. Image Process. **27**(10), 4838–4849 (2018)
23. Xie, S., Tu, Z.: Holistically-nested edge detection. In: IEEE International Conference on Computer Vision (ICCV), pp. 1395-1403 (2015)
24. Yan, Q., Xu, L., Shi, J., Jia, J.: Hierarchical saliency detection. In: 2013 IEEE Conference on Computer Vision and Pattern Recognition, pp. 1155–1162 (2013)
25. Yang, H., Huang, C., Wang, F., Song, K., Yin, Z.: Robust semantic template matching using a superpixel region binary descriptor. IEEE Trans. Image Process. **28**(6), 3061–3074 (2019)
26. Zhang, J., Sclaroff, S., Lin, Z., Shen, X., Price, B., Mech, R.: Minimum barrier salient object detection at 80 fps. In: 2015 IEEE International Conference on Computer Vision (ICCV), pp. 1404–1412 (2015)
27. Zhang, Y., Li, X., Gao, X., Zhang, C.: A simple algorithm of superpixel segmentation with boundary constraint. IEEE Trans. Circuits Syst. Video Technol. **27**(7), 1502–1514 (2017)
28. Zheng, Y., Zheng, P.: Hand tracking based on adaptive kernel bandwidth mean shift. In: 2016 IEEE Information Technology, Networking, Electronic and Automation Control Conference, pp. 548–552 (2016)
29. Zhu, W., Liang, S., Wei, Y., Sun, J.: Saliency optimization from robust background detection. In: 2014 IEEE Conference on Computer Vision and Pattern Recognition, pp. 2814–2821 (2014)

Visualization

Referenced Based Color Transfer for Medical Volume Rendering

Sudarshan Devkota$^{(\boxtimes)}$ and Sumanta Pattanaik

University of Central Florida, Orlando, FL, USA
sudarshan.devkota93@knights.ucf.edu, sumant@cs.ucf.edu

Abstract. The benefits of medical imaging are enormous. Medical images provide considerable amounts of anatomical information and this facilitates medical practitioners in performing effective disease diagnosis and deciding upon the best course of medical treatment. A transition from traditional monochromatic medical images like CT scans, X-Rays, or MRI images to a colored 3D representation of the anatomical structure could further aid medical professionals in extracting valuable medical information. The proposed framework in our research starts with performing color transfer by finding deep semantic correspondence between two medical images: a colored reference image, and a monochromatic CT scan or an MRI image. We extend this idea of reference based colorization technique to perform colored volume rendering from a stack of grayscale medical images. Furthermore, we also propose to use an effective reference image recommendation system to aid for selection of good reference images. With our approach, we successfully perform colored medical volume visualization and essentially eliminate the painstaking process of user interaction with a transfer function to obtain color parameters for volume rendering.

Keywords: Color transfer · Volume rendering · Medical imaging

1 Introduction

In the last decade, several techniques have been proposed for colorization of images and videos. While some of these techniques involve propagating colored scribbles taken from users to achieve the final colorized result [17,20], another category involves example based colorization that seeks to transfer color properties from a reference image to a target image [13,25]. In an example based technique, establishment of semantic similarities between the images plays a crucial role in performing accurate color transfer. Due to large variations in structural content or appearance, establishing semantic similarities could be challenging with matching methods based on low level hand-crafted features like intensity patch features, Haar features, HOG features, SIFT features, etc. A recent work performed by Liao et al. [18] demonstrated that multi-level features

© Springer Nature Switzerland AG 2020
G. Bebis et al. (Eds.): ISVC 2020, LNCS 12509, pp. 197–208, 2020.
https://doi.org/10.1007/978-3-030-64556-4_16

obtained using deep neural networks are robust in finding high level semantic correspondence between images, thus reducing the limitation of using hand-crafted features.

In our work, we take an approach similar to the one used by Liao et al., leveraging a pretrained network like VGG-19 [23] as the feature extractor network and using multi level features to establish deep correspondence between images. While most of their approach serves as a base to our implementation, we extend it to color transfer for medical data and medical volume rendering with direct volume rendering technique. Specifically, we perform colorization of monochromatic MRI images and CT scans with a specific set of reference images and perform medical volume visualization with the colored version of medical images.

Medical Volume Visualization provides meaningful information from the rendered three-dimensional structure. Moreover, the shift from grayscale volume visualization, where each voxel constitutes a single intensity value, to a colored 3D volume, where each voxel has RGB components, further provides improved visualization of the anatomical structures.

To perform a colored 3D rendering, each voxel must have $RGBA$ value, where RGB defines the color channels and A is the opacity channel. Voxels that have a low alpha value will appear transparent while voxels with high alpha value will appear opaque. One essential step in traditional volume rendering technique is to design proper transfer functions, where a user interacts with a volume renderer by modifying values in the transfer function in order to obtain best color and opacity parameters in the final rendered volume. This work essentially involves trial-and-error interaction with the transfer function, and can be tedious and time consuming. With our proposed system, we obtain the color values with reference based colorization technique, and for the alpha channel, we use the luminance values of each voxel as the alpha value during volume rendering.

In brief, our major technical contributions are:

- We experimentally verify the effectiveness of multi-level feature extraction to establish deep correspondence and to eventually perform color transfer between two medical images, where one is a colored reference image, and other is a CT scan or a MRI image.
- We extend color transfer with deep image analogy for medical volume visualization. Our approach essentially removes tedious user interaction with transfer function to obtain color parameters for volume rendering.

2   Related Work

In this section we review the work that has been performed in the following two sectors: Color Transfer and Volume Rendering.

2.1   Colorization

One of the novel techniques on color transfer which was proposed by Levin et al. required color scribbling by users on top of the grayscale images and then using an optimization technique for colorization of the input image [17]. There have been several advancements on this pioneering work. Qu et al. extended their idea for colorization of manga which contains different pattern and intensity continuous regions [20]. These work showed some promising results but one of the drawbacks of these methods is that they require proper scribbling with intense manual effort.

In recent years, with capabilities of Deep Neural Networks, different learning based techniques have been proposed for automatic colorization, which do not require any user effort. Cheng et al. [4] used a deep neural network to colorize an image where they pose the colorization problem as a regression problem. With comparatively larger set of data, Zhang et al. [26], Larsson et al. [16] and Iizuka et al. [12] used Convolutional Neural Networks (CNNs) to perform automatic colorization, where the three methods differ in terms of loss functions and CNN architectures. The first two methods used classification loss, while the third one used regression loss. While all of these networks are learned from large-scale data, there have been other works [10,18] that perform color transfer from a single colored reference image to a grayscale image. These methods utilize pretrained networks like VGG-19 for extracting deep features from the images. These deep features are used to find reliable correspondence between the images which is further leveraged to perform attribute transfer like style and color. While the work we perform is primarily based on Liao et al.'s [18] work on visual attribute transfer, we extend their idea to perform color transfer with various guided image filters, and focus our work towards medical dataset. We further extend our work for medical volume rendering.

2.2 Volume Rendering

In the last decade, research in volume rendering has expanded to a wide variety of applications. Conventional volume rendering pipeline utilizes either one dimensional or multidimensional transfer functions [14,15,21] for volume rendering. Volume rendering with multidimensional transfer functions than 1D transfer functions have been immensely successful in producing better results, however, with the introduction of more features for classification of voxels, it makes interaction between users and the multidimensional transfer function more complex.

In an attempt to take a different approach to volume rendering, a certain number of works [3,11,24] have utilized the capabilities of machine learning techniques by introducing a new pipeline for volume visualization. The majority of these methods, however, require a significantly large amount of training data to produce quality results. In our method, we require a comparatively smaller set of reference images to obtain the color properties for volume rendering. Furthermore, our work only focuses on coloring part of 1D transfer function by automatic mapping of intensity to color without any user effort. Obtaining opacity parameters from a transfer function also plays a significant role in direct volume rendering, but we are not addressing that in our work.

Pipeline.pdf

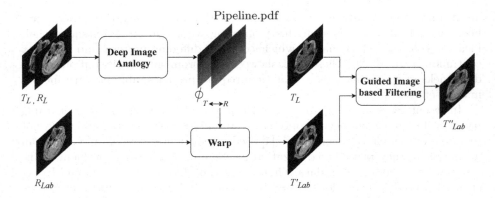

Fig. 1. Our proposed system pipeline consists of two stages. In the first stage, we perform deep image analogy on two input images T_L and R_{Lab} to obtain the reconstructed output T'_{Lab}. Then, in the second stage, we use guided image based filtering technique to perform colorization of image T_L with the help of reconstructed output T'_{Lab}

3   Dataset

The Visible Human Project (VHP) [1] provides a publicly available dataset that contains cross-sectional cryosection, CT scans, and MRI images from one male cadaver and one female cadaver. In our work, we take 33 MRI samples of head, 328 CT scans of thorax and abdomen, and 696 color cryosections from Visible Human Male to perform color transfer on the monochromatic MRI images. Among the color cryosection images, 40 of them are from male-head, and remaining 656 images are from male-thorax and abdomen. Here, the monochromatic images are our target images, and all of the color cryosection slices form the database of reference images.

4   Methodology

Our end goal is to automatically transfer color or tone to a stack of monochromatic medical images from semantically similar reference images and to finally render a 3D volume using the colored image stack. Therefore, there are two parts to our problem: automatic reference based color transfer and medical volume rendering.

In our approach to tackle the first problem, we use a state of the art dense correspondence algorithm like Deep Image Analogy [18] which finds a semantically meaningful dense correspondence between two input images. The reason behind establishing a dense correspondence is to perform color transfer between semantically similar regions of reference image and target image. Since, the reference images that we are using here are frozen cross sections of the human body, we can argue that the range of colors present in the reference image will be sufficient for colorization of target images.

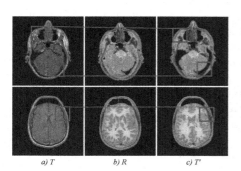

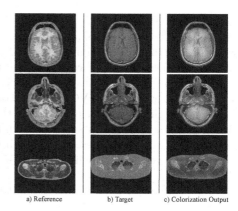

Fig. 2. First column (target images): two MRI slices of Visible Human [1] Head. Second column (reference images): cross-sectional cryosections of Visible Human Head. Third column: Reconstructed output T' obtained after performing visual attribute transfer with Deep Image Analogy. We can see unwanted distortions (indicated by red squares) in the output image that are not present in the target images.

Fig. 3. With the use of FGS filter [19], we obtain the final colorized version (third column) of the target grayscale medical images presented in the second column with the reference images presented in the first column.

4.1 Deep Image Analogy

Using Deep Image Analogy [18], given that there are two input images T and R, we can construct an image T', which is semantically similar to T but contains the visual attributes of R. T' is the reconstructed result after transfer of visual attributes like color, texture, and style. Liao et al. performed two major steps in their work for dense matching. In the first step, their implementation computes features of two input images T and R at different intermediate layers of a pre-trained CNN that is trained on image recognition tasks. In the second step, they use the PatchMatch algorithm [2] in deep feature domain rather than in image domain to find deep correspondence between those images. The final output after these two steps is a bidirectional similarity mapping function $\phi_{T \leftrightarrow R}$ between those two images. PatchMatch is a randomized correspondence algorithm which finds an approximate nearest neighbor field (NNF) between two images. The algorithm has three main components: **initialization, propagation** and **random search**, where it first initializes NNF as a function $f : \mathbb{R}^2 \to \mathbb{R}^2$ of random offsets. This is followed by an iterative process, where good patch offsets are propagated to adjacent pixels and and finally, a random search is performed in the neighborhood of the best offset.

The pretrained network used by Liao et al. [18] to obtain feature representations of an image is the original VGG-19 [23] network that has been pre-trained on the colored ImageNet dataset [22]. However, finding good semantic similarity between two images is difficult when one of them is grayscale and the other is color. Furthermore, original VGG-19 has a comparatively poor performance when it comes to image recognition on grayscale images [9]. So, in order to minimize the difference in performance, we use a gray-VGG-19 as the feature extractor network. Gray-VGG19 was trained only using the luminance channel of images in the ImageNet dataset and the performance evaluation of gray-VGG-19 shows that it exhibits superior performance to original VGG-19 when both of these networks are tested on gray images. Original VGG-19 tested on gray images achieves 83.63%, while gray-VGG-19 achieves 89.39% on the Top-5 Class accuracy [9].

The system pipeline to perform automatic color transfer is shown in Fig. 1. We propose our system with CIE Lab color space which is perceptually linear and it expresses color as three values L, a, and b. Here, L denotes Luminance, and a and b denote Chrominance values. Thus each image can be divided into three channels: a single luminance channel and two chrominance channels. Our system takes two images: a grayscale target image and a color reference image, which can be denoted as $T_L \in \mathbb{R}^{h*w*1}$ and $R_{Lab} \in \mathbb{R}^{h*w*3}$ respectively. Here, h and w are the height and width of the input images. The output from deep image analogy is a bidirectional mapping function between the two images which is a spatial warping function defined with bidirectional correspondences. The bidirectional mapping functions can be denoted as $\phi_{T \leftrightarrow R}$, which returns the transformed pixel location for a given source location p. It consists of a forward mapping function $\phi_{T \rightarrow R}$, that maps pixels from T to R, and a reverse mapping function $\phi_{R \rightarrow T}$, that maps pixels from R to T. Using the mapping function $\phi_{R \rightarrow T}$, we map the image R_{Lab} to image T'_{Lab}. In other words, T'_{Lab} is the reconstructed result obtained after warping the image R_{Lab} with the mapping function $\phi_{R \rightarrow T}$.

Figure 2c) shows the reconstructed output images that were obtained after performing deep image analogy on the given target and reference images in Fig. 2a) and Fig. 2b). We can observe that the reconstructed result T'_{Lab} not only transferred color but other attributes like style and texture that were extracted from the reference image R_{Lab}. The results also contain distortions that are unwanted in our final colored image. In a field like medical imaging, edges and corners are key features and the overall structural details must be preserved when performing any kind of image manipulation.

In our approach to tackle this problem, where we need to maintain the semantic structure from the target image T_L, preserve color, and disregard other visual details from the reference image, we performed guided image based filtering technique to obtain the final colored image T''_{Lab}. Guided image based edge preserving filters like Domain-Transform (DT) filter [7], the Guided Filter (GF) [8], the Weighted Least Square Filter (WLS) [5] and the Fast Global Smoother (FGS) filter [19] are designed to perform smoothing of an image while preserving the edges using the content of the guide image. Specifically, we use the Fast Global Smoother [19] to smooth both input image T_L and T'_{Lab} with the guidance T_L. More on this is explained in the following section.

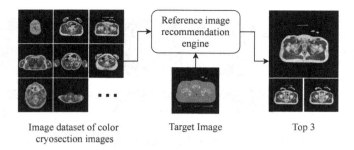

Image dataset of color   Target Image   Top 3
cryosection images

Fig. 4. Pipeline of reference image retrieval system, where the recommendation engine takes two inputs: a monochromatic target image, and 696 color cryosection images from Visible Human head, thorax and abdomen. The output of the recommendation engine are the top three reference images which share similar semantic content with the target image.

4.2 Colorization Using Guided Image Filters

As seen in Fig. 2, the reconstructed output after performing Deep Image Analogy contains unwanted structural distortions that were introduced from the reference image. Since our goal is to only transfer color from the reference image, we resorted to using guided image based edge preserving smoothing filters to preserve the color and structural details of the target image while removing other visual artifacts from image T'_{Lab}. One such filter is the Fast Global Smoother (FGS) [19], which performs spatially inhomogeneous edge-preserving smoothing. To be more specific, we performed

$$T''_{Lab} = fgs(T'_{Lab}, T_L) - fgs(T_{Lab}, T_L) + T_{Lab} \tag{1}$$

where function $fgs(.)$, which is a short-hand notation for the Fast Global Smoothing filter, takes two input images: a source image, and a guide image whose edges guide the smoothing operation for source image. First we perform the edge aware smoothing operation on images T'_{Lab} and T_{Lab} with guide image T_L to get smoothened output $fgs(T'_{Lab}, T_L)$ and $fgs(T_{Lab}, T_L)$, then we add the differences between these two filtered output to image T_{Lab} to get the final colored image $T"_{Lab}$. Here, since the target image T_{Lab} is a grayscale image, its chromatic color channels T_a and T_b contain true neutral gray values, i.e zero values.

Figure 3c) shows the colorization result obtained from Eq. 1. We can observe that the final colorized version of the target images are free from undesirable distortions and attributes that were previously being introduced from the reference image.

4.3 Reference Image Retrieval

To aid for selection of good reference images, we propose to use a robust image retrieval algorithm that automatically recommends the best reference images for

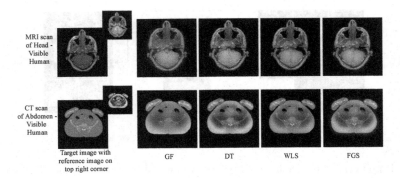

Fig. 5. Comparison of results obtained after performing Deep Image Analogy followed by Colorization using Guided Image filters. First column: Target images with reference image on the top right corner of each target image. Second column: Colorized result with GF [8], where radius $r = 16$, regularization term $\epsilon = 2$ Third column: Colorized result with DT filter [7], where sigma spatial $\sigma_s = 8$, sigma range(color) $\sigma_r = 200$ Fourth column: Colorized result with WLS filter [5], where lambda $\lambda = 0.2$, alpha $\alpha = 1.8$ Fifth column: Colorized result with FGS filter [19], where lambda $\lambda = 32$, sigma range $\sigma_r = 200$. Note that the reconstructed output obtained after performing Deep Image Analogy is not shown in the figure above.

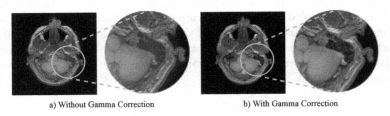

a) Without Gamma Correction   b) With Gamma Correction

Fig. 6. Comparison of results obtained a) without gamma correction and b) with gamma correction. The circular image in the right-side of each image shows a closer view of the region present inside the blue circle. With gamma correction, the colored image appears more detailed and at the same time, color spilling out of the edges is also reduced. (Color figure online)

performing color transfer. Figure 4 shows the pipeline of the reference image recommendation system. The inputs to the recommendation engine are the dataset of our reference images which contain 696 frozen cross-section slices of Visible Human Male and a single monochromatic query image. Ideally, the image suggested by the recommendation engine is expected to have similar semantic structure as the query image.

Content based Image Retrieval techniques that use deep neural networks exploit the property of pretrained CNN networks, where the lower layers (layers closer to the input) of the network encode low-level details of an image and the higher layers are more sensitive towards high-level details, that is, content of an image. Since the features obtained from the higher layers provide a good representation of the content of an image, it is common to use these features, which are also called descriptors, to evaluate semantic similarity between two images.

A similar work on image retrieval has been performed by [9] where they obtain features of reference images and a query image from two different layers of gray-VGG-19 network and finally compute a similarity score to rank the images. We adopt a similar technique, where we first feed all of our reference images to VGG-19 network and pre-compute their feature vector from the first fully connected layer F_c^6. In the second step we feed our target image through the network to obtain its features from the same fully connected layer of VGG-19 network.

Let f_{R_i} denote the feature vector of ith reference image and , f_T denote the feature vector of the target image. To obtain the measure of semantic similarity between two images, we compute cosine similarity, as given by Eq. 2, between these feature vectors for each reference-target image pair R_i, T. We use this similarity score to obtain the best reference image for performing color transfer.

$$d(f_{R_i}, f_t) = \frac{f_{R_i}.f_t}{||f_{R_i}|| \times ||f_t||} \qquad (2)$$

4.4   Direct Volume Rendering

After obtaining the colored images, we perform volume visualization using 3D-slicer [6], which is an open source medical image computing platform. 3D-slicer provides various tools for biomedical research and GPU-based Direct Volume Rendering is one of them. Typically, the final volume is rendered using a stack of medical images, where ray-casting is performed on the volumetric medical data.

5   Results

As mentioned in Sect. 4.2, to remove the unwanted artifacts introduced from reference image to target image, we performed guided image filtering on the reconstructed output from Deep Image Analogy. Figure 5 shows the comparison of results that were obtained after performing colorization with different guided image filters. We obtain the output in the same way as mentioned in Eq. 1 where the Fast Global Smoothing filter (FGS) is replaced by other filters: Guided filter (GF), Domain Transform filter (DT), and Weighted Least Square filter (WLS). A comparison between the four filters provided by Min et al. [19] shows that fgs provides the speed advantage over the other three filters, and unlike GF and DT filters, it is not prone to halo effect. Due to these benefits, the FGS filter is the preferred filter in our colorization pipeline.

5.1   Gamma Correction

With color transfer, in addition to ensuring that all the semantic structures present in the grayscale image are preserved in the final colored image, we also

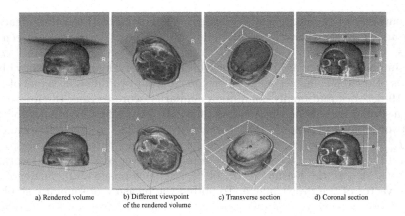

a) Rendered volume   b) Different viewpoint   c) Transverse section   d) Coronal section
                      of the rendered volume

Fig. 7. Volume visualization using 3D slicer for top half of Visible Human Head. First row: Volume is rendered with 33 monochromatic MRI images. Second row: Volume is rendered with corresponding colored versions of medical images that are used to render the volume displayed in the first row.

aim to have our colorized result look as natural as possible. In some of the resulting images that we obtained after performing color transfer, the image seemed to lack proper contrast making the image appear to have a washed-out effect. Furthermore, it was noticed that, in some regions of those images, color was spilling out of the edges. This may happen due to excessive smoothing of image with guided image filters. An example of this can be seen in Fig. 6. So, to improve the vividness of the result, we use gamma correction which is simple non-linear operation defined by the power law transformation as given in Eq. 3.

$$I_{in} = \alpha I_{out}^{\gamma} \tag{3}$$

Specifically, after obtaining the reconstructed image from deep image analogy, we perform gamma encoding on both target and the reconstructed image, where we use a gamma value of $\gamma = 1/2$. This is followed by colorization using guided image filters, and finally we perform gamma decoding with gamma value of $\gamma = 2$ to obtain the resulting colored image. With gamma correction, not only the color content spilling out of the edges was suppressed, but also the vividness of the image was improved to a certain extent, making the image look comparatively more sharp and detailed.

5.2   Volume Visualization

Since there is no ground-truth for this task, we only present qualitative results here that we obtained in our work. After obtaining the colored version of all the monochromatic medical images, we use the GPU based ray-casting module provided in 3D slicer for volume visualization. First row in Fig. 7 shows the volume rendered using a stack of grayscale medical images while the second row shows the volume rendered using colored medical images.

In Fig. 7, the first row displays the rendered volume for the top half of the human head, where we use 33 MRI scans obtained from the Visible Human Dataset. In the second row of Fig. 7, we present a similar viewpoint of the volume rendered in the first row, but in this case, the volume visualization is rather performed with colored versions of MRI images and CT scans.

To perform visual inspection on the quality of the rendered volume we also compare the transverse and coronal section between grayscale volume and colored volume as shown in Fig. 7c) and 7d). We can see that the structure of grayscale volume is well preserved in the final colored volume. More results are presented in our full paper which is available here: graphics.cs.ucf.edu/.

6   Conclusion

In our work, we have managed to introduce a new pipeline for medical volume visualization. With our proposed pipeline, we completely eliminate the tedious work of interacting with a volume renderer where a user has to experiment with different values on a transfer function to generate plausible color in the rendered volume. We also believe that our approach will be very helpful for a variety of applications in the medical community.

References

1. Ackerman, M.J.: The visible human project. Proc. IEEE **86**(3), 504–511 (1998)
2. Barnes, C., Shechtman, E., Goldman, D.B., Finkelstein, A.: The generalized Patch-Match correspondence algorithm. In: European Conference on Computer Vision, September 2010
3. Berger, M., Li, J., Levine, J.A.: A generative model for volume rendering. IEEE Trans. Visual Comput. Graphics **25**(4), 1636–1650 (2019)
4. Cheng, Z., Yang, Q., Sheng, B.: Deep colorization. In: Proceedings of the 2015 IEEE International Conference on Computer Vision (ICCV), ICCV 2015, pp. 415–423. IEEE Computer Society, USA (2015)
5. Farbman, Z., Fattal, R., Lischinski, D., Szeliski, R.: Edge-preserving decompositions for multi-scale tone and detail manipulation. ACM Trans. Graph. **27**(3), 1–10 (2008)
6. Fedorov, A., et al.: 3D slicer as an image computing platform for the quantitative imaging network. Magn. Reson. Imaging **30**, 1323–1341 (2012)
7. Gastal, E.S.L., Oliveira, M.M.: Domain transform for edge-aware image and video processing. ACM Trans. Graph. **30**(4) (2011)
8. He, K., Sun, J., Tang, X.: Guided image filtering. In: Daniilidis, K., Maragos, P., Paragios, N. (eds.) ECCV 2010. LNCS, vol. 6311, pp. 1–14. Springer, Heidelberg (2010). https://doi.org/10.1007/978-3-642-15549-9_1
9. He, M., Chen, D., Liao, J., Sander, P.V., Yuan, L.: Deep exemplar-based colorization. ACM Trans. Graph. **37**, 4 (2018)
10. He, M., Liao, J., Yuan, L., Sander, P.V.: Neural color transfer between images. arXiv abs/1710.00756 (2017)

11. Hong, F., Liu, C., Yuan, X.: DNN-VolVis: interactive volume visualization supported by deep neural network. In: 2019 IEEE Pacific Visualization Symposium (PacificVis), pp. 282–291 (2019)
12. Iizuka, S., Simo-Serra, E., Ishikawa, H.: Let there be color! joint end-to-end learning of global and local image priors for automatic image colorization with simultaneous classification. ACM Trans. Graph. **35**(4), 1–11 (2016)
13. Irony, R., Cohen-Or, D., Lischinski, D.: Colorization by example. In: Proceedings of the Sixteenth Eurographics Conference on Rendering Techniques, EGSR 2005, Goslar, DEU, pp. 201–210. Eurographics Association (2005)
14. Kindlmann, G., Durkin, J.W.: Semi-automatic generation of transfer functions for direct volume rendering. In: Proceedings of the 1998 IEEE Symposium on Volume Visualization, VVS 1998, New York, NY, USA, pp. 79–86. Association for Computing Machinery (1998)
15. Kniss, J., Kindlmann, G., Hansen, C.: Multidimensional transfer functions for interactive volume rendering. IEEE Trans. Visual Comput. Graphics **8**(3), 270–285 (2002)
16. Larsson, G., Maire, M., Shakhnarovich, G.: Learning representations for automatic colorization. In: Leibe, B., Matas, J., Sebe, N., Welling, M. (eds.) ECCV 2016. LNCS, vol. 9908, pp. 577–593. Springer, Cham (2016). https://doi.org/10.1007/978-3-319-46493-0_35
17. Levin, A., Lischinski, D., Weiss, Y.: Colorization using optimization. In: ACM SIGGRAPH 2004 Papers, SIGGRAPH 2004, New York, NY, USA, pp. 689–694. Association for Computing Machinery (2004)
18. Liao, J., Yao, Y., Yuan, L., Hua, G., Kang, S.B.: Visual attribute transfer through deep image analogy. ACM Trans. Graph. **36**(4) (2017)
19. Min, D., Choi, S., Lu, J., Ham, B., Sohn, K., Do, M.: Fast global image smoothing based on weighted least squares. IEEE Trans. Image Process. **23**, 5638–5653 (2014)
20. Qu, Y., Wong, T.T., Heng, P.A.: Manga colorization. ACM Trans. Graph. **25**(3), 1214–1220 (2006)
21. Roettger, S., Bauer, M., Stamminger, M.: Spatialized transfer functions. In: Brodlie, K., Duke, D., Joy, K. (eds.) EUROVIS 2005: Eurographics/IEEE VGTC Symposium on Visualization. The Eurographics Association (2005)
22. Russakovsky, O., et al.: ImageNet large scale visual recognition challenge. Int. J. Comput. Vision **115**(3), 211–252 (2015). https://doi.org/10.1007/s11263-015-0816-y
23. Simonyan, K., Zisserman, A.: Very deep convolutional networks for large-scale image recognition. arXiv 1409.1556 (2014)
24. He, T., Hong, L., Kaufman, A., Pfister, H.: Generation of transfer functions with stochastic search techniques. In: Proceedings of Seventh Annual IEEE Visualization 1996, pp. 227–234 (1996)
25. Welsh, T., Ashikhmin, M., Mueller, K.: Transferring color to greyscale images. ACM Trans. Graph. **21**(3), 277–280 (2002)
26. Zhang, R., Isola, P., Efros, A.A.: Colorful image colorization. In: Leibe, B., Matas, J., Sebe, N., Welling, M. (eds.) ECCV 2016. LNCS, vol. 9907, pp. 649–666. Springer, Cham (2016). https://doi.org/10.1007/978-3-319-46487-9_40

An Empirical Methodological Study of Evaluation Methods Applied to Educational Timetabling Visualizations

Wanderley de Souza Alencar[1]([✉]) [ID], Walid Abdala Rfaei Jradi[1] [ID],
Hugo Alexandre Dantas do Nascimento[1] [ID], Juliana Paula Felix[1] [ID],
and Fabrízzio Alphonsus Alves de Melo Nunes Soares[1,2] [ID]

[1] Instituto de Informática, Universidade Federal de Goiás, Goiânia, GO, Brazil
`wanderleyalencar@ufg.br, walid.jradi@gmail.com, hadn@inf.ufg.br,`
`jufelix16@gmail.com`
[2] Department of Computer Science, Southern Oregon University, Ashland, OR, USA
`soaresf@sou.edu`
`http://www.inf.ufg.br`
`http://www.sou.edu`

Abstract. The conception, and usage, of methods designed to evaluate information visualizations is a challenge that goes along with the development of these visualizations. In the scientific literature there is a myriad of proposals for such methods. However, none of them was able to pacify the field or establish itself as a *de facto* standard, due to difficulties like: (a) the complexity of its usage; (b) high financial and time costs; and (c) the need of a large number of raters to guarantee the reliability of the results. One way to circumvent such adversities is the usage of *Heuristic Evaluation* given its simplicity, low cost of application and the quality of reached results. This article intends to conduct an *empirical methodological study* about the use of three of such methods (Zuk *et al.*, Forsell & Johansson and *Wall et al.*) for evaluation of visualizations in the context of Educational Timetabling Problems. Five different visualizations were evaluated using the original methods and versions modified by the current authors (where an *importance factor* was assigned to each statement being evaluated, as well as the rater's *level of confidence*) in order to improve their efficiency when measuring the quality of visualizations. The experimental results demonstrated that for the two first heuristics, only the modification on the *importance* of the statements proved to be (statistically) relevant. For the third one, both factors did not induce different results.

Keywords: Information visualization evaluation · Heuristic Evaluation · Educational Timetabling Problems · Combinatorial problems · NP-Hard · User interface

G. Bebis et al. (Eds.): ISVC 2020, LNCS 12509, pp. 209–223, 2020.
https://doi.org/10.1007/978-3-030-64556-4_17

1   Introduction

It is well known, and accepted, by the Information Visualization (IV) scientific community that assessing the *quality* and/or *usefulness* of a visualization is not a trivial task, as showed by several works [4,14,20,23]. Some of the difficulties involved includes determining whether a given visualization is able to: (1) positively contribute to the understanding and analysis of the data [14,20]; (2) induce significant *insights*[1]; and (3) be expressive enough, easy to *memorize* and *aesthetically* appropriate [10]

Considering the evaluation of interactive visualizations, Xiaozhou Zhou *et al.* [24] list three main difficulties: (1) the semantics meaning significantly differs between distinct types of databases and to build an uniform evaluation system is not trivial; (2) the subjective influence of cognitive process of each individual is remarkable. This includes person's knowledge structure and the familiarity on the field and technology. In the course of cognition, even the psychological and physiological state of an individual has a significant influence on cognition performance; (3) the number of visual elements in the interactive visualization is excessive and a high linkage relationship is present, which leads to an increase in the visual complexity. Therefore, the creation and evaluation of a visualization interface that comprises a separate set of visual elements is impossible.

There are currently two major lines, or general approaches, when evaluating a visualization: (1) **Generalist**: applies assessment instruments that are *independent* of the problem domain, evaluating sufficiently generic and high-level characteristics of the visualization. Some studies [5,8] are examples; (2) **Specific Problem Domain**: as the name says, this kind of evaluation is tightly coupled to the problem's characteristics, not being applicable in other contexts [12].

Following the second line, a common approach is the so called *task-based*. It consists of recording the accuracy and the time consumed to carry out a well-defined list of *tasks*, conducted by a carefully selected group of users, as shown by [2,18]. This approach aims to answer the following general question: *"Are users able to use the visualization for the understanding of the underlying data/information, and correctly and efficiently perform the proposed tasks?"*.

Based on the critical analysis of several contemporary methodologies for evaluating visualizations, the current paper performs an *empirical methodological study* of evaluation methods when applied to *Educational Timetabling Problems* (Ed-TTPs) [15]. Such problems arrive from the need of conceiving and presenting timetables for educational institutions (schools, universities, etc.). Hamed Babaei *et al.* [3] point out that this *big* class of problems can be divided in: 1. High-School Timetabling Problem (HS-TTP); 2. University Timetabling Problems (U-TTP), including Course (UC-TTP) and Examination (UE-TTP).

The remainder of this paper is organized as follows: Section 2 presents the main works in information visualization evaluation field and provides a critical

---

[1] Chris North [17] clarifies that the ability to measure whether a given visualization can induce insights, or not, is subjective and individual. Also, it is known that insights are characterized by being *complex*, *deep*, *qualitative*, *unexpected* and *relevant*. In another words, an insight can not simply be directly extracted from the visualization.

analysis on them. Section 3 details the empirical methodological study aimed to compare three different evaluation methods when applied in the context of Ed-TTPs. Section 4 reports the experimentation process and records the conclusions from the evaluation of three visualizations extracted from the scientific literature of the area. Finally, Sect. 6 synthesizes the conclusions obtained by this work and points out to potential future research.

2 Literature Review

This section presents a brief review of the literature on scientific works related to the topic under analysis, with an emphasis on publications from the last twenty years. Even with this restriction, the number of studies is vast and, therefore, only those with high affinity with the approach here proposed are discussed.

In 2012, Heidi Lam *et al.* [14] examined 850 selected publications from 1995–2010 and identified seven scenarios that defined the practical application of information visualization evaluations (IV-Eval) in that period. The most frequent types of evaluation are aimed at measuring people's task performance (also known as *task-based* evaluation), user experience and quality/performance of algorithms. Expanding this previous study, Tobias Isenberg *et al.* [13] reviewed 581 papers to analyze the practice in the context of evaluation visualizations (data and information). They concluded that, in general, the level of evaluation reporting is low. Some found pitfalls were: (1) the goals of the evaluation are not explicit; (2) participants do not belong to the target audience; (3) the strategy and the method of analysis are not appropriate; (4) the level of rigor is low. The authors of the present study observe that, until the current days, these pitfalls are still noticed in the reports of IV evaluation.

Steven R. Gomez *et al.* [9] devised an evaluation method that combines *insight-based* and *task-based* methodologies, called LITE (*Layered Insight- and Task-based Evaluation*). Experimentation was carried out on a *visual analytics* system that required the user to carry out both research on the data set as well as the analysis of this data in order to identify broader patterns. As *general guidelines* for the visualization designers, the authors suggested that: (1) low-level tasks must be chosen in order to not steer participants toward insights; (2) ordering effects must be mitigated by counterbalancing the ordering of visualizations in the *insight* component of LITE; (3) it must be considered the complexity of the data and participant expertise when choosing insight characteristics to measure; (4) the details of the process of coding insights have to be reported: who are the coders, how well did they agree, and how were disagreements resolved into one score.

Right after these studies and going beyond the *task-based* approach, John Stasko [20] conceived the idea that a visualization should be evaluated by its *value*, a metric to measure the broader benefits that a visualization can generate. He says that a "*Visualization should ideally provide broader, more holistic benefits to a person about a data set, giving a **big picture** understanding of the data and spurring insights beyond specific data case values.*" (emphasis added).

Thus, the *value* goes beyond visualizations' ability to answer questions about the data. It is at the heart of visualizations' the aptitude to allow a true understanding of the data, the creation of a holistic scope and an innate sense of context, evidencing the importance of data in forming a general overview. Stasko defines that the *value* (V) of a visualization is expressed by the Eq. (1):

$$V = I + C + E + T \tag{1}$$

where, I (*insights*) measures the discovery of *insights* or *insightful questions* about the data, C (*confidence*) represents the level of conviction, trust and knowledge about the data, its domain and the context, E (*essence*) conveys the general essence or perception of the data, and T (*time*) indicates the total time required to answer a wide variety of questions about the data.

The aforementioned study uses a qualitative analysis bias, as there is no specification about a measurement method (a quantitative approach) related to the previous four components. Based on it, Emilly Wall *et al.* [23] propose a *Heuristic Evaluation* (HE) [16] – a method in which experts employ experimental-based rules to assess the usability of user interfaces in independent steps and report issues – which goal is to evaluate interactive visualizations, seeking a methodology that: (1) is low cost in terms of time and resources required for its usage; (2) allows measuring the usefulness of the visualization in addition to that provided by a *task-based* approach; (3) is practical and relatively easy to use; and (4) admits comparison between different visualization applications.

To make the proposed methodology (called ICE-T) viable, the components were decomposed into *guidelines* and these were defined by low-level heuristics expressed by a set of statements, that follows the Likert scale, from *Strongly Disagree* to *Strongly Agree*. After experimentation involving fifteen researchers and three visualizations, the authors concluded that the methodology was promising for the evaluation of interactive visualizations, highlighting that they obtained results consistent with a qualitative assessment carried out previously. They also call attention to the fact that only five raters would be enough to obtain the same results, demonstrating its applicability to real-world problems.

The ability of experts in an HE to identify usability problems in a visualization application – when compared to using a group of non-experts in the same task – was subject of a study by Beatriz Santos *et al.* [19]. They concluded that the use of experts employing HE, such as those proposed by Camilla Forsell *et al.* [6,7], Torre Zuk *et al.* [25] and Jakob Nielsen [16], was able to identify most of the problems later reported by a larger amount of non-experts, which subsidized the choice made by [23]. Following another path, M. Tory and T. Möller [22] argue that *expert feedback* can be a complement to HE and a mechanism that helps understand high-level cognitive tasks.

Also focusing on (dynamic) interactive visualizations (DIV) interfaces, Xiauzhou *et al.* [24] present a new quantitative method based on eye-tracking (visual momentum – VM). The authors argue that the performed experiments proved there are a positive effect on reducing cognitive load in DIVs and, therefore, VM can be used, with reliability and convenience to evaluate a visual interface. M. A. Hearst *et al.* [11] argue that there is a mutual influence between conducting assessments using HE and *Query-Based Scoring* and that the usage of both can contribute to improve the quality of the visualization evaluation process.

2.1 Critical Analysis of Previous Methodologies

The work of Emilly Wall *et al.* [23], based on Stasko's seminal idea [20], signals strength for applicability in other real-world contexts, considering that it requires a small number of evaluators to obtain results equivalent to those obtained by the application of a qualitative evaluation method. It is characterized, therefore, as a low cost application methodology. However, as highlighted by the authors of the article, the methodology does not serve as a panacea, and should be used as a complementary approach to the application of other assessment techniques. Another drawback is that its validation was done using only three visualizations, thus lacking a large scale experimentation that could involve other problem domains in order to reinforce its validity.

The work of Steven R. Gomez *et al.* [9] is relevant for identifying and presenting four general guidelines applicable to visualization assessments, as well as for emphasizing the usefulness of combining *insight* and *task-based* evaluation approaches. Just like the previous work, it also needs a broader application, with more case studies and different designs.

Despite its highlighted qualities for the evaluation of (dynamic) interactive visualizations, the approach proposed by M. A. Hearst *et al.* [11] has, as a drawback, the (current) high cost of the equipment involved in the experiments, ultimately making extremely difficult its adoption in large-scale in real-world scenarios.

The evidence presented in the studies of Beatriz Santos *et al.* [19] and M. Tory and T. Möller [22] reinforces the idea that the proper use of strategies based on heuristic evaluation, subsidized by the guidelines of Steven R. Gomez *et al.* [9], induces and allows the conduction of empirical studies to compare different visualization assessment methods. The present work compares three heuristic-based methods available in the literature to measure their effectiveness to estimate the quality of visualizations when applied to *Educational Timetabling Problems*. The next section details how the empirical study was coined.

3 Proposed Empirical Methodological Study

Inspired by the research listed at Sect. 2.1, the present paper proposes and performs an empirical study to compare three heuristic evaluation methods: (1) Zuk *et al.* [25], with thirteen statements to measure the quality of the visualization; (2) Forsell and Johansson [7], which uses ten statements; and (3) Wall *et al.* [23] employ twenty one statements.

The three methods were chosen because they are well known and, despite sharing some common concepts, investigate complementary aspects for evaluating information visualization applications. The study is structured in three phases, as shown in Fig. 1.

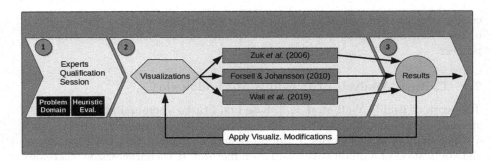

Fig. 1. Proposed empirical methodological study structure.

1. **Expert Qualification Session**: In order to uniform the knowledge of the evaluating specialists (raters), in this phase a session is held in which are provided the main theoretical-practical foundations about *Heuristic Evaluation* (HE) and the target problem domain *Educational Timetabling Problems* (Ed-TTPs). In addition, its opened space for the exchange of experiences between the participants. The authors of this article conduct the meeting and make notes to plan, and improve, future experiments;

2. **Individual Heuristic Evaluation Session**: Using as keystone the three HEs revisited in the previous phase, the specialists assign a score for each statement, based in a natural numeric scale. The scores can vary from 1 (minimum) to 5 (five), being possible to indicate that the statement is *Not Applicable* (N/A) and, therefore, no score is attributed to it. This was done to make the evaluation simpler, more natural, homogeneous and, later, to make feasible better statistical treatment;

3. **Results and Analysis**: Finally, after compiling the assigned scores, the final results of each visualization are generated. This is followed by a statistical analysis aimed at identifying the level of confidence in the result.

It is important to note that in Phase 2, in the original heuristics, all statements were considered to be of equal importance. However, this approach make it difficult for factors resulting from the particularities of the problem domain to be observed during the visualization evaluation process. Thus, to address this issue, the authors of this article (specialists in educational timetabling problems), in a phase prior to those mentioned, defined the relative importance (weight) of each statement of all heuristics used when applied in the context of Ed-TTPs. In the experiments, the weights can vary in the range 0 (minimum) to 6 (maximum). They were employed in Scenarios 3 and 4, as depicted by Table 1. These scenarios are described at the beginning of Sect. 5.

The current authors also define that for all statements in the Phase 2, each rater must record his/her confidence in the score, expressed by one value in the set $\mathcal{S}_C = \{1, 2, 4\}$, where 1 means *small*, 2 *medium* and 4 *total* confidence. Rater's confidence is employed to weight his/her evaluation using the factors $\frac{1}{4}$, $\frac{1}{2}$ and 1, respectively, to multiply the rater's score.

Table 1. Statement weights per heuristic adopted in Scenarios 3 and 4.

Heuristic method	Statement number																				
	1	2	3	4	5	6	7	8	9	10	11	12	13	14	15	16	17	18	19	20	21
Zuk *et al.*	4	3	3	3	3	3	3	6	6	4	4	6	4	–	–	–	–	–	–	–	–
Forsell & Johansson	6	2	2	2	6	6	6	2	4	4	–	–	–	–	–	–	–	–	–	–	–
Wall *et al.*	4	2	2	2	2	2	2	2	4	4	4	4	4	6	6	4	4	6	6	4	4

Typically the phases 1–3 are applied in this sequence and only once each, since it is considered in this scenario that the visualization being evaluated is in use and cannot be changed, that is, it is a process of evaluation carried out after the definitive visualization implementation.

However, according to the purpose of the assessment, phases 2 and 3 can be applied repetitively, during the process of developing/evaluating a new visualization. In this case, after each application cycle, the visualization can be improved to eliminate the identified problems and implement suggestions provided by the raters. At the end of this process the results are considered the definitive ones.

The next section details how the empirical study was carried out according to these guidelines.

4   Experiment Description

This section describes the application of the empirical methodological study presented in Sect. 3, aiming to check if the approach:

1. identifies differences between the three heuristic-based methods, regarding the measure of the quality of the evaluated visualizations;
2. whether the modifications applied by the authors of this article benefited the original heuristics, improving their efficiency when measuring the quality of visualizations in *Educational Timetabling Problems* (Ed-TTPs) context;
3. is capable of assisting decision-making by professionals involved in the problem domain.

Initially, an explanatory text was sent to fifteen specialists, all them involved in Information Visualization (IV) research projects, explaining the motivations for the carried out study and inviting them to take part in the planned experimentation. Ten accepted the invitation: seven men and three women, aged between 30 and 52 years. Of these, five participants are professors in higher education, three are PhD candidates and two have a master degree in Computer Science. Among the participants, four are also experts in the problem domain (Ed-TTPs) and the others have good knowledge in this field.

The visualizations used in the experiments were obtained from the following sources in the literature:

216   W. S. Alencar et al.

VisT2D – *Traditional 2D-Table*: Shown in Fig. 2a, this type of visualization is widely used in the area of Ed-TTPs. It displays a column to represent the days of the week, another for the possible event times and one column per group (a class) of involved students.

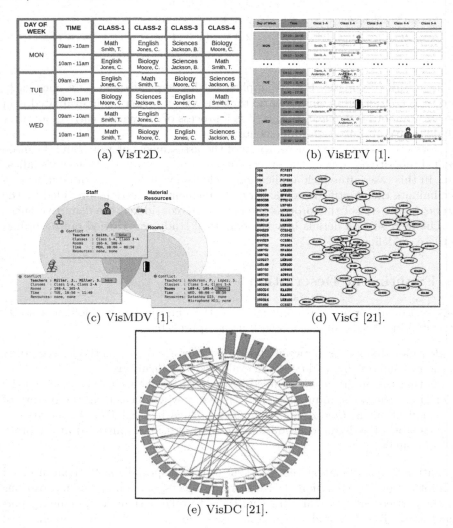

(a) VisT2D.

(b) VisETV [1].

(c) VisMDV [1].

(d) VisG [21].

(e) VisDC [21].

Fig. 2. Visualization of educational timetabling used in this study.

VisETV – *Enhanced Tabular Visualization* (ETV): Extracted from [1] and depicted in Fig. 2b. It is based on the VisT2D approach, but extends it to highlight the elements of the problem involved in the *conflicts* (or *clashes*). A *cell* contains information about one lecture. If it's in light gray, this indicates the absence of any conflict. Two cells can be connected through a colored pair of points and a bidirectional arc, pointing to a *real/apparent* conflict between them. The color of the points/arc makes the distinction. A *teacher*, a *door*, a *technical staff member* and a *datashow* represent, respectively, a conflict in: (1) the teacher's timetable; (2) a room, being used simultaneously by two or more classes; (3) a technical staff member's timetable; and (4) a material resource.

VisMDV – *Multilayer Diagram Visualization*: Also presented in [1] and illustrated in Fig. 2c, it resembles the *Venn Diagram*, although it is distinct because it considers that the sets involved are in *different layers* in the visualization, since each one is associated to one of the categories of resources involved in a conflict (staff and material resources). As a result, the intersection of sets is reinterpreted: instead of indicating elements in common to two sets, it means that a conflict involves elements associated with those two categories. The rooms are considered a special subcategory of the material resources that deserve differentiated treatment and, therefore, appear as a separated subset. The user, clicking a conflict icon, opens an correspondent pop-up window, which is an artistic representation that, in order to avoid visual pollution and due to space constraints, omits the *technical staff member* and *material resource* conflict pop-up windows.

VisCG – *Cluster Graph View*: Registered in [21] and presented in Fig. 2d. It shows a cluster graph whose *nodes* represent students or exams of some subject. An *arc* connecting a subject to a student indicates that he(she) must take that exam, showing possible conflicts.

VisDC – *Daisy Chart View*: Also registered in [21] and presented in the Fig. 2e. In it, the boxes represent students or subjects and the *edges* denote the relationship that the student must take the exam of that subject. The histograms show the number of existing associations for each element (student or subject) of the semicircle on which the user is *focusing* at that moment.

5 Experimental Results

Due to COVID-19 pandemic, Phase 1 was performed in a remote session. In Phase 2, as aforementioned, the evaluations were conducted providing a questionnaire in a numeric scale format, from 1 to 5, and 0 when *Not Applicable*, and answers collected through an individually shared spreadsheet. The raters were not required to provide answers in a specific order. Although we estimated five hours to perform evaluation process, we provided one week to all raters.

In Phase 3, four different scenarios were used to confront the evaluations: (*Scenario 1*) Ignore statement's weights and rater's self-declaration confidence; (*Scenario 2*) Ignore statement's weights and take in account rater's confidence; (*Scenario 3*) Take in account statement's weight and ignore rater's confidence; (*Scenario 4*) Take in account statement's weight and rater's confidence.

The Fig. 3 presents our results for all three heuristics, in scenarios 1 to 4, in which we compare all five visualizations. Although our result is an average result of all raters, since each heuristic has a different amount of statements to evaluate, we normalized our results to values between 0 (zero) and 10 (ten) to allow a comparison of results in the same scale. Equations 2 and 3 present how scores are computed.

$$Score_r = \frac{\sum_{s=1}^{|S|} (weight_s \times confidence_s \times score_s)}{|S|} \times 10, \qquad (2)$$

$$Score_v = \frac{\sum_{r=1}^{|R|} Score_r}{|R|}, \qquad (3)$$

where $Score_r$, $Score_s$ and $Score_v$ are raters (r), statements (s) and visualizations (v) scores, respectively. The weights of the statements and raters confidence score are $weight_s$ and $confidence_s$, in this order. The values $|R|$ and $|S|$ are the number of raters and heuristic statements.

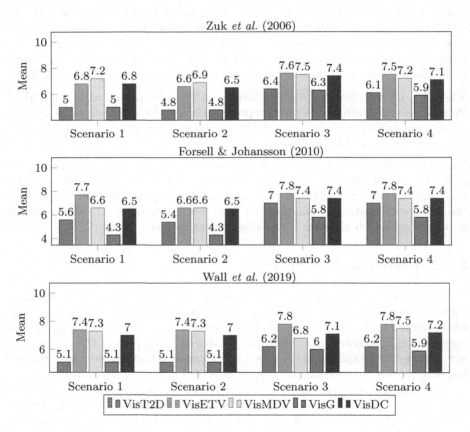

Fig. 3. Comparison of the evaluation of five visualizations in four different scenarios and three heuristics (Zuk *et al.*, Forsell & Johansson *et al.* e Wall *et al.*).

In the application of Zuk *et al.* [25], it was possible to conclude that, regardless the visualization considered, the insertion of the raters' confidence did not generate statistical difference in the results of the evaluations. Nevertheless, the insertion of the statement weights in the problem domain generated statistical difference and, therefore, was relevant in the final results of the evaluations.

When analyzing the application of Forsell & Johansson [7], despite the slight numerical differences regarding the previous heuristic, the same conclusion is obtained: the raters' confidence did not generate statistical difference, but the insertion of the statements weights performed by the authors did.

Applying Wall *et al.* [23], it was possible to infer that, in any scenario, neither the raters' confidence nor the weighting of the statements were able to induce statistical difference in the results evaluations. Therefore, in the scope of this study, Scenario 4 proved to be unnecessary. Another unique fact is that, in any scenario, the VisETV visualization is the one with the best evaluation, as well as the VisMDV and VisDC occupied the second or third places.

From the comparison of these facts, it was possible to realize that for the first two heuristics, only the weights of the statements proved to be statistically relevant. This was expected by the present authors, since invited raters are researchers in IV, which contributed to a high confidence in their answers.

In order to support our conclusions, we conducted an hypothesis test, in which heuristic methods and scenarios can be considered independent variables, while raters score is the dependent variable. However, heuristic and scenarios were divided in experiments to avoid a multivariate analysis. Initially we applied a *normality test* to each experiment group (heuristic) via Lilliefors test and Shapiro-Wilk tests and both reported that our results follow a normal distribution. Therefore we conducted an ANOVA (Analysis of Variance) to verify statistical difference between scenarios considering 0.05 of significance. Table 2 presents ANOVA results for each comparison.

Table 2. Hypothesis test results (ANOVA).

Heuristic method	Scenario 1 vs 2		Scenario 1 vs 3		Scenario 1 vs 4	
	F-Stat	P-Value	F-Stat	P-Value	F-Stat	P-Value
Zuk *et al.* (2006)	0.39	0.5331	8.93	**0.0036**	5.09	**0.0265**
Forsel & Johanssen (2010)	0.32	0.5734	8.29	**0.0050**	8.22	**0.0052**
Wall *et al.* (2019)	0.01	0.9417	1.33	0.2513	3.04	0.0849

As we can see in Table 2, Scenario 1 vs. 2 has show no statistical difference for all heuristic methods. This show that the level of confidence that a rater has in each question did not provide any improvement in our results. This was also expected, since we invited a group of researchers in IV to evaluate.

Scenario 1 vs. 3 show statistical difference for Zuk and Forsel heuristics, meaning that the weights assigned by rater performs a significant change in the result and can be helpful when selecting a visualization for timetabling. And although scenarios 1 vs. 4 also show statistical difference for Zuk and Forsell, this is a consequence of Scenario 3, since Scenario 4 is a combination of Scenarios 2 and 3. Finally, no statistical difference was presented for scenarios 1 vs. 3 and 1 vs. 4. In this sense the timetabling specialist weights did not provide any improvement to the evaluation process. Wall *et al.* has about a double of statements to evaluate, which probably buffered the effect of weights. In this sense, this heuristic is more robust and require a strong variation of the specialist defined weight.

At the end of the evaluations, the authors informally asked the raters to express their perceptions about the process. The most frequent observations, although not majority, were the following: (1) In Zuk *et al.* it was hardest to identify, in certain visualizations, whether the assessment for some of the statements should be marked with *Not Applicable*, e.g., *Color perception varies with size of colored item* in the VisG visualization; (2) Forsell & Johansson's statements were considered more *abstract* than those of other heuristics and, therefore, took more time for evaluation and score assignment, as it was necessary to revisit the visualization several times; (3) Due to the number of statements, Wall *et al.* is the most expensive to fulfill and, consequently, the most time consuming.

6   Conclusions and Future Works

This article designed and conducted an empirical methodological study aimed to compare results of the application of three heuristic methods for the evaluation of visualizations available in the scientific literature in the area of Information Visualization, namely: Zuk *et al.*, Forsell & Johansson, Wall *et al.* The three methods were applied to evaluate five different views, also extracted from scientific articles [1,21], related to *Educational Timetabling Problems* (Ed-TTPs) context. The defined goals were the following:

(1) to identify differences between the three heuristic-based methods, regarding the measure of the quality of the evaluated visualizations;
(2) to check if the modifications applied by the authors of this article benefited the original heuristics, improving their efficiency when measuring the quality of visualizations in *Educational Timetabling Problems* (Ed-TTPs) context;
(3) to verify whether the empirical methodological study is capable of assisting decision-making by professionals involved in Ed-TTPs.

Going beyond the simple application of the heuristic methods as they were conceived, the present authors introduced changes that aimed to provide greater adherence of the evaluation process to the particular characteristics of Ed-TTPs. This was accomplished through the definition of the relative importance between each of the statements to be evaluated, expressed by means of an *weight* for the statement. Another modification, similar to that employed by Wall *et al.*, was to collect the raters' declaration of confidence for each statement of heuristics.

From the carried out experiments, it was realized that only the association of weights with the statements, performed by the authors of this study – who are Ed-TTPs specialists – had statistical relevance during the application of the heuristics of Zuk *et al.* and Forsell & Johansson. The raters' self-declaration of confidence for each statement was irrelevant and, therefore, can be ignored. This phenomenon was already expected, given the experience of the raters in IV field (a high confidence in the answers). When applying Wall *et al.*, it was possible to infer that, in any scenario, neither the rater's confidence nor the weighting of the statements were able to induce statistical difference in the evaluations. Hence, the scenario four was proved unnecessary. A relevant fact is that, in any scenario, the VisETV visualization is the one best evaluated, with VisMDV and VisDC occupying the second and third places, alternately.

As future works, we intend to: (1) perform a similar study involving a greater number of users, including non-specialists in IV and Ed-TTP; (2) design and apply a heuristic evaluation method focusing on Ed-TTP visualizations.

Acknowledgements. The first author is a PhD candidate and thanks the Brazilian research supporting agency FAPEG for scholarships. The others authors thanks CAPES.

References

1. de Souza Alencar, W., do Nascimento, H.A.D., Jradi, W.A.R., Soares, F.A.A.M.N., Felix, J.P.: Information visualization for highlighting conflicts in educational timetabling problems. In: Bebis, G., et al. (eds.) ISVC 2019. LNCS, vol. 11844, pp. 275–288. Springer, Cham (2019). https://doi.org/10.1007/978-3-030-33720-9_21
2. Amar, R., Stasko, J.: A knowledge task-based framework for design and evaluation of information visualizations. In: IEEE Symposium on Information Visualization, pp. 143–150. IEEE (2004). https://doi.org/10.1109/INFVIS.2004.10
3. Babaei, H., Karimpour, J., Hadidi, A.: A survey of approaches for university course timetabling problem. Comput. Indust. Eng. **86**, 43–59 (2015). https://doi.org/10.1016/j.cie.2014.11.010
4. Carpendale, S.: Evaluating information visualizations. In: Kerren, A., Stasko, J.T., Fekete, J.-D., North, C. (eds.) Information Visualization. LNCS, vol. 4950, pp. 19–45. Springer, Heidelberg (2008). https://doi.org/10.1007/978-3-540-70956-5_2
5. Elmqvist, N., Yi, J.S.: Patterns for visualization evaluation. Inform. Vis. **14**(3), 250–269 (2015). https://doi.org/10.1177/1473871613513228
6. Forsell, C.: A guide to scientific evaluation in information visualization. In: Proceedings of the 2010 14th International Conference Information Visualisation, IV 2010, pp. 162–169. IEEE Computer Society, USA (2010). https://doi.org/10.1109/IV.2010.33
7. Forsell, C., Johansson, J.: An heuristic set for evaluation in information visualization. In: Proceedings of the International Conference on Advanced Visual Interfaces, AVI 2010, pp. 199–206. ACM, New York (2010). https://doi.org/10.1145/1842993.1843029
8. Fu, X., Wang, Y., Dong, H., Cui, W., Zhang, H.: Visualization assessment: a machine learning approach. In: Proceedings of the 2019 IEEE Visualization Conference (VIS 2019), pp. 126–130. IEEE (2019). https://doi.org/10.1109/VISUAL.2019.8933570

9. Gomez, S.R., Guo, H., Ziemkiewicz, C., Laidlaw, D.H.: An insight and task-based methodology for evaluating spatiotemporal visual analytics. In: Proceedings of the IEEE Symposium on Visual Analytics Science and Technology 2014, pp. 9–14. IEEE (2014). https://doi.org/10.1109/VAST.2014.7042482

10. Harrison, L., Reinecke, K., Chang, R.: Infographic aesthetics: designing for the first impression. In: Proceedings of the ACM Conference on Human Factors in Computing Systems, pp. 1186–1190. ACM (2015). https://doi.org/10.1145/2702123.2702545

11. Hearst, M.A., Laskowski, P., Silva, L.: Evaluating information visualization via the interplay of heuristic evaluation and question-based scoring. In: Proceedings of the 2016 CHI Conference on Human Factors in Computing Systems, CHI 2016, pp. 5028–5033. ACM, New York (2016). https://doi.org/10.1145/2858036.2858280

12. Hermawati, S., Lawson, G.: Establishing usability heuristics for heuristics evaluation in a specific domain: is there a consensus? Appl. Ergon. **56**, 34–51 (2016). https://doi.org/10.1016/j.apergo.2015.11.016

13. Isenberg, T., Isenberg, P., Chen, J., Sedlmair, M., Möller, T.: A systematic review on the practice of evaluating visualization. IEEE Trans. Vis. Comput. Graphics **19**, 2818–2827 (2013). https://doi.org/10.1109/TVCG.2013.126

14. Lam, H., Bertini, E., Isenberg, P., Plaisant, C., Carpendale, S.: Empirical studies in information visualization: seven scenarios. IEEE Trans. Vis. Comput. Graphics **18**, 1520–1536 (2012). https://doi.org/10.1109/TVCG.2011.279

15. Mühlenthaler, M.: Fairness in Academic Course Timetabling. Lecture Notes in Economics and Mathematical Systems, vol. 678. Springer, Cham (2015). https://doi.org/10.1007/978-3-319-12799-6

16. Nielsen, J.: Finding usability problems through heuristic evaluation. In: Proceedings of the SIGCHI Conference on Human Factors in Computing Systems, CHI 1992, pp. 37–380. ACM (1992). https://doi.org/10.1145/142750.142834

17. North, C.: Toward measuring visualization insight. IEEE Comput. Graph. Appl. **26**(3), 6–9 (2006). https://doi.org/10.1109/MCG.2006.70

18. Saket, B., Endert, A., Stasko, J.: Beyond usability and performance: a review of user experience-focused evaluations in visualization. In: Proceedings of the Sixth Workshop on Beyond Time and Errors on Novel Evaluation Methods for Visualization, BELIV 2016, pp. 133–142. ACM (2016). https://doi.org/10.1145/2993901.2993903

19. Santos, B.S., Silva, S.S., Dias, P.: Heuristic evaluation in visualization: an empirical study (position paper). In: 2018 IEEE Evaluation and Beyond-Methodological Approaches for Visualization, pp. 78–85 (2018). https://doi.org/10.1109/beliv.2018.8634108

20. Stasko, J.: Value-driven evaluation of visualizations. In: Lam, H., Isenberg, P. (eds.) Proceedings of the Fifth Workshop on Beyond Time and Errors: Novel Evaluation Methods for Visualizations, BELIV 2014, pp. 46–53. ACM, New York (2014). https://doi.org/10.1145/2669557.2669579

21. Thomas, J.J., Khader, A.T., Belaton, B.: Visualization techniques on the examination timetabling pre-processing data. In: 2009 Sixth International Conference on Computer Graphics, Imaging and Visualization, pp. 454–458. IEEE (2009). https://doi.org/10.1109/CGIV.2009.23

22. Tory, M., Moller, T.: Evaluating visualizations: do expert reviews work? IEEE Comput. Graph. Appl. **25**(5), 8–11 (2005). https://doi.org/10.1109/MCG.2005.102

23. Wall, E., et al.: A heuristic approach to value-driven evaluation of visualizations. IEEE Trans. Vis. Comput. Graphics **25**, 491–500 (2019). https://doi.org/10.1109/TVCG.2018.2865146
24. Zhou, X., Xue, C., Zhou, L., Yafeng, N.: An evaluation method of visualization using visual momentum based on eye-tracking data. Int. J. Pattern Recognit. Artif. Intell. **32**(5), 1850016 (2018). https://doi.org/10.1142/S0218001418500167
25. Zuk, T., Schlesier, L., Neumann, P., Hancock, M.S., Carpendale, S.: Heuristics for information visualization evaluation. In: Proceedings of the 2006 AVI Workshop on BEyond Time and Errors, BELIV 2006, pp. 1–6. ACM (2006). https://doi.org/10.1145/1168149.1168162

Real-Time Contrast Enhancement for 3D Medical Images Using Histogram Equalization

Karen Lucknavalai and Jürgen P. Schulze[✉]

University of California San Diego, La Jolla, CA, USA
jschulze@ucsd.edu

Abstract. Medical professionals rely on medical imaging to help diagnose and treat patients. It is therefore important for them to be able to see all the details captured in the images. Often the use of contrast enhancement or noise reduction techniques are used to help improve the image quality. This paper introduces a real-time implementation of 3D Contrast Limited Adaptive Histogram Equalization (CLAHE) to enhance 3D medical image stacks, or volumes. This algorithm can be used interactively by medical doctors to help visualize the 3D medical volumes and prepare for surgery. It also introduces two novel extensions to the algorithm to allow a user to interactively decide on what region to focus the enhancement: Focused CLAHE and Masked CLAHE. Focused CLAHE applies the 3D CLAHE algorithm to a specified block of the entire medical volume and Masked CLAHE applies the algorithm to a selected organ or organs. These three contributions can be used, to not only help improve the visualization of 3D medical image stacks, but also to provide that contrast enhancement in real-time.

Keywords: Volume rendering · Medical imaging · High dynamic range

1 Introduction

Medical imaging, such as computed tomography (CT) and magnetic resonance (MR) imaging is critical when it comes to helping doctors diagnose patients and prepare for surgeries. Diagnoses are typically done by radiologists, while surgeries are planned by surgeons. Radiologists typically view and study medical images one slice at a time on special high-contrast 2D monitors. Surgeons use the diagnosis they are given by the radiologist, and sometimes also look at the medical image stacks, on their own computers which are standard laptop or desktop computers with regular 2D monitors. Given that viewing 2D image stacks from the CT and MR scans on a monitor is a considerable difference from the reality they experience in an actual surgery, it seems advantageous to be able to view and interact with this 3D data in a 3D environment, and at the highest image quality their displays can reproduce.

© Springer Nature Switzerland AG 2020
G. Bebis et al. (Eds.): ISVC 2020, LNCS 12509, pp. 224–235, 2020.
https://doi.org/10.1007/978-3-030-64556-4_18

The reason radiologists use special high contrast monitors is that CT and MR data are typically generated with a single luminance data point per pixel at 12 bit dynamic range. Standard monitors only have a dynamic range of 8 bit for luminance values, which are typically displayed as grayscale values.

The goal for our work was to maximize the available contrast in the data for virtual reality (VR) headsets. These often have an even smaller dynamic range than desktop monitors, which made the work even more important for us. But the findings in this paper apply to regular monitors equally well, as long as the goal is to display the CT or MR image stack in its entirety with volume rendering techniques.

This paper offers three novel contributions. First it introduces a real-time implementation of 3D Contrast Limited Adaptive Histogram Equalization (CLAHE). This allows medical professionals to interactively enhance the contrast of a medial volume or image stack within a 3D viewer. It also introduces two new extensions to the real-time algorithm, which give the user more flexibility and control over the contrast enhancement. The first extension is a focused version, which applies the contrast enhancement algorithm to a specified block of the medical volume. The second extension is a masked version which applies the algorithm to a particular organ or organs.

2   Related Work

2.1   Medical Images

MR scanner data is stored in DICOM files as a series of 12 bit grayscale images with each slice of the scan stored as a separate image. In order to display as much of the detail as possible, special high dynamic range (HDR) grayscale monitors were developed. These monitors are based on the Grayscale Standard Display Function, which was developed based on the number of gray values the human eye can detect [5, 7].

Numerous DICOM viewers have been developed that allow a user to view DICOM files on their available display. Most of these are 2D viewers, which allow a user to view an MRI scan one slice at a time. The interaction available generally includes zooming in and out of the image, the ability to take measurements, and perhaps apply some preset filters to the image to increase or decrease the contrast. There are some 3D DICOM viewers that create a 3D visual representation of the 2D slices that can then be viewed on the available 2D display. In general, the interaction with these viewers is the same as their 2D counterparts. There have been some more recent developments using virtual and augmented reality (AR) to display and interact with 3D scans in an immersive environment. However, they are still in development and are all limited to displaying within the 8 bit standard dynamic range. While HDR grayscale displays found a hardware solution to display the details in medical scans, the same solution is not currently available on laptops or in AR and VR headsets. Overcoming this mismatch, and enhancing the contrast of the 3D visualization of these medical images in real-time is the focus of this paper.

2.2   Contrast Enhancement Techniques

Image processing techniques have been around for decades. One method that has sparked a lot of research is histogram equalization (HE) [4]. This method was developed in the 1970s and has the goal of increasing the global contrast of an image, and is especially useful when applied to images that are either over or under exposed. HE works by redistributing pixel values for an image throughout the entire dynamic range, and has been shown to produce particularly good results in x-ray images [2].

Histogram equalization enhances the contrast based on the pixel distribution of the entire image, which may lead to areas that still appear over or underexposed. Adaptive Histogram Equalization (AHE) was developed to help combat this effect and improve the contrast of these local regions. AHE creates local histograms for each of the pixels in an image, so that the final enhancement adapts to these smaller image sections. This is done by dividing the image into Contextual Regions (CR) and bi-linearly interpolate between these local histograms to generate the final image [6, 9].

A drawback to both Histogram Equalization and Adaptive Histogram Equalization is the possibility of magnifying noise within the original image. Contrast Limited Histogram Equalization aims to counteract this problem by limiting the contrast amplification. This is done by clipping the histogram at a predefined value, or clip limit, which in turn reduces the final contrast of the image [9]. Contrast Limited Adaptive Histogram Equalization (CLAHE) combines the advantages of the Contrast Limited approach to limit contrast and noise, as well as the ability to decrease the over and underexposed regions in the final image with Adaptive Histogram Equalization [12]. This combination of methods provides multiple parameters that allow for flexibility and control over the final enhancement of the image. Adjusting the number of CRs changes the amount of detail enhanced in the final image whereas the changing the clip limit affects the overall contrast and enhancement of the final image.

2.3   Medical Imaging Enhancement

Since Histogram Equalization is both an effective and simple method for contrast enhancement, it is a popular choice to enhance medical images. CLAHE has a track record for providing good contrast enhancements for a variety of medical images, and has been shown to be effective and helpful for the doctors diagnosis, and interaction with the medical images [8, 10]. With the development and availability of 3D visualization, multiple papers have taken to adapting 2D methods to 3D. Amorim [1] extended CLAHE for 3D volumes by creating local histograms for a sub-volume of the medical volume, and tri-linearly interpolating between these local histograms. These results while impressive are not fast enough for real-time applications. This work takes this 3D CLAHE method and develops it for real-time applications.

3   Implementation

We started by developing a Python version of the original 2D CLAHE algorithm, and the 3D extension by Amorim [1,12]. The first step in CLAHE is to create a look-up table. This look-up table (LUT) is used to convert the dynamic range of the input image into the desired output dynamic range. This is done with a simple linear mapping shown in Eq. 1, where this equation is applied for each of the gray values in the original input image. The $inMin$ and $inMax$ are the maximum and minimum values of the input image, together making up the input dynamic range. $numBins$ refers to the number of gray values within the desired output dynamic range. This LUT will be the size of the input image dynamic range and contain the mappings between the original dynamic range to the desired dynamic range. This LUT and the mapping used to generate it is where the dynamic range disparity is handled.

$$LUT[inGrayVal] = \left\lfloor \frac{inGrayVal - inMin}{binSize} \right\rfloor$$
$$binSize = \frac{1 + inMax - inMin}{numBins} \tag{1}$$

After this LUT is generated, the local histograms are created. This is done by dividing the image or volume into smaller sections or CRs. Local histograms are then created for these sections where each histogram counts the number of times each of the possible gray values occur within a particular CR. Once the Histograms have been generated for their respective regions, the histograms are clipped based on a clip value. Any gray values that occur more times than this clip value within a CR are redistributed evenly throughout that histogram. This redistribution limits the amount of times a particular gray value can occur, which in turn limits the resulting contrast of the final image. This is done with the goal of reducing the amount of noise in the final image. The clip limit presented in [12] was calculated as given in Eq. 2. This one $clipValue$ is used to clip all the histograms such that there is no more than $clipValue$ pixels with a particular gray value in any of the CRs.

$$clipValue = clipLimit \cdot \frac{(sizeCRx \cdot sizeCRy)}{numBins} \quad , \quad cliLimit \in [1, \infty) \tag{2}$$

The $clipLimit$ is a user inputted value that must be larger than 1. A value of 1 corresponds to a completely uniform distribution of pixels and visually results in an unaltered image. As the clip limit increases, the contrast is also increased. If, however, the $clipValue$ is larger than the count for the most common gray value in a CR, the histogram will not be clipped and the clip Limit will have no effect on the image. Figure 1 shows the histograms and resulting images for the example case of using just one CR for the image. The value for the clip limit can be thought of as how far away the histograms can stray from a uniform distribution. Through experimentation, values between 2 and 8 seem to give a good range of results, but the results do vary between different amounts of CRs and different sized images.

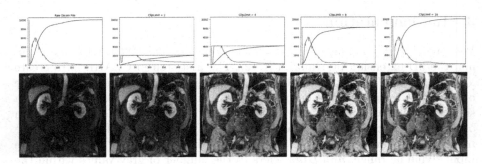

Fig. 1. Resulting Images and plots of the histogram (in red), CDF (in blue), and *clipValue* (in green). Using a single Contextual Region for the entire image and varying values for the *clipValue* calculated with Eq. 2. (Color figure online)

This clip limit is constant throughout the adaptive equalization process. Meaning that the same *clipValue* is used for every local histogram. So it is possible that the clip value only clips some of the histograms. We implemented a more adaptive approach to the clip limit in which it is treated as a percentage of the most frequently occurring value in a particular CR (Eq. 3. With this approach the *clipLimit* ranges between [0, 1], with a value of 1 corresponding to the fully enhanced contrast, and the smaller the value corresponding to less contrast in the final image. It is important to place a lower bound on the *clipValue* since it would be impossible to re-distribute the values of the histogram if they were clipped below a uniform distribution. The *minClipVal* or lower bound is found utilizing the original formula for the *clipValue* and 1.1 as the clip limit because the closer the *clipValue* is to a uniform distribution, the harder it gets to re-distribute the histogram values. Figure 2 shows the results of this approach for varying clip values on a DICOM slice, again using 4 × 4 CRs.

$$clipValue = max\big(minClipVal, \ clipLimit \cdot max(hist_{currCR})\big)$$
$$minClipVal = 1.1 \cdot \frac{(sizeCRx \cdot sizeCRy)}{numBins}, \quad clipLimit \in [0, 1] \qquad (3)$$

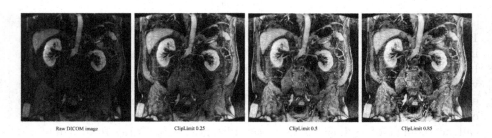

Fig. 2. Applying CLAHE to a slice of an MRI DICOM with an increasing *clipLimit* where *clipValue* is calculated with Eq. 3.

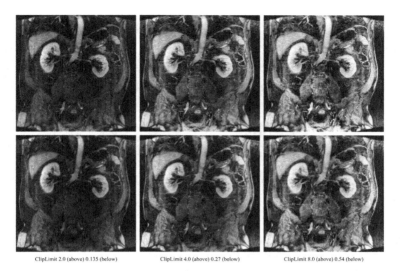

ClipLimit 2.0 (above) 0.135 (below)   ClipLimit 4.0 (above) 0.27 (below)   ClipLimit 8.0 (above) 0.54 (below)

Fig. 3. Comparison between using the *clipValue* as calculated in the original CLAHE paper (Eq. 2, with the presented adaptive/local approach (Eq. 3).

The difference between these two approaches is subtle. The original approach treats the clip value as a global clip on the histograms, which results in a smooth transition between the raw image and the CLAHE enhanced image. On the other hand, the percentage approach depends on the local histograms, which results in a local *clipValue* that adjusts the contrast of each local region individually. Figure 3 shows the comparison between these two approaches using 4×4 CRs on a single DICOM slice. To make the comparisons as close and fair as possible, the clip limit used in the original global method is equivalent to the average clip limit applied in the local approach. So the overall contrast is about the same for these sets of images; however, differences can be seen between the two sets of images. The original method seems to over expose the center bottom of the images especially in middle and right images. Whereas the details in this region are better preserved in the local approach. The rest of the results presented will be using this local approach to the clip limit.

Once the histograms have been clipped, the cumulative distribution function is calculated for each histogram to create the mapping between the original gray value and the CLAHE enhanced gray value. The final pixel value is determined by bi-linearly interpolating between the 4 neighboring CR mappings in the 2D case, and tri-linearly interpolating between the 8 neighboring CR mappings in the 3D case. The results of the 3D implementation of CLAHE can be seen in Fig. 4. All the 2D images shown are from DICOM slices which are 512×512 pixels, and the Volumes are on the full $512 \times 512 \times 116$ DICOM volume.

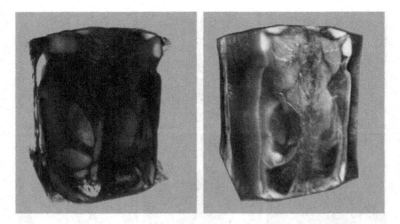

Fig. 4. Comparison between the original DICOM volume on the left, alongside the CLAHE enhanced volume on the right.

3.1   Optimizing for Real-Time Interaction

The initial implementation was done in Python because of its simplicity when working with images. However, it became clear that the speed limitations of the language would be unacceptable for a real-time application. Running the algorithm on just a DICOM slice would take about 2.2 s, and the entire volume took about 5 min. These are nowhere near acceptable run-times for a real-time application. The fist change to speed up the computation was to re-implement the algorithms in C++. This change alone produced a considerable improvement: computing the entire volume went from 5 min to 3 s, which was still not fast enough for real-time. To further optimize, we transferred the algorithm onto the GPU using GLSL Compute Shaders.

Using GLSL Compute Shaders provides a significant speed up since they are computed in parallel on the GPU. But only a few of them can be done in lockstep due to hardware constraints. Since the GPU allocates the computations the user has little control over the how the computations are completed or the order in which they are computed. So if a particular block of code needs to be completed by all inputs before moving onto something else, it is safest to place that block of code in its own shader. This is especially crucial for any global data that needs to be accessed in parallel between the threads or used for future computations.

The first step in the 3D CLAHE algorithm is computing the LUT to map from HDR to SDR. The equation for calculating this mapping is straightforward (Eq. 1). However, in order to compute this table, we need to know what the max and min values of the volume are. In Python, this was calculated with a function call. In C++, a double nested for loop is needed to loop over every single pixel in the volume. With compute shaders, it is calculated with one dispatch call to run a single compute shader that processes each pixel in the entire volume.

Once the Max and Min values for the volume are computed, a separate compute shader can then be called to compute the LUT. Computing the histograms can similarly be done with a single shader. Clipping the histograms and redistributing the pixels is less straightforward. The algorithm works by evenly re-distributing the pixels that are above the clip value, which means that the amount of pixels above this value, or the number of excess pixels, needs to be known before they can be re-distributed. As a result, the process of clipping the histogram needs to be done through multiple shader executions - the first to calculate the number of excess pixels in each histogram, and a second to re-distribute those evenly throughout the histogram.

The next step is to calculate the mapping from the original gray value to the new histogram equalized gray value. This is done by calculating the Cumulative Distribution Function for each histogram. This is the only portion of the algorithm that not optimized through compute shaders. To be done efficiently, Cumulative Distribution Functions should be calculated in a sequential order. This is, unfortunately, not easy to make efficient with compute shaders. After dispatching the compute shader, there is no explicit control over the order in which those groups, and therefore indices, are being processed. So it is possible that the CDF value for index 100 gets computed before the value for index 1. This is a problem because the value for index 100 is dependent on the values calculated for index 1 through index 99. To ensure that these values were calculated sequentially, they were instead computed via CPU based multi-threading, with one thread per histogram.

The last and final step is interpolating between these mappings to process each pixel in the volume and generate the final 3D enhanced volume. Overall, changing from Python to compute shaders decreased the computation time to the point that these could be completed in real-time. This will allow for the user to vary the parameters and interact the results in real-time.

4   Results

4.1   Run-Time Results

The initial CLAHE implementation in Python was prohibitively slow for a real-time application, even in the 2D case, so it was in need of optimization. The differences in language speed alone can clearly be seen through the speed up in run-times for the Python and C++ implementations. The improvement between C++ and the GLSL compute shader implementation, while not as drastic, does offer a significant boost in getting the algorithm to run in real-time. The average measured run-times for the Python, C++ and GLSL implementations can be seen in Table 1, and the data used was a $512 \times 512 \times 116$ DICOM volume.

4.2   Extensions

In an effort to provide more focused and varied control of the contrast enhancement, I implemented two new versions of a selective application of the 3D CLAHE algorithm; Focused CLAHE and Masked CLAHE.

Table 1. The average computation time in seconds for the Python, C++ and GPU based CLAHE methods, calculated on a laptop with an Intel HD Graphics 620 Graphics Card.

	Python (secs)	C++ (secs)	GLSL (secs)
2D	2.201	0.025	–
2D focused	3.228	0.019	–
3D	400	3.092	1.165
3D focused	–	0.333	0.189

Focused CLAHE: Focused CLAHE allows the user to focus the contrast enhancement on a particular region of the image or volume. This is accomplished by extracting the desired region from the original image or volume, and applying the CLAHE algorithm on just that extracted region. When working with a smaller portion of the entire image or volume, the number of CRs has a large impact on the results. The more regions used, the more specialized those mappings become which further enhances the images, sometimes to the point that any noise in the original image is also enhanced. The affect of just varying the number of CRs can be seen in Fig. 5. All these results are applied to the same $240x240$ pixels with a clip limit of 0.75. With all other factors held constant, it can be seen that the increased number of CRs also enhances the noise.

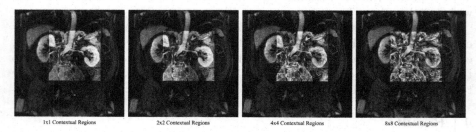

1x1 Contextual Regions   2x2 Contextual Regions   4x4 Contextual Regions   8x8 Contextual Regions

Fig. 5. Comparing the number of Contextual Regions for a focused region in a DICOM slice.

To help reduce the amount of noise in the final image, instead of letting the user choose the number of CRs in addition to the area CLAHE is applied to, we decided to calculate the number of CRs to use based on number of pixels in the desired focused region. Based on visual inspection and trial and error, we found that using one CR for every 100 pixels seems to produce a good balance between adaptive enhancement without too much noise. The results from the 3D version of this Focused CLAHE method can be seen in Fig. 6. The size and placement of the focused region can be manipulated by the user, with the results shown in real-time. The dispatch calls to create the histograms for Focused CLAHE are based only on the size of the region. However, the call to interpolate and create the entire volume still needs to be based on the full volume dimensions to produce a complete volume.

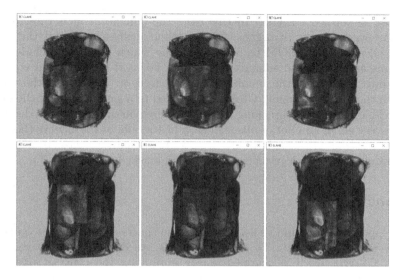

Fig. 6. Two different viewpoints of the DICOM volume with Focused CLAHE applied to different regions of the volume. These images show the flexibility of Focused CLAHE in that the user can adjust both the size and placement of the focused region.

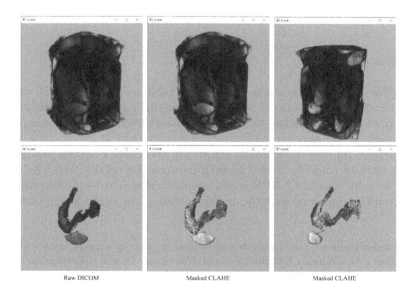

Fig. 7. The first column of images show the raw DICOM file displayed as a part of the entire volume, and the organs alone. The next four images show two different views of the DICOM volume and organs after applying Masked CLAHE.

Masked CLAHE: A second method to focus the enhancement on a region of interest is Masked CLAHE. In this case, the enhancement is directed to a particular organ or set of organs. This method utilizes masks of the organs for each slice in the DICOM to help determine which pixels to include in the histograms and apply the enhancement to. In Focused CLAHE, the volume is divided into CRs, with the number of CRs based on the size of the focused region. In the Masked version, CLAHE is applied to a small region of the overall volume. This means that breaking that masked region into CRs runs the risk of having a very small number of pixels in each histogram, or not having those CRs be evenly distributed throughout the organs. As a result, we chose to implement this Masked version with just one CR for each masked organ (Fig. 7).

5   Conclusions

We developed an algorithm to help improve the contrast of MRI data on typical monitors and VR displays. To accomplish this, we developed a 3D version of CLAHE. CLAHE itself is geared towards improving the contrast of medical imaging, and the 3D version further improves that enhancement for medical volumes. We optimized the 3D CLAHE computations for real-time interaction by computing them with compute shaders. We then extended 3D CLAHE to focus on a particular region of the volume - Focused CLAHE, and Masked CLAHE, in which the user can enhance the contrast of a particular organ. With our GPU-based implementation, all of these computations can be done in real-time to enable the user to interact with the different methods.

6   Future Work

Our current algorithm uses a linear look-up table to map the HDR values to the standard dynamic range. The simplicity of this method is beneficial to the overall speed of the algorithm, but it may be possible to use a better compression method such as the Accelerated Bilateral Filter method [3].

To further improve the CLAHE algorithm, the Local Contrast Modification CLAHE method could be added to help improve the results [11]. The current method used in Masked CLAHE is not adaptive. It should be investigated if the results could be improved with the addition of adaptive methods and using more than one CR.

Acknowledgements. This research was funded in part by a grant from The Leona M. and Harry B. Helmsley Charitable Trust. We thank Trevor Hedstrom for his help with the implementation of the shader version of the algorithm.

References

1. Amorim, P., Moraes, T., Silva, J., Pedrini, H.: 3D adaptive histogram equalization method for medical volumes. In: VISIGRAPP (2018)
2. Dorothy, R., Joany, R.M., Rathish, R.J., Prabha, S.S., Rajendran, S.: Image enhancement by histogram equalization. Int. J. Nano Corros. Sci. Eng. **2**, 21–30 (2015)
3. Durand, F., Dorsey, J.: Fast bilateral filtering for the display of high-dynamic-range images. ACM Trans. Graph. **21**(3), 257–266 (2002). https://doi.org/10.1145/566654.566574
4. Hall, E.L.: Almost uniform distributions for computer image enhancement. IEEE Trans. Comput. **C-23**, 207–208 (1974)
5. Kimpe, T., Tuytschaever, T.: Increasing the number of gray shades in medical display systems–how much is enough? J. Digit. Imaging **20**(4), 422–432 (2007). https://doi.org/10.1007/s10278-006-1052-3
6. Leszczynski, K.W., Shalev, S.: A robust algorithm for contrast enhancement by local histogram modification. Image Vis. Comput. **7**(3), 205–209 (1989). https://doi.org/10.1016/0262-8856(89)90045-0
7. Li, M., Wilson, D., Wong, M., Xthona, A.: The evolution of display technologies in PACS applications. Comput. Med. Imaging Graph. **27**, 175–84 (2003). https://doi.org/10.1016/S0895-6111(02)00072-1
8. Pizer, S.M., Johnston, R.E., Ericksen, J.P., Yankaskas, B.C., Muller, K.E.: Contrast-limited adaptive histogram equalization: speed and effectiveness. In: Proceedings of the First Conference on Visualization in Biomedical Computing, pp. 337–345, May 1990. https://doi.org/10.1109/VBC.1990.109340
9. Pizer, S.M., et al.: Adaptive histogram equalization and its variations. Comput. Vision Graph. Image Process. **39**(3), 355–368 (1987). https://doi.org/10.1016/S0734-189X(87)80186-X
10. Pizer, S.M., Austin, J.D., Perry., J.R., Safrit, H.D., Zimmerman, J.B.: Adaptive histogram equalization for automatic contrast enhancement of medical images. In: III, S.J.D., Schneider, R.H. (eds.) Application of Optical Instrumentation in Medicine XIV and Picture Archiving and Communication Systems, vol. 0626, pp. 242–250. International Society for Optics and Photonics, SPIE (1986). https://doi.org/10.1117/12.975399
11. Mohan, S., Ravishankar, M.: Modified contrast limited adaptive histogram equalization based on local contrast enhancement for mammogram images. In: Das, V.V., Chaba, Y. (eds.) Mobile Communication and Power Engineering. CCIS, vol. 296, pp. 397–403. Springer, Heidelberg (2013). https://doi.org/10.1007/978-3-642-35864-7_60
12. Zuiderveld, K.: Contrast Limited Adaptive Histogram Equalization, pp. 474–485. Academic Press Professional Inc, Cambridge (1994)

Flow Map Processing by Space-Time Deformation

Thomas Wilde$^{(\boxtimes)}$, Christian Rössl, and Holger Theisel

Otto-von-Guericke University Magdeburg, Magdeburg, Germany
`thomas@isg.cs.uni-magdeburg.de`

Abstract. In Flow Visualization, the consideration of flow maps instead of velocity fields has recently moved into the focus of research. We present an approach to transforming standard techniques in vector field processing – like smoothing, modeling, deformation – to flow maps. This requires a solution to the fundamental problem that – contrary to vector fields – a specific modification of the flow map is, in general, not a flow map anymore. We introduce a concept that enables the modification of discrete sampling of a flow map while enforcing the flow map properties. Based on this, we present approaches for flow map deformation that are applied to a 2D time-dependent flow field.

Keywords: Flow visualization · Flow map · Unsteady vector fields

1 Introduction

In Flow Visualization, a subfield of Scientific Visualization, vector fields describing the velocity of a flow are usually in the focus of interest. In addition to just visualizing vector fields, there are also established approaches to model, construct, deform, simplify, and compress vector fields. We call these approaches *vector field processing* and consider them as an inevitable part of Flow Visualization. In recent years, Flow Visualization techniques that do not focus on the velocity field but the *flow map* have gained increased interest. This is motivated by the fact that the flow map directly encodes all particle trajectories (path lines) without the necessity of numerical integration. Flow maps are complex data structures: they are computationally expensive, high-dimensional, have highly connected data, and strong gradients [19]. Considering flow maps is challenging but rewarding. This brings up the question for the systematic *processing of flow maps*, similar to vector field processing. The main challenge for flow map processing is the complexity of flow maps and another fundamental problem: a small local modification would destroy inherent flow map properties, and therefore the result is not a flow map anymore. To tackle this problem, we present the following main contributions: first, we give solid foundations to characterize properties of general flow maps. Afterward, we introduce a concept for modification techniques that keep these properties and apply this to a benchmark data set.

© Springer Nature Switzerland AG 2020
G. Bebis et al. (Eds.): ISVC 2020, LNCS 12509, pp. 236–247, 2020.
https://doi.org/10.1007/978-3-030-64556-4_19

2   Related Work

Vector Field Design: Vector fields have been of research interest over the past decades in various fields. Theisel [16] presents an early approach to designing 2D steady vector fields based on a set of control polygons and extracted topologic features. Weinkauf et al. [18] extend this to a solution based on topological skeletons of vector fields to 3D. Zhang et al. [20,21] present an interactive design system that uses similar metaphors by placing singularities in the field. Chen et al. [4] go a step further and contribute an element-based framework for designing unsteady vector fields on manifold surfaces. Recently Baeza [1] presented a new approach to the extraction of time-dependent vector field topology. For a more complete overview, we refer to the work of Vaxman[17]. Several authors utilize vector fields to solve other problems, e.g., von Funck et al. [5,6] present vector field based shape deformations. We formulate our approach for flow map modification similarly.

Flow Maps: Several papers use the Lagrangian point of view for flow visualization - they directly or indirectly use flow maps. The majority of state-of-the-art flow visualization techniques are based on advection and therefore utilize at least parts of the flow map [3,12–14]. Hlawatsch et al. [9] perform a concatenation of short-time flow maps for fast parallel computation of path lines. Hummel et al. [11] give an error estimation for this kind of path line computation on short-time flow maps. Wilde et al. [19] present a distance function based on the full 5D flow map used to extract closed surfaces with recirculation behavior. Hofmann [10] introduces a generic vector operator that is also capable of computing sparse samplings on recirculation surfaces. One of the most prominent tools for the visualization of unsteady flow behavior are FTLE fields, as described by Haller et al. [7]. FTLE indicates the separation of colocated particles and is based on the spatial flow map gradient.

3   Flow Maps and Velocity Fields

Notation: We depict scalar values by lower case letters, e.g., time t, vectorial data is denoted by lower case bold letters, e.g. position x, an uppercase letter describes a set of elements or an area, e.g. S. We use a tilde for modified values, e.g., $\tilde{\phi}$.

Definitions: We denote a *time-dependent vector field* **v**, evaluated at position x and time t as:

$$\mathbf{v} : D \times T_t \to \mathbb{R}^n \ : \ (\mathbf{x}, t) \to \mathbf{v}(\mathbf{x}, t) \tag{1}$$

where $D \subseteq \mathbb{R}^n$ is the spatial domain, and $T_t = [t_s, t_e]$ is the finite time interval in which we define the velocity field. Furthermore, $\mathbf{v} \in C^1$, i.e., **v** is sufficiently smooth. In practice, both the spatial and temporal domains are limited to a bounded region and a time interval. The path of a massless particle that is advected by the underlying velocity field is called a *path line*. We compute a path line starting at $\mathbf{x}_0$ and time t_0 by integrating **v** over a time interval

$t \in [t_0, t_0 + \tau] \subseteq T$. The corresponding *flow map* for the vector field $\mathbf{v}(\mathrm{x}, t)$ is given by:

$$\phi_\tau^t : D \times T_t \times T_\tau \to D : (\mathrm{x}, t, \tau) \to \phi(\mathrm{x}, t, \tau) \tag{2}$$

with $T_\tau = [\tau_s, \tau_e]$. ϕ maps a particle seeded at position x and time t to its destination. τ denotes the integration time, i.e., the time which passes between particle seeding and reaching its destination. We write the flow map equivalently as $\phi = \phi(\mathrm{x}) = \phi_\tau^t$, whenever position x, starting time t, or integration time τ are clear from the context. The flow map encodes path lines. A path line starting at x_0 and t_0 can be computed by an evaluation of $\phi(\mathrm{x}_0, t_0, \tau)$ over a time interval $\tau \in [\tau_0, \tau_1] \subseteq T_\tau$. The time derivative with respect to τ is the direction in which a massless particle currently moves and is defined as:

$$\phi_\tau(\mathrm{x}, t, \tau) = \frac{\delta}{\delta \tau} \phi(\mathrm{x}, t, \tau) \tag{3}$$

Properties and Relations: A map $D \times T_t \times T_\tau \to D$ must fulfill the following properties to be a flow map:

$$\phi(\mathrm{x}, t, 0) = \mathrm{x} \tag{4}$$

$$\phi(\phi(\mathrm{x}, t, \tau_1), t + \tau_1, \tau_2) = \phi(\mathrm{x}, t, \tau_1 + \tau_2) \tag{5}$$

$$\phi(\phi(\mathrm{x}, t, \tau_1), t + \tau_1, -\tau_1) = \mathrm{x} \tag{6}$$

for all $\mathrm{x} \in D, t \in T_t, t + \tau_1 \in T_t, t + \tau_1 + \tau_2 \in T_t$. Equation (4) denotes the flow map's *identity* for the particular case $\tau = 0$, i.e., a particle is mapped to its starting position if there is no integration time. Equation (5) describes the flow map's *additivity*, i.e., the particle moves on its path line in several small consecutive steps or one big step. Equation (6) denotes the *inversion* of the flow map, which is a particular case of additivity. If τ is inverted, a massless particle has to move backward on its path, which also means it will reach its starting position again. Assuming a velocity field $\mathbf{v}(\mathrm{x}, t)$ and the corresponding flow map $\phi(\mathrm{x}, t, \tau)$ are given, both smooth and continuous. The following relations hold:

$$\phi_\tau(\mathrm{x}, t, 0) = \mathbf{v}(\mathrm{x}, t) \tag{7}$$

$$\phi_\tau(\mathrm{x}, t, \tau) = \mathbf{v}(\phi(\mathrm{x}, t, \tau), t + \tau) \tag{8}$$

i.e., the velocity field is the partial derivative of the flow map with respect to the integration time τ. The flow map $\phi_\tau^t(\mathrm{x})$ is a function mapping $\phi : \mathbb{R}^{n+2} \to \mathbb{R}^n$, where n denotes the number of spatial dimensions. The remaining two dimensions are the starting time t and integration time τ. In practice, the use of 2D or 3D unsteady flows is common. In this paper, we also use the 1D case ($\phi : \mathbb{R}^3 \to \mathbb{R}$) to clarify concepts. However, all presented flow map properties and concepts hold for higher dimensions.

4   Flow Map Modification

This section introduces the theoretical background for modifying flow maps based on a space deformation. Afterward, we develop a shape-based method, which implements this approach and could be the basis for an interactive transformation tool. The flow map explicitly encodes the path lines. We use them to illustrate the presented ideas and concepts for the 1D and 2D cases.

Modification Based on Space Deformation: Given a flow map ϕ, we want to apply a local modification in space-time such that the new map $\widetilde{\phi}$ is a flow map again. The mapping of positions in space, at selected domain locations in space-time, must be modified. An example may be to pick a path line and locally change its shape. Due to continuity reasons, a modification must also affect the region near the modified path line, i.e., we also have to change the shape of adjacent path lines, but in a certain distance (in space-time), all remaining path lines are untouched. We can model such behavior by defining a space deformation. A space deformation $\mathbf{y} : \mathbb{R}^{n+1} \to \mathbb{R}^n$ maps a point (x, t) in space-time to the new point $\mathbf{y}(\mathrm{x}, t)$. We expect $\mathbf{y}$ to be local, continuous, and invertible:

<u>Local:</u> it affects only a region of the space-time domain, unless $\mathbf{y}$ is the identity
<u>Continuous:</u> $\mathbf{y}$ is at least C^1
<u>Invertible:</u> $\nabla_{\mathrm{x}}\mathbf{y}$ does have full rank, i.e., the inverse map $\mathbf{y}^{-1}$ is well-defined.
We compute the new flow map $\widetilde{\phi}$ from ϕ and $\mathbf{y}$ by:

$$\widetilde{\phi}(\mathrm{x}, t, \tau) = \mathbf{y}(\phi(\mathbf{y}^{-1}(\mathrm{x}, t), t, \tau), t + \tau) \tag{9}$$

Note that $\widetilde{\phi}$ is a flow map as well; we give a proof for this in the appendix. The transformation from ϕ to $\widetilde{\phi}$ is local in space-double-time, i.e., position x, time t, and integration time τ. If both $\mathbf{y}(\mathrm{x}, t)$ and $\mathbf{y}(\phi(\mathbf{y}^{-1}(\mathrm{x}, t), t, \tau), t + \tau)$ are the identity, we have $\widetilde{\phi} = \phi$. A modification must preserve, all flow map defining properties (Sect. 3). Flow maps are high dimensional and have highly connected data, i.e., it is not possible to change the flow map in a small area without breaking the global flow map properties. A small change always has a global impact in the space-time domain. This makes modifications of flow maps a challenging task. In the following, we propose an approach to solving this task, divided into two steps:

1. Define a local area (in space-time) to perform a modification.
2. Globally identify all influenced areas and adapt them.

4.1   Definition of Modification Area

For an interactive manipulation of flow maps, we follow a metaphor using interactive shape modeling by deformations [2,5] and adapt this to flow map modeling. We define the shape S in space-time, with n dimensions in space and 1 dimension in time; therefore, $S \subset D \times T_{t+\tau}$. All possible $(t + \tau)$-combinations have to be covered, i.e., $T_{t+\tau} = T_t \cup T_\tau = [t_0 - \tau_e, t_0 + 2\tau_e]$. S describes an area of effect, in which the modification is performed. It is placed interactively at a user-defined location. We divide the shape into three regions:

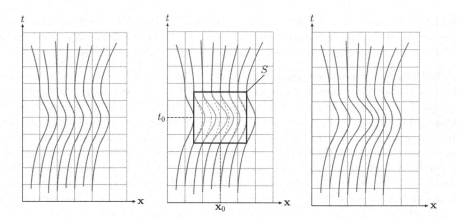

Fig. 1. Left: original path lines. Middle: process of modification, it is strongest in the middle of S. Right: smooth modified path lines.

1. an inner region, with a rigid modification
2. an outer region, where no modification takes place
3. an intermediate region, where the deformation is computed by an energy minimization to ensure continuity and other useful properties.

We define a local space deformation $\mathbf{y}$ by setting the following values for the modification shape S: $\mathbf{x}_0, t_0, r_1, r_2, r_t, \mathbf{d}_0$. Here $(\mathbf{x}_0, t_0)$ denotes the center position of S in space-time, $\mathbf{d}_0$ denotes a transformation vector. Furthermore we demand $0 \leq r_1 < r_2$, $0 < r_t$, $\|\mathbf{d}_0\| < r_2 - r_1$. Then we define a space deformation as

$$\mathbf{y}(\mathbf{x}, t) = \mathbf{x} + \lambda \mathbf{d}_0 \tag{10}$$

$$\lambda = \lambda_s \lambda_t, \qquad \lambda_s = (s_\mathbf{x}^3 + 3s_\mathbf{x}^2(1 - s_\mathbf{x})), \qquad \lambda_t = (s_t^3 + 3s_t^2(1 - s_t)) \tag{11}$$

$$r = \|\mathbf{x} - \mathbf{x}_0\| \tag{12}$$

$$s_\mathbf{x} = \begin{cases} 1 & r < r_1 \\ \frac{r - r_2}{r_1 - r_2} & r_1 \leq r \leq r_2 \\ 0 & r > r_2 \end{cases} \quad s_t = \begin{cases} 1 - \frac{|t - t_0|}{r_t} & |t - t_0| < r_t \\ 0 & \text{else} \end{cases} \tag{13}$$

λ is a scaling factor for the deformation, defined in the dependency of S. λ is 0 next to the border (no modification) and 1 at the center (full modification) of S. Figure 2 (left) gives an illustration of S for the 1D case. This definition of the modification shape S leads to a smooth transition from original to modified areas in the ϕ domain. Figure 1 gives an example of a modification of path lines for the 1D case. We place S at a specific location $(\mathbf{x}_0, t_0)$, e.g., guided by the user. Figure 1 (left) shows path lines extracted from the flow map. Note that they are defined in space-time and do *not* necessarily start or end at the same time t. Figure 1 (middle) illustrates a modification in the form of a translation in a positive x direction. We show the modified path line pieces in orange; the pieces stay inside of S. Outside of the modification shape $\mathbf{y}$ maps to the identity, i.e., $\tilde{\phi} = \phi$. This also holds for the particular case $\tau = 0$. Figure 1 (right) shows

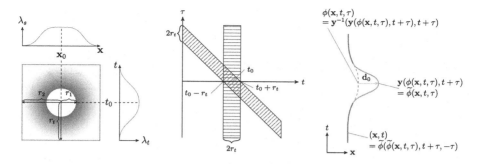

Fig. 2. Left: Illustration of the modification shape S for the 1D case. Middle: Areas with (t, τ)-pairs in which ϕ has to be updated. Right: The effect of $\mathbf{y}$ for two locations on a single path line.

the final result. Note that by construction, $\mathbf{y}$ is C^1 continuous and invertible. However, the inverse $\mathbf{y}^{-1}$ does not have a simple formula. Because of this, we numerically precompute $\mathbf{y}^{-1}$ on a uniform grid in a space-time box with the same size as S.

4.2   Local Modification and Global Adaption

Having defined the space deformation $\mathbf{y}$, we have to update the flow map ϕ accordingly by applying Eq. (9). Since $\mathbf{y}$ is local, i.e., only in a specific area, it is not the identity, $\tilde{\phi}$ is local as well. To ensure the flow map properties, we need to identify the parts, which need to be adapted in the process of a local modification. These parts can be classified into two groups:

1. parts mapping from *inside* S to its *outside*, i.e. $\phi(\mathbf{x}, t, \tau) \notin S$ with $(\mathbf{x}, t) \in S$
2. parts mapping to the *inside* of S, i.e., $\phi(\mathbf{x}, t, \tau) \in S$

Keep in mind that S is defined in space-time. Therefore the terms *inside* and *outside* also refer to space-time. For the spatial part, we have to check if a location x or its mapping $\phi(\mathbf{x}, t, \tau)$ belongs to S. Regarding the double-time dimensions, only specific (t, τ)-combinations are relevant. The new flow map must be computed only for (t, τ)-pairs with $(t_0 - r_t) \leq (t + \tau) \leq (t_0 + r_t)$. Figure 2 (middle) illustrates the relevant parts in (t, τ) domain. Regarding a single path line from the example given in Fig. 1, the flow map needs to be adapted for all locations on this path line, where a (t, τ)-pair maps into the modification area S. Figure 2 (right) illustrates this adaption for two locations on a path line. If $\phi(\mathbf{x}, t, \tau)$ is modified, $\phi(\phi(\mathbf{x}, t, \tau), t + \tau, -\tau)$ has to be adapted as well.

4.3   Discretization of the Flow Map

ϕ is defined as a continuous map, describing particle trajectories in flows from the Lagrangian reference frame. In practice, it is discretized in space and time.

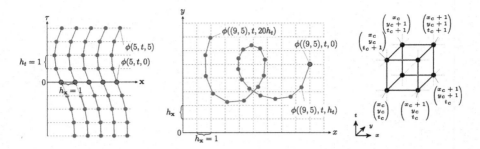

Fig. 3. Left: Sampled path lines for different x, fixed t, and consecutive τ in 1D. Middle: A path line for a fixed x, fixed t, and consecutive τ in 2D. Green circles denote (x, t)-coordinates of samples. Blue circles indicate τ-coordinates and mapping destinations. Right: Illustration of a lookup-cell in (x, y, t)-space. (Color figure online)

We discretize the domain over a regular grid. For the discretization scheme, we require the parameters h_x and h_t. They denote the constant distance between two samples in the spatial dimensions, e.g. (x, y) and the temporal dimensions t and τ. This discretization of the domain results in a single *slice* for each (t, τ)-combination, containing the spatial grid samples. We perform an integration in the underlying vector field for each discrete (x, t, τ)-sample. The corresponding trajectory endpoint is stored for this sample and builds a single entry in the discretized flow map. This way, we get a discrete approximation of the flow map in each dimension. Figure 3 gives an example of the 1D and 2D cases. The access to the flow map entries is given by (x, t, τ)-coordinates for each sample. Furthermore, each sample gets a unique *ID*. Flow map values between discrete samples are obtained by linear interpolation of the corresponding neighboring samples. Path lines for a fixed $(x, t, 0)$-position can be extracted by reading the entries for consecutive τ-coordinates.

Modification of the Discrete Flow Map: When we perform the modification on the discrete flow map, we have to adapt the discrete samples' entries. As stated out, we classify the involved samples into two groups:

1. samples located *inside* the modification area S mapping *outside*
2. samples mapping *into* the modification area S .

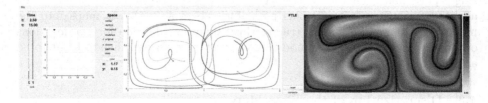

Fig. 4. The path line explorer. Left: (t, τ)-space selection. Middle: random path lines. Right: FTLE visualization. Path lines originate at the dots.

The first group are the samples covered by the modification area S and are therefore easy to identify. The members of the second group are not so easily identifiable. Potentially we have to check all samples with a suitable (t, τ)-combination (see Fig. 2), for each modification. But in general, only a small group of samples maps into S. To cope with this problem, we introduce a further data structure.

Lookup-Cells for Fast Sample Retrieval: Based the flow map sampling, we divide the discretization into *lookup-cells*, defined by (x, t)-coordinates, i.e., we omit one temporal coordinate τ. The adjacent samples of a location in (x, t)-space build the vertices of the surrounding lookup-cell. For the 2D, case a lookup-cell C at the sample (x_c, t_c) is given by the following coordinates:

$$C_{(\mathrm{x}_c, t_c)} := (x_c, y_c, t_c), \quad (x_c + 1, y_c, t_c), \quad (x_c, y_c + 1, t_c), \quad (x_c + 1, y_c + 1, t_c),$$
$$(x_c, y_c, t_c + 1), (x_c + 1, y_c, t_c + 1), (x_c, y_c + 1, t_c + 1), (x_c + 1, y_c + 1, t_c + 1).$$

Figure 3 (right) gives an illustration. $2^{(n+1)}$ neighboring samples make up a cell. Vice versa, each discrete sample is part of up to $2^{(n+1)}$ adjacent cells. Each lookup-cell $C_{(\mathrm{x}_c, t_c)}$ holds the *IDs* of samples mapping into its volume in discretized space-time. The set P of these samples for a single cell is given by:

$$P_{C_{(\mathrm{x}_c, t_c)}} := \{(\mathrm{x}, t, \tau) \mid \phi(\mathrm{x}, t, \tau) \in C_{(\mathrm{x}_c, t_c)}\} \ \ with \ \ t_c \leq (t + \tau) \leq t_c + 1$$

This way, fast retrieval of all parts that need to be adapted is possible. The temporal domain of the lookup-cells covers the whole (t, τ)-space, i.e., $T_t \times T_\tau$.

5   Implementation

After precomputing the complete flow map in a particular resolution, we can reformulate standard visualization approaches based on path line integration as a simple array lookup. Based on this, we implemented an interactive exploration tool for unsteady 2D flows. Since the path line starting at (x, t) in a parametrization of τ is just $\phi(\mathrm{x}, t, \tau)$, we can compute every point by a quadrilinear interpolation in the sampled flow map. Note that this way, the path line's accuracy does *not* depend on the path line's sampling density: even for a sparse sampling, the points on the path line are correct (up to the accuracy of the initial flow map sampling). This is contrary to a numerical integration of path lines where the integration's step size influences the integration error. Besides the exploration via path lines, we also implemented a visualization via FTLE fields. The FTLE is a widely used scalar value that characterizes the separation of neighboring particles over time. For further information about FTLE, we refer to the work of Haller et al. [7,8] and Shadden et al. [15]. The FTLE field as well can be computed by a straightforward lookup in the discretized flow map. Given t and τ, we determine the FTLE field at the same spatial resolution as the sampled flow map. For this, we compute the flow map derivatives by central differences. Figure 4 shows a snapshot of our interactive viewer. The values t and τ are modified either by sliders or by interactively moving around in the (t, τ)-space. According to this, we update the path lines and the FTLE fields in interactive real-time. We implemented a toolset based on the concepts presented in this paper for interactive flow map modification.

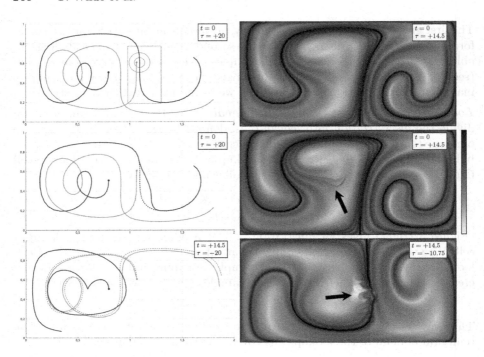

Fig. 5. Path lines and FTLE fields after modification with the translation tool.

6   Results and Discussion

We show the results as plots of selected path lines and FTLE fields. Timings were taken on an Intel Core i7-8700K CPU running 3.70 GHz with 32 GB of RAM. We executed all algorithms on a single core. The data set we use is the DOUBLE GYRE, a synthetic periodic 2D unsteady vector field introduced by Shadden et al. [15]. The DOUBLE GYRE is one of the most used benchmarks in Flow Visualization. Figure 4 shows path lines and the FTLE field for $t = 2.5$ and $\tau = 15$ for the DOUBLE GYRE. To obtain the discretized flow map, we sampled the domain with a resolution of 256×128 for $(x, y) \in [0.0, 2.0] \times [0.0, 1.0]$. We discretized the temporal dimension $t \in [0.0, 20.0]$ by 80 samples and $\tau \in [-20.0, 20.0]$ by 160 samples. This sums up to approximately $4.2 \cdot 10^8$ samples, leading to a memory usage of 6.5 GB for the discretized flow map. In a pre-computation step, we perform a second-order Runge-Kutta integration for each sample; this took about 70 min. In another pre-computation step, we compute the lookup-cells; this takes approx. 30 s and costs additional 1.6 GB of RAM. We show results for two different interactive modification tools.

Translation Tool: The first one performs a simple translation of flow map entries and is presented in Fig. 5. Top row shows path lines and FTLE field before modification. Top left also shows the modification tool with its inner and outer region by two black circles and the modified domain parts' spatial extent by

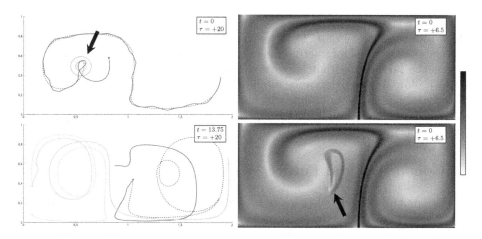

Fig. 6. Path lines and FTLE fields after modification with the rotation tool.

a red rectangle. The modification was manually performed in 56 repeated small translation steps in the area of $1.0 \leq x \leq 1.3$, $0.2 \leq y \leq 0.8$, $14.25 \leq t + \tau \leq 15.5$. In each step, about $5.2 \cdot 10^5$ entries were adapted, which took 0.13 s in average. After the process, $5.9 \cdot 10^6$ flow map entries were modified in total. The overall interactive modification took about 1.5 min. Figure 5 middle left shows a blue path line, which passes the modified area and an orange one, that is not influenced. Dashed lines indicate the original trajectories before modification. Middle right shows an FTLE field that differs from the original one. Path lines starting in the region marked with a white arrow at $t = 0$ will pass the modified area after $\tau = 14.5$. The global influence of the modification is even more evident in the images in the bottom row. Path lines starting in the modified area, with respect to space-time, take a different path over the whole integration time. This effect is also visible in the FTLE field. Please note, we decided to show only two carefully selected path lines to avoid visual clutter. The selected ones and the shown (t, τ)-combinations give a good impression of the global influence of (pseudo-)local modifications.

Rotation Tool: The second tool performs a clockwise rotation of entries around the center of the modification area. Figure 6 shows the modification performed on consecutive locations along the whole trajectory in space-time for a fixed $t = 0$ of the blue path line shown top left. We modified the flow map in the vicinity of the whole blue path line. This can also be seen with the green and yellow path lines shown bottom left, which start next to the blue line in space-time and take rather different paths. The arrow marks the modification tool, which is currently placed at time $t + \tau = 6.5$. The FTLE fields in the right column show the effect of modification at this specific location. All points starting in the area marked with a white arrow with $t = 0$ and $tau = 6.5$ map into the modified region. The modification was manually performed in 66 consecutive steps at different locations in space-time. On average, in each step $3.3 \cdot 10^6$ entries were adapted, which took an average of 0.71 s. The time needed for adaption is noticeable but still sufficient for an interactive process. The reason for the higher processing time is the larger area that is covered by the rotation tool. After the process, $3.9 \cdot 10^7$ flow map entries were modified in total. This means almost 10% of all samples had to be adapted, which clearly shows the high connectivity and complexity of the underlying flow map. The overall interactive modification with the rotation tool took about 3.0 min.

7   Conclusion and Future Work

Flow maps are a highly complex but powerful tool for flow representation. We expect flow map processing to be of more interest in future research. This will lead to more knowledge, a better understanding, new algorithms, and new applications considering the flow map. With this work, we want to go a step further in this direction. Flow map processing opens up new possibilities for efficient and effective Flow Visualization. In Sect. 3, we gave a compact overview of flow map properties and their relations to vector fields. In Sect. 4, we introduced an approach for flow map modifications based on space deformation. Although we stick to the 1D and 2D cases to explain, all presented concepts are valid for any dimension. We presented an implementation in Sect. 5 and 6. Future research could be related to more and better (interactive) tools for flow map processing, e.g., for smoothing, deformation, construction or simplification. Furthermore, better techniques to visualize the global behavior of flow maps in space-double-time are necessary. In the presented results, we modify the flow map of a 2D unsteady flow. Effectively this modification takes place in a highly connected 4D domain (x, y, t, τ). Due to the data's high connectivity, this can lead to unexpected results in areas currently not visible. This will even be a bigger problem for 3D flows and needs to be addressed in future research.

Acknowledgement. This work was partially supported by DFG grant TH 692/17-1

Appendix

Lemma. *If ϕ is flow map, then $\widetilde{\phi}$ defined by Eq. 9 is a flow map as well.*

Proof. To show that $\widetilde{\phi}$ is a glow map, we need to show the identity (Eq. 4) and additivity (Eq. 5) of $\widetilde{\phi}$:

$$\widetilde{\phi}(\mathbf{x}, t, 0) = \mathbf{y}(\phi(\mathbf{y}^{-1}(\mathbf{x}, t), t, 0), t) = \mathbf{y}(\mathbf{y}^{-1}(\mathbf{x}, t), t) = \mathbf{x}$$

$$\widetilde{\phi}(\widetilde{\phi}(\mathbf{x}, t, \tau_1), t + \tau_1, \tau_2)$$
$$= \mathbf{y}(\phi(\mathbf{y}^{-1}(\mathbf{y}(\phi(\mathbf{y}^{-1}(\mathbf{x}, t), t, \tau_1), t + \tau_1), t + \tau_1), t + \tau_1, \tau_2), t + \tau_1 + \tau_2)$$
$$= \mathbf{y}(\phi(\mathbf{y}^{-1}(\mathbf{x}, t), t, \tau_1 + \tau_2), t + \tau_1 + \tau_2) = \widetilde{\phi}(\mathbf{x}, t, \tau_1 + \tau_2) \qquad \square$$

References

1. Baeza, I., Günther, T.: Vector field topology of time-dependent flows in a steady reference frame. IEEE Trans. Visual Comput. Graphics **26**(1), 280–290 (2019)
2. Botsch, M., Kobbelt, L.: An intuitive framework for real-time freeform modeling. ACM Trans. Graph. **23**(3), 630–634 (2004)
3. Bujack, R., Middel, A.: State of the art in flow visualization in the environmental sciences. Environ. Earth Sci. **79**(2), 1–10 (2020). https://doi.org/10.1007/s12665-019-8800-4
4. Chen, G., Kwatra, V., Wei, L., Hansen, C.D., Zhang, E.: Design of 2D time-varying vector fields. IEEE Trans. Visual Comput. Graphics **18**(10), 1717–1730 (2012)
5. Von Funck, W., Theisel, H., Seidel, H.P.: Vector field based shape deformations. Trans. Graph. **25**(3), 1118–1125 (2006). (Proc. ACM SIGGRAPH)
6. Von Funck, W., Theisel, H., Seidel, H.P.: Explicit control of vector field based shape deformations. In: Proceedings of Pacific Graphics 2007 (2007)
7. Haller, G., Yuan, G.: Lagrangian coherent structures and mixing in 2D turbulence. Physica D **147**(3–4), 352–370 (2000)
8. Haller, G.: Lagrangian coherent structures. Annu. Rev. Fluid Mech. **47**, 137–162 (2015). https://doi.org/10.1146/annurev-fluid-010313-141322
9. Hlawatsch, M., Sadlo, F., Weiskopf, D.: Hierarchical line integration. IEEE Trans. Visual Comput. Graphics **17**(8), 1148–1163 (2011)
10. Hofmann, L., Sadlo, F.: The dependent vectors operator. CG Forum (2019)
11. Hummel, M., Bujack, R., Joy, K.I., Garth, C.: Error estimates for lagrangian flow field representations. In: 18th Eurographics Conference on Visualization (2016)
12. Laramee, R.S., Hauser, H., Doleisch, H., Vrolijk, B., Post, F.H., Weiskopf, D.: The state of the art in flow visualization: dense and texture-based techniques. In: Computer Graphics Forum (2004)
13. Laramee, R.S., Hauser, H., Zhao, L., Post, F.H.: Topology-based flow visualization, the state of the art. In: Hauser, H., Hagen, H., Theisel, H. (eds.) Topology-Based Methods in Visualization. Springer, Heidelberg (2007). https://doi.org/10.1007/978-3-540-70823-0_1
14. Salzbrunn, T., Wischgoll, T., Jänicke, H., Scheuermann, G.: The state of the art in flow visualization: partition-based techniques. In: Simulation and Visualization 2008 Proceedings (2008)
15. Shadden, S.C., Lekien, F., Marsden, J.E.: Definition and properties of Lagrangian coherent structures from finite-time Lyapunov exponents in two-dimensional aperiodic flows. Physica D: Nonlinear Phenom. **212**(3), 271–304 (2005). ISSN 0167-2789. https://doi.org/10.1016/j.physd.2005.10.007
16. Theisel, H.: Designing 2D vector fields of arbitrary topology. In: Computer Graphics Forum (Proceedings of Eurographics 2002), vol. 21 (2002)
17. Vaxman, A., et al.: Directional field synthesis, design, and processing. In: Computer Graphics Forum (2016)
18. Weinkauf, T., Theisel, H., Hege, H.C., Seidel, H.P.: Topological construction and visualization of higher order 3D vector fields. In: Computer Graphics Forum (2004)
19. Wilde, T., Rössl, C., Theisel, H.: Recirculation surfaces for flow visualization. IEEE Trans. Visual Comput. Graphics **25**(1), 946–955 (2018). (Proc. IEEE SciVis)
20. Zhang, E., Hays, J., Turk, G.: Interactive tensor field design and visualization on surfaces. IEEE Trans. Visual Comput. Graphics **13**(1), 94–107 (2007)
21. Zhang, E., Mischaikow, K., Turk, G.: Vector field design on surfaces. ACM Trans. Graph. **25**(4), 1294–1326 (2006)

GenExplorer: Visualizing and Comparing Gene Expression Levels via Differential Charts

Chau Pham$^{(\boxtimes)}$ ⃝, Vung Pham ⃝, and Tommy Dang ⃝

Texas Tech University, Texas, TX 79409, USA
{chaupham,vung.pham,tommy.dang}@ttu.edu

Abstract. This paper describes a visual interface for analyzing gene expression data generated from multiple biological samples under different controlled conditions. The tasks are to provide a comprehensive overview of thousands of genes under different states and have an intuitive way to narrow down genes with common behaviors. Our method involves using multidimensional projections and differential charts to help users analyze different data sets via a web-based interface. Incorporating these charts and other visualization techniques into our final design makes the application accessible to genetics analysts, as demonstrated in the two use cases in plant and cancer researches. We further discuss the feedback from domain experts and the limitations of our approach to accommodate gene exploration tasks.

Keywords: Gene expression · Abiotic stress · Cancer research · Differential charts · Venn diagram · Multidimensional projection

1 Introduction

Gene expression data generated from multiple samples are interesting and essential to the analysis of biological processes. The most common use of gene expression analysis is to compare expression levels of genes under different controlled conditions. For example, a table composed of expression values across all the libraries corresponding to the same *Arabidopsis Identificator* may contain many test conditions such as gene mutations. The mutations mean altering the DNA sequence that makes genes express differently compared to the natural conditions (wild type or WT) [11]. Another example, to study suppression of spontaneous carcinogenesis for curing cancer, different cross-bred mice were monitored and analyzed [3]. The experimental results require to compare and inspect samples of mice in different conditions.

Analyzing these data is nevertheless challenging due to the large number of genes that express significantly different under different conditions. With a lot of genes and many filter conditions, it is not trivial to make an overview and narrow down to the subset of genes of interest. Meanwhile, the development of user-friendly tools has not developed at the same pace with increasing Gene expression data. A dedicated interactive tool allowing to display and compare

© Springer Nature Switzerland AG 2020
G. Bebis et al. (Eds.): ISVC 2020, LNCS 12509, pp. 248–259, 2020.
https://doi.org/10.1007/978-3-030-64556-4_20

genes in sets of controlled conditions and also to insert humans into the discovery loop is desirable and essential to biologists. To ease the burden, we build an interactive website for tackling the problems discussed above.

The greatest practical challenge is to represent a vast amount of genes in a meaningful way and provide powerful filters for the biologist so that they can concentrate on a smaller set of interesting genes. In our work, we represent each condition test as a time series and show a pair of conditions simultaneously as a comparison chart. The chart then is colored to highlight the difference between the two test conditions. With many conditions, we have many pairs of normal and controlled conditions or comparison charts. For each chart, there is a filter button with four possible statuses (up-regulated, down-regulated, no change, both up and down-regulated) and a slider to support the filter process. Contributions of this work are listed as the following:

– We identify a list of important tasks for analyzing and understanding the genetics data through close collaborations and weekly conversations with the domain experts.
– We develop an interactive visual interface to handle a large amount of gene expression data. The interface contains various visual components to support different analysis tasks. We focus on representing the difference in values across a gene's conditions to highlight the up and down-regulated. An interactive Venn diagram and multidimensional projections are integrated into the application to visualize the high-level relationships among genes.
– Two case studies and expert feedback demonstrate how the system design evolved and how it can be used in biological analysis workflow.

2   Related Work

2.1   Gene Expression Analytics

There has been an extensive study on genetics visualizations in the literature, and various visualizations have been proposed to analyze and visualize genetics datasets. Meyer et al. presented MizBee [22], a multiscale synteny browser with interactive views of the hierarchical data to support the exploration of relationship types. Rutter et al. introduced visualization tools named *bigPint* [27], which mainly integrated parallel coordinate and scatter plot into an R package to work with RNA-seq datasets. The tools can identify genes of interest and patterns that may not otherwise detect with traditional modeling. Specifically, users can create modern and effective plots for large multivariate datasets, quickly examine the variability between all samples in the datasets, and assess the differences between treatment groups and replicate groups. *ReactionFlow* [6] focused pathway analysis allows analysts to filter, cluster, and select pathway components across linked views. It also supports researchers to analyze the complex nature of biological pathways [7], such as structural and causal relationships amongst proteins and biochemical reactions within a given pathway [17].

In other work, Reyes et al. proposed *GENAVi* [26], a web application for gene expression normalization, analysis, and visualization. The tool can help biologists in terms of normalization and differential expression analysis of human or mouse feature count level RNA-Seq data. It also provides some useful visualizations as a clustered heatmap and volcano plots. A thorough comparison of existing tools for gene expression normalization and analysis is also presented to highlight the common features supported by various tools. These tools also support a wide range of normalization methods [20] and differential expression analysis via user-friendly interfaces that allow genetics analysts to load their experimental data and perform RNA-seq analysis [18] of their own. Differential expression analysis aims to identify a subset of genes expressing significantly different under the test conditions [29]. In Sect. 3.1, we will discuss the unique features supported by our proposed prototype.

2.2   Serial Data Visualization

This section provides a quick overview of the most related researches on representing long sequential data. The first one is TensorBoard [30]. It is a browser-based application that presents training parameters, metrics, hyperparameters, and any statistics as time series. Javed et al. [14] survey a variety of line graph techniques involving multiple time series display and provide guidelines to find suitable methods when dealing with a temporal visualization application. Also, Moritz and Fisher proposed DenseLines [24] to calculate a discrete density representation of time series. Besides, Gogolou et al. examined how line- and color-encoding techniques affect what time series we perceive as similar. Specifically, the work compared three representative techniques, namely line charts, horizon graphs, and color fields. In contrast to the popular left to right metaphor, Weber et al. presented an approach to visualize time-series data based on spirals called Spiral Graph [33]. The technique supports both the visualization of nominal and quantitative data based on a similar visual metaphor and helps the human in the ability to detect underlying cyclic processes.

This project adopts a differential chart design to highlight the differences between the two charts with comparable data. We apply differential line graph visualization techniques instead of other methods to display the long sequences of gene expression data. The time aspect is considered as the gene names in ascending order according to the base condition. For this section's brevity, we defer further details regarding the difference between our approach and the existing ones in Sect. 6.

3   Research Methodology and Requirements

In this work, we adapted Data-Users-Tasks Design Triangle framework proposed by Miksch and Aigner [23]. We focused on tackling the three following questions.

- What kinds of data are the users working with? (data)
- Who are the users of the Visual Analytics solution(s)? (users)
- What are the (general) tasks of the users? (tasks)

3.1   Motivation

The goal of differential expression analysis is to identify genes whose expression differs under different conditions. For example, statistical testing can be used to decide whether differences in the read count of a given gene are greater than what would be expected is just due to chance, or it is worth further analysis. Another example is that some transcripts are being produced at a significantly higher or lower number in the tumor tissue than the healthy one. These differences in transcript production in aggregate comprise the differential expression that we want to focus on for the visualization task. Specifically, we consider two conditions in gene expressions: The base condition (blue curve on the top panel of Fig. 1) and the test condition (black curve, the second graph). Genetics analysts care more about the differences in expression rather than their absolute values [32]. In other words, finding genes that are differentially expressed between conditions is an essential part of understanding the molecular basis [29]. Thus, in differential expression analysis, we take the normalized read count data and perform statistical analysis to discover interesting changes in quantity between experimental groups and the controlled groups in terms of expression levels. As an attempt to make a focal point on the difference, we combine the expression values in two conditions into a single chart as depicted in Fig. 1).

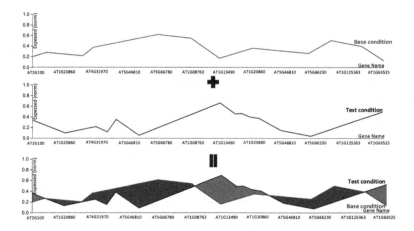

Fig. 1. The Differential Chart is generated by overlaying two conditions and then coloring in green (*up-regulated* genes) vs. orange (*down-regulated* genes). (Color figure online)

3.2   Data

In this work, we focused on RNA-Seq data in genetic fields. Domain experts provide the data that includes cancer datasets containing replicates of mice genetics in both normal and test condition for *p53* cancer (we defer the further details in Sect. 5). There has been intensive work on differential expression analysis methods from RNA-Seq data, such as DESeq2 [20]. The differential expression analysis usually involves five steps, one of which is the normalization step for raw read count data [5]. The normalization of RNA-Seq data has proven essential to ensure accurate inferences and replication of findings. Generally, we need an appropriate approach to dealing with data issues such as differences in library preparation across samples, sequencing errors, mapping and annotation bias, gene length, and sequencing depth. Such unwanted noises impede the accuracy of statistical inferences and, in turn, mislead the analysis results. Thus, thoughtful considerations are needed in determining how to normalize the raw data [1].

3.3   Users

Experts in the genetic area are the primary users of this tool. Therefore, a detailed understanding of what biologists expect and are interested in the tool is the top priority [4] to develop and design an effective visual analytics solution. Furthermore, we also consider the visual solution designs so that casual users who do not have a solid background in the fields can also use the tool.

3.4   Visualization Tasks

Shneiderman's mantra [28] suggests three-step processes for information visualization: "overview first, zoom and filter, and then details-on-demand". Moreover, information systems should allow users to perform analysis tasks that capture the requirements from a specific application domain [2]. In gene expression analysis, a comprehensive understanding of tasks performed by domain researchers plays an important role in the design and implementation of an effective visualization tool. Through close collaborations with domain experts, we have identified a set of important tasks for analyzing the gene expression data:

- **T1:** Overview: Provide a holistic overview of gene expression data under different controlled conditions [15].
- **T2:** Details on Demand: The selected set of genes are expanded for further comparisons under different controlled conditions [2].
- **T3:** Filter and Rank genes by various criteria [12].
- **T4:** Classify genes based on their expression data and represent the relationship among gene groups in an interactive manner [15].
- **T5:** Download the set of interest genes with the respective expression values for reporting and reproducibility of analysis.

4   *GenExplorer* Designs and Visual Components

4.1   Charts

We use differential charts to show the visual comparisons of how genes express under the test vs. natural conditions. In particular, gene names are listed from left to right while their normalized expressed values are projected vertically. The solid black curve represents expressed value across genes for a conditioned test. These genes are sorted in ascending order according to the base condition for easier to compare across conditions.

4.2   Control Panel

Mode Selection. There are various comparison modes (depending on the input data) in the control panel: *WT(s) Comparison*: Compare each conditioned test w.r.t the optimal condition: wild type (WT). *Custom Mode*: Users can choose to analyze and compare any pair of conditions (visualization task **T2**).

Filter Buttons and Sliders. We collectively use a button and a slider to define the condition and the threshold of significant differences. Figure 2 shows four possible filtering selections for each pair of test conditions: *wtlp6* vs. *wthp6* in this case of the plant genes are under two different conditions (low Phosphate vs. high Phosphate and *pH 6 medium*). The green background allows us to get all the up-regulated genes in the test condition more than the threshold set by the slider below. Similarly, with the orange (Fig. 2c), we get all the down-regulated genes more than 0.1. The gray (Fig. 2d) background helps to filter non-expressed genes.

Fig. 2. Possible selections for comparing *wtlp5* vs. *wthp6* with a slider threshold of 0.1.

Preset Table. We pre-calculate the number of genes that satisfied the slider settings for each filtering combination and report them in *Preset Table*. On the top are the most popular combinations. When selecting any row of the data table, other visualizations are updated based on the new filters (**T3**).

Overview Panel. This panel provides the supervised vs. unsupervised summaries of the data sets. In the supervised mode, the Venn diagram highlights various gene collections (which are labeled, such as EXP for expression factors, from an independent experiment by the domain experts) and how they intersect (**T1**). The Venn diagram is interactive: users can also select any overlapping area to narrow down a subset of common genes for further analysis. From the Venn diagram in Fig. 3(a), we can see an overlap between the *EXP* set and the *LowCPM* set. We can also confirm that *DE* set (Differently Expressed Genes) is a complete subset of *EXP* set (Expressed Genes). It is also clear that our focus gene *STOP1* belongs to the *EXP* set. Notably, *LowLog2Fold*, which contains the log fold change ranging from −0.5 to 0.5, has overlapped with other sets when it should have no overlap.

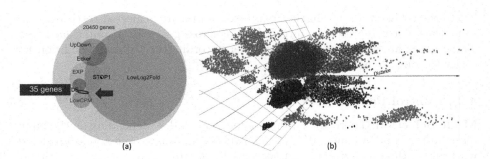

Fig. 3. Overview panel in two modes: (a) Supervised: Gene collections via lab experiments, and (b) Unsupervised: Gene clusters via k-means on expression levels.

In the unsupervised mode, genes are first clustered (using k-means algorithm) based on their expression values on the input conditions. Then, we apply multidimensional projection techniques, such as Principle Component Analysis [13], t-SNE [31], or UMAP [21] to project the high-dimensional data into the lower dimensional space (from 12D to 3D in this case). Now, it is interesting to compare and verify if the gene collections obtained from two independent approaches are consistent (visualization task **T4**).

4.3   Data Table

The Data Table and the charts show only 500 genes at a time. To navigate more genes satisfied filtering conditions, users simply click on *Next/Previous* buttons. We can opt to show the raw data (vs. normalized data) by checking the *Raw data* checkbox. Users can export the current data table as *csv* file by clicking on the *Export Table* button for reporting and reproducibility purpose (**T5**).

5   Evaluation

5.1   Use Case 1: Plant Genetics

For this case study, we investigate 20,450 plant genes experimented under 12 conditions, with *STOP1* mutant. The tested conditions are abbreviated as *wt*: wild type, *stop1*: knock-out mutant background for the transcription factor, *hp*: high phosphate supply (1 mM), *lp*: low phosphate supply (0 mM), *Al*: Al stress pH 5. *Fe*: Fe excess supplied to the medium pH 5. We first investigate the differently expressed genes (the *DE* red circle from the Venn diagram). Figure 4 shows 210 genes in this DE set: most of these genes are in green (up-regulated). Especially in the high *Fe* soil (the bottom chart), these 210 DE genes expressed much more compared to the natural condition.

To filter all higher values of STOP1 mutant condition compared to its responding wild type, we go to the third tab in the control panel. Figure 5

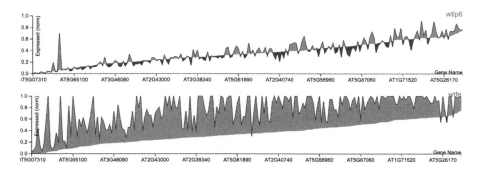

Fig. 4. Differently Expressed Genes (the DE set) on the *wtfe* vs. *wtlp6* conditions.

shows the example where the filtered genes up-regulated in the *s1lp6* condition, but down-regulated in the *s1fe* condition, with the thresholds of 0.15 (we get a list of 9 genes in this case). These observations are important to biologists who want to control the plant behaviors by adjusting their environment settings.

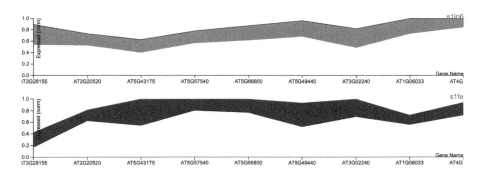

Fig. 5. Genes with up/down regulations at least 15% in STOP1 vs. wild type condition.

5.2 Use Case 2: Cancer Gene Expression

In our second use case, the cancer data, provided by *University Medical Center*, contains multi-replicates of mice in both normal and test conditions. For this dataset, the first column is the *symbol*, the next four columns are the *replicate 1* conditions, including the base condition, *Wild Type 1* (*WT1*). The last four columns are the corresponding conditions for *replicate 2*. Using the filters, we narrow down to the list of genes that are not expressed on *P53KO-O1* but highly expressed on *p53KO-O-CAS1* and *p53KO-O-RAS1*. Figure 6 depicted the 24 genes that satisfy the filtering conditions above. It turns out that most of them are up-regulated in *p53KO-O-CAS1* and *p53KO-O-RAS1* conditions.

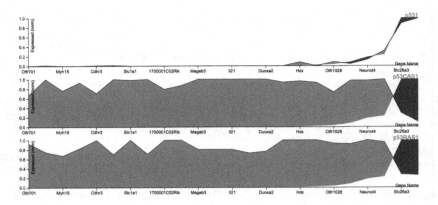

Fig. 6. Visualizing 24 genes which are not expressed on *P53KO-O1* but highly expressed on *p53KO-O-CAS1* and *p53KO-O-RAS1* conditions.

6 Discussion

6.1 Comparisons to Other Tools

Table 1. Summary of our *GenExplorer* vs. existing gene expression visualizations.

	GenExplorer	START	iDEP	DEBrowser	DEGUST	DEIVA	DEApp	GENAVi
Hosting								
GUI	✓	✓	✓	✓	✓	✓	✓	✓
URL hosted	✓	✓	✓	No	✓	✓	✓	✓
Active	✓	✓	✓	✓	✓	✓	✓	✓
run from R	No	✓	No	✓	No	No	✓	✓
Open source	✓	✓	✓	✓	✓	✓	✓	✓
Docker	No	No	✓	No	No	No	No	✓
User data								
Upload	✓	✓	✓	✓	✓	✓	✓	✓
Prefiltering	✓	No	✓	✓	✓	No	✓	✓
Bulk Feature Selection	✓	No	No	No	No	✓	No	✓
Normalization	✓	✓	✓	✓	No	No	✓	✓
Visualization								
T1: Overview	✓	✓	✓	✓	✓	✓	✓	✓
T2: Detail comparison	✓	No	No	✓	✓	✓	✓	✓
T3: Ranking&Filtering	✓	✓	✓	✓	✓	✓	✓	✓
T4: Gene relations	✓	No	No	No	No	No	No	No
T5: Exporting&Reporting	✓	No	✓	No	No	No	No	✓

To show the advantages and the disadvantages of our technique, we make an overview comparison between our work and other prominent tools, namely START [25], iDEP [9], DEBrowser [16], DEGUST [8], DEIVA [10], DEApp [19], and GENAVi [26] as in Table 1. These tools, including ours, have similar functionality to one another in some aspects. For the comparison, we split into different criteria, such as Hosting, User Data [26], and Visualization.

6.2 Expert Feedback

We solicited qualitative responses about *GenExplorer* from four experts from two genetics research domains: Functional Genomics of abiotic stress and cancer drug development. All have at least ten years of experience in their research domain. The informal study started with a quick description (around 10–15 min) of the main visual components and their basic functionalities to familiarize users with the main GUI of *GenExplorer*. Then the experts are free to use *GenExplorer* for their own analysis before providing feedback. We got some useful comments from experts in the domain. In general, they are interested in the interactive Venn Diagram and expect to have an option for uploading simultaneously many different input files to the Venn diagram. Some gave advice on the layout and asked for an option to transpose the line graph. Others focused on the line graph and had comments on the normalization as they suggested to have more options for this task, e.g., adding the z-score normalization.

One expert in cancer research commented: "The Preset Table gives a quick idea about the popularity of various combinations of filtering conditions under the given threshold of the master slider". And the colors should be updated to red (for increase) vs. blue (for decrease) instead of green vs. orange. We are iteratively working with these scientists to improve the prototype and make it accessible to wider audiences working in the genetics domains.

7 Conclusion

This paper presents a simple but efficient way of comparing gene expression data under different test conditions. The application is designed to handle a large number of genes, focusing on the variances of gene expression data under different controlled conditions. Interactive features are supported to help users navigate a large number of genes and narrow down smaller sets of genes of interests. The work has been developed through close collaborations with experts in two genetics application domains: Plant genetics and cancer gene expression. The results show that the application may shed light on experiment results by providing interactive tools for biologists to analyze potential genes of interests.

The demo video, web application, and source codes of our work are available on our *Github* at https://git.io/JJT0i. In future work, we will integrate more normalization options and continue to work with the experts to improve the visualization tasks.

References

1. Abbas-Aghababazadeh, F., Li, Q., Fridley, B.L.: Comparison of normalization approaches for gene expression studies completed with high-throughput sequencing. PLoS ONE **13**(10), 1–21 (2018). https://doi.org/10.1371/journal.pone.0206312

2. Amar, R., Eagan, J., Stasko, J.: Low-level components of analytic activity in information visualization. In: Proceedings of the IEEE Symposium on Information Visualization, pp. 15–24 (2005)
3. Awasthi, S., et al.: Rlip depletion prevents spontaneous neoplasia in TP53 null mice. Proc. Natl. Acad. Sci. **115**(15), 3918–3923 (2018). https://doi.org/10.1073/pnas.1719586115. https://www.pnas.org/content/115/15/3918
4. Collins, C., et al.: Guidance in the human-machine analytics process. Visual Inform. **2**(3), 166–180 (2018). https://doi.org/10.1016/j.visinf.2018.09.003. http://www.sciencedirect.com/science/article/pii/S2468502X1830041X
5. Costa-Silva, J., Domingues, D., Lopes, F.: RNA-Seq differential expression analysis: an extended review and a software tool. PLoS ONE **12**, e0190152 (2017). https://doi.org/10.1371/journal.pone.0190152
6. Dang, T.N., Murray, P., Aurisano, J., Forbes, A.G.: Reactionflow: an interactive visualization tool for causality analysis in biological pathways. BMC Proc. **9**(6), S6 (2015). https://doi.org/10.1186/1753-6561-9-S6-S6
7. Dang, T.N., Murray, P., Forbes, A.G.: PathwayMatrix: visualizing binary relationships between proteins in biological pathways. BMC Proc. **9**(6), S3 (2015). https://doi.org/10.1186/1753-6561-9-S6-S3
8. drpowell: Degust tool. http://victorian-bioinformatics-consortium.github.io/degust/
9. Ge, S.X., Son, E.W., Yao, R.: iDEP: an integrated web application for differential expression and pathway analysis of RNA-Seq data. BMC Bioinform. **19**(1), 534 (2018). https://doi.org/10.1186/s12859-018-2486-6
10. Harshbarger, J., Kratz, A., Carninci, P.: DEIVA: a web application for interactive visual analysis of differential gene expression profiles. BMC Genom. **18**(1), 47 (2017). https://doi.org/10.1186/s12864-016-3396-5
11. Herrera-Estrella, L.: My journey into the birth of plant transgenesis and its impact on modern plant biology. Plant Biotechnol. J. (2020). https://doi.org/10.1111/pbi.13319. https://onlinelibrary.wiley.com/doi/abs/10.1111/pbi.13319
12. Hochheiser, H., Shneiderman, B.: Dynamic query tools for time series data sets: timebox widgets for interactive exploration. Inf. Visual. **3**(1), 1–18 (2004). https://doi.org/10.1145/993176.993177. http://dx.doi.org/10.1145/993176.993177
13. Hotelling, H.: Analysis of a complex of statistical variables into principal components. J. Educ. Psychol. **24**(6), 417 (1933)
14. Javed, W., McDonnel, B., Elmqvist, N.: Graphical perception of multiple time series. IEEE Trans. Visual Comput. Graphics **16**(6), 927–934 (2010). https://doi.org/10.1109/TVCG.2010.162
15. Keim, D.A.: Information visualization and visual data mining. IEEE Trans. Visual Comput. Graphics **1**, 1–8 (2002)
16. Kucukural, A., Yukselen, O., Ozata, D.M., Moore, M.J., Garber, M.: DEBrowser: interactive differential expression analysis and visualization tool for count data. BMC Genom. **20**(1), 6 (2019). https://doi.org/10.1186/s12864-018-5362-x
17. Lex, A., et al.: Entourage: visualizing relationships between biological pathways using contextual subsets. IEEE Trans. Visual Comput. Graphics **19**(12), 2536–2545 (2013). http://entourage.caleydo.org
18. Li, P., Piao, Y., Shon, H.S., Ryu, K.H.: Comparing the normalization methods for the differential analysis of Illumina high-throughput RNA-Seq data. BMC Bioinform. **16**(1), 347 (2015). https://doi.org/10.1186/s12859-015-0778-7
19. Li, Y., Andrade, J.: DEApp: an interactive web interface for differential expression analysis of next generation sequence data. Source Code Biol. Med. **12**(1), 2 (2017). https://doi.org/10.1186/s13029-017-0063-4

20. Love, M.I., Huber, W., Anders, S.: Moderated estimation of fold change and dispersion for RNA-Seq data with DESeq2. Genome Biol. **15**(12), 550 (2014). https://doi.org/10.1186/s13059-014-0550-8
21. McInnes, L., Healy, J., Melville, J.: UMAP: uniform manifold approximation and projection for dimension reduction (2018)
22. Meyer, M., Munzner, T., Pfister, H.: MizBee: a multiscale synteny browser. IEEE Trans. Visual Comput. Graphics **15**(6), 897–904 (2009). https://doi.org/10.1109/TVCG.2009.167
23. Miksch, S., Aigner, W.: A matter of time: applying a data-users-tasks design triangle to visual analytics of time-oriented data. Comput. Graph. **38**, 286–290 (2014). https://doi.org/10.1016/j.cag.2013.11.002
24. Moritz, D., Fisher, D.: Visualizing a million time series with the density line chart. arXiv abs/1808.06019 (2018)
25. Nelson, J.W., Sklenar, J., Barnes, A.P., Minnier, J.: The START app: a web-based RNAseq analysis and visualization resource. Bioinformatics **33**(3), 447–449 (2017). https://doi.org/10.1093/bioinformatics/btw624. 28171615[pmid]
26. Reyes, A.L.P., et al.: GENAVi: a shiny web application for gene expression normalization, analysis and visualization. BMC Genom. **20**(1), 745 (2019). https://doi.org/10.1186/s12864-019-6073-7
27. Rutter, L., Moran Lauter, A.N., Graham, M.A., Cook, D.: Visualization methods for differential expression analysis. BMC Bioinform. **20**(1), 458 (2019). https://doi.org/10.1186/s12859-019-2968-1
28. Shneiderman, B.: Designing the User Interface: Strategies for Effective Human-Computer Interaction, 3rd edn. Addison-Wesley Longman Publishing Co., Boston (1997)
29. Soneson, C., Delorenzi, M.: A comparison of methods for differential expression analysis of RNA-Seq data. BMC Bioinform. **14**(1), 91 (2013). https://doi.org/10.1186/1471-2105-14-91
30. tensorboard: Tensorbtensorboard: Tensorflow's visualization toolkit. https://www.tensorflow.org/tensorboard
31. Van Der Maaten, L., Hinton, G.: Visualizing data using t-SNE. J. Mach. Learn. Res. **9**, 2579–2605 (2008)
32. Wang, T., Li, B., Nelson, C.E., Nabavi, S.: Comparative analysis of differential gene expression analysis tools for single-cell RNA sequencing data. BMC Bioinform. **20**(1), 40 (2019). https://doi.org/10.1186/s12859-019-2599-6
33. Weber, M., Alexa, M., Müller, W.: Visualizing time-series on spirals. In: Proceedings of the IEEE Symposium on Information Visualization 2001 (INFOVIS 2001), INFOVIS 2001, p. 7. IEEE Computer Society, USA (2001)

Video Analysis and Event Recognition

An Event-Based Hierarchical Method for Customer Activity Recognition in Retail Stores

Jiahao Wen[1]([✉]), Luis Guillen[2], Muhammad Alfian Amrizal[2], Toru Abe[3], and Takuo Suganuma[3]

[1] Graduate School of Information Sciences, Tohoku University, Sendai, Japan
jh-wen@ci.cc.tohoku.ac.jp
[2] Research Institute of Electrical Communication, Tohoku University, Sendai, Japan
[3] Cyberscience Center, Tohoku University, Sendai, Japan

Abstract. Customer Activity (CA) provides valuable information for marketing. CA is a collective name of customer information from on-the-spot observation in retail environments. Existing methods of Customer Activity Recognition (CAR) recognize CA by specialized end-to-end (e2e) models. Consequently, when marketing requires changing recognition targets, specialized e2e models are not reconfigurable to fit different marketing demands unless rebuilding the models entirely. Besides, redundant computation in the existing CAR system leads to low efficiency. Also, the low maintainability of the CAR system results in lots of modifications when updating methods in the system. In this research, we decompose behaviors into several primitive units called "event". We propose an event-based CAR method to achieve reconfigurability and design a hierarchy to solve issues about redundancy and maintainability. The evaluation results show that our proposed method can adapt and perform better than existing methods, which fits different marketing demands.

Keywords: Retail environments · Customer activities · Activity recognition · Hierarchical activity model

1 Introduction

1.1 Background

In retail stores, various customer information is required to support marketing. Traditional retail only uses the purchase information to analyze purchasing behavior from the records [1]. However, purchase records only reveal results instead of the process of deciding the purchase. As this process would probably reveal the reasons for purchase, it is valuable for marketing analysis. Therefore, a solution called "smart retail" installs ubiquitous cameras to collect the shopping process data. Moreover, despite the large size of real-time data, machine learning models can efficiently and accurately handle them to get information about

© Springer Nature Switzerland AG 2020
G. Bebis et al. (Eds.): ISVC 2020, LNCS 12509, pp. 263–275, 2020.
https://doi.org/10.1007/978-3-030-64556-4_21

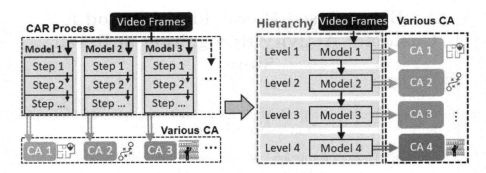

Fig. 1. Structure of existing CAR system (left) and proposed CAR system (right)

the shopping process [1–5]. In this research, the shopping process information is named "Customer Activity" (CA). CA is a collective name of customer information from on-the-spot observation in retail environments. Usually, CA contains information, among others, of the customer's location, trajectory, behavior.

1.2   Problems in Existing CAR System

Many methods [6] have been proposed for Customer Activity Recognition (CAR). They recognize various CAs mainly from the visual input [1–5,7–13]. However, none of them describe the structure of their CAR systems. Therefore, there is no way to infer the compatibility with other CAR systems, as shown on the left side of Fig. 1. Since the CAR system serves marketing, it should satisfy the malleability of different demands.

Problem 1: Models are Not Reconfigurable
The recognition targets vary in different development phases and conditions. Thus, different CAR results are required. However, these CAR methods mainly use machine learning-based end-to-end (e2e) models to recognize CA from video frames, specialized e2e models make the model impossible to be reconfigured for different target recognition. For instance, a model can recognize if a customer is selecting products. But if the requirements change so that the model is required to recognize whether a customer is selecting products either by a single or both hands, the original model is no longer useful. Consequently, new training data should be collected to train the model again, which is time-consuming.

Problem 2: System has Redundant Computation
As shown in Fig. 1, all models share the same visual input. Therefore, there might be some similar steps in different models during processing video frames. For example, common models for customer behavior recognition include locating customers in the frame, which is also computed by the people detection model. Thus, the computation of locating customers is repeated. This leads to redundancy in the CAR system, which results in low efficiency.

Problem 3: System has Low Maintainability

To achieve better performance of the CAR system, it is necessary to update the system to utilize different methods in different situations. But, the existing CAR systems do not have a clear division of tasks in their CAR models, and the output CA is not uncategorized, which leads to the existence of some common steps in different models. Therefore, updating methods in the system should modify all these common steps, which results in the system's low maintainability.

1.3   Solutions

In this paper, we categorize output CA in existing methods. According to the CA category, we design a four-level hierarchy, as shown in Fig. 1, which specifies the division of CAR tasks. While the hierarchy solves Problems 2 and 3, we propose a reconfigurable behavior recognition method based on the hierarchy to solve Problem 1.

Solution to Problem 1: Though CAR of every type of CA should be reconfigurable, in this research, we only achieve a reconfigurable method for customer behavior recognition. To design a reconfigurable model in this structure, we decompose a complex behavior into the permutation and combination of several primitive units, called "event". The proposed method recognizes events instead of behaviors. Therefore, redefining the permutation and combination of events can easily reconfigure behavior outputs.

Solution to Problem 2: Visual data is processed level by level in the hierarchy in Fig. 1. Each level receives its previous level's output as its input. Therefore, every level processes different types of data, which means no repeated process. Thus, redundant computation can be avoided by this hierarchy.

Solution to Problem 3: According to Table 1, we categorize various CAs into several levels, which provides a clear division of tasks. This avoids common steps between models. Therefore, updating any level does not influence the other levels. In other words, the hierarchy solves Problem 3.

We evaluate the hierarchy by adapting to three different marketing demands. The results show that our proposed hierarchy can fit different marketing demands easier than existing methods.

2   Related Work

The related work on CAR is categorized in Table 1 by the output of those methods. It reveals that current methods mostly detect/recognize the object's location, movement, and customer behavior. The column of "Content" refers to the detailed classification of outputs. These methods achieved good performance in their particular cases. However, once the CAR system is built with these methods to get outputs of each category, it forms the structure on the left side of Fig. 1, because of incompatible methods and sharing the same visual data as input. Therefore, it leads to the three problems explained above.

Table 1. Output CAs in existing methods

Category	Content	Related methods
Object's location	Body (region of the whole body)	[1–3, 7–19]
	Body part (hands, arms)	[1, 5]
	Other object (product, basket, etc.)	[1, 5]
Object's movement	Object/Pixel's motion feature	[1–3, 5, 10, 11]
	Object's trajectory	[13]
Customer behavior	Passing by/No interest	[1, 10]
	Viewing the shelf	[1, 3]
	Turn to the shelf	[1]
	Pick a product from shelf	[1, 2, 10, 11, 13]
	Pick nothing from shelf (Touch)	[1, 2, 11]
	Return a product to the shelf	[1, 10, 11]
	Put a product into cart/basket	[1]
	Holding a product	[3]
	Browsing a product on the hand	[2, 3]
	Fit next to you & check how it looks & try on & take off (in clothes shop)	[2]

For methods in the category "Customer Behavior", their models require time-consuming training, and the trained models are specialized, which means Problem 1 "Models are not reconfigurable".

On the other hand, most methods in the category "customer behavior" contain the computation of locating and tracking customers, which has been done in methods of the other two categories. This leads to Problem 2 "System has redundant computation".

In addition, these methods do not have a clear division of tasks, which results in incompatibility with other methods. In [3], it even regards the location of hand which is position information as customer behavior because the output CAs are not categorized. Therefore, updating methods in a system consists of these methods is difficult. This refers to Problem 3 "System has low maintainability".

3   Proposal

To solve Problems 2 and 3, we design a hierarchical structure to specify the division of CAR tasks and categorize CAs. After the hierarchy, we introduce our proposed method for reconfigurable behavior recognition, which is the solution to Problem 1.

3.1   Hierarchy

In Table 1, we categorize the output CAs and notice that existing CAR methods mainly output object location, object trajectory, and customer behavior. Apart

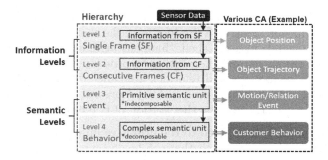

Fig. 2. Proposed hierarchy

from these three types of outputs, we add a new data type called "event", representing primitive units of behaviors. With "event" and three types of data of existing methods, we design a hierarchy in Fig. 2. It includes "Single Frame", "Consecutive Frame", "Event", and "Behavior". Among them, level 1 "Single Frame", which is in the top place, is the most basic. Data flows through levels from top to bottom. Therefore, each level receives output CA from its previous level as the input.

In the hierarchy, we assume that level 1 and 2 are information levels, which extract objective information from the sensor data. Level 3 and 4 are semantic levels, which learn to understand the information from level 1 and 2 subjectively. Therefore, level 1 and 2 output data of successive values, which represent the data observed from the objective world, while level 3 and 4 provide discrete values, which compress the redundant part of data together to show the comprehension of the objective information.

Level 1 "Single Frame": This most basic level of the hierarchy refers to the information that can be extracted from a single frame. For example, the output CA can be the objects' position. The object refers to any object in the frame, such as the content in Table 1. Thus, the model for extracting information from a single frame is supposed to be implemented into this level. For the case of object detection, a model of detecting objects from sensor data should be implemented.

Level 2 "Consecutive Frame": This level refers to the information extracted from consecutive frames, such as the content in Table 1. Compared to level 1, this level tends to find the relation of data, which has been extracted in level 1, between several frames. Usually, the pixel-based method, such as optical flow estimation, and the coordinate-based tracking method are implemented into this level.

Level 3 "Event": This level is inspired by [20] that defines human behavior as a composition of multiple events. An event refers to a single low-level spatiotemporal entity that cannot be further decomposed. Thus, we utilize the name "event" and define it as a primitive semantic unit that cannot be decomposed. In this research, an event can be the motion of one object or relation between several objects. Moreover, behavior is regarded as the composition of several events. For instance, the behavior "Pick up a product from the shelf" can be decomposed as the motion "put hands into the shelf" happens at first, then, the motion "take out hands from the shelf" and the relation "a product is following hands" occur concurrently. These motions and relations are called "Event". Therefore, there are two types of events, motion events (ME) represent the motion of an object, and relation events (RE) describe the relation of two objects.

Level 4 "Behavior": Compared to the primitive unit "event", the behavior is defined as a complex semantic unit that can be decomposed as several events. As its name implies, this level is supposed to do tasks about behavior recognition.

Compared to the existing CAR system's structure, this hierarchy specifies a clear division of tasks. Level 1 and 2 are responsible for extracting objective information from sensor data. Then, level 3 and 4 comprehend the objective information to get a semantic understanding of the data. Each level outputs one type of CA. Figure 2 shows the example outputs of each level. Each level processes different data types, and the computation for a particular type of CA is integrated into one level. Thus, this design avoids redundant computation and makes the methods in different levels independent. Therefore, updating the methods of any level does not influence the other levels, which shows high maintainability.

Besides, the proposed hierarchy does not specify methods in each level. Therefore, as long as the method completes each level's work, any method can be utilized in this level.

3.2   Event-Based Method: Level 3

The hierarchy solves Problems 2 and 3. In the hierarchy, we define the behavior recognition as recognizing events and matching a particular combination of events to recognize the behavior. To solve Problem 1, we propose a reconfigurable customer behavior recognition method based on events. We assume the input is objects' trajectories, which is the objective information from level 2. Therefore, our method is supposed to comprehend trajectory information to get MEs and REs. Understanding objective information to get semantic units requires a process to transfer successive values into discrete values. Thus, we separate the method into trajectory segmentation and symbolization.

Trajectory Segmentation: It means dividing the trajectory into several segments. If a part of the trajectory has a similar direction, it is regarded as a segment. For MEs and REs, different methods of trajectory segmentation are applied due to their different properties.

For MEs, they require that each segment has a similar direction. Thus, we apply DynMDL [21] to divide the trajectory by direction. For REs, the segment should include a similar part of two trajectories. Therefore, we design a value named "difference" to describe the similarity of two trajectories. We accumulate each corresponding point's distance in two trajectories. The average accumulated

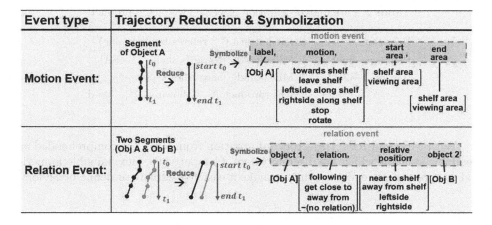

Fig. 3. Trajectory reduction and symbolization

distance is considered as the difference between the two trajectories. The trajectories are divided according to their difference value. Additionally, to reduce computation, we only handle the trajectories of some specific objects.

Trajectory Symbolization: The object moves in a similar direction in each segment. To compress the information and make it readable, we symbolize the segment into a four-dimension vector. As shown in Fig. 3, each segment is firstly reduced to a vector of the start and end. Then, the vector is symbolized to get MEs and REs.

(**ME**)**Label:** An object's identity, which can be the name or id of an object.
(**ME**)**Motion:** An object's moving direction. Thus, it is determined by the vector's direction. The "left-side/right-side" is one's left/right side when facing the shelf. These symbols represent the direction relative to the shelf because a behavior consists of events, and all the behaviors in existing methods are related to the product shelf.
(**ME**)**Start Area & End Area:** The located area of the reduced vector's endpoints. Each frame is divided into two areas, viewing area (VA) and shelf area (SA). VA includes the area where the customer is close enough to the shelf to interact with products on the shelf. SA includes the region of the whole shelf and all products on the shelf.

(**RE**)**Label of object 1 & 2:** The label of two objects.
(**RE**)**Relation:** The relation of two objects. We design three types of relations. However, only the "following" is implemented currently, which means an object is following another one. Another two relations refer to an object is getting close to/away from another one.
(**RE**)**Relative Position:** The relative position of two objects. The product shelf is the reference in the comparison. Compared to object 2, object 1 can be nearer to/away from the shelf. When the distance to the shelf is similar, object 1 can be on the left-side/right-side of object 2 from the shelf's view.

Table 2. Formulated definition of behavior "pick a product"

Behavior	Event pattern ([*] referes to any value)
Pick a product	1. ME: [hand], [towards shelf], [*→SA]
(Order: 1→2&3)	2. ME: [hand], [leave shelf], [SA→*]
	3. RE: [product A], [following], [*], [hand]

With MEs and REs, trajectory information from level 2 is comprehended as readable symbols which are discrete values. Compared to unexplainable numerical features, these readable symbols make it easier to explain or define behaviors.

3.3 Event-Based Method: Level 4

To achieve reconfigurable behavior recognition, we decompose behaviors into events and match these events instead of recognizing behaviors from pixel features. Therefore, changing the composed events can easily reconfigure behavior recognition. In level 4, we predefine behaviors as event patterns, and match the composed events from the results of level 3.

In Fig. 4, yellow blocks show that each behavior is predefined as a particular pattern of events. "→" specifies the chronological order of events. Events on the left side of the arrow happen at first. "&" means adjacent events occur concurrently. To arrange all events, we use the timeline because events happen in chronological order. Figure 4 shows that we match event patterns from events in the timeline to recognize behaviors.

Table 2 shows the formulated definition of behavior "pick a product". Firstly, ME 1 occurs, which is explained as "A hand is moving towards shelf from any area to the shelf area". Then, ME 2 happens, which represents "A hand is leaving the shelf from the shelf area to any area". Concurrently, RE 3 happens, which means "The product A is following hand at any relative position". Figure 4 shows an example of matching "pick a product" from timelines. For the timeline, the latest event $i+2$ matches ME 2, and $i+3$ matches RE 3. Since the latest events

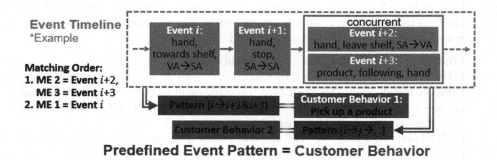

Fig. 4. Define & match customer behavior by event pattern (Color figure online)

are matched, the algorithm continues matching previous events. Then, ME 1 is matched by event i. The behavior "Pick a product" is recognized.

Behaviors are decomposed as events. Therefore, even with the same events, we can recognize another behavior by changing the order of the composed events. Namely, with this event-based method, we achieve a reconfigurable customer behavior recognition, which solves Problem 1.

4 Evaluation

4.1 Implementation Experiment

For level 1, we use top-view video as the input to avoid occlusion. Unfortunately, we did not find any existing dataset about the top-view video for customer behaviors. Therefore, we build a retail laboratory environment to collect top-view videos to evaluate our proposed method. Figure 5 shows that an RGB camera takes images from the above of the shelf. Camera frames are divided into the viewing area and shelf area. Videos are collected at a public activity, where random participants are requested to pick at least one provided product from the shelf. Besides, we assume that each participant does not interact with another person. Eventually, 19 videos from 19 participants, including 10648 frames with the FPS of 30, are collected and manually labeled for evaluation. Considering the various products, we choose four kinds of products which include two hard objects and two soft objects. Finally, person, hand, and four products are labeled.

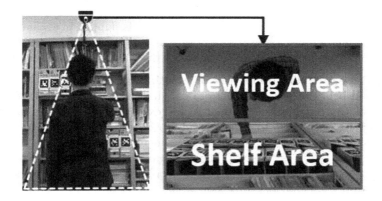

Fig. 5. Camera installation and input image

Table 3. Event patterns of six common behaviors

Step	Behavior	Event pattern ([*] referes to any value)
Step 1	Walking: walking in VA (1)	1. ME: [person], not [stop], [VA→VA]
	Viewing: stop and view products (1)	1. ME: [person], [stop], [VA→VA]
	Browse: browse a product on hands (1,2)	1. ME: [person], [*], [VA→VA] 2. RE: [A], [following], [*], [hand]
	Pick: pick a product out of shelf (1→2,3)	1. ME: [hand], [towards shelf], [*→SA] 2. ME: [hand], [leave shelf], [SA→*] 3. RE: [A], [following], [*], [hand]
	Touch: pick nothing out of shelf (1→2)	1. ME: [hand], [towards shelf], [*→SA] 2. ME: [hand], [leave shelf], [SA→*]
	Return: return a product to shelf (1,2→3)	1. ME: [hand], [towards shelf], [*→SA] 2. RE: [A], [following], [*], [hand] 3. ME: [hand], [leave shelf], [SA→*]
Step 2	Selecting: select products in SA (1)	1. ME: [person], [*], [*→SA]
Step 3	Select by one hand (1,2)	1. ME: [person], [*], [*→SA] 2. ME: [hand], [*], [VA→VA]
	Select by both hands (1)	1. ME: [person], [*], [*→SA]

4.2   Evaluation Steps

To evaluate our proposed event-based method without the influence of level 1 and 2, we use the labeled bounding boxes as the output of level 1 instead of training an object detection model. Namely, level 1 is skipped in evaluation steps. To evaluate our proposed method's performance in meeting different marketing demands, we designed three steps to simulate the change in marketing demands.

Step 1. Recognize six behaviors of existing methods
Six common behaviors are chosen from existing methods in step 1 of Table 3. The symbol "A" refers to the product A. For existing methods, these six behaviors should be annotated to train models to do recognition. In our proposed method, only four events shown in Table 3 in red color are required to define these behaviors. ME 1 in "browse" can be regarded as the union set of ME 1 in "walking" and ME 1 in "viewing". The F1 score of the proposed method reaches 94.71% (Total 153 behaviors, precision = 95.32%, recall = 94.11%).

Step 2. Add a new behavior "selecting"
Suppose that the marketing demand requires recognizing a new behavior "selecting", which is defined as the customer is selecting products with hands in SA, but there is still nothing in his hand. Existing methods should collect new training data to train their models again. However, we only need to define this new behavior as Table 3. "Selecting" is defined as "The whole person's region moves from any area to shelf area". We use the region of the whole person (including arms) because the region of the hand may be invisible when it is occluded by the

shelf. The F1 score of the proposed method reaches 95.10% (Total 178 behaviors, precision = 95.79%, recall = 94.45%).

Step 3. Extract details from "selecting"
In this case, details are required about "selecting", such as selecting products by one hand or both hands. Existing methods require re-training the model with new training data. However, we only need to redefine event patterns as Table 3. If a hand is found outside the shelf when the whole person's region (including arms) is still in SA, it means another hand is inside the shelf, namely "select by one hand". Otherwise, it is "select by both hands". The F1 score reaches 94.94% (Total 181 behaviors, precision = 95.64%, recall = 94.30%).

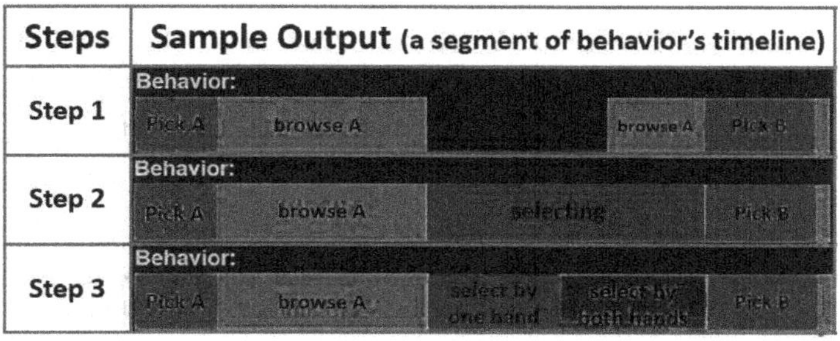

Steps	Sample Output (a segment of behavior's timeline)
Step 1	**Behavior:** Pick A · browse A · browse A · Pick B
Step 2	**Behavior:** Pick A · browse A · selecting · Pick B
Step 3	**Behavior:** Pick A · browse A · select by one hand · select by both hands · Pick B

Fig. 6. Behavior timeline of each step

Figure 6 shows the behavior timeline of each step within the same period. We can see that the proposed method reveals more details to meet the change in marketing demands. However, the specialized models in existing methods cannot be reconfigured to meet different demands. To sum up, the evaluation results show good accuracy and reconfigurable behavior recognition, it indicates that our proposed method can be reconfigured to meet different marketing demands.

5 Conclusion

The existing CAR system cannot adapt to different marketing demands when the recognition target changes or the recognition methods require updates. The specialized models are not reconfigurable, making it hard to adapt to the change of recognition target. The redundant computation in the system causes low efficiency. The low maintainability of the system results in the difficulty in fitting the update of recognition methods. In this research, we design a four-level hierarchy and an event-based method for reconfigurable customer behavior recognition to solve these three problems. The evaluation shows that the proposed method can easily reconfigure behavior outputs compared to existing methods, which adapt to different marketing demands.

References

1. Liu, J., Gu, Y., Kamijo, S.: Customer behavior recognition in retail store from surveillance camera. In: 2015 IEEE International Symposium on Multimedia (ISM), pp. 154–159. IEEE (2015)
2. Popa, M.C., Rothkrantz, L.J., Wiggers, P., Shan, C.: Shopping behavior recognition using a language modeling analogy. Pattern Recogn. Lett. **34**(15), 1879–1889 (2013)
3. Yamamoto, J., Inoue, K., Yoshioka, M.: Investigation of customer behavior analysis based on top-view depth camera. In: 2017 IEEE Winter Applications of Computer Vision Workshops (WACVW), pp. 67–74. IEEE (2017)
4. Generosi, A., Ceccacci, S., Mengoni, M.: A deep learning-based system to track and analyze customer behavior in retail store. In: 2018 IEEE 8th International Conference on Consumer Electronics-Berlin (ICCE-Berlin), pp. 1–6. IEEE (2018)
5. Merad, D., Drap, P., Lufimpu-Luviya, Y., Iguernaissi, R., Fertil, B.: Purchase behavior analysis through gaze and gesture observation. Pattern Recogn. Lett. **81**, 21–29 (2016)
6. Hernandez, D.A.M., Nalbach, O., Werth, D.: How computer vision provides physical retail with a better view on customers. In: 2019 IEEE 21st Conference on Business Informatics (CBI), vol. 1, pp. 462–471. IEEE (2019)
7. Lee, K., Choo, C.Y., See, H.Q., Tan, Z.J., Lee, Y.: Human detection using histogram of oriented gradients and human body ratio estimation. In: 2010 3rd International Conference on Computer Science and Information Technology, vol. 4, pp. 18–22. IEEE (2010)
8. Zhang, S., Wang, X.: Human detection and object tracking based on histograms of oriented gradients. In: 2013 Ninth International Conference on Natural Computation (ICNC), pp. 1349–1353. IEEE (2013)
9. Ahmad, M., Ahmed, I., Recognition in Intelligent Ullah, K., Khan, I., Khattak, A., Adnan, A.: Person detection from overhead view: a survey. Int. J. Adv. Comput. Sci. Appl. **10**(4), 567–577 (2019)
10. Frontoni, E., Raspa, P., Mancini, A., Zingaretti, P., Placidi, V.: Customers' activity recognition in intelligent retail environments. In: Petrosino, A., Maddalena, L., Pala, P. (eds.) ICIAP 2013. LNCS, vol. 8158, pp. 509–516. Springer, Heidelberg (2013). https://doi.org/10.1007/978-3-642-41190-8_55
11. Liciotti, D., Contigiani, M., Frontoni, E., Mancini, A., Zingaretti, P., Placidi, V.: Shopper analytics: a customer activity recognition system using a distributed RGB-D camera network. In: Distante, C., Battiato, S., Cavallaro, A. (eds.) VAAM 2014. LNCS, vol. 8811, pp. 146–157. Springer, Cham (2014). https://doi.org/10.1007/978-3-319-12811-5_11
12. Sturari, M., Liciotti, D., Pierdicca, R., Frontoni, E., Mancini, A., Contigiani, M., Zingaretti, P.: Robust and affordable retail customer profiling by vision and radio beacon sensor fusion. Pattern Recogn. Lett. **81**, 30–40 (2016)
13. Popa, M.C., Gritti, T., Rothkrantz, L.J.M., Shan, C., Wiggers, P.: Detecting customers' buying events on a real-life database. In: Real, P., Diaz-Pernil, D., Molina-Abril, H., Berciano, A., Kropatsch, W. (eds.) CAIP 2011. LNCS, vol. 6854, pp. 17–25. Springer, Heidelberg (2011). https://doi.org/10.1007/978-3-642-23672-3_3
14. Zheng, Z., Chen, Y., Chen, S., Sun, L., Chen, D.: Location-aware POI recommendation for indoor space by exploiting WiFi logs. Mob. Inf. Syst. **2017** (2017)
15. Chen, Y., Zheng, Z., Chen, S., Sun, L., Chen, D.: Mining customer preference in physical stores from interaction behavior. IEEE Access **5**, 17436–17449 (2017)

16. Lacic, E., Kowald, D., Traub, M., Luzhnica, G., Simon, J., Lex, E.: Tackling cold-start users in recommender systems with indoor positioning systems. In: RecSys Posters (2015)
17. Christodoulou, P., Christodoulou, K., Andreou, A.S.: A real-time targeted recommender system for supermarkets (2017)
18. So, W.T., Yada, K.: A framework of recommendation system based on in-store behavior. In: Proceedings of the 4th Multidisciplinary International Social Networks Conference, pp. 1–4 (2017)
19. de Sousa Silva, D.V., de Santana Silva, R., Ara, F., et al.: Recommending stores for shopping mall customers with recstore. J. Inf. Data Manag. **9**(3), 197 (2018)
20. Candamo, J., Shreve, M., Goldgof, D.B., Sapper, D.B., Kasturi, R.: Understanding transit scenes: a survey on human behavior-recognition algorithms. IEEE Trans. Intell. Transp. Syst. **11**(1), 206–224 (2009)
21. Leal, E., Gruenwald, L.: DynMDL: a parallel trajectory segmentation algorithm. In: 2018 IEEE International Congress on Big Data (BigData Congress), pp. 215–218 (2018)

Fully Autonomous UAV-Based Action Recognition System Using Aerial Imagery

Han Peng[iD] and Abolfazl Razi[✉]

Northern Arizona University, Flagstaff, AZ 86011, USA
{hp263,Abolfazl.Razi}@nau.edu

Abstract. Human action recognition is an important topic in artificial intelligence with a wide range of applications including surveillance systems, search-and-rescue operations, human-computer interaction, etc. However, most of the current action recognition systems utilize videos captured by stationary cameras. Another emerging technology is the use of unmanned ground and aerial vehicles (UAV/UGV) for different tasks such as transportation, traffic control, border patrolling, wild-life monitoring, etc. This technology has become more popular in recent years due to its affordability, high maneuverability, and limited human interventions. However, there does not exist an efficient action recognition algorithm for UAV-based monitoring platforms. This paper considers UAV-based video action recognition by addressing the key issues of aerial imaging systems such as camera motion and vibration, low resolution, and tiny human size. In particular, we propose an automated deep learning-based action recognition system which includes the three stages of video stabilization using the SURF feature selection and Lucas-Kanade method, human action area detection using faster region-based convolutional neural networks (R-CNN), and action recognition. We propose a novel structure that extends and modifies the InceptionResNet-v2 architecture by combining a 3D CNN architecture and a residual network for action recognition. We achieve an average accuracy of 85.83% for the entire-video-level recognition when applying our algorithm to the popular UCF-ARG aerial imaging dataset. This accuracy significantly improves upon the state-of-the-art accuracy by a margin of 17%.

Keywords: Drone video · Human detection · Action recognition · Deep learning · Unmanned aerial systems

1 Introduction

Video-based action recognition, an integral part of a class of AI platforms, is typically designed for capturing human behaviors and using them in support of

This material is based upon the work supported by the National Science Foundation under Grant No. 1755984. This work is also partially supported by the Arizona Board of Regents (ABOR) under Grant No. 1003329.

G. Bebis et al. (Eds.): ISVC 2020, LNCS 12509, pp. 276–290, 2020.
https://doi.org/10.1007/978-3-030-64556-4_22

decision making systems [20]. Most traditional video-based action recognition systems use stationary ground cameras to collect video information. Recently, the use of unmanned aerial vehicles (UAVs) has become commonplace in many applications, and video-based action recognition systems is not an exception. Researchers have already tried to develop human action recognition systems using stationary cameras in various fields such as security system [12], visual surveillance [7], human-computer interaction [22], etc. However, the UAV-based human action recognition has not yet received the deserved attention from the research community. Implementing UAV-based human action recognition systems can revolutionize the current practice in many applications, since drones provide several advantages over the ground-based monitoring systems. Some of the advantages include flexible and faster access, on-demand video streaming with adjustable resolution, focus and angle of view, and less human intervention and lower risk in harsh and extreme environments, only to name a few. That is the main reason that the UAV-based monitoring systems are experiencing an exponential growth in recent years [19,25]. Recognizing human actions by processing captured video frames using static platforms is known to be a challenging task due to its computational complexity, the intrinsic variability between the actions of the same class, challenges related to determining the start and end points of each action, and dealing with mixed actions, and complications of background removal. This task becomes even more challenging when applied to UAV-based monitoring systems due to facing additional problems such as motion-related blurriness, camera vibration, varying angles of view, and tiny object sizes.

This paper proposes an end-to-end system for UAV-based action recognition by solving the aforementioned issues. More specifically, we use non-overlapping 16-frame video segments for clip-based action classification purpose. In this regard, we extract labeled 16-frame video segments from the benchmark UCF-ARG dataset [1] to develop a training dataset for action recognition. Likewise, we use clip-level classification along with majority voting for the ultimate video-level action recognition.

The contribution of the proposed works is two-fold: i) we proposed a fully autonomous UAV-based human action recognition system that enables the UAVs to precisely detect and recognize human actions while accommodating aerial imaging artifacts; ii) we introduced a novel architecture for neural networks that combines a 3D convolutional network with a residual network, which substantially improves the performance of the 3D CNNs [27]. More specifically, our proposed method when applied to the UCF-ARG dataset, achieves the classification success rate (CSR) of 73.72% for the clip-level 5-class action recognition problem. This translates to entire-video-level accuracy of 85.83% which shows a substantial improvement over the current state of the art methods with 68% accuracy [18].

2   Related Works

In recent years, deep learning methods have become popular in many regression and classification tasks, due to their superior performance in capturing intricate relations through stacked hidden layers, generalizability, and eliminating the need for handcrafted feature extraction methods [2]. There exist three mainstream methods in using deep learning for video-based action recognition. The first approach is using two-stream methods [26], where two separate CNN structures are used to extract temporal and spatial features from the video, and then the results are integrated to classify the action. The second approach is 3D convolutional neural networks (*C3D networks*) [28] by considering videos as 3D input, where the time is the 3rd dimension. In this approach, a 3D convolutional neural network is used to process videos with no pre-processing. The third mainstream approach is using the *long short-term recurrent convolutional neural network* (LRCN) [8], where a CNN architecture is used to extract spatial features from the image sequences and output fixed-length vectors, and then a *long short term memory* (LSTM) is used to learn from the sequenced information. There are some recent and ongoing researches that achieve even higher action recognition accuracies building upon these works, including (i) *fusion stream* [10] which develops two-stream method by inserting multiple fusion layers into both spatial and temporal streams instead of fusing the results at the last step, (ii) spatio-temporal residual networks (ST-ResNet) [9] which adds residual connections into both spatial and temporal domains so it can captures partial-temporal information in both streams separately, (iii) *pseudo 3D CovNet* [21] which uses the idea of decoupling 3D CovNet into two parts: a 2D spatial convolution filter to extract spatial information and a 1D temporal convolution filter to extract temporal information and then uses P3D to replace the residual unit in ResNet. However, these methods perform reasonably well for stationary platforms but do not accommodate the key requirements of aerial imaging when subjected to shaking, vibration, and varying angle of views.

Although human action recognition and UAV-based monitoring systems are both well-studied topics, there are very few works that bridge these two distinct research areas to develop an end-to-end solution for efficient UAV-based action recognition. Burghouts et al. [6] proposed a focus-of-attention mechanism to perform the human action recognition that includes tracking, human detection and a per-track analysis. However, their method with its basic configuration achieves only 57% accuracy for the UCF-ARG dataset when the entire video is utilized. Hazar et al. [18] used a two-phase method along with the scene stabilization algorithm. Their method involves human detection through human vs non-human modeling as well as the human action modeling, where the modeling part is performed offline and the recognition part is performed on the fly in the inference phase. However, this method is not good enough since it achieves only 68% accuracy for the UCF-ARG dataset.

As mentioned earlier, the majority of action recognition methods are suitable for stationary cameras and fail in solving the issues of aerial imaging such as video instability, small object size, and varying angle of view. The few recent attempts for developing UAV-based human action recognition systems have considered this problem and produced some interesting results, but their performance is still far from satisfactory highlighting the need for more efficient methods.

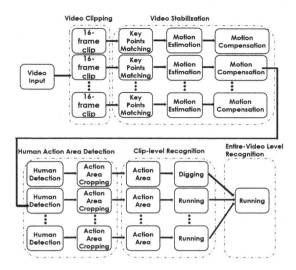

Fig. 1. Conceptual block diagram of the proposed UAV-based human action recognition.

In this paper, we propose a fully autonomous human action recognition system to boost the performance of the action recognition accuracy for aerial videos using video stabilization, human detection, and deep neural networks.

3   Methods

Our end-to-end solution includes three steps of (i) video stabilization, (ii) human detection, and (iii) human action recognition, while taking necessary considerations to solve challenges associated with UAV-based video streaming (see Fig. 1). Due to the flight instability and motion dynamics of commercial UAVs, aerial videos typically suffer from issues like vibration and camera motion. Therefore, using video stabilization is a critical need to obtain a stabled video appropriate for further processing. Furthermore, videos captured by drones usually include large areas that contain no information and the targets of interests (humans in this context) are tiny and barely noticeable. The human detection stage should be powerful enough to exclude unnecessary regions and video segments in order to focus only on the areas with recognizable human objects. In the following sections, we elucidate the details of each step.

3.1   Video Stabilization

We use a frame-by-frame method for video stabilization. The overall idea is to extract key points from one frame and then finding the corresponding nodes in the following frame that exhibit consistent spatial shift, and this continues until we reach the last frame. Then we quantify the averaged frame by frame motions in terms of 3D trajectories represented by a transformation. The obtained cumulative trajectory is smoothed out to represent the actual motions, while the difference between the original and smoothed trajectories are considered video instability and is used to eliminate the vibration from the video by proper shifting. The following are the details of each step.

Keypoints Extraction Using the *Speeded Up Robust Features* (SURF). We first use the SURF method to extract key points from the frames. SURF [4] is a low-complexity image feature detection method that is an accelerated version of the *scale-invariant feature transform* (SIFT) [16] to extract local image descriptors. Using a light-weight algorithm such as SURF is highly desirable for one-the-fly feature extraction by the drones.

Track Keypoints to Next Frame. In the next step, we use the *Lucas-Kanade optical flow* [17] to find the mapping between keypoints among the consecutive frames and quantify their relative motions. This method assumes that the displacement of the image content between two adjacent moments (frames) is small and approximately constant near the point p under consideration. Therefore, the optical flow equation can be applied to all pixels in a window centered at p and the local image flow (velocity) vector (V_x, V_y) can be written in a matrix form $Av = b$, where we have

$$A = \begin{bmatrix} I_x(p_1) & I_y(p_1) \\ I_x(p_2) & I_y(p_2) \\ \vdots & \vdots \\ I_x(p_n) & I_y(p_n) \end{bmatrix}, v = \begin{bmatrix} V_x \\ V_y \end{bmatrix}, b = \begin{bmatrix} -I_t(p_1) \\ -I_t(p_2) \\ \vdots \\ -I_t(p_n) \end{bmatrix}, \tag{1}$$

and $p_1, p_2, \ldots, p_n$ are the pixels inside the window, and $I_x(p_i), I_y(p_i), I_t(p_i)$ denote the partial derivatives of the image I with respect to position x, y and time t, evaluated at point p_i at the current time.

This over-determined system which has more equations than unknowns, can be solved using the least squares method by

$$v = (A^T A)^{-1} A^T b \tag{2}$$

which provides the following results for the averaged relative 2D motions between the two consecutive frames:

$$\begin{bmatrix} V_x \\ V_y \end{bmatrix} = \begin{bmatrix} \sum_i I_x(p_i)^2 & \sum_i I_x(p_i)I_y(p_i) \\ \sum_i I_y(p_i)I_x(p_i) & \sum_i I_y(p_i)^2 \end{bmatrix}^{-1} \\ \cdot \begin{bmatrix} -\sum_i I_x(p_i)I_t(p_i) \\ -\sum_i I_y(p_i)I_t(p_i) \end{bmatrix} \tag{3}$$

where the summations are over n points $p_1, p_2, \ldots, p_n$.

Motion Estimation. Suppose that F_i, and F_{i+1} are the two adjacent frames, and $P_i = \{p_1^i, p_2^i, \ldots, p_n^i\}$ and $P_{i+1} = \{p_1^{i+1}, p_2^{i+1}, \ldots, p_n^{i+1}\}$ are the set of

---

Algorithm 1: Video stabilization Using a method based on SURF and Lucas-Kanade optical flow.

Input: Unstable video
Output: Stabilized video
Initialization:
1. Read the first frame as PreviousIMG;
2. detect the keypoint using SURF as PreviousPts;
3. Set i = 1; set nF = the number of frames.
4. **while** $i \neq nF$ **do**

    5. Set $i \leftarrow i + 1$

    6. Read the i_{th} frame as CurrentIMG;

    7. Track and match PreviousPts from PreviousIMG to obtain CurrentPts
       in CurrentIMG using Lucas-Kanade optical flow;

    8. Calculate T_i, the i_{th} transformation matrix between PreviousPts and
       CurrentPts using equation (5);

    9. Find keypoints in the ith frame using SURF as PreviousPts;

end
10. Compute trajectory using cumulative sum of transformations as trajectory;
11. Smooth out the trajectory using convolution calculation using *Hanning window*;
12. Calculate the difference between the original and the smoothed trajectories and apply the difference to transformation matrix;
13. Apply the new transformation matrix to each frames and generate stable video;
14. Return stabilized video.

---

matched points between frames F_i and F_{i+1}, respectively, and T is the transformation matrix between the two frames. Then, we can state:

$$\begin{bmatrix} \mathbf{x}_j^{i+1} \\ y_j^{i+1} \\ 1 \end{bmatrix} = T_i \begin{bmatrix} x_j^i \\ y_j^i \\ 1 \end{bmatrix} \tag{4}$$

$$T_i = \begin{bmatrix} S_i \cdot \cos \Delta\theta_i & -S_i \cdot \sin \Delta\theta_i & \Delta x_i \\ S_i \cdot \sin \Delta\theta_i & S_i \cdot \cos \Delta\theta_i & \Delta y_i \\ 0 & 0 & 1 \end{bmatrix}, \tag{5}$$

where (x_j^i, y_j^i) is the coordinate of point p_j^i, $\Delta\theta_i$ is the rotation angle, S_i is the scale factor, and Δx_i and Δy_i are the translation motion vectors in horizontal and vertical directions between frames F_i, and F_{i+1}. No motion in the 3rd dimension is assumed ($z_i = 1$). Here, we use the cumulative sum of Δx_i, Δy_i, and $\Delta\theta_i$ to produce the motion trajectories specified by $x_i = \sum_{k=1}^{i} \Delta x_k, y_i = \sum_{k=1}^{i} \Delta y_k, \theta_i = \sum_{k=1}^{i} \Delta\theta_k$.

Trajectory Smoothing. Finally, we use a *Hanning* window to smooth out the obtained cumulative motion trajectories. Hanning window has no side lobes and is defined as:

$$w[n] = 0.5 \left[1 - \cos\left(\frac{2\pi n}{N}\right) \right] = \sin^2\left(\frac{\pi n}{N}\right), \qquad (6)$$

where N is the window size. The following algorithm summarizes the stabilization algorithm.

3.2   Human Action Area Detection

Since the video taken by a UAV contains lots of irrelevant information, to achieve higher accuracies it is desirable to focus on areas where the humans are located. In deep learning, there are two main types of object detection methods: one-stage methods and two-stage methods. The two-stage methods firstly identify a large pool of candidate regions which may or may not contain the object and then use a classification method (e.g. CNN) to classify these regions of interest (ROI) to verify if there exists an object or not. Two-stage methods require a longer time but achieve better results. The most successful implementations of the two-stage methods use fast R-CNN [11] and faster R-CNN [24]. The one-stage methods (e.g., single shot multi-box detector (SSD) [15] and you only look once (YOLOV3) [23]) use a similar approach, but skip the region proposal stage and execute the detection process directly over a dense sampling of possible locations. This approach requires only a single pass through the neural network and predicts all the bounding boxes at the same time. Thus the one-stage methods can realize a faster detection speed but with a lower accuracy. In our problem, the detection accuracy is considered more important than the execution speed, therefore a two-stage method is more suitable. Therefore, we applied a two-stage method based the faster R-CNN for human detection.

3.3   Action Recognition

The last stage of the proposed end-to-end system deals with the action recognition. Inspired by the success of *Inception-ResNet-v2* [27] in image classification, we developed a new architecture for action recognition by modifying and extending the Inception-ResNet-v2 method to a 3D version, which called Inception-ResNet-3D.

Inception-ResNet-v2 is a combination of two recent networks, namely the *residual connections* [13] and the *Inception architecture* [27]. The Inception-ResNet-3D network architecture is shown in Fig. 2, which extends the original 2D architecture to a 3D version by using 3D convolutional neural network, and reducing the filter sizes while maintaining the overall architecture (i.e., the number and the order of the layers, pooling approaches, activation functions, etc.) unchanged.

Note that the Inception-ResNet-V2 has three main parts including (i) stem block, (ii) Inception-ResNet A, B, C blocks, and (iii) reduction A, B, C blocks. In the 3D stem block of the revised version (Fig. 2), all kernels with dimensions (h, w) are extended to 3D kernels of size (h, w, d), where the 3r dimensional d equals to the first two dimensions, i.e. $h = w = d$. Also, the number of output

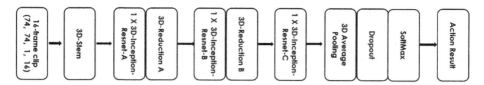

Fig. 2. The architecture of the modified 3D InceptionResNet-v2 networks. The modified blocks and parameters are shown with blue color. (Color figure online)

filters in the convolution layers are divided by 8. For instance, the number of filters 32 is replaced with 4 in the first layer of the 3D stem block.

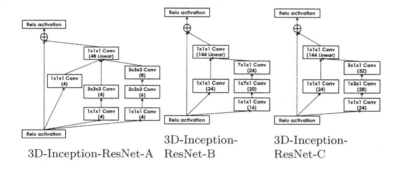

Fig. 3. The schematic for interior grid modules of the Inception-ResNet-3D

The interior module of the network includes 3D-Inception-Resnet-A, 3D-Inception-Resnet-B, and 3D-Inception-Resnet-C blocks as shown in Fig. 3. Instead of using 5 Inception-Resnet-A, 10 Inception-Resnet-B, and 5 Inception-Resnet-C for each block, we use only 1 of each type per block to reduce the parameter size. For the 3D reduction A and B blocks, all the kernels of size (h, w) are extended to 3D versions (h, w, d). Unlike the Inception Resnet A, B, C blocks, here the size of the 3rd dimension here is $d = 1$. The number of filters for each block is reduced by 8. Finally, the average pooling size is $(2, 2, 2)$ in our 3D-Inception-ResNet network.

4   Experiments

In this section, the performance of the proposed method for fully autonomous UAV-based human activity recognition is assessed. We first describe the used dataset, and then provide a quantitative analysis of the proposed approach along with comparisons with the state of the art methods.

4.1   Dataset Description

UCF-ARG dataset is a benchmark dataset for action recognition which includes a set of hard-to-distinguish tasks based on videos taken by stationary ground and mobile aerial cameras [1]. More specifically, this dataset includes actions performed by 12 actors recorded by a ground camera, a rooftop camera at a height of 100 feet, and a UAV-mounted camera. Here, we only use the aerial videos. This dataset contains 10 human action classes: *boxing, carrying, clapping, digging, jogging, open-close trunk, running, throwing, walking,* and *waving.* Except for the *open-close trunk,* all other actions are performed 4 times by each actor in different directions, while the *open-close trunk* is performed only 3 times by each actor. Since most of the former research projects on human detection and human action recognition, focused on 5 classes: *digging, running, throwing, walking,* and *waving* [3,6,18], we choose the same set of classes for a fair and meaningful comparison.

4.2   Implementation Details

Video Stabilization. For the SURF feature point detection method, we used the python cv2 package with the hessian Threshold 500. For the *Lucas-Kanade optical flow* method, we use the iterative Lucas-Kanade algorithm with pyramids, following the implementation details presented in [5]. Since the video clips include only 16 frames, we wouldn't expect that clips include multiple camera motion episodes. Therefore, we set the *Hanning* window size to 16, which is equal to the number of frames to realize a global stabilization rather than local short-term stabilization.

Human Detection. A pre-trained faster R-CNN model with implementation details of a version previously applied to the COCO dataset [14] is used for human detection. We consider that a clip contains a valid action, if a human subject is detected in at least one frame. Otherwise, the clip is not used for the further processing of action detection. The size and the width-height ratio of the *rectangular* box containing a human subject can be different from one frame to another. To avoid the issue of bias to the object size that can reduce the performance of the human action recognition, we extend the detected *rectangular* box to the smallest *square* box that encompasses all the identified *rectangular* boxes. We crop the video frames to include only the extracted boxes for enhanced accuracy in the action recognition. Therefore, the action recognition stage that is applied to the reproduced 16-frame video clips is scale-invariant and rotation-invariant with respect to the human objects. If more than one humans are detected, we choose the one closer to the center of the frame.

Data Augmentation. Since the data size is limited and noting the imbalanced number of recordings for different classes (e.g., the number of video clips for the *running* classes is about 1/3 of other classes because of shorter videos), we implemented data augmentation before applying the Inception-ResNet-3D network. More specifically, to solve the imbalanced number of samples, we produced

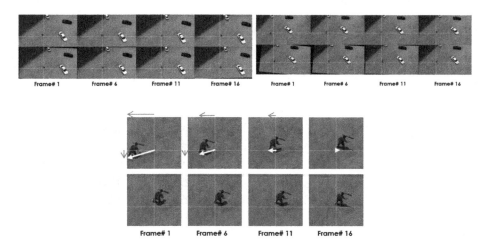

Fig. 4. Two examples of video stabilization result for actions: (a) *digging*, (b) *throwing* (original size), (c) *throwing* (zoomed-in view). In each sub-figure, the top row shows sample frames of the original 16-frame clip, and the bottom row shows the stabilized video clip. The relative human position to a fixed point (represented by the intersection of green lines) varies from one frame to another in the original video clip, while remaining constant in the stabilized video. (Color figure online)

two extra sets of video clips for the *running* class by adding videos with altered blurriness and sharpness effects. Likewise, to increase the number of samples, we produce two new video clips by horizontal flipping and adding Gaussian Noise with zero mean and unit variance to the original video frames. Consequently, the number of training samples increased by a factor of 6 for the *running* class and doubled for other classes.

Human Action Recognition. To realize a uniform input size, we resized the video frames into (74, 74) since the detected human boxes typically fit into 74 pixel by 74 pixel image segments. For a fair comparison with other works [6,18], a *leave-one-out cross-validation* (LOO CV) is used to split the dataset into training and test sets, where each test is corresponding to one person. The dropout rate of 0.5 is used in our method. The popular *Adam* optimizer is used with the learning rate of 0.001 and *decay* = 0. The network is trained for the clip-level samples. The entire-video-level action recognition is based on applying the majority voting to the obtained clip-level labels.

Table 1. Comparison of the performance of the proposed method with the state of the art in terms of action recognition accuracy per test video.

Test set	Burghouts et al. [6]	Hazar et al. [18]	Our method	
			16-frame level	Entire-Video level
1		65%	68.7%	**75%**
2		55%	71.5%	**80%**
3		75%	77.5%	**90%**
4		55%	71.7%	**80%**
5		85%	75.9%	**95%**
6		35%	78.2%	**80%**
7		60%	68.2%	**85%**
8		70%	72.5%	**90%**
9		60%	66.2%	**75%**
10		85%	77.4%	**95%**
11		75%	82.1%	**90%**
12		90%	82.7%	**95%**
Average	57%	68%	73.72%	**85.83%**

4.3   Result

Figure 4 presents the video stabilization stage for two exemplary actions: *digging* and *throwing*. The top row in each sub-figure shows the original frames while the bottom row shows the stabilized frames. The green lines points to a fixed point close to the human object in the video frames. We can see that the human moves considerably with respect to the intersections of the green lines from one frame to another in the original video, while remaining stationary in the stabilized video frames. This indicates that the video stabilization part is successful in eliminating the camera vibration and motion effects. The figures illustrate that a small vibration in the UAV camera can translate to a large shift of the human object in the entire video which can be multiple times of a human size. Since this effect is not clearly visible in the original videos, we show the zoomed-in version of the *throwing* action. The shift in the human object location can cause a severe performance degradation in the action classification if not properly addressed. Therefore, video stabilization is a necessary step of the proposed method for aerial imaging.

Table 1 presents the action recognition accuracy of the proposed method as well as the two state of the art methods [6,18] which use the same dataset (UCF-ARG). The results are provided per test (i.e. a sample recording) for the proposed method and Hazar et al. [18], but only the average accuracy is available for Burghouts et al. [6]. The results confirm that the proposed method improves upon both methods with a significant margin. If we consider the clip-level results, our method achieves an average accuracy of 68% which is significantly higher than the Burghouts et al. [6] method with accuracy 57% and the Hazar et al. [18] method with accuracy 68%. The achieved gain is even higher if we consider the ultimate result of the entire-video-level action recognition which achieves the high accuracy of 85.83%. It significantly improves the state of the art results by more than 17% increase in the action recognition accuracy.

Table 2. Comparison of the performance of the proposed method with the state of the art in terms of action recognition accuracy per class.

Test set	Burghouts et al. [6]	Hazar et al. [18]	Our method	
			16-frame level	Entire-video level
Digging	50%	79%	68.91%	**81.25%**
Running	**91%**	67%	77.39%	89.58%
Throwing	33%	69%	62.57%	**72.92%**
Walking	75%	67%	83.83%	**95.83%**
Waving	33%	56%	75.91%	**89.58%**
Average	57%	68%	73.72%	**85.83%**

Similar results are presented in Table 2 in terms of average action recognition accuracy per class for the three methods. Again the achieved gain is higher for the entire-video-level classification as expected. Our method consistently outperforms the competitor methods with a significant margin. The only exception is the *running class*, where our method with accuracy 89.58% slightly under-performs the [6] method with an accuracy of 91%. Perhaps a better video augmentation method can help improve the accuracy for this class. The higher gain is achieved for the *waving* class that improves the best method by 33.58%.

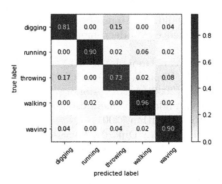

Fig. 5. The confusion matrix of the multi-level action classification for the proposed method.

Figure 5 shows the confusion matrix for all classes, where we can see that the *running, walking,* and *waving* actions are well classified with the accuracy above 90%. However, the *digging* and *throwing* actions relatively lower accuracies of 81% and 73%. The potential reason is that these two classes may have some similar action components in the utilized 16-frame video clips.

5 Conclusion and Discussion

Noting the lack of an effective action recognition algorithm which is capable of accommodating specific requirements of aerial monitoring systems, in this paper, we proposed an end-to-end system for UAV-based action recognition. The proposed method includes three stages of video stabilization, action area detection, and action recognition, where the video stabilization solves the camera motion and vibration issue, and the action area detection deals with the small human sizes in aerial images. Also, the classification algorithm is trained for top-view images, where action recognition is more challenging than the front-view and side-view. Our experiment results show that our algorithm achieves a very high accuracy of 85.83% when applied to the benchmark UCF-ARG dataset. This accuracy is significantly higher than the previously reported accuracy of 68% (by a margin of 17%), therefore it is appropriate for aerial monitoring systems for action recognition tasks.

References

1. Nagendran, A., Harper, D.: UCF-ARG dataset, University of Central Florida (2010). http://crcv.ucf.edu/data/UCF-ARG.php
2. Abiodun, O.I., Jantan, A., Omolara, A.E., Dada, K.V., Mohamed, N.A., Arshad, H.: State-of-the-art in artificial neural network applications: a survey. Heliyon 4(11), e00938 (2018)
3. AlDahoul, N., Sabri, M., Qalid, A., Mansoor, A.M.: Real-time human detection for aerial captured video sequences via deep models. Comput. Intell. Neurosci. **2018** (2018)
4. Bay, H., Tuytelaars, T., Van Gool, L.: SURF: speeded up robust features. In: Leonardis, A., Bischof, H., Pinz, A. (eds.) ECCV 2006. LNCS, vol. 3951, pp. 404–417. Springer, Heidelberg (2006). https://doi.org/10.1007/11744023_32
5. Bouguet, J.Y., et al.: Pyramidal implementation of the affine lucas kanade feature tracker description of the algorithm (2001)
6. Burghouts, G., van Eekeren, A., Dijk, J.: Focus-of-attention for human activity recognition from UAVs. In: Electro-Optical and Infrared Systems: Technology and Applications XI, vol. 9249 (2014)
7. Danafar, S., Gheissari, N.: Action recognition for surveillance applications using optic flow and SVM. In: Asian Conference on Computer Vision (2007)
8. Donahue, J., et al.: Long-term recurrent convolutional networks for visual recognition and description. In: Proceedings of the IEEE Conference on Computer Vision and Pattern Recognition, pp. 2625–2634 (2015)

9. Feichtenhofer, C., Pinz, A., Wildes, R.P.: Spatiotemporal multiplier networks for video action recognition. In: Proceedings of the IEEE Conference on Computer Vision and Pattern Recognition, pp. 4768–4777 (2017)
10. Feichtenhofer, C., Pinz, A., Zisserman, A.: Convolutional two-stream network fusion for video action recognition. In: Proceedings of the IEEE Conference on Computer Vision and Pattern Recognition, pp. 1933–1941 (2016)
11. Girshick, R.: Fast R-CNN. In: Proceedings of the IEEE International Conference on Computer Vision, pp. 1440–1448 (2015)
12. Han, S., Achar, M., Lee, S., Peña-Mora, F.: Empirical assessment of a RGB-D sensor on motion capture and action recognition for construction worker monitoring. Visual. Eng. 1(1), 6 (2013)
13. He, K., Zhang, X., Ren, S., Sun, J.: Deep residual learning for image recognition. In: 2016 IEEE Conference on Computer Vision and Pattern Recognition (CVPR), pp. 770–778, June 2016. https://doi.org/10.1109/CVPR.2016.90
14. Lin, T.-Y., et al.: Microsoft COCO: common objects in context. In: Fleet, D., Pajdla, T., Schiele, B., Tuytelaars, T. (eds.) ECCV 2014. LNCS, vol. 8693, pp. 740–755. Springer, Cham (2014). https://doi.org/10.1007/978-3-319-10602-1_48
15. Liu, W., et al.: SSD: single shot MultiBox detector. In: Leibe, B., Matas, J., Sebe, N., Welling, M. (eds.) ECCV 2016. LNCS, vol. 9905, pp. 21–37. Springer, Cham (2016). https://doi.org/10.1007/978-3-319-46448-0_2
16. Lowe, D.G., et al.: Object recognition from local scale-invariant features. In: ICCV, vol. 99, pp. 1150–1157 (1999)
17. Lucas, B.D., Kanade, T., et al.: An iterative image registration technique with an application to stereo vision (1981)
18. Mliki, H., Bouhlel, F., Hammami, M.: Human activity recognition from UAV-captured video sequences. Pattern Recogn. 100, 107140 (2020)
19. Peng, H., Razi, A., Afghah, F., Ashdown, J.: A unified framework for joint mobility prediction and object profiling of drones in UAV networks. J. Commun. Netw. 20(5), 434–442 (2018)
20. Poppe, R.: A survey on vision-based human action recognition. Image Vis. Comput. 28(6), 976–990 (2010)
21. Qiu, Z., Yao, T., Mei, T.: Learning spatio-temporal representation with pseudo-3D residual networks. In: Proceedings of the IEEE International Conference on Computer Vision, pp. 5533–5541 (2017)
22. Rautaray, S.S., Agrawal, A.: Vision based hand gesture recognition for human computer interaction: a survey. Artif. Intell. Rev. 43(1), 1–54 (2012). https://doi.org/10.1007/s10462-012-9356-9
23. Redmon, J., Farhadi, A.: Yolov3: an incremental improvement. arXiv preprint arXiv:1804.02767 (2018)
24. Ren, S., He, K., Girshick, R., Sun, J.: Faster R-CNN: towards real-time object detection with region proposal networks. In: Advances in Neural Information Processing Systems, pp. 91–99 (2015)
25. Shamsoshoara, A., Afghah, F., Razi, A., Mousavi, S., Ashdown, J., Turk, K.: An autonomous spectrum management scheme for unmanned aerial vehicle networks in disaster relief operations. IEEE Access 8, 58064–58079 (2020)
26. Simonyan, K., Zisserman, A.: Two-stream convolutional networks for action recognition in videos. In: Advances in Neural Information Processing Systems 27, pp. 568–576 (2014)

27. Szegedy, C., Ioffe, S., Vanhoucke, V., Alemi, A.A.: Inception-v4, inception-resnet and the impact of residual connections on learning. In: Thirty-First AAAI Conference on Artificial Intelligence (2017)
28. Tran, D., Bourdev, L., Fergus, R., Torresani, L., Paluri, M.: Learning spatiotemporal features with 3D convolutional networks. In: Proceedings of the IEEE International Conference on Computer Vision, pp. 4489–4497 (2015)

Hierarchical Action Classification with Network Pruning

Mahdi Davoodikakhki$^{(\boxtimes)}$ ⓘ and KangKang Yin$^{(\boxtimes)}$ ⓘ

Simon Fraser University, Burnaby, Canada
{mahdid,kkyin}@sfu.ca

Abstract. Research on human action classification has made significant progresses in the past few years. Most deep learning methods focus on improving performance by adding more network components. We propose, however, to better utilize auxiliary mechanisms, including hierarchical classification, network pruning, and skeleton-based preprocessing, to boost the model robustness and performance. We test the effectiveness of our method on three commonly used testing datasets: NTU RGB+D 60, NTU RGB+D 120, and Northwestern-UCLA Multiview Action 3D. Our experiments show that our method can achieve either comparable or better performance than state-of-the-art methods on all three datasets. In particular, our method sets up a new baseline for NTU 120, the largest dataset among the three. We also analyze our method with extensive comparisons and ablation studies.

Keywords: Human action recognition · Human action classification · Hierarchical classification · Network pruning

1 Introduction

Human action classification and recognition has many important applications, such as autonomous driving, smart surveillance, patient monitoring, and interactive games. Despite extensive research on this topic in recent years, human-level performance is still out of reach. Image classification, however, has achieved human-level performance a few years ago. There are many challenges in human action recognition. First, there are high intra-class variations and inter-class similarities. A powerful deep learning model and a large amount of training data are necessary to achieve good performance. Second, the qualities of input videos vary greatly. There are multiple benchmark datasets, and in this work we focus on captured indoor videos in lab environments. Third, multiple data types and representations can be captured with the video data or extracted from the videos. Skeleton data, for example, should be used whenever possible.

We propose to extend the Inflated ResNet architecture with hierarchical classification for better feature learning at different scales. Iterative pruning is then incorporated for a further performance boost. We also use skeleton data, captured or extracted, to crop out irrelevant background so the learning can focus

© Springer Nature Switzerland AG 2020
G. Bebis et al. (Eds.): ISVC 2020, LNCS 12509, pp. 291–305, 2020.
https://doi.org/10.1007/978-3-030-64556-4_23

on human activities. These mechanisms combined compare favorably to other state-of-the-art methods in the field.

In summary, our main contributions include: (a) We show that Inflated ResNet coupled with hierarchical classification can boost the performance of the baseline model. (b) We show that iterative pruning can help improve the performance even further. (c) We also show that 2D/3D skeleton data, when available, could be used to crop videos in a preprocessing stage to increase the classification accuracy in most cases. (d) We evaluate our method extensively on three datasets. Our method sets up a new baseline for the NTU RGB+D 120 dataset for future research in this field.

2   Related Work

There is a large body of prior work related to our work. Due to the limited space, we only summarize the most relevant and most recent papers here.

2.1   Human Action Classification

Most human action classification methods work on either RGB image sequences and/or skeleton data. Our method uses both 2D skeletons and video inputs for classification, so we will review and compare with state-of-the-art methods from both categories. However, we only use skeletons for preprocessing to crop out irrelevant backgrounds, and not for classification.

Skeleton-Based Action Classification. For skeleton-based classification, traditional CNN (Convolutional Neural Networks) methods can still be used after converting skeleton data into 2D images. Example works include TSRJI [3], Skelemotion [4], and Enhanced Viz. [21]. RNN (Recurrent Neural Networks) and its two common variations LSTM (Long Short-Term Memories) and GRU (Gated Recurrent Units) can also be used to interpret skeleton sequences. Their ability to learn long and short-term memories help achieve good results. Example works include TS-LSTM [16] and EleAtt-GRU [33]. Most advanced methods, however, are based on Graph Convolutional Networks (GCN), which can model sparse joint connections. Example works include MS-G3D Net [23], FGCN [32], and GVFE+AS-GCN with DH-TCN [24].

Video-Based Action Classification. Most state-of-the-art video-based classification methods are based on CNN. Inflated 3D ConvNet (I3D) and Inflated ResNet proposed by [6] became the foundation of many advanced algorithms, such as MMTM [13], Glimpse Clouds [2], Action Machine [34], and PGCN [27]. Such networks inflate 2D kernels of convolutional filters and pooling layers along the temporal domain to process 3D spatio-temporal information. In addition, Glimpse Clouds [2] extracts attention glimpses from each frame and uses the penultimate feature maps to estimate 2D joint positions and encourage glimpses to focus on the people in the scene. Action Machine [34] extracts Region of Interests (RoI), which are human bounding boxes, for better pose estimation and classification over these regions. The skeleton classification results are then fused with video-based classification to boost the performance further. PGCN [27] performs graph convolutions over RGB features extracted around 2D joints rather than over the joint positions to improve the video-based classification performance, which is then also fused with skeleton-based classification scores. Our baseline network is similar to that of Glimpse Clouds [2], and our cropping preprocess is inspired by Action Machine [34].

In addition to video and skeleton input, various other data types can be used for input or intermediate feature representations. For instance, PoseMap [20] extracts pose estimation maps from the RGB frames. 3D optical flow can also be estimated for classification [1]. RGB and optical flow classifications can be fused to further boost performance [28]. MMTM [13] uses a combination of depth, optical flow, and skeleton data with RGB frames as input for different datasets. Different fusion strategies have also been investigated, such as MMTM [13] and [25] that fuse features from intermediate layers for the next layers or final classification.

2.2   Hierarchical Classification and Loss Functions

Hierarchical classification and loss functions facilitate learning the most important features in different scales. One straightforward way to apply hierarchical classification is to learn on different resolutions of the same set of images, such as [14] for skin lesion classification. Semantic graphs can be constructed to form hierarchical relations among classes for text classification [31]. Our approach is mainly inspired by related works in image classification that use features from intermediate layers for the main classification as well, by accumulating loss functions from all participating layers [12,29].

2.3   Network Pruning

Over-parameterization is a well-known property of deep neural networks. Network pruning is usually used to improve generalization and achieve more compact models for low-resource applications [9,22]. There are multiple choices to implement pruning and the fine-tuning after pruning. One option is to use one-shot pruning [17], but usually unimportant filters in convolutional layers are iteratively located and deleted. After each pruning iteration, the network can be re-trained from scratch with reinitialized weights [9,22]. Our pruning method is similar to [9], as we also iteratively prune filters with the lowest $l2$ norms. The difference is that we retrain with inherited weights, similar to [17].

3   Our Methods

We present our video preprocessing procedures including cropping and projecting 3D skeletons to 2D in Sect. 3.1. We describe our modified ResNet network architecture in Sect. 3.2. We then detail the hierarchical classification and network pruning in Sects. 3.3 and 3.4, respectively.

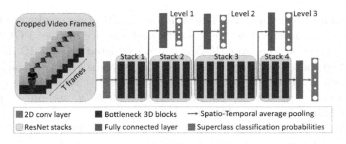

Fig. 1. Structure of our neural network.

3.1 Video Preprocessing

Raw action videos usually contain not only human subjects, but also surrounding objects and background environments, most of which are irrelevant to the performed actions. Neural networks can overfit to such noises instead of focusing on human actions. Inspired by [34], we also crop the raw videos to focus on human skeletons inside.

We use 2D skeletons and joint positions in pixels for cropping. 2D skeleton data can be captured together with the videos, or extracted by pose estimation algorithms such as OpenPose [5], or computed from 3D skeletons as we will explain shortly. We first extract the skeleton bounding boxes, and then enlarge them by a factor of 10% on all four sides and cap them at frame borders, in order to leave a margin for errors and retain relevant information of surrounding areas. After cropping, we rescale all the video frames to a resolution of 256×256 as input to our neural network.

For datasets that provide 3D skeleton data, we project the 3D skeletons onto the image plane as 2D skeletons using Eq. 1, as illustrated in Fig. 2. We denote the 2D and 3D skeletons as $S_p \in R^{T \times J \times 2}$ and $S \in R^{T \times J \times 3}$, respectively, where T is the number of frames and J is the number of joints. We denote the individual channels in skeleton data as S_{px}, S_{py} for 2D pixel positions, and S_x, S_y, S_z for 3D world coordinates. $b_x = 320$ and $b_y = 240$ are bias values that correspond to the image centers for the N-UCLA dataset. c_x, c_y are coefficients that can be solved for from Eq. 1. We randomly sample ten frames from ten different N-UCLA dataset video clips and manually estimate the pixel position S_{px} and S_{py} of 5 end-effector joints (head, hands, and feet). A least squares fit returns $c_x = 554.84$ and $c_y = 583.68$. We found that these coefficients work well for the all video frames in the N-UCLA dataset.

$$S_p = \begin{bmatrix} S_{px} \\ S_{py} \end{bmatrix} = \begin{bmatrix} c_x \times \frac{S_x}{S_z} + b_x \\ c_y \times \frac{S_y}{S_z} + b_y \end{bmatrix} \rightarrow \begin{bmatrix} c_x \\ c_y \end{bmatrix} = \begin{bmatrix} (S_{px} - b_x) \times \frac{S_z}{S_x} \\ (S_{py} - b_y) \times \frac{S_z}{S_y} \end{bmatrix} \tag{1}$$

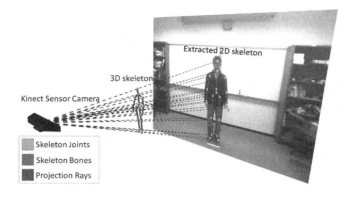

Fig. 2. Projection of a 3D skeleton onto the image plane as a 2D skeleton.

3.2 Modified ResNet Architecture

Our baseline network is the Inflated ResNet from Glimpse Clouds [2], which was created according to the inflation procedure introduced in [6]. The Inflated ResNet is a variation of ResNet developed by [11]. It is also similar to the I3D network in [34]. In Inflated ResNet, 2D convolutional kernels, except the first one, are converted into 3D kernels, to make them suitable for video input. We perform experiments on different variations of Inflated ResNet in Sect. 4.2, and find the Inflated ResNet50 to be the best architecture for our task.

Our baseline network consists of four main ResNet stacks of convolutional layers, each consisting of multiple bottleneck building blocks. We label them as stacks 1 to 4 in Fig. 1 for hierarchical classification. More specifically, we modify the baseline network after each ResNet stack by averaging the extracted features over the spatial and temporal domain, and then passing them to a fully-connected linear layer and a softmax layer to obtain multiple levels of classification probabilities.

3.3 Hierarchical Classification

We employ hierarchical classification to encourage our neural network to learn important features at different scales. For each ResNet stack, we enforce a superclass constraint for each action. That is, a fully-connected linear classifier assigns each action to a superclass after each ResNet stack. Each superclass contains the same number of original action classes to keep the learned hierarchy balanced. We use up to four ResNet stacks for hierarchical classification. The final structure of our network is shown in Fig. 1. We train the classifiers in two passes. The first pass trains the network with a cross-entropy loss only after the last stack. We then compute the confusion matrix C from the trained network for assigning the superclasses as described next.

We define a graph with N nodes, each corresponding to one of the original action classes. We then cluster them into superclasses as follows. Edge e_{ij} denotes a connection between node i and j $(i < j)$, with its cost defined as $e_{ij} = c_{ij} + c_{ji}$, where c_{ij} is the corresponding element of the confusion matrix C. We denote the assigned superclass for each action class as $s_i^l \in \{1, ..., N/M_l\}$, where $i \in \{1, ..., N\}$ is the action class index, $l \in \{1, ..., L\}$ is the stack index, and hyperparameter M_l is the number of superclasses of stack l. The bigger l is, the larger M_l is. That is, front stacks have fewer number of superclasses which only need to find the most distinguishable features to classify the actions. The rear stacks, however, need to concentrate more on finer details to differentiate actions into more categories. We also denote the set of assigned superclasses for level l as $S_l = \{s_1^l, ..., s_N^l\}$. For each level l, we aim to minimize the sum of edge costs among all superclasses:

$$\forall l \in \{1, ..., L\} \quad \min_{S_l} \sum_{i,j} e_{ij}, \quad i, j \in \{1, ..., N\}, s_i^l \neq s_j^l \tag{2}$$

Fig. 3. N-UCLA: all 10 action classes and the derived superclasses.

We use a simple greedy algorithm to minimize the total edge cost. We initialize the superclass assignments randomly but evenly. At each optimization step we swap two superclass assignments that decrease the cost function the most. We continue this procedure until no more deduction can be achieved. We run the greedy optimization 1000 times and then choose the solution with the lowest cost. More advanced optimization algorithms, such as genetic algorithms or deep learning methods, can be used as well. But our early experiments showed similar performance among different algorithms. So we choose the simple greedy algorithm in the end.

The optimized superclass assignments help classify the original action classes into similar groups. For the NTU 60 dataset, all mutual classes with two persons in action are classified into the same level-1 superclass. Most medical actions are in the other superclass. Figure 3 shows the superclasses for the N-UCLA dataset. All class pairs in the level-3 superclass are similar. For instance the "carry" and "walk around" classes or the "throw" and "drop trash" classes.

Hierarchical Loss Function. After the first pass of training, we denote the predicted classification probabilities by each ResNet stack as $\tilde{y}_l$. We also denote the ground truth and the superclass assignments from the greedy algorithm as y_l. We then train the network for a second time, using a cross-entropy loss

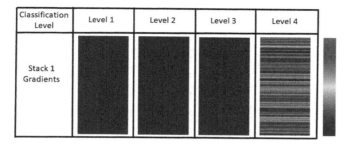

Classification Level	Level 1	Level 2	Level 3	Level 4
Stack 1 Gradients				

Fig. 4. Averaged and normalized absolute gradients in the last convolutional layer of stack 1, backpropagated from different levels of classifiers. The gradients are computed from the first 500 clips of NTU 60. Pure red indicates 1 and pure blue indicates 0. (Color figure online)

$Loss_l(y_l, \tilde{y}_l)$ after each stack. The total loss is a weighted sum of the loss for each stack:

$$Loss = \sum_{l \in \{1,...,L\}} w_l \times Loss_l(y_l, \tilde{y}_l), \tag{3}$$

Generally speaking, we use bigger weights w_l for latter stacks. This is because the prior stacks tend to extract low-level features less important for the final classification. In Fig. 4 we show the normalized and averaged absolute gradients backpropagated from each classifier to the last convolutional layer of stack 1, when using equal weights $(1, 1, 1, 1)$ for all ResNet stacks. Note that gradients from latter stacks are richer than those of the previous stacks. We also experiment with different weighting schemes, some of which are shown in Table 1.

3.4 Network Pruning

We apply network pruning to further improve the accuracy and generalization ability of our model. We also tried to apply dropout but did not find it beneficial in our experiments. We employ two iterative pruning methods while keeping the hierarchical classification approach intact.

For both pruning methods, we find the $p\%$ of the convolutional filters with the lowest $l2$ norm and zero them out. The first method prunes the bottom $p\%$ of filters in all convolutional layers of the ResNet stacks; while the second method prunes the bottom $p\%$ of filters in each layer of the ResNet stacks independently. We compare different choices of p values on the NTU 60 dataset using the first pruning method in Table 2. We will use 10% for all our experiments in Sect. 4. The pruning can be carried out iteratively for multiple passes. We perform pruning until we observe reductions in testing performance for two consecutive steps. We will show more pruning results for up to seven passes in Tables 8, 9 and 10 in our ablation studies.

Table 1. Different weighting schemes of the hierarchical loss function on NTU 60.

Superclass weights	Cross-subject	Cross-view
$\frac{1}{27}, \frac{1}{9}, \frac{1}{3}, 1$	95.07%	98.41%
$\frac{1}{8}, \frac{1}{4}, \frac{1}{2}, 1$	**95.45%**	**98.59%**
$1, 1, 1, 1$	95.31%	98.01%
$1, \frac{1}{2}, \frac{1}{4}, \frac{1}{8}$	93.91%	97.20%
$1, \frac{1}{3}, \frac{1}{9}, \frac{1}{27}$	93.22%	97.24%

Table 2. Different pruning ratios and passes on the NTU 60 cross-subject benchmark.

Pruning passes	5% pruning	10% pruning	15% pruning
Pass 1 pruning	94.84%	95.52%	95.08%
Pass 2 pruning	95.17%	95.61%	95.21%
Pass 3 pruning	94.92%	95.60%	95.00%
Pass 4 pruning	94.87%	**95.66%**	95.10%

4 Experiments

4.1 Implementation Details

Our network is based on the Inflated ResNet50 as described in Sect. 3.2. We train our network for 20 epochs, with an adaptive learning rate initially set to 0.0001. We divide the learning rate by 10 when the validation loss has not improved for two consecutive epochs. We use a pruning ratio of 10% at each pruning pass.

We preprocess all input videos with cropping and rescaling as described in Sect. 3.1. In addition, we flip all the video frames horizontally with a probability of 50%. For both training and testing, we partition each video clip into eight equal segments and uniformly sample eight frames as the input frames, with the location of the first frame randomly chosen within the first segment. For training we also randomly crop a fixed 224 × 224 square from all input frames to feed into our network, but at test time we crop a square of the same size at the center of each frame. We also shuffle the training data at the beginning of each epoch. For testing, five sets of frames are sampled from the eight segments of each clip as input to the network, and the final classification probabilities are averaged similar to [2]. 10% of the test data is randomly chosen as the validation data.

4.2 Network Architecture

We perform experiments to search for the best Inflated ResNet architecture as shown in Table 3. The original ResNet has five variations: ResNet18, ResNet34, ResNet50, ResNet101 and ResNet152. We do experiments on the inflated version of the first four variations, as ResNet152 is unnecessarily big for our datasets.

We note that the Inflated ResNet34 has more parameters than the Inflated ResNet50, as they are made of different building blocks. We refer the readers to [6] for more details of the inflation procedure. From Table 3 we conclude that the Inflated ResNet50 is the best baseline model to use for our further experiments.

Table 3. Different Inflated ResNet architectures on NTU 60.

Architecture	#Parameters	Cross-subject	Cross-view
ResNet18	33.7M	93.83%	97.87%
ResNet34	64.0M	93.91%	97.69%
ResNet50	46.8M	**95.25%**	**98.34%**
ResNet101	85.8M	95.19%	98.09%

4.3 Hyperparameters

The number of superclasses for each level of the hierarchical classification is one important hyperparameter of our model. However, when the original number of action classes is big, such as 60 for NTU 60, there are too many combinations of these parameters for all the classification levels. We thus chose some representative combinations, some of which are shown in Table 4, to test for NTU 60. We have also performed experiments on different weighting schemes for the hierarchical loss function in Table 1, and different pruning ratios in Table 2.

Table 4. Different superclass sizes for level 1–3 classification on the NTU 60 dataset.

Superclasses	Cross-subject	Cross-view
2/6/20	**95.45%**	**98.59%**
3/10/30	95.25%	98.34%
4/12/30	95.25%	98.38%
5/15/30	95.20%	98.29%
6/12/30	95.39%	98.28%
10/20/30	95.04%	98.38%

4.4 Comparisons

We evaluate our method and compare with other state-of-the-art methods on three commonly used datasets.

Datasets. NTU RGB+D 60 (NTU 60) contains more than 56000 video clips [26]. 2D and 3D skeleton data, as well as depth, are also available. There are 60 action classes, and two evaluation benchmarks: cross-view and cross-subject. We choose 2, 6, 20 as the number of superclasses for levels 1–3 classification respectively, according to Table 4. We use weights $(\frac{1}{8}, \frac{1}{4}, \frac{1}{2}, 1)$ for the hierarchical loss function, according to Table 1.

Table 5. Comparison on NTU 60. – indicates no results available.

Method	Year	Pose input	RGB input	Cross-view	Cross-subject
Glimpse Clouds [2]	2018		✓	93.2%	86.6%
FGCN [32]	2020	✓		96.25%	90.22%
MS-G3D Net [23]	2020	✓		96.2%	91.5%
PoseMap [20]	2018	✓	✓	95.26%	91.71%
MMTM [13]	2019	✓	✓	–	91.99%
Action Machine [34]	2019		✓	97.2%	94.3%
PGCN [27]	2019	✓	✓	–	**96.4%**
Ours	2020	✓	✓	**98.79%**	95.66%

NTU RGB+D 120 (NTU 120) adds 60 new action classes to the original NTU 60 dataset [18]. It contains more than 114000 video clips in total and provides two benchmarks: cross-setup and cross-subject. As the number of action classes is doubled compared with that of NTU 60, we use 4, 12, 40 as the number of superclasses for levels 1–3 classification. We still use $(\frac{1}{8}, \frac{1}{4}, \frac{1}{2}, 1)$ for weighting the hierarchical loss function.

Table 6. Comparison on NTU 120. * indicates results obtained from author-released code. – indicates no results available.

Method	Year	Pose input	RGB input	Cross-setup	Cross-subject
Action Machine [34]	2019		✓	–	–
TSRJI [3]	2019	✓		62.8%	67.9%
PoseMap from Papers with Code [19]	2018	✓	✓	66.9%	64.6%
SkeleMotion [4]	2019	✓		66.9%	67.7%
GVFE + AS-GCN with DH-TCN [24]	2019	✓		79.8%	78.3%
Glimpse Clouds [2]	2018		✓	83.84%*	83.52%*
FGCN [32]	2020	✓		87.4%	85.4%
MS-G3D Net [23]	2020	✓		88.4%	86.9%
Ours	2020	✓	✓	**94.54%**	**93.69%**

Northwestern-UCLA Multiview Action 3D (N-UCLA) contains 1494 video sequences, together with depth and 3D skeleton data [30]. Each action is recorded simultaneously with three Kinect cameras. We convert the 3D skeleton data into

2D skeletons using the projection method described in Sect. 3.1. We use three view-based benchmarks where each view is used for testing and the other two for training. There are 10 different actions in this dataset. We thus choose 2 and 5 as the number of superclasses for the level-2 and level-3 classifiers, respectively. We do not need the level-1 classifier for hierarchical classification anymore. We use weights $(\frac{1}{16}, \frac{1}{4}, 1)$ for the hierarchical loss function. As the size of this dataset is small, we use the pre-trained network on NTU 60 cross-subject benchmark to initialize the network training on N-UCLA.

Table 7. Comparison on N-UCLA. – indicates no results available. The pre-trained column indicates if the model was pre-trained on ImageNet and/or a bigger human action dataset.

Method	Year	Pre-trained	Pose input	RGB input	View1	View2	View3	Average
PoseMap [20]	2018	✓	✓	✓	–	–	–	–
Ensemble TS-LSTM [16]	2017		✓		–	–	89.22%	–
EleAtt-GRU(aug.) [33]	2018	✓	✓		–	–	90.7%	–
Enhanced Viz. [21]	2017	✓	✓		–	–	92.61%	–
Glimpse Clouds [2]	2018	✓		✓	83.4%	89.5%	90.1%	87.6%
FGCN [32]	2020		✓		–	–	95.3%	–
Action Machine [34]	2019	✓		✓	88.3%	**92.2%**	96.5%	92.3%
Ours	2020	✓	✓	✓	**91.10%**	91.95%	**98.92%**	**93.99%**

Table 8. Ablation study on NTU 60. The baseline model refers to the inflated ResNet50 network trained without hierarchical loss using the original videos. The full model refers to the baseline network trained with the hierarchical loss using cropped video input.

Method	Pruning altogether		Pruning by layers	
	Cross-subject	Cross-view	Cross-subject	Cross-view
baseline	89.13%	94.39%	89.13%	94.39%
baseline + cropping	95.29%	98.34%	95.29%	98.34%
full model	95.45%	98.59%	95.45%	98.59%
full model + 1-pass pruning	95.52%	98.61%	95.37%	98.66%
full model + 2-pass pruning	95.61%	98.60%	95.50%	98.63%
full model + 3-pass pruning	95.60%	**98.65%**	**95.64%**	98.74%
full model + 4-pass pruning	**95.66%**	–	–	**98.79%**

Performance. Tables 5, 6 and 7 show the comparison results. Our method scores the highest or close to the highest for all three datasets. We report the accuracy for prior work by either directly taking numbers reported in the original paper, or running author-released code if relevant performance was not reported in the original papers. For fair comparisons, we check if a method uses RGB input

Table 9. Ablation study on NTU 120 dataset.

Method	Pruning altogether		Pruning by layers	
	Cross-subject	Cross-setup	Cross-subject	Cross-setup
baseline	84.64%	86.20%	84.64%	86.20%
baseline + cropping	92.48%	93.99%	92.48%	93.99%
baseline + hierarchical loss	86.17%	86.98%	86.17%	86.98%
full model	92.95%	94.25%	92.95%	94.25%
full model + 1-pass pruning	93.48%	94.12%	93.19%	**94.54%**
full model + 2-pass pruning	93.55%	94.31%	**93.56%**	–
full model + 3-pass pruning	**93.69%**	**94.42%**	–	–

or pose input or both. We also mark if a method uses pre-trained models on ImageNet and/or a bigger human action dataset to initialize the network for training on small datasets.

We detail the performance gains of the video cropping preprocess, the hierarchical classification, and the multipass network pruning components with ablation studies shown in Tables 8, 9 and 10. The hierarchical classification is proved to be beneficial in all cases after cropping. Without cropping, the hierarchical classification alone is also able to gain performance as shown in the third row of Table 9 for NTU 120. We continue the network pruning iterations until we observe lowered performance from the best one achieved so far in two consecutive steps. The network pruning is helpful in most cases. The cropping preprocess yields large performance gains in all cases.

Table 10. Ablation study on N-UCLA dataset. The "Viewn" columns indicate the camera view used for testing and the other two views are used for training.

Method	Pruning altogether			Pruning by layers		
	View1	View2	View3	View1	View2	View3
baseline	77.76%	70.73%	97.00%	77.76%	70.73%	97.00%
baseline + cropping	88.78%	89.00%	98.50%	88.78%	89.00%	98.50%
full model	88.78%	**89.98%**	**98.92%**	88.78%	89.98%	**98.92%**
full model + 1-pass pruning	89.75%	–	–	88.39%	88.39%	–
full model + 2-pass pruning	**90.14%**	–	–	**91.10%**	88.39%	–
full model + 3-pass pruning	–	–	–	–	91.36%	–
full model + 4-pass pruning	–	–	–	–	90.37%	–
full model + 5-pass pruning	–	–	–	–	**91.95%**	–

5   Conclusions

We have augmented the Inflated ResNet50 architecture with hierarchical classification, iterative network pruning, and skeleton-based cropping. These components are simple to implement and effective in improving the classification accuracy for human action datasets captured in lab environments. The performance of our system is either comparable or better than the other top-ranking algorithms in the field. Our work has set up a new baseline for the NTU 120 dataset, which is the largest dataset of its kind.

5.1   Limitations and Future Work

Our choices of hyperparameters, such as the number of superclasses for each classification level, number of iterations for the pruning, and weights in the hierarchical loss function, are all set by either heuristics and/or manual searching. There is no guarantee that these parameters are optimal. Automatic search algorithms that are not computationally prohibitive are desirable.

We have used the skeleton data only for video preprocessing in this work. GCN-based skeleton classification algorithms, however, can be easily incorporated to further boost the performance of our system. We could simply fuse the classification results of the two algorithms, or implement an integrated two-stream system from both the video stream and the skeleton stream.

We have mainly focused on NTU RGB+D type of datasets that were captured in lab settings together with 2D/3D skeletons of reasonable quality. For future work, we would like to incorporate outdoor datasets or datasets obtained from the Internet, such as the Kinetics dataset [15]. Such datasets are usually more heterogeneous and of much lower quality. 2D skeletons extracted by pose estimation algorithms such as OpenPose [5] are also less trustworthy. Large-scale pretraining using super large neural network models is likely needed as suggested by [7,8,10].

References

1. Ballin, G., Munaro, M., Menegatti, E.: Human action recognition from RGB-D frames based on real-time 3D optical flow estimation. In: Chella, A., Pirrone, R., Sorbello, R., Jóhannsdóttir, K.R. (eds.) Biologically Inspired Cognitive Architectures 2012. AISC, vol. 196, pp. 65–74. Springer, Heidelberg (2013). https://doi.org/10.1007/978-3-642-34274-5_17
2. Baradel, F., Wolf, C., Mille, J., Taylor, G.W.: Glimpse clouds: human activity recognition from unstructured feature points. In: CVPR, pp. 469–478. IEEE (2018)
3. Caetano, C., Bremond, F., Schwartz, W.R.: Skeleton image representation for 3D action recognition based on tree structure and reference joints. In: SIBGRAPI. IEEE (2019)
4. Caetano, C., Sena, J., Bremond, F., Dos Santos, J.A., Schwartz, W.R.: SkeleMotion: a new representation of skeleton joint sequences based on motion information for 3D action recognition. In: IEEE International Conference on Advanced Video and Signal Based Surveillance. IEEE (2019)

5. Cao, Z., Simon, T., Wei, S.E., Sheikh, Y.: Realtime multi-person 2D pose estimation using part affinity fields. In: CVPR, pp. 1302–1310. IEEE (2017)
6. Carreira, J., Zisserman, A.: Quo vadis, action recognition? A new model and the kinetics dataset. In: CVPR, pp. 4724–4733. IEEE (2017)
7. Duan, H., Zhao, Y., Xiong, Y., Liu, W., Lin, D.: Omni-sourced webly-supervised learning for video recognition. arXiv:2003.13042 (2020)
8. Feichtenhofer, C., Fan, H., Malik, J., He, K.: SlowFast networks for video recognition. In: ICCV, pp. 6201–6210. IEEE (2019)
9. Frankle, J., Carbin, M.: The lottery ticket hypothesis: finding sparse, trainable neural networks. In: International Conference on Learning Representations (2019)
10. Ghadiyaram, D., Tran, D., Mahajan, D.: Large-scale weakly-supervised pre-training for video action recognition. In: CVPR, pp. 12038–12047. IEEE (2019)
11. He, K., Zhang, X., Ren, S., Sun, J.: Deep residual learning for image recognition. In: CVPR, pp. 770–778. IEEE (2016)
12. Huang, G., Chen, D., Li, T., Wu, F., van der Maaten, L., Weinberger, K.: Multi-scale dense networks for resource efficient image classification. In: International Conference on Learning Representations (2018)
13. Joze, H.R.V., Shaban, A., Iuzzolino, M.L., Koishida, K.: MMTM: multimodal transfer module for CNN fusion. arXiv:1911.08670 (2019)
14. Kawahara, J., Hamarneh, G.: Multi-resolution-tract CNN with hybrid pretrained and skin-lesion trained layers. In: Wang, L., Adeli, E., Wang, Q., Shi, Y., Suk, H.-I. (eds.) MLMI 2016. LNCS, vol. 10019, pp. 164–171. Springer, Cham (2016). https://doi.org/10.1007/978-3-319-47157-0_20
15. Kay, W., et al.: The kinetics human action video dataset. arXiv:1705.06950 (2017)
16. Lee, I., Kim, D., Kang, S., Lee, S.: Ensemble deep learning for skeleton-based action recognition using temporal sliding LSTM networks. In: ICCV, pp. 1012–1020. IEEE (2017)
17. Li, H., Kadav, A., Durdanovic, I., Samet, H., Graf, H.P.: Pruning filters for efficient convnets. In: International Conference on Learning Representations (2017)
18. Liu, J., Shahroudy, A., Perez, M.L., Wang, G., Duan, L.Y., Chichung, A.K.: NTU RGB+D 120: a large-scale benchmark for 3D human activity understanding. IEEE Trans. Pattern Anal. Mach. Intell. **42**(10), 2684–2701 (2019)
19. Liu, M., Yuan, J.: Recognizing human actions as the evolution of pose estimation maps. https://paperswithcode.com/paper/recognizing-human-actions-as-the-evolution-of. Accessed 12 May 2020
20. Liu, M., Yuan, J.: Recognizing human actions as the evolution of pose estimation maps. In: CVPR, pp. 1159–1168. IEEE (2018)
21. Liu, M., Liu, H., Chen, C.: Enhanced skeleton visualization for view invariant human action recognition. Pattern Recogn. **68**, 346–362 (2017)
22. Liu, Z., Sun, M., Zhou, T., Huang, G., Darrell, T.: Rethinking the value of network pruning. In: International Conference on Learning Representations (2019)
23. Liu, Z., Zhang, H., Chen, Z., Wang, Z., Ouyang, W.: Disentangling and unifying graph convolutions for skeleton-based action recognition. arXiv:2003.14111 (2020)
24. Papadopoulos, K., Ghorbel, E., Aouada, D., Ottersten, B.: Vertex feature encoding and hierarchical temporal modeling in a spatial-temporal graph convolutional network for action recognition. arXiv:1912.09745 (2019)
25. Perez-Rua, J.M., Vielzeuf, V., Pateux, S., Baccouche, M., Jurie, F.: MFAS: multimodal fusion architecture search. In: CVPR, pp. 6959–6968. IEEE (2019)
26. Shahroudy, A., Liu, J., Ng, T., Wang, G.: NTU RGB+D: a large scale dataset for 3D human activity analysis. In: CVPR, pp. 1010–1019. IEEE (2016)

27. Shi, L., Zhang, Y., Cheng, J., Lu, H.Q.: Action recognition via pose-based graph convolutional networks with intermediate dense supervision. arXiv:1911.12509 (2019)
28. Simonyan, K., Zisserman, A.: Two-stream convolutional networks for action recognition in videos. In: Proceedings of the International Conference on Neural Information Processing Systems, vol. 1, pp. 568–576. MIT Press (2014)
29. Szegedy, C., et al.: Going deeper with convolutions. In: CVPR, pp. 1–9. IEEE (2015)
30. Wang, J., Nie, X., Xia, Y., Wu, Y., Zhu, S.: Cross-view action modeling, learning, and recognition. In: CVPR, pp. 2649–2656. IEEE (2014)
31. Wu, C., Tygert, M., LeCun, Y.: A hierarchical loss and its problems when classifying non-hierarchically. PLoS ONE **14**(12), e0226222 (2019)
32. Yang, H., et al.: Feedback graph convolutional network for skeleton-based action recognition. arXiv:2003.07564 (2020)
33. Zhang, P., Xue, J., Lan, C., Zeng, W., Gao, Z., Zheng, N.: Adding attentiveness to the neurons in recurrent neural networks. In: Ferrari, V., Hebert, M., Sminchisescu, C., Weiss, Y. (eds.) ECCV 2018. LNCS, vol. 11213, pp. 136–152. Springer, Cham (2018). https://doi.org/10.1007/978-3-030-01240-3_9
34. Zhu, J., Zou, W., Zheng, Z., Xu, L., Huang, G.: Action machine: toward person-centric action recognition in videos. IEEE Sig. Process. Lett. **26**, 1633–1637 (2019)

An Approach Towards Action Recognition Using Part Based Hierarchical Fusion

Aditya Agarwal[(✉)] and Bipasha Sen[(✉)]

Microsoft, Hyderabad, India
{adiagar,bise}@microsoft.com

Abstract. The human body can be represented as an articulation of rigid and hinged joints which can be combined to form the parts of the body. Human actions can be thought of as a collective action of these parts. Hence, learning an effective spatio-temporal representation of the collective motion of these parts is key to action recognition. In this work, we propose an end-to-end pipeline for the task of human action recognition on video sequences using 2D joint trajectories estimated from a pose estimation framework. We use a Hierarchical Bidirectional Long Short Term Memory Network (HBLSTM) to model the spatio-temporal dependencies of the motion by fusing the pose based joint trajectories in a part based hierarchical fashion. To denote the effectiveness of our proposed approach, we compare its performance with six comparative architectures based on our model and also with several other methods on the widely used KTH and Weizmann action recognition datasets.

Keywords: Action recognition · Hierarchical Bidirectional Long Short Term Memory Network · Part based fusion

1 Introduction

Human action recognition is a prominent field of research in computer vision with its wide applications in the areas of robotics, video search and retrieval, intelligent surveillance systems, automated driving, human computer interaction etc. Despite the extensive research on action recognition in the vision community, the problem still poses a significant challenge due to large variations and complexities, e.g., occlusion, appearance, low frame-rate, camera angle and motion, illumination, cluttered background, intra-class variations, and so on.

Traditionally, the spatio-temporal structure has been modeled using hand-crafted features and actions recognized using well defined discriminative networks. These methods usually start by detecting the spatio-temporal interest points [1] and then using local representations to describe these points. In [2], Histogram of Oriented Gradients (HOG) [3] and Histogram of Optical Flow

---

A. Agarwal and B. Sen—These authors contributed equally to the work.

© Springer Nature Switzerland AG 2020
G. Bebis et al. (Eds.): ISVC 2020, LNCS 12509, pp. 306–318, 2020.
https://doi.org/10.1007/978-3-030-64556-4_24

(HOF) [4] were extracted at each spatio-temporal interest point and then features were encoded with Bag of Features (BoF). [5] proposed a method to extract dense trajectories by sampling and tracking dense points from each frame in multiple scales. They also extracted HOG, HOF and Motion Boundary Histogram (MBH) at each point whose combination further boosted the performance. In [6], dense trajectories were employed in a joint learning framework to simultaneously identify the spatial and temporal extents of the actions of interest in training videos. A combination of handcrafted and deeply learnt features was proposed in Trajectory-Pooled Deep-Convolutional Descriptors (TDD) [7] which proved to be successful. Deep Trajectory Descriptor (DTD) [8] for action recognition extracts dense trajectories from multiple consecutive frames and then projects them onto a two-dimensional plane to characterize the relative motion in frames. Despite encouraging results for action recognition on several datasets, these approaches suffer from variations of view point and scale, subject and appearance. Statistical and handcrafted features work well on recognizing simple actions but not complex actions involving multiple simultaneous sub-actions. Moreover, they are designed to be optimal for a specific task.

Recent advances in human pose estimation using deep learning [9–14] and the availability of depth sensors [15–18] have led to accurate representations of high level features. Studies show that high-level features extracted using current pose estimation algorithms already outperform state of the art low level representations based on hand crafted features implicating their potential in action recognition. In this work, we use a pose estimation framework based on Convolutional Neural Networks (CNN) in tandem with a robust object detection framework to deal with variations in scale and viewpoint to obtain a 2D representation of joint locations. The object detection algorithm filters frames that do not contain the object of interest and are therefore non-discriminative for the task of action recognition.

Human body can be articulated as a system of rigid and hinged joints [19]. These joints can be combined to form the limbs and the trunk. Human actions can be thought of as a collective action of these limbs and the trunk. Human action recognition is considered a time series problem where the characteristics of the body posture and its dynamics are extracted over time to represent the action [20–22]. [23] proposed a hierarchical approach on a trajectory of 2D skeleton joint coordinates. In this work, we propose a part based hierarchical action recognition pipeline on raw video sequences. We use a pose estimation framework to estimate a trajectory of 2D joint coordinates. These are combined in a part based hierarchical fashion using Hierarchical Bidirectional Long Short Term Memory (HBLSTM) networks to encode the spatio-temporal dependencies in the video sequence. The encoded representation is then fed to a discriminative network to classify the action.

The major contributions of this work are two-fold,

1. Designing a pipeline for pose based action recognition using a part-based hierarchical approach on raw video sequences. We handle the common

issues of occlusion, camera zoom-motion-angle variations and eliminate non-discriminative frames while learning robust joint coordinates.
2. To validate the effectiveness of the proposed approach, we compare its performance with six other comparative architectures based on our model.

The rest of the paper is organized as follows, Sect. 2 defines our proposed pipeline and explains each component in detail. Section 3 talks about the experimental details and the evaluation results. Section 4 presents the conclusion and future work.

2   Proposed Approach

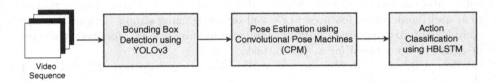

Fig. 1. Proposed pipeline

Figure 1 depicts the proposed pipeline which consists of three modules that are connected sequentially:

1. Bounding Box Detection using YOLOv3 [24]
2. Pose Estimation using CPMs [12]
3. Action Classification using HBLSTM (Sect. 2.3)

A video sequence can be denoted as

$$F = [f_1, ..., f_T], f_t \in R^{160 \times 120 \times 1}, \tag{1}$$

where each frame f_t represents a single channel image. The proposed pipeline works in a supervised fashion. Frames of fixed dimension $\in R^{160 \times 120}$ (for Weizmann, dimension $\in R^{180 \times 144}$) are extracted from the input video sequence. An object detection algorithm is used to obtain an initial estimate of human's presence in the image. The purpose of the object detection module is two folds,

1. Generate accurate pose coordinates when dealing with changing camera zoom-motion-angles.
2. Select frames containing the human action and discard the remaining frames as they are non-discriminative for the task of action recognition.

We use a pose estimation framework based on CNNs to generate an estimate of human joints in the extracted bounding boxes. 2D coordinates of 14 joint locations (head, neck, wrist, elbow, shoulder, hip, knee, and ankle) are extracted for every frame representing the joint trajectories for the entire video sequence.

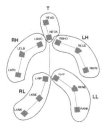

Fig. 2. Part representations of the joint coordinates.

In the subsequent sections, we describe each of the modules in detail.
The proposed model is based on HBLSTMs that takes 2D joint trajectories
as input. HBLSTMs can learn across multiple levels of temporal hierarchy. As
shown in Fig. 5, the first recurrent layer encodes the representation of 5 body
parts, namely, Right Hand (RH), Left Hand (LH), Right Leg (RL), Left Leg (LL)
and Trunk (T) (Fig. 2). The next set of layers encodes the part representations
into Upper Right (RHT), Upper Left (LHT), Lower Right (RLT), and Lower
Left (LLT) vectors by fusing the encoded representation of T with RH, LH, RL,
and LL respectively. The subsequent layers generate the encoded representation
of Upper (U) and Lower (L) bodies followed by the encoded representation of
the entire body. Finally, a dense layer followed by a softmax layer is added to
classify the action.

2.1 Bounding Box Detection

We use an object detection algorithm to obtain an initial estimate of human's
presence in the image. YOLOv3 [24] is an efficient object detection algorithm
pretrained on the ImageNet [25] and MSCOCO [26] datasets. It uses 53 successive
3×3 and 1×1 convolutional layers. The input to the bounding box algorithm
is the grey scaled image frames of fixed dimension $\in R^{160 \times 120}$ (for Weizmann,

Fig. 3. The result of bounding box. (a) Shows the result on two frames with varying
camera zoom. (b) Shows the result on the frame with missing person.

dimension $\in R^{180 \times 144}$) extracted from the video sequences in the KTH and Weizmann action recognition datasets. The network predicts 4 coordinates for each bounding box t_x, t_y, t_w and t_h. We have modified the code to produce bounding boxes only for those frames that have been labeled as a person and the remaining frames are discarded. Figure 3 shows a typical output of the YOLOv3 algorithm. The reason behind using bounding box detection is two-fold,

1. It filters out all frames that do not contain human action and is non-discriminative for the task of action recognition.
2. It deals with camera zoom-motion-angle and generates accurate pose estimates.

2.2 Pose Estimation

Convolutional Pose Machines (CPMs) [12] were introduced for the task of articulated pose estimation. CPMs consist of a sequence of convolutional neural networks that repeatedly produce 2D belief maps for the location of each part. At each stage in a CPM, image features and belief maps produced in the previous stage are used as inputs producing increasingly refined locations of each part (Eq. 2). CPMs are based on pose inference machines [27] with the key difference being that prediction and image feature computation modules of a pose machine are replaced by deep convolutional architecture allowing for both image and contextual representations to be learned directly from the data.

$$g_t(x'_z, \psi_t(z, b_{t-1})) \rightarrow \{b_t^p(Y_p = z)\}_{p \in \{0...P+1\}} \tag{2}$$

Fig. 4. Extracted pose coordinates using Convolutional Pose Machines

We operate CPMs directly on the bounding boxes generated from the previous stage to produce 2D joint coordinates. CPMs consist of five convolutional layers followed by two 1×1 convolutional layers and the input images being cropped to dimension 368×368. The bounding boxes extracted have a maximum dimension of 160×120 pixels for KTH and 180×144 pixels for Weizmann. Thus, the bounding boxes are first scaled while maintaining the aspect ratio and grey padded on either side to obtain the required dimension of 368×368. Figure 4 shows a typical output generated by CPM on a single frame. A 14×2 representation is obtained for every frame which denotes the x, y coordinates of the 14 joints in the frame. The coordinates of the frames are aggregated over the entire video sequence to obtain a joint trajectory of dimension $R^{T \times 28 \times 1}$, T denoting the number of frames in the input video sequence.

2.3   Hierarchical Bidirectional Long Short Term Memory

We denote a video sequence as $X = [x_1, ..., x_T]$, with each frame x_t denoting the $2D$ coordinates of 14 joints. We work in a supervised classification setting with a training set,

$$\chi = \{(X_i, y_i)\}_{i=1}^{N} \in R^{T \times 28 \times 1} \times \{1, ..., C\} \tag{3}$$

where X_i is a training video sequence and y_i is its class label (from one of the C possible classes).

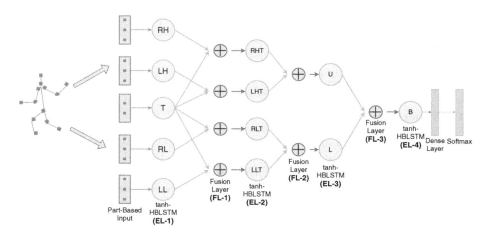

Fig. 5. Proposed part based hierarchical architecture. *EL* and *FL* denote *Encoding Layer* and *Fusion Layer* respectively.

Human body can be decomposed into five parts - two arms, two legs and a trunk (Fig. 2) and the global action can be modeled as the collective motion of these five parts. Benefitting from the LSTM's ability to model contextual dependencies from temporal sequences, we propose a Hierarchical Bidirectional LSTM (HBLSTM) for the task of pose based action recognition (Fig. 5). For the ith encoding layer, given the inputs $I_{i,j}^t$ as trajectories of part j at i^{th} layer for time t, the corresponding encoded representation is expressed as

$$h_{i,j}^t = \overrightarrow{h_{i,j}^t} \oplus \overleftarrow{h_{i,j}^t} \tag{4}$$

where $\overrightarrow{h_{i,j}^t}$ and $\overleftarrow{h_{i,j}^t}$ are the forward and backward layers passes respectively with tanh activations [28].

For the fusion layer at time t, the newly fused p^{th} representation as the input for the $(i+1)^{th}$ encoding layer is:

$$I_{i+1,p}^t = h_{i,j}^t \oplus h_{i,k}^t \tag{5}$$

where $h_{i,j}^t$ is the concatenated hidden representation of the jth part in i^{th} encoding layer and $h_{i,k}^t$ is for the kth part in i^{th} layer.

The encoded representation of the entire body is given by the Tth unit of the last (4th) encoding layer, $h_{4,body}^T$, which is given as input to the dense layer. The output of the dense layer is expressed as:

$$O = v_{h_{4,body}^t} \cdot h_{4,body}^T + b_{h_{4,body}^t} \tag{6}$$

O is given as input to the softmax layer. A softmax activation is applied to get the class probabilities as,

$$p(c_k) = \frac{e^{O_k}}{\sum_{j=1}^{C} e^{O_j}} \tag{7}$$

where C is the number of classes.

3   Experimental Details

3.1   Experimental Dataset

As the proposed method aims to classify human actions in a video, we train the model on two of the most commonly used human actions dataset - KTH [29] and Weizmann [30] and evaluate its performance using the commonly used leave-one-out cross validation scheme based on the subjects. The data is prepared by sampling 25 consecutive frames of 2D joint coordinates estimated from Sect. 2.2 denoting a single human action $\in R^{25 \times 28}$.

KTH Dataset. The KTH dataset contains six types of human actions: walking, jogging, running, boxing, hand-waving and hand-clapping performed by 25 subjects in four different scenarios: indoors, outdoors, outdoors with variations in scale, and outdoors with changes in clothing. The videos are on an average four seconds in duration with a static frame rate of 25 fps. Additionally, every sequence has an action that is performed 3 or 4 times, with a total of 2391 shorter subsequences. The sequences are taken over homogenous backgrounds and are sampled at a spatial resolution of 160×120 pixels.

Weizmann Dataset. The Weizmann dataset provided by [30] consists of 10 actions: bending, jumping, jumping jack, jumping in place, running, galloping sideways, skipping, walking, one-hand-waving and two-hands-waving. The dataset consists of 90 low resolution videos performed by 9 different subjects with a static frame rate of 25 fps and are sampled at a spatial resolution of 180×144 pixels.

3.2   Class Imbalance

We observed that for some of the video sequences belonging to the action recognition classes in the KTH dataset, the subject acting appears for a short duration of time in the video and thus the video is largely composed of frames that are non-discriminative for the given task. The number of frames in the KTH dataset per class for all video sequences is shown in Table 1. After preprocessing the frames using the object detection approach mentioned in Sect. 2.1, the number of bounding box frames for the classes jogging, running, and walking reduce drastically as the frames that don't contain the human as the object of interest are discarded. We notice that the number of frames for the remaining classes largely remains the same as can be seen from Table 1. We augment the dataset by adding a moving window of size 10 to handle the class imbalance problem. Table 1 shows the number of sequences before and after data augmentation for each class.

Table 1. Class imbalance on the six action classes in the KTH dataset. *no-objdm* and *w-objdm* denote the number of frames before and after processing by object detection module. *no-daug* and *w-daug* denote the number of sequences before and after data augmentation.

Classes	Frames		Sequences	
	no-objdm	w-objdm	no-daug	w-daug
boxing	45187	45074	1848	**4401**
hand-clapping	42667	42448	1744	**4141**
hand-waving	53678	53291	2187	**5220**
jogging	43884	**18812**	800	**1779**
running	38505	**13001**	563	**1198**
walking	65795	32774	1343	**3122**

3.3 Origin Shift of Pose Coordinates

The 2D pose coordinates estimated by the CPMs are anchored w.r.t. the top left position in the rectangular bounding box. Given that human actions are independent of their absolute spatial positions, we shift the pose coordinates with respect to the new origin at the center of the body. The new origin (O) is computed as the centroid of the pose coordinates belonging to head (P_{head}), left hip (P_{lhip}) and right hip (P_{rhip}) and is denoted as:

$$O = \frac{(P_{head} + P_{lhip} + P_{rhip})}{3} \tag{8}$$

The joint coordinates are shifted w.r.t the new origin as:

$$P'_{N,x}, P'_{N,y} = (P_{N,x}, P_{N,y}) - (O_x, O_y) \tag{9}$$

where P' and P denote the new and old pose coordinates respectively. Shifting the origin improved our action recognition rates by an average of ∼5%.

3.4 Experimental Results

Comparative Architectures. To denote the effectiveness of our proposed architecture, we compare its performance with six other architectures based on deep RNN. Our first architecture is a Deep Bidirectional RNN (**DBRNN**) which is one of the most commonly used models in sequence classification problems. To denote the importance of LSTM units in modeling long term contextual dependencies and the role of backward connections in modeling the future context, we compare a Deep Unidirectional LSTM (**DULSTM**) and a Deep Bidirectional LSTM (**DBLSTM**). These architectures operate directly on the trajectories of 2D pose coordinates.

To denote the importance of hierarchical connections, we compare a Point based Hierarchical BLSTM model (**PointHBLSTM**) that first obtains an encoded representation of all the frames in a sequence and then encodes them temporally to obtain a representation of the entire sequence.

Table 2. Average recognition rates with different experiments on the augmented dataset from Sect. 3.2 using the leave-one-out cross validation scheme.

Methods	KTH	Weizman
DBRNN	82.4%	81.2%
DULSTM	89.8%	91.7%
DBLSTM	92.7%	94.8%
PointHBLSTM	94.1%	96.6%
PartHBLSTM$_1$	98.9%	99.9%
PartHBLSTM$_2$	98.4%	99.7%
Proposed approach	**99.3%**	**100%**

To denote the effectiveness of part based hierarchical fusion, we build three similar part based models with different part based fusion. In the first part based model (**PartHBLSTM$_1$**), the encoded representation of upper body is obtained from the encoded representation of right hand, trunk and left hand and the lower body from encoded representation of left and right leg. The encoded representation of upper and lower bodies are then combined to get an encoded representation of the whole body. In the second part based model (**PartHBLSTM$_2$**), the encoded representation of left and right bodies are combined to obtain an encoded representation of the whole. Finally, we achieve the best evaluation result on the proposed approach shown in Fig. 5.

The number of learnable layers in all the experiments has been kept the same with small modifications to parameters to ensure best average performance.

Evaluation on KTH and Wiezman. Similar to many evaluation approaches on the KTH [29] and Weizmann [30] dataset, we carried out our experiments using the leave-one-out cross validation strategy [31] (i.e. all subjects except one were used for training and the learned model was evaluated on the remaining one) on the datasets described in Sect. 3.1. Average accuracy on the comparative architectures are reported in Table 2 and the average accuracy on the proposed model along with the existing approaches are reported in Table 3.

We achieve full separation between different actions and that a slight misclassification occurs between similar actions (i.e. between "hand-clapping" and "hand-waving" and between "running" and "jogging") in the KTH dataset. The classification accuracy is averaged over all selections of test data to achieve a recognition rate of **99.3%** and **100%** on the KTH and Weizmann dataset respectively using the proposed approach. We show that our proposed approach outperforms the state of the art on both KTH and Weizmann dataset for the task of action recognition.

Table 3. Recognition rates against different approaches on the KTH dataset.

Existing Methods	KTH	Weizman
Schuldt *et al.* [29]	71.72%	–
Fathi *et al.* [32]	90.5%	99.9%
Baccouche *et al.* [33]	94.39%	94.58%
Gorelick *et al.* [34]	–	97.83%
Gilbert *et al.* [35]	96.7%	–
Mona *et al.* [36]	97.89%	–
Proposed approach	**99.3%**	**100%**

4   Conclusion and Future Work

In this work, we present a pipeline for the task of human action recognition in videos. Using an object detection approach, we first estimate the presence of human and discard remaining frames as they are non-discriminative for the task of action recognition. We use a pose estimation framework to generate the trajectory of joint coordinates and combine them in a part-based hierarchical fashion to obtain a global representation of the entire video sequence. We showed that adding part based hierarchical fusion helps us achieve better results over other comparative architectures. Experimental evaluation on the KTH and Weizmann action recognition dataset show that our proposed approach outperforms the existing state of the art approaches on these datasets.

Future work includes applying the proposed system on more complex and larger datasets, such as UCF101 [37] and HMDB51 [38]. We are also exploring the use of appearance features in distinguishing between actions with similar motion but distinguishable appearance which is a limitation of the current approach.

References

1. Laptev, L.: Space-time interest points. In: Proceedings of the Ninth IEEE International Conference on Computer Vision, vol. 1, pp. 432–439 (2003)
2. Poppe, R.: A survey on vision-based human action recognition. Image Vis. Comput. **28**, 976–990 (2010)
3. Dalal, N., Triggs, B., Schmid, C.: Human detection using oriented histograms of flow and appearance. In: Leonardis, A., Bischof, H., Pinz, A. (eds.) ECCV 2006. LNCS, vol. 3952, pp. 428–441. Springer, Heidelberg (2006). https://doi.org/10.1007/11744047_33
4. Perš, J., Sulić, V., Kristan, M., Perše, M., Polanec, K., Kovačič, S.: Histograms of optical flow for efficient representation of body motion. Pattern Recogn. Lett. **31**, 1369–1376 (2010)
5. Wang, H., Kläser, A., Schmid, C., Liu, C.: Action recognition by dense trajectories. In: CVPR 2011, pp. 3169–3176 (2011)
6. Zhou, Z., Shi, F., Wu, W.: Learning spatial and temporal extents of human actions for action detection. IEEE Trans. Multimed. **17**(1), 512–525 (2015)
7. Wang, L., Qiao, Y., Tang, X.: Action recognition with trajectory-pooled deep-convolutional descriptors. In: 2015 IEEE Conference on Computer Vision and Pattern Recognition (CVPR) (2015)
8. Shi, Y., Zeng, W., Huang, T., Wang, Y.: Learning deep trajectory descriptor for action recognition in videos using deep neural networks. In: 2015 IEEE International Conference on Multimedia and Expo (ICME), pp. 1–6 (2015)
9. Toshev, A., Szegedy, C.: DeepPose: human pose estimation via deep neural networks. In: 2014 IEEE Conference on Computer Vision and Pattern Recognition (2014)
10. Brau, E., Jiang, H.: 3D human pose estimation via deep learning from 2D annotations. In: 2016 Fourth International Conference on 3D Vision (3DV), pp. 582–591 (2016)
11. Newell, A., Yang, K., Deng, J.: Stacked hourglass networks for human pose estimation. In: Leibe, B., Matas, J., Sebe, N., Welling, M. (eds.) ECCV 2016. LNCS, vol. 9912, pp. 483–499. Springer, Cham (2016). https://doi.org/10.1007/978-3-319-46484-8_29
12. Wei, S.E., Ramakrishna, V., Kanade, T., Sheikh, Y.: Convolutional pose machines (2016)
13. Cao, Z., Hidalgo, G., Simon, T., Wei, S.E., Sheikh, Y.: OpenPose: realtime multi-person 2D pose estimation using part affinity fields (2018)
14. Güler, R.A., Neverova, N., Kokkinos, I.: DensePose: dense human pose estimation in the wild (2018)
15. Shotton, J., et al.: Real-time human pose recognition in parts from single depth images. In: CVPR 2011, pp. 1297–1304 (2011)
16. Ye, M., Zhang, Q., Wang, L., Zhu, J., Yang, R., Gall, J.: A survey on human motion analysis from depth data. In: Grzegorzek, M., Theobalt, C., Koch, R., Kolb, A. (eds.) Time-of-Flight and Depth Imaging. Sensors, Algorithms, and Applications. LNCS, vol. 8200, pp. 149–187. Springer, Heidelberg (2013). https://doi.org/10.1007/978-3-642-44964-2_8
17. Siddiqui, M., Medioni, G.: Human pose estimation from a single view point, real-time range sensor. In: 2010 IEEE Computer Society Conference on Computer Vision and Pattern Recognition - Workshops, pp. 1–8 (2010)

18. Plagemann, C., Ganapathi, V., Koller, D., Thrun, S.: Real-time identification and localization of body parts from depth images. In: 2010 IEEE International Conference on Robotics and Automation, pp. 3108–3113 (2010)
19. Vemulapalli, R., Arrate, F., Chellappa, R.: Human action recognition by representing 3D skeletons as points in a lie group. In: 2014 IEEE Conference on Computer Vision and Pattern Recognition, pp. 588–595 (2014)
20. Gong, D., Medioni, G., Zhao, X.: Structured time series analysis for human action segmentation and recognition. IEEE Trans. Pattern Anal. Mach. Intell. **36**, 1414–1427 (2014)
21. Zhang, Y., Zhang, Y., Zhang, Z., Bao, J., Song, Y.: Human activity recognition based on time series analysis using U-Net (2018)
22. Kim, H., Kim, I.: Human activity recognition as time-series analysis. Math. Probl. Eng. **2015**, 1–9 (2015)
23. Du, Y., Wang, W., Wang, L.: Hierarchical recurrent neural network for skeleton based action recognition. In: 2015 IEEE Conference on Computer Vision and Pattern Recognition (CVPR), pp. 1110–1118 (2015)
24. Redmon, J., Farhadi, A.: YOLOv3: an incremental improvement (2018)
25. Deng, J., Dong, W., Socher, R., Li, L.J., Li, K., Fei-Fei, L.: ImageNet: a large-scale hierarchical image database. In: CVPR 2009 (2009)
26. Lin, T.-Y., et al.: Microsoft COCO: common objects in context. In: Fleet, D., Pajdla, T., Schiele, B., Tuytelaars, T. (eds.) ECCV 2014. LNCS, vol. 8693, pp. 740–755. Springer, Cham (2014). https://doi.org/10.1007/978-3-319-10602-1_48
27. Ramakrishna, V., Munoz, D., Hebert, M., Andrew Bagnell, J., Sheikh, Y.: Pose machines: articulated pose estimation via inference machines. In: Fleet, D., Pajdla, T., Schiele, B., Tuytelaars, T. (eds.) ECCV 2014. LNCS, vol. 8690, pp. 33–47. Springer, Cham (2014). https://doi.org/10.1007/978-3-319-10605-2_3
28. Schuster, M., Paliwal, K.K.: Bidirectional recurrent neural networks. IEEE Trans. Sig. Process. **45**, 2673–2681 (1997)
29. Schuldt, C., Laptev, I., Caputo, B.: Recognizing human actions: a local SVM approach. In: 2004 Proceedings of the 17th International Conference on Pattern Recognition, ICPR 2004, vol. 3, pp. 32–36 (2004)
30. Blank, M., Gorelick, L., Shechtman, E., Irani, M., Basri, R.: Actions as space-time shapes. In: The Tenth IEEE International Conference on Computer Vision (ICCV 2005), pp. 1395–1402 (2005)
31. Gao, Z., Chen, M., Hauptmann, A.G., Cai, A.: Comparing evaluation protocols on the KTH dataset. In: Salah, A.A., Gevers, T., Sebe, N., Vinciarelli, A. (eds.) HBU 2010. LNCS, vol. 6219, pp. 88–100. Springer, Heidelberg (2010). https://doi.org/10.1007/978-3-642-14715-9_10
32. Fathi, A., Mori, G.: Action recognition by learning mid-level motion features. In: 2008 IEEE Conference on Computer Vision and Pattern Recognition, pp. 1–8 (2008)
33. Baccouche, M., Mamalet, F., Wolf, C., Garcia, C., Baskurt, A.: Sequential deep learning for human action recognition. In: Salah, A.A., Lepri, B. (eds.) HBU 2011. LNCS, vol. 7065, pp. 29–39. Springer, Heidelberg (2011). https://doi.org/10.1007/978-3-642-25446-8_4
34. Gorelick, L., Blank, M., Shechtman, E., Irani, M., Basri, R.: Actions as space-time shapes. IEEE Trans. Pattern Anal. Mach. Intell. **29**, 2247–2253 (2007)
35. Gilbert, A., Illingworth, J., Bowden, R.: Fast realistic multi-action recognition using mined dense spatio-temporal features, pp. 925–931 (2009)
36. Moussa, M.M., Hamayed, E., Fayek, M.B., El Nemr, H.A.: An enhanced method for human action recognition. J. Adv. Res. **6**, 163–169 (2015)

37. Soomro, K., Zamir, A.R., Shah, M.: UCF101: a dataset of 101 human actions classes from videos in the wild (2012)
38. Kuehne, H., Jhuang, H., Garrote, E., Poggio, T., Serre, T.: HMDB: a large video database for human motion recognition. In: 2011 International Conference on Computer Vision, pp. 2556–2563 (2011)

ST: Computational Bioimaging

Ensemble Convolutional Neural Networks for the Detection of Microscopic Fusarium Oxysporum

Josh Daniel L. Ong$^{(\boxtimes)}$, Erinn Giannice T. Abigan, Luis Gabriel Cajucom, Patricia Angela R. Abu, and Ma. Regina Justina E. Estuar

Ateneo de Manila University, Quezon City, Philippines
{josh.ong,erinn.abigan,luis.cajucom}@obf.ateneo.edu,
{pabu,restuar}@ateneo.edu

Abstract. The Panama disease has been reported to wipe out banana plantations due to the fungal pathogen known as Fusarium oxysporum f. sp. Cubense Tropical Race 4, or Foc TR4. Currently, there are no proven methods to control the spread of the disease. This study aims to develop an early detection model for Foc TR4 to minimize damages to infected plantations. In line with this, CNN models using the ResNet50 architecture were utilized towards the classification of the presence of Foc TR4 in a given microscopy image of a soil sample. Fungi samples were lab-cultivated, and images were taken using a lab microscope with three distinct microscopy configurations in LPO magnification. The initial results have shown that brightfield and darkfield images are generally more helpful in the automatic classification of fungi. Gradient-weighted Class Activation Mapping (Grad-CAM) was used to validate the decision processes of the individual CNN models. The proposed ensemble model shows promising results that achieved an accuracy of 91.46%. The model is beneficial as a low-cost preliminary test that could be performed on areas that are suspected to be infected with the pathogen given that the exported models can easily be implemented in a mobile system.

Keywords: Fusarium oxysporum f. sp. cubense · Model stacking · Ensemble learning · Convolutional neural networks

1 Introduction

The banana is the one of the most popular fruits in the world. In 2009, it was one of the most valuable export products for countries such as the Philippines [13]. However, farmers who choose to grow the fruit have to face the risk of the disease known as the Fusarium wilt. With no long-term solution to combat the disease, infected plantations are destroyed or abandoned to prevent further spread of the disease. Even drastic measures such as burning the soil does not guarantee that the disease will not reinfect future crops planted on it [12]. In addition to being able to survive in soil for extended periods of time, the pathogen behind the

© Springer Nature Switzerland AG 2020
G. Bebis et al. (Eds.): ISVC 2020, LNCS 12509, pp. 321–332, 2020.
https://doi.org/10.1007/978-3-030-64556-4_25

disease can also survive through other hosts without showing any apparent signs of infection [4]. The best solution to combat the disease would be to develop a new banana cultivar that is genetically resistant to the pathogen [12]. As of writing, there are four known strains of the pathogen: Race 1, 2, 3, and 4. Historically, the Gros Michel cultivar was the most popular banana grown and traded, but Fusarium wilt caused by Race 1 eventually pushed producers to transition to growing Cavendish bananas instead [4]. Race 2 affected plantains of the Bluggoe subgroup while Race 3 did not infect bananas at all. In 1989 however, a new strain of Foc has been discovered in Taiwan that threatened the Cavendish cultivar. Known as Tropical Race 4, it has quickly spread across Southeast Asia and some regions in West Asia despite swift efforts to contain the disease [14]. Even today, the Fusarium wilt still stands as a critical issue, forcing farmers to relocate as healthy soil becomes progressively scarce [2].

The Fusarium wilt is caused by a fungal pathogen named Fusarium oxysporum f. sp. cubense (Foc) [8]. When it colonizes a host plant, it first enters the roots. Eventually, the host plant's vascular tissues are compromised. This causes the host to limit nutrient intake from infected tissue, resulting in wilt and eventual plant death [4]. Visible symptoms induced by the wilt only appear at this stage of the colonization. As such, when a plant has been shown to be infected with the Fusarium wilt, nearby asymptomatic plants are most likely to be infected as well. Hence, there is a need for a method that would aid in the earlier detection of the pathogen.

As with other kinds of fungi, features of Foc are visible on a microscopic level. While there are microscopic structures that could be identified as belonging to Foc, these are not unique to the species of oxysporum. There are structures that are similar to the ones belonging to other species of Fusarium as well as other genera of fungi entirely [8]. Because of this, studies have recommended that additional tests such as Polymerase chain reaction (PCR) should be performed when attempting to classify fungal samples as Foc. However, these tests require expensive equipment and materials [6] and are thus inaccessible to small-scale banana producers whose farms are the most susceptible to the disease [2].

There have been other studies on the automatic detection of Foc TR4 and other plant diseases, but these are largely focused on analyzing the leaves of the potentially infected plants. Although this is a proven method for identifying plant diseases, this would be only possible in the later stages of Fusarium wilt. Automatic detection can instead be done on images of possibly infected soil samples taken using a microscope. For this task, convolutional neural networks (CNNs) can be trained to classify these images.

The purpose of this study is to create a model that would accurately classify whether a given image of a microscopic soil sample contains Foc TR4, Foc, other fungi, or no fungi at all. The dataset contains images, each of which have been captured using three different microscopy techniques. Three CNN models will be trained separately to classify these respectively. An ensemble model will also be evaluated against the performance of the individual CNN models. The ResNet50 architecture will be used for the CNN models.

2 Related Literature

Multiple studies have been done in order to automatically identify Fusarium wilt and other plant diseases. Ferentinos [7] utilized various CNN architectures such as AlexNet and VGGNet to classify various diseases based on leaf images. The performance achieved by the CNN models in the study justifies the use of deep neural networks for image classification. While training the model itself may be computationally expensive, using the trained model to make predictions is not. This prompts Ferentinos to suggest possible applications for the model as a low-cost solution in plant disease detection [7]. Using a dataset of 87,848 leaf images containing 58 different classes, Ferentinos was able to train a VGGNet model to attain an accuracy of 99.53%.

Estuar, Lim, and Alampay [5] proposed the use of multiple sensors in order to augment the use of leaf analysis in predicting the spread of the pathogen in the soil. Using soil sensors, weather data, and leaf images, they were able to create a predictive model to map out areas possibly infected with the disease. The study also produced an autoencoder that was able to learn and generate features of infected leaves with a success rate of 91% for non-infected leaves and 78% for infected leaves.

In a different study, Lim and Estuar [10] proposed using CNNs to detect Foc in microscopy images of soil. Using a dataset that was created by the authors themselves, the resulting models were able to perform well. While the initial number of images was few, data augmentation was performed on the images in order to artificially populate the dataset as well as to make the model dependent on the morphological features of the pathogen. The models in the study were able to achieve F1 scores of 1.0, and these results were validated using Local Interpretable Model-agnostic Explanations (LIME).

3 Methodology

In this study, images of various fungal samples were taken by lab microscopes using three different microscopy techniques and are used to train three CNN models. Figure 1 shows an overview of the entire experiment setup. The models will then be assessed using select performance metrics such as accuracy, precision, recall, f1-score, and confusion matrices. To validate the features learned by the model against known features of the pathogen based on literature, Gradient-weighted Class Activation Mapping (Grad-CAM) visualizations will be generated [15]. An ensemble model using the three trained CNN models will also be created. The performance of which will be compared to the performance of the individual CNN models. The experiment utilizes the Python programming language with the TensorFlow and Keras deep learning libraries. The Grad-CAM implementation that will be used is a modified version of Petsiuk's [11] implementation.

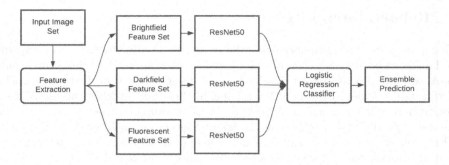

Fig. 1. Overview of the methodology

Fig. 2. Example of an image set: (a) Brightfield (b) Darkfield (c) Fluorescent

3.1   Data Collection and Data Description

The dataset is made up of images from the Cloud-based Intelligent Total Analysis System (CITAS) project taken by the project's biology team using a lab microscope with three different microscopy configurations: brightfield, darkfield, and fluorescent. An image set contains three images, one for each microscopy technique used. An example of this can be seen in Fig. 2.

Moreover, the samples used in the data collection process have been categorized into three distinct labels: Foc TR4, Foc non-TR4, and Fungi. Images were then captured from soil sample slides containing these fungi. Settings for the microscope camera remained unchanged throughout the entire collection period as to reduce variations in image characteristics. Captures that did not contain any fungal features whatsoever were labeled as "Clean." For this study, the dataset used is comprised of 1,352 Clean image sets, 771 Foc TR4 image sets, 876 Foc non-TR4 image sets, and 598 Fungi image sets.

It is worth noting that each microscopy technique appears to emphasize features in the captured sample area differently. For this reason, models may learn different features when looking at each type of image. To confirm this idea, Grad-CAM visualizations will be generated in order to verify the learned features across all microscopy techniques.

3.2   Image Sampling

The images were organized by microscopy technique and label. The dataset consists of three subsets, one for each microscopy technique. Although separate, these subsets were shuffled simultaneously to preserve the image set relationship. To balance out the dataset, a number of clean image sets were removed from the dataset for this experiment. Once parsed into arrays, the dataset was randomly split into two subsets: 66% for the training set and 33% for the test set. Furthermore, the images were downsized from their original resolution of 2048px × 1536px to 256px × 192px primarily to reduce computational costs. The original aspect ratio of the image was preserved in order to retain information such as shapes of important features [17].

3.3   Modelling

In this study, the ResNet50 and MobileNet deep learning architectures will be assessed. For the final framework, separate models will be trained to learn features from each one of the microscopy techniques, as outlined in Fig. 1. In this experiment, the weights of the network were randomly initialized. The models were trained on the training set generated from the dataset outlined in Sect. 3.1 for 50 epochs with a batch size of 16.

Ensemble Learning. The dataset is assembled in a manner that allows for the implementation of ensemble learning. Ensemble learning models are algorithms that produce new predictions by combining predictions from a set of classifiers [3]. Generally, an ensemble classifier will achieve a better performance if the individual classifiers fulfill the necessary conditions outlined by Diettrich, Hansen, and Salamon [3,9] in their studies: 1) The member classifiers must be accurate in that they outperform random guessing and 2) the member classifiers must be diverse in that they make different errors on new data points. The latter condition is fulfilled in this study through the property of the dataset itself being diverse in that the images were taken using three different techniques.

For this experiment, an ensemble method known as model stacking is used to take advantage of the full set of images for each classification. Model stacking is a method in where predictions from a set of models are used as inputs for a second-level model to generate a final prediction [16]. This method is selected since stacked models perform better when the individual models are dissimilar [1]. A Logistic Regression model using default parameters will be trained on the predictions of the three models on the training set. Since each set contains three distinct types of images of the same sample area, all three classifiers are expected to be diverse after being trained.

3.4   Model Evaluation

The performance of each trained CNN model will be evaluated using popular performance metrics, namely: accuracy, precision, recall, and f1-score. These metrics will be generated using the scikit-learn package. Furthermore, the use of model interpretability methods are necessary in order to visualize and validate the decision processes of the neural networks. For this experiment, Gradient-weighted Class Activation Mapping (Grad-CAM) will be used to verify that the learned features match what is described in Foc literature. Lastly, the performance of the final ensemble model will be compared to that of the individual CNNs as well as to that of a MobileNet implementation with similar parameters using the same metrics.

4   Results and Discussion

Table 1 lists the performances of the individual CNN models in terms of Precision (Pr), Recall (Re), F1-score (F1) and Accuracy. From Table 1, the individual CNN models performed differently from each other. Based on performance in terms of accuracy, brightfield and darkfield images are generally more helpful in classifying the type of fungi than fluorescent images. The performance metrics used to assess the individual models are outlined in Table 2.

Table 1. Model performance overview

Model	Pr	Re	F1	Test accuracy
ResNet50 brightfield model	0.78	0.78	0.77	78.12%
ResNet50 darkfield model	0.75	0.75	0.74	74.92%
ResNet50 fluorescent model	0.65	0.66	0.65	65.85%
ResNet50 ensemble	0.91	0.91	0.91	**91.46%**
MobileNet model	0.65	0.64	0.63	64.45%
MobileNet ensemble	0.84	0.85	0.84	84.53%

4.1   ResNet50 Individual Model Evaluation

Brightfield Model. Individually, the brightfield model performed the best among the three CNNs with an accuracy of 78.12%. Table 2 shows that the model was able to classify Clean and Foc non-TR4 images relatively well with F1-scores of 0.83 and 0.87 for these labels respectively. On the other hand, the performance of the model in identifying Foc TR4 images needs improvement. With a recall of 0.58, it was able to correctly predict over half of the Foc TR4 images in the test set.

Darkfield Model. The darkfield model performed similarly to the brightfield model with an accuracy of 74.92%. Table 2 shows that the model is slightly better at classifying Foc non-TR4 images with a near perfect recall score of 0.97. However, a corresponding precision score of 0.81 suggests that the model has a tendency of mislabeling other images as Foc non-TR4.

Table 2. Individual model classification report

Label	Brightfield model			Darkfield model			Fluorescent model		
	Pr	*Re*	*F1*	*Pr*	*Re*	*F1*	*Pr*	*Re*	*F1*
Clean	0.77	0.91	0.83	0.76	0.65	0.70	0.71	0.87	0.78
Foc TR4	0.72	0.58	0.64	0.64	0.69	0.66	0.67	0.64	0.65
Foc non-TR4	0.82	0.91	0.87	0.81	0.97	0.88	0.65	0.58	0.61
Other fungi	0.79	0.63	0.70	0.87	0.67	0.70	0.60	0.51	0.55

Fluorescent Model. The fluorescent model attained an accuracy of 65.85% on the test set. Table 2 shows that the model performs poorly outside of labeling Clean images, having obtained F1-scores of around 0.6 for the non-clean labels. A possible explanation for this is that the model may have been overly dependent on the color exhibited by fluorescence instead of morphological characteristics found in the images to make predictions.

The individual models have shown to perform well in classifying certain labels, namely Clean and Foc non-TR4. However, both the metrics and the confusion matrix shows that the models struggle to predict Foc TR4 and Fungi images. Among the three models, the highest accuracy scores for these labels alone are 65.7% and 67.5%. This is possibly due to the nature of Foc TR4 fungal structures being similar to Foc non-TR4 and the Fungi label containing images of a wide variety of different fungal species.

Grad-CAM Validation. Both the brightfield and darkfield models appear to have learned to detect fungal structures and shapes within the images. Examples of this can be seen in Figs. 3 and 4. The saliency maps generated by Grad-CAM in Figs. 3a and 4a shows that the model focused on empty areas when classifying images as clean. For the rest of the classes, the model accentuates fungal structures even when these structures are not immediately visible. This is shown in Figs. 3c and 4c.

Upon inspection of the saliency maps for the fluorescent model, the model does not appear to have considered all of the fungal structures in a given image. Figure 5 shows that while the model highlights some structures in the images, there does not appear to be any consistency in its selection.

4.2 ResNet50 Ensemble Model Evaluation

In the same image set, there exists instances where the three individual CNNs do not have the same prediction. An example of this is shown in Fig. 6, where a Clean image set was mislabeled by both the darkfield and the fluorescent model. This suggests that all three models have learned features unique to their respective microscopy types. To validate this, a logistic regression model has been trained on the training set predictions of the individual models, thereby creating an ensemble model.

Table 3. Ensemble model classification report

Label	Pr	Re	F1
Clean	0.91	0.91	0.91
Foc TR4	0.83	0.91	0.87
Foc non-TR4	0.94	0.96	0.95
Other fungi	0.89	0.75	0.81

The performance of the ensemble model is outlined in Tables 1 and 3. Evidently, the ensemble model achieved an accuracy of 91.46% which is significantly higher than the best performing individual model. In Table 3, the model seems to perform well across all classes except for "Other Fungi." This is to be expected given the broad range of varying fungal species and the limited samples available in the dataset for each of these.

Furthermore, the ensemble model was able to correctly predict the image set shown in Fig. 6 despite differing predictions from the individual classifiers. To reinforce this, a second example can be observed in Fig. 7 which the ensemble model was also able to successfully label.

4.3   Comparison to MobileNet

A MobileNet network was also trained in order to evaluate the performance of the ResNet50-based ensemble network. The MobileNet was trained with parameters similar to the ones used in training the ResNet50 models. Table 1 outlines two approaches done using MobileNet. In the first approach, an instance of MobileNet was trained on all the images with no regard for the technique used in capturing the image. The second approach involved using the proposed ensemble framework but with MobileNet models as the member classifiers.

MobileNet with All Images. The MobileNet trained on all image types from the dataset performed only as well as the ResNet50 trained on fluorescent images exclusively. However, the confusion matrix generated from the predictions of this model shows that the model was not able to accurately predict more than half of the Foc TR4 and Fungi images on the test set, only being able to correctly predict 49.1% and 39.8% of the classes, respectively. The model instead had a tendency to mislabel those images as Clean and Foc non-TR4. This is due to similarities between Foc TR4 and Foc non-TR4 as well as the nature of the Fungi label as discussed earlier.

Ensemble MobileNet. Unlike in the previous approach, the ensemble framework with MobileNet was able to achieve an accuracy score similar to the one achieved by the ResNet50 ensemble. An explanation for the slightly lower accuracy may be attributed to the lower performance of the MobileNet member

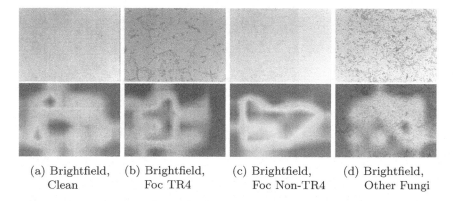

(a) Brightfield,   (b) Brightfield,   (c) Brightfield,   (d) Brightfield,
    Clean   Foc TR4   Foc Non-TR4   Other Fungi

Fig. 3. Grad-CAM visualizations for correctly identified brightfield images

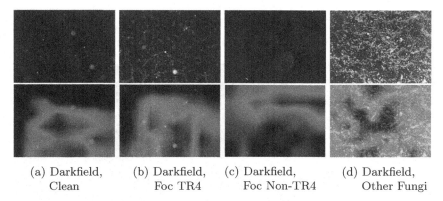

(a) Darkfield,   (b) Darkfield,   (c) Darkfield,   (d) Darkfield,
    Clean   Foc TR4   Foc Non-TR4   Other Fungi

Fig. 4. Grad-CAM visualizations for correctly identified darkfield images

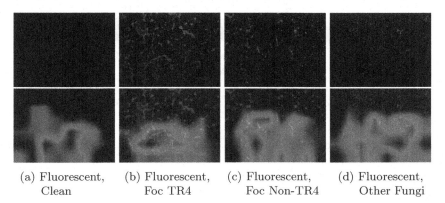

(a) Fluorescent,   (b) Fluorescent,   (c) Fluorescent,   (d) Fluorescent,
    Clean   Foc TR4   Foc Non-TR4   Other Fungi

Fig. 5. Grad-CAM visualizations for correctly identified fluorescent images

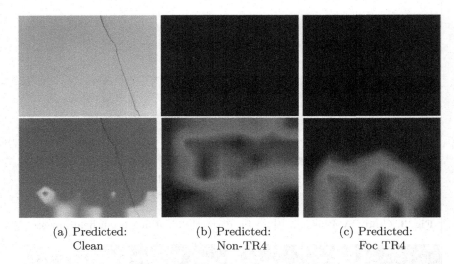

(a) Predicted: Clean	(b) Predicted: Non-TR4	(c) Predicted: Foc TR4

Fig. 6. A clean image set labeled differently by the member classifiers

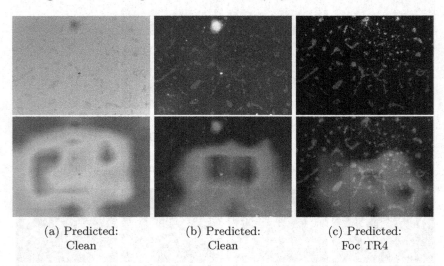

(a) Predicted: Clean	(b) Predicted: Clean	(c) Predicted: Foc TR4

Fig. 7. A Foc TR4 image set labeled differently by the member classifiers

classifiers. For instance, the MobileNet model trained on darkfield models was only able to achieve an accuracy score of 50.91%. This is an indication that the individual models need further tuning to achieve performance similar to the ResNet50 models.

5 Conclusions

Multiple convolutional neural network models have been created in order to detect the presence of fungi in a given image of a soil sample under a microscope. Each unique capture of a soil sample was taken using three distinct microscopy techniques: brightfield, darkfield, and fluorescent. The dataset was divided by microscopy technique, and separate CNN models were trained on each of the subsets. The initial results have shown that brightfield and darkfield images are generally more helpful in the automatic classification of fungi. Gradient-weighted Class Activation Mapping (Grad-CAM) was used to validate the decision processes of the individual CNN models. The ensemble model, though achieving an accuracy of 91.46% in this experiment, is not a surefire method in determining the presence of Foc. This can be further validated by testing the model on images captured from actual field samples. Moreover, better performance may be achieved by exploring methods such as pre-processing on the input images, transfer learning using pre-trained models, using different CNN architectures, using diverse member classifiers for the ensemble framework, or other ensemble learning methods. However, the proposed model is beneficial as a low-cost preliminary test that could be performed on areas that are suspected to be infected with the pathogen given that the exported models can easily be implemented in a mobile system.

Acknowledgments. The authors would like to acknowledge the Ateneo Center for Computing Competency and Research (ACCCRe), the Philippine-California Advanced Research Institutes - Cloud-based Intelligent Total Analysis System (PCARI-CITAS) Project, the Commission on Higher Education (CHED), and the Department of Science and Technology - Science Education Institute (DOST-SEI) for supporting this research.

References

1. Breiman, L.: Stacked regressions. Mach. Learn. **24**, 49–64 (1996). https://doi.org/10.1007/BF00117832
2. Cayon, M.: Dreaded banana disease spreads to other mindanao plantations, March 2020. https://businessmirror.com.ph/2020/02/03/dreaded-banana-disease-spreads-to-other-mindanao-plantations/
3. Dietterich, T.G.: Ensemble methods in machine learning. In: Kittler, J., Roli, F. (eds.) MCS 2000. LNCS, vol. 1857, pp. 1–15. Springer, Heidelberg (2000). https://doi.org/10.1007/3-540-45014-9_1
4. Dita, M., Barquero, M., Heck, D., Mizubuti, E.S., Staver, C.P.: Fusarium wilt of banana: current knowledge on epidemiology and research needs towards sustainable management. Front. Plant Sci. **9**(9), 1468 (2018)
5. Estuar, M.R.J.E., Lim, H.P.M., Alampay, R.B.: Towards the development of a multidimensional multisensor spatiotemporal model for disease detection and spread. Int. J. Biotech. Recent Adv. (2018). https://doi.org/10.18689/2639-4529.a1.002
6. Fakruddin, M., et al.: Nucleic acid amplification: alternative methods of polymerase chain reaction. J. Pharm. Bioallied Sci. **5**(4), 245–252 (2013)
7. Ferentinos, K.P.: Deep learning models for plant disease detection and diagnosis. Comput. Electron. Agric. **145**, 311–318 (2018)

8. Fourie, G., Steenkamp, E.T., Ploetz, R.C., Gordon, T.R., Viljoen, A.: Current status of the taxonomic position of Fusarium oxysporum formae specialis cubense within the Fusarium oxysporum complex. Infect. Genet. Evol. **11**, 533–542 (2011)

9. Hansen, L.K., Salamon, P.: Neural network ensembles. IEEE Trans. Pattern Anal. Mach. Intell. **12**(10), 993–1001 (1990)

10. Lim, H.P.M., Estuar, M.R.J.E.: Microscopic fusarium detection and verification with convolutional neural networks. In: Proceedings of the 2018 International Conference on Machine Learning Technologies, ICMLT 2018, pp. 48–52. Association for Computing Machinery, New York (2018). https://doi.org/10.1145/3231884.3231892

11. Petsiuk, V.: Keras implementation of gradcam, October 2019. https://github.com/eclique/keras-gradcam

12. Ploetz, R.C.: Panama disease: a classic and destructive disease of banana. Plant Health Prog. **1**, 10 (2000)

13. Ploetz, R.C.: Fusarium wilt of banana. Phytopathology **105**, 1512–1521 (2015)

14. Reynolds, M.: A fungus could wipe out the banana forever, August 2019. https://www.wired.com/story/fungus-could-wipe-out-banana-forever/

15. Selvaraju, R.R., Cogswell, M., Das, A., Vedantam, R., Parikh, D., Batra, D.: Grad-CAM: visual explanations from deep networks via gradient-based localization, December 2019

16. Sill, J., Takacs, G., Mackey, L., Lin, D.: Feature-weighted linear stacking, November 2009

17. Zheng, L., Zhao, Y., Wang, S., Wang, J., Tian, Q.: Good practice in CNN feature transfer, April 2016

Offline Versus Online Triplet Mining Based on Extreme Distances of Histopathology Patches

Milad Sikaroudi[1], Benyamin Ghojogh[2], Amir Safarpoor[1],
Fakhri Karray[2], Mark Crowley[2], and Hamid R. Tizhoosh[1]([✉])

[1] KIMIA Lab, University of Waterloo, Waterloo, ON, Canada
{msikaroudi,asafarpo,tizhoosh}@uwaterloo.ca
[2] Department of Electrical and Computer Engineering, University of Waterloo,
Waterloo, ON, Canada
{bghojogh,mcrowley,karray}@uwaterloo.ca

Abstract. We analyze the effect of offline and online triplet mining for colorectal cancer (CRC) histopathology dataset containing 100,000 patches. We consider the extreme, i.e., farthest and nearest patches to a given anchor, both in online and offline mining. While many works focus solely on selecting the triplets online (batch-wise), we also study the effect of extreme distances and neighbor patches before training in an offline fashion. We analyze extreme cases' impacts in terms of embedding distance for offline versus online mining, including easy positive, batch semi-hard, batch hard triplet mining, neighborhood component analysis loss, its proxy version, and distance weighted sampling. We also investigate online approaches based on extreme distance and comprehensively compare offline, and online mining performance based on the data patterns and explain offline mining as a tractable generalization of the online mining with large mini-batch size. As well, we discuss the relations of different colorectal tissue types in terms of extreme distances. We found that offline and online mining approaches have comparable performances for a specific architecture, such as ResNet-18 in this study. Moreover, we found the assorted case, including different extreme distances, is promising, especially in the online approach.

Keywords: Histopathology · Triplet mining · Extreme distances · Online mining · Offline mining · Triplet network

1 Introduction

With the advent of the deep learning methods, image analysis algorithms leveled and, in some cases, surpassed human expert performance. But due to the lack of interpretability, the deep model decision is not transparent enough. Additionally,

---

The first two authors contributed equally to this work.

© Springer Nature Switzerland AG 2020
G. Bebis et al. (Eds.): ISVC 2020, LNCS 12509, pp. 333–345, 2020.
https://doi.org/10.1007/978-3-030-64556-4_26

these models need a massive amount of the labeled data, which can be expensive and time consuming for medical data [1]. To address the interpretability issue, one may evaluate the performance by enabling consensus, for example, by retrieving similar cases. An embedding framework, such as the triplet loss, can be applied for training models to overcome the expensive label requirement, where either soft or hard similarities can be used [2]. In triplet loss, triplets of anchor-positive-negative instances are considered where the anchor and positive instances belong to the same class or are similar. Still, the negative instance belongs to another class or is dissimilar to them. Triplet loss aims to decrease and increase the intra-class and inter-class variances of embeddings, respectively, by pulling the anchor and positive closer and pushing the negative away [3].

Since the introduction of the triplet loss, many updated versions have been proposed to increase efficiency and improve generalization. Furthermore, considering beneficial aspects of these algorithms, such as unsupervised feature learning, data efficiency, and better generalization, the triplet techniques are applied to many other applications, like representation learning in pathology images [2,4–6] and other medical applications [7]. Schroff et al. [8] proposed a method to encode images into a space with distances reflecting the dissimilarity between instances. They trained a deep neural network using triplets, including similar and dissimilar cases.

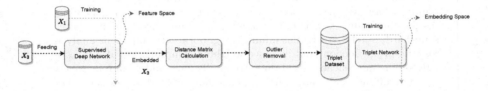

Fig. 1. Block diagram for the offline triplet mining approach.

Later, a new family of algorithms emerged to address shortcomings of the triplet loss by selecting more decent triplets with the notion of the similarity for the network while training. These efforts, such as Batch All (BA) [9], Batch Semi-Hard (BSH) [8], Batch Hard (BH) [10,11], Neighborhood Components Analysis (NCA) [12], Proxy-NCA (PNCA) [13,14], Easy Positive (EP) [15], and Distance Weighted Sampling (DWS) [16] fall into *online triplet mining* category where triplets are created and altered during training within each batch. As the online methods rely on mini-batches of data, they may not reflect the data neighborhood correctly; thus, they can result in a sub-optimal solution. In the *offline triplet mining*, a triplet dataset is created before the training session, while all training samples are taken into account. As a result, in this study, we investigate four offline and five online approaches based on four different extreme cases imposed on the positive and negative samples for triplet generation. Our contributions in this work are two-fold. For the first contribution, we have investigated four online methods and the existing approaches, and five offline methods, based on extreme cases. Secondly, we will compare different triplet mining methods for histopathology data to analyze them based on their patterns.

The remainder of this paper is organized as follows. Section 2 introduces the proposed offline triplet mining methods. In Sect. 3, we review the online triplet mining methods and propose new online strategies based on extreme distances. The experiments and comparisons are reported in Sect. 4. Finally, Sect. 5 concludes the paper and reports the possible future work.

Notations: Consider a training dataset X where x^i denotes an instance in the i-th class. Let b and c denote the mini-batch size and the number of classes, respectively, and $\mathcal{D}$ be a distance metric function, e.g., squared ℓ_2 norm. The sample triplet size per class in batch is $w := \lfloor b/c \rfloor$. We denote the anchor, positive, and negative instance in the i-th class by x_a^i, x_p^i, and x_n^i, respectively, and their deep embeddings by y_a^i, y_p^i, and y_n^i, respectively.

2 Offline Triplet Mining

In the offline triplet mining approach, the processing of data is not performed during the triplet network training but beforehand. The extreme distances are calculated only once on the whole training dataset, not in the mini-batches. The histopathology patterns in the input space cannot be distinguished, especially for the visually similar tissues [17]. Hence, we work on the extreme distances in the feature space trained using the class labels. The block diagram of the proposed offline triplet mining is depicted in Fig. 1. In the following, we explain the steps of mining in detail.

Training Supervised Feature Space: We first train a feature space in a supervised manner. For example, a deep network with a cross-entropy loss function can be used for training this space where the embedding of the one-to-last layer is extracted. We want the feature space to use the labels to better discriminate classes by increasing their inter-class distances. Hence, We use a set of training data, call it X_1, for training the supervised network.

Distance Matrix in the Feature Space: After training the supervised network, we embed another set of the training data, denoted by X_2 (where $X_1 \cup X_2 = X$ and $X_1 \cap X_2 = \varnothing$), in the feature space. We compute a distance matrix on the embedded data in the feature space. Therefore, using a distance matrix, we can find cases with extreme distances. We consider every $x \in X_2$ as an anchor in a triplet where its nearest or farthest neighbors from the same and other classes are considered as its positive and negative instances, respectively. We have four different cases with extreme distances, i.e., Easiest Positive and Easiest Negative (EPEN), Easiest Positive and Hardest Negative (EPHN), Hardest Positive, and Easiest Negative (HPEN), and Hardest Positive and Hardest Negative (HPHN). We also have the *assorted* case where one of the extreme cases is randomly selected for a triplet.

There might exist some outliers in data whose embeddings fall much apart from others. In that case, merely one single outlier may become the hardest negative for all anchors. We prevent this issue by a statistical test [18], where for every data instance in X_1 embedded in the feature space, the distances from other instances are standardized using the Z-score normalization. We consider the instances having distances above the 99-th percentile (i.e., normalized distances above the threshold 2.3263 according to the standard normal table) as outliers and ignore them.

Training the Triplet Network: After preparing the triplets in any extreme case, a triplet network [8] is trained using the triplets for learning an embedding space for better discrimination of dissimilar instances holding similar instances close enough. We call the spaces learned by the supervised and triplet networks as the feature space and embedding space, respectively (see Fig. 1).

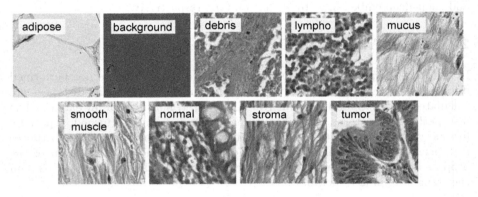

Fig. 2. Example patches for the different tissue types in the large CRC dataset.

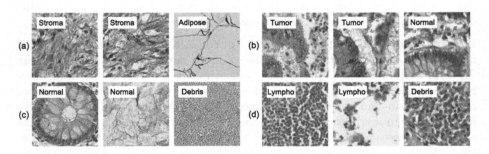

Fig. 3. Examples for extreme distance triplets: (a) EPEN, (b) EPHN, (c) HPEN, and (d) HPHN.

3 Online Triplet Mining

In the online triplet mining approach, data processing is performed during the training phase and in the mini-batch of data. In other words, the triplets are found in the mini-batch of data and not fed as a triplet-form input to the network. There exist several online mining methods in the literature which are introduced in the following. We also propose several new online mining methods based on extreme distances of data instances in the mini-batch.

Batch All [9]: One of the online methods which consider all anchor-positive and anchor-negative in the mini-batch. Its loss function is in the regular triplet loss format, summed over all the triplets in the mini-batch, formulated as

$$\mathcal{L}_{\text{BA}} := \sum_{i=1}^{c} \sum_{j=1, j \neq i}^{c} \sum_{a=1}^{w} \sum_{p=1, p \neq a}^{w} \sum_{n=1}^{w} \left[m + \mathcal{D}(y_a^i, y_p^i) - \mathcal{D}(y_a^i, y_n^j) \right]_+, \qquad (1)$$

where m is the margin between positives and negatives and $[.]_+ := \max(., 0)$ is the standard Hinge loss.

Batch Semi-hard [8]: The hardest (nearest) negative instance in the mini-batch, which is farther than the positive, is selected. Its loss function is

$$\mathcal{L}_{\text{BSH}} := \sum_{i=1}^{c} \sum_{a=1}^{w} \sum_{\substack{p=1 \\ p \neq a}}^{w} \left[m + \mathcal{D}(y_a^i, y_p^i) \right.$$

$$\left. - \min_{\substack{j \in \{1, \dots, c\} \setminus \{i\} \\ n \in \{1, \dots, w\}}} \{\mathcal{D}(y_a^i, y_n^j) | \mathcal{D}(y_a^i, y_n^j) > \mathcal{D}(y_a^i, y_p^i)\} \right]_+. \qquad (2)$$

Batch Hard [10]: The Hardest Positive and Hardest Negative (HPHN), which are the farthest positive and nearest negative in the mini-batch, are selected. Hence, its loss function is

$$\mathcal{L}_{\text{BH}} := \sum_{i=1}^{c} \sum_{a=1}^{w} \left[m + \max_{p \in \{1, \dots, w\} \setminus \{a\}} \mathcal{D}(y_a^i, y_p^i) - \min_{\substack{j \in \{1, \dots, c\} \setminus \{i\} \\ n \in \{1, \dots, w\}}} \mathcal{D}(y_a^i, y_n^j) \right]_+. \qquad (3)$$

NCA [12]: The softmax form [19] instead of the regular triplet loss [8] is used. It considers all possible negatives in the mini-batch for an anchor by

$$\mathcal{L}_{\text{NCA}} := - \sum_{i=1}^{c} \sum_{a=1}^{w} \ln \left(\frac{\exp(-\mathcal{D}(y_a^i, y_p^i))}{\sum_{j=1, j \neq i}^{c} \sum_{n=1}^{w} \exp(-\mathcal{D}(y_a^i, y_n^j))} \right), \qquad (4)$$

where $\ln(.)$ is the natural logarithm and $\exp(.)$ is the exponential power operator.

Proxy-NCA [13]: A set of proxies $\mathcal{P}$, e.g., the center of classes, with the cardinality of the number of classes is used. An embedding y is assigned to a proxy

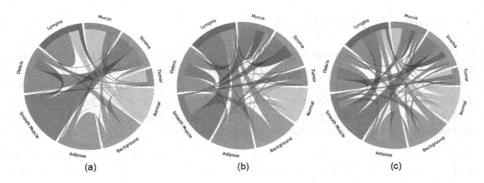

Fig. 4. Chord diagrams of the negatives in the offline mining based on extreme distances: (a) nearest negatives (EPHN & HPHN), (b) farthest negatives (EPEN & HPEN), and (c) *assorted*. The flow from i to j means that i takes j as a negative.

as $\Pi(y) := \arg\min_{\pi \in \mathcal{P}} \mathcal{D}(y, \pi)$ for memory efficiency. PNCA uses the proxies of positive and negatives in the NCA loss:

$$\mathcal{L}_{\text{PNCA}} := -\sum_{i=1}^{c}\sum_{a=1}^{w} \ln \Big(\frac{\exp\big(-\mathcal{D}(y_a^i, \Pi(y_p^i))\big)}{\sum_{j=1, j\neq i}^{c}\sum_{n=1}^{w} \exp\big(-\mathcal{D}(y_a^i, \Pi(y_n^j))\big)} \Big). \qquad (5)$$

Easy Positive [15]: Let $y_{ep}^i := \arg\min_{p \in \{1,...,w\}\setminus\{a\}} \mathcal{D}(y_a^i, y_p^i)$ be the easiest (nearest) positive for the anchor. If the embeddings are normalized and fall on a unit hyper-sphere, the loss in EP method is

$$\mathcal{L}_{\text{EP}} := -\sum_{i=1}^{c}\sum_{a=1}^{w} \ln \Big(\frac{\exp(y_a^{i\top} y_{ep}^i)}{\exp(y_a^{i\top} y_{ep}^i) + \sum_{j=1, j\neq i}^{c}\sum_{n=1}^{w} \exp(y_a^{i\top} y_n^i)} \Big). \qquad (6)$$

Our experiments showed that for the colorectal cancer (CRC) histopathology dataset [20], the performance improves if the inner products in Eq. (6) are replaced with minus distances. We call the EP method with distances by EP-D whose loss function is

$$\mathcal{L}_{\text{EP-D}} := -\sum_{i=1}^{c}\sum_{a=1}^{w} \ln \Big(\frac{\exp(-\mathcal{D}(y_a^i, y_{ep}^i))}{\exp(-\mathcal{D}(y_a^i, y_{ep}^i)) + \sum_{j=1, j\neq i}^{c}\sum_{n=1}^{w} \exp(-\mathcal{D}(y_a^i, y_n^i))} \Big). \qquad (7)$$

Distance Weighted Sampling [16]: The distribution of the pairwise distances is proportional to $q(\mathcal{D}(y_1, y_2)) := \mathcal{D}(y_1, y_2)^{p-2}(1 - 0.25\mathcal{D}(y_1, y_2)^2)^{(n-3)/2}$ [16]. For a triplet, the negative sample is drawn as $n^* \sim \mathbb{P}(n|a) \propto \min(\lambda, q^{-1}(\mathcal{D}(y_a^i, y_n^j))), \forall j \neq i$. The loss function in the DWS method is

$$\mathcal{L}_{\text{DWS}} := \sum_{i=1}^{c}\sum_{a=1}^{w}\sum_{p=1, p\neq a}^{w} \Big[m + \mathcal{D}(y_a^i, y_p^i) - \mathcal{D}(y_a^i, y_{n^*}) \Big]_+. \qquad (8)$$

Table 1. Results of offline triplet mining on the training and test data

	Train					Test				
	R@1	R@4	R@8	R@16	Acc.	R@1	R@4	R@8	R@16	Acc.
EPEN	92.60	97.66	98.85	99.48	95.87	89.86	96.78	98.20	99.11	94.58
EPHN	**94.82**	**98.46**	**99.27**	**99.70**	**97.10**	**94.50**	**98.41**	**99.25**	**99.67**	**97.21**
HPEN	93.22	96.93	97.71	98.35	96.16	87.11	97.01	98.83	99.59	94.10
HPHN	81.62	89.73	93.15	95.78	91.19	42.71	71.07	86.13	95.32	71.25
assorted	86.40	93.65	95.93	97.66	92.53	88.56	97.31	98.95	99.52	94.60

Table 2. Results of online triplet mining on the training and test data

	Train					Test				
	R@1	R@4	R@8	R@16	Acc.	R@1	R@4	R@8	R@16	Acc.
BA [9]	95.13	98.45	99.20	99.60	97.73	82.42	93.94	96.93	98.58	90.85
BSH [8]	95.83	98.77	**99.42**	99.65	98.00	84.70	94.78	97.34	98.75	91.74
HPHN [10]	91.52	97.14	98.60	99.34	96.09	**86.65**	95.80	97.81	99.04	93.20
NCA [12]	**96.45**	**98.92**	99.40	**99.69**	**98.40**	78.93	92.58	96.39	98.47	89.65
PNCA [13]	93.59	98.06	99.04	99.53	97.08	80.45	93.02	96.34	98.42	88.72
EP [15]	84.30	94.30	96.94	98.38	92.78	74.00	90.35	95.00	97.93	85.88
EP-D	86.11	95.90	97.86	99.00	93.30	77.23	92.14	96.18	98.49	87.95
DWS [16]	84.43	94.78	97.27	98.59	92.25	83.74	94.36	96.72	98.33	92.20
EPEN	87.44	95.89	97.84	98.90	94.03	85.48	95.40	97.65	98.92	92.57
EPHN	95.44	98.68	99.22	99.57	97.90	85.34	94.80	97.49	98.81	91.77
HPEN	89.53	96.67	98.21	99.15	95.04	85.38	95.30	97.55	98.82	92.56
assorted	93.73	97.98	99.02	99.57	97.12	86.57	**96.18**	**98.25**	**99.30**	**93.44**

Extreme Distances: We propose four additional online methods based on extreme distances. We consider every instance once as an anchor in the mini-batch and take its nearest/farthest same-class instance as the easiest/hardest positive and its nearest/farthest other-class instance as the hardest/easiest negative instance. Hence, four different cases, i.e., EPEN, EPHN, HPEN, and HPHN, exist. Inspiration for the extreme values, especially the farthest, was the opposition-based learning [21,22]. HPHN is equivalent to BH, which has already been explained. We can also have a mixture of these four cases (i.e., *assorted* case) where for every anchor in the mini-batch, one of the cases is randomly considered. The proposed online mining loss functions are as follows:

$$\mathcal{L}_{\text{EPEN}} := \sum_{i=1}^{c} \sum_{a=1}^{w} \left[m + \min_{p \in \{1,\ldots,w\}\setminus\{a\}} \mathcal{D}(y_a^i, y_p^i) - \max_{\substack{j \in \{1,\ldots,c\}\setminus\{i\} \\ n \in \{1,\ldots,w\}}} \mathcal{D}(y_a^i, y_n^j) \right]_+, \quad (9)$$

$$\mathcal{L}_{\text{EPHN}} := \sum_{i=1}^{c} \sum_{a=1}^{w} \left[m + \min_{p \in \{1,\dots,w\} \setminus \{a\}} \mathcal{D}(y_a^i, y_p^i) - \min_{\substack{j \in \{1,\dots,c\} \setminus \{i\} \\ n \in \{1,\dots,w\}}} \mathcal{D}(y_a^i, y_n^j) \right]_+, \quad (10)$$

$$\mathcal{L}_{\text{HPEN}} := \sum_{i=1}^{c} \sum_{a=1}^{w} \left[m + \max_{p \in \{1,\dots,w\} \setminus \{a\}} \mathcal{D}(y_a^i, y_p^i) - \max_{\substack{j \in \{1,\dots,c\} \setminus \{i\} \\ n \in \{1,\dots,w\}}} \mathcal{D}(y_a^i, y_n^j) \right]_+, \quad (11)$$

$$\mathcal{L}_{\text{Assorted}} := \sum_{i=1}^{c} \sum_{a=1}^{w} \left[m + \min/\max_{p \in \{1,\dots,w\} \setminus \{a\}} \mathcal{D}(y_a^i, y_p^i) - \min/\max_{\substack{j \in \{1,\dots,c\} \setminus \{i\} \\ n \in \{1,\dots,w\}}} \mathcal{D}(y_a^i, y_n^j) \right]_+, \\ (12)$$

where min/max denotes random selection between the minimum and maximum operators.

4   Experiments and Comparisons

Dataset: We used the large colorectal cancer (CRC) histopathology dataset [20] with 100,000 stain-normalized 224 × 224 patches. The large CRC dataset includes nine classes of tissues, namely adipose, background, debris, lymphocytes (lymph), mucus, smooth muscle, normal colon mucosa (normal), cancer-associated stroma, and colorectal adenocarcinoma epithelium (tumor). Some example patches for these tissue types are illustrated in Fig. 2.

Experimental Setup: We split the data into 70K, 15K, 15K set of patches, respectively, for X_1, X_2, and the test data, denoted by X_t. We used ResNet-18 [23] as the backbone of both the supervised network and the triplet network. For the sake of a fair comparison, the mini-batch size in offline and online mining approaches was set to 48 (16 sets of triplets) and 45 (5 samples per each of the 9 classes), respectively, which are roughly equal. The learning rate, the maximum number of epochs, and the margin in triplet loss were 10^{-5}, 50, and 0.25, respectively. The feature-length and embedding spaces were both 128.

Offline Patches with Extreme Distance: Figure 3 depicts some examples for the offline created triplets with extreme distances in the feature space. The nearest/farthest positives and negatives are visually similar/dissimilar to the anchor patches, as expected. It shows that the learned feature space is a satisfactory subspace for feature extraction, which is reasonably compatible with visual patterns.

Relation of the Colorectal Tissues: The chord diagrams of negatives with extreme distances in offline mining are illustrated in Fig. 4. In both the nearest and farthest negatives, the background and normal tissues have not been negatives of any anchor. Some stroma and debris patches are the nearest negatives for smooth muscle, as well as adipose for background patches, and lymph, mucus,

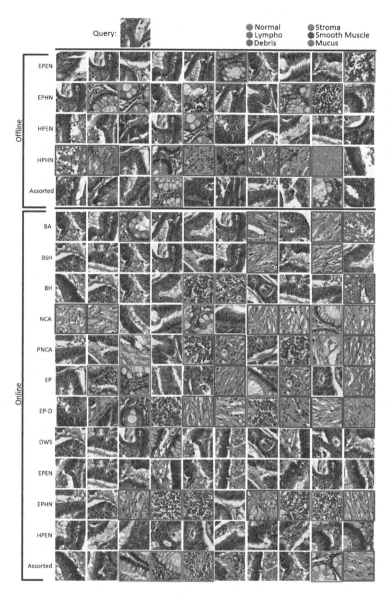

Fig. 5. The top 10 retrievals (left to right) of a tumor patch query for different loss functions. The patches with no frame are tumor patches.

and tumor for normal patches. It stems from the fact that these patches' patterns are hard to discriminate, especially tumor versus normal and stroma and debris versus smooth muscle. In farthest negatives, lymph, debris, mucus, stroma, and tumor are negatives of smooth muscle, as well as debris, smooth muscle, and lymph for adipose texture, and adipose and smooth muscle for normal patches. It is meaningful since they have different patterns. Different types of negatives are selected in the *assorted* case, which is a mixture of the nearest and farthest negative patches. It gives more variety to the triplets so that the network sees different cases in training.

Offline versus Online Embedding: The evaluation of the embedding spaces found by different offline and online methods are reported in Tables 1 and 2, respectively. The Recall@ (with ranks 1, 4, 8, and 16) and closest neighbor accuracy metrics are reported.

In offline mining, HPHN has the weakest performance on both training and test sets, showing whether the architecture or embedding dimensionality is small for these strictly hard cases or the network might be under-parameterized. We performed another experiment and used ResNet-50 to see whether a more complicated architecture would help [10]. The results showed that for the same maximum number of epochs, either would increase embedding dimensionality to 512 or utilizing the ResNet-50 architecture increased the accuracy by 4%. The test accuracy in online mining is not as promising as in offline mining because in online mining we only select a small portion of each class in a mini-batch. The chance of having the most dissimilar/similar patches in a mini-batch is much lower than the case we select triplets in an offline manner. In other words, mining in mini-batches definitely depends upon a representative population of every class in each batch. Besides, the slightly higher training accuracy of the online manner compared to offline mining can be a herald of overfitting in online mining. Tables 1 and 2 show that the easiest negatives have comparable results. It is because the histopathology patches (specifically this dataset) may have small intra-class variance for most of the tissue types (e.g., lympho tissue) and large intra-class variance for some others (e.g., normal tissue). Moreover, there is a small inter-class variance in these patches (with similar patterns, e.g., the tumor and normal tissue types are visually similar); hence, using the easy negatives would not drop the performance drastically. Moreover, as seen in Fig. 4, the hardest negatives might not be perfect candidates for negative patches in histopathology data because many patches from different tissue types erroneously include shared textures in the patching stage [20]. In addition to this, the small inter-class variety, explains why the hardest negatives struggle in reaching the best performance, as also reported in [10]. Furthermore, literature has shown that the triplets created based on the easiest extreme distances can avoid over-clustering and yield to better performance [15], which can also be acknowledged by our results. The *assorted* approach also has decent performance. Because both the inter-class and intra-class variances are considered. Finally, offline and online ways can be compared in terms of batch size. Increasing the batch size can cause the training of the network to be intractable [13]. On the contrary, a larger batch size implies a better statistical population of data to have a decent representative of every class. An ideal method has a large batch size without sacrificing the tractability. The online approaches can be considered as a special case of offline mining where the mini-batch size is the number of all instances. The offline approach is tractable because of making the triplets in pre-processing. As the Tables 1 and 2 show, the offline and online mining approaches have comparable performances. The promising performance of online approach has already been investigated by the literature. Here, we also show the promising performance of the offline approach which is because of a good statistical representation for working on the whole data population. In addition, Table 2 shows that the assorted case can result in acceptable embedding because of containing different cases of extreme distances of histopathology patches.

Retrieval of Histopathology Patches: Finally, in Fig. 5, we report the top retrievals for a sample tumor query [24]. As the figure shows, EPEN, HPEN, and *assorted* cases have the smallest false retrievals among the offline methods. In online mining, BSH, DWS, EPEN, and HPEN have the best performance. These findings coincide with Tables 1 and 2 results showing these methods had better performance. Comparing the offline and online methods in Fig. 5 shows that more number of online approaches than offline ones have false retrievals demonstrating that offline methods benefit from a better statistical population of data.

5   Conclusion and Future Direction

In this paper, we comprehensively analyzed the offline and online approaches for colorectal histopathology data. We investigated twelve online and five offline mining approaches, including the state-of-the-art triplet mining methods and extreme distance cases. We explained the performance of offline and online mining in terms of histopathology data patterns. The offline mining was interpreted as a tractable generalization of the online mining where the statistical population of data is better captured for triplet mining. We also explored the relation of the colorectal tissues in terms of extreme distances.

One possible future direction is to improve upon the existing triplet sampling methods, such as [16], for online mining and applying that on the histopathology data. One can consider dynamic updates of probabilistic density functions of the mini-batches to sample triplets from the embedding space. This dynamic sampling may improve embedding of histopathology data by exploring more of the embedding space in a stochastic manner.

References

1. Tizhoosh, H.R., Pantanowitz, L.: Artificial intelligence and digital pathology: challenges and opportunities. J. Pathol. Inform. **9**, 38 (2018)
2. Sikaroudi, M., Safarpoor, A., Ghojogh, B., Shafiei, S., Crowley, M., Tizhoosh, H.: Supervision and source domain impact on representation learning: a histopathology case study. In: 2020 International Conference of the IEEE Engineering in Medicine and Biology Society (EMBC). IEEE (2020)

3. Ghojogh, B., Sikaroudi, M., Shafiei, S., Tizhoosh, H., Karray, F., Crowley, M.: Fisher discriminant triplet and contrastive losses for training Siamese networks. In: 2020 International Joint Conference on Neural Networks (IJCNN). IEEE (2020)
4. Teh, E.W., Taylor, G.W.: Metric learning for patch classification in digital pathology. In: Medical Imaging with Deep Learning (MIDL) Conference (2019)
5. Koch, G., Zemel, R., Salakhutdinov, R.: Siamese neural networks for one-shot image recognition. In: ICML Deep Learning Workshop, vol. 2 (2015)
6. Medela, A., et al.: Few shot learning in histopathological images: reducing the need of labeled data on biological datasets. In: IEEE 16th International Symposium on Biomedical Imaging (ISBI 2019), 1860–1864. IEEE (2019)
7. Wang, J., Fang, Z., Lang, N., Yuan, H., Su, M.Y., Baldi, P.: A multi-resolution approach for spinal metastasis detection using deep Siamese neural networks. Comput. Biol. Med. **84**, 137–146 (2017)
8. Schroff, F., Kalenichenko, D., Philbin, J.: FaceNet: a unified embedding for face recognition and clustering. In: Proceedings of the IEEE Conference on Computer Vision and Pattern Recognition, pp. 815–823 (2015)
9. Ding, S., Lin, L., Wang, G., Chao, H.: Deep feature learning with relative distance comparison for person re-identification. Pattern Recogn. **48**(10), 2993–3003 (2015)
10. Hermans, A., Beyer, L., Leibe, B.: In defense of the triplet loss for person re-identification. arXiv preprint arXiv:1703.07737 (2017)
11. Peng, T., Boxberg, M., Weichert, W., Navab, N., Marr, C.: Multi-task learning of a deep K-nearest neighbour network for histopathological image classification and retrieval. In: Shen, D., et al. (eds.) MICCAI 2019. LNCS, vol. 11764, pp. 676–684. Springer, Cham (2019). https://doi.org/10.1007/978-3-030-32239-7_75
12. Goldberger, J., Hinton, G.E., Roweis, S.T., Salakhutdinov, R.R.: Neighbourhood components analysis. In: Advances in Neural Information Processing Systems, pp. 513–520 (2005)
13. Movshovitz-Attias, Y., Toshev, A., Leung, T.K., Ioffe, S., Singh, S.: No fuss distance metric learning using proxies. In: Proceedings of the IEEE International Conference on Computer Vision, pp. 360–368 (2017)
14. Teh, E.W., Taylor, G.W.: Learning with less data via weakly labeled patch classification in digital pathology. In: IEEE 17th International Symposium on Biomedical Imaging (ISBI 2020), pp. 471–475. IEEE (2020)
15. Xuan, H., Stylianou, A., Pless, R.: Improved embeddings with easy positive triplet mining. In: The IEEE Winter Conference on Applications of Computer Vision, pp. 2474–2482 (2020)
16. Wu, C.Y., Manmatha, R., Smola, A.J., Krahenbuhl, P.: Sampling matters in deep embedding learning. In: Proceedings of the IEEE International Conference on Computer Vision, pp. 2840–2848 (2017)
17. Jimenez-del Toro, O., et al.: Analysis of histopathology images: from traditional machine learning to deep learning. In: Biomedical Texture Analysis, pp. 281–314. Elsevier (2017)
18. Aggarwal, C.C.: Outlier Analysis, 2nd edn. Springer, Cham (2017). https://doi.org/10.1007/978-3-319-47578-3
19. Ye, M., Zhang, X., Yuen, P.C., Chang, S.F.: Unsupervised embedding learning via invariant and spreading instance feature. In: Proceedings of the IEEE Conference on Computer Vision and Pattern Recognition, pp. 6210–6219 (2019)
20. Kather, J.N., et al.: Predicting survival from colorectal cancer histology slides using deep learning: a retrospective multicenter study. PLoS Med. **16**(1), e1002730 (2019)

21. Tizhoosh, H.R.: Opposition-based learning: a new scheme for machine intelligence. In: International Conference on Computational Intelligence for Modelling, Control and Automation and International Conference on Intelligent Agents, Web Technologies and Internet Commerce (CIMCA-IAWTIC 2006), vol. 1, pp. 695–701. IEEE (2005)

22. Tizhoosh, H.R., Ventresca, M.: Oppositional Concepts in Computational Intelligence, vol. 155. Springer, Heidelberg (2008). https://doi.org/10.1007/978-3-540-70829-2

23. He, K., Zhang, X., Ren, S., Sun, J.: Deep residual learning for image recognition. In: Proceedings of the IEEE Conference on Computer Vision and Pattern Recognition, pp. 770–778 (2016)

24. Kalra, S., et al.: Pan-cancer diagnostic consensus through searching archival histopathology images using artificial intelligence. NPJ Digit. Med. Nat. **3**(1), 1–15 (2020)

Multi-label Classification of Panoramic Radiographic Images Using a Convolutional Neural Network

Leonardo S. Campos⊙ and Denis H. P. Salvadeo$^{(\boxtimes)}$ ⊙

São Paulo State University (UNESP), Rio Claro, SP 13506-900, Brazil
leonardo.souzacampos@hotmail.com, denis.salvadeo@unesp.br

Abstract. Dentistry is one of the areas which mostly present potential for application of machine learning techniques, such as convolutional neural networks (CNNs). This potential derives from the fact that several of the typical diagnosis methods on dentistry are based on image analysis, such as diverse types of X-ray images. Typically, these analyses require an empiric and specialized assessment by the professional. In this sense, machine learning can contribute with tools to aid the professionals in dentistry, such as image classification, whose objective is to classify and identify patterns and classes on a set of images. The objective of this current study is to develop an algorithm based on a convolutional neural network with the skill to identify independently six specific classes on the images and classify them accordingly on panoramic X-ray images, also known as orthopantomography. The six independent classes are: Presence of all 28 teeth, restoration, braces, dental prosthesis, images with more than 32 teeth and images with missing teeth. The workflow was based on a DOE (Design of experiments) study, considering the neural network architecture variables as factors, in order to identify the most significant ones, which ones mostly contribute to improve the fitness of the network, and the interactions between these in order to optimize the network architecture, based on the F1 and recall scores. Obtained results are promising, considering that for the optimal network architecture, F1 and Recall scores of 87% and 86%, respectively, were obtained.

Keywords: Panoramic radiography · Image classification · Convolutional neural network · Dentistry images

1 Introduction

One of the fields on which the advances in Machine learning, and specifically Artificial Neural Networks, can considerably contribute to the society is regarding medical applications and diagnosis.

In this specific domain of diagnosis, one of the main architectures which can substantially contribute to professionals are the convolutional neural networks (CNNs), whose main output is the skill to identify visual features and patterns on images, taking conclusions based on the identification and interaction between these features.

© Springer Nature Switzerland AG 2020
G. Bebis et al. (Eds.): ISVC 2020, LNCS 12509, pp. 346–358, 2020.
https://doi.org/10.1007/978-3-030-64556-4_27

The capability driven by these architectures aid the diagnosis of diseases in early stages, allowing the professional to drive a treatment in early stages. One of the areas of health which is currently a big focus of studies in the area of machine learning is dentistry, which relies on several diagnostic tools based on images.

In dentistry, radiographic images are fundamental data sources to aid diagnosis. Radiography is the record of an image produced by the passage of an X-ray source through an object (Quinn and Sigl 1980). X-ray images are used in dental medicine to check the condition of the teeth, gums, jaws and bone structure of a mouth (Quinn and Sigl 1980). Without X-rays, dentists would not be able to detect many dental problems until they become severe. This way, the radiographic examination helps the dentist to discover the cause of the problem at an early stage, allowing them to outline the best treatment plan for the patient (Paewinsky et al. 2005).

Among the main kinds of X-rays radiographies utilized for this purpose, the panoramic radiography, also known as orthopantomography, is an extraoral X-ray image, allowing the obtention of fundamental information for the diagnosis of anomalies in dental medicine (Amer and Aqel 2015). Orthopantomographic examination allows for the visualization of dental irregularities, such as: teeth included, bone abnormalities, cysts, tumors, cancers, infections, post-accident fractures, temporomandibular joint disorders that cause pain in the ear, face, neck and head (Oliveira and Proença 2011).

X-ray images are pervasively used by dentists to analyze the dental structure and to define a patient's treatment plan. However, due to the lack of adequate automated resources to aid the analysis of dental X-ray images, X-ray analysis relies on mostly the dentist's experience and visual perception (Wang et al. 2016). Other details in dental X-rays that make it difficult to analyze these images are: variations of patient-to-patient teeth, artifacts used for restorations and prostheses, poor image qualities caused by certain conditions (such as noise, low contrast, homogeneity in regions close to objects of interest), space existing by a missing tooth, and limitation of acquisition methods; all these challenges result in unsuccessful development of automated computer tools to aid dental diagnosis, avoiding completely automatic analysis (Amer and Aqel 2015).

Regarding this matter, a series of studies were performed regarding the development of tools to aid in two main steps of automated analysis of orthopantomography images: Image segmentation and image classification.

Image segmentation is the process of partitioning a digital image into multiple regions (pixel set) or objects, in order to make an image representation simpler, and to facilitate its analysis (Silva et al. 2018).

Silva et al. (2018) performed a study whose objective was to apply ten segmentation techniques divided in five main categories, namely Region-based, thresholding based, clustering-based, boundary-based and watershed and compare their performances on image segmentation. The authors identified that the majority of the studies on this matter used a very small dataset, below 100 images. So, a much bigger database was generated, composed of 1500 panoramic X-ray images, acquired at the diagnostic imaging center of the Southwest State University of Bahia (UESB), Brazil. Besides increasing the size of dataset, authors considered a sampling aiming to account for significant structural variations in relation to: the teeth, the number of teeth, existence of restorations, existence of implants, existence of braces, existence of supernumerary teeth and the size of the mouth and jaws. The obtained results showed that local thresholding methods (method from Niblack (1985)) obtained the biggest performance on segmenting teeth, with a 83% score in Recall and 82% in specificity metrics.

On the other hand, image classification is the process of detecting specific features on an image and classifying these images on categories, based on these attributes, which is the actual focus of this study. For classification tasks in dental images we can highlight the following relevant works.

Sukegawa et al. (2020) applied a model based on CNN to classify types of implants from panoramic radiographic images, reaching about 90% accuracy.

Singh and Sehgal (2020) used a CNN to classify the canine, incisor, molar and premolar classes. They reported reaching more than 90% accuracy on panoramic radiographic images. Tian et al. (2019) also considered the same classes, achieving more than 95% accuracy in classification using convolutional neural networks in three-dimensional models.

Lee et al. (2018) used a CNN to classify teeth with or without caries from radiographic images, reporting an accuracy of more than 80%.

Welikala et al. (2020) made use of a CNN for detecting and classifying lesions of some types of oral lesions (such as cancer, keratosis) from photographic images, having achieved an F1 score of over 87% in the classification of images with lesions.

Muramatsu et al. (2020) applied an object detection CNN model, alongside fourfold cross-validation method, with the capability of identifying four tooth types and three tooth restoration conditions. Obtained accuracies for tooth types and tooth conditions were, respectively, 93.2% and 98.0%.

1.1 Contributions and Objective

The aim of this work is to provide a tool, using machine learning techniques, namely Convolutional Neural Networks, capable of analyze an orthopantomography and identify specific features on the digital image which can contribute to the diagnosis of possible diseases or identification of features for large-scale segregation and public health measures and policies.

This tool would be useful, for example, in large-scale diagnosis of dental health in regions with poor access to dental services. This automated tool would help identify individuals which require professional treatments or identify patterns of anomalies/diseases in a specific population, allowing the identification of variables that contribute to a population having better buccal health than others.

The proposed algorithm would have the objective to identify independently 6 specific categories: Images with all standard 28 teeth, images with restoration, images with dental appliances, images with dental implants and images with more than 32 teeth (milks teeth).

As the main contribution of this work, this is the first work that aims to detect these categories.

The following sections will describe, sequentially, the architecture of the convolutional neural network, the performed experimental setup and the obtained results. Section 2 will focus on the CNN architecture, such as the kind of neural network applied, the considered sequence of layers and type of activation functions and the convergence criteria. Section 3 will focus on the experimental setup, structured as a full-factorial

DOE (design of experiments) in order to determine the most significant factors which contribute to improve the fitness metrics and their interactions. Section 4 will discuss the obtained experimental results and perform the analysis of the considered factors, their interaction regarding recall and F1 scores and finally choosing the best CNN architecture based on the fitness scores. Finally, Sect. 5 concludes this paper.

2   CNN Architecture

The CNN (Convolutional Neural Network) (Goodfellow et al. 2016) working principle is based on detecting pixel patterns, namely features, on the images and, by grouping these features in higher layers, using image processing procedures called convolution and pooling, understanding their correlation to known outputs, using hidden layers for training. By doing so, one can train a network with a set of images and use the model to predict an unseen image in one of the categories the image was trained, in case of a classification network.

The mechanics of a CNN is mainly based on the human vision itself, on which we correlate a series of small visual features in bigger ones, until we correlate that features to a specific category. For example, we differentiate a dog and a cat based on the nose shape, ear shape, tongue, hair color, etcetera. The combination of these specific characteristics, namely features in the CNN environment, lead us to the conclusion and correct classification of the animal.

2.1   Baseline Architecture

The architecture for this analysis was based on a sequence of Convolutional/Pooling layers, followed by two fully connected hidden layers of neurons. The output layer was a group of 6 sigmoid neurons, as the 6 outputs are independent of each other.

Between each hidden layer, a dropout rate of 50% was added. This procedure has the objective of improving the accuracy of the network on predicting unseen data, as long as avoiding overfitting. As to compensate for the high dropout rate, a higher number of neurons were applied on each hidden layer. The number of neurons on the first hidden layer was defined based on the number of pixels after the last convolution/pooling layer and linearization, as defined by the equation below:

$$N_{hidden\ layer} = \frac{2}{3} \frac{\left(l_{image} * w_{image}\right)}{Dropout\ rate} * C, \tag{1}$$

where l_{image} and w_{image} stand, respectively, for the length and width of the image after the last pooling layer. C stands for the hidden layer size coefficient, whose role is to propitiate the orthogonal manipulation of the number of neurons in each hidden layer in the experiment which will be described in Sect. 3.3.

As can be noticed based on Eq. 1, the application of a dropout rate of 50% leads to the double quantity of neurons on the layer in comparison to a layer on which the dropout was not applied. This implementation aimed to compensate for the reduction of active neurons on the forward propagation process due to dropout implementation.

On the second hidden layer, the number of neurons was defined as 50% the quantity of neurons of the first hidden layer. The activation function set for both the hidden layers was the Softmax, also known as linear rectifier. No dropout was applied between convolutional layers.

In order to avoid overfitting of the network, an early-stopping method was applied on the network. The monitored variable was the loss function of the test/validation set, with the patience being used as a variable for study. In other words, the following procedure occurs during training and test of each epoch: (1) The 1050 training images were used on training of the network, applying the respective dropouts; (2) The lastly trained network on each epoch was used to predict the test/validation set of 450 images versus their real output, without considering the dropouts for the estimation; (3) The obtained validation loss is compared to the N previous epochs. If the validation loss is smaller than all the N previous losses, the training keeps going (back to step 1), otherwise the training is finished.

Patience, named N in the previous paragraph, is a numeric value which stands for the maximum number of epochs the model is trained after which the monitored variable, in this case the binary cross entropy of the six categories, is not reduced. In this study, a maximum patience of 5 epochs will be considered.

In order to perform the training, the Keras.layers library was applied for the generation of the CNN itself and the keras.preprocessing.image was applied for the preprocessing of the images, which will be detailed in the next Section.

3   Experimental Setup

The objective of this Section is to describe the dataset considered for the setup, as long as the image augmentation transformations applied in order to improve the classification, and posteriorly the structure of the full-factorial DOE (design of experiments) study performed in order to analyze the architecture factors.

As will be described in Sect. 3.3, the chosen factors of the experiment are variables which impact directly on the architecture of the network: The resolution of the input image, the quantity of hidden layers and the quantity of neurons in each of the hidden layers. As y's of the analysis, both the F1 score and recall metrics of the system will be considered.

3.1   Dataset

For this study, the same dataset generated on Silva et al. (2018) was used. The main advantage of using this dataset is the size of the dataset, containing a total of 1500 images of panoramic X-ray images, and its variation, once the images included, such as mentioned in the introduction, significant structural variations in the images. The six categories and the respective amount of images belonging to each category can be observed on Table 1.

The images were generated using an Orthographos XG5/XG 5DS/Ceph, manufactured by Sirona Dental Systems GmbH. They were acquired by the Diagnostic Imaging

Table 1. Extra-oral X-ray image categories.

Category	Description	Qty. of images
All_teeth	Images with at least 28 teeth	645
Restoration	Images on which restoration is perceived	865
Braces	Images on which dental braces are perceived	278
Implant	Images on which implants are perceived	120
More_32	Images on which at least 32 teeth are perceived	170
Missing_teeth	Images on which missing teeth are perceived and less than 28 teeth	732

Center of Southwest State University of Bahia. The radiographic images used for this research were coded in order not to identify the patient in the study (Silva et al. 2018).

The categories are independent from each other, with exception of All_teeth, which is always true if more_32 is true and All_teeth is always false if Missing_teeth is true. Thus, the classifier must have skill to classify each of the six categories independently, as each image may belong to more than one category. Examples of X-ray images on which one or more of the categories mentioned above can be observed in Fig. 1.

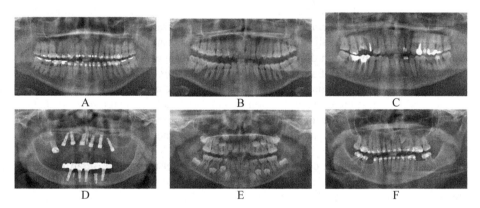

Fig. 1. Samples from dataset. A. All teeth, braces and restoration. B. All teeth, without braces or restoration. C. All teeth, with restoration and without braces. D. Implants. E. More than 32 teeth. F. Missing teeth and braces.

For the experiments, the dataset was divided in train and test/validation data in a ratio of 70%–30%, totalizing 1050 images for training and 450 images for test. The same dataset and division were applied posteriorly to train all the CNN architectures equally, as to avoid noise from splitting on the performance metrics of the trained NNs.

During the splitting of the dataset, the images were fully randomized, to avoid unbalance between categories, although the original dataset presents a considerably high unbalance. The most common category, **restoration**, is present in 865 of the 1500 images, while **implant** is present in only 120 samples out of 1500. This may compromise the skill of the model on classifying these specific categories with small population, implant and more_32.

3.2 Database Image Augmentation

In order to enhance the training process, the ImageDataGenerator from the preprocessing library from Keras was applied. This function performs random transformations in the training images based on defined ranges. These transformations can be rotation, shear, horizontal and vertical flipping, zooming and so on. By doing so, the training is enhanced as the network is less biased by positions and sizes of features. Thus, in each epoch of training, a random transformation is applied on each of the training images. Though, for each epoch, the input neurons are different from the previous epoch, despite the output layer results are the same.

For this application, the following transformations were applied on the image dataset: Horizontal flipping, shear, varying from -20% to $+20\%$ and zooming, varying from -20% to $+20\%$.

3.3 CNN Architecture Variables

The accuracy of the CNN highly depends on the architecture variables chosen. Though, each application itself would present a specific set of variables which optimize the accuracy considering the specific application. Among the variables which impact on the overall performance of the fit, three factors were chosen: number of image input size, number of neurons in each hidden layer and number of layers.

The study has a shape of a balanced full-factorial DOE (design of experiments), as three independent factors (Image input size, Hidden layers, neurons per layer) are varied symmetrically amidst the eight architectures. This study allows a significance analysis of the factors, as long as the interactions between factors in the overall accuracy of the fitting. Table 2 displays the architecture of every tested network, as a function of the three independent factors.

As can be observed, the convolutional layers were set to 5 for all input images of 498×282 pixels, while the convolutional layers were set to 6 to all input images of 996×282. This means that with one extra layer, the last layer after the last pooling layer for architectures V5 to V8 have the same input size after the last pooling layer, compared to networks V1 to V4.

4 Results

This section will be divided in two main steps: Initially, a DOE analysis will be performed, in order to identify the best architecture and the factors which generated an increase in the overall fit metrics. For this analysis, two metrics will be considered: The F1 score and the recall.

Table 2. Architecture variants of tested networks.

Network ID	Image input size	Conv. layers	Hidden layers	Hidden layer size coefficient C	Neurons on first hidden layer	Neurons on second hidden layer
V1	498 × 282	5	1	0.8	144	–
V2	498 × 282	5	1	1.2	220	–
V3	498 × 282	5	2	0.8	144	72
V4	498 × 282	5	2	1.2	220	110
V5	996 × 564	6	1	0.8	144	–
V6	996 × 564	6	1	1.2	220	–
V7	996 × 564	6	2	0.8	144	72
V8	996 × 564	6	2	1.2	220	110

4.1 Neural Network Performance DOE Analysis

The objective of this section is to compare qualitatively and quantitatively the performance of the Neural network fitting, as a function of the three factors: Initial image size, number of hidden layers and number of neurons. The graph below (Fig. 2) shows the variability chart of the network F1 score, as function of the factors.

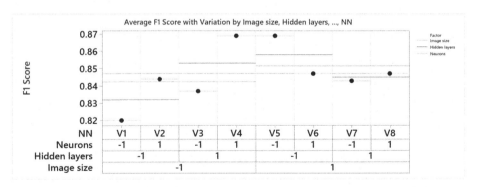

Fig. 2. Variability chart of the obtained F1 score.

Two networks achieved a similar weighted F1 score of 0.869, networks V4 and V5. The variability shows an interaction between the image size and the two remaining factors. When the image is on level - 1 (498 × 282), both the increase of hidden layers and number of neurons on each individual layer enhance the overall performance of the fit.

Figures 3 and 4 shows respectively the Pareto plot of estimates and interaction plot of factors. As can be observed, the most significant factor which contributed to increase the F1 accuracy was the interaction between size of input image and number of neurons in the hidden layer. When the number of neurons is larger, increasing the image size increases the F1 score of the model, while decreasing the F1 score when the input image is smaller.

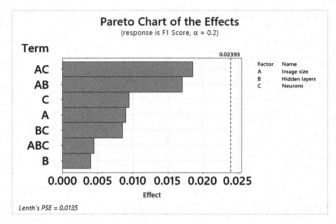

Fig. 3. Pareto plot of F1 score effect estimates.

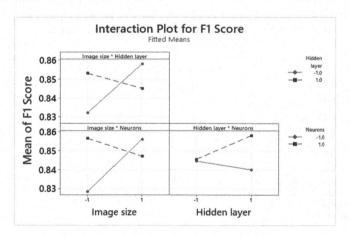

Fig. 4. Interaction plot between network factors.

The second evaluated metric was the recall performance of the model. The recall metric was used as, for medical purposes, it means that it has a bigger true positive or, in other words, it accurately classified the population of true positives, which makes sense on having the skill to accurately predict all real diseases/features.

Figure 5 compares the recall performance of the neural network models as function of the three factors. As can be observed, there is a clear effect of the number of neurons on the overall recall score. The **increase** of the number of neurons on the hidden layers tends to **decrease** the overall recall score of the model. This means that the models with fewer neurons on the hidden layers presented lower probability of false negative results, which is desired in case of diagnosis of diseases and identification of specific features on the X-ray medical images. The main effect being the number of neurons in the hidden layer can also be observed in the Pareto chart of recall effects, on Fig. 6.

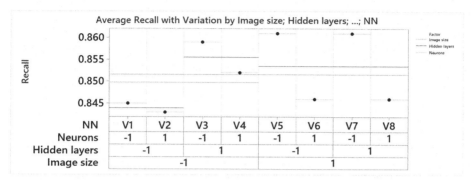

Fig. 5. Variability chart of the recall performance of the model.

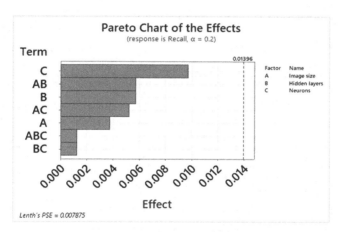

Fig. 6. Pareto plot of recall effect estimates.

As a consequence, CNN V5 would be chosen for its performance, considering the tradeoff between the F1 score and the less probability of false negatives. Table 3 shows all the compiled results based on category for each of the neural network models. The color scale compares, for each metric (precision, recall and F1 score) on each neural network architecture, the performance of classification comparing the six classes. This scale was implemented to evaluate if there are any categories which achieved better results independently of the CNN architecture. As can be stated, the implant category had a high precision score in all networks, but usually accompanied by poor F1 score.

Table 3. Precision, recall and F1 score for all tested architectures.

	V1			V2			V3		
	precision	recall	F1 score	precision	recall	F1 score	precision	recall	F1 score
All_teeth	0.762	0.890	0.821	0.806	0.916	0.858	0.840	0.796	0.817
Restoration	0.782	0.957	0.861	0.869	0.849	0.859	0.808	0.915	0.858
Appliance	0.841	0.885	0.863	0.873	0.885	0.879	0.893	0.859	0.876
Implant	0.960	0.585	0.727	0.868	0.805	0.835	0.895	0.829	0.861
More_32	0.938	0.682	0.789	0.733	0.750	0.742	0.761	0.795	0.778
Missing	0.821	0.739	0.778	0.868	0.784	0.824	0.781	0.867	0.822
micro avg	0.802	0.845	0.823	0.845	0.843	0.844	0.816	0.859	0.837
macro avg	0.851	0.790	0.806	0.836	0.831	0.833	0.830	0.844	0.835
weighted avg	0.810	0.845	0.820	0.848	0.843	0.844	0.818	0.859	0.837
samples avg	0.800	0.829	0.803	0.844	0.841	0.832	0.828	0.858	0.832
	V4			**V5**			**V6**		
	precision	recall	F1 score	precision	recall	F1 score	precision	recall	F1 score
All_teeth	0.848	0.937	0.891	0.864	0.864	0.864	0.827	0.901	0.862
Restoration	0.920	0.806	0.860	0.878	0.868	0.873	0.846	0.876	0.861
Appliance	0.957	0.859	0.905	0.958	0.885	0.920	0.941	0.821	0.877
Implant	0.912	0.756	0.827	0.943	0.805	0.868	0.960	0.585	0.727
More_32	0.761	0.795	0.778	0.868	0.750	0.805	0.850	0.773	0.810
Missing	0.890	0.858	0.874	0.853	0.876	0.864	0.835	0.835	0.835
micro avg	0.887	0.852	0.869	0.877	0.861	0.869	0.850	0.846	0.848
macro avg	0.881	0.835	0.856	0.894	0.841	0.866	0.877	0.798	0.829
weighted avg	0.891	0.852	0.869	0.878	0.861	0.869	0.854	0.846	0.847
samples avg	0.888	0.852	0.861	0.883	0.862	0.863	0.848	0.835	0.832
	V7			**V8**					
	precision	recall	F1 score	precision	recall	F1 score			
All_teeth	0.822	0.822	0.822	0.827	0.901	0.862			
Restoration	0.805	0.926	0.861	0.846	0.876	0.861			
Appliance	0.932	0.885	0.908	0.941	0.821	0.877			
Implant	0.875	0.854	0.864	0.960	0.585	0.727			
More_32	0.814	0.795	0.805	0.850	0.773	0.810			
Missing	0.818	0.826	0.822	0.835	0.835	0.835			
micro avg	0.827	0.861	0.844	0.850	0.846	0.848			
macro avg	0.844	0.851	0.847	0.877	0.798	0.829			
weighted avg	0.828	0.861	0.843	0.854	0.846	0.847			
samples avg	0.836	0.861	0.837	0.848	0.835	0.832			

5 Conclusion

This study had the objective of designing a convolutional neural network (CNN) to accurately and independently classify six classes on a set of X-ray orthopantomography images. The six considered classes were: All teeth, restoration, presence of braces, presence of dental implants, more than 32 teeth and missing teeth.

In order to optimize the architecture of the CNN, a DOE (design of experiments) study was performed in order to optimize the design factors of the network. The most noticeable result of this analysis was that for all levels of image size and number of hidden layers, the increase in the number of neurons generated a decrease in the recall metrics of the classification, which is undesirable, considering that false negatives have a very big impact on medical applications.

The most promising architecture presented an overall **F1 score** performance of **87%** and **86%** in recall score, which are promising results, considering the initial stage of development of the algorithm.

In the future, besides efforts in the direction of improving the diagnosis performance and improving metrics of the CNN architecture, studies must include disease diagnosis, such as presence of caries, bacterial plaque, among others, as to contribute to large scale diagnosis, aiming political policies and statistical behavioral studies.

References

Amer, Y.Y., Aqel, M.J.: An efficient segmentation algorithm for panoramic dental images. Procedia Comput. Sci. **65**, 718–725 (2015)

Lee, J.-H., et al.: Detection and diagnosis of dental caries using a deep learning-based convolutional neural network algorithm. J. Dent. **77**, 106–111 (2018)

Goodfellow, I., Bengio, Y., Courville, A.: Deep Learning. MIT Press, Cambridge (2016)

Oliveira, J., Proença, H.: Caries detection in panoramic dental X-ray images. In: Tavares, J., Jorge, R. (eds.) Computational Vision and Medical Image Processing. COMPUTMETHODS, vol. 19, pp. 175–190. Springer, Dordrecht (2011)

Muramatsu, C., et al.: Tooth detection and classification on panoramic radiographs for automatic dental chart filing: improved classification by multi-sized input data. Oral Radiol. 1–7 (2020)

Niblack, W.: An Introduction to Digital Image Processing, 1st edn. Strandberg Publishing Company, Birkerød (1985)

Paewinsky, E., Pfeiffer, H., Brinkmann, B.: Quantification of secondary dentine formation from orthopantomograms – a contribution to forensic age estimation methods in adults. Int. J. Legal Med. **119**(1), 27–30 (2005)

Quinn, R.A., Sigl, C.C.: Radiography in modern industry (1980)

Silva, G., Oliveira, L., Pithon, M.: Automatic segmenting teeth in X-ray images: trends, a novel data set, benchmarking and future perspectives. Expert Syst. Appl. **107**, 15–31 (2018)

Sukegawa, S., et al.: Deep neural networks for dental implant system classification. Biomolecules **10**(7), 984 (2020)

Singh, P., Sehgal, P.: Numbering and classification of panoramic dental images using 6-layer convolutional neural network. Pattern Recogn. Image Anal. **30**(1), 125–133 (2020)

Tian, S., et al.: Automatic classification and segmentation of teeth on 3D dental model using hierarchical deep learning networks. IEEE Access **7**, 84817–84828 (2019)

Wang, C.W., et al.: A benchmark for comparison of dental radiography analysis algorithms. Med. Image Anal. **31**, 63–76 (2016)

Welikala, R.A., et al.: Automated detection and classification of oral lesions using deep learning for early detection of oral cancer. IEEE Access **8**, 132677–132693 (2020)

Ink Marker Segmentation in Histopathology Images Using Deep Learning

Danial Maleki, Mehdi Afshari, Morteza Babaie[ID], and H. R. Tizhoosh[(✉)][ID]

Kimia Lab, University of Waterloo, Waterloo, Canada
{dmaleki,m4afshar,mbabaie,tizhoosh}@uwaterloo.ca

Abstract. Due to the recent advancements in machine vision, digital pathology has gained significant attention. Histopathology images are distinctly rich in visual information. The tissue glass slide images are utilized for disease diagnosis. Researchers study many methods to process histopathology images and facilitate fast and reliable diagnosis; therefore, the availability of high-quality slides becomes paramount. The quality of the images can be negatively affected when the glass slides are ink-marked by pathologists to delineate regions of interest. As an example, in one of the largest public histopathology datasets, The Cancer Genome Atlas (TCGA), approximately 12% of the digitized slides are affected by manual delineations through ink markings. To process these open-access slide images and other repositories for the design and validation of new methods, an algorithm to detect the marked regions of the images is essential to avoid confusing tissue pixels with ink-colored pixels for computer methods. In this study, we propose to segment the ink-marked areas of pathology patches through a deep network. A dataset from 79 whole slide images with $4,305$ patches was created and different networks were trained. Finally, the results showed an FPN model with the EffiecentNet-B3 as the backbone was found to be the superior configuration with an F1 score of 94.53%.

Keywords: Histopathology · Whole slide images · Convolutional neural networks · Ink marker segmentation · U-Net · FPN · Artifact removal

1 Introduction

The definitive diagnosis of numerous diseases is possible through meticulous visual inspection by a trained pathologist, an examination that requires considerable time and effort while inevitably being prone to error. Computer vision and machine learning can assist the pathologists to reduce their workload and

This work was supported by an NSERC-CRD Grant on "Design and Development of Devices and Procedures for Recognizing Artefacts and Foreign Tissue Origin for Diagnostic Pathology".

G. Bebis et al. (Eds.): ISVC 2020, LNCS 12509, pp. 359–368, 2020.
https://doi.org/10.1007/978-3-030-64556-4_28

to increase the diagnostic accuracy [6]. Computer-assisted diagnosis necessitates the digitization of biopsy glass slides. In some cases, pathologists use ink markers to highlight parts of glass slides for a variety of purposes such as educational and diagnosis hints. Once the slides are digitized, marker signs naturally appear in the digital images as well. Consequently, computer methods are potentially prone to mistaking marker colored regions for tissue information [1].

The pathology slides contain valuable information in high resolution; therefore, rejection of an entire slide because of some ink markings may not be a feasible approach. To enable reliable processing with images with marker signs, we have used deep learning models to detect and removed different marker colors. Several deep learning strategies have been explored to generate a mask that extracts the ink marker areas automatically. The aim of this task is to distinguish between the tissue areas and the areas that are colorized through the marker's ink. Elimination of areas that have marker signs is useful since in most cases areas that are covered by marker are of less importance (therefore overpainted by the pathologists to show something more important). As a result, discarding these areas may generally not affect the tissue relevant for diagnosis. Moreover, removing manual markings can help to generate a considerable number of proper patches without the presence of the marker artifacts for the benefit of many machine learning algorithms.

Smart software for digital scanners is another potential application of this research. The focus depth of whole slide scanners must be adjusted for different tissue regions due to variable tissue thickness. Focus points on the marker area will considerably affect the scan quality. Avoiding to set focus points on the marker places from a pre-scan image, could boost the automated scanning process and hence improve the lab workflow in digital pathology [3].

Three main challenges concerning the detection of ink-marking areas should be addressed. The first one is that these markings can be drawn by pens with different colors. The worst case in this regard occurs when ink markers have a color similar to the tissue such as red or pink. The second problem is the composition of inconsistent patterns and ink markers' shapes/symbols. They can be letters, circles, or other shapes such as arrows and dots. The third issue is that ink markers can be created/seen at different transparency levels. In addition, markers may cross the tissue regions, mark outside or around the tissue, which can affect the observed color of the marker. A combination of these scenarios in a single image makes the discovery of marked regions a challenging task [23].

Traditional methods, such as thresholding, may not be accurate enough because of the difficulties mentioned above. An automatic approach that is capable of overcoming these issues is the goal of this study. The advent of deep learning has led to multiple breakthroughs in different domains. One of these domains is medical imaging which consists of numerous tasks including classification, image search, and segmentation [2,13]. In this work, a comparative study of deep network segmentation models (U-net and FPN) that can generate a mask of areas that contain ink markers is presented. The areas that include ink marker are determined, and then a binary mask of the detected regions is generated. By having this mask, no trace of markers may appear in the patch selection phase avoiding the loss of tissue information. The method is accurate, tolerant and requires only a limited number of images for training. The final network as well as the created dataset are available to download for academic purposes.

2   Related Work

Ink marker segmentation could be considered as a part of the pre-processing of histopathology images. The main goal of pre-processing methods is to prepare high-quality images for the training procedure. Most of the pre-processing methods for histopathology images ignore the presence of ink marker in images. Taqi et al. [21] investigated various types of artifacts that may appear in histopathological images and how could one differentiate an artifact and a tissue segement. The presence of these artifacts may render images useless for computer aided diagnosis when accessing existing repositories. Rastogi et al. [17] demonstrated that the presence of artifact can be a major pitfall. The artifacts may occur in different stages of the process. Therefore, it is essential to identify the presence of artifacts. Janowczyk et al. [8] mentioned that variability of histopathology images can mislead the diagnostic algorithms. Stain normalization using sparse autoencoders has been proposed to avoid the problem. However, the presence of ink markers as an artifact has not been discussed in these studies.

A few techniques are developed for the detection and removal of the ink marker signs in histopathology images. These methods could be categorized into two following types. The first type is the image processing methods based on traditional algorithms. Most of the techniques that are proposed to remove marker signs use thresholding techniques combined with mathematical morphology operations. In this approach, different types of color space, filters, and thresholds for different ink marker colors have been used[1]. HistoQC is a tool presented for the quality control of WSIs which discovers artifacts and outputs outliers. The method was validated using open-access dataset of TCGA and the results were verified by pathologists. However, the precision of the outlier detection of the method is not high enough which can result in loss of valuable data [9]. Mostly, these methods are not fully automated. Due to the high variation of the markers' color and intensity, thresholds fail in different images. As a result, the manual setting of the thresholds or other parameters for each image may be required.

The second method type is deep learning. Recent improvements in deep learning enable the modeling of complex data distributions. One of the well-known tasks that are done using deep learning techniques is image segmentation and reconstruction. Venkatesh et al. [23] used CycleGan for the reconstruction of a marker removed WSI. Sharib et al. [1] separated tiles that were contaminated with markers with a binary classification network and fed the tiles with marker

---

[1] https://github.com/deroneriksson/python-wsi-preprocessing/blob/master/docs/ wsi-preprocessing-in-python/index.md.

signs to a YOLO3 network [18] to detect the marker areas. Finally, for the restoration of the original non-marked tiles, CycleGAN was used [24].

2.1 Segmentation Models

U-Net has been developed to segment biomedical images [19]. The network architecture has two major parts. The first part is the encoding path which is used to capture the image context. In this part, convolutional layers are applied which followed by max-pooling layers. The second part uses transposed convolution layers and up-sampling layers to construct an image with the same size as the input image. The main goal is to add skip connections from the down-sampling part to the second part as an up-sampling part which can help the model to have better localization information. The down-sampling layers output is then concatenated with the input of up-sampling layers. Figure 1 shows the proposed configuration when U-Net architecture is used. For the pathology practice, U-Net has been utilized for a wide range of applications, for instance for epithelial tissue segmentation [4] and cell nuclei segmentation [16].

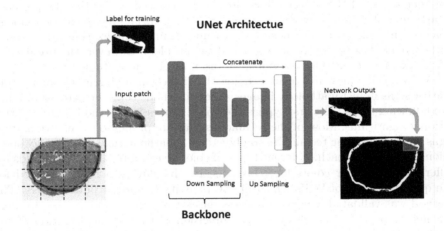

Fig. 1. Overall structure of the proposed method for segmentation of ink marked images using U-Net architecture network. Blue boxes show the CNN layers. (Color figure online)

Feature Pyramid Network (FPN) [14] like U-Net has two parts. The first part which is a bottom-up pathway has a convolutional network as backbone. The output of each stage in this part will be used as a skip connection for enriching the second part layers. The second part of the model, which is named top-down pathway, uses transposed convolution and up-sampling layers to up-sample features. Afterward, FPN concatenates each stage in this pathway with skip connections from the bottom-up pathway. In the end, the network concatenates the output of each stage after feeding each of them to the convolutional layer with a kernel size of three and predicts the segmentation for the input image. Figure 2 shows the FPN architecture used in this study.

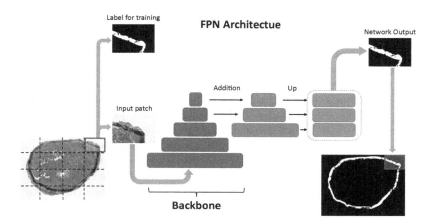

Fig. 2. The proposed architecture (blue/green/orange boxes show the CNN layers). (Color figure online)

2.2 Transfer Learning

Providing large sets of labeled data in medical imaging is expensive [10]. Recently, transfer learning has become a feasible in the medical imaging domain [11]. Transfer learning helps to build new models in a shorter time requiring a rather small number of training samples. In computer vision, transfer learning is mainly implemented through the use of pre-trained models. A pre-trained model is a network that is trained on a large dataset for a similar task. A pre-trained model which was trained on the ImageNet dataset [5] with more than 14 million images for the encoding pathway that can extract features by using a few images from a new domain for the segmentation task. For instance, in EffiecientNet [20] the main idea is to find an optimal baseline network using Neural Architecture Search (NAS) with respect to a trade-off between accuracy and FLOPS (Floating-point Operations Per Second) and then scale the depth, width and resolution through an equation. By changing the parameter in the formula, different network settings can be achieved that have different FLOPS and accuracy levels.

In ResNet [7], using skip connections is the main idea. Skip connections between ResNet blocks help the network to perform the backward propagation of the loss better and to prevent gradient vanishing that is a common problem in very deep networks.

3   Method

The goal of this study is a fully automatic Convolutional Neural Network (CNN) that generates a binary mask with the same size of the input image. Two of the most popular architectures for the medical image segmentation namely U-Net and FPN, are chosen and investigated in this paper. These networks achieved success in many segmentation tasks mainly due to skipping connections from the down-sampling pathways to the up-sampling pathways. On the other hand, due to the limited number of training samples, transfer learning approach is utilized by using a pre-trained network as the backbone of segmentation models. Different backbone networks are compared to discover a suitable pre-trained network for the segmentation task. Selected backbones are EfficientNet and ResNet.

In this study, our network uses a combination of two types of cost functions. One of them is the Dice loss function and the other one is the Focal loss function [15]. The dice loss function principally measures the overlap between two binary samples. The measurement range is 0 to 1 where a dice coefficient value of 1 denotes a perfect match between two samples which in this case would be the target and the network output. The dice loss function can be calculated as follows:

$$\text{Dice} = \frac{2|Output \cap Target|}{|Output| + |Target|},\tag{1}$$

where $|output \cap target|$ denotes the common pixels between output and target and $|output|$ shows the number of pixels in output (and likewise for target).

The second term of the cost function is the focal loss. The distribution of each class pixels in the data is imbalanced which serves the definition of focal loss term. The term avoids the complication of correct pixels number and the total number of pixels. Relatively speaking, uncomplicated examples are well classified; therefore, these examples contribute to the loss rather in a minor fashion. The focal loss function can be described as:

$$FL(p_t) = -(1 - p_t)^\gamma \log(p_t).\tag{2}$$

In this formula, γ is a tunable parameter. This controlling element defines the steepness of the function shape. Parameter p_t is the probability of the background class. The term puts more emphasis on hard samples while reduces loss for well-classified examples.

4   Experiments and Results

To train the model, 89 ink marked TCGA [22] slides were selected visually through diverse body parts. The ground truth masks (ink marker areas) of selected slides are created manually. Then, each WSI has been patched into images with the size of 256 × 256 pixels at 1× magnification. The total number of 4,305 patches are extracted from 89 annotated slides to train the model. We applied 8-fold cross validation to train and test our model. Therefore, training, validation, and test data are set to 70%, 15% and 15% from the randomly

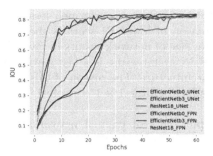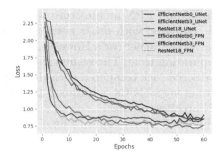

Fig. 3. Jaccard index (left) and loss function values (right) for validation data.

selected patches, respectively. The encoder pathway is the pre-trained model and different models are trained using the Adam optimizer [12] with the learning rate set to 0.00001. Each model is trained for 60 epochs with one Nvidia Tesla V100 GPU. The maximum training time of a network is roughly 160 s per epoch. On the other hand, the minimum training time is 60 s per epoch for the smallest size network as U-Net architecture and EfficientNet-B0 backbone. Two evaluation criteria are used. The first one is the Jaccard index defined as:

$$\text{Jaccard index} = \frac{|Output \cap Target|}{|Output \cup Target|}. \tag{3}$$

The second one is the F1-score which measures the sensitivity and specificity together. As discussed in the method section, the proposed model can adapt to different architectures and backbones. FPN and U-Net are used for the architecture and EfficienNet-B0, EfficeinetNet-B3 and ResNet-18 are used for the encoder part. Figure 3 (left) shows the Jaccard index for all training scenarios over the training process. The vertical axis shows trained epochs and the horizontal axis shows the Jaccard index for the validation data. The Jaccard index trend shows the fastest learning trend of FPN architecture with ResNet backbone with respect to number of epochs. Our study shows that ResNet-18 with FPN architecture has the steepest slope at the starting epochs, but at the end, other backbones show better performance. UNet architecture with EfficientNet-B0 and EfficientNet-B3 show similar trends as the slowest learners with respect to the number of training epochs. All networks reach a considerably high Jaccard index at the end of training process. Comparison among the validation loss values are shown in Fig. 3 (right) for all architectures and backbones. As expected, the loss value over epochs has correlation with Jaccard criterion. Figure 3 (left) shows the importance of architecture based on loss. Different architectures show varied behaviour in the course of loss value trends. FPN architecture has lower loss value in comparison with UNet architecture through all epochs.

Table 1 shows the evaluation on the test set (average of 8-fold cross validations) of the trained models on the presented dataset. In the ink marker segmentation problem, FPN architecture shows better performance comparing U-Net architecture. FPN architecture with ResNet-18 backbone performed less accurate compared with other networks. The reason of lower F1-score is the lower capacity of the network. However, the smaller size of network results in favorable computation time. The results shows that FPN architecture is a fast learner for the desired task compared with the U-Net architecture. The reason of this faster learning trend is the additional part that appears after 1×1 convolution that FPN architecture has.

Figure 4 shows some sample input-output pairs of trained networks. The samples include different colors, intensities, and overlaps with the tissue.

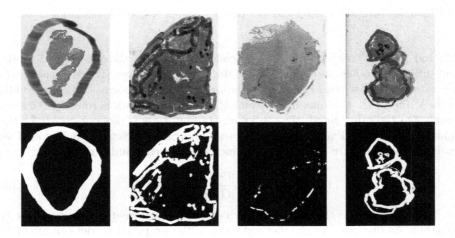

Fig. 4. WSIs (top) and ground-truths (bottom): The network segmentation is applied on individual patches and then combined to a complete image.

Table 1. Evaluation of results for Jaccard index and F1-score and execution times

Base	Backbone	Metrics		
		IoU	F1 score	Time (s)
U-Net	EfficientNet-B0	0.8244	0.9128	0.0238
	EfficientNet-B3	0.8251	0.9227	0.029
	ResNet-18	0.8234	0.9091	0.0195
FPN	EfficientNet-B0	0.8326	0.9312	0.028
	EfficientNet-B3	0.8354	0.9453	0.0352
	ResNet-18	0.8154	0.8912	0.0217
Baseline (See footnote 1)	–	0.6512	0.7312	0.0189

5   Conclusions

A fully automatic deep model to generate a binary mask of areas that have ink markers on archived WSIs is proposed and evaluated in this study. The investigated method is capable of the extraction of ink markers with different colors and different shapes and intensities. Calculation of two evaluation metrics including the Jaccard index and F1-score showed the efficiency of the method. Removing ink markings helps to use all archived WSIs that have ink highlights for research instead of discarding them. As well, this method can be added to digital scanners to apply the ink removal during the image acquisition.

References

1. Ali, S., Alham, N.K., Verrill, C., Rittscher, J.: Ink removal from histopathology whole slide images by combining classification, detection and image generation models. arXiv preprint arXiv:1905.04385 (2019)
2. Babaie, M., et al.: Classification and retrieval of digital pathology scans: a new dataset. In: The IEEE Conference on Computer Vision and Pattern Recognition (CVPR) Workshops, July 2017
3. Babaie, M., Tizhoosh, H.R.: Deep features for tissue-fold detection in histopathology images. arXiv preprint arXiv:1903.07011 (2019)
4. Bulten, W., Hulsbergen-van de Kaa, C.A., van der Laak, J., Litjens, G.J., et al.: Automated segmentation of epithelial tissue in prostatectomy slides using deep learning. In: Medical Imaging 2018: Digital Pathology, vol. 10581, p. 105810S. International Society for Optics and Photonics (2018)
5. Deng, J., Dong, W., Socher, R., Li, L.J., Li, K., Fei-Fei, L.: ImageNet: a large-scale hierarchical image database. In: 2009 IEEE Conference on Computer Vision and Pattern Recognition, pp. 248–255. IEEE (2009)
6. Fuchs, T.J., Buhmann, J.M.: Computational pathology: challenges and promises for tissue analysis. Comput. Med. Imaging Graph. $35(7-8)$, 515–530 (2011)
7. He, K., Zhang, X., Ren, S., Sun, J.: Deep residual learning for image recognition. In: Proceedings of the IEEE Conference on Computer Vision and Pattern Recognition, pp. 770–778 (2016)
8. Janowczyk, A., Basavanhally, A., Madabhushi, A.: Stain normalization using sparse autoencoders (StaNoSA): application to digital pathology. Comput. Med. Imaging Graph. **57**, 50–61 (2017)
9. Janowczyk, A., Zuo, R., Gilmore, H., Feldman, M., Madabhushi, A.: HistoQC: an open-source quality control tool for digital pathology slides. JCO Clin. Cancer Inform. **3**, 1–7 (2019)
10. Kalra, S., et al.: Pan-cancer diagnostic consensus through searching archival histopathology images using artificial intelligence. arXiv preprint arXiv:1911.08736 (2019)
11. Kieffer, B., Babaie, M., Kalra, S., Tizhoosh, H.R.: Convolutional neural networks for histopathology image classification: training vs. using pre-trained networks. In: 2017 Seventh International Conference on Image Processing Theory, Tools and Applications (IPTA), pp. 1–6. IEEE (2017)
12. Kingma, D.P., Ba, J.: Adam: a method for stochastic optimization. arXiv preprint arXiv:1412.6980 (2014)

13. Kumar, M.D., Babaie, M., Tizhoosh, H.R.: Deep barcodes for fast retrieval of histopathology scans. In: 2018 International Joint Conference on Neural Networks (IJCNN), pp. 1–8, July 2018. https://doi.org/10.1109/IJCNN.2018.8489574

14. Lin, T.Y., Dollár, P., Girshick, R., He, K., Hariharan, B., Belongie, S.: Feature pyramid networks for object detection. In: Proceedings of the IEEE Conference on Computer Vision and Pattern Recognition, pp. 2117–2125 (2017)

15. Lin, T.Y., Goyal, P., Girshick, R., He, K., Dollár, P.: Focal loss for dense object detection. In: Proceedings of the IEEE International Conference on Computer Vision, pp. 2980–2988 (2017)

16. Naylor, P., Laé, M., Reyal, F., Walter, T.: Segmentation of nuclei in histopathology images by deep regression of the distance map. IEEE Trans. Med. Imaging **38**(2), 448–459 (2018)

17. Rastogi, V., Puri, N., Arora, S., Kaur, G., Yadav, L., Sharma, R.: Artefacts: a diagnostic dilemma-a review. J. Clin. Diagn. Res. (JCDR) **7**(10), 2408 (2013)

18. Redmon, J., Farhadi, A.: YOLOv3: an incremental improvement. arXiv preprint arXiv:1804.02767 (2018)

19. Ronneberger, O., Fischer, P., Brox, T.: U-Net: convolutional networks for biomedical image segmentation. In: Navab, N., Hornegger, J., Wells, W.M., Frangi, A.F. (eds.) MICCAI 2015. LNCS, vol. 9351, pp. 234–241. Springer, Cham (2015). https://doi.org/10.1007/978-3-319-24574-4_28

20. Tan, M., Le, Q.V.: EfficientNet: rethinking model scaling for convolutional neural networks. arXiv preprint arXiv:1905.11946 (2019)

21. Taqi, S.A., Sami, S.A., Sami, L.B., Zaki, S.A.: A review of artifacts in histopathology. J. Oral Maxillofac. Pathol. (JOMFP) **22**(2), 279 (2018)

22. Tomczak, K., Czerwińska, P., Wiznerowicz, M.: The cancer genome atlas (TCGA): an immeasurable source of knowledge. Contemp. Oncol. **19**(1A), A68 (2015)

23. Venkatesh, B., Shah, T., Chen, A., Ghafurian, S.: Restoration of marker occluded hematoxylin and eosin stained whole slide histology images using generative adversarial networks. arXiv preprint arXiv:1910.06428 (2019)

24. Zhu, J.Y., Park, T., Isola, P., Efros, A.A.: Unpaired image-to-image translation using cycle-consistent adversarial networks. In: Proceedings of the IEEE International Conference on Computer Vision, pp. 2223–2232 (2017)

P-FideNet: *Plasmodium Falciparum* Identification Neural Network

Daniel Cruz[1(✉)], Maíla Claro[2], Rodrigo Veras[2], Luis Vogado[2], Helano Portela[2], Nayara Moura[1], and Daniel Luz[1]

[1] Federal Institute of Education, Science and Technology of Piauí (IFPI), Picos, PI, Brazil
danielknunes@gmail.com, naayaraholanda@gmail.com, daniel.luz@ufpi.edu.br
[2] Department of Computing, Federal University of Piauí (UFPI), Teresina, PI, Brazil
claromaila@gmail.com, rveras@ufpi.edu.br, lhvogado@gmail.com, helano38@gmail.com

Abstract. Malaria is a blood disease caused by the *Plasmodium* parasites transmitted through the bite of *female Anopheles* mosquito. The identification of the parasitized blood cells is a laborious and challenging task as it involves very complex and time consuming methods such as spotting the parasite in the blood and counting the number of the parasites. This examination can be arduous for large-scale diagnoses, resulting in poor quality. This paper presents a new Convolutional Neural Network (CNN) architecture named P-FideNet aimed at the detection of Malaria. The proposed CNN model can be used to solve image classification problems of blood cells infected or not by parasite X. This tool makes the process of analysis by the specialist faster and more accurate. Comparative tests were carried out with state-of-the-art works, and P-FideNet achieved 98.53% recall, 98.88% accuracy and 99% precision.

Keywords: Convolutional neural network · Malaria · *Plasmodium falciparum*

1 Introduction

During the last decade, specialists from the most diverse fields, such as biology, computer science, statistics, and others, started to contribute to more complex and precise image analysis methods. They aim to help diagnose diseases, such as Leukemia, skin cancer, and Malaria [13].

Malaria is an infectious disease transmitted by parasitic mosquitoes. The transmission includes infection of red blood cells (RBCs) in humans and other organisms by protists of some genera. Among the most common and deadly types of malaria are the variants *Plasmodium Falciparum* and *Plasmodium Vivax*, the first being the most harmful type of the disease [20].

The last report from the World Health Organization (WHO), published in 2019, presented data collected globally, referring to malaria infections and deaths from

G. Bebis et al. (Eds.): ISVC 2020, LNCS 12509, pp. 369–380, 2020.
https://doi.org/10.1007/978-3-030-64556-4_29

2018. That year, there were an estimated 228 million confirmed malaria cases in 80 countries, 405.000 of which resulted in the deaths of infected people worldwide [20]. According to specialists, children under the age of 5 are the most vulnerable. They correspond to 61% of the estimated number of deaths. The disease transmitted by *Plasmodium Falciparum* has a high incidence in Africa, followed by Southeast Asia and the Eastern Mediterranean regions. About $3.1 billion has been invested worldwide in strategies to control and eliminate Malaria [12].

According to Das et al. [2], early diagnosis of malaria is the essential method for its control, since it enables to perform the treatment before further progression of the transmission. However, malaria symptoms are often indistinguishable from symptoms caused by diseases such as viral hepatitis, dengue, leptospirosis, and others, making its diagnosis challenging.

There is a manual method for malaria diagnosis widely used due to its low cost and ability to detect all malaria species. This method is commonly used to discover the severity of malaria, test malaria drugs, and identify any parasites left after treatment [19]. Manual malaria detection and classification are composed of factors that, even well performed, are still subject to human variations and failures, caused by fatigue or repetitive work. In recent years, the automatic detection of malaria in digital images has been a relevant research topic.

This study aims to improve the analysis method for *Plasmodium Falciparum* identification, making it more accurate, faster, and reducing the demand for professionals and costs involved in the diagnosis. Thus, this work proposes implementing a CNN-based approach to automate the identification of the *Plasmodium Falciparum* parasite, providing a solution capable of extinguishing from the final process the variations of human analysis. This fact is important because results that are subject to the physical and emotional state of the professional may change according to the long periods of continuous work [3].

The remainder of the paper is organized as follows. Section 2 presents related works. Section 3 describes the materials and methods used in this study as a basis for images, evaluation metrics, and the proposed CNN model. Section 4 presents the results obtained, and Sect. 5 contains a discussion about these results. Finally, we present a conclusion and future work in Sect. 6.

2 Related Works

We carried out a literature review looking for state of the art papers related to computer-aided diagnosis applications to detect cells infected by the malaria parasite. The survey aimed to identify and classify the works available in the literature based on the techniques employed, image dataset, year of publication, and relevance.

We searched using three strings: malaria classification, malaria detection, and blood smear malaria detection in three databases of scientific publications: Scopus, Web of Science, and IEEE Xplore. We then selected works published after 2015 in the engineering and computer science fields. As a result, we obtained 327 papers. Subsequently, we analyzed the title and abstract to eliminate repeated documents and non-automatic classification methods. Another important detail that we evaluated was using the same image dataset that we use to develop our approach; the NIH Malaria Dataset is maintained by the National Library of Medicine[1]. The use of the same dataset enables direct comparison with our method. Table 1 presents the works found in the literature, demonstrating the methods used and the results.

Table 1. Summary of works found in the literature in terms of the year of publication, method and accuracy result, applied to dataset with 27558 images.

Authors	Year	Method (s)	Accuracy (%)
Liang et al. [10]	2016	Customized CNN	97.37
Fatima and Farid [4]	2019	Customized CNN	91.80
Rajaraman et al. [17]	2019	Customized CNN, VGG-19 SqueezeNet, Inception, Resnetv2	99.32
Kashtriya et al. [9]	2019	OSICNN	98.30
Masud et al. [11]	2020	Customized CNN	97.30

In Liang et al. [10], the authors carry out the implementation of a CNN to malaria detection. For comparison purposes, the authors applied the Transfer Learning technique (TL) on well known CNNs. This technique is usually used in small databases to save time for training and overcome a lack of data at the expense of performance, which can be lower, but at an acceptable rate. The CNN architecture proposed obtained an accuracy of 97.37% while with TL's application, the accuracy obtained was 91.99%.

Aiming to solve the same problem, Fatima and Farid [4] have developed an algorithm that pre-processes the images. The algorithm also performs the separation of the classes to evidence the healthy and infected cells. The rest of the process employs standard neural network techniques.

When evaluating the performance of custom CNNs and pre-trained models, Rajaraman et al. [17] implemented models considered ideal for solving malaria detection. From the CNN architectures used, the models built with VGG-19 [18] and SqueezeNet [7] brought the best results in terms of performance metrics. Among these models, VGG-19 [18] stands out with the best accuracy, achieving the value of 99.32%

Kashitriya et al. [9] proposed a CNN model named *Optimized Step-Increase CNN* (OSICNN). This CNN classifies images of red blood cells taken from thin blood smear samples of infected and non-infected malaria parasites. The proposed OSICNN model consists of four convolutional layers and demonstrates similar results compared to other state-of-the-art models.

---

[1] https://lhncbc.nlm.nih.gov.

Masud et al. [11] implemented a CNN to detect malaria. The model was developed guided by the learning rate, and performance evaluation was considered to measure the improvement in the method's results. In this study, the authors chose to use the optimizer Stochastic Gradient Descent (SGD) to perform the model's training and optimization, focusing on minimizing logarithmic loss. The combination of SGD and the Cyclical Learning Rate (CLR) technique makes the method faster and results in model convergence. The authors compared their results, where they obtained an accuracy of 97.30%, with other results, which used models such as Resnet50 [5] and VGG-16 [18] but obtained lower results than their model.

3 Materials and Methods

This paper aims to present a CNN model to diagnose blood cells infected with malaria. To develop the architecture proposed in this work, we rely on convolutional neural networks that have been recently shown to have the most promising results in detecting malaria, according to studies found in the literature.

3.1 Image Dataset

The image dataset employed in our method's development is the NIH Malaria dataset provided by the National Library of Medicine[2] [16]. This image dataset is pre-processed and labeled, which enables it to be used for research purposes. These images were obtained by capturing and digitizing the images with specific equipment to provide good image quality in the final result. The images were analyzed and labeled by specialists in the field and finally became a dataset.

The NIH Malaria dataset is the same employed in the methods proposed by the authors cited in Sect. 2. The images were obtained with the use of a microscope and a camera coupled to it. The data set consists of 27558 images from blood cells. The dataset is well balanced with healthy, parasitic cells. The Figs. 2 and 1 show examples of infected and non-infected cells.

Fig. 1. Samples of healthy cells.

Both samples were stained with the GIesma Stain Solution to highlight the image features and facilitate their classification. For the labeling, the objects considered include artifacts or staining impurities to make the analysis as accurate as possible.

---

[2] https://lhncbc.nlm.nih.gov.

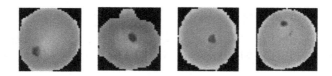

Fig. 2. Samples of cells infected by *Plasmodium falciparum*.

3.2 Evaluation Metrics

To evaluate the classification results, we calculate the confusion matrix values: True Positive (TP) - number of images correctly classified as infected by malaria; False Positive (FP) - number of healthy images incorrectly classified as infected; False Negative (FN) - number of infected images incorrectly classified as healthy and True Negative (TN) - number of images correctly classified as healthy [1].

Based on these values, we calculated precision (P), Recall (R), *f1-score* and Accuracy (ACC) [14]. The equations of these evaluation metrics are represented as following: Eqs. 1, 2, 3 and 4, respectively.

$$P = \frac{TP}{TP + FP} \tag{1}$$

$$R = \frac{TP}{TP + FN} \tag{2}$$

$$f1\text{-}score = 2 * \frac{P * R}{P + R} \tag{3}$$

$$ACC = \frac{TP + TN}{TP + TN + FP + FN} \tag{4}$$

Another metric used in this study was the loss function (*Loss*). This metric can describe how far the method is from the ideal prediction model and therefore quantifies the 'cost' or 'loss' by accepting the prediction generated by the current parameters of the model [8]. The Eq. 5 describes how the loss function is calculated.

$$\frac{1}{N} \sum_{i=1}^{N} \sum_{j=1}^{M} y_{ij} \log p_{ij} \tag{5}$$

The 5 equation indicates that N is the number of samples or instances, M is the number of possible labels, y_{ij} is a binary index where the label j is or is not the correct label classification for an instance i and p_{ij} is the probability of the model to assign the label j to the instance i. A perfect classifier would have a loss of *log* value precisely zero.

3.3   Proposed Method

The proposed method implemented a customized CNN architecture to provide a viable solution to the classification of cell images infected by *Plasmodium Falciparum*. The simplified model was based on the networks VGG-16 and VGG-19 [18].

Figure 3 presents the structure of the developed model. The data used in the experiments were 50 × 50 RGB images. Therefore, the input shape parameter was defined as (50, 50, 3). The image is submitted to a 0.25 dropout layer, followed by a convolutional layer. We have three central convolutional layers values 32, 64, and 128, respectively. In sequence, a MaxPooling layer, dropout of the same value as the previous one, and flatten are applied. Finally, we have two fully connected layers; between them, there is another 0.5 dropout layer. This model has similar features as in sequential architectures presented in related works.

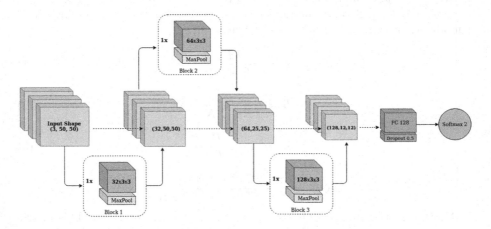

Fig. 3. P-FideNet architecture flowchart.

The P-FideNet was built to solve a binary classification problem. However, the CNN architectures used as the baseline were initially created to solve the competition problem ImageNet dataset (available at the *website MatConv-Net*[3]), which possesses 1000 classes. So, the networks were used initially without their FC layers, which are responsible for the classification. For that, a custom layer was introduced with binary output. We also added a flatten layer to restructure the data to 2D dimension, and two dense layers, one with Relu activation. And the last (output) layer, we defined the activation as softmax.

To finally get the model compiled, we define the loss function as categorical cross-entropy, and we used the Adam Optimizer to tune the CNN parameters.

---

[3] http://www.vlfeat.org/matconvnet/.

4   Results

The NIH Malaria dataset images were arranged in three folds, composed of 22046 images for training (80% of the whole dataset), 2756 for testing, and 2756 for validation. The arrangement kept the initial disposition of two classes, being them, infected and non-infected. The images were randomly divided in both cases, maintaining the balance between the number of images per category. The experiments performed in this study were implemented in Python 3.6 using the libraries Keras 2.3.0, MatplotLib 3.1.1, and Tensorflow 1.14. We also used Google Colab to run some tests.

Table 2. Parameter settings for the CNN models used in the experiments.

Parameter	Value
Epochs	75
Batch size	32
Error function	Binary cross entropy
Learning rate	0.005

We compare the results obtained with our proposed architecture with some other architectures to define the best approach. For this, we chose CNNs architectures that presented excellent results in the ImageNet contest. We picked the architectures with a relatively low number of parameters compared to other sequential architectures such as VGG-16 and VGG-19 [18], ResNet50 [5], and DenseNet [6]. Each model has its peculiarities and has been adapted for this work, using the settings detailed in Table 2. It is essential to point out that the networks used for comparison used the pre-trained weights from ImageNet.

Table 3 depicts the results of the CNNs from state of the art and P-FideNet. The proposed model achieved a better performance overall than the other CNNs, besides having a smaller amount of parameters, making the model much less computationally expensive. According to the results, we can notice that the number of parameters is 39 times lower than ResNet-50, for example. P-FideNet obtained 98.88% of accuracy and precision of 99%.

To better understand the results obtained for the proposed model in terms of accuracy and loss, we plot the charts of Fig. 4. According to these charts, we notice that the validation and training curves' similarity for accuracy and loss. This result proves that the model is stable and robust. It is also observed that the gap between training and validation loss, as well as accuracy, reduces significantly over the epochs, indicating a faster model convergence.

Figure 5 depicts examples of labeling mistakes made by the pathologist. According to Rahman et al. [15], such images were classified as free from malaria and strongly indicated the specialist's identification mistakes when labeling the dataset. To support this statement, Rahman et al. [15]. had the false positives

Table 3. Comparison among the results of P-FideNet against the ones obtained by related methods.

Model	P (%)	R (%)	F1-score (%)	Acc (%)	Num. param
DenseNet-121	95.12	95.00	94.76	95.10	7,825,473
ResNet-50	96.00	95.89	96.90	95.21	24,638,339
VGG-16	98.10	98.53	98.59	98.60	15,240,513
VGG-19	96.10	97.30	96.98	97.80	20,550,209
P-FideNet	**99.00**	**98.57**	**98.88**	**98.88**	631,778

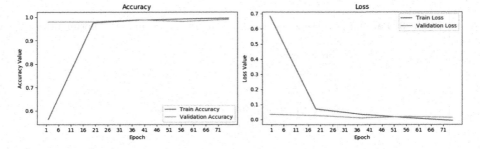

Fig. 4. Training and validation loss and accuracy.

found in the VGG-16 network of his experiment evaluated by another patholo- gist. After the evaluation, it was concluded that 38% of the false-positive blood cells are wrong, showing the apparent formation of malaria parasites while being labeled as non-infected.

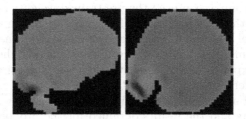

Fig. 5. Images of infected cells wrongly labelled by a pathologist as non-infected.

Based on this statement, we can conclude that a similar error rate can be found for false negatives. This fact might be due to a large number of blood cell images to be analyzed to compose the NIH dataset.

Due to this fact, the P-FideNet model was applied in a practical test case to perform the prediction of some samples. The trained model to predict a label of a sample of images demonstrated in Fig. 6, we have the images along with their actual label and its prediction (1 for infected and 0 for healthy).

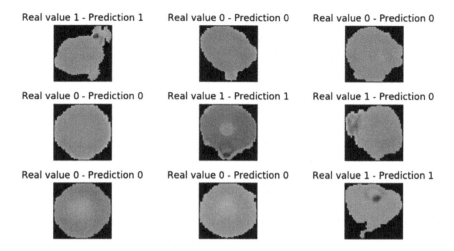

Fig. 6. Image samples along with their real label and our model prediction.

The model was tested with a larger number of images. We performed three experiments with five tests. When performed with only a few hundred images, the model kept at the rate of 100% hits in their predictions. In a scenario with thousands of images, the model still has an accuracy rate close to 100%.

5   Discussion

When using a CNN to classify the NIH Malaria Dataset images to bring much faster and more accurate results than the manual method, we can find that the P-FideNet obtained high-level results like the networks compared in the experiments. From these results, the P-FideNet got 98.88% accuracy. From all the other networks compared, the only one that came close to this result was the VGG-16.

We compared the results of our proposed method and those obtained by studies in the state of the art that address the same problem. This comparison becomes more effective as the methods involved use the same image dataset and comparing the metrics they have in common. This comparison is detailed in Table 4.

According to Table 4, Rajaraman et al. [17] work achieved a higher result in precision, accuracy, and f1-score metrics. Thus, we made a statistical evaluation using the Student's T-test with a significance level of 5% and found that the results obtained by P-FideNet and Rajaraman et al. [17] are statistically equivalent. Therefore, we can conclude that P-FideNet, although less complex (it has

Table 4. Proposed method results compared with the state-of-the-art.

Author	P (%)	R (%)	*F1-score* (%)	Acc (%)
Liang et al. [10]	97.73	97.75	97.36	97.37
Fatima and Farid [4]	94.66	88.60	91.53	91.80
Rajaraman et al. [17]	**99.84**	–	**99.50**	**99.51**
Kashtriya et al. [9]	–	–	–	98.30
Masud et al. [11]	97.00	97.00	97.00	97.30
Proposed method	99.00	**98.57**	98.88	98.88

about 12 to 39 times fewer parameters compared to other CNNs architectures), achieves results comparable to pre-trained architectures. This model is interesting to apply to mobile devices due to its low number of parameters. That is not the case in the work of Rajaraman et al. [17] whose uses two architectures as a model, VGG-19 and SqueezeNet.

This comparative study highlights important aspects that make a greater understanding of the architectures used and the best way to take advantage of their features. Also, the P-FideNet was submitted to predict a small sample of data. The P-FideNet achieved excellent results, demonstrating that P-FideNet can provide a viable solution to the Malaria classification problem.

6 Conclusion and Future Works

Malaria is a disease that has taken millions of lives around the world. The automation of the analysis process provides a more accurate diagnosis of this disease, which can benefit health care in areas with few resources and serve as a second opinion for other test cases.

In this paper, we presented a new CNN architecture, the P-FideNet, to improve the classification of malaria in images of red blood cells. It has been shown that by using different Convolutional Neural Network architectures, we can improve the comparison between them and optimize the classification process. The proposed model, the P-FideNet, reaches an accuracy of 98.88% that achieves a high classification level.

Thus, we notice that the use of Convolutional Neural Networks is outstanding, as this is a technique that has resulted in great relevance to computational vision problems. It is entirely possible to obtain a very high performance compared to other traditional Machine Learning methods.

For future works, we must improve the method by working on the following aspects: the analysis of the neural network to understand weak points and provide an increase in the current results. Expand the existing dataset by applying data augmentation techniques, for instance. Include more images of cells selected by pathologists so that a more effective evaluation can be made. Another methodology to be applied will be the migration of the current model to device-oriented architectures such as the MobileNet as the low number of parameters of our architecture allows it.

References

1. Chimieski, B.F., Fagundes, R.D.R.: Association and classification data mining algorithms comparison over medical datasets. J. Health Inform. **5**(2), 44–51 (2013)
2. Das, D.K., Ghosh, M., Pal, M., Maiti, A.K., Chakraborty, C.: Machine learning approach for automated screening of malaria parasite using light microscopic images. Micron **45**, 97–106 (2013)
3. Doi, K.: Current status and future potential of computer-aided diagnosis in medical imaging. Br. J. Radiol. **78**(suppl_1), s3–s19 (2005)
4. Fatima, T., Farid, M.S.: Automatic detection of plasmodium parasites from microscopic blood images. J. Parasit. Dis. **44**(1), 69–78 (2020). https://doi.org/10.1007/s12639-019-01163-x
5. He, K., Zhang, X., Ren, S., Sun, J.: Deep residual learning for image recognition. In: Proceedings of the IEEE Conference on Computer Vision and Pattern Recognition, pp. 770–778 (2016)
6. Huang, G., Liu, Z., Van Der Maaten, L., Weinberger, K.Q.: Densely connected convolutional networks. In: Proceedings of the IEEE Conference on Computer Vision and Pattern Recognition, pp. 4700–4708 (2017)
7. Iandola, F.N., Han, S., Moskewicz, M.W., Ashraf, K., Dally, W.J., Keutzer, K.: SqueezeNet: AlexNet-level accuracy with 50x fewer parameters and 0.5 MB model size. arXiv preprint arXiv:1602.07360 (2016)
8. Janocha, K., Czarnecki, W.M.: On loss functions for deep neural networks in classification. arXiv preprint arXiv:1702.05659 (2017)
9. Kashtriya, V., Doegar, A., Gupta, V., Kashtriya, P.: Identifying malaria infection in red blood cells using optimized step-increase convolutional neural network model **8**, 813–818 (2019)
10. Liang, Z., et al.: CNN-based image analysis for malaria diagnosis. In: 2016 IEEE International Conference on Bioinformatics and Biomedicine (BIBM), pp. 493–496. IEEE (2016)
11. Masud, M., et al.: Leveraging deep learning techniques for malaria parasite detection using mobile application. Wirel. Commun. Mob. Comput. **2020**, 5–13 (2020)
12. World Health Organization, et al.: World malaria report 2014. Who, Geneva. Fecha de consulta **23**, 247 (2018)
13. Pedrini, H., Schwartz, W.R.: Análise de imagens digitais: princípios, algoritmos e aplicações. Thomson Learning (2008)
14. Powers, D.: Evaluation: from precision, recall and f-factor to roc, informedness, markedness & correlation. Technical report SIE-07-001. School of Informatics and Engineering, Flinders University, Adelaide, Australia (2016)
15. Rahman, A., et al.: Improving malaria parasite detection from red blood cell using deep convolutional neural networks. arXiv preprint arXiv:1907.10418 (2019)
16. Rajaraman, S., et al.: Pre-trained convolutional neural networks as feature extractors toward improved malaria parasite detection in thin blood smear images. PeerJ **6**, e4568 (2018)
17. Rajaraman, S., Jaeger, S., Antani, S.K.: Performance evaluation of deep neural ensembles toward malaria parasite detection in thin-blood smear images. PeerJ **7**, e6977 (2019)

18. Simonyan, K., Zisserman, A.: Very deep convolutional networks for large-scale image recognition. arXiv preprint arXiv:1409.1556 (2014)
19. Warhurst, D., Williams, J.: ACP broadsheet no 148. July 1996. Laboratory diagnosis of malaria. J. Clin. Pathol. **49**(7), 533 (1996)
20. WHO: World malaria report 2019. World Health Organization (2020)

Applications

Lightless Fields: Enhancement and Denoising of Light-Deficient Light Fields

Carson Vogt[1($\boxtimes$)], Geng Lyu[2($\boxtimes$)], and Kartic Subr[2($\boxtimes$)]

[1] Heriot-Watt University, Edinburgh, UK
crv3@hw.ac.uk
[2] University of Edinburgh, Edinburgh, UK
lvgengbuaa@gmail.com, K.subr@ed.ac.uk

Abstract. Modern focused light field cameras are capable of capturing video at over 160 frames per second, but in so doing sacrifice shutter speed. Outside of laboratory environments, lighting can be problematic resulting in noisy light fields and poor depth reconstruction. To enhance and denoise modern focused light field cameras, we create a unique deep neural network that allows for the full light field to be processed at once, eliminates stitching artifacts, and takes advantage of feature redundancy between neighboring microlenses. We show that our double U-Net network, ENH-W, significantly outperforms several popular architectures and light field denoising methods in both visual and depth metrics.

Keywords: Focused light field camera · Deep learning · Low light

1 Introduction

Light deficiency results in undesirable visual noise which can have further detrimental effects on image processing techniques such as depth estimation and feature matching. Larger pixels or high gain can sometimes improve the performance of imaging sensors in low light. While the trade-offs involved in adjusting variables such as exposure value for light-deficient photography are well understood [13] and computational cameras have been built to address some of these problems [14], there is very little work that investigates the problem of light deficiency in light field photography. Most relevant work falls into the general category of denoising light fields [1,3]. Noise introduced by light deficiency is particularly undesirable in computational imaging since the computational processes could become unstable due to this noise. Light field capture forms a special case where the resulting data is processed computationally for viewing in the form of the "total focus" image [9,26] or for depth estimation [6]. Both of these reconstruction pipelines are sensitive to noise, making the investigation of light-deficient light fields both important and relevant. In this work we investigate the problem of simultaneously enhancing light fields to improve visual quality as well as the quality of depth estimation from the enhanced light fields. We use supervised learning to train deep neural networks (DNN) to take

© Springer Nature Switzerland AG 2020
G. Bebis et al. (Eds.): ISVC 2020, LNCS 12509, pp. 383–396, 2020.
https://doi.org/10.1007/978-3-030-64556-4_30

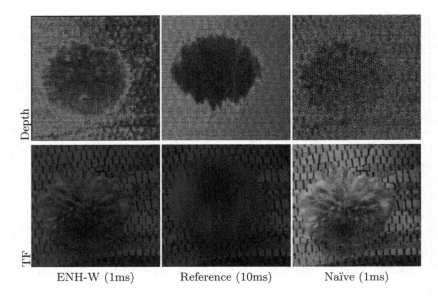

Fig. 1. Motivation: The ability of our approach to cope with low-light scenarios enables improved depth estimation and rendering with adjustable brightness. Methods like histogram equalization arbitrarily brighten while denoising methods like BM3D can hinder depth estimation.

advantage of inherent redundancies to improve robustness to noise introduced by insufficient light. We train our network on a custom dataset created by capturing a set of short exposures and a reference long exposure for a number of static scenes with a focused light field camera. In the next section we cover some relevant background. In Sect. 3 we explain our method and training, followed by experiments performed and results in Sect. 4. Finally, we discuss these results in Sect. 5.

2   Related Work

Initial research into light fields required light field sampling in the form of gantries or camera arrays [17]. Hand-held light field cameras were proposed relatively recently, being introduced in their current form in [7,23]. Light field cameras come in two main types: the standard and the focused light field camera. Both have a microlens array placed between the main lens and the image sensor. For standard light field cameras, the microlenses are focused at the back of the main lens, resulting in unfocused microlens images. Processing this light field requires an initial rendering step consisting of sampling a pixel from each lens with a fixed stride, and de-hexing with a 1D interpolation. This yields a grid of sub aperture images (SAIs) and we refer to this as the SAI parametrization. Most research focuses on this type of light field.

We work with a focused light field camera [27]. In this case the microlenses are focused on the image created by the main lens. This allows for a much higher resolution rendering of the scene relative to image sensor size [8]. However, this method requires an accurate depth map for rendering. Large and focused microlenses means that depth can be estimated directly from microlens images without further processing unlike the standard light field camera.

Image denoising is a well-studied area. BM3D is a successful technique with the original target being traditional 2D images [4]. This was extended to video with VBM4D [21]. Alain and Smolic [1] build on BM3D to take advantage of the redundancies found in light field SAIs with LFBM5D. In their results, they report that VBM4D performs better than other light field denoising techniques on a stack of SAIs. These findings are corroborated in [3] who develop a CNN for the purpose of denoising SAIs. Learning-based burst denoising techniques have also been proposed, such as in [10], which utilizes a Recurrent Neural Network (RNN) to denoise a series of exposures, and [22] which predicts kernels for alignment and denoising of a series of input frames.

Low-light imaging is a difficult problem and a considerable amount of research exists for traditional photography. While histogram equalization (HE) is a fast and simple method that is commonly used, many sophisticated non-learning techniques exist. Low-light Image Enhancement (LIME) estimates a refined illumination map based on a structural prior and initial illumination map [11], with generally very good results in adverse lighting. A number of deep learning techniques have been applied to low-light photography including autoencoders with LLNet to simultaneously learn brightening and denoising [19]. Low-light Convolutional Neural Network (LLCNN) is a fully convolutional network with a structure inspired by feature extraction methods found in ResNet [29]. To emphasize texture retention in the image the authors train the network with an SSIM loss. More recently, Chen reports comparing two networks, the U-Net and Context Aggregation Network (CAN) noting a decrease in mean PSNR and SSIM when using CAN [2].

Much work has been done in processing SAI parametrized light fields, thanks in large part to the availability of consumer grade cameras like the Lytro Illum for which there exists established support, such as the Light Field Toolbox [5]. DNN based approaches have been investigated for this category of light field [3], though all of these methods require conversion from the light field MLA to SAI parametrization whereas we propose to operate directly on the MLA.

In our work, we propose a two part network that not only takes inspiration from low-light and denoising methods, but utilizes the unique structure of the light field. The first part of our network learns a mapping from neighboring microlenses to a target microlens. Unlike some burst denoising techniques, our method does not require any stabilization. The second part refines the input. We go on to analyze the effects of applying other denoising and enhancement networks to a focused light field MLA directly as well as how our network performs relative to SAI-based denoising methods.

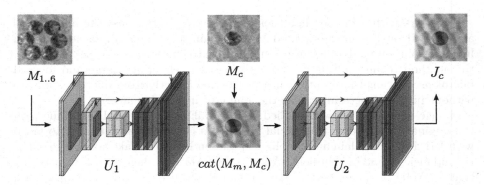

Fig. 2. Network diagram for ENH-W. U_1 takes the angular data in the form of neighboring microlenses, $M_{1..N}$, then warp and merges it to the central microlens. The output of U_1 is M_m. The input to U_2 is the concatenation of M_m and M_c. The output of U_2 is the enhanced central microlens, J_c

3   Method

The light field is defined as a 4D function of radiance given by

$$F = f(u, v, s, t) \tag{1}$$

where (u, v), and (s, t) represent two planes that define the direction of a particular ray. By convention, the (u, v) plane represents the angular or camera plane, while the (s, t) plane represents the imaging plane [17]. Unlike the standard light field camera, we consider that each microlens image for a focused light field camera lies on the (u, v) plane and the pixels of each microlens are spatial samples. Using a standard light field camera rendering with a 40 megapixel Lytro Illum yields 512×512 pixel SAI images. Using the same technique with a 4.2 megapixel Raytrix R5 yields 100×100 pixels. However, using the depth-based rendering techniques for focused light field cameras introduced in [20], "total focus" (T) images up to 1024×1024 pixels can be rendered. Because of this the resulting T image for a MLA light field, I, is a function of the depth map and microlens array images:

$$T = r(D(I), I) \tag{2}$$

where D is the estimated depth map for the entire MLA. Noise present in I will precipitate through D and therefore affect T. To fully take advantage of the focused light field camera, we perform enhancement directly on the MLA utilizing deep learning. We introduce a two part network that first learns a mapping between neighboring microlenses then refines the result. We refer to the network as ENH-W.

3.1   Network

The foundation of our network is the U-Net [28] which has proven successful in low-light image enhancement as shown in [2] as it preserves high frequency data, learns an encoding for the input, and can be loaded with the full light field to the GPU. Structures for U-Nets are limited with pooling restricted by the very low resolution of the individual microlenses at 24×24 pixels. The number of layers is restricted by the amount of memory of our GPU and the relatively high resolution of the full light field, 2048×2048 pixels in our case. We are able to size a U-Net that can both be loaded to the GPU with the full light field as well as preserve the data of the individual microlenses. Using two U-Nets, we combine them to create the network shown in Fig. 2. The inputs to these two sections differs and a separate loss is used for each. We refer to the first section of the network as U_1 and the second as U_2

Prior to being fed to the network, the light field is multiplied by an amplification factor α similar to [2] defined as

$$\alpha = \frac{S_{max}}{S_{cap}} \tag{3}$$

where S_{max} is the target shutter speed brightness level, and S_{cap} is the shutter speed of the captured light field. The low-light MLA is multiplied by this value before enhancement. The α parameter allows us to provide the network with the target exposure level.

Because the MLA is made up of hexagonally packed microlenses, each microlens has a maximum of six immediate neighbors, $M_{1..N}$. U_1 learns a mapping from neighboring microlenses, and effectively warps and merges $M_{1..N}$ to a central microlens, M_c. M_c is omitted from the input to U_1 to force the network to learn the angular warping. We refer to the meta data output of U_1 as M_m.

U_2 is the refinement step of the network. While U_1 combines the features from neighboring lenses, U_2 takes as input the concatenation of M_c and M_m. The output of U_2 is the final enhanced central microlens, J_c. The total loss for ENH-W is defined as

$$Loss_{total} = MSE(M_m, L_c) + MSE(J_c, L_c) \tag{4}$$

where MSE is the Mean-Squared Error, and L_c is the target, central microlens of the reference light field. The final enhanced MLA light field is given as

$$I_{enhanced} = \sum_{i=1}^{H} U_2(cat(U_1(cat_{j=1}^{N} M_j), M_i)) \tag{5}$$

where H is the total number of microlenses in I, and cat refers to a concatenation along the color channels.

3.2 Training

The final structure for both U_1 and U_2 is based on the results in Fig. 3 a and consists of two pooling layers. There are 64 channels for the first convolution block, 128 for the second, and 256 for the bottleneck. Kernel size is set to 3 for all layers apart from the transposed convolutions in upsampling with kernel size 2.

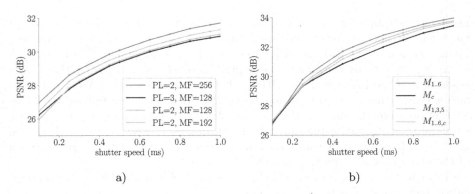

Fig. 3. In a) we compare different U-Net structures. The best performing U-Net from this test makes up the two U-Nets of ENH-W. In this case MF refers to the maximum number of feature channels in the network which occurs at the bottleneck, and PL refers to the number of pooling layers. In b) we compare the effects of different angular inputs to U_1.

Initial weight values are set to default with PyTorch [25]. Optimization is carried out with the Adam optimizer [18]. The learning rate is initially set to 10^{-4}, which reduces to 10^{-5} after 3 epochs, and 10^{-6} after 5 epochs. Training continues for a total of 10 epochs with a batch size of 8 for all networks. Training was done on a GeForce GTX Titan X (Maxwell) GPU with Intel i5-7600 CPU.

For training, we split our light fields into 128×128 pixel MLA patches, where $M_{1..N}$ becomes a stack of MLA patches of dimension $H \times W \times NC$ with each MLA patch centered on the neighbor microlens. Splitting the light field into patches is also a technique that has been proven in [16] as a way of increasing the number of samples and speeding up training. At run time, we pass the full 2048×2048 pixel light field into the network.

4   Experiments and Results

4.1   Low-Light Dataset

All of our experiments are conducted using a Raytrix R5 focused light field camera. The MLA is 2048×2048 pixels and consists of approximately 8700 usable microlenses with synthesized, total focus images rendered at up to 1024×1024 pixels. The camera requires special hardware to operate, as such movement was limited leading us to focus on smaller scenes which allowed us to capture light fields with dense depth coverage.

Light fields of static scenes were collected by varying the shutter speed of the camera to simulate lower light scenarios. We took a wide range of shutter speeds for each scene, with the minimum at 0.01 milliseconds, and the maximum at 30 milliseconds. We chose a reference shutter speed of 10 milliseconds based on

Table 1. The average results of each method for all light fields and shutter speeds are compared against the reference light fields. PSNR/SSIM are compared for light fields as well as the rendered total focus (TF) and sub-aperture images. Training and run times are given for the networks, as well as whether or not the full light field can fit into memory.

Method	PSNR (dB)			SSIM			BadPix (%)			Net details	
	LF	TF	SAI	LF	TF	SAI	0.1	0.3	0.7	Run(s)	Full LF
ENH-W (Ours)	**31.40**	**30.89**	**30.79**	**0.958**	**0.934**	**0.929**	**21.42**	**6.35**	**0.81**	0.75	✓
ENH	30.55	30.34	30.28	0.950	0.912	0.913	27.98	11.10	1.97	0.023	✓
ENH-S	30.96	30.49	30.43	0.954	0.926	0.924	24.54	8.18	1.28	0.62	✓
DBPN	29.17	28.73	28.65	0.943	0.911	0.910	27.45	10.01	1.65	0.063	✗
DBD	29.47	28.88	28.93	0.944	0.908	0.911	28.10	10.27	1.41	1.74	✗
LLCNN	29.27	28.98	29.08	0.938	0.882	0.889	34.84	16.39	3.17	**0.0052**	✗
HE	13.91	14.90	14.62	0.581	0.520	0.528	37.30	15.39	2.05	0.034	✓
HE-BM3D	14.51	15.58	15.42	0.663	0.709	0.672	41.13	19.08	2.83	139	✓

the best average depth reconstruction quality generated during collection. Depth was calculated per microlens using the Plenoptic 2.0 Toolbox [24].

After cropping, our training dataset consists of 307,675 samples and our test set contains 17,311 samples. All of this was taken from 40 light fields. A further 13 light fields were used for all of the experiments.

4.2   Experiments

Because little to no research exists on applying deep learning to the 4D light field MLA, we train a number of networks to compare against. In total we train six networks on our dataset. ENH and ENH-W are covered in Sect. 3.1. ENH-S is equal in structure to ENH but takes the concatenation of $M_{1..6}$ and M_c as input. LLCNN was designed specifically for low-light enhancement, and utilizes short residual connections and no pooling layers. DBPN was originally designed for image super resolution. Rather than having a compressing encoder/decoder structure, it alternates up and down sampling to allow the network to learn from error feedback in the upsampling process [12]. Deep Burst Denoising (DBD) is introduced in [10] and requires a pretraining step for single microlenses before using $M_{1..6,c}$ as input. Each network is trained on the same data with the same starting parameters discussed in Sect. 3.2. We compare the results of different rendering methods using the standard metrics PSNR and SSIM. For depth we utilize the BadPix metric. BadPix is defined in [15], and we adapt as

$$BadPix(\tau) = |D_{reference} - D_{enhanced}| > \tau \qquad (6)$$

where τ is a particular threshold.

In Fig. 3a) we show the comparisons between different U-Net structures that make up ENH. For each U-Net tested we varied the number of feature channels per layer where the bottleneck portion of the network contained the most channels, referred to in the figure as MF. We also varied the number of pooling layers,

PL. Figure 3b) shows the results of using different numbers of angular inputs. We vary the inputs to U_1 to include only the central microlens input, M_c, the central plus all neighboring microlenses $M_{1..6,c}$, all neighbors only, $M_{1..6}$, and finally three neighbors only $M_{1,3,5}$.

Table 1 shows results between methods as an average of each metric across all shutter speeds. It also shows run times for the networks, as well as whether or not the network accepts the full light field as input, or if the light field must be cropped and stitched together after enhancement.

While our method operates on the MLA produced by a focused light field camera, prominent state-of-the-art light field denoising techniques are SAI-based. These methods were not designed with low-light in mind, therefore we add white Gaussian noise to our reference validation data and denoise the MLA with BM3D and SAIs with VBM4D and LFBM5D. For both VBM4D and LFBM5D we pass all SAIs for a particular light field in at once. For our camera configuration, this equates to 144 SAIs per light field. As in [10], the network is trained with simulated Gaussian noise. We also train and test against the popular denoising network, DnCNN [30].

Table 2. State-of-the-art denoising methods were not designed to operate on low-light data, and as such it is uninformative to compare them on low-light data. Instead, we add white Gaussian noise to the refence data at various σ. In this case, BM3D, DnCNN, and Ours are applied to the MLA then rendered as SAIs, while VBM4D and LFBM5D are applied to the rendered, noisy SAIs.

Additive White Gaussian Noise SAI Comparison								
	PSNR(dB)				SSIM			
	$\sigma = 15$	$\sigma = 25$	$\sigma = 50$	$\sigma = 75$	$\sigma = 15$	$\sigma = 25$	$\sigma = 50$	$\sigma = 75$
ENH-W (Ours)	**33.96**	**32.65**	**30.39**	**28.97**	**0.970**	**0.958**	**0.926**	**0.897**
DnCNN	31.14	29.95	28.03	26.37	0.955	0.936	0.894	0.851
LFBM5D	25.32	19.30	14.04	12.15	0.782	0.489	0.227	0.151
VBM4D	28.67	24.87	19.14	16.63	0.894	0.783	0.547	0.424
BM3D	**32.73**	**27.90**	**17.14**	**13.87**	**0.948**	**0.898**	**0.400**	**0.219**

Figures 4, 5, and 6 demonstrate the computed results of the light fields from the highest performing networks according to Table 1. This includes the input light field, ENH-W, DBPN, DBD, and the reference light field, Ref. The input light field in this case is captured at a shutter speed of 0.25 ms.

5   Discussion

The structure of focused light field cameras means we can render high resolution 2D images from relatively small image sensors. To do so the MLA must remain intact. It is tempting to apply generic 2D-based denoising techniques to the light

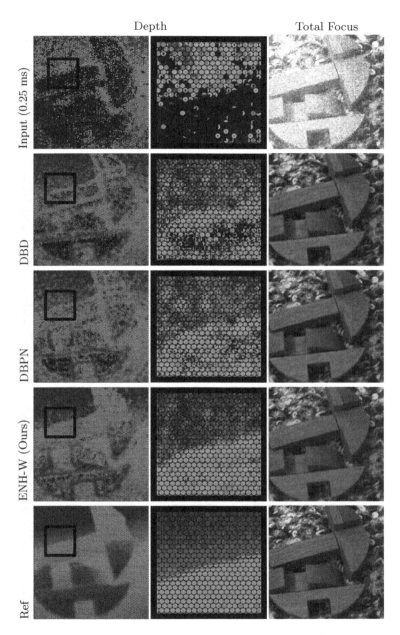

Fig. 4. A depth map is estimated via Plenoptic 2.0 Toolbox (left). Closer inspection (center) shows clearly that our method performs significantly better than other methods. The right column shows the resulting T image.

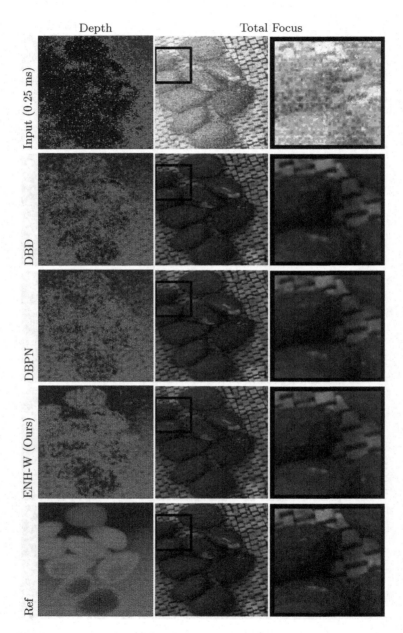

Fig. 5. Improvements to the MLA manifest directly as improvements in the total focus images. We can see significant noise in the Input images, with increased noise caused by poor depth resulting in incorrect patch sizes being sampled from microlenses.

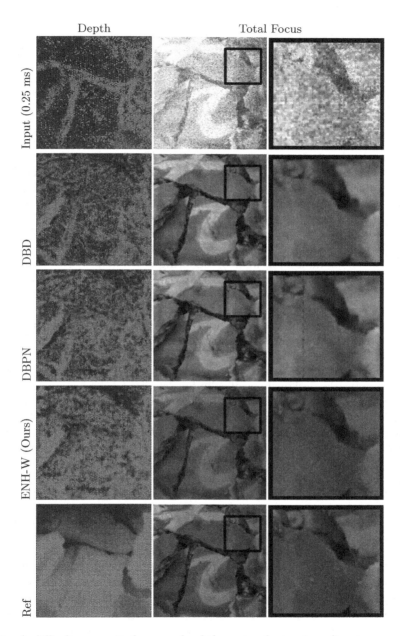

Fig. 6. A difficult scene, it shows each of the networks to struggling to recover the full color of the scene. Methods that require the light field to be cropped show clear artifacts in the synthesized views, highlighted in the far right column. DBPN suffers the most as the light field had to be divided into the most pieces due to the network's memory usage.

field MLA though we have found that these techniques can have a harmful effect on the MLA as excessive blurring removes high-frequency detail from microlenses used for depth estimation. We can see this in Table 1 where we show the results from using HE and BM3D to denoise it. While the visual metrics improve with BM3D, the resulting BadPix metrics show that BM3D actually worsens the depth estimation. While HE is not visually competitive, it is worth showing the sensitivities particular to the MLA-based light field.

ENH-S in Table 1 shows that the addition of angular information to the input of ENH can drastically improve the quality of J_c as shown by both the visual and depth metrics. In the case of ENH-W Fig. 3b) shows that the network performs best with only $M_{1..6}$ as input to U_1, and performs worse when $M_{1..6,c}$ is the input. We believe that by removing M_c from the U_1 input the network is encouraged to warp and merge the neighboring microlenses, taking advantage of scene features captured in neighboring microlenses. We also tested using M_c as the input to both U_1 and U_2 but saw little improvement over ENH. ENH-W shows particularly significant improvements in the depth metrics for all three BadPix threshold values. As well, by adopting the double U-Net architecture, we are able to overcome the limitations on U-Net architecture created by the light field structure as well as being able to keep the full light field on GPU. This comes at a cost of slower run times, especially compared to LLCNN.

Because current state-of-the-art light field denoising techniques do not take low-light into account and only apply to SAIs, we show that our architecture significantly improves visual metrics of SAIs in Table 2. The results here show that our network performs better than popular light field denoising techniques and other networks designed specifically for denoising.

Figures 4, 5, and 6 show that our method clearly outperforms others, though it still struggles with recovering all of the color for a scene. We see that, especially compared with DBPN in Fig. 6, by loading the full light field we avoid any chance of stitching artifacts.

6   Conclusion

As light field video becomes popular for the visual aspects such as total focus images and practical aspects such as depth maps, higher frame rates will mean shorter exposures. In this work, we have introduced a network architecture that takes into account the high resolution of the full MLA light field and low resolution of the individual microlenses. We presented a two part neural network we refer to as ENH-W that first learns an angular mapping between neighboring microlenses then uses the results of this mapping to enhance a target microlens. Future work would involve looking into different loss functions that could further leverage the MLA structure.

References

1. Alain, M., Smolic, A.: Light field denoising by sparse 5D transform domain collaborative filtering. In: IEEE International Workshop on Multimedia Signal Processing (2017)
2. Chen, C., Chen, Q., Xu, J., Koltun, V.: Learning to see in the dark. In: Computer Vision and Pattern Recognition (2018)
3. Chen, J., Hou, J., Chau, L.: Light field denoising via anisotropic parallax analysis in a CNN framework. IEEE Signal Process. Lett. **25**, 1403–1407 (2018)
4. Dabov, K., Foi, A., Katkovnik, V., Egiazarian, K.: Image denoising by sparse 3D transform-domain collaborative filtering. IEEE Trans. Image Process. **16**, 2080–2095 (2007)
5. Dansereau, D.G., Pizarro, O., Williams, S.B.: Decoding, calibration and rectification for lenslet-based plenoptic cameras. In: Computer Vision and Pattern Recognition (2013)
6. Fleischmann, O., Koch, R.: Lens-based depth estimation for multi-focus plenoptic cameras. In: Jiang, X., Hornegger, J., Koch, R. (eds.) GCPR 2014. LNCS, vol. 8753, pp. 410–420. Springer, Cham (2014). https://doi.org/10.1007/978-3-319-11752-2_33
7. Georgiev, T., Intwala, C.: Light field camera design for integral view photography. Adobe Technical report (2006)
8. Georgiev, T., Lumsdaine, A.: Reducing plenoptic camera artifacts. In: Computer Graphics Forum (2010)
9. Georgiev, T., Lumsdaine, A.: The multi-focus plenoptic camera. In: SPIE Electronic Imaging (2012)
10. Godard, C., Matzen, K., Uyttendaele, M.: Deep burst denoising. In: European Conference on Computer Vision (2018)
11. Guo, X., Li, Y., Ling, H.: LIME: a method for low-light image enhancement. In: Proceedings of the 24th ACM International Conference on Multimedia (2016)
12. Haris, M., Shakhnarovich, G., Ukita, N.: Deep back-projection networks for super-resolution. In: Computer Vision and Pattern Recognition (2018)
13. Hasinoff, S.W., Kutulakos, K.N.: Light-efficient photography. IEEE Trans. Pattern Anal. Mach. Intell. **33**, 2203–2214 (2011)
14. Hasinoff, S.W., et al.: Burst photography for high dynamic range and low-light imaging on mobile cameras. ACM Trans. Graph. **35**, 1–12 (2016)
15. Honauer, K., Johannsen, O., Kondermann, D., Goldluecke, B.: A dataset and evaluation methodology for depth estimation on 4D light fields. In: Lai, S.-H., Lepetit, V., Nishino, K., Sato, Y. (eds.) ACCV 2016. LNCS, vol. 10113, pp. 19–34. Springer, Cham (2017). https://doi.org/10.1007/978-3-319-54187-7_2
16. Kalantari, N.K., Wang, T., Ramamoorthi, R.: Learning-based view synthesis for light field cameras. In: SIGGRAPH Asia (2016)
17. Levoy, M., Hanrahan, P.,: Light field rendering. In: SIGGRAPH (1996)
18. Kingma, D.P., Ba, J.: Adam: a method for stochastic optimization. In: International Conference on Learning Representations (2015)
19. Lore, K.G., Akintayo, A., Sarkar, S.: LLNet: a deep autoencoder approach to natural low-light image enhancement. Pattern Recogn. **61**, 650–662 (2016)
20. Lumsdaine, A., Georgiev, T.: The focused Plenoptic camera. In: International Conference on Computational Photography (2009)
21. Maggioni, M., Boracchi, G., Foi, A., Egiazarian, K.: Video denoising, deblocking and enhancement through separable 4-D nonlocal spatiotemporal transforms. IEEE Trans. Image Process. **21**, 3952–3966 (2012)

22. Mildenhall, B., Barron, J.T., Chen, J., Sharlet, D., Ng, R., Carroll, R.: Burst denoising with kernel prediction networks. In: Computer Vision and Pattern Recognition (2018)
23. Ng, R., Levoy, M., Bredif, M., Duval, G., Horowitz, M., Hanrahan, P.: Light field photography with a hand-held Plenoptic camera. Computer Science Technical Report (2005)
24. Palmieri, L., Op Het Veld, R., Koch, R.: The plenoptic 2.0 toolbox: benchmarking of depth estimation methods for MLA-based focused plenoptic cameras. In: International Conference on Image Processing (2018)
25. Paszke, A., et al.: Automatic differentiation in PyTorch. In: Neural Information Processing Systems (2017)
26. Perwass, C., Wietzke, L.: Single lens 3D-camera with extended depth-of-field. In: Proceedings of SPIE (2012)
27. Raytrix. https://www.raytrix.de
28. Ronneberger, O., Fischer, P., Brox, T.: U-Net: convolutional networks for biomedical image segmentation. In: Navab, N., Hornegger, J., Wells, W.M., Frangi, A.F. (eds.) MICCAI 2015. LNCS, vol. 9351, pp. 234–241. Springer, Cham (2015). https://doi.org/10.1007/978-3-319-24574-4_28
29. Tao, L., Zhu, C., Xiang, G., Li, Y., Jia, H., Xie, X.: LLCNN: a convolutional neural network for low-light image enhancement. In: Visual Communications and Image Processing (2017)
30. Zhang, K., Zuo, W., Chen, Y., Meng, D., Zhang, L.: Beyond a Gaussian denoiser: residual learning of deep CNN for image denoising. Transactions on Image Processing **26**, 3142–3155 (2017)

FA3D: Fast and Accurate 3D Object Detection

Selameab S. Demilew$^{(\boxtimes)}$, Hamed H. Aghdam, Robert Laganière,
and Emil M. Petriu

University of Ottawa, Ottawa, Canada
{sdemi032,h.aghdam,laganier,petriu}@uottawa.ca

Abstract. Fast and accurate detection of objects, in 3D, is one of the
critical components in an advanced driver assistance system. In this
paper, we aim to develop an accurate 3D object detector that runs in
near real-time on low-end embedded systems. We propose an efficient
framework that converts raw point cloud into a 3D occupancy cuboid
and detects cars using a deep convolutional neural network. Even though
the complexity of our proposed model is high, it runs at 7.27 FPS on
a Jetson Xavier and at 57.83 FPS on a high-end workstation that is
18% and 43% faster than the fastest published method while having
a comparable performance with state-of-the-art models on the KITTI
dataset. We conduct a comprehensive error analysis on our model and
show that two quantities are the principal sources of error among nine
predicted attributes. Our source code is available at https://github.com/
Selameab/FA3D.

Keywords: 3D object detection · Deep neural networks · Smart and
autonomous vehicles

1 Introduction

Detecting 3D objects in road scenes is vital for autonomous cars and an important safety function in advanced driver assistance systems (ADAS). High-end
computational resources are an indispensable part of autonomous vehicles to
process the massive amount of data in real-time and make decisions. In contrast, regular cars utilize low-end embedded systems with limited computational
power. With the advent of cost-effective and accurate LiDAR sensors, there is
a growing demand for integrating these sensors with contemporary cars (*e.g.*
mounting on bumpers) to perform various tasks such as detecting vulnerable
road users (*e.g.* pedestrians, cyclists), and vehicles. Hence, LiDAR point clouds
have to be processed using low-end embedded systems to make this technology
widely accessible in cars.

As opposed to images, points in raw LiDAR scans are not sampled from a
regular grid. Most detection networks address this problem by applying quantization techniques and converting the point cloud into 3D grids. VoxelNet [26],

© Springer Nature Switzerland AG 2020
G. Bebis et al. (Eds.): ISVC 2020, LNCS 12509, pp. 397–409, 2020.
https://doi.org/10.1007/978-3-030-64556-4_31

SECOND [23] and SA-SSD [5] create 3D voxels where each voxel may contain zero or more points. While a voxel in VoxelNet and SECOND may contain more than one 3D point, SA-SSD retains only one point inside each voxel. Instead of voxels, PointPillars [8] creates vertical pillars where each pillar covers the entire vertical axis and contains up to 100 points.

Even though SA-SSD has outperformed other methods on the KITTI 3D object detection benchmark [4], it has major practical drawbacks. Specifically, its reliance on 3D sparse convolutions makes its execution time highly dependent on the point cloud's density. In other words, if a car uses a LiDAR sensor with 128 channels (*i.e.* scan lines) or utilizes multiple LiDAR sensors, the density of the point cloud will increase several times and negatively impact the execution time of SA-SSD.

Likewise, the pillar representation utilized by PointPillars depends on the number of pillars and the number of points inside each pillar. Moreover, pillars are only generated from the data within the field-of-view (FOV) of the camera. Even though $12K$ pillars suffice to cover the points inside FOV, it will become less accurate on denser point clouds and larger FOVs. To deal with this problem, we must increase the number of pillars, and in turn increase the runtime of the model. Besides, although 100 points per pillar (suggested by the authors) is crucial to model close objects accurately, it is redundant in distant objects since LiDAR readings become sparser as one moves away from the sensor. Among all the methods reported on the KITTI dataset, PointPillars is the fastest model where the PyTorch implementation can process 40 frames per second on a high-end GPU. Despite that, both of the above representations will potentially fail to detect objects using embedded systems in real-time on denser and larger (*i.e.* larger FOVs) point clouds. PIXOR [25] and PIXOR++[24] have previously used 3D occupancy grids that are faster to compute compared to voxels and pillar, but had significantly lower performance.

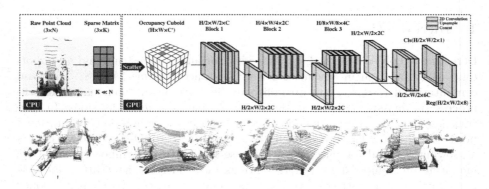

Fig. 1. Architecture of FA3D (top) and predictions on the validation set (bottom).

Contribution: In this paper, we propose a fast and deep 3D detection network that utilizes 3D occupancy grids to encode point clouds, and not only is more accurate than PointPillars, but also the fastest deep 3D detection network reported on the KITTI dataset. More importantly, we do not improve the execution time by sacrificing the expressive power of the neural network. Instead, we utilize an input encoding that is multiple times faster to compute and a few times faster to transfer to GPUs. Our main gain in the execution time is primarily due to these two factors and not by designing a less flexible (*i.e.* smaller) network. Moreover, we present a few techniques to properly train an accurate 3D detection network using this input representation.

Furthermore, we show that our network's performance is comparable to more computational approaches when we evaluate at intersection-over-union (IoU) threshold of 0.5 instead of 0.7. As we will explain in our experiments, the differences in predictions whose IoU are more than 0.7, and whose IoU are in [0.5, 0.7] are negligible in practical applications. Last but not least, we assess our model extensively from different perspectives, carefully analyze the error and demonstrate that the central source of the error in most models boils down to two factors. Improving these two factors will significantly improve the results.

We will start by explaining the state-of-the-art in Sect. 2. The proposed network and fast input representation will be explained in Sect. 3, and we will comprehensively analyze the performance of our method in Sect. 4. Finally, Sect. 5 concludes the paper and provides a guideline for future work.

2   Related Work

Object Detection from Point Clouds: Early works in 3D object detection use handcrafted projections of the point cloud. MV3D [2] and AVOD [7] generate range view (RV) and bird's eye view (BEV) projections that capture point cloud density, height, and intensity. PIXOR [25] voxelizes the input using a simple and effective occupancy cuboid. The height information is encoded along the channel axis, while the spatial axes of the pseudo-image capture the remaining two dimensions. Also, it augments the pseudo-image with an extra channel carrying the reflectance information. VoxelNet [26] and SECOND [23], on the other hand, divide the space into a grid of voxels and apply a Voxel Feature Encoding layer (a smaller form of PointNet [17]) to map the input into a higher dimension and more informative space. Next, they apply a set of 2D and 3D convolutions to classify and regress 3D bounding boxes. PointPillars [8] improves the runtime of [23] by removing the 3D convolutions, using a smaller PointNet encoder and a single bin along the height axis in its voxel representation. Similarly, Patch Refinement [9] uses voxel representation at two different resolutions. It stacks two convolutional networks where the second network refines estimates by fusing the information from the first network with higher resolution voxels. As it turns out, this method is not computationally efficient since it requires encoding two different voxel-based representations and detects objects in two stages. SA-SSD [5] implemented an auxiliary network that reverts intermediate convolutional feature maps into point-wise representations to help the backbone capture structural information in the point cloud. They also propose a part-sensitive warping operation that aligns confidence scores to predicted boxes.

Point-based 3D object detectors work directly on points rather than dividing the point cloud into a gird. Point RCNN [18] employs an expensive per-point segmentation to classify all the points as either foreground or background. Next, they crop the area around foreground points along with corresponding features learned from the previous stage for classifying and refining 3D bounding boxes. Fast Point R-CNN [3], on the contrary, replaces the first proposal generation stage with a faster VoxelRPN that resembles [26]. [15] adopts an engineered sampling strategy for proposing candidate regions. In general, two-stage 2D object detection networks have had better performance, while single-stage detectors offered higher frame rates. Similar observations are made in the 3D object detection literature. Currently, PointPillars [8], a single-stage method, reports the shortest runtime at 16ms on a GTX-1080 GPU.

Multimodal 3D Object Detection: Several attempts have been made to fuse point cloud and images to increase the performance. [10,11,22] run two concurrent streams for each modality and perform a late-fusion at the feature level. [16,21] use PointNet to regress boxes on point cloud crops generated from 2D image proposals. PointPainting [20] also decorates points with a class vector that is computed using an image-only semantic segmentation network.

Currently, LiDAR-only methods outperform fusion-based methods in detecting cars and pedestrians. We hypothesize that the KITTI dataset is not big and diverse enough to learn a robust joint representation. In addition to that, fusion methods usually run slower due to the additional computation required for reading and processing images by another sub-network. For these reasons, we opt for using only LiDAR data in this paper.

3   Proposed Method

In this section, we explain our proposed fast and accurate framework for 3D object detection using point clouds. We achieve the highest processing speed reported on the KITTI dataset and maintain state-of-the-art results using a computationally more efficient input representation that is 6 times faster than computing a voxel representation (Sect. 4).

Input Representation: Denoting the ith 3D point in a LiDAR point cloud using $p_i = (x_i, y_i, z_i)$, our goal is to transform the point cloud $\mathbf{P} = \{p_0, \ldots, p_i, p_{N-1}\}$ composed of N points into a regular 3D grid representation. Assuming that $\mathbf{P}$ is bounded within (x_{min}, x_{max}), (y_{min}, y_{max}) and (z_{min}, z_{max}) along x, y and z axes respectively, we compute a *sparse* occupancy matrix $\mathbf{M}$ using the quantization factors $(\delta x, \delta y, \delta z)$. In this paper, we utilize dictionary of keys representation to encode $\mathbf{M}$ where the i_{th} point updates $\mathbf{M}$ using:

$$\mathbf{M}\big[\lfloor \frac{x_i}{\delta x} \rfloor, \lfloor \frac{y_i}{\delta y} \rfloor, \lfloor \frac{z_i}{\delta z} \rfloor \big] = 1 \qquad i = 0 \ldots N - 1 \tag{1}$$

In this equation, $[\lfloor \frac{x_i}{\delta x} \rfloor, \lfloor \frac{y_i}{\delta y} \rfloor, \lfloor \frac{z_i}{\delta z} \rfloor]$ is analogous to the bin index of p_i after quantization. Dictionary of keys ensures the minimal representation for matrix $\mathbf{M}$ as it only allocates one entry for all points that fall into the same cell. Nevertheless, it is also possible to utilize the coordinate-list representation for this purpose. It should be noted that 99.88% of cells are empty (*i.e.* zero) in the dense representation of $\mathbf{M}$. Thus, our representation significantly reduces the amount of data transferred from the CPU to the GPU or embedded neural network accelerator. The sparse matrix $\mathbf{M}$ is scattered into a dense matrix on the GPU.

In addition to the computational efficiency of the above representation, it is also invariant to LiDAR scanning errors to some extent. In other words, assuming ± 3 cm scanning error in the LiDAR point cloud, a point will potentially fall into the same cell in $\mathbf{M}$ if the scanning repeats several times that in the sequel will generate identical $\mathbf{M}$ regardless of the scanning error.

Architecture: We base our backbone, illustrated in Fig. 1, on the widely used architecture of [8,23]. The input to our model is a sparse occupancy matrix that first transforms into a dense occupancy cuboid of size $H \times W \times C'$. Subsequently, it passes through three convolutional blocks with regular 2D convolutions. The first convolution in a block has a stride of 2 to reduce the spatial dimensions while all consecutive convolutions have a stride of 1. We apply the nearest-neighbor upsampling followed by a convolution operation to the outputs of Block 2 and Block 3. The feature map from Block 1 is passed through a convolution without upsampling because it has the same spatial dimensions as the target map. Next, we concatenate feature maps from all three blocks. Concatenating feature maps from different levels improves the flow of gradients to intermediate layers and eliminates the need for residual blocks. Finally, 1×1 convolutions are applied to compute classification and regression outputs.

We employ a batch normalization layer [8,23] between each convolution and activation layer. However, our empirical findings show that similar performance can be achieved without batch normalization in our network. It is worth mentioning that we do not use residual blocks [6] as they increase the computational complexity of our model due to 1×1 residual connections. Likewise, achieving a comparable performance using feature pyramid networks (FPNs) [12] was not possible with similar computational complexity as our network.

Loss: For a ground truth box with label $l = (x_g, y_g, z_g, h_g, w_g, l_g, \theta_g)$, we compute a corresponding target t $= (\Delta\text{x}, \Delta\text{y}, \Delta\text{z}, \Delta\text{h}, \Delta\text{w}, \Delta\text{l}, \Delta\theta_x, \Delta\theta_y)$ as:

$$\Delta x = \frac{(x_g - x_a)}{\sqrt{l_a{}^2 + w_a{}^2}} \qquad \Delta y = \frac{(y_g - y_a)}{h_a} \qquad \Delta z = \frac{(z_g - z_a)}{\sqrt{l_a{}^2 + w_a{}^2}}$$

$$\Delta h = \log \frac{h_g}{h_a} \qquad \Delta w = \log \frac{w_g}{w_a} \qquad \Delta l = \log \frac{l_g}{l_a}$$

$$\Delta\theta_x = \cos(\theta_g - \theta_a) \qquad \Delta\theta_y = \sin(\theta_g - \theta_a) \qquad\qquad (2)$$

where x_a, y_a, z_a are offsets and h_a, w_a, l_a are dimensions of the anchor. The proposed network is trained by minimizing the weighted sum of classification and regression losses. We use focal loss [13] with $\alpha = 0.75$ and $\gamma = 1.0$ for the classification head and smooth L1 loss for the regression head.

$$\mathcal{L}_{cls} = -\sum_{i\in pos} \alpha \cdot (1-\hat{c}_i)^\gamma \log(\hat{c}_i) - \sum_{i\in neg} (1-\alpha) \cdot (\hat{c}_i)^\gamma \log(1-\hat{c}_i) \qquad (3)$$

$$\mathcal{L}_{reg} = -\sum_{i\in pos} \sum_{m\in(x,y,z,h,w,l,C_\theta,S_\theta)} L_{1(smooth)}(m_i - \hat{m}_i) \qquad (4)$$

$$\mathcal{L} = \frac{1}{N}\left(\mathcal{L}_{cls} + \alpha\mathcal{L}_{reg}\right) + \lambda||\mathbf{W}||_2^2 \qquad (5)$$

where α is the weight of the regression loss, λ is the weight decay, $\mathbf{W}$ is the parameter vector, and $\hat{c}_i$ and N are the predicted confidence and number of positive anchors, respectively.

4   Experiments

Dataset and Evaluation Metric: We evaluate our proposed network (FA3D) on KITTI [4] dataset. The KITTI dataset contains 7,481 training samples with annotations and 7,518 testing samples without labels. We follow the common practice and split the training set into training and validation splits [1,14] containing 3,712 training samples and 3,769 validation samples. We report our results on cars, pedestrians, and cyclists. Based on the discovery in [19], the official KITTI evaluation kit was recently updated to use 40 samples for computing the average precision (AP). In addition to the official KITTI evaluation, we compute the average precision at the intersection-over-union (IoU) threshold of 0.5. As we will explain shortly, this assessment is better suited for gauging the performance of object detection models in the context of advanced driver assistance systems.

Implementation Details: Similar to [8,23,26], we bound the point cloud within a region of $[-40, 40] \times [-1, 3] \times [0, 70]$ m for car and a region of $[-20, 20] \times [-0.5, 2.5] \times [0, 48]$ m for pedestrians and cyclists. This covers 98% of labeled ground truth boxes in the KITTI dataset. To generate the binary occupancy cuboid, we set δ_x and δ_z to 0.16 and δ_y to 0.1. Thus, the resulting occupancy cuboid will be of size $H = 500$, $W = 440$ and $C' = 40$.

Anchors. Anchors are matched based on their relative offset from the center of ground truth boxes. For a ground truth box $\mathbf{G}$ with height h, width w and centered at (x, y), an anchor $\mathbf{A}$ is positive if its *center* falls in $[x - \frac{w}{4}, x + \frac{w}{4}]$ and $[y - \frac{h}{4}, y + \frac{h}{4}]$. All remaining anchors will become negative.

Augmentation: Augmentation is important in reducing overfitting on small datasets such as KITTI. Similar to [23], we create a dictionary of the ground-truth boxes in the training set. During training, we randomly sample five to ten instances for Cars, eight samples for Pedestrians and eight samples for Cyclists, and add them to the point cloud after collision testing. Additionally, ground truth boxes are rotated and translated using values drawn from the uniform distribution $\mathcal{U}(-\frac{\pi}{15}, \frac{\pi}{15})$ and the normal distribution $\mathcal{N}(0, 0.25)$, respectively. The scene is also randomly flipped with a probability of 0.5. Finally, the scene is scaled randomly in the range of $[0.95, 1.05]$, translated by $\mathcal{N}(0, 0.2)$ and rotated by $\mathcal{U}(-\frac{\pi}{4}, \frac{\pi}{4})$. In all the cases, ground-truth boxes are adjusted accordingly.

Network Parameters and Training Procedure: The width of all convolutions in the same block is identical where the widths of Block 1, Block 2, and Block 3 (Fig. 1) are $C = 64$, $2C$ and $4C$, respectively. The first block is composed of four convolution layers, and each of the next two blocks contains six convolution layers. Moreover, the stride of the first convolution layer in each block is two. The output from each block is upsampled to 250×200 using nearest-neighbor interpolation followed by convolution with $2C$ kernels. The model is trained using the Adam optimizer for 200 epochs using the batch size 2, the learning rate $2e-3$ and the regularization coefficient $\lambda = 1e-4$ (see Eq. 4).

Post-processing: During inference, we keep all boxes with prediction scores higher than 0.3 followed by a fast distance-based non-maxima suppression (NMS). We use a threshold of 1.5 m, but results are similar for a wide range of values. Computing the distance is faster than computing the IoU, and we empirically found that they produce similar results.

4.1   Pragmatic Evaluation

We evaluate the performance of our method on detecting cars using the validation set at two different IoU thresholds. As Table 1 shows, our approach performs on par with state-of-the-art methods on BEV and 3D object detection. Moreover, it surpasses PointPillars, the fastest published method, on the *Easy* and *Moderate* difficulty levels. Compared to the highest-scoring approaches on the KITTI Leaderboard, our model has a similar AP on *Hard* but slightly lower on the other two levels. Besides, we evaluate our network on Pedestrian and Cyclists in Table 2. Our model detects cyclists more accurately than PointPillars, and its performance is moderately lower on pedestrians. Note that SA-SSD has only reported results on detecting cars, and its detection accuracy on Pedestrian and Cyclists is not evaluated.

From a practical standpoint, predicting very tight 3D bounding boxes has a negligible benefit for modules in the pipeline, such as the motion planner. Figure 2 illustrates the effect of a slight offset (*difference*) between the ground-truth box and the predicted box on IoU considering various scenarios. In all configurations, the IoU drops below 0.7 for an offset of 0.4 m and below 0.5 for an offset of 0.8 m. Since our method is deigned for fast processing on low-end embedded devices for ADAS applications, not complex autonomous functions, the 0.4 to 0.8 offset error is still admissible. Thus, evaluating at IoU threshold 0.5 is promising for the real-world use cases of ADAS. Also, human-annotated datasets such as KITTI may contain noisy labels, and models with high performance at a high IoU are more likely to overfit to the annotation error. Figure 3 illustrates a few examples of incorrect annotations where the ground-truth bounding box is relatively off.

Table 1. Evaluation on KITTI validation set (cars). **E:** easy, **M:** moderate. **H:** hard.

| | BEV | | | | | | 3D | | | | | |
| | IOU = 0.5 | | | IOU = 0.7 | | | IOU = 0.5 | | | IOU = 0.7 | | |
	E	M	H	E	M	H	E	M	H	E	M	H
Point Pillars	94.81	93.78	93.11	91.49	87.2	85.81	94.79	93.39	92.33	86.00	75.66	72.56
Point RCNN	98.87	94.81	92.39	95.61	88.94	86.51	98.86	94.73	92.27	91.86	82.13	77.89
SA-SSD	99.24	96.25	93.70	96.50	92.62	90.08	99.23	96.19	93.64	92.89	84.16	81.26
Ours	95.94	94.31	93.65	94.63	88.10	85.49	95.90	94.07	91.71	87.35	75.47	71.97

Table 2. Evaluation on KITTI validation set (Pedestrians and Cyclists)

| | BEV | | | | | | 3D | | | | | |
| | Pedestrian | | | Cyclist | | | Pedestrian | | | Cyclist | | |
	E	M	H	E	M	H	E	M	H	E	M	H
Point pillars	71.21	65.55	60.22	85.51	65.22	61.1	63.36	57.78	52.1	83.72	61.57	57.57
Ours	70.72	63.13	56.85	90.55	66.29	62.89	63.45	55.78	49.09	82.73	60.23	56.86

When deploying a model, the confidence threshold is usually set to a value that maximizes the F_1 score. Hence, it is more practical to compare the methods based on their maximum F_1 score instead of APs. To this end, we compute the maximum F_1 score for our method as well as state-of-the-art methods and compare them in Table 3. We observe that the performance of highly computational methods such as SA-SSD is comparable to the proposed network while our method is significantly faster.

Table 3. Maximum F1 Score

| Method | IOU = 0.5 | | | IOU = 0.7 | | |
	E	M	H	E	M	H
PointPillars	94.73	91.53	90.00	91.41	86.60	85.09
Point RCNN	96.62	91.11	89.98	93.60	87.22	86.34
SA-SSD	97.01	93.02	91.88	95.58	89.74	88.45
Ours	95.86	91.47	89.44	93.61	87.54	85.41

Table 4. Comparing the latency of our proposed method with PointPillars on Jetson Xavier using different power settings and a high-end workstation

| Device | Point pillars (ms) | | | | Our method (ms) | | | |
	Enc.	Network	Post	fps	Enc.	Network	Post	fps
Jetson (Max-N)	3.71	139.73	19.05	6.15	0.62	125.26	11.60	7.27
Jeston (15W)	6.45	248.41	29.37	3.08	1.31	242.96	15.38	3.85
Jetson (30W-All)	5.44	195.06	27.60	4.38	1.32	184.26	15.35	4.97
Workstation	4.08	15.69	5.02	40.45	0.48	14.34	2.47	57.83

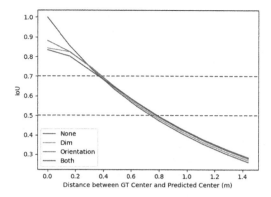

Fig. 2. Effect of small perturbations on IoU: *None* - ground truth and prediction are identical, *Dim* - slight variation between ground truth and prediction in dimension, *Orientation* - prediction has slight perturbation in orientation, *Both* - both dimension and orientation are different

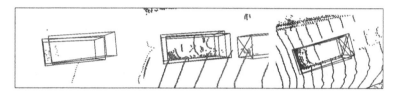

Fig. 3. Noisy Labels in the KITTI Dataset: *Green* - Ground Truth and *Red* - Predictions (Color figure online)

4.2   Runtime Analysis

We benchmark our model on a modern GPU and an embedded computing board. The first machine is a high-end workstation equipped with a Core-i7 CPU and a GTX 2080 Ti graphics card while the embedded board is a Jetson AGX Xavier with an 8-core ARM processor and 512-core Volta GPU. It is worth mentioning that we have NOT optimized our model using TensorRT to make a fair comparison with PointPillars. The inference procedure is broken down into encoding, forward pass, and post-processing and the latency of each stage is measured. Table 4 shows the results on the Jetson with various power models and the high-end workstation. First, our approach is faster than PointPillars in all three stages including encoding, forward pass, and post-processing. Specifically, our encoding method requires 3.09 ms less time (on MAX-N) that makes it 5.98 times faster than pillar encoding. Second, the forward pass takes 14.47 ms that makes it 1.12 times faster. Finally, the post-processing in our model finishes 7.45 ms faster than PointPillars making it 1.64 times faster. Overall, our model is slightly more accurate than PointPillars and processes 7.27 point clouds per second, which is 1.12 more frames compared to PointPillars. According to the official results, our method is the fastest network reported on the KITTI dataset until now.

Furthermore, we showed that considering the point estimate in precision-recall curves, the F_1 score of our method is only about 2% lower than SA-SSD that is several times slower than the proposed method.

4.3 Error Analysis

In this section, we analyze the contribution of the classification and regression heads to the overall *error* of the model. Specifically, we replace the output of the classification head with actual labels and use the predictions of the regression head to localize bounding boxes. This way, we remove all false positives and add all false negatives to the prediction. Results are presented in Table 5.

Table 5. The effect of classification head on the error.

| | BEV | | | | | | 3D | | | | | |
| | IOU = 0.5 | | | IOU = 0.7 | | | IOU = 0.5 | | | IOU = 0.7 | | |
	E	M	H	E	M	H	E	M	H	E	M	H
Original	95.94	94.31	93.65	94.63	88.10	85.49	95.90	94.07	91.71	87.35	75.47	71.97
GT Class.	97.47	97.42	97.41	96.18	90.55	88.11	97.42	97.27	94.79	88.19	77.07	74.44

Ideally, the APs must be 100% after replacing the classification head with the ground-truth labels. However, the results suggest that even using a precise classification, the regression head is not still able to localize the bounding boxes accurately. In other words, the improvement in APs is not significant, even using a perfect classification head. Therefore, we come to a conclusion that the regression head must have a profound impact on the results.

To study this, we selectively replace each output of the regression head with ground truth values. The results are detailed in Table 6. For instance, the third row in this table states that we replace the predicted x and y values with the ground-truth values and use them along with *predicted z, w, h, l, θ* to localize bounding boxes.

Table 6. The effect of regression head on the error.

| Quantity | BEV | | | | | | 3D | | | | | |
| | IOU = 0.5 | | | IOU = 0.7 | | | IOU = 0.5 | | | IOU = 0.7 | | |
	E	M	H	E	M	H	E	M	H	E	M	H
Original (Cls)	97.47	97.42	97.41	96.18	90.55	88.11	97.42	97.27	94.79	88.19	77.07	74.44
x	97.48	97.45	97.44	96.56	91.12	91.07	97.48	97.35	94.87	91.41	80.50	78.04
xy	99.97	97.45	97.44	96.57	93.45	91.07	99.97	97.44	97.43	95.51	87.37	87.16
xyz	99.99	97.48	97.48	97.26	96.89	94.43	99.99	97.49	97.48	96.74	93.52	91.09
xyzw	99.99	97.48	97.48	97.41	97.07	97.08	99.99	97.48	97.48	97.14	94.03	93.97
xyzwh	99.99	99.98	99.98	99.90	99.56	97.09	99.99	99.98	99.98	99.89	99.56	97.09
xyzwhl	99.99	99.98	98.98	99.99	99.96	99.95	99.99	99.98	99.98	99.99	99.96	99.95
xyzwhl θ	100	100	100	100	100	100	100	100	100	100	100	100

As it turns out, predicting x (*i.e.* the left to right axis) more accurately will improve the results dramatically. Likewise, predicting z values (forward axis) precisely will have a significant impact on the accuracy. The third important regression output is y values as they improve the results on both BEV and 3D metrics. In contrast, replacing w, h, l and θ with ground truth values has little impact on the BEV detection accuracy. The results suggest that our network has already generalized well on these four quantities.

In sum, the KITTI dataset is small and our proposed method overfits on the dataset (even using augmentation). However, the classification head and most of the regression values generalize well and the main source of error boils down to regressing x, z, and y values. We argue that using a better augmentation or larger dataset will potentially improve the generalization of these three quantities.

5   Conclusion

In this work, we proposed a fast and accurate 3D object detector that is 18% and 43% faster than the fastest published method in this area on Jetson Xavier and a high-end workstation, respectively. Our proposed network utilizes a computationally efficient, yet expressive input representation that reduces the time required for encoding the point cloud and copying to GPU. One of the main advantages of our method is that we do not gain time improvement by designing a smaller or more biased network. Quite the contrary, our model is complex and highly flexible. In addition to detailed accuracy and runtime experiments, we also analyzed the predictions and identified two predicted quantities that have the highest impact on the detection error.

References

1. Chen, X., et al.: 3D object proposals for accurate object class detection. In: Cortes, C., Lawrence, N.D., Lee, D.D., Sugiyama, M., Garnett, R. (eds.) Advances in Neural Information Processing Systems, vol. 28, pp. 424–432. Curran Associates, Inc. (2015)
2. Chen, X., Ma, H., Wan, J., Li, B., Xia, T.: Multi-view 3D object detection network for autonomous driving (2017)
3. Chen, Y., Liu, S., Shen, X., Jia, J.: Fast point R-CNN. In: Proceedings of the IEEE International Conference on Computer Vision, October 2019, pp. 9774–9783 (2019)
4. Geiger, A., Lenz, P., Stiller, C., Urtasun, R.: Vision meets robotics: the KITTI dataset. Int. J. Robot. Res. **32**, 1–6 (2013)
5. He, C., Zeng, H., Huang, J., Hua, X.S., Zhang, L.: Structure aware single-stage 3D object detection from point cloud. In: IEEE Conference on Computer Vision and Pattern Recognition, vol. 1 (2020)

6. He, K., Zhang, X., Ren, S., Sun, J.: Deep residual learning for image recognition. In: Proceedings of the IEEE Conference on Computer Vision and Pattern Recognition, pp. 770–778 (2016)
7. Ku, J., Mozifian, M., Lee, J., Harakeh, A., Waslander, S.L.: Joint 3D proposal generation and object detection from view aggregation. In: IEEE International Conference on Intelligent Robots and Systems, pp. 5750–5757 (2018)
8. Lang, A.H., Vora, S., Caesar, H., Zhou, L., Yang, J., Beijbom, O.: Pointpillars: fast encoders for object detection from point clouds. In: Proceedings of the IEEE Computer Society Conference on Computer Vision and Pattern Recognition, June 2019, pp. 12689–12697 (2019)
9. Lehner, J., Mitterecker, A., Adler, T., Hofmarcher, M., Nessler, B., Hochreiter, S.: Patch refinement - localized 3D object detection. In: NeurIPS 2019 (2019)
10. Liang, M., Bin, Y., CHen, Y., Hu, R., Urtaun, R.: Multi-task multi-sensor fusion for 3D object detection (2019)
11. Liang, M., Yang, B., Wang, S., Urtasun, R.: Deep continuous fusion for multi-sensor 3D object detection. In: Ferrari, V., Hebert, M., Sminchisescu, C., Weiss, Y. (eds.) ECCV 2018. LNCS, vol. 11220, pp. 663–678. Springer, Cham (2018). https://doi.org/10.1007/978-3-030-01270-0_39
12. Lin, T.Y., Dollár, P., Girshick, R., He, K., Hariharan, B., Belongie, S.: Feature pyramid networks for object detection. In: Proceedings of the IEEE Conference on Computer Vision and Pattern Recognition, pp. 2117–2125 (2017)
13. Lin, T.Y., Goyal, P., Girshick, R., He, K., Dollar, P.: Focal loss for dense object detection. IEEE Trans. Pattern Anal. Mach. Intell. **42**(2), 318–327 (2020)
14. Mousavian, A., Anguelov, D., Košecká, J., Flynn, J.: 3D bounding box estimation using deep learning and geometry. In: Proceedings - 30th IEEE Conference on Computer Vision and Pattern Recognition, CVPR 2017, pp. 5632–5640 (2017)
15. Ngiam, J., et al.: StarNet: targeted computation for object detection in point clouds (2019)
16. Qi, C.R., Liu, W., Wu, C., Su, H., Guibas, L.J.: Frustum PointNets for 3D object detection from RGB-D data. In: Proceedings of the IEEE Computer Society Conference on Computer Vision and Pattern Recognition, pp. 918–927 (2018)
17. Qi, C.R., Su, H., Mo, K., Guibas, L.J.: PointNet: Deep learning on point sets for 3D classification and segmentation. In: Proceedings - 30th IEEE Conference on Computer Vision and Pattern Recognition, CVPR 2017, January 2017, pp. 77–85 (2017)
18. Shi, S., Wang, X., Li, H.: PointRCNN: 3D object proposal generation and detection from point cloud. In: Proceedings of the IEEE Computer Society Conference on Computer Vision and Pattern Recognition, June 2019, pp. 770–779 (2019)
19. Simonelli, A., Bulo, S.R., Porzi, L., Lopez-Antequera, M., Kontschieder, P.: Disentangling monocular 3D object detection. In: Proceedings of the IEEE International Conference on Computer Vision, October 2019, pp. 1991–1999 (2019)
20. Vora, S., Lang, A.H., Helou, B., Beijbom, O.: PointPainting: sequential fusion for 3D object detection (2019)
21. Wang, Z., Jia, K.: Frustum ConvNet: sliding frustums to aggregate local point-wise features for Amodal. In: IEEE International Conference on Intelligent Robots and Systems, pp. 1742–1749 (2019)
22. Wang, Z., Zhan, W., Tomizuka, M.: Fusing bird's eye view LIDAR point cloud and front view camera image for 3D object detection. In: IEEE Intelligent Vehicles Symposium, Proceedings, June 2018, pp. 834–839 (2018)
23. Yan, Y., Mao, Y., Li, B.: Second: Sparsely embedded convolutional detection. Sensors (Switzerland) **18**(10), 1–17 (2018)

24. Yang, B., Liang, M., Urtasun, R.: HDNET : Exploiting HD maps for 3D object detection (CoRL), pp. 1–10 (2018)
25. Yang, B., Luo, W., Urtasun, R.: PIXOR: real-time 3D object detection from point clouds. In: Proceedings of the IEEE Computer Society Conference on Computer Vision and Pattern Recognition, pp. 7652–7660 (2018)
26. Zhou, Y., Tuzel, O.: VoxelNet: end-to-end learning for point cloud based 3D object detection. In: Proceedings of the IEEE Computer Society Conference on Computer Vision and Pattern Recognition, pp. 4490–4499 (2018)

Generalized Inverted Dirichlet Optimal Predictor for Image Inpainting

Omar Graja[✉], Fatma Najar[✉], and Nizar Bouguila[✉]

Concordia Institute for Information and Systems Engineering (CIISE),
Concordia University, Montreal, QC, Canada
omar.graja@mail.concordia.ca, f_najar@encs.concordia.ca,
nizar.bouguila@concordia.ca

Abstract. Predicting a given pixel from surrounding neighbouring pixels is of great interest for several image processing tasks. Previous works focused on developing different Gaussian based models. Simultaneously, in real-world applications, the image texture and clutter are usually known to be non-Gaussian. In this paper, we develop a pixel prediction framework based on a finite generalized inverted Dirichlet (GID) mixture model that has proven its efficiency in several machine learning applications. We propose a GID optimal predictor, and we learn its parameters using a likelihood-based approach combined with the Newton-Raphson method. We demonstrate the efficiency of our proposed approach through a challenging application, namely image inpainting, and we compare the experimental results with related-work methods.

Keywords: Generalized inverted Dirichlet · Mixture models · Optimal predictor · Image pixel prediction · Image inpainting

1 Introduction

Pixel prediction has shown to be one of the most needed tool to perform several applications in image processing such as anomaly detection [18,31], object detection [8,17], edge detection [28], video compression [7,24], semantic segmentation [27,36], image restoration [11,32] and keypoint prediction [37]. Meanwhile, pixel prediction is represented by approximating the predicted pixel using its neighbors. For that, it is usually represented by a linear or a non-linear combination of the neighboring pixels plus an error value [29,38]. In this paper, inspired by the work proposed in [20], we take the optimal predictor of x_n as the conditional expectation $E\big(x_{ij} \mid \forall x_{i'j'} \in N_{i,j}\big)$, where $x_{i'j'}$ are the neighbors of x_{ij} within the set of pixels $N_{i,j}$.

Exploiting the ease of analytical derivations, the authors in [40] derived optimal predictors for Gaussian distribution and mixture of Gaussians. However, the field of non-Gaussian distributions exhibited an exciting expansion in terms of mathematical theorems [23,35]. Yet, a large number of researchers proved that Gaussian assumption is generally inappropriate and other alternative distributions are more effective in modeling data than Gaussian distribution by unveiling

G. Bebis et al. (Eds.): ISVC 2020, LNCS 12509, pp. 410–421, 2020.
https://doi.org/10.1007/978-3-030-64556-4_32

more appropriate patterns and correlations among data features [4–6,10]. In our recent work [19], we proved that finite inverted Dirichlet mixture model effectively represents positive vectors [3,9,39]. However, it suffers from significant drawbacks such as its minimal, strictly positive covariance structure. Therefore, to overcome this limitation, we consider applying the generalized inverted Dirichlet which belongs to Liouville family of distributions [22]. This distribution provides a more decent representation of the variability of the data [12]. Indeed, considering the fact that generalized inverted Dirichlet could be factorized into a set of inverted Beta distributions [13], gives more flexibility for modeling data in real-world applications.

In this work, we derive a novel optimal predictor based on generalized inverted Dirichlet distribution which results in a linear combination of the neighboring pixels. Meanwhile, we evaluate the proposed approach on image inpainting application. We choose a publicly available dataset namely Paris StreetView to validate our approach [16]. For the purpose of proving the efficiency of our proposed optimal predictor, we consider two types of pixel discarding. The first pixel removal is random, whereas, in the second experiment, we discard lines from the image. We use a 3rd order non-symmetrical half-plane casual (NSHP) neighborhood system to compute the missing pixel [11]. Finally, we perform two image comparison metrics to evaluate our proposed model and compare it to other similar optimal based predictors.

The rest of the paper is organized as follows: in Sect. 2, we describe our prediction model, and we derive the analytical expression of the GID optimal predictor. In Sect. 3, we consider the image inpainting application on Paris StreetView dataset with two different data masks to demonstrate the effectiveness of the proposed predictor, and we discuss the experimental results. Finally, a summary is provided in Sect. 4.

2   GID Prediction Model

The generalized inverted Dirichlet mixture model has shown high flexibility for modeling and clustering positive vectors. In this section, we start by reviewing the finite GID mixture model. Then, we introduce the parameters learning through the EM algorithm and, later, we extend this model to the prediction.

2.1   Mixture of Generalized Inverted Dirichlet Distributions

Let $\mathcal{X} = (\boldsymbol{X}_1, \ldots, \boldsymbol{X}_N)$ be a set of N d-dimensional positive vectors where each vector $\boldsymbol{X}_i$ follows a mixture of K generalized inverted Dirichlet (GID) distributions characterized by parameters $\boldsymbol{\theta}_j = (\boldsymbol{\alpha}_j, \boldsymbol{\beta}_j)$ and mixing weight π_j of the jth component.

$$P(\boldsymbol{X}_i | \Theta) = \sum_{j=1}^{K} \pi_j P(\boldsymbol{X}_i | \boldsymbol{\theta}_j) \tag{1}$$

where $\Theta = (\boldsymbol{\theta}_1, \ldots, \boldsymbol{\theta}_K, \pi_1, \ldots, \pi_K)$ represents the GID mixture model parameters and $P(\boldsymbol{X}_i|\boldsymbol{\theta}_j)$ is the generalized inverted Dirichlet distribution, which has the following form [26]:

$$P(\boldsymbol{X}_i|\boldsymbol{\theta}_j) = \prod_{l=1}^{d} \frac{\Gamma(\alpha_{jl} + \beta_{jl})}{\Gamma(\alpha_{jl})\Gamma(\beta_{jl})} \frac{X_j^{\alpha_{jl}-1}}{(1 + \sum_{s=1}^{l} X_{is})^{\gamma_{jl}}} \tag{2}$$

where $\gamma_{jl} = \beta_{jl} + \alpha_{jl} - \beta_{jl+1}$, for $l = 1, \ldots, d$ ($\beta_{jd+1} = 1$). It is to be noted that the GID is reduced to the inverted Dirichlet distribution when the parameter γ_{jl} is set to zero ($\gamma_{j1} = \cdots = \gamma_{jd} = 0$).

The flexibility of the generalized inverted Dirichlet is by dint of the concept of "Force of mortality" of the population where we introduce, here, a doubly non-central Y independent-variables defined as

$$Y_{i1} = 1, \quad Y_{jl} = \frac{X_{il}}{T_{il-1}}, \quad l > 1 \tag{3}$$

where $T_{il} = 1 + X_{i1} + X_{i2} + \cdots + X_{il-1}, \quad l = 1, \ldots, d$

The characteristic function underlying the $\mathcal{Y} = (\boldsymbol{Y}_1, \ldots, \boldsymbol{Y}_N)$ independent variables follows a product of 2-parameters inverted Beta distribution, where $\theta_l = (\alpha_l, \beta_l)$

$$P(\boldsymbol{Y}_i|\boldsymbol{\theta}) = \prod_{l=1}^{d} P_{IBeta}(Y_{il}|\theta_l) \tag{4}$$

In which the probability of inverted Beta is given by:

$$P_{IBeta}(Y_{il}|\theta_l) = \frac{\Gamma(\alpha_l + \beta_l)}{\Gamma(\alpha_l)\Gamma(\beta_l)} \frac{Y_{il}^{\alpha_l}}{(1 + Y_{il})^{\alpha_l + \beta_l}} \tag{5}$$

Many characteristics of the distribution are defined in [30]. We mention some interesting statistics for this distribution.

First, the mixed moments such as the nth moment is given by:

$$E(Y^n) = \frac{\Gamma(\alpha + \beta)\Gamma(\beta - n)}{\Gamma(\alpha)\Gamma(\beta)} \tag{6}$$

where $\beta - n$ is positive.

Then, the covariance between two variable Y_1 and Y_2 is defined as:

$$COV(Y_1, Y_2) = \frac{(\alpha_1 - 1)(\alpha_2 - 1)}{(\alpha_1\alpha_2 - 1)(\beta_1 - 1)(\beta_2 - 1)} \tag{7}$$

The covariance between two features for inverted Beta is always positive, which means that both they tend to increase or decrease together.

Finally, the variance of a variable Y is conveyed by:

$$VAR(Y) = \frac{(\alpha - 1)(\alpha + \beta - 2)}{(\beta - 1)^2(\beta - 2)} \tag{8}$$

2.2   Likelihood-Based Learning

Theoretically, a plethora of literature agrees on the effectiveness of the likelihood-based approach for estimating the mixture parameters. One of the well-known methodologies is the Expectation-Maximization technique [15], beginning with a tuned initialization for the set of parameters to the expectation step where the posterior is inferred (named often as "responsibilities"), then the iterations are proceeded to update the required variables until convergence. The heart of the matter comes with estimating the parameters based on the second derivative of the log-likelihood function with regards to each parameter. First, we introduce the log-likelihood as follows:

$$\log P(\mathcal{Y}|\Theta) = \sum_{i=1}^{N} \log \left[\sum_{j=1}^{K} \pi_j \prod_{l=1}^{d} P_{IBeta}(Y_{il}|\theta_{jl}) \right] \tag{9}$$

Initializing Process. As a first step, an unsupervised-method, namely "K-means," is applied to obtain the initial K clusters. Consequently, for each cluster, the method-of-moments is implemented to get the initial α_j and β_j parameters of each component j. The mixing weight is set in the initial phase as the number of elements in each cluster divided by the total number of vectors. As mentioned earlier, with conditionally independent features, the GID is converted by the inverted Beta distribution factorization. Thus, given the moments of inverted Beta distribution [2], the initial α_{jl_0} and β_{jl_0} are deduced by

$$\alpha_{jl_0} = \frac{\mu_{jl}^2(1 + \mu_{jl}) + \mu_{jl}\sigma_{jl}^2}{\sigma_{jl}^2} \tag{10}$$

$$\beta_{jl_0} = \frac{\mu_{jl}(1 + \mu_{jl}) + 2\sigma_{jl}^2}{\sigma_{jl}^2} \tag{11}$$

where μ_{jl} is the mean and σ_{jl} is the standard-deviation, $j = 1, \ldots, K$, $l = 1, \ldots, D$.

Expecting the Responsibilities. The responsibilities or posterior probabilities play an essential role in the likelihood-based estimation technique. It affects the update of the parameters in the next following step using the current parameter value.

$$P(j|\mathbf{Y}_i) = \frac{\pi_j P(\mathbf{Y}_i|\boldsymbol{\theta}_j)}{\sum_{m=1}^{K} \pi_m P(\mathbf{Y}_i|\boldsymbol{\theta}_m)} \tag{12}$$

Maximizing and Upgrading the GID Parameters. At the beginning, we set the gradient of log-likelihood function with respect to the mixing weight parameter equals to zero:

$$\frac{\partial \log P(\mathcal{Y}, \Theta)}{\partial \pi_j} = 0 \tag{13}$$

Then, we obtain the update formula for π_j, for $j = 1, \ldots, K$ as

$$\pi_j = \frac{1}{N} \sum_{i=1}^{N} P(j|\boldsymbol{Y}_i) \tag{14}$$

where $P(j|\boldsymbol{Y}_i)$ is the posterior computed in the E-step.

To learn the parameters $\boldsymbol{\alpha}_j$ and $\boldsymbol{\beta}_j$, the Fisher scoring algorithm [25] is used. Thus, we need to calculate the first and the second derivatives of the log-likelihood function based on the following update [1]:

$$\alpha_{jl}^{t+1} = \alpha_{jl}^{t} - \left(\frac{\partial^2}{\partial \alpha_{jl}^2} \log P(\mathcal{Y}, \Theta) \right)^{-1} \times \frac{\partial}{\partial \alpha_{jl}} \log P(\mathcal{Y}, \Theta) \tag{15}$$

$$\beta_{jl}^{t+1} = \beta_{jl}^{t} - \left(\frac{\partial^2}{\partial \beta_{jl}^2} \log P(\mathcal{Y}, \Theta) \right)^{-1} \times \frac{\partial}{\partial \beta_{jl}} \log P(\mathcal{Y}, \Theta) \tag{16}$$

The first derivatives of $\log P(\mathcal{Y}, \Theta)$ are given by:

$$\frac{\partial}{\partial \alpha_{jl}} \log P(\mathcal{Y}, \Theta) = \sum_{i=1}^{N} P(j|\boldsymbol{Y}_i) \Big(P_{IBeta}(Y_{il}|\theta_{jl}) [\Psi(\alpha_{jl} + \beta_{jl}) - \Psi(\alpha_{jl}) + \log Y_{il}$$
$$- \log(1 + Y_{il})] \Big), \tag{17}$$

$$\frac{\partial}{\partial \beta_{jl}} \log P(\mathcal{Y}, \Theta) = \sum_{i=1}^{N} P(j|\boldsymbol{Y}_i) \Big(P_{IBeta}(Y_{il}|\theta_{jl}) [\Psi(\alpha_{jl} + \beta_{jl}) - \Psi(\alpha_{jl}) - \log(1 + Y_{il})] \Big) \tag{18}$$

The second derivative with respect to α_{jl} is given by:

$$\frac{\partial^2}{\partial^2 \alpha_{jl}} \log P(\mathcal{Y}, \Theta) = \sum_{i=1}^{N} P(j|\boldsymbol{Y}_i) \Big(\frac{\partial P_{IBeta}(Y_{il}|\theta_{jl})}{\partial \alpha_{jl}} [\Psi(\alpha_{jl} + \beta_{jl}) - \Psi(\alpha_{jl})$$
$$- \log(1 + Y_{il})] + P_{IBeta}(Y_{il}|\theta_{jl}) [\Psi'(\alpha_{jl} + \beta_{jl}) - \Psi'(\alpha_{jl})] \Big), \tag{19}$$

The second derivative w.r.t β_{jl} is obtained through the same development.

2.3   GID Optimal Predictor

In this section, we present our novel non-linear optimal predictor method based on generalized inverted Dirichlet distribution. We consider the conditional expectation property to predict one random variable from the other neighboring variables.

We consider p data points $(X_i, X_{i+1}, \ldots, X_{i+p-1})$, knowing their values, we predict the neighboring data point $\hat{X}_{i+p}$ on the base of minimizing the *mean squared error* (MSE). Therefore, we model the joint density of X_{i+p} and its neighbors using the generalized inverted Dirichlet. We take $i = 0$ and we derive the equations.

$$X \sim GID(\theta) \tag{20}$$

Considering generalized inverted Dirichlet properties [22], the conditional random variable Y_p follows an inverted Beta distribution:

$$Y_p = \frac{X_p}{T_{p-1}} | X_{p-1}, \ldots, X_1, X_0 \sim IB(\alpha_p, \beta_p) \tag{21}$$

Consequently, the conditional probability density function of X_p is

$$X_p \mid X_{p-1}, \ldots, X_0 \sim T_{p-1} IB(\alpha_p, \beta_p) \tag{22}$$

where $T_{p-1} = 1 + \sum_{k=1}^{p-1} X_k$.

Hence, the conditional expectation expression of X_p is expressed as follows.

$$E(X_p \mid X_{p-1}, X_1, \ldots, X_0) = T_{p-1} \frac{\alpha_p}{\beta_p - 1} \tag{23}$$

In the case of mixture models, the optimal predictor expression can be derived directly by following steps defined in [19] (more details are in [40]):

$$\hat{X}_p = E(X_p \mid X_{p-1}, \ldots, X_0) \tag{24}$$

$$\hat{X}_p = \int X_p P(X_p \mid X_{p-1}, \ldots, X_0) \, dX_p$$
$$= \sum_{j=1}^{K} \pi'_j E_j(X_j \mid X_{j-1}, \ldots, X_0) \tag{25}$$

where

$$\pi'_j = \pi_j \frac{\int P_j(X_p, \ldots, X_0) \, dX_p}{\int P(X_p, \ldots, X_0) \, dX_p} \tag{26}$$

$$\pi'_j = \pi_j \frac{P_j(X_{p-1}, \ldots, X_0)}{\sum_{j=1}^{K} \pi_j P_j(X_{p-1}, \ldots, X_0)} \tag{27}$$

Finally, the GID optimal predictor is resumed in the following linear combination of X_p neighbors:

$$\hat{X}_p = \sum_{j=1}^{K} \pi'_j \left(1 + \sum_{k=1}^{p-1} X_k \right) \frac{\alpha_p}{\beta_p - 1} \tag{28}$$

3   Experimental Results

Image inpainting is the process of restoring deteriorating, damaged or missing parts of an image to produce a complete picture. It is an active area of image processing research [32–34] where machine learning has exciting results comparable to artists' results. Mainly, in this process, we will be completing a missing pixel by an approximated value that depends on its neighborhood. In our work, we use the 3rd order non-symmetrical half-plane casual neighborhood system [19,21]. We apply the model on a publicly available dataset; Paris StreetView [16]. Then, we compare it with the widely used mixture of Gaussian predictor, generalized Dirichlet mixture predictor and inverted Dirichlet mixture predictor. We are not trying to restore the ground-truth image, our goal is to get an output image that is close enough or similar to the ground-truth. Therefore, we use the structural similarity index (SSIM) [11] to gauge the differences between the predicted images and the original ones. We also perform signal to noise ratio (PSNR) [14] to evaluate the performance of the models.

We reduce the size of the original images to 256 × 256 to minimize the complexity of computing the model's parameters. We train the model on 70% of the database and we test on the rest. We apply two types of masks. The first one is randomly distributed as shown in Fig. 1a. And, for the second one, we discard lines of the images, as in Fig. 1b. Finally, we compute the SSIM and PSNR of each test image with its corresponding ground-truth, and we average all over the test set.

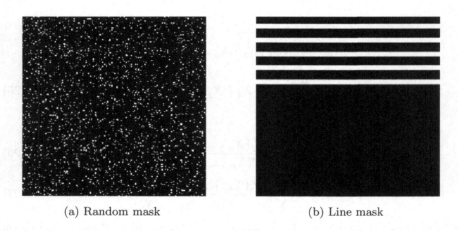

(a) Random mask   (b) Line mask

Fig. 1. Types of image mask

As we mentioned earlier, we discard around 15% of the pixels randomly. Figure 2 reveals that the difference between models' prediction is undetectable visually. Moreover, Table 1 shows that the difference between the models is not significant. There is a slight advantage for the use of GIDM model compared

Fig. 2. Models' performance on random masked images. 1st column is for the ground truth images, 2nd column is for the masked images, 3rd column is for the GM prediction, 4th column is for the DM prediction, 5th column is for the IDM prediction, 6th column is for the GIDM prediction

to the others. Thus, we conclude that this approach of models' evaluation is not appropriate. For that, we decide to remove slightly thick lines of pixels and re-evaluate the models.

To evaluate the models' performance, we used TensorFlow to calculate the PSNR and Skimage python package for the SSIM metric.

After discarding lines from the images, we are able to generate back again the missing pixels, and Fig. 3 demonstrates that GIDM is the most efficient model among all the others. This is also clear in Table 2, where we can notice in the chosen images that GIDM is the most accurate re-generator of discarded pixels. Therefore, our work has shown that image data is better represented by

Table 1. Models' evaluation for the randomly masked images.

	PSNR	SSIM
GM	21.832	0.853
DM	25.963	0.878
IDM	25.672	0.875
GIDM	26.126	0.887

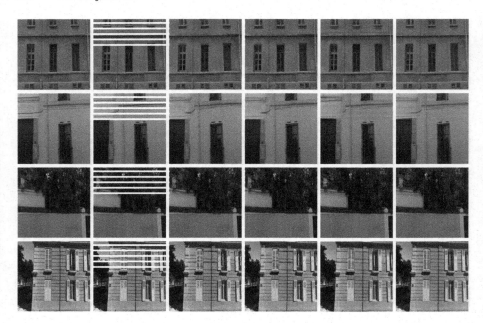

Fig. 3. Models' performance on line masked images. 1ˢᵗ column is for the ground truth images, 2ⁿᵈ column is for the masked images, 3ʳᵈ column is for the GM prediction, 4ᵗʰ column is for the DM prediction, 5ᵗʰ column is for the IDM prediction, 6ᵗʰ column is for the GIDM prediction

Table 2. Models' evaluation for the line masked images.

	PSNR	SSIM
GM	20.366	0.833
DM	25.851	0.856
IDM	27.673	0.868
GIDM	29.398	0.891

generalized inverted Dirichlet. It is noteworthy to mention that these models' performance is hugely dependent on the size of the masks, the hyper-parameters, the type and order of the neighbouring system.

4   Conclusion

In this paper, we have developed a new optimal predictor based on finite generalized inverted Dirichlet mixtures. The GID demonstrates its efficiency in representing positive vectors due to its statistical characteristics through its covariance structure.

We learnt the model parameters using MLE approach with Newton Raphson method, and we considered the NSHP neighbouring system to compute the predicted pixel. We evaluated the GID optimal predictor on image inpainting and we compared the proposed model to other similar related works. The experimental results demonstrate its capability that offers reliable prediction and modeling potential.

References

1. Al Mashrgy, M., Bdiri, T., Bouguila, N.: Robust simultaneous positive data clustering and unsupervised feature selection using generalized inverted dirichlet mixture models. Knowl. Based Syst. **59**, 182–195 (2014)
2. Mashrgy, M.A., Bouguila, N.: A fully Bayesian framework for positive data clustering. In: Laalaoui, Y., Bouguila, N. (eds.) Artificial Intelligence Applications in Information and Communication Technologies. SCI, vol. 607, pp. 147–164. Springer, Cham (2015). https://doi.org/10.1007/978-3-319-19833-0_7
3. Bdiri, T., Bouguila, N.: An infinite mixture of inverted Dirichlet distributions. In: Lu, B.-L., Zhang, L., Kwok, J. (eds.) ICONIP 2011. LNCS, vol. 7063, pp. 71–78. Springer, Heidelberg (2011). https://doi.org/10.1007/978-3-642-24958-7_9
4. Bdiri, T., Bouguila, N.: Learning inverted dirichlet mixtures for positive data clustering. In: Kuznetsov, S.O., Ślezak, D., Hepting, D.H., Mirkin, B.G. (eds.) RSFD-GrC 2011. LNCS (LNAI), vol. 6743, pp. 265–272. Springer, Heidelberg (2011). https://doi.org/10.1007/978-3-642-21881-1_42
5. Bdiri, T., Bouguila, N.: Positive vectors clustering using inverted dirichlet finite mixture models. Expert Syst. Appl. **39**(2), 1869–1882 (2012)
6. Bdiri, T., Bouguila, N.: Bayesian learning of inverted dirichlet mixtures for SVM kernels generation. Neural Comput. Appl. **23**(5), 1443–1458 (2013)
7. Bdiri, T., Bouguila, N., Ziou, D.: Visual scenes categorization using a flexible hierarchical mixture model supporting users ontology. In: 25th IEEE International Conference on Tools with Artificial Intelligence, ICTAI 2013, Herndon, VA, USA, 4–6 November 2013, pp. 262–267. IEEE Computer Society (2013)
8. Bdiri, T., Bouguila, N., Ziou, D.: Object clustering and recognition using multi-finite mixtures for semantic classes and hierarchy modeling. Expert Syst. Appl. **41**(4), 1218–1235 (2014)
9. Bdiri, T., Bouguila, N., Ziou, D.: A statistical framework for online learning using adjustable model selection criteria. Eng. Appl. Artif. Intell. **49**, 19–42 (2016)
10. Bdiri, T., Bouguila, N., Ziou, D.: Variational Bayesian inference for infinite generalized inverted dirichlet mixtures with feature selection and its application to clustering. Appl. Intell. **44**(3), 507–525 (2016). https://doi.org/10.1007/s10489-015-0714-6
11. Bouguila, N.: Non-gaussian mixture image models prediction. In: 2008 15th IEEE International Conference on Image Processing, pp. 2580–2583. IEEE (2008)
12. Bourouis, S., Al Mashrgy, M., Bouguila, N.: Bayesian learning of finite generalized inverted dirichlet mixtures: application to object classification and forgery detection. Expert Syst. Appl. **41**(5), 2329–2336 (2014)
13. Boutemedjet, S., Bouguila, N., Ziou, D.: A hybrid feature extraction selection approach for high-dimensional non-Gaussian data clustering. IEEE Trans. Pattern Anal. Mach. Intell. **31**(8), 1429–1443 (2008)

14. Channoufi, I., Bourouis, S., Bouguila, N., Hamrouni, K.: Image and video denoising by combining unsupervised bounded generalized gaussian mixture modeling and spatial information. Multimedia Tools Appl. **77**(19), 25591–25606 (2018). https://doi.org/10.1007/s11042-018-5808-9

15. Dempster, A.P., Laird, N.M., Rubin, D.B.: Maximum likelihood from incomplete data via the EM algorithm. J. Roy. Stat. Soc. Ser. B (Methodol.) **39**(1), 1–22 (1977)

16. Doersch, C., Singh, S., Gupta, A., Sivic, J., Efros, A.A.: What makes Paris look like Paris? ACM Trans. Graph. (SIGGRAPH) **31**(4), 101:1–101:9 (2012)

17. Elguebaly, T., Bouguila, N.: Finite asymmetric generalized Gaussian mixture models learning for infrared object detection. Comput. Vis. Image Underst. **117**(12), 1659–1671 (2013)

18. Fan, W., Bouguila, N.: Topic novelty detection using infinite variational inverted dirichlet mixture models. In: Li, T., et al. (eds.) 14th IEEE International Conference on Machine Learning and Applications, ICMLA 2015, Miami, FL, USA, 9–11 December 2015, pp. 70–75. IEEE (2015)

19. Graja, O., Bouguila, N.: Finite inverted dirichlet mixture optimal pixel predictor. In: 2019 IEEE Global Conference on Signal and Information Processing (GlobalSIP), pp. 1–5. IEEE (2019)

20. Grimmett, G., Grimmett, G.R., Stirzaker, D., et al.: Probability and Random Processes. Oxford University Press, New York (2001)

21. Guidara, R., Hosseini, S., Deville, Y.: Maximum likelihood blind image separation using nonsymmetrical half-plane Markov random fields. IEEE Trans. Image Process. **18**(11), 2435–2450 (2009)

22. Gupta, A., Song, D.: Generalized liouville distribution. Comput. Math. Appl. **32**(2), 103–109 (1996)

23. Kotz, S., Balakrishnan, N., Johnson, N.L.: Continuous multivariate distributions, Volume 1: Models and applications. Wiley, Hoboken (2004)

24. Li, Y., Sayood, K.: Lossless video sequence compression using adaptive prediction. IEEE Trans. Image Process. **16**(4), 997–1007 (2007)

25. Lindley, D., Rao, C.R.: Advanced statistical methods in biometric research. (1953)

26. Lingappaiah, G.: On the generalised inverted dirichlet distribution. Demostratio Mathematica **9**(3), 423–433 (1976)

27. Long, J., Shelhamer, E., Darrell, T.: Fully convolutional networks for semantic segmentation. In: Proceedings of the IEEE Conference on Computer Vision and Pattern Recognition, pp. 3431–3440 (2015)

28. Maini, R., Aggarwal, H.: Study and comparison of various image edge detection techniques. Int. J. Image Process. (IJIP) **3**(1), 1–11 (2009)

29. Makhoul, J.: Linear prediction: a tutorial review. Proc. IEEE **63**(4), 561–580 (1975)

30. Mathai, A., Moschopoulos, P.: A multivariate inverted beta model. Statistica **57**, 189–198 (1997)

31. Matteoli, S., Diani, M., Corsini, G.: A tutorial overview of anomaly detection in hyperspectral images. IEEE Aerosp. Electron. Syst. Mag. **25**(7), 5–28 (2010)

32. Mosleh, A., Bouguila, N., Hamza, A.B.: Bandlet-based sparsity regularization in video inpainting. J. Vis. Commun. Image Represent. **25**(5), 855–863 (2014)

33. Mosleh, A., Bouguila, N., Hamza, A.B.: A video completion method based on bandlet transform. In: Proceedings of the 2011 IEEE International Conference on Multimedia and Expo, ICME 2011, Barcelona, Catalonia, Spain, 11–15 July 2011, pp. 1–6. IEEE Computer Society (2011)

34. Mosleh, A., Bouguila, N., Hamza, A.B.: Automatic inpainting scheme for video text detection and removal. IEEE Trans. Image Process. **22**(11), 4460–4472 (2013)

35. Ng, K.W., Tian, G.L., Tang, M.L.: Dirichlet and Related Distributions: Theory, Methods and Applications, vol. 888. Wiley, Hoboken (2011)
36. Sefidpour, A., Bouguila, N.: Spatial color image segmentation based on finite non-Gaussian mixture models. Expert Syst. Appl. **39**(10), 8993–9001 (2012)
37. Simon, T., Joo, H., Matthews, I., Sheikh, Y.: Hand keypoint detection in single images using multiview bootstrapping. In: Proceedings of the IEEE conference on Computer Vision and Pattern Recognition, pp. 1145–1153 (2017)
38. Therrien, C.W., Quatieri, T.F., Dudgeon, D.E.: Statistical model-based algorithms for image analysis. Proc. IEEE **74**(4), 532–551 (1986)
39. Tirdad, P., Bouguila, N., Ziou, D.: Variational learning of finite inverted dirichlet mixture models and applications. In: Laalaoui, Y., Bouguila, N. (eds.) Artificial Intelligence Applications in Information and Communication Technologies. SCI, vol. 607, pp. 119–145. Springer, Cham (2015). https://doi.org/10.1007/978-3-319-19833-0_6
40. Zhang, J., Ma, D.: Nonlinear prediction for gaussian mixture image models. IEEE Trans. Image Process. **13**(6), 836–847 (2004)

BVNet: A 3D End-to-End Model Based on Point Cloud

Nuo Cheng[1,2(✉)], Xiaohan Li[2], Shengguang Lei[2], and Pu Li[1]

[1] Process Optimization Group, Technische Universität Ilmenau,
98693 Ilmenau, Germany
nuocheng1992@gmail.com, Pu.li@tu-ilmenau.de
[2] LiangDao GmbH, 12099 Berlin, Germany
{xiaohao.li,shengguang.lei}@liangdao.de

Abstract. Point cloud LiDAR data are increasingly used for detecting road situations for autonomous driving. The most important issues here are the detection accuracy and the processing time. In this study, we propose a new model which can improve the detection performance based on point cloud. A well-known difficulty in processing 3D point cloud is that the point data are unordered. To address this problem, we define 3D point cloud features in the grid cells of the bird's view according to the distribution of the points. In particular, we introduce the average and standard deviation of the heights as well as a distance-related density of the points as new features inside a cell. The resulting feature map is fed into a conventional neural network to obtain the outcomes, thus realizing an end-to-end real-time detection framework, called BVNet (**B**ird's-**V**iew-**N**et). The proposed model is tested on the KITTI benchmark suit and the results show considerable improvement for the detection accuracy compared with the models without the newly introduced features.

Keywords: Autonomous driving · Point cloud · Feature extraction · 3D object detection · CNN · KITTI

1 Introduction

Object detection plays an important role in an advanced driver assistance system (ADAS). Compared with 2D images, 3D data have many advantages because of its depth information. However, with the rapid hardware development, the improvement of the performance of 3D object detection based on deep learning is not as fast as that of 2D object detection. For example, in the tests of the KITTI benchmark suite[1], the performance gap of the average precision between 2D and 3D models for car detection is higher than 10%. Therefore, improving the 3D detection precision remains a significant challenge.

---

[1] http://www.cvlibs.net/datasets/kitti/eval_3dobject.php.

© Springer Nature Switzerland AG 2020
G. Bebis et al. (Eds.): ISVC 2020, LNCS 12509, pp. 422–435, 2020.
https://doi.org/10.1007/978-3-030-64556-4_33

The available 2D object detection methods can be classified into two approaches: the one-stage methods [13,18–20] and the two-stage methods [6–8,21]. A two-stage method first trains a region proposal network (RPN) to generate several interested regions, and then performs the classification and regression of the bounding boxes. On the other hand, the one-stage detection method predicts bounding boxes and object categories in one step. The latest versions of the software using these two approaches both show extremely high performance [8,20].

With the fast development and wide application of LiDAR, 3D detection-based point cloud data becomes more and more important. Point cloud gives 3D information which can be used for 3D object detection. However, unlike the 2D arrangement of pixels in an image, the data points of a 3D point cloud are unordered. For this reason, point cloud cannot be processed directly by a typical convolutional architecture. Currently, the existing 3D detection methods could be classified into three categories to solve this problem.

First, the unordered point cloud is processed using a symmetric function. Qi et al. were the first to propose a detection method based on point cloud called PointNet [16,17]. In [15] they applied it for detecting objects for autonomous driving and tested on the KITTI benchmark suite. However, this method needs a pre-processing using a 2D image and a 2D detection model. Therefore, the precision of this method depends on the performance of the 2D detection approach. In addition, it is difficult to achieve a real-time detection, since successively running the 2D and 3D detection models will take a large amount of computation time.

Using PointNet [16,17] as the backbone network, PointRCNN [22] has recently shown higher performance on the KITTI Benchmark Suite. It is the first two-stage 3D object detection approach with raw point cloud as input. However, in the first detection stage, a bounding box is needed for each foreground point of the detected object, which requires high computation expense. In addition, PointNet [16,17] does not show high-speed performance on large-scale point cloud [15,17]. Furthermore, PointRCNN is not suitable to detect large objects such as trucks and special vehicles.

Second, unordered point cloud is projected to a 2D image before processing. Chen et al. [3] proposed another highly ranked model (MV3D) by projecting LiDAR point cloud to a bird's eye view map. In this way, unordered 3D points are transferred into a 2D image which is further processed for object detection. After that, more and more detection models [1–4,10,11,24,25,28] were proposed to extract features on the bird's eye view map to improve the quality of the object detection. Table 1 shows the features extracted in the grid cells by these detection models. Some models [1,2,4,11,24,25,28] extract features based only on the bird's eye view map and others combine it together with image [3,10]. The features mostly extracted are the height, intensity and density of the point cloud for each grid cell. Although 2D approaches could achieve a high frame-rate, the average precision is low [1,2,4,11,24,25,28].

Third, unordered point cloud is transformed to voxels. The basic idea is to divide the point cloud into many small voxels and uses a 3D-CNN to extract features. VoxelNet [29] was developed based on this idea. In comparison to the models shown in Table 1, VoxelNet achieves a high average precision but cannot be used for real-time detection (only 4 fps on TitanX GPU [29]).

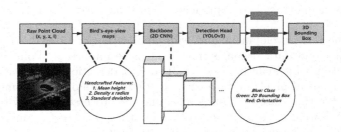

Fig. 1. BVNet Pipeline. We present a sample detection model. The input is raw point cloud from Velodyne HDL-64 LiDAR. The output is 3D bounding box with classes. We connect three new handcrafted features with modified State-of-the-Art 2D detector. (Color figure online)

From the hardware implementation point of view, the first and the third approaches discussed above cannot be readily applied in real circumstances due to the fact that they usually run in GPUs [9,14,15,17,22,23,26,29]. High performance GPUs consume a large amount of power and thus are difficult to run stably for vehicle-mounted detection systems. Existing dedicated hardware or embedded devices (e.g. Huawei Atlas 200 and 300 etc.) support 2D-detectors better than 3D-detectors[2]. In such cases, the second approach is suitable.

In addition, detection of multiple objects for autonomous driving is required. Compared with 3D detectors, 2D detectors are more appropriate for addressing multi-classification problems [18–20]. 3D detectors such as MV3D [3] and PointRCNN [22] can only detect a single category at a time. Therefore, it is favorable to use the second approach, i.e. to project the point cloud to a 2D image and combine it with an efficient 2D detection model, and finally convert the 2D results back into the 3D detection results. However, the shortcoming of this approach is that the height information is lost. Therefore, proper measures have to be taken to compensate the height information in the case of autonomous driving.

In this study, we propose a simple 3D detection model, BVNet (**B**ird's-**V**iew-**N**et), which is only based on raw point cloud, to achieve real-time detection for multi-categories for autonomous driving. The proposed BVNet pipeline is shown in Fig. 1, being a detection method based on the bird's eye view map. Unlike the models listed in Table 1, we introduce the average and standard deviation of the heights as new features inside each cell. In addition, we define a distance-related density feature of the points. The backbone detection network in BVNet

---

[2] Huawei atlas support: https://support.huawei.com/enterprise/en.

is an extended CNN based on the Complex-YOLO [24,25] and YOLOv3 [20]. The proposed BVNet is evaluated on the KITTI benchmark suite[3]. Compared with the models in Table 1, better results in terms of accuracy are achieved by using our model. In addition, in comparison to models with 3D approaches like PointNet [16,17] and VoxelNet [29], we can achieve similarly accurate results for detecting cars with considerably lower computation time.

Table 1. Features extracted by different detection models

Models	Features			Number of the height feature maps	Camera
MV3D [3]	Max intensity	Density	Max height	M	+
Complex-YOLO [25]	Max intensity	Density	Max height	1	−
AVOD [10]	−	Density	Max height	5	+
YOLO3D [1,4]	−	Density	Max height	1	−
RT3D [28]	Mean height	Min height	Max height	3	−
BirdNet [2]	Mean Intensity	Density	Max height	1	−

2   Proposed Model

2.1   Introduction of New Features

We consider the point cloud data from Velodyne HDL64 Lidar [5]. At first, we represent the point cloud by projecting it to a bird's eye view map. The detection range is selected as 60 m × 60 m × 3.25 m. Inspired by Complex-YOLO [24,25], we discretize and project the raw point cloud into a 2D grid cell with the resolution of 8 cm. Therefore, the final size of the grid map is 768 × 768.

Since the features of the cells used for detection are important, we introduce following three new features to improve the performance for detection.

First, as mentioned in the last section, the models listed in Table 1 extract the maximum height information of the point cloud inside grid cells as a feature. However, the measurement of the maximum height by Lidar may include noises. In order to reduce the influence of the noises, we use the average height of each grid cell, as follows:

$$f_h = \frac{h_{mean}}{3.25} \tag{1}$$

where h_{mean} is the average of the height values at the points reflecting the object under consideration,and the 3.25 is the maximum height of the points.

Second, it is a well-known fact that the raw point cloud will become sparser as the distance increases. It means that the detection accuracy will be lowered if the cloud data are taken from a large distance. To address this problem, we introduce a distance-related density of the point cloud as a new feature. To this end, we multiply the grid density by the Euclidean distance between the grid cell and the origin point (i.e. the LiDAR sensor position), as shown in Fig. 2. For this purpose, we modify the normalized density formula $min(\frac{log(N+1)}{log64})$ used in MV3D [3], as follows:

$$r = \sqrt{(x_{grid} - x_{origin})^2 + (y_{grid} - y_{origin})^2} \tag{2}$$

$$\vartheta = N \times r \tag{3}$$

$$f_d = min(1.0, \frac{log(\vartheta + 1) - a}{b}) \tag{4}$$

where N is the number of points in the grid cell, x_{grid}, y_{grid} denote the coordinates of the grid cell and (x_{origin}, y_{origin}) is defined as $(0, 0)$. Figure 3 shows the distribution of the values of $log(\vartheta + 1)$, based on which, it can be found that most of the values are between 3.0 to 9.0. Thus, in the normalized density formula (4), we take $a = 3, b = 6$. Attention should be paid that for different LiDAR data, different values for a and b should be chosen.

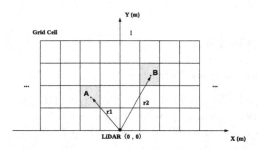

Fig. 2. For the two grid cells (A and B) in this bird's eye view map, we multiply the number of point clouds in each grid by r1 and r2 to balance the point clouds sparse region.

Third, some detection models [2,3,24,25] extract the intensity as a feature inside a grid cell. However, based on the BirdNet's experimental results [2], it is found that only using this feature, the intensity of point cloud is extremely unstable. Thus, using the intensity as a feature can improve a little or nothing of the detection performance. Therefore, we propose to use the standard deviation of the height of the point cloud as a new feature to replace the intensity. This is because the main disadvantage of bird's-eye-view-based detection models is the loss of the height information. However, it is difficult to reflect the distribution of point clouds on the Z-axis only by the mean point cloud height of each grid cell. However, the standard deviation can supplement the distribution of the point clouds in the cell, which is computed as follows

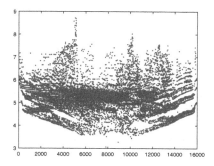

Fig. 3. The distribution of the distance-related density of the point cloud (The horizontal ordinate is the number of point cloud and the vertical ordinate is the values of $log(\vartheta + 1)$).

$$S_n = \sqrt{\frac{1}{N}\sum_{i=1}^{N}(h_i - h_{mean})^2} \qquad (5)$$

where h_i is the height values of the points. However, the standard deviation in most grids may be too small (e.g. $0 - 0.1$. To make the distribution of the standard deviation smooth between the cells, we normalize the standard deviation by

$$f_{std} = \sqrt{1 - (\frac{S_n}{max(S_n)} - 1)^2} \qquad (6)$$

Finally, the three newly introduced features f_d, f_h, f_{std} are used as inputs to the CNN, as shown in Fig. 1.

2.2 Network Architecture

Our BVNet model uses a modified Darknet53 [20] architecture as the backbone, which can predict not only the dimension and classes of the bounding boxes, but also the orientation. Figure 4 shows the complete network structure. Because the BVNet consists of feature pyramid networks [12], it extracts features from three different scales of a feature map. The down-sampling steps of the three scales are 8, 16 and 32, respectively. In addition, as YOLOv3 [20], BVNet also has 5 residual modules, which extends the network to 53 layers.

Orientation Prediction. In the past two years, many methods [1,4,24,25] were proposed to modify YOLO [18–20] to enable it to predict orientation. YOLO3D [1] and YOLO4D [4] can predict the offset of orientation and compute the mean squared error between the ground truth and the predicted orientation directly in the loss function expressed as $\sum_{i=0}^{s^2}\sum_{j=0}^{B} L_{ij}^{obj}(\theta_i - \theta_i')^2$, where θ_i is the predicted

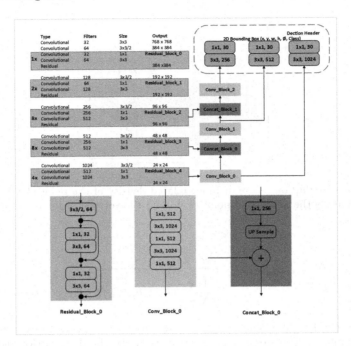

Fig. 4. The detection backbone is the same as YOLOv3's and we add an orientation regression at the end, so that the network can predict the orientation of the object. The bottom shows the residual block, the convolutional block and the feature pyramid network of the network, respectively.

orientation and θ'_i is the ground truth orientation of the bounding box. However, since using one value could create singularities, in Complex-YOLO [24,25], the Grid-RPN approach in YOLOv2 [19] was modified by adding two responsible regression parameters (t_{im}, t_{re}): $b_\theta = arg(|z| e^{ib_\theta}) = arctan_2(t_{im}, t_{re})$. In BVNet, We employ this modified method so that it can predict the orientation of bounding boxes.

Loss Function. The loss function $\mathcal{L}$ of our network is based on YOLOv3 [20] and Complex-YOLO [25] and the ground true boxes are defined by (x, y, w, h, θ, class):

$$\mathcal{L}_{BVNet} = \mathcal{L}_{YOLOv3} + \mathcal{L}_{Complex-YOLO} \tag{7}$$

$$\mathcal{L}_{BVNet} = \lambda_{coord} \sum_{i=0}^{N \times N} \sum_{j=0}^{K} 1_{ij}^{obj}[(t_x - t_x')^2 + (t_y - t_y')^2]$$

$$+\lambda_{coord} \sum_{i=0}^{N \times N} \sum_{j=0}^{K} 1_{ij}^{obj}[(t_w - t_w')^2 + (t_h - t_h')^2]$$

$$+\lambda_{coord} \sum_{i=0}^{N \times N} \sum_{j=0}^{K} 1_{ij}^{obj}[(t_{re} - t_{re}')^2 + (t_{im} - t_{im}')^2] \tag{8}$$

$$-\sum_{i=0}^{N \times N} \sum_{j=0}^{K} 1_{ij}^{obj}[c_i'log(c_i) + (1 - c_i')log(1 - c_i)]$$

$$-\lambda_{noobj} \sum_{i=0}^{N \times N} \sum_{j=0}^{K} 1_{ij}^{noobj}[c_i'log(c_i) + (1 - c_i')log(1 - c_i)]$$

$$-\sum_{i=0}^{N \times N} 1_{ij}^{obj} \sum_{c \in classes} [P_i'(c)log(P_i(c)) + (1 - P_i'(c))log(1 - P_i(c))]$$

where λ_{coord} is the weight of the coordinate loss. λ is used to control the imbalance of the predicted bounding boxes with and without objects inside. $t_x, t_y, t_w, t_h, t_{re}, t_{im}$ are the predicted values of the 2D bounding box. $t_x', t_y', t_w', t_h', t_{re}', t_{im}'$ are the truth values of the 2D bounding box. c is the confidence of the prediction bounding box. P_i is the probability of the object class. Cross entropy is used here to calculate the loss. 1_{ij}^{obj} takes the value of 0 and 1 based on whether there is a ground truth box in the i-th and j-th location (i.e.,1 if there is a ground truth box, and 0 otherwise). In contrast, 1_{ij}^{noobj} takes the value of 0 if there is no object, and 1 otherwise.

Anchor Box Calculation. As reported above, YOLOv3 [20] uses a feature pyramid network [12] to detect objects on three different scale feature maps. For each feature map, an object detector predicts three anchors on every grid cell. The size of the anchors is calculated in different datasets by the k-means clustering. Since the position of Lidar is fixed, the size of the object in the bird's view map does not change with distance, we use the predefined length and width from cars, cyclists and pedestrians to determine the sizes of the 3 anchors in each grid cell, with width, and length of $(1.6, 3.9)$, $(0.6, 1.76)$ and $(0.6, 0.8)$ meters [11], respectively.

Detection Header Network. We predict 3 bounding boxes in each grid cell on one feature map. The dimension of the tensor is $[3 \times (6 + 1 + N_{class})]$, where 6 stands for the number of bounding box offsets, 1 stand for the confidence prediction, and N_{class} is the number of the classes. In our model, we choose three KITTI-classes (i.e., car, pedestrian and cyclist) to perform the detection.

3D Bounding Box Regression. A 2D bounding box is obtained through our improved detection model. Quit a few methods [24,25] transfer 2D bounding boxes to 3D by a predefined height for each class. However, this method cannot accurately generate the 3D bounding boxes. In order to improve the accuracy, we take the maximum average height from the 2D bounding box as the height of the 3D bounding box.

3   Training and Experiments

3.1   KITTI Dataset

The KITTI dataset [5] (with 7,481 samples for the training and 7,518 samples for testing) is used to test our model. We follow the frequently used method [14,17] to divide the KITTI training dataset into train split (3712 samples) and validation split (3769 samples).

3.2   Optimization of Feature Maps

As stated in the second section, we at first extract the features on the bird's eye view map. Figure 5(a) and (b) show the density map from our model and that from Complex-YOLO [25]/MV3D's [3]. It can be seen that since we use a distance-related density of point cloud instead of the normally used density, the improvement is obvious.

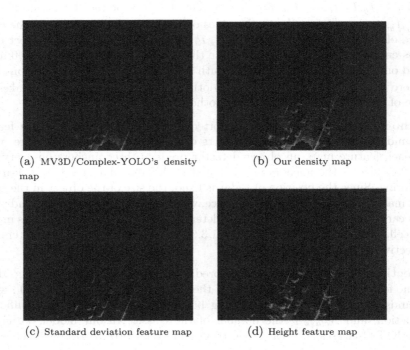

(a) MV3D/Complex-YOLO's density map

(b) Our density map

(c) Standard deviation feature map

(d) Height feature map

Fig. 5. Comparison of different feature maps

In addition, Fig. 5(c) and (d) show the mean height and the standard deviation feature map. It is shown that, compared with the height and the density feature map, the deviation feature map provides the contour of the object better and remove some useless points. Finally, we encode the three features as RGB (**R**ed-**G**reen-**B**lue) and fed them into the CNN.

3.3   Training and Implementation

Our model is trained by the stochastic gradient descent method with a weight decay of 0.0005 and a momentum of 0.9. Since the backbone network is based on YOLOv3 [20], the training parameters are taken as the same as YOLOv3's. We trained the network for 500 epochs, with a batch size of 4.

At the first few epochs, we used a small learning rate to ensure the convergence (0.001), and then we scaled the learning rate up in the middle epochs (0.005). In order to avoid gradient divergence, we slowly reduce the learning rate at the end of the training (0.005 to 0.001). Batch normalization for regularization is performed and Leaky ReLU is used as the activation function. To remove overlapped bounding boxes, we use the non-maximal suppression (NMS) on the bird's eye view maps with a threshold of 0.4.

The training environment used is Ubuntu 16.04 with an NVIDIA 2080ti GPU and an i7-9700K 3.6 GHz CPU. During the training, we randomly crop and flip the bird's eye view maps for data augmentation. The total training time is around 50 h.

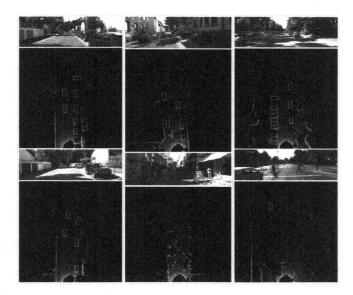

Fig. 6. Visualization of BVNet results. Examples of detection results of BVNet on KITTI validation set. (red: car, blue: pedestrian, pink: Cyclist) (Color figure online)

3.4 Result Evaluation

We evaluate our model by following the KITTI evaluation protocol, where the IoU thresholds for the car class is 0.7 and for others are 0.5. Results are given on the validation set. The average precision (AP) is used to compare the performances of different models.

Bird's Eye View Map Detection Performance on Validation Set using Different Features as Input. We use our detection network to test all extracted features on the bird's view map. We trained each network for 150 epochs. The combinations of features are listed in Table 1. All the methods are tested on our validation dataset. Our method is compared with Complex-YOLO [25], YOLO3D [1,4] and BirdNet [2], which are based only on bird's-eye-view map feature extraction. It can be seen that our model shows the best performance. (see Table 2 and Fig. 6).

Table 2. Results of testing different features on the validation dataset.

Features			Car	Pedestrian	Cyclist
Max intensity	Max height	Density	78.18	42.21	61.81
Mean intensity	Max height	Density	78.77	**42.57**	61.21
–	Max height	Density	76.21	41.78	60.00
Max height	Mean height	Min height	72.94	38.92	56.89
Our features			**82.78**	42.50	**63.71**

Evaluation of the Bird's View Map with other State-of-the-Art Models. All other results are taken from the KITTI benchmark suite[3]. Following the KITTI setting, we also divide the results into three difficulty regimes: easy, moderate and hard. For the car class, our model uses a 2D detector and shows similar performance compared with the models using a 3D detector. On the other hand, BVNet has an advantage in terms of efficiency (see Table 3).

Table 3. Results of bird's view detection

Method	Modality	Speed	Car			Pedestrian			Cyclist		
			Easy	Moderate	Hard	Easy	Moderate	Hard	Easy	Moderate	Hard
MV3D [3]	Lid. + Img.	360 ms	86.62	78.93	69.80	–	–	–	–	–	–
VoxelNet [29]	LiDAR	230 ms	89.35	76.26	77.39	46.13	40.74	38.11	66.70	54.76	50.55
F-PointNet [15]	LiDAR	170 ms	91.17	84.67	74.77	**57.13**	**49.57**	**45.48**	77.26	61.37	53.78
PointRCNN [22]	LiDAR	100 ms	**92.13**	87.36	**82.72**	54.77	46.13	42.84	82.56	67.24	60.28
F-ConvNet [26]	LiDAR	470 ms	91.51	85.84	76.11	57.04	48.96	44.33	**84.16**	**68.88**	60.05
PointRGCN [27]	LiDAR	260 ms	91.63	**87.49**	80.73	–	–	–	–	–	–
Ours	LiDAR	**50 ms**	89.45	84.65	78.52	48.97	42.53	38.12	73.87	64.68	**60.98**

3.5 Failure Cases

Although our model results in an improved detection performance, it shows some failure cases. The most error cases are road signs and trees mistakenly detected as pedestrians. The reason is due to the fact that the three handcrafted features for these classes are too similar. In practical applications, this issue can be addressed by using target tracking after the detection so as to remove such false bounding boxes.

4 Conclusion

In this paper, we propose BVNet, an end-to-end model based on point cloud only. We compensate the loss of height information on the bird's eye view map with newly introduced features to improve the detection accuracy. In addition, since our backbone network is YOLOv3 [20] which is able to detect objects of multiple classes, our model can also be easily extended for detecting new classes. Moreover, since BVNet only uses point cloud coordinate information to extract features, it works not only on Velodyne HDL-64 LiDAR, our model can also be adapted to various LiDAR (e.g. Innovusion LiDAR or Ibeo LiDAR etc.) with different parameters. Furthermore, since we use the classical 2D network as the backbone, our model can be readily applied to real autopilot.

References

1. Ali, W., Abdelkarim, S., Zidan, M., Zahran, M., El Sallab, A.: Yolo3D: end-to-end real-time 3D oriented object bounding box detection from lidar point cloud. In: Proceedings of the European Conference on Computer Vision (ECCV) (2018)
2. Beltran, J., Guindel, C., Moreno, F.M., Cruzado, D., Garcia, F., De La Escalera, A.: Birdnet: a 3D object detection framework from lidar information. In: 2018 21st International Conference on Intelligent Transportation Systems (ITSC), pp. 3517–3523. IEEE (2018)
3. Chen, X., Kundu, K., Zhang, Z., Ma, H., Fidler, S., Urtasun, R.: Monocular 3D object detection for autonomous driving. In: Proceedings of the IEEE Conference on Computer Vision and Pattern Recognition, pp. 2147–2156 (2016)
4. El Sallab, A., Sobh, I., Zidan, M., Zahran, M., Abdelkarim, S.: Yolo4D: a spatio-temporal approach for real-time multi-object detection and classification from lidar point clouds (2018)
5. Geiger, A., Lenz, P., Urtasun, R.: Are we ready for autonomous driving? The kitti vision benchmark suite. In: 2012 IEEE Conference on Computer Vision and Pattern Recognition, pp. 3354–3361. IEEE (2012)
6. Girshick, R.: Fast R-CNN. In: Proceedings of the IEEE International Conference on Computer Vision, pp. 1440–1448 (2015)
7. Girshick, R., Donahue, J., Darrell, T., Malik, J.: Rich feature hierarchies for accurate object detection and semantic segmentation. In: The IEEE Conference on Computer Vision and Pattern Recognition CVPR, June 2014
8. He, K., Gkioxari, G., Dollár, P., Girshick, R.: Mask R-CNN. In: Proceedings of the IEEE International Conference on Computer Vision, pp. 2961–2969 (2017)

9. Jiang, M., Wu, Y., Zhao, T., Zhao, Z., Lu, C.: Pointsift: a sift-like network module for 3D point cloud semantic segmentation. arXiv preprint arXiv:1807.00652 (2018)
10. Ku, J., Mozifian, M., Lee, J., Harakeh, A., Waslander, S.L.: Joint 3D proposal generation and object detection from view aggregation. In: 2018 IEEE/RSJ International Conference on Intelligent Robots and Systems (IROS), pp. 1–8. IEEE (2018)
11. Lang, A.H., Vora, S., Caesar, H., Zhou, L., Yang, J., Beijbom, O.: Pointpillars: fast encoders for object detection from point clouds. In: Proceedings of the IEEE Conference on Computer Vision and Pattern Recognition, pp. 12697–12705 (2019)
12. Lin, T.Y., Dollár, P., Girshick, R., He, K., Hariharan, B., Belongie, S.: Feature pyramid networks for object detection. In: Proceedings of the IEEE Conference on Computer Vision and Pattern Recognition, pp. 2117–2125 (2017)
13. Liu, W., et al.: SSD: single shot MultiBox detector. In: Leibe, B., Matas, J., Sebe, N., Welling, M. (eds.) ECCV 2016. LNCS, vol. 9905, pp. 21–37. Springer, Cham (2016). https://doi.org/10.1007/978-3-319-46448-0_2
14. Qi, C.R., Litany, O., He, K., Guibas, L.J.: Deep hough voting for 3D object detection in point clouds. In: Proceedings of the IEEE International Conference on Computer Vision, pp. 9277–9286 (2019)
15. Qi, C.R., Liu, W., Wu, C., Su, H., Guibas, L.J.: Frustum pointnets for 3D object detection from RGB-D data. In: Proceedings of the IEEE Conference on Computer Vision and Pattern Recognition, pp. 918–927 (2018)
16. Qi, C.R., Su, H., Mo, K., Guibas, L.J.: Pointnet: deep learning on point sets for 3D classification and segmentation. In: Proceedings of the IEEE Conference on Computer Vision and Pattern Recognition, pp. 652–660 (2017)
17. Qi, C.R., Yi, L., Su, H., Guibas, L.J.: Pointnet++: deep hierarchical feature learning on point sets in a metric space. In: Advances in Neural Information Processing Systems, pp. 5099–5108 (2017)
18. Redmon, J., Divvala, S., Girshick, R., Farhadi, A.: You only look once: unified, real-time object detection. In: The IEEE Conference on Computer Vision and Pattern Recognition, CVPR, June 2016
19. Redmon, J., Farhadi, A.: Yolo9000: better, faster, stronger. In: The IEEE Conference on Computer Vision and Pattern Recognition, CVPR, July 2017
20. Redmon, J., Farhadi, A.: Yolov3: an incremental improvement. arXiv preprint arXiv:1804.02767 (2018)
21. Ren, S., He, K., Girshick, R., Sun, J.: Faster R-CNN: towards real-time object detection with region proposal networks. In: Advances in Neural Information Processing Systems, pp. 91–99 (2015)
22. Shi, S., Wang, X., Li, H.: Pointrcnn: 3D object proposal generation and detection from point cloud. In: The IEEE Conference on Computer Vision and Pattern Recognition, CVPR, June 2019
23. Shi, S., Wang, Z., Wang, X., Li, H.: Part-A^ 2 net: 3D part-aware and aggregation neural network for object detection from point cloud. arXiv preprint arXiv:1907.03670 (2019)
24. Simon, M., et al.: Complexer-yolo: real-time 3D object detection and tracking on semantic point clouds. In: Proceedings of the IEEE Conference on Computer Vision and Pattern Recognition Workshops (2019)
25. Simony, M., Milzy, S., Amendey, K., Gross, H.M.: Complex-yolo: an Euler-region-proposal for real-time 3D object detection on point clouds. In: Proceedings of the European Conference on Computer Vision (ECCV) (2018)
26. Wang, Z., Jia, K.: Frustum convnet: sliding frustums to aggregate local point-wise features for amodal 3D object detection. arXiv preprint arXiv:1903.01864 (2019)

27. Zarzar, J., Giancola, S., Ghanem, B.: PointRGCN: graph convolution networks for 3D vehicles detection refinement. arXiv preprint arXiv:1911.12236 (2019)
28. Zeng, Y., et al.: Rt3D: real-time 3D vehicle detection in lidar point cloud for autonomous driving. IEEE Robot. Autom. Lett. **3**(4), 3434–3440 (2018)
29. Zhou, Y., Tuzel, O.: Voxelnet: end-to-end learning for point cloud based 3D object detection. In: Proceedings of the IEEE Conference on Computer Vision and Pattern Recognition, pp. 4490–4499 (2018)

Evaluating Single Image Dehazing
Methods Under Realistic Sunlight Haze

Zahra Anvari[(✉)] and Vassilis Athitsos

VLM Research Lab Computer Science and Engineering Department,
University of Texas at Arlington, Arlington, Texas, USA
zahra.anvari@mavs.uta.edu, athitsos@cse.uta.edu

Abstract. Haze can degrade the visibility and the image quality drastically, thus degrading the performance of computer vision tasks such
as object detection. Single image dehazing is a challenging and ill-posed
problem, despite being widely studied. Most existing methods assume
that haze has a uniform/homogeneous distribution and haze can have
a single color, *i.e.* grayish white color similar to smoke, while in reality
haze can be distributed non-uniformly with different patterns and colors. In this paper, we focus on haze created by sunlight as it is one of
the most prevalent types of haze in the wild. Sunlight can generate non-
uniformly distributed haze with drastic density changes due to sun rays
and also a spectrum of haze color due to sunlight color changes during
the day. This presents a new challenge to image dehazing methods. For
these methods to be practical, this problem needs to be addressed. To
quantify the challenges and assess the performance of these methods, we
present a sunlight haze benchmark dataset, Sun-Haze, containing 107
hazy images with different types of haze created by sunlight having a
variety of intensity and color. We evaluate a representative set of state-
of-the-art image dehazing methods on this benchmark dataset in terms
of standard metrics such as PSNR, SSIM, CIEDE2000, PI and NIQE.
Our results provide information on limitations of current methods, and
on the practicality of their underlying assumptions.

Keywords: Image dehazing · Image reconstruction · Contrast
enhancement

1 Introduction

Haze is an atmospheric phenomenon that can cause poor visibility, low contrast, and image quality degradation. Haze can decrease the performance of
different computer vision tasks, such as object detection [17,20], semantic segmentation [18], face detection, clustering, dataset creation [5,15,16,23,24], *etc.*
Therefore, haze removal has drawn a great deal of attention over the past decade.

© Springer Nature Switzerland AG 2020
G. Bebis et al. (Eds.): ISVC 2020, LNCS 12509, pp. 436–447, 2020.
https://doi.org/10.1007/978-3-030-64556-4_34

However, haze removal is still a challenging and ill-posed problem and most existing methods make assumptions that may not hold in reality. For example, most existing methods and datasets assume that i) haze has a uniform and homogeneous distribution in the entire image, and ii) haze can only have a single color, *i.e.* grayish white similar to the color of smoke or pollution. However, in reality, haze density can change non-homogeneously throughout an image and it can vary in pattern and color. Figure 1 shows a few sample images of different haze datasets that are widely used to test image dehazing methods. As one can see, haze is monochromatic and homogeneous in all these images. These datasets are created synthetically and do not look realistic, which may limit the practicality of dehazing methods.

  (a) SOTS indoor   (b) SOTS outdoor   (c) NYU   (d) Middlebury

Fig. 1. Sample hazy images of the datasets widely used to test image dehazing methods, SOTS test dataset [14], NYU dataset [4], and Middlebury [4].

In this paper, we focus on haze created by sunlight, which present a unique challenge to dehazing methods. The reason we focus on sunlight is that haze created by sunlight is one of the most prevalent types of haze for outdoor and indoor settings, and yet it has not received enough attention. To the best of our knowledge, our work is the first work that focuses on sunlight haze.

Haze created by sunlight has multiple unique features: i) it can drastically vary in between sun rays throughout an image, ii) it can corrupt some parts of an image more than another, meaning haze density drastically varies, iii) it can have an spectrum of colors, due to the sunlight color changes during the day, and iv) it has a unique gradually diminishing pattern.

To quantify the challenges and assess the performance of state-of-the-art dehazing methods, we present a sunlight haze benchmark dataset, Sun-Haze, containing 107 hazy images with different haze density, coverage, and color, caused by sunlight. Figure 2 presents some sample hazy images of Sun-Haze. We describe our dataset in the next section in detail.

Since the ground truth/haze-free image of a hazy image can be a variety of clean images, for instance images with different contrast or lighting, having only a single image as the ground truth might not be a fair representative and it lacks flexibility and practicality. Thus we build our dataset on top of MIT-Adobe FiveK dataset [9] which includes images retouched by five experts. The retouched images are clean images that we can employ as ground truth. Therefore, our dataset contains six ground truth images per hazy image, including

Fig. 2. Sample hazy images of Sun-Haze

the original one before adding haze. This provides us with the opportunity to compare existing methods more widely, fairly and more importantly in a more practical way.

Our evaluation of the current state-of-the-art methods shows that there is no clear winner and all these dehazing methods have difficulties in generalizing well to the haze created by sunlight, especially when dealing with haze with a different color.

In summary, this paper presents the following contributions:

- We present a sunlight haze benchmark dataset, Sun-Haze, that contains 107 hazy images caused by sunlight, along with six ground truth images (five retouched by five experts and one original image before being retouched) per hazy image.
- We perform an extensive analysis to evaluate current state-of-the-art dehazing methods over Sun-Haze in terms of both reference-based and no-reference-based metrics.
- We show that existing dehazing methods cannot generalize well when there is sunlight haze, in particular when we have sunlight color changes.

The rest of this paper is organized as follows. Section 2 explains our dataset, Sun-Haze. Section 3 describes a representative set of state-of-the-art dehazing methods to evaluate on our Sun-Haze dataset. Section 4 presents our evaluation results and discussion.

2   Sun-Haze Dataset

In this section, we describe how we created our hazy dataset, called Sun-Haze. This dataset is built on top of MIT-Adobe FiveK dataset [9]. MIT-Adobe FiveK dataset contains 5,000 photos taken by photographers with SLR cameras. These photos are all in RAW format, meaning that all the information recorded by the camera sensors, *i.e.* metadata, is preserved. These photos are captured from different scenes, subjects, and during various lighting conditions. These photographs are retouched to obtain a visually pleasing renditions by five photography experts using *Adobe Lightroom* [1].

To create our own dataset, we carefully selected a subset of 107 images from MIT-Adobe FiveK dataset, and added sunlight haze to them. We selected images that would create a realistic image after adding the sunlight haze. For example, we did not select night time images, or indoor images with no windows.

To add sunlight haze and mimic the real sunlight haze effect, we utilized *Adobe Photoshop* [2] and *Luminar 4* [3] which are photo editing applications. They enable us to add realistic sunlight haze. To produce realistic sunlight haze effect, we carefully used different parameters in Luminar 4, such as sunlight length, number of sunlight rays, intensity, penetration, and warmth. Increasing intensity would create a thicker and more dense haze effect. Increasing penetration would expand the sunlight haze effect to a broader region of the image. Increasing sunlight warmth creates a golden yellow type of haze, which enables us to create realistic sunlight color changes during the day. We also added sunlight haze from different angles to further diversify our dataset. To create sunset/sunrise haze effect, we used Adobe Photoshop and professionally added a gradient sunlight haze effect.

Sun-Haze dataset includes 107 outdoor and indoor images with sunlight haze professionally added. It also includes the original image (before retouch) as well as five retouched images (retouched by five experts) per hazy image, that serve as the ground truth images for each hazy image. Therefore each hazy image in our dataset has six ground truth images, enabling us to evaluate dehazing methods more widely and in a more practical way (since the ground truth of a hazy image could be a variety of clean/haze-free images). We will make our dataset public, and we hope that this dataset can help other researchers to test dehazing methods in a more practical and realistic way.

3 Dehazing Methods

In this section, we describe a representative of existing dehazing methods from the earliest ones to the current state-of-the-art methods. We can categorize the dehazing methods into the following categories (Note that some of the methods might fall into multiple categories):

- **Prior-Based:** Prior-based methods, also known as prior information-based methods, are mainly based on the parameter estimation of atmospheric scattering model by utilizing the priors, such as dark channel priors [12], color attenuation prior [26], haze-line prior [7,8]. The physical scattering model consists of the transmission map and the atmospheric light, and it is formulated as follows:

$$I(x) = J(x)t(x) + A(1 - t(x)) \qquad (1)$$

where $I(x)$ is the hazy image, $J(x)$ is the haze-free image or the scene radiance, $t(x)$ is the medium transmission map, and A is the global atmospheric light on each x pixel coordinates.

- **Learning-Based:** On the other hand, some methods utilize the deep convolutional neural networks to estimate the transmission map indirectly [10,22]. Some work employ deep convolutional neural networks to jointly estimate the parameters of the physical scattering model, *i.e.* atmospheric light and the transmission map [25,27].
- **Paired/Unpaired Supervision:** Paired single image dehazing methods need the haze-free/ground truth of each hazy image for training [13,19], while unpaired dehazing methods do not require the haze-free pair of the hazy images [6,11].
- **Adversarial-Based:** Some image dehazing methods utilize generative adversarial networks for image dehazing and learn transmission map and atmospheric light simultaneously in the generators. Some data-driven methods use adversarial training to solve the dehazing problem without using priors. Some recently proposed methods use image-to-image translation techniques to tackle the image dehazing problem through adversarial training [6,11,19]. Xitong *et al.* proposed a joint model that learns to perform physical-model based disentanglement by adversarial training [25].

Table 1 represents a description of the methods that we evaluated. As one can observe, we selected a variety of methods from different categories. Next, we will describe these methods in more detail.

Table 1. Description of the evaluated existing methods.

Method	Paired vs. unpaired	Prior-based	Learning-based	Adversarial-based
DCP [12]	NA	✓		
MSCNN [22]	Paired	✓	✓	
DehazeNet [10]	Paired	✓	✓	
AODNet [13]	Paired	✓	✓	
EPDN [19]	Paired		✓	✓
Dehaze-GLCGAN [6]	Unpaired		✓	✓
CycleDehaze [11]	Unpaired		✓	✓

3.1 DCP

Early dehazing methods are mostly prior-based methods, DCP [12] is one of those prior-based dehazing methods [12,29] which estimates the transmission map by investigating the dark channel prior. DCP utilizes dark channel prior to more reliably calculate the transmission matrix. With dark channel prior, the thickness of haze is estimated and removed by the atmospheric scattering model.

Moreover, this method is proposed based on experimental statistics of experiments on haze-free images, which shows at least one color channel has some pixels with very low intensities in most of non-haze patches. However, DCP has poor performance on dehazing the sky images and is computationally intensive.

3.2   MSCNN

The performance of prior-based image dehazing methods is limited by hand-designed features, such as the dark channel, color disparity and maximum contrast, with complex fusion schemes. Unlike the previous methods, MSCNN [22] is a learning-based dehazing method. The authors proposed a multi-scale deep neural network for single-image dehazing by learning the mapping between hazy images and their corresponding transmission maps.

This method contains two sub-networks called coarse-scale and fine-scale, to estimate the transmission map. The coarse-scale network estimates the transmission map based on the entire image. The results are further improved locally by the fine-scale network.

3.3   DehazeNet

DehazeNet [10] takes advantage of both priors and the power of convolutional neural networks. DehazeNet proposed an end-to-end system for medium transmission estimation. It takes a hazy image as input, and outputs its medium transmission map that is later used to recover a haze-free image via atmospheric scattering model. In addition, DehazeNet proposed a CNN-based deep network, which its layers are specially designed to embody the established priors in image dehazing. Authors also proposed a nonlinear activation function called Bilateral Rectified Linear Unit (BReLU), to improve the quality of recovered haze-free image.

In short, DehazeNet modified the classic CNN model by adding feature extraction and non-linear regression layers. These modifications distinguish DehazeNet from other CNN-based models.

3.4   AOD-Net

AOD-Net [13] is an end-to-end dehazing network which is based on estimating the transmission map through reformulating the atmospheric scattering model. Instead of estimating the transmission matrix and the atmospheric light separately, AODNet directly generates the clean image through a light-weight CNN. AOD-Net can be easily embedded with Faster R-CNN [21] and improve the object detection performance on hazy images with a large margin.

3.5   EPDN

EPDN [19] is a recently proposed GAN-based single image dehazing method. In this work they reduced the image dehazing problem to a **paired** image-to-image translation problem and proposed an enhanced Pix2pix Dehazing network based on a generative adversarial network. This network contains generators, discriminators, and two enhancing blocks to produce a realistic dehazed image on the fine scale.

The enhancer contains two enhancing blocks based on the receptive field model, which reinforces the dehazing effect in both color and details. The GAN is jointly trained with the enhancer.

3.6   CycleDehaze

CycleDehaze [28] is an end-to-end single image dehazing method which does not require pairs of hazy and corresponding ground truth images for training, *i.e.* they train the network by feeding clean and hazy images in an unpaired manner.

This method enhances CycleGAN formulation by combining cycle-consistency and perceptual loss to improve the quality of textural information recovery and generate more visually pleasing and realistic haze-free images.

3.7   Dehaze-GLCGAN

Dehaze-GLCGAN [6] is another GAN-based single image dehazing method based on a global-local dehazing mechanism. They cast the image dehazing problem as an **unpaired** image-to-image translation problem, which means that, similar to CycleDehaze [11], pairs of hazy images and the corresponding ground truth images are not required for the training process.

They proposed a dehazing Global-Local Cycle-consistent Generative Adversarial Network. The generator network of Dehaze-GLCGAN combines an encoder-decoder architecture with residual blocks to better recover the haze-free scene. They also proposed a global-local discriminator structure to deal with spatially varying haze.

4   Results and Discussion

In this section, we present the quantitative and qualitative evaluation results and then discuss the performance of the dehazing methods over Sun-Haze dataset.

4.1   Quantitative Evaluation

In this section, the Sun-Haze dataset is used to perform a comprehensive quantitative evaluation of several state-of-the-art single image dehazing methods, as described in Sect. 3.

We used several metrics to evaluate these dehazing methods, including reference-based and no-reference-based metrics. These metrics are:

- **PSNR:** This metric provides a pixel-wise evaluation and is capable of indicating the effectiveness of haze removal. It measures the ratio between the maximum possible value of a signal and the power of distorting noise that affects the quality of its representation.
- **SSIM:** It is a perceptual metric for measuring the structural similarity between two images.
- **CIEDE2000:** It measures the color difference between hazy and dehazed images.
- **NIQE:** It is a well-known no-reference image quality assessment metric for evaluating real image restoration without requiring the ground-truth.

Table 2. Results over Sun-Haze dataset. We performed separate analysis for different ground truth images. The images retouched by 5 experts and the original image before retouch are considered as ground truth/haze free. We also present results for the no-reference metrics.

Ground truth	Metric	DCP	MSCNN	Dehazenet	AOD-Net	EPDN	Dehaze-GLCGAN	CycleDehaze
Expert A	PSNR	11.01	**16.48**	15.62	14.83	15.88	14.38	15.53
	SSIM	0.641	0.773	0.733	0.698	0.784	**0.789**	0.778
	CIEDE	34.76	**23.46**	27.55	30.26	26.29	24.37	26.62
Expert B	PSNR	11.28	16.33	15.13	14.15	14.96	15.12	15.38
	SSIM	0.655	0.763	0.709	0.676	0.761	**0.801**	0.763
	CIEDE	32.66	25.43	30.90	34.33	31.64	**22.03**	26.49
Expert C	PSNR	11.32	**16.57**	15.49	14.49	15.44	14.74	15.23
	SSIM	0.643	0.746	0.703	0.670	0.756	**0.782**	0.737
	CIEDE	33.22	24.57	28.84	31.93	28.73	**23.98**	28.98
Expert D	PSNR	11.43	14.91	13.75	12.82	13.55	**14.93**	14.35
	SSIM	0.649	0.722	0.667	0.632	0.713	**0.781**	0.728
	CIEDE	30.87	29.10	34.76	38.87	36.28	**22.36**	28.67
Expert E	PSNR	11.32	15.27	13.86	12.99	13.56	**15.32**	14.84
	SSIM	0.640	0.719	0.660	0.626	0.704	**0.780**	0.733
	CIEDE	33.07	28.56	34.38	38.11	35.88	**22.30**	28.13
Original image	PSNR	11.40	**19.10**	17.78	16.89	17.96	14.57	16.39
	SSIM	0.686	**0.867**	0.814	0.782	0.857	0.810	0.834
	CIEDE	36.10	**18.44**	23.95	26.63	22.72	24.46	23.46
Average	PSNR	11.34	**17.51**	16.28	15.37	16.32	14.73	15.73
	SSIM	0.651	0.765	0.721	0.680	0.763	**0.799**	0.762
	CIEDE	33.45	24.93	30.06	33.36	30.26	**23.25**	27.06
No reference	NIQE	5.35	4.06	4.08	**3.93**	4.13	4.09	4.60
No reference	PI	3.71	3.25	3.25	3.02	3.04	**2.93**	4.08

– **PI:** Perceptual Index measures the quality of the reconstructed images based on human perception. A lower perceptual index indicates better perceptual quality. The perceptual quality of an image is the degree to which the image looks like a natural image. This metric is a no-reference quality measurement metric which means that it does not require a ground truth image.

The larger values of PSNR, SSIM and the smaller values of CIEDE2000, NIQE, and PI indicate better dehazing and perceptual quality.

Table 2 shows the quantitative results of evaluating the dehazing methods in terms of PSNR and SSIM, CIEDE2000, NIQE, and PI. We conducted multiple experiments to evaluate the dehazing and generalization capability of the dehazing techniques.

We used our Sun-Haze dataset as the hazy images and the retouched images by five experts as well as the original image as the ground truth for each experiment. The best results are depicted in bold. We also highlighted the top three best results. The green highlights represent the best results, yellow the second best and pink the third best results.

As one can observe, on average MSCNN achieved best PSNR of 17.51 and the second best SSIM and CIEDE2000. GLCGAN outperformed other methods in terms of SSIM, CIEDE2000, and PI by a very small margin. AOD-Net achieved the best NIQE of 3.93 which is very comparable with the second and third best results.

As you can see, no method is superior to other methods in all five measurements and the best results are only slightly better than the second and third best results. This suggests that current methods cannot generalize well to remove haze caused by sunlight.

4.2   Qualitative Evaluation

Figure 3 depicts five hazy images from Sun-Haze dataset, and the dehazing results yielded by AOD-Net [13], Dehaze-GLCGAN [6], DehazeNet [10], MSCNN [22], and EPDN [19]. In this figure we have five pairs of rows. In each pair the top row shows a hazy image followed by the results of five dehazing methods mentioned above and the second row shows the five experts' retouched images and the untouched original image to compare with.

Qualitatively, most methods were unable to remove the sunlight haze without introducing color shifting or artifacts. EPDN, which is a paired image-to-image translation technique, has mainly learned to remove haze through increasing the color intensity at different channels, thus the dehazed images look visibly darker and the sunlight haze more yellow or orange than the original hazy image. EPDN also introduced artifacts to some of the generated images while partially removing haze. It also created the halo effect near edges.

Other methods also were unable to generalize to remove sunlight haze and they removed haze partially and improved the visibility to a small extent. For instance, even though AOD-Net, Dehaze-GLCGAN, Dehazenet, and MSCNN could recover the image structure similar to EPDN, they introduced color shifting and artifacts which are not visually pleasing and made the haze even more prominent.

Dehaze-GLCGAN achieved the best/highest structural similarity index and recovered the image structure well but introduced artifacts and overexposure in particular where the sun rays lie.

In conclusion, these methods were unable to generalize well to remove sunlight haze, and performed even more poorly in sunset hazy images which embody more varicolored haze. This questions the underlying assumptions of these methods and their practicality in real-world scenarios. Therefore, for dehazing methods to be practical they need to be trained and tested using more realistic and practical datasets which include a variety of realistic haze patterns and colors.

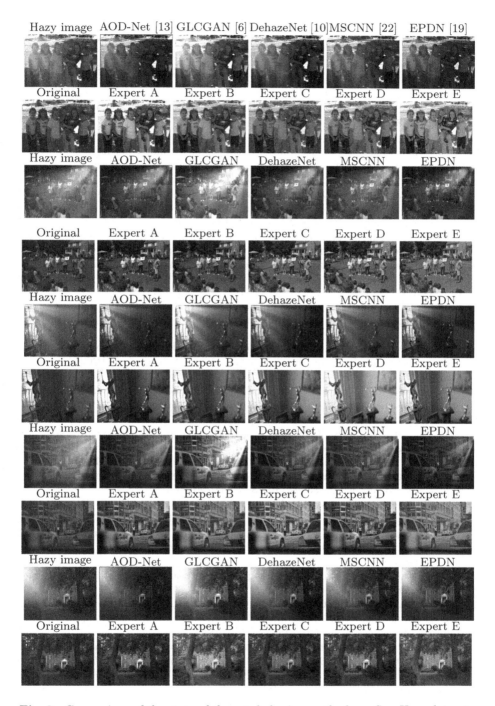

Fig. 3. Comparison of the state-of-the-art de-hazing methods on Sun-Haze dataset.

Acknowledgments. We would like to thank the ISVC'20 anonymous reviewers for their valuable feedback. This work is partially supported by National Science Foundation grant IIS-1565328. Any opinions, findings, and conclusions or recommendations expressed in this publication are those of the authors, and do not necessarily reflect the views of the National Science Foundation.

References

1. Adobe lightroom. https://www.adobe.com/products/photoshop-lightroom.html
2. Adobe photoshop. https://www.adobe.com/products/photoshop.html
3. Luminar 4. https://skylum.com/luminar
4. Ancuti, C., Ancuti, C.O., De Vleeschouwer, C.: D-hazy: a dataset to evaluate quantitatively dehazing algorithms. In: 2016 IEEE International Conference on Image Processing (ICIP), pp. 2226–2230. IEEE (2016)
5. Anvari, Z., Athitsos, V.: A pipeline for automated face dataset creation from unlabeled images. In: Proceedings of the 12th ACM International Conference on PErvasive Technologies Related to Assistive Environments, pp. 227–235 (2019)
6. Anvari, Z., Athitsos, V.: Dehaze-GLCGAN: unpaired single image de-hazing via adversarial training. arXiv preprint arXiv:2008.06632 (2020)
7. Berman, D., Avidan, S., et al.: Non-local image dehazing. In: Proceedings of the IEEE Conference on Computer Vision and Pattern Recognition, pp. 1674–1682 (2016)
8. Berman, D., Treibitz, T., Avidan, S.: Air-light estimation using haze-lines. In: 2017 IEEE International Conference on Computational Photography (ICCP), pp. 1–9. IEEE (2017)
9. Bychkovsky, V., Paris, S., Chan, E., Durand, F.: Learning photographic global tonal adjustment with a database of input/output image pairs. In: CVPR 2011, pp. 97–104. IEEE (2011)
10. Cai, B., Xu, X., Jia, K., Qing, C., Tao, D.: Dehazenet: an end-to-end system for single image haze removal. IEEE Trans. Image Process. **25**(11), 5187–5198 (2016)
11. Engin, D., Genç, A., Kemal Ekenel, H.: Cycle-dehaze: enhanced cyclegan for single image dehazing. In: Proceedings of the IEEE Conference on Computer Vision and Pattern Recognition Workshops, pp. 825–833 (2018)
12. He, K., Sun, J., Tang, X.: Single image haze removal using dark channel prior. IEEE Trans. Pattern Anal. Mach. Intell. **33**(12), 2341–2353 (2010)
13. Li, B., Peng, X., Wang, Z., Xu, J., Feng, D.: Aod-net: all-in-one dehazing network. In: Proceedings of the IEEE International Conference on Computer Vision, pp. 4770–4778 (2017)
14. Li, B., et al.: Benchmarking single-image dehazing and beyond. IEEE Trans. Image Process. **28**(1), 492–505 (2018)
15. Lin, W.A., Chen, J.C., Castillo, C.D., Chellappa, R.: Deep density clustering of unconstrained faces. In: Proceedings of the IEEE Conference on Computer Vision and Pattern Recognition, pp. 8128–8137 (2018)
16. Lin, W.A., Chen, J.C., Chellappa, R.: A proximity-aware hierarchical clustering of faces. In: 2017 12th IEEE International Conference on Automatic Face & Gesture Recognition (FG 2017), pp. 294–301. IEEE (2017)
17. Liu, W., et al.: SSD: single shot MultiBox detector. In: Leibe, B., Matas, J., Sebe, N., Welling, M. (eds.) ECCV 2016. LNCS, vol. 9905, pp. 21–37. Springer, Cham (2016). https://doi.org/10.1007/978-3-319-46448-0_2

18. Long, J., Shelhamer, E., Darrell, T.: Fully convolutional networks for semantic segmentation. In: Proceedings of the IEEE Conference on Computer Vision and Pattern Recognition, pp. 3431–3440 (2015)
19. Qu, Y., Chen, Y., Huang, J., Xie, Y.: Enhanced pix2pix dehazing network. In: Proceedings of the IEEE Conference on Computer Vision and Pattern Recognition, pp. 8160–8168 (2019)
20. Redmon, J., Divvala, S., Girshick, R., Farhadi, A.: You only look once: unified, real-time object detection. In: Proceedings of the IEEE Conference on Computer Vision and Pattern Recognition, pp. 779–788 (2016)
21. Ren, S., He, K., Girshick, R., Sun, J.: Faster R-CNN: towards real-time object detection with region proposal networks. In: Advances in Neural Information Processing Systems, pp. 91–99 (2015)
22. Ren, W., Liu, S., Zhang, H., Pan, J., Cao, X., Yang, M.-H.: Single image dehazing via multi-scale convolutional neural Networks. In: Leibe, B., Matas, J., Sebe, N., Welling, M. (eds.) ECCV 2016. LNCS, vol. 9906, pp. 154–169. Springer, Cham (2016). https://doi.org/10.1007/978-3-319-46475-6_10
23. Schroff, F., Kalenichenko, D., Philbin, J.: Facenet: a unified embedding for face recognition and clustering. In: Proceedings of the IEEE Conference on Computer Vision and Pattern Recognition, pp. 815–823 (2015)
24. Yang, S., Luo, P., Loy, C.C., Tang, X.: Wider face: a face detection benchmark. In: Proceedings of the IEEE Conference on Computer Vision and Pattern Recognition, pp. 5525–5533 (2016)
25. Yang, X., Xu, Z., Luo, J.: Towards perceptual image dehazing by physics-based disentanglement and adversarial training. In: Thirty-second AAAI Conference on Artificial Intelligence (2018)
26. Zhang, T., Shao, C., Wang, X.: Atmospheric scattering-based multiple images fog removal. In: 2011 4th International Congress on Image and Signal Processing, vol. 1, pp. 108–112. IEEE (2011)
27. Zhu, H., Peng, X., Chandrasekhar, V., Li, L., Lim, J.H.: Dehazegan: when image dehazing meets differential programming. In: IJCAI, pp. 1234–1240 (2018)
28. Zhu, J.Y., Park, T., Isola, P., Efros, A.A.: Unpaired image-to-image translation using cycle-consistent adversarial networks. In: Proceedings of the IEEE International Conference on Computer Vision, pp. 2223–2232 (2017)
29. Zhu, Q., Mai, J., Shao, L.: A fast single image haze removal algorithm using color attenuation prior. IEEE Trans. Image Process. **24**(11), 3522–3533 (2015)

Biometrics

Deep Partial Occlusion Facial Expression Recognition via Improved CNN

Yujian Chen and Shiguang Liu[✉]

College of Intelligence and Computing, Tianjin University,
Tianjin 300350, People's Republic of China
lsg@tju.edu.cn

Abstract. Facial expression recognition (FER) can indicate a person's emotion state, that is of great importance in virtual human modelling and communication. However, FER suffers from a partial occlusion problem when applied under an unconstrained environment. In this paper, we propose to use facial expressions with partial occlusion for FER. This differs from the most conventional FER problems which assume that facial images are detected without any occlusion. To this end, by reconstructing the partially occluded facial expression database, we propose a 20-layer "VGG + residual" CNN network based on the improved VGG16 network, and adapt a hybrid feature strategy to parallelize the Gabor filter with the above CNN. We also optimize the components of the model by LMCL and momentum SGD. The results are then combined with a certain weight to get the classification results. The advantages of this method are demonstrated by multiple sets of experiments and cross-database tests.

Keywords: Facial expression recognition · CNN · Gabor · LMCL · SGD

1 Introduction

Expressions can be defined as a facial change that corresponds to a person's internal emotional state, intention or social interaction. The rich and small changes in the face can denote a variety of expressions [24]. Facial expression recognition (FER), i.e., calculation of the changes in muscles, morphology and key features of a person's face by computer, is a very active and challenging area that plays an important role in virtual human modelling and communication [4,11,15]. It has also been widely used in social robots, safe driving, public monitoring, polygraph technology, interactive games, etc., which attracted much attention in recent years [14].

Most recent research [3,10] in this area has focused on unconstrained FER by CNN. The CNN model exhibits excellent performance on this task because it is based on a combination of low-level features to find advanced features that are capable of extracting features which are robust to the changes in the training data (if sufficient changes of samples are included).

Supported by the Natural Science Foundation of China under grant nos. 61672375 and 61170118.

© Springer Nature Switzerland AG 2020
G. Bebis et al. (Eds.): ISVC 2020, LNCS 12509, pp. 451–462, 2020.
https://doi.org/10.1007/978-3-030-64556-4_35

Fig. 1. Systematic occlusion (a), temporary occlusion (b), mixed occlusion (c), and other special occlusions (d).

However, in our unrestricted real life, the scenes are likely to have partial occlusion of the face. As shown in Fig. 1, facial occlusion includes systemic occlusion, temporary occlusion, mixed occlusion, and other special occlusions [19,25]. The presence of partial occlusion of the face can have two effects on facial expression recognition: first, occlusion can significantly change the visual appearance of the face, seriously affecting the performance of the FER system; secondly, occlusion can result in inaccurate feature positions or inaccurate face alignment, which increases the difficulty of extracting discriminant features from occluded faces. Partial occlusion of the face has become one of the main limitations of developing a robust FER system.

Therefore, in this work, we show that some facial occlusions still have problems for unconstrained facial recognition. This is because that most databases used for training do not provide samples of occluded faces to learn how to handle them. One way to solve this problem is to train the CNN model with a data set that contains more occluded faces. However, this task can be challenging because the main source of facial images is usually the internet, where there are fewer marked faces with occlusion.

With this in mind, we manually occluded the mouth and eyes of the KDEF [5] and JAFFE [13] datasets and added them as occluded samples. Based on the improvement of VGG16, a 20-layer deep CN network with two residual blocks is designed, which can solve the problem of degradation of deep networks. In the network, by fedding the image of the occluded eyes and mouth into the network for training, the model can adapt to different occlusion areas, and the strong occlusion feature is learned from the unoccluded area. Excellent results have been achieved in training and testing. In order to solve the problem of cross-database verification caused by insufficient amount and insufficient feature extraction of partially occluded facial expressions data. We combine the Gabor filter and CNN and obtain their respective classification results through parallel processing. We then combine the above two parts according to a certain weight to produce the final classification vector. Secondly, the traditional Softmax Loss in deep CNN can make the calculation of the model more stable, that is beneficial for optimizing the distance between classes. It is weaker, however, for the optimization class distance and the feature distinguishing ability is also insufficient. To solve this problem in our FER system, we applied the latest, validated and well-functioning LMCL (Large Margin Cosine Loss) [21] to our model and optimized the classification results. We also use momentum SGD (Stochastic Gradient Descent) to optimize the traditional SGD, thus speeding up the gradient descent optimization process. Through comparative experiments, we evaluated the relationship of the recognition rates in different conditions.

2 Related Work

The study of facial expressions began in the 19th century. In 1872, Darwin described the connection and difference of facial expressions between humanity and animals [20].

In recent years, the latest research and development of convolutional neural networks [12,22] has greatly improved the effects of various computer vision tasks, which has made DCNN a mainstream machine learning method for computer vision. As one of the most common computer vision tasks, facial expression recognition has been widely studied and become a new hot research direction. The early research was based on traditional methods and shallow models of low-level features, and today's facial expression recognition has made great progress under the impetus of DCNN. However, most of the previous researches on facial expression recognition are based on the premise of unobstructed conditions in the laboratory. In real life, there are often various occlusions on the face, which has become a major problem of FER. The bottlenecks and challenges of the system have also attracted attention of more and more researchers.

2.1 Facial Expression Recognition Without Occlusion

Most of the related researches are based on FER without occlusion under laboratory constraints. Traditionally, Facial Action Coding System (FACS) [3] expresses different emotions by describing subtle changes in facial expressions, which can better describe the details of facial expressions.

In terms of deep learning methods, Liu et al. [10] proposed a new method called elevated deep confidence network (BDBN). Their experiments were performed in Cohn-Kanade and JAFFE, with the accuracy of 96.7% and 68.0%, respectively. However, this method ignores the correlation between different facial areas.

2.2   Facial Expression Recognition with Partial Occlusion

As mentioned above, in the early investigation of facial expression recognition, no research has been reported on overcoming facial occlusion. Nevertheless, due to the recognition of the great influence of facial occlusion on facial expressions, many studies have begun to try face facial expression recognition with partial occlusion. It can be seen from the existing research that FER methods under partial occlusion can be divided into two categories, traditional methods and deep learning methods.

Traditional Methods. Kotsia et al. [9] used Gabor wavelet texture information extraction based on discriminant non-negative matrix factorization and shape-based methods to classify partial occlusion images. Hammal and Arguin [6] proposed the improved transferable belief model (TBM) for FER under partial occlusions. But the recognition of sadness is not high (25%). FER based on traditional methods are often affected by the extraction of more occluded physical features.

Deep Learning Methods. Zoltan et al. [26] used an 8-layer CNN for action unit detection to detect self-occlusion caused by large attitude changes in 3D pose data, but it may not be the best to use CNN alone. Brink and Vadapalli [1] proposed a hybrid model by combining the variable processing model and CNN. This model greatly reduces the error rate of feature extraction, but they do not pay more attention to occlusion expression recognition. Cheng et al. [2] proposed the deep structure of facial expression recognition with partial occlusion, and extracted features from face images using the Gabor filter as input to 3-layer deep Boltzmann machine for sentiment classification. The accuracy reaches up to 82%. The performance of this work still has room to improve, and the amount of database used is only 213, which is not enough for learning the deep structure. Lu et al. [23] proposed a Wasserstein Generative Adversarial Network-based method to perform occluded FER. This method consists of a generator G and two discriminators D1 and D2. FER is completed by introducing the classification loss into D2.

3   Method

The flow chart of the models is shown in Fig. 2. We propose a two part model structure. Given source images, we first use the improved CNN network and the Gabor filter for parallel processing, and then combine the two resulting vectors by weighting to obtain the classification result. The first part is a 20-layer CNN. The input is a 256×256 image, which is preprocessed and then fed to the VGG16, followed by a 4-layer residual network at the back of the network. In the second part, we combine the traditional Gabor filter with Adaboost to construct another processing classifier. Finally, the classification results of the two parts are combined by a certain weight (DCNN + Gabor). In addition, we use LMCL to optimize the traditional Softmax Loss, and use the SGD with momentum to optimize the traditional SGD, and the results of our model classification are further optimized.

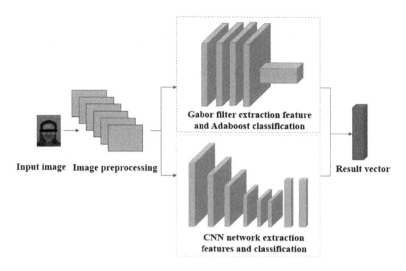

Fig. 2. Overview of our approach.

3.1 Data Set

We first constructed partial occlusion dataset for occlusion of the eyes and mouth using the public no-occlusion data sets JAFFE [13] and KDEF [5], then classify it as 7 expressions (i.e., angry, disgusted, fearful, happy, sad, surprised and neutral) for comparative testing. We denote their abbreviations as AN, DI, FE, HA, SA, SU and NE, respectively. We will process all the images into 256×256 and perform a series of data preprocessing, including standardizing the space and augmented data and generating synthetic images by artificially rotating real images [17].

3.2 CNN Network with Residual Block

As shown in Fig. 3, the first part of our models is based on the VGG16 [18] architecture, which consists of 13 convolutional layers and 3 fully connected layers, where the convolutional layer is divided by 5 max-pooling layers. Note that the filter size of all convolutional layers is 3×3 and the step size is 1 for padding. The input is a preprocessed image that passes through multiple convolutional layers, pooling layers and two residual blocks. Then, after processing through the fully connected layer and Softmax, a seven-dimensional output vector is obtained. Finally, the resulting expression is judged based on the probability value.

During training facial expressions, when the number of network layers is deepened, it may cause gradient dispersion or gradient explosion problems. This problem may be solved through regularization, however, another one still remain unsolved, i.e., the degradation of the network. Although the number of network layers increases, the accuracy of the training set is saturated or even decreased. To this end, He et al. [7] proposed a residual network and proved to achieve

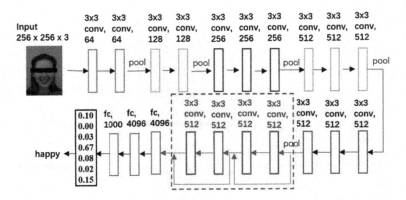

Fig. 3. Illustration of the proposed network.

good results in deep networks. Inspired by their work, we add a 4-layer residual network to VGG16 to improve the network. It can solve the problem of degradation of a deep network, so that the model can make good use of the depth of the network, and the learning of the training set is more sufficient.

The residual block transfers the input x by adding a jump connection between every two layers. The residual map $F(x)$ is constructed at the same time. Finally, $F(x)$ is summed with x to obtain the result map $H(x)$. The optimization of the network can also avoid the instability of the training error when the network is deepened, which can help alleviate the problem of gradient disappearance and gradient explosion, and also ensure the good performance of the network and avoid the network becoming "bloated".

3.3   Hybrid Model Structure Combined with Gabor Filter

The second part of our model structure is a facial expression recognition system based on the Gabor filter and the Adaboost classifier. The Gabor filter can be regarded as a feature filter that can better imitate the human visual system. It can well describe the feature information of facial expression images, including texture features, edge features and directional features. The process of this model is described below.

Image Preprocessing. We mainly perform two pre-processing steps, i.e., gray normalization and geometric normalization. First, the Sobel operator [8] is used to extract the edge of the facial feature region, and the automatic threshold binarization method [16] is employed to obtain the segmentation graph of the facial features. PCA (Principal Component Analysis) is introduced to select true facial features, combined with the constraints of a priori relationship between facial features and face size. We can obtain important position parts such as nose, eyes, mouth, cheeks, lower bars and foreheads. Then, the feature images corresponding to the feature regions are extracted from the facial expression image.

Feature Extraction. In this paper, Gabor filter banks with different scales and different directions are used. Different parameters are selected according to actual requirements, and they are convoluted with the preprocessed image to obtain the filtered Gabor features. Specifically, the filter bank used here includes a total of 40 filters consisting of 5 different scales and 8 different directional Gabor filters.

Feature Selection and Expression Classification. Due to the characteristics of the Gabor filter, the feature dimension obtained after passing through the Gabor filter bank will be very large, and if it is directly passed as input to the classifier, the amount of computation will be very large. And the high-dimensional feature vector contains more redundant information, which will have a great impact on the final classification accuracy. Therefore, Adaboost is used for feature selection and the classifier. The weak learner is the classification and regression tree (CART). Through each round of adjustment of the sample weights, we learn 10 weak learners in series, and finally get a series of classifier parameters and weak learners. The weight value is then combined with the weight value according to a certain strategy to obtain the final classification result.

As shown in Fig. 2, we obtain a hybrid structure consisting of the CNN method and the Gabor method. By linearly combining the resulting vectors obtained by the above two models, the final classification result can be obtained. By experiments, the weight of the model structure of CNN and that of the Gabor filter model are set as 0.6 and 0.4, respectively.

3.4 Component Optimization for Deep Networks

In the optimization of the model structure, we replace the traditional Softmax Loss with LMCL, so that the loss function has great feature classification ability to optimize the classification accuracy. We also improve the traditional SGD as the momentum SGD in order to greatly accelerate the convergence process of the model.

4 Experiments

In this section, we introduce the experimental environment, data sets, model frameworks, and training processes, etc. We performed the experiments using the model described above.

4.1 Implementation

Our model is based on the Tensorflow framework, which uses the GPU (Graphics Processing Unit) for parallel computing. We run our method under a 6G discrete graphics card. The experimental data set is a mixed data set of KDEF and JAFFE using artificial occlusion. Among them, the 90% of the total data are

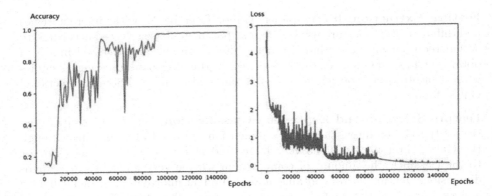

Fig. 4. The testing accuracy (left) and testing loss (right).

served as training set, and the remaining is test set. The size of each image is processed to 256 × 256. After a series of pre-processing, the image is fed into the model for iterative training.

As shown in the left image of Fig. 4, the total iteration of testing reaches more than 100,000 times. In the beginning, the accuracy of the testing was low. After about 1000 rounds of fine-tuning, the accuracy quickly rises to be around 50%. Then the accuracy fluctuated and reaches about 90% after about 5000 iterations. Finally, after constant fluctuations and small adjustments, the accuracy of the testing set can reach higher values. When the testing iteration is approximating 90,000 times, the testing accuracy reaches a peak. Corresponding to this stage, as shown in the right image of Fig. 4, the loss value of the testing is also decreasing until it reaches a minimum at the 90,000th iteration.

Table 1. The confusion matrix of our model on the KDEF database.

%	AN			DI			FE			HA			SA			SU			NE		
	NO	EY	MO	NO	EY	MO	NO	EY	MO	NO	EY	MO	NO	EY	MO	NO	EY	MO	NO	EY	MO
AN	83.5	80.5	80.2	5.9	10.7	9.2	1.1	0	0	0	0	0	6.4	9.1	7.5	1.0	2.5	0	0	0	0
DI	8.9	7.0	6.4	86.1	80.6	81.9	0	0	0	0.1	0	0	2.4	1.6	2.6	0	0.7	3.1	0	0	0
FE	0	1.5	4.7	0	0	0	91.8	89.1	86.0	1.5	4.7	7.6	0	0	0	3.2	2.5	4.4	0	0	0
HA	0	0	0	0	0	0	5.2	5.9	5.1	98.3	95.3	88.5	1.5	2.4	5.6	0	0	0	1.6	0.5	0.9
SA	7.3	11.0	8.7	7.6	7.0	5.9	1.9	5.0	8.9	0	0	3.9	89.6	86.9	85.9	0	1.1	1.5	2.6	0.8	
SU	0	0	0	0	0	0	0	0	0	0	0	0	0	0	0.5	95.8	90.3	91.4	1.3	3.4	2.7
NE	0	0	0	0	0	0	0	0	0	0.1	0	0	0	0	0.5	0	1.0	0	95.9	93.5	95.6

4.2 Experimental Results and Analysis

KDEF. As shown in Table 1, the accuracy of 91.6%, 88.3 and 87.5% was obtained in the cases of no-occlusion, occlusion of the eyes and occlusion of the mouth, respectively. Note that the average accuracy of the JAFFE dataset is slightly smaller than KDEF, but the overall law is consistent, which is not

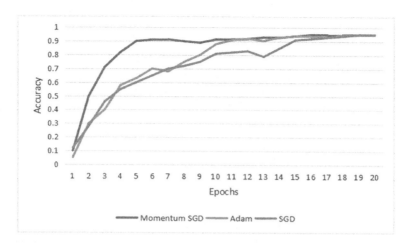

Fig. 5. Convergence time of different optimization algorithms.

listed here. It can be found that, in general, mouth occlusion will have a greater impact than eye occlusion, which also means that the mouth is more important in expression recognition. Mouth occlusion has a greater impact on the recognition accuracy of expressions of angry, fearful, happy and sad, while eye occlusion has a greater impact on the recognition accuracy of disgusted, surprised and neutral expressions.

Specifically, for angry, disgusted and sad, these three types of expressions are more likely to be confused when judged; happy is the expression with the highest accuracy. Relatively speaking, some happy expressions are recognized as fearful. This may be due to that these two expressions have some similarities in the change of facial morphology; neutral is not easily misjudged by other expressions, and their accuracy is relatively high and more stable under various circumstances; surprise is more likely to be misjudged as fearful and angry.

4.3   Evaluation of the Effects of Different Optimization Algorithms

In order to evaluate the performance of SGD, we select SGD, Adam and RMSProp for comparison and perform the above mentioned DCNN with Gabor. As shown in Fig. 5, the results show that there is great improvement in terms of the accuracy of training. Note that the improvement may be restricted by the amount of training data. Moreover, the training speed and gradient reduction process of the whole model have been greatly optimized.

4.4   Comparison with the State-of-the-Arts

As shown in Fig. 6 and Fig. 7, we can find that our experimental results are effective and robust, especially under occlusion compared with LGBPHS, Deep Nonlinear Network Structure, Gabor and DNMF.

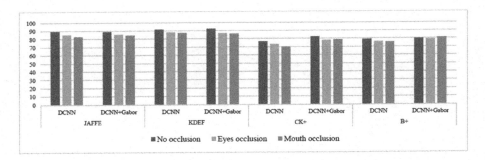

Fig. 6. Comparison among different methods in cross-data validation.

JAFFE Dataset. It can be observed from the results that all seven methods have higher precision under no-occlusion, both exceed 85%. Our approach has slight advantage, up to 89.5%. Under partial occlusion, each method has a different degree of reduction, especially the occlusion of the mouth. The results show that our method has excellent accuracy in eye occlusion and mouth occlusion, which arrive 85.5% and 83.1%, respectively. The accuracy is slightly lower than no occlusion condition, but is superior to all other methods. Among other methods, the Gabor method achieves better results in the case of no occlusion. As for partial occlusion, the unmodified VGG16 and LGBPHS perform slightly lower than other methods.

KDEF Dataset. We found that the accuracy under the KDEF dataset is higher than that under JAFFE, and the improvement of the model brings the improvement of accuracy, which shows that the improvement of our algorithm is effective. This may be owing to more explicit representation of the KDEF dataset and the larger amount of data than JAFFE.

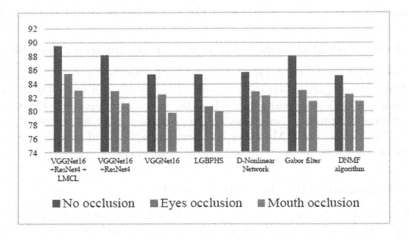

Fig. 7. Comparison between the proposed method and other methods in JAFFE.

5   Conclusion and Future Work

This paper has proposed a novel deep learning method for FER with various partial occlusion. We first reconstructed the facial expression data set under partial occlusion and perform preprocessing. We developed a novel "VGG + residual" CNN network based on the improved VGG16 network, and adapt a hybrid feature strategy to parallelize the Gabor filter with the above CNN. We used LMCL and momentum SGD to improve the traditional methods. Our model can greatly accomplish FER under various partial occlusion and achieve higher recognition accuracy than the state-of-the-arts. We have found out from the statistical results that the mouth occlusion has greater impact on the resulting recognition accuracy than that of eye occlusion.

Our method is not without limitation. The amount of the partially occluded facial expression data is not large enough. We will introduce more challenging partially occluded facial expression data under natural state into our data set. The recognition accuracy and efficiency still have room for improvement. It may work by introducing more advanced optimization strategies into our network. We will also attempt to apply our method in virtual human modelling systems. It would endow a virtual human more ability to "see" one's emotion by accurately recognizing various facial expressions, and thereby benefit the communication in the virtual world.

References

1. Brink, H., Vadapalli, H.B.: Deformable part models with CNN features for facial landmark detection under occlusion. In: ACM Press the South African Institute of Computer Scientists and Information Technologists, pp. 681–685 (2017)
2. Cheng, Y., Jiang, B., Jia, K.: A deep structure for facial expression recognition under partial occlusion. In: IEEE Tenth International Conference on Intelligent Information Hiding and Multimedia Signal Processing, pp. 211–214 (2014)
3. Ekman, P., Friesen, W.V.: Constants across cultures in the face and emotion. J. Pers. Soc. Psychol. **17**(2), 124–129 (1971)
4. García-Rojas, A., et al.: Emotional face expression profiles supported by virtual human ontology: research articles. Comput. Animation Virtual Worlds **17**(3–4), 259–269 (2006)
5. Goeleven, E., De-Raedt, R., Leyman, L., Verschuere, B.: The Karolinska directed emotional faces: a validation study. Cogn. Emot. **22**(6), 1094–1118 (2008)
6. Hammal, Z., Arguin, M.: Comparing a novel model based on the transferable belief model with humans during the recognition of partially occluded facial expressions. J. Vis. **9**(2), 22–28 (2009)
7. He, K., Zhang, X., Ren, S., Sun, J.: Deep residual learning for image recognition. In: IEEE Conference on Computer Vision and Pattern Recognition, pp. 1–12 (2015)
8. Kanopoulos, N., Vasanthavada, N., Baker, R.L.: Design of an image edge detection filter using the Sobel operator. IEEE J. Solid State Circuits **23**(2), 358–367 (1988)
9. Kotsia, I., Zafeiriou, S., Pitas, I.: Texture and shape information fusion for facial expression and facial action unit recognition. Pattern Recogn. **41**(3), 833–851 (2008)

10. Liu, P., Han, S., Meng, Z., Tong, Y.: Facial expression recognition via a boosted deep belief network. In: IEEE Conference on Computer Vision and Pattern Recognition, pp. 1–8 (2014)
11. Liu, S., Yang, X., Wang, Z., Xiao, Z., Zhang, J.: Real-time facial expression transfer with single video camera. Comput. Animation Virtual Worlds 27(3–4), 301–310 (2016)
12. Liu, W., Wen, Y., Yu, Z., Yang, M.: Large-margin softmax loss for convolutional neural networks. In: International Conference on Machine Learning, pp. 507–516 (2016)
13. Lyons, M.J., Akamatsu, S., Kamachi, M.: Coding facial expressions with Gabor wavelets. In: IEEE International Conference on Automatic Face and Gesture Recognition, pp. 200–205 (1998)
14. Pantic, M., Rothkrantz, L.J.M.: Automatic analysis of facial expressions the state of the art. IEEE Trans. Pattern Anal. Mach. Intell. 22(12), 1424–1445 (2000)
15. Qiao, F., Yao, N., Jiao, Z., Li, Z.: Emotional facial expression transfer from a single image via generative adversarial nets. Comput. Animation Virtual Worlds 29(6), e1819 (2018)
16. Shi, J., Ray, N., Zhang, H.: Shape based local thresholding for binarization of document images. Pattern Recogn. Lett. 33(1), 24–32 (2012)
17. Simard, P., Steinkraus, D., Platt, J.C.: Best practices for convolutional neural networks applied to visual document analysis. In: International Conference on Document Analysis and Recognition, pp. 958–963 (2003)
18. Simonyan, K., Zisserman, A.: Very deep convolutional networks for large-scale image recognition. In: International Conference of Learning Representation, pp. 1409–1417 (2014)
19. Towner, H., Slater, M.: Reconstruction and recognition of occluded facial expressions using PCA. In: Paiva, A.C.R., Prada, R., Picard, R.W. (eds.) ACII 2007. LNCS, vol. 4738, pp. 36–47. Springer, Heidelberg (2007). https://doi.org/10.1007/978-3-540-74889-2_4
20. Wallace, C.: A note on Darwins work on the expression of the emotions in man and animals. J. Abnorm. Psychol. Soc. Psychol. 16(5), 356–366 (1921)
21. Wang, H.: Cosface large margin cosine loss for deep face recognition. In: IEEE Conference on Computer Vision and Pattern Recognition, pp. 1801–1807 (2018)
22. Wen, Y., Zhang, K., Li, Z., Qiao, Yu.: A discriminative feature learning approach for deep face recognition. In: Leibe, B., Matas, J., Sebe, N., Welling, M. (eds.) ECCV 2016. LNCS, vol. 9911, pp. 499–515. Springer, Cham (2016). https://doi.org/10.1007/978-3-319-46478-7_31
23. Yang, L., Wang, S., Zhao, W., Zhao, Y.: Wgan-based robust occluded facial expression recognition. IEEE Access 7, 93594–93610 (2019)
24. Zhang, L., Brijesh, V., Dian, T., Vinod, C.: Facial expression analysis under partial occlusion: a survey. ACM Comput. Surv. 51(2), 1–49 (2018)
25. Zhuo, J., Chen, Z., Lai, J., Wang, G.: Occluded person re-identification. In: International Conference on Multimedia and Expo, pp. 1–6 (2018)
26. Tősér, Z., Jeni, L.A., Lőrincz, A., Cohn, J.F.: Deep learning for facial action unit detection under large head poses. In: Hua, G., Jégou, H. (eds.) ECCV 2016. LNCS, vol. 9915, pp. 359–371. Springer, Cham (2016). https://doi.org/10.1007/978-3-319-49409-8_29

Towards an Effective Approach for Face Recognition with DCGANs Data Augmentation

Sirine Ammar[1,2(✉)], Thierry Bouwmans[2], Nizar Zaghden[3], and Mahmoud Neji[1]

[1] Laboratoire MIRACL, Université de Sfax, Sfax, Tunisie
[2] Laboratoire MIA, Université de La Rochelle, La Rochelle, France
ammarsirine3@gmail.com
[3] SETIT (ISBS), Université de Sfax, Sfax, Tunisie

Abstract. Deep Convolutional Neural Networks (DCNNs) are widely used to extract high-dimensional features in various image recognition tasks [1] and have shown significant performance in face recognition. However, accurate real-time face recognition remains a challenge, mainly due to the high computation cost associated with the use of DCNNs and the need to balance precision requirements with time and resource restrictions. Besides, the supervised training process of DCNNs requires a large number of labeled samples. Aiming at solving the problem of data insufficiency, this study proposes a Deep Convolutional Generative Adversarial Net (DCGAN) based solution to increase the face dataset by generating synthetic images. Our proposed face recognition approach is based on FaceNet model. First, we perform face detection using MTCNN. After, a 128-D face embedding is extracted to quantify each face and a Support Vector Machine (SVM) is applied on top of the embeddings to recognize faces. In the experiment part, both LFW database and Chokepoint video database showed that our proposed approach with DCGANs data augmentation has improved the face recognition performance.

Keywords: DCNNs · DCGANs · Face recognition · FaceNet · MTCNN

1 Introduction

Despite the outstanding progress reached in face recognition using CNN, it still encounters challenging issues, such as the difficulty in obtaining sufficient learning images, since CNNs require a lot of data for learning. Generally, a large amount of training samples is useful to achieve high recognition accuracy. But, due to the lack of labeled samples, obtaining accurate results is difficult. Collecting such a dataset is not only time consuming, but also impractical. To solve this issue, an effective method is proposed is the technique of data augmentation, which generates virtual samples to increase the size of the training dataset,

© Springer Nature Switzerland AG 2020
G. Bebis et al. (Eds.): ISVC 2020, LNCS 12509, pp. 463–475, 2020.
https://doi.org/10.1007/978-3-030-64556-4_36

improve the accuracy and robustness of a classifier and reduce overfitting. A common method to enlarge the training data is to apply affine transformation (translation, rotation, brightness changes, filtering operations, adding gaussian noise). However, the produced images represent a high correlation with the original images. In addition, the structural images distribution is complex and mixed. To deal with these problems, Generative Adversarial Network (GAN) may be a possible choice. In this paper, we introduce one specific generative model, called, DCGAN to increase the face image dataset by generating human faces. The proposed approach efficiently expands the training data, mitigating the effects of misalignment, pose variations, lighting changes and over-fitting. Due to the large amount of parameters in DCGANs, they need a large amount of training samples. By adding more images, DCGAN's performance would be improved.

As compared to traditional machine learning methods, Deep Learning (DL) technologies have shown favorable performances in terms of accuracy and speed of image processing. Existing deep learning-based face recognition models employ a classification layer [2,3] on an ensemble of known identities. A middle bottleneck layer is considered as a vector mapping that generalizes recognition over all identities used for training. The disadvantages of this method are its indirect nature and its inefficiency. By using a bottleneck layer, the dimension of face representation remains very high. Some recent works use PCA to reduce this dimensionality [2], but this is a linear transformation that can be easily learnt in one layer of the network. Unlike these algorithms, FaceNet uses a loss function with a triplet based on LMNN [4] to directly train its output to be a compact 128-D encoding. In this paper, we propose a face recognition approach based on FaceNet model to directly learn a mapping from facial images to a compact euclidean space, in which distances correspond to a face similarity measure. Then, face verification, recognition and clustering can be simply performed with conventional methods with previously extracted encodings as feature vectors. Compared to conventional DL methods that use an intermediate bottleneck layer, our approach directly employs a trained DCNN to optimize the embedding itself. Triplets of approximately aligned matched / unmatched face patches are used for training, generated using online triplet mining. FaceNet allows a much greater representation efficiency.

The paper is organized as follows. In Sect. 2, we summarize the different data augmentation and face recognition techniques. Section 3 briefly presents the DCGAN architecture. Section 4 describes the FaceNet model and the triplet loss. Our proposed approach is described in Sect. 5. Section 6 presents the qualitative and quantitative results. Finally, we conclude the paper in Sect. 7.

2   Related Works

2.1   Image Data Augmentation Techniques

In this section, we present the methods based on image synthesis and augmentation that had the greatest effect. Collecting more training data allows a stronger generalization ability of the trained model. However, getting a large database with correctly labeled data is difficult and expensive. Therefore, data augmentation methods have emerged that generate large number of samples using affine transformations. Vincent et al. [5] introduced Gaussian noise, Masking noise and Salt-and-pepper noise to produce more corrupted images for training Stacked Denoising Autoencoders. Howard et al. [6] adopted flipping and cropping to enlarge the training dataset, even incorporated the original face image and its mirror to well represent the face. Xie et al. [7] added Gaussian noise to generate large number of noisy images. Wu et al. [8] introduced methods such as color casting, vignetting and lens distortion. Jiang et al. [9] proposed an efficient 3D reconstruction method to generate face images with different poses, illuminations and expressions. Mohammadzade and Hatzinakos [10] proposed an expression subspace projection algorithm to synthesize new expression images for each person. Seyyedsalehi et al. [11] generated visual face images with different expressions by using non-linear manifold separator neural network (NMSNN). Also, Shan et al. [12] proposed a landmark perturbation method to expand the training data to cope with mis-alignment. However, only face image's eye coordinates are perturbed with eightneighbor. Lv et al. [13] proposed a landmark perturbation and four synthesis methods (hairstyles, poses, glasses, illuminations). In this paper, we apply DCGANs as data augmentation method. The faces produced by DCGANs enlarge the training dataset, which alleviates the impacts of misalignment, pose and illumination changes.

2.2   Face Recognition

The conventional face recognition process includes face detection, face alignment (or pre-processing), feature representation (extraction) and classification. Among them, feature representation is the most basic step. Many approaches have been proposed for face representation. Ammar et al. [14] proposed a human identification system that combines both color, texture and shape features with some soft-biometric traits (hair color, skin tone, eyes color, face shape, etc.) to identify humans through their faces by making use of local and global features. In 2020, Ammar et al. [15] reviewed and classified the approaches that have been explored and evaluated in the field of face recognition into three categories: holistic, hybrid [16] and local. In 2017, Johannes and Armin [17] have demonstrated that eigenfaces are better than fisherfaces and LBP histograms for face representation. In 2016, LBP, Pyramid of Local Binary Pattern (PLBP) and Rotation Invariant Local Binary Pattern (RILBP) are evaluated by Khoi et al. [18] for face retrieval. Compared to conventional face recognition methods, CNNs are trained with a network-based data-driven method by combining both feature extraction and classification. Schroff et al. [19] propose the FaceNet model to learn a mapping from a face image to an euclidean space embedding, in which the distance of two faces measures their similarity. An angular margin penalty is proposed by Liu et al. [20] to simultaneously apply extra intra-class compactness and inter-class difference. An additive angular margin (ArcFace) loss function is presented by Deng et al. [21] to obtain more discriminative feature embeddings learned by CNNs to recognize faces. CNNs trained on 2-D facial images is fine-tuned with 3-D facial scans to perform well for 3-D face recognition. The 3-D context is invariant to the camouflage/make-up/lightening situations. Tornincasa et al. [22] use differential geometry to extract pertinent discriminant features from the query faces. Dagnes et al. [23] present an algorithm to capture face motion by calculating a minimal optimized marker layout. In Vankayala-pati et al. [24], radon and wavelet transforms are used for non-linear features extraction that are robust to changes in facial expression and illumination. In 2015, two DNN architectures [25] are proposed for face recognition, mentioned as DeepID3, which are reconstructed from the stacked convolutions of VGG and the inception layers of GoogLeNet. DeepID3 achieved high performance on iden-tification tasks. Zhu et al. [26] employ a DNN to distort faces at different views to a canonical frontal view. A CNN is learned that categorizes each face as cor-responding to a known identity. PCA and SVMs are applied for face verification. In Taigman et al. [3], faces are aligned to a general 3D shape model. A multi-class network is trained to recognize faces on more than 4000 identities. In Sun et al. [25,27], a compact and relatively inexpensive network is presented for the computation. A set of 25 of these networks is used, each performed on a separate facial patch. Using a combination of classification and verification loss, the net-works are trained. The verification loss is similar to the triplet loss we employ [4,28], that aims to minimize the distance between faces of the same identity and imposes a margin between the distance of faces of different identities. A DeepID model is implemented by Sun et al. [29] which contains multiple CNNs, allowing to use a strong feature extractor. DeepID takes as input facial patches as well as features extracted from several face positions. Sun et al. [27] extend DeepID to DeepID2, which includes both identification and verification signals for increasing inter-class variations whereas reducing intra-class variations. Sun et al. [2] proposed DeepID2+ to increase the performance by adding supervision information to all convolutional layers. Simonyan et al. [30] propose a VGG-16 architecture, which requires fewer training data than DeepFace and FaceNet and uses a simpler network than DeepID2. However, the construction of such a huge dataset exceeds the capabilities of most academic groups.

In this paper, we propose a face recognition approach based on FaceNet model with DCGANs data augmentation, that can deal with the above dis-cussed issues. Like other current works [3,29], our method is an entirely data-driven approach that directly learns its representation from the pixels of the face. Rather than using engineered features, we obtain a large dataset of labeled faces using DCGANs to achieve pose and illumination invariances. Our work based on FaceNet combines the output of a DCNN and an SVM for classification.

3 DCGANs

In this paper, we exploit the ability of DCGAN's generator [31] to artificially gen-erate more facial images similar to the original faces in the training dataset. The idea is to simultaneously train two adversarial neural networks. The first network is a discriminator that learns to determine weather the sample comes from the data distribution. The other is a generative model that aims to generate "fake" images that attempts to fool the discriminator. After several stages of training, the optimization will achieve a stable point where the discriminator will difficult to discern whether the data was "fake" or not. Mathematically, the training process of DCGANs can be seen as a minimax game. The generator G(z) takes a sampled input z from a uniform distribution. The discriminator D(.) takes x as input, being either images, from the database or output of generator G(z). During training, the discriminator tries to distinguish between selected database and G(z), i.e. attempts to maximize, log(D(x))+log(1-D(G(z))). Simultaneously, the generator attempts to deceive the discriminator by minimizing log(1-D(G(z))). The optimization will achieve a point of equilibrium where the discriminator is unable to distinguish between x and G(z), after multiple steps of training. The generator takes a noise vector as input, followed by a fully connected layer containing 8192 neurons and resized to the dimension of $4 \times 4 \times 1024$. Next, 4 transposed convolutional layers are used with stride of 2 and padding resulting in a reduction of the channels and an up-sampling of the features by factor of 2. The output image's size is of $64 \times 64 \times 3$. The input image with dimension $64 \times 64 \times 3$ is transmitted through 4 consecutive convolutional layers with the final output of dimension $4 \times 4 \times 512$. The last fully connected layer produces final output classes by a softmax activation function. It generates the probability that x is sampled from the true distribution. The final classification is done by attributing the class with the highest probability to a given image.

4   FaceNet

4.1   FaceNet Model

FaceNet is proposed by Schroff et al. [19] to successfully manage face detection and verification. FaceNet network transforms the face image into a 128-D euclidean space. It aims to identify the similarities and differences on the image dataset when is trained for triplet loss. The encodings are used as feature vectors for face verification and identification. The distance for the "same" samples would be much less than that between non similar random images. FaceNet [19] generally consists of two different basic architectures based on CNNs. The first category adds $1 \times 1 \times d$ convolutional layers between the standard convolutional layers of the Zeiler & Fergus [32] architecture, then gets a 22 layers NN1 model. The second category consists of Inception models based on GoogLeNet [33]. The inception network contains 4 branches from the left to right. It employs convolution with 1×1 filters as well as 3×3 and 5×5 filters and a 3×3 max pooling layer. Each branch uses a 1×1 convolution to achieve time complexity reduction. FaceNet model uses triplet loss function that allows vectors for the same identity to become more similar, while vectors of different identities should become less similar. The key advantage of this model is that it trains a neural network, which directly optimize the embedding itself rather than extracting them from a middle bottleneck layer as in conventional DL approaches.

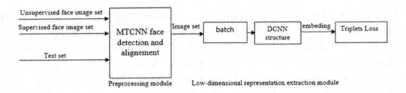

Fig. 1. FaceNet model structure, which consists of two modules: preprocessing and extraction of low-dimensional representation.

The most important part of the FaceNet model is the end-to-end learning of the entire system. The triplet loss allows directly reflecting what we want to perform in face verification, identification and categorization. The triplet loss of [27] assists to project all faces with a similar identity onto a single point in the embedding space. Figure 1 presents the structure of the FaceNet model.

4.2 Triplet Loss

To train a face recognition model, each input batch of data contains three images, the anchor, the positive sample and the negative sample. The triplet loss aims to minimize the distance between the anchor and the positive sample, which signifies the same person; also, to maximize the distance between the encodings of the anchor and the negative sample, which signifies a different identity. Triplet loss function is one of the best ways to learn a good 128-D encoding for each face. The anchor image represents the reference image used to calculate the triplet loss. Let's $f(x) \in \mathbb{R}^d$, where $f(x)$ represents the embedding which maps an image x into a d-dimensional euclidean space. This encoding is restrained to live on the d-dimensional hypersphere, *i.e.* $\|f(x)\|_2 = 1$. This loss is motivated in [4] in the context of the nearest neighbors clustering. A baseline image (anchor) x_i^a of a one person must be closer to all other images x_i^p of the "same" person than to any image x_i^n of a different person. Thus, this equation must be satisfied

$$\|f(x_i^a) - f(x_i^p)\|_2^2 + \alpha < \|f(x_i^a) - f(x_i^n)\|_2^2 \tag{1}$$

$$\forall (f(x_i^a), f(x_i^p), f(x_i^n)) \in \tau \tag{2}$$

where α is a margin that is imposed to achieve a better separation between positive and negative samples. Let N be the cardinality of τ, the set of all possible triplets in the training set. The generation of all possible triplets results in numerous triplets that should reach the restriction in Eq. 1. The process minimizes a loss on triplets that measures triplet satisfaction. These triplets would lead to a slower convergence.

5 Proposed Approach

Our proposed approach is based on DCGANs for data augmentation and FaceNet model for face classification. Sometimes a small number of data is used for CNN. By adding more images, CNN would become more efficient. In this paper, we address the problem of sample collection difficulties using data augmentation through the application of DCGANs. Thus, we add similar images which are created by DCGANs to the training face dataset as data augmentation. We assume that generated images have similar CNN features and work as similar images. In addition, we compare our DCGANs data augmentation method for face identification with the work of Pei et al. [34] who use standard data augmentation techniques. Furthermore, we present an approach based on both OpenCv and DL for face recognition. Our system starts by detecting regions of the face quickly and accurately, preprocessing and cropping the faces by computing face landmarks using MTCNN face detector, extracting 128-d face embeddings using FaceNet algorithm, training a face recognition model on the embeddings and finally applying SVM to classify faces in images and video streams. Our face recognition pipeline is presented in Fig. 2. First, we input an image or video frame to our face recognition system. Given the input image, we detect the location of a face in the image using a cascaded face landmark detector called Multi-task CNN (MTCNN). MTCNN [35] consists of three layers of deep convolutional networks, to detect and align the sample set. MTCNN integrates both joint face detection and alignment by multi-task learning. It consists of three stages. First, it generates candidate windows quickly through a shallow CNN. Next, the windows is refined by rejecting a large amount of non-faces windows via a more complex CNN. Finally, it uses a more performant CNN to refine the result and display the position of facial landmarks. The face is preprocessed and aligned by computing facial landmarks. MTCNN aims to construct the image pyramid of the corresponding face image. Face landmarks include five feature points, the nose, left eye, right eye, left mouth and the right mouth. Next, each face is represented by a DNN on a 128-D unit hypersphere based on FaceNet

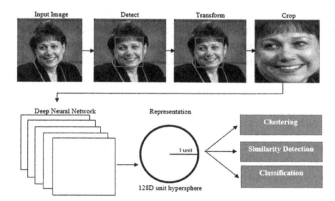

Fig. 2. An overview of the proposed face recognition pipeline.

model [19]. This method uses DCNN to map face images to an euclidean space where distances match to the face similarity measures. Compared with other representations of faces, this embedding has the benefit that a greater distance between two face embeddings signifies that the faces are probably not identical. The last step of our face identification model is to train a classifier based on the encodings previously produced. The network is trained so that the embedding space (squared L2 distances) directly corresponds to the face similarity. The faces of the same person have small distances and the faces of different identities have great distances. Once this embedding has been created, face verification can be simply done by thresholding the distance between the two points in this space. SVM was applied for the classification.

6   Results and Discussions

6.1   Datasets

Labeled Faces in the Wild (LFW) Dataset. The LFW dataset [36] is the standard benchmark for face verification/recognition, which includes 13,233 face images of 5,749 subjects. These images include changes in lighting, pose and facial expression. This dataset has a limitation is that only 1,680 identities out of a total of 5,749 subjects have more than one face image. A subset of the dataset consisting of 3137 images belonging to 62 subjects was used during our experiments, by selecting the subjects with 20 or more images.

Chokepoint Dataset. The Chokepoint video dataset [37] is designed for verification/identification of people in real world surveillance situations. Faces have variations in terms of pose, lighting, sharpness, as well as mis-alignment. It consists of 25 identities (19 men and 6 women) in portal 1 and 29 identities (23 men and 6 women) in portal 2. We used portal 1 for our experiments.

6.2   Evaluation

In our experiments, we first recognize faces in still images, then move on to the recognition of faces in videos. A label encoder is loaded that contains the "name" for the people our model can identify. Weak detections are rejected and the faces ROI are extracted to recognize people. The proposed method using DCGAN's generated images is compared to the work of Pei et al. [34] based on conventional data augmentation techniques (Translation, rotation, brightness change and filtering) and VGG-16 model for face identification. We added 100, 250 and 500 generated images per one class for LFW dataset [36] and 100 generated images per class on Chokepoint dataset [37].

Quality of Generated Images. In this paper, we trained a DCGAN model on two face datasets, the LFW dataset [36] and the Chokepoint video dataset [37]. Several quality images were produced. Various unrealistic images that could not be seen faces were generated. This emergence of many unrealistic images is caused by the lack of training images for DCGANs. Realistic and unrealistic images are picked up through our subjective assessment. The criterion was whether we could see them as human faces or not. Then, we add realistic images per one class on both datasets.

Results. As shown in Table 1, the more training samples are used, the higher the accuracy and performance of the model is. By adding 100 images per class, the results show that our method based on DCGANs data augmentation achieves an accuracy of 78.1% with LFW dataset[36]. After a period of collecting more data, the accuracy improves to 89.5%. Furthermore, with adding 500 samples per class, the accuracy can achieve 92.12%. Table 3 shows that the face recognition accuracy increases with 0.47 % when adding only 100 images per class using the Chokepoint video dataset [37]. Next, we compared our DCGANs data augmentation method with standard techniques. Results summarized in Table 2 & Table 4 show that our approach which combines DCGANs data augmentation and FaceNet model for face recognition is more effective than other methods. To verify the effectiveness of our approach based on FaceNet model, it is compared with traditional face recognition methods such as Principal Component Analysis (PCA) and Local Binary Patterns Histogram (LBPH). Experimental results show the effectiveness of our approach with DCGANs data augmentation compared to LBPH and PCA methods using only a small amount of samples. The proposed approach also outperforms the work of Pei et al. [34] based on VGG-16 model for face recognition and geometric transformations and filtering methods for data augmentation. Our approach also gives more accuracy than using VGG-16 model with DCGANs data augmentation with a difference of 7.86% and 12.11% using LFW dataset [36] and Chokepoint dataset [37], respectively. In Fig. 3(a), we can see that the face is correctly recognized with only 93.86% confidence when using the Chokepoint dataset [37]; however, this confidence is higher when applying data augmentation with DCGANs achieving 95,76% as shown in Fig. 3(b). It is shown that our approach has improved the face recognition performance with better recognition results.

Table 1. Face recognition accuracy with data augmentation using the proposed method.

	Number of augmented samples per class			
	+0	+100	+250	+500
LFW dataset [36]	0.64	0.781	0.895	**0.9212**

Table 2. Recognition performance with different methods using 62 classes from LFW dataset [36].

PCA method	50%
LBPH method	37%
CNN with geometric transformation and brightness augmentation method [34]	69.21%
CNN with filter operation augmentation method [34]	81.94%
CNN with DCGANs augmentation method	84.26%
Proposed approach with geometric transformation and brightness augmentation method	70.94%
Proposed approach with filter operation augmentation method	86.57%
Proposed approach with DCGANs augmentation method	**92.12%**

Table 3. Face recognition accuracy with data augmentation using the proposed method.

	Number of augmented samples per class	
	+0	+100
Chokepoint dataset [37]	94.71%	**95.18%**

Table 4. Recognition performance with different methods using portal 1 from Chokepoint dataset [37].

PCA method	50.4%
LBPH method	34.09%
CNN with geometric transformation and brightness augmentation method [34]	72.66%
CNN with filter operation augmentation method [34]	70.83%
CNN with DCGANs augmentation method	83.07%
Proposed approach with geometric transformation and brightness augmentation method	75.26%
Proposed approach with filter operation augmentation method	82.18%
Proposed approach with DCGANs augmentation method	**95.18%**

(a) Without data augmentation (b) With data augmentation

Fig. 3. Face confidence using Chokepoint dataset [37].

7 Conclusion

In this paper, first, we show how DCGANs data augmentation can be used to efficiently generate synthetic face images, to train an effective face recognition system, as an alternative to expensive data labeling and collection. Second, we describe a face recognition method based on FaceNet model as a way of obtaining more robust face representations that handles lighting, occlusion and pose. Our method directly learns an embedding into an euclidean space, instead of using a bottleneck layer. Another strength of our model is that it only requires minimum alignment (tight crops of the face region) which improves performance slightly. Our approach outperforms standard data augmentation methods and VGG-16 network with high recognition results. Further studies are needed to obtain more realistic generated images to further improve the recognition performance.

References

1. Ammar, S., Bouwmans, T., Zaghden, N., Neji, M.: Deep detector classifier (DeepDC) for moving objects segmentation and classification in video surveillance. IET Image Proc. **14**(8), 1490–1501 (2020)
2. Sun, Y., Wang, X., Tang, X.: Deeply learned face representations are sparse, selective, and robust. In: International Conference on Computer Vision and Pattern Recognition (CVPR), pp. 2892–2900 (2015)
3. Taigman Y., Yang M., Ranzato M., and Wolf L. Deepface: Closing the gap to human-level performance in face verification. In: IEEE Conference on Computer Vision and Pattern Recognition, pp. 1701–1708 (2014)
4. Weinberger, K.Q., Blitzer, J., Saul, L.K.: Distance metric learning for large margin nearset neighbor classification. J. Mach. Learn. Res. Adv. Neural Inf. Process. Syst. **10**(9), 207–244 (2009)
5. Vincent, P., Larochelle, H., Lajoie, I., Bengio, Y., Manzagol, P.: Stacked denoising autoencoders: learning useful representations in a deep network with a local denoising criterion. J. Mach. Learn. Res. **11**, 3371–3408 (2010)
6. Howard A.G.: Some improvements on deep convolutional neural network based image classification. arXiv:1312.5402 (2013)
7. Xie, J., Xu, L., Chen, E.: Image denoising and inpainting with deep neural networks. Adv. Neural Inf. Process. Syst. **1**, 341–349 (2012)
8. Wu, R., Yan, S., Shan, Y., Dang, Q., Sun, G.: Deep image: scaling up image recognition. arXiv preprint arXiv:1501.02876, January 2015
9. Jiang, D., Hu, Y., Yan, S., Zhang, L., Zhang, H., Gao, W.: Efficient 3d reconstruction for face recognition. Pattern Recon. **38**(6), 787–798 (2005)
10. Mohammadzade, H., Hatzinakos, D.: Projection into expression subspaces for face recognition from single sample per person. IEEE Trans. Affective Comput. **4**(1), 69–82 (2013)
11. Seyyedsalehi, S.Z., Seyyedsalehi, S.A.: Simultaneous learning of nonlinear manifolds based on the bottleneck neural network. Neural Process. Lett. **40**(2), 191–209 (2014)
12. Shan, S., Chang, Y., Gao, W., Cao, B., Yang, P.: Curse of mis-alignment in face recognition: problem and a novel mis-alignment learning solution. In: International Conference on Automatic Face and Gesture Recognition, pp. 314–320 (2004)

13. Lv, J., Shao, X., Huang, J., Zhou, X., Zhou, X.: Data augmentation for face recognition. Neurocomputing **230**(22), 184–196 (2017)
14. Ammar, S., Zaghden, N., Neji, M.: A framework for people re-identification in multi-camera surveillance systems. In: International Association for Development of the Information Society (2017)
15. Ammar, S., Bouwmans, T., Zaghden, N., Neji, M.: From moving objects detection to classification and recognition : A review for smart cities. Homes to Cities using Internet of Things, Handbook on Towards Smart World. CRC Press (2020)
16. Zaghden, N., Mullot, R., Alimi A.: A proposal of a robust system for historical document images indexing. Int. J. Comput. Appl. **11**(2) (2010)
17. Johannes, R., Armin, S.: Face recognition with machine learning in opencv fusion of the results with the localization data of an acoustic camera for speaker identification. ArXiv, abs/1707.00835 (2017)
18. Khoi, P., Thien, L.H., Viet, V.H.: Face retrieval based on local binary pattern and its variants: a comprehensive study. Adv. Comput. Sci. Appl. **7**, 249–258 (2016)
19. Schroff, F., Kalenichenko, D., Philbin, J.: Facenet: A unified embedding for face recognition and clustering. In: Proceedings of the IEEE Conference on Computer Vision and Pattern Recognition, vol. 7, no. 12, pp. 815–823 (2015)
20. Liu, W., Wren, Y., Yu, Z., Li, M., Raj, B., Song, L.: Sphereface: deep hypersphere embedding for face recognition. In: Proceedings of the IEEE Conference on Computer Vision and Pattern Recognition, vol. 22, no. 25, pp. 212–220 (2017)
21. Deng, J., Guo, J., Xue, N., Zafeiriou, S.: Arcface: Additive angular margin loss for deep face recognition. In: Proceedings of the IEEE Conference on Computer Vision and Pattern Recognition, vol. 16, no. 20, pp. 4690–4699 (2019)
22. Tornincasa, S., Vezzetti, E., Moos, S., Violante, M.G., Marcolin, F., Dagnes, N., Ulrich, L., Tregnaghi, G.F.: 3d facial action units and expression recognition using a crisp logic. Comput. Aided Des. Appl. **16**, 256–268 (2019)
23. Dagnes, N., et al.: Optimal marker set assessment for motion capture of 3d mimic facial movements. J. Biomech. **93**, 86–93 (2019)
24. Vankayalapati, H.D., Kyamakya, K.: Nonlinear feature extraction approaches with application to face recognition over large databases. Int. Workshop Nonlinear Dyn. Synchron. **20**(2), 44–48 (2009)
25. Sun, Y., Liang, D., Wang, X., Tang, X.: Deepid3: face recognition with very deep neural networks. arXiv, bs/1502.00873 (2015)
26. Zhu, Z., Luo, P., Wang, X., Tang, X.: Recover canonical-view faces in the wild with deep neural networks. ArXiv, abs/1404.3543:5325–5334 (2014)
27. Sun, Y., Chen, Y., Wang, X., Tang, X.: Deep learning face representation by joint identification-verification. In: NIPS'14: International Conference on Neural Information Processing Systems, vol. 2, pp. 1988–1996, December 2008
28. Schultz, M., Joachims, T.: Learning a distance metric from relative comparisons. In: Thrun, S., Saul, L., Schölkopf, B. (eds.) NIPS, vol. 2, pp. 41–48 (2004)
29. Sun, Y., Wang, X., Tang, X.: Deep learning face representation from predicting 10,000 classes. IEEE Conf. Comput. Vis. Pattern Recogn. **23**(28), 1891–1898 (2014)
30. Simonyan, K., Zisserman, K.: Very deep convolutional networks for large-scale image recognition. arXiv, pp 1409–1556 (2014)
31. Radford, A., Metz, L., Chintala, S.: Unsupervised representation learning with deep convolutional generative adversarial networks. CoRR, pp. 1–9 (2015)
32. Zeiler, M.D., Fergus, R.: Visualizing and understanding convolutional networks. In: European Conference on Computer Vision, pp. 818–833 (2014)
33. Szegedy, C., et al.: Going deeper with convolutions. In: IEEE Conference on Computer Vision and Pattern Recognition (CVPR), pp. 1–9 (2015)

34. Pei, Z., Xu, H., Zhang, Y., Guo, M.: Face recognition via deep learning using data augmentation based on orthogonal experiments. Electronics **8**(10), 1088 (2019)
35. Zhang, K., Zhang, Z., Li, Z., Qiao, Y.: Joint face detection and alignment using multitask cascaded convolutional networks. IEEE Signal Process. Lett. **23**(10), 1499–1503 (2016)
36. Huang, G.B., Ramesh, M., Tamara, B., Learned-Miller, E.: Labeled faces in the wild: a database for studying face recognition in unconstrained environments. University of Massachusetts, Amherst, 07(49), October 2008
37. Wong, Y., Chen, S., Mau, S., Sanderson, C., Lovell, B.C.: Patch-based probabilistic image quality assessment for face selection and improved video-based face recognition. In: Computer Vision and Pattern Recognition, pp. 81–88, June 2011

Controlled AutoEncoders to Generate Faces from Voices

Hao Liang$^{(\boxtimes)}$, Lulan Yu$^{(\boxtimes)}$, Guikang Xu$^{(\boxtimes)}$, Bhiksha Raj$^{(\boxtimes)}$, and Rita Singh$^{(\boxtimes)}$

Carnegie Mellon University, Pittsburgh, PA 15213, USA
hliang2@andrew.cmu.edu, {lulany,guikangx}@alumni.cmu.edu, {bhiksha,rsingh}@cs.cmu.edu

Abstract. Multiple studies in the past have shown that there is a strong correlation between human vocal characteristics and facial features. However, existing approaches generate faces simply from voice, without exploring the set of features that contribute to these observed correlations. A computational methodology to explore this can be devised by rephrasing the question to: "how much would a target face have to change in order to be perceived as the originator of a source voice?" With this in perspective, we propose a framework to morph a target face in response to a given voice in a way that facial features are implicitly guided by learned voice-face correlation in this paper. Our framework includes a guided autoencoder that converts one face to another, controlled by a unique model-conditioning component called a *gating controller* which modifies the reconstructed face based on input voice recordings. We evaluate the framework on VoxCelab and VGGFace datasets through human subjects and face retrieval. Various experiments demonstrate the effectiveness of our proposed model.

Keywords: Controlled autoencoder, Face generation, Speech-face association learning, Voice-face biometric matching

1 Introduction

Curiosity has long driven humans to picture what someone else looks like upon hearing his/her voice. One of the assumptions, presumably made based on millennia of experience, is that there exists a statistical relation between what a person *looks* like, and what they *sound* like [1]. Some of these relations are immediately obvious, *e.g.* we expect the visage that goes with old-sounding voices to look old, and that of female voices to be female. Besides these obvious covariates, however, it may be expected that there are other unapparent dependencies between human vocal characteristics and facial features, since humans are able to associate faces with voices with surprising accuracy [2].

In trying to visualize the face behind a voice, however, we do not generally begin *de novo*, drawing up the face from whole cloth. Indeed, if one were to try

© Springer Nature Switzerland AG 2020
G. Bebis et al. (Eds.): ISVC 2020, LNCS 12509, pp. 476–487, 2020.
https://doi.org/10.1007/978-3-030-64556-4_37

to imagine the source of a sound such as voice with no prior information at all, it is highly unlikely that one would picture anything resembling a face. Therefore, we visualize faces based on two hypotheses:

- First, that in identifying the sound as a human voice, we draw upon the general shape of human faces, rather than any physical object that could produce the sound, and
- Second, that we draw upon an actual imagined face and make the modifications we deem necessary to match the voice.

The problem of *automatically* guessing speakers' faces from voice recordings has recently gained some popularity (or notereity, depending on the reader's perspective) [3–5]. The proposed approaches have taken two paths. The first, "matching" approach finds the most suitable face from a collection [6,7], which is fundamentally restricted by the selection of faces it can choose from and cannot generate entirely novel faces. The second, "generation" approach attempts to *synthesize* the facial image [3]. The approach embodies the first of our two hypotheses above: the proposed solutions learn a generic statistical model for the relationship between voices and face-like images, which they use to generate faces from novel voices. However, learning such statistical models is fraught with challenge. As [8] discover, direct modelling of statistical dependencies can result in models that often do not generate images that are even facelike. More sophisticated approaches do manage to generate face-like imagery, but these often show distortions [9,10]. While one may nevertheless try to produce better-quality visualizations, these techniques are dependent more on the well-known ability of GANs and similar models to hallucinate near-perfect faces [10,11], than on any dependence of these faces on all but the highest-level aspects of the voice, such as gender and age. Even so, they will still suffer problems such as *mode collapse* (whereby all voices end up producing the same face)[3,12], and lack of variety in the generated faces [11].

In this paper we take a different approach based on the second of our hypotheses above: that it may be easier to generate realistic facsimiles of a speaker's face if one were to begin with an initial template of an actual face and only make the minimal changes necessary to it (retaining as many features from the input face as possible), to make it match the voice. Accordingly, we propose a new model that begins with an initial "proposal" face image, and makes adjustments to it according to information extracted from the voice.

Our proposed model, which we will refer to as a *controlled AutoEncoder* (CAE), comprises two components. The primary component is a scaffolding based on a U-net-like [13] autoencoder, which takes in the proposal face and outputs a redrawn face. In the absence of other signals, the network must regenerate the input proposal face. The second component, which accepts the voice input, is a gating *controller* that modifies the parameters of the decoder based on information derived from the voice, to modify the generated face to match the voice. While being trained, the model also includes a discriminative component that is used to optimize the parameters of the network. The entire model is learned using a set of losses that simultaneously capture the degree of match to the target (speaker's) face and deviation from the proposal face. The CAE has several advantages over prior models. Being fundamentally an autoencoder, the output does not diverge from a face. As a morphing mechanism, rather than a genreating one, it does not face problems such as mode collapse. Diversity of output may be obtained simply by changing the proposal face.

Experimental results show that our model performs well under several evaluation metrics, including human subjective evaluation, feature similarity and face retrieval performance.

2   The Controlled AutoEncoder Model

The purpose of our model is to modify an input "proposal" face image to best match a given voice. The model has two components: an autoencoder based on a U-net-like [13] structure that derives a latent representation of the proposal face and attempts to reconstruct the latter from it, and a gating *controller* that modifies the parameters of the decoder based on the input speech signal. We describe the two below.

2.1   The AutoEncoder Scaffold

The main scaffold of our model is an autoencoder that derives a latent representation from the proposal face and reconstructs it from this representation. We specifically choose the U-net structure [13] for reasons we will shortly explain. The U-net includes an *encoder* that comprises a sequence of downsampling convolutional layers, ending finally in a simple, low-dimensional representation of the input image. This is followed by a *decoder* that comprises a sequence of upsampling *transpose-convolutional* layers that recreate the input image from the latent representation. The structure of the entire network is symmetric around its central latent-representation layer – corresponding to each layer of the encoder is a complementary decoder layer that is at an identical distance (or depth) from the central latent-representation layer, and has the same size as its encoder complement.

What distinguishes the U-net from conventional autoencoders is that the U-net also includes *direct* "skip" connections from each encoder layer to its complementary decoder layer. This is particularly relevant to our model, since it provides a pathway for information about the details of the face to be retained, while permitting high-level latent characteristics to be modified.

The blue components of Fig. 1 illustrate the U-net AE scaffolding of our model.

In our implementation the encoder consists of 4 convolutional layers with 64,128,256 and 512 output channels. All convolutional filters are size 3×3. Convolutional layers followed by maxpooling layers of size 2×2, with stride 2. The decoder is the mirror image of the encoder, sans the pooling layers. The transpose convolution in the decoder has a stride of size 2. Input images are rescaled to $3 \times 64 \times 64$ and output images too are the same size.

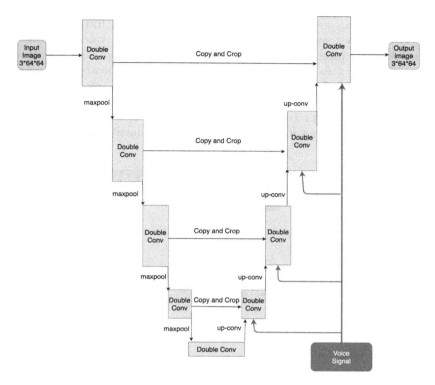

Fig. 1. The controlled AE model architecture. DoubelConv represents a layer with two convolutional neural networks, with a batchnorm layer appending to each of them.

2.2 The Gating Controller

The gating controller modifies the *trasverse convolutional filters* of the decoder, based on the voice signal.

In our setup, the voice recordings, duly endpointed, are first transformed into a 64-dimensional log mel-spectrographic representation, computed using an analysis window of 25 ms and a frameshift of 10 ms. The resulting spectrographic representation is fed to an *embedding* network, which produces a 64-dimensional embedding of the voice signal. The voice embedding is subsequently input, in parallel, to a number of linear layers, one each corresponding to each layer of the decoder. The linear layer corresponding to each decoder layer produces as many outputs as the number of convolutional filter parameters in the decoder layer. The outputs of the linear layer are passed through a sigmoid activation. The outputs of the sigmoid multiply the parameters of the filters, thereby modifying them.

The pink components of Fig. 1 illustrate the overall operation of the gating controller. Figure 2 shows the details of the gating control for *one* of the decoder layers. The dotted lines in the figure show paths to other layers.

The embedding network is a key component of this framework, as it is intended to extract speaker-specific information from the voice. For our work we employ an architecture derived from [10], where it was found to be effective for biometric voice-to-face matching. Table 1 shows the architecture of the embedding network. It too is a convolutional network t_0 t_1 *etc.* are the lengths (temporal) of the input after each layer, which compresses the input length with a stride of 2. We found it most effective to pre-train the voice embedding network, using the DimNet framework from [10], and to subsequently fix the network.

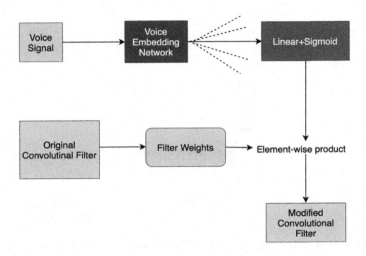

Fig. 2. The gating controller

3   Training and Inference

3.1   Training the Network

The network is trained on a collection of training instances, where each instance comprises an original face, a target voice and the corresponding target face. We optimize the parameters of the network to try to ensure that the output of the U-net stays close to its input, while simultaneously capturing the identity of the speaker. To support this, during the learning phase, we include two additional components, that work on the image produced by the model:

– A binary *discriminator* that is intended to ensure that the generated images are facelike. The architecture for which is also described in Table 1.
– A multi-class *classifier* which tries to enforce the visual identity of the speaker on the generated face. The classifier is a shared structure with the discriminator, with the exception that the final representation layer of the discriminator forks off into a multi-class softmax layer with as many outputs as we have subjects in the training data.

Table 1. Detailed network architecture. In voice embedding network, Conv $3_{/2,1}$ denotes a 1D convolutional layer with kernel size 3, stride 2 and padding 1. BN denotes batchnorm. In discriminator/classifier, Conv $1 \times 1_{/1,1}$ denotes a 2D convolutional layer with kernel size 1×1, stride 1 and padding 0. They share these structures, and for the last layer, discriminator has: FC 64×1, Sigmoid as activation, and output shape is 1. Classifier has: FC $64 \times k$, Softmax as activation, and output shape is k.

Voice embedding network			Discriminator/Classifier		
Layer	Act.	Output shape	Layer	Act.	Output shape
Input	-	$64 \times t_0$	Input	-	$3 \times 64 \times 64$
Conv $3_{/2,1}$	BN+ReLU	$256 \times t_1$	Conv $1 \times 1_{/1,0}$	LReLU	$32 \times 64 \times 64$
Conv $3_{/2,1}$	BN+ReLU	$384 \times t_2$	Conv $3 \times 3_{/2,1}$	LReLU	$64 \times 32 \times 32$
Conv $3_{/2,1}$	BN+ReLU	$576 \times t_3$	Conv $3 \times 3_{/2,1}$	LReLU	$128 \times 16 \times 16$
Conv $3_{/2,1}$	BN+ReLU	$864 \times t_4$	Conv $3 \times 3_{/2,1}$	LReLU	$256 \times 8 \times 8$
Conv $3_{/2,1}$	BN+ReLU	$64 \times t_5$	Conv $3 \times 3_{/2,1}$	LReLU	$512 \times 4 \times 4$
AvgPool $3_{/2,1}$	-	64×1	Conv $4 \times 4_{/1,0}$	LReLU	$64 \times 1 \times 1$

We employ a number of losses to train the network. We explain these below. In the explanation we represent real faces with f, synthetic faces with $\hat{f}$, voice with v, and identity label with I. In terms of model components, we use G to represent the generator (the scaffolding), D for the discriminator, and C for classifier.

- **L1-norm loss**: $L_{L1}(f_1, f_2)$ computes the total L_1 norm of the error between the RGB values of two face images f_1 and f_2.
- **Classifier loss**: $L_c(f, I)$ is the cross-entropy between the classifier's output and a one-hot representation of the identity of the speaker.
- **Discriminator loss**: $L_d(f, I)$ computes a binary cross entropy between the discriminator output and a binary label that specifies if the image input to the discriminator is synthetic or real.

The actual training paradigm, which is inspired by [6,10], StarGAN [14] and CycleGAN [15], tries to simultaneously satisfy multiple objectives.

First, the output of the generator must be similar to the target face, $i.e.$ $G(f_a, v_b) \approx f_b$, where f_a denotes the face image of original identity A and v_b denotes the voice embedding of target identity B. In addition, the generated face should resemble the original identity, $i.e.$ $G(f_a, v_b) \approx f_a$. Likewise, the generator should be capable of generating the original face back when taking the fake image B and voice of A as input, $i.e.$ $G(G(f_a, v_b), v_a) = f_a$. The functionality of the discriminator is determining if an input image is synthetic or natural, $i.e.$ $D(f) = 1, D(\hat{f}) = 0$. The goal of the classifier is to determine if the image produced in response to a voice is indeed the face of the target, i.e. is $C(\hat{f_B}) = B$. With the aforementioned building blocks, the complete training process as is explained in Algorithm 1.

Algorithm 1. Training algorithm of Our model

Input: A set of voice recordings and labels(V, I_v). A set of labeled face images with labels(F, I_f). A pre-trained fixed voice embedding network E(v) tuned under a speaker recognition task.

Output: Generator parameters θ_g

1: **while** not converge **do**
2:     Randomly sample a face image from F (f_A, I_A);
3:     Randomly sample a voice recording from V (v_B, I_B);
4:     Retrieve the corresponding face image of B (f_B, I_B);
5:     Retrieve the corresponding voice recording of A (v_A, I_A);
6:     Get voice embedding $e_B = E(v_B)$;
7:     Update the discriminator D(f; θ_d) with loss
         $\Delta_{\theta_d}(L_d(G(f_A, e_B; \theta_d), 0) + L_d(f_A, 1))$;
8:     Update the classifier C(f; θ_c) with loss
         $\Delta_{\theta_c}(L_c(C(f_A; \theta_c), I_A))$;
9:     Get fake face of B $\hat{f}_B = G(f_A, e_B; \theta_g)$;
10:    Get voice embedding $e_A = E(v_A)$;
11:    Update the generator with loss
         $\Delta_{\theta_g}(\lambda_1 L_{L1}(\hat{f}_B, f_A) + \lambda_2 L_{L1}(\hat{f}_B, f_B) + \lambda_3 L_c(C(\hat{f}_B; \theta_c), I_B) + \lambda_4 L_d(D(\hat{f}_B; \theta_d), 1)$
         $+ \lambda_5 L_{L1}(G(\hat{f}_b, e_A; \theta_g), f_A))$;
12: **end while**
13: **return** θ_g

3.2 Inference

During the inference time, a proposal face image f_a and a target voice's embedding v_b are injected to the generator network, and a face image $\hat{f}$ is synthesized.

4 Experiments

4.1 Dataset

In this paper, we chose VoxCeleb [16] and VGGFace [17] datasets, given that there exists intersection on the celebrity identities presented in the two datasets. Specifically, 149,354 voice recordings and 139,572 face images of 1,225 subjects are found in the intersection in total.

4.2 Experiments

We used Adam optimizer with batch size 1. Note that it makes no sense using a value of batch size other than 1. The reason being, in our proposed framework, each pair of voice and face is unique, thus it requires a unique set of network weights to perform generation. After grid search, we finalized the learning rate to be 0.0002, $\beta_1 = 0.5$, and $\beta_2 = 0.999$. Also, we trained the discriminator and generator with ratio 1:1, using $\lambda_1 = 1$, $\lambda_2 = 10$, $\lambda_3 = 1$, $\lambda_4 = 1$, $\lambda_5 = 10$. Results for this part are illustrated in Fig. 3.

To validate the model indeed performs as we expect, we present visualizations of the following settings:

- **Fix the proposal face, change the input voice.** This is to confirm our model's ability of generating different faces based on the same proposal face.
- **Fix the input voice, change the proposal face.** This is to confirm our model's ability of generating the target face based on different proposal faces.

Example results are shown in Fig. 3(e) and 3(f) respectively. Results are random selections from our data and are not cherry picked. We can confirm that our model is able to generate a target face by performing necessary modifications to the proposal faces. Figures 3(a), 3(b), 3(c), 3(d) also compare faces generated from voices by our CAE to those generated by the technique from [10], which is currently a state of the art. For example, the faces in the upper left corner of (a), (b), (c), (d) represent the original input face, corresponding face of the target voice, generated face using our model, generated face using [10] respectively.

4.3 Evaluation

Evaluation of generative models like GANs models is always tricky and several methods have been proposed [18] for it. Considering the speciality of our task which requires the output image to keep features from both faces, however, classification error [10], Fréchet Inception Distance (FID) [19] and reconstruction error, which are the most common evaluation metrics, are not good options. Instead, we resort to human subjective votes – one of the most mature and solid method – as our first evaluation metric, and *retrieval* as our second.

Human Subjective Evaluation. The human subject method is broadly adopted in many generative models [20–23] because of its intuitiveness and reliability when the number of samples becomes large. In this task, we conducted human subjective evaluation through interviews. To ensure the feasibility and reliability, the interviewers were first asked to finish a real-image mapping, which contains two images and their corresponding voices, and map the images with the voices. A 89% mapping accuracy was obtained from 20 subjects, performing 100 tests each, validating our conjecture: human subjective mapping between voices and images is reliable and robust. Next, they were shown a generated face image that was synthesized with our model, its corresponding voice audio, and another randomly generated face image which has the same gender, then asked to map the voice to one of the two images.

All the interviewers were asked to rate in total 100 rounds of tests. Finally, a 72% mapping accuracy was achieved. Based on the result, we are convinced we have reached our goal – to generate a face behind a voice by only modifying necessary features from a proposal face (Table 2).

Feature Similarity and Face Retrieval. To make our results more convincing, we adopted the evaluation strategies from [3]. We reused the face embedding network we got from our training to get three 64-dimensional feature vectors for

484   H. Liang et al.

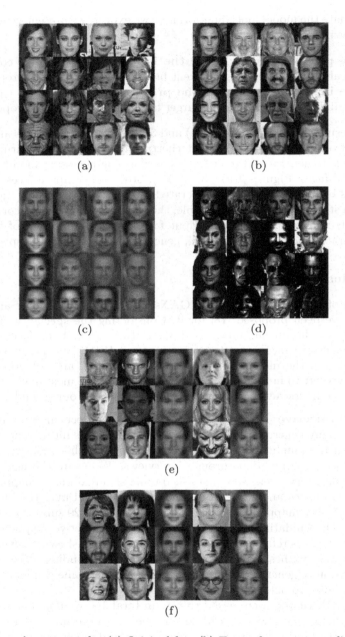

Fig. 3. Experiment results (a) Original face (b) Target face corresponding to input voice (c) Generated face using CAE (d) Generated face using [10] (e) the first column shows the proposal face. subsequent pairs show target and generated faces. (f) The first column shows the target face. Subsequent pairs show proposal and generated faces. (Best viewed in color). (Color figure online)

Fig. 4. Face retrieval results. The first column corresponds to the target face, the second column corresponds to the generated face, and the following five columns correspond to the retrieval results, in ranked order. (Best viewed in color). (Color figure online)

Table 2. Human subjective evaluation accuracy. Random guess is set up as a baseline, which is 50%.

Task	Accuracy (%)
Real image maping	89
Generated image mapping(CAE)	**72**
Random	50

the generated face images, original input image and the corresponding image of the voice respectively. Then we calculated the cosine similarity between the generated image's embedding vector and the other two. The result is shown in Table 3, indicating out results complete the goal of maintaining features from both faces.

Table 3. Feature cosine similarity. Here g_C, A, B denotes generated face image from our model(CAE), input image and corresponding face image of input voice respectively.

Mapping pair	Cos
g_C, A	**0.32**
g_C, B	**0.42**
Random mapping	0.21

In addition to this, we also utilized face retrieval, where we reused the classifier we obtained from training again and injected the generated face image as input, and got top 5 faces retrieved, i.e. whose corresponding value in the output vector of classifier lies in top 5. If the original face was in the top 5, we marked it as a successful retrieval. The successful ratios of our model was **21%**, in a 500 images retrieval task. Some samples are shown in Fig. 4.

5   Conclusion

We presented a novel model, the Controlled AutoEncoder, for modifying human face images to match input voices. The model uses conditioning voice input as a *controller*, to modify output images. While this is seen to work well in the setting of conditional production of face images, we believe the model has wider applicability in other problems, which we are investigating. Within the proposed framework too, much room remains for improvement. Current results seem to indicate that the entire face is modified, as opposed to specific components of it. We are conducting investigations into whether finer control may be exercised over this process.

References

1. Zhu, L.L., Beauchamp, M.: Mouth and voice: a relationship between visual and auditory preference in the human superior temporal sulcus. J. Neurosci. Official J. Soc. Neurosci. **37**, 02 (2017)
2. Kim, C., Shin, H.V., Oh, T.-H., Kaspar, A., Elgharib, M., Matusik, W.: On learning associations of faces and voices. In: Proceedings of Asian Conference on Computer Vision (ACCV) (2018)
3. Oh, T.-H., et al.: Speech2face: learning the face behind a voice. In: Proceedings of the IEEE/CVF Conference on Computer Vision and Pattern Recognition (CVPR), June 2019
4. Sadoughi, N., Busso, C.: Speech-driven expressive talking lips with conditional sequential generative adversarial networks. CoRR, vol. abs/1806.00154 (2018)
5. Wiles, C., Koepke, A., Zisserman, A.: X2face: a network for controlling face generation by using images, audio, and pose codes. In: European Conference on Computer Vision (2018)
6. Wen, Y., Ismail, M.A., Liu, W., Raj, B., Singh, R.: Disjoint mapping network for cross-modal matching of voices and faces. In: International Conference on Learning Representations (2019)
7. Nagrani, A., Albanie, S., Zisserman, A.: Seeing voices and hearing faces: cross-modal biometric matching. In: IEEE Conference on Computer Vision and Pattern Recognition (2018)
8. Duarte, A., et al.: "Wav2pix: speech-conditioned face generation using generative adversarial networks. In: 2019 IEEE International Conference on Acoustics, Speech and Signal Processing (ICASSP). IEEE (2019)
9. Li, H., Li, B., Tan, S., Huang, J.: Detection of deep network generated images using disparities in color components. arXiv e-prints, p. arXiv:1808.07276, August 2018
10. Wen, Y., Raj, B., Singh, R.: Face reconstruction from voice using generative adversarial networks. In: Advances in Neural Information Processing Systems, pp. 5266–5275 (2019)
11. Bian, Y., Wang, J., Jun, J.J., Xie, X.-Q.: Deep convolutional generative adversarial network (dcgan) models for screening and design of small molecules targeting cannabinoid receptors. Molecular pharmaceutics **16**(11), 4451–4460 (2019)
12. Chen, H., Lu, C.: Nested variance estimating vae/gan for face generation. In: International Joint Conference on Neural Networks (IJCNN) 2019, pp. 1–8 (2019)

13. Ronneberger, O., Fischer, P., Brox, T.: U-Net: convolutional networks for biomedical image segmentation. In: Navab, N., Hornegger, J., Wells, W.M., Frangi, A.F. (eds.) MICCAI 2015. LNCS, vol. 9351, pp. 234–241. Springer, Cham (2015). https://doi.org/10.1007/978-3-319-24574-4_28
14. Choi, Y., Choi, M., Kim, M., Ha, J.-W., Kim, S., Choo, J.: Stargan: unified generative adversarial networks for multi-domain image-to-image translation. In: Proceedings of the IEEE Conference on Computer Vision and Pattern Recognition (2018)
15. Zhu, J., Park, T., Isola, P., Efros, A.A.: Unpaired image-to-image translation using cycle-consistent adversarial networks. In: IEEE International Conference on Computer Vision (ICCV) 2017, pp. 2242–2251 (2017)
16. Nagrani, A., Chung, J.S., Zisserman, A.: Voxceleb: a large-scale speaker identification dataset. In: INTERSPEECH (2017)
17. Parkhi, O.M., Vedaldi, A., Zisserman, A., et al.: Deep face recognition. In: bmvc, vol. 1, no. 3, p. 6 (2015)
18. Borji, A.: Pros and cons of gan evaluation measures. Comput. Vision Image Understanding **179**, 41–65 (2019)
19. Heusel, M., Ramsauer, H., Unterthiner, T., Nessler, B., Hochreiter, S.: Gans trained by a two time-scale update rule converge to a local nash equilibrium. In: Advances in Neural Information Processing Systems 30, pp. 6626–6637 (2017)
20. Zhou, S., Gordon, M.L., Krishna, R., Narcomey, A., Li, F., Bernstein, M.: HYPE: a benchmark for human eye perceptual evaluation of generative models. In: Advances in Neural Information Processing Systems 32: Annual Conference on Neural Information Processing Systems 2019, NeurIPS 2019, 8–14 December 2019, Vancouver, BC, Canada, pp. 3444–3456 (2019)
21. Bau, D., et al.: Gan dissection: visualizing and understanding generative adversarial networks. In: Proceedings of the International Conference on Learning Representations (ICLR) (2019)
22. Lin, K., Li, D., He, X., Zhang, Z., Sun, M.-T.: Adversarial ranking for language generation, ser. NIPS'17, pp. 3158–3168 (2017)
23. Yu, L., Zhang, W., Wang, J., Yu, Y.: Seqgan: sequence generative adversarial nets with policy gradient. In: Proceedings of the Thirty-First AAAI Conference on Artificial Intelligence, ser. AAAI 2017. AAAI Press, pp. 2852–2858 (2017)

Gender and Age Estimation Without Facial Information from Still Images

Georgia Chatzitzisi[1], Michalis Vrigkas[2(✉)], and Christophoros Nikou[1]

[1] Department of Computer Science and Engineering, University of Ioannina,
Ioannina, Greece
{gchatzizisi,cnikou}@uoi.gr
[2] Department of Communication and Digital Media, University of Western
Macedonia, Kastoria, Greece
mvrigkas@uowm.gr

Abstract. In this paper, the task of gender and age recognition is performed on pedestrian still images, which are usually captured in-the-wild with no near face-frontal information. Moreover, another difficulty originates from the underlying class imbalance in real examples, especially for the age estimation problem. The scope of the paper is to examine how different loss functions in convolutional neural networks (CNN) perform under the class imbalance problem. For this purpose, as a backbone, we employ the Residual Network (ResNet). On top of that, we attempt to benefit from appearance-based attributes, which are inherently present in the available data. We incorporate this knowledge in an autoencoder, which we attach to our baseline CNN for the combined model to jointly learn the features and increase the classification accuracy. Finally, all of our experiments are evaluated on two publicly available datasets.

Keywords: Gender classification · Age estimation · Deep imbalanced learning

1 Introduction

Gender and age classification has been studied in the literature over the last decade and recently has gained much more interest due to the large availability of data [2, 7, 12]. In recent years, deep learning methods, such as CNNs, have been gradually applied to age estimation and have achieved better results than hand-crafted features. Yi et al. [20] introduced a relatively shallow CNN architecture and a multi-scale analysis strategy to learn in an end-to-end manner the age label of a facial image. Niu et al. [11] formulated the age estimation problem as an ordinal regression problem using a series of binary classification tasks. Chen et al. [2] proposed a ranking-CNN framework, in which a series of basic CNNs were employed and their binary outputs were aggregated. A separate CNN for each ordinal age group was learned, allowing each sub-CNN to capture different patterns for different age groups.

© Springer Nature Switzerland AG 2020
G. Bebis et al. (Eds.): ISVC 2020, LNCS 12509, pp. 488–500, 2020.
https://doi.org/10.1007/978-3-030-64556-4_38

Several hybrid methods predicting age and gender simultaneously with other facial attributes have also been reported in the literature [5]. Levi *et al.* [8] were the among first to use a CNN architecture for the problem of age and gender classification with a relatively shallow architecture. Rodriguez *et al.* [13] introduced the visual attention mechanism to discover the most informative and reliable parts in a face image for improving age and gender classification. Dual *et al.* [4] integrated a CNN for feature extraction and an extreme learning machine (ELM) [6] for classifying the intermediate results. It is yet another popular idea to make use of body-part information and jointly utilize global CNN features with person, object and, scene attributes [18].

Visual attention mechanism has also been used in pedestrian attribute recognition. Sarfraz *et al.* [17] introduced a model with view guidance to make view-specific attribute predictions to overcome the variance of patterns from different angles. In [16], Sarafianos *et al.* extracted and aggregated visual attention masks at different scales and establish a weighted-variant of the focal loss to handle both under-represented or uncertain attributes. Although attention-based methods improve recognition accuracy, they are attribute-agnostic and fail to consider the attribute-specific information.

Other approaches are regarded as relation-based and exploit semantic relations to assist attribute recognition. Wang *et al.* [19] proposed a CNN-RNN based framework to exploit the interdependence and correlation among attributes. In [15], Sarafianos *et al.* leveraged curriculum learning, by learning first the strongly correlated attributes in a multi-task learning setup and then used transfer learning to additionally learn the weakly-correlated attributes. However, these methods require manually defined rules, e.g., prediction order and attribute groups, which are hard to determine in real-world applications.

In practice, numerous factors affect the classification performance and make the task of gender and age classification far from trivial. Datasets with gender and age annotations are usually captured in-the-wild, where often no near-frontal information is available. Also, images are taken under different illumination conditions and different camera viewing angles, providing poor visual quality. To this end, we employ CNNs and we conduct all of the experiments with the ResNet architecture as the backbone [1]. Another concern about CNNs is that they require datasets to be composed of balanced class distributions. However, datasets with gender and age labels are inherently imbalanced. To examine how a loss function affects the performance of a model, we study the performance of four different loss functions. Having the ResNet architecture as the baseline, an autoencoder is added in parallel to benefit from the appearance-based attributes, and the whole network is trained end-to-end. We consider that this combined model can learn more powerful relationships among the attributes and potentially lead in a better performance.

2 Methodology

In this work, we focus on recognizing the gender and age attributes, which are physical, adhered human characteristics belonging to the soft biometrics. Our method relies on still images of pedestrians without the presence of clear-shot face-frontal information. We opt for a three-stage strategy; (i) we first only consider the problem of gender classification, (ii) then the problem of age classification, and (iii) finally, the problem of multi-label classification, where we try to predict both attributes simultaneously. The main challenge we focused on is the class imbalanced distributions, which are inherently present in the available datasets. For all experiments, we use the ResNet50 architecture [1] as the backbone to investigate how four different loss functions perform under the class imbalance problem. Its power comes from its special architecture, which comprises of skip or shortcut connections to jump over the stacked convolutional layers. Finally, we build a model, adding an autoencoder on top of the ResNet, which we feed with appearance-based attributes. We consider that a combined model can leverage this additional information to make more accurate predictions.

2.1   Gender Classification

Consider there are N pedestrian images $\mathcal{X} = \{x_i\}_{i=1}^{N}$, labeled with the gender attribute $y_i \in \{0, 1\}$. The features extracted from the ResNet are pooled and passed through a binary classifier to determine the pedestrian's gender. Our approach employs a global average pooling, which takes the average of each of the feature maps obtained from the ResNet. The output of the model is one neuron with the sigmoid activation function, representing the probability of the pedestrian being "male" or "female".

In the presence of class imbalance, the loss due to the frequent class may dominate total loss and cause instability. Hence, to see how different loss functions perform under the class imbalance problem, we explore the performance of four different loss functions. The first one is the standard binary cross-entropy, formulated as:

$$L_{bce} = -y \log \hat{y} - (1 - y) \log(1 - \hat{y}), \tag{1}$$

where y and $\hat{y}$ are the ground truth and predicted labels, respectively. Such a loss function ignores completely the class imbalance, assigning the same weight to the two classes. Aiming to alleviate this problem, we employ a weighted-variant of the binary cross-entropy, called the binary focal loss [10], defined as:

$$L_{bfl} = -y (1 - \hat{y})^{\gamma} \log \hat{y} - (1 - y) \hat{y}^{\gamma} \log(1 - \hat{y}), \tag{2}$$

where $\gamma \geq 0$ is a focusing parameter. Focal loss is a cross-entropy loss that weighs the contribution of each example to the loss based on the classification error. With this strategy, the loss is made to implicitly focus on the problematic cases by extending the range in which an example receives low loss. For instance, when $\gamma = 2$, an example classified with $\hat{y} = 0.9$ would have 100× lower loss and with $\hat{y} = 0.968$ it would have 1000× lower loss compared with cross-entropy. Finally, we also employ two variants of the binary cross-entropy and the binary focal loss. These two variants are the weighted binary cross-entropy and the weighted binary focal loss and are respectively defined as:

$$L_{wbce} = -w \left[y \log \hat{y} + (1 - y) \log(1 - \hat{y}) \right], \tag{3}$$

$$L_{wbfl} = -w \left[y \, (1 - \hat{y})^{\gamma} \log \hat{y} + (1 - y) \, \hat{y}^{\gamma} \log(1 - \hat{y}) \right], \tag{4}$$

$$w = \begin{cases} \frac{1}{1 - p_f} & \text{if} \quad y = 0 \\ \frac{1}{p_f} & \text{if} \quad y = 1 \end{cases}, \tag{5}$$

where w is the loss weight according to the gender label and p_f is the proportion of the females in the training set.

For the problem of gender recognition, we developed a model that can benefit from annotations already present in the available data. Specifically, instead of treating an image independently, we consider inference with help from additional attributes. We claim that introducing this kind of information into a model, gender prediction would be performed with more confidence. For instance, most datasets provide attributes related to pedestrian appearance, upper and lower body clothing styles, and accessories. We incorporate these attributes in a binary vector, hence, each pedestrian image x_i is assigned with an K-length binary vector y_i, where $y_{il} \in \{0, 1\}$ denotes the presence of the k-th attribute in x_i. Then, we employ an autoencoder to learn the "compressed" representation of the original attribute input vector. The autoencoder is a one-hidden-layer neural network, with the size of the "bottleneck" layer and the size of the output layer to be the same as the size of the input vector (=K). The problem that the autoencoder is trying to solve is a multi-label classification problem hence, we use the sigmoid activation function for each of the output neurons. We also employ the binary cross-entropy loss of Eq. (1) and the binary focal loss of Eq. (2) slightly modified to account for all K attributes:

$$L_{ae} = - \sum_{k=1}^{K} \left[y_k \log \hat{y}_k + (1 - y_k) \log(1 - \hat{y}_k) \right], \tag{6}$$

$$L_{ae} = - \sum_{k=1}^{K} \left[y \, (1 - \hat{y})^{\gamma} \log \hat{y} + (1 - y) \, \hat{y}^{\gamma} \log(1 - \hat{y}) \right], \tag{7}$$

where K is the number of attributes and y_k, $\hat{y}_k$ are the ground truth and predicted labels for the k-th attribute.

The features from the autoencoder's bottleneck layer are concatenated with the features obtained from the last fully connected layer of ResNet to form a new model. At the top, we add a binary classifier and we train this combined model, which we call ResNet+AE, with the best performing loss function from the

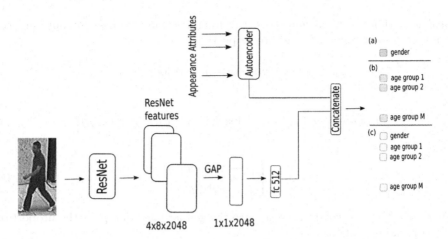

Fig. 1. The ResNet+AE model for (a) gender classification, (b) age classification and (c) multi-label classification.

single-ResNet architecture. The illustration of the ResNet+AE model is depicted in Fig. 1(a). This combined model is trained end-to-end and the overall loss is a combination of the autoencoder's loss and the loss arising from the ResNet:

$$L_{combined} = L_{ae} + L_{ResNet}. \tag{8}$$

where L_{ae} is one of the Eqs. (6), (7) and L_{ResNet} is one of the Eqs. (1), (2), (3), or (4), whichever performs the best in the case of gender classification.

2.2 Age Classification

We also study the problem of age recognition, where the model should predict one of M classes corresponding to M age categories. The age label vector is a one-hot vector y, and each element of that vector is represented as $y_m \in \{0, 1\}$, with $m = 1, \cdots, M$. We now employ the ResNet architecture, with the difference that the top classifier now predicts one of M possible classes. The M output neurons use the softmax activation function, to model a probability distribution consisting of M probabilities.

For the problem of age classification, we adopt the categorical cross-entropy loss, formulated as:

$$L_{cce} = -\sum_{i=1}^{M} y_i \log \hat{y}_i. \tag{9}$$

where M is the number of classes, and y_i, $\hat{y}_i$ are the one-hot encoded ground truth and predicted labels for the i-th class. Since the ground-truth labels are one-hot encoded only the positive class keeps its term in the loss, discarding the elements of the summation which are zero due to zero target labels. In addition to the categorical cross-entropy loss, we also explore the performance of the categorical focal loss and their weighted variants, which can be extended to the multi-class case easily:

$$L_{cfl} = -\sum_{i=1}^{M} y_i \left(1 - \hat{y}_i\right)^{\gamma} \log \hat{y}_i \,, \tag{10}$$

$$L_{wcce} = -\sum_{i=1}^{M} w_i \, y_i \, \log \hat{y} \,, \tag{11}$$

$$L_{wcfl} = \sum_{i=1}^{M} -w_i \, y \left(1 - \hat{y}\right)^{\gamma} \, \log \hat{y} \,, \tag{12}$$

where the weighting factor $w_i = \frac{n_{\mathrm{argmax}_{i \in \{1, \cdots, M\}} n_i}}{n_i}$ is the weight loss assigned to the age group i and n_i is the number of examples of the i-th age group in the training set. Finally, $n_{\mathrm{argmax}_{i \in \{1, \cdots, M\}} n_i}$ is the number of examples of the most representative class. Besides, we conduct experiments with the combined model for the problem of age recognition, which is depicted in Fig. 1(b). The overall loss is the summation of the loss originating from the autoencoder and the loss originating from the ResNet and it is in the form of Eq. (8).

2.3 Multi-label Classification

Finally, we consider the multi-label recognition problem, in which both attributes, gender and age, are predicted simultaneously. Now, each pedestrian image is labeled with a $(M+1)$-length vector, with the first element referring to the pedestrian's gender and the remaining M referring to the pedestrian's age range. For the multi-label recognition problem, we use the sigmoid activation function for the $M + 1$ output neurons and conduct experiments with the four loss functions, which for the multi-label case are reformulated as:

$$L_{bce} = -\sum_{i=1}^{M+1} y_i \log \hat{y}_i + (1 - y_i) \log(1 - \hat{y}_i) \,, \tag{13}$$

$$L_{bfl} = -\sum_{i=1}^{M+1} y_i \left(1 - \hat{y}_i\right)^{\gamma} \log \hat{y}_i + (1 - y_i) \, \hat{y}_i^{\gamma} \, \log(1 - \hat{y}_i) \,, \tag{14}$$

$$L_{wbce} = -\sum_{i=1}^{M+1} w_i \left[y_i \log \hat{y}_i + (1 - y_i) \log(1 - \hat{y}_i) \right] , \tag{15}$$

$$L_{wbfl} = - \sum_{i=1}^{M+1} w_i \left[y_i \left(1 - \hat{y}_i\right)^\gamma \log \hat{y}_i + (1 - y_i) \, \hat{y}_i{}^\gamma \log(1 - \hat{y}_i) \right], \qquad (16)$$

$$w_i = \begin{cases} e^{p_i} & \text{if} \quad y = 0 \\ e^{1-p_i} & \text{if} \quad y = 1 \end{cases}, \qquad (17)$$

where y_i, $\hat{y}_i$ are the ground truth and predicted labels for the i-th attribute, respectively, w_i is the loss weight assigned to attribute i and p_i is the proportion of the positive labels for the attribute i in the training set. The multi-label case is depicted in Fig. 1(c).

3   Experimental Results

To demonstrate the effectiveness of the proposed method, we compared with several state-of-the-art methods in two publicly available benchmark datasets. PEdesTrian Attribute (PETA) [3] dataset merges 10 consists of 19,000 images, each annotated with 61 binary attributes. PETA dataset is randomly partitioned into three parts, of which 9,500 for training, 1,900 for validation, and 7,600 for testing. Images are all captured from far view field and they exhibit large differences in terms of lighting conditions, camera viewing angles, image resolutions, background complexity, and indoor/outdoor environment. RAP v2 (Richly Annotated Pedestrian) [9] dataset has in total 84,928 images and image resolutions range from 36×92 to 344×554. Each image is annotated with 69 binary attributes.

For the problem of gender recognition, we used five metrics, namely accuracy, precision, recall, F1 score, and mean accuracy. Accuracy quantifies the fraction of predictions the model got right. For the problem of age classification, we similarly use the accuracy, precision, recall, and F1 score, slightly modified, since age classification is a multi-class problem. In this case, accuracy quantifies how often predictions match the true labels by checking if the index of the maximal true label is equal to the index of the maximal predicted label. Finally, for the problem of multi-label recognition, accuracy, precision, recall, and F1 score are calculated per-sample.

Finally, we used the pre-trained ResNet50 architecture, which has already been trained on the ImageNet dataset [14]. All images were pre-processed and resized to 256×128 since pedestrian images are usually rectangular. To avoid overfitting, we employed some of the commonly used data augmentation techniques. As for the optimizer, we used the mini-batch stochastic gradient descent with momentum set to 0.9 and early stopping when the validation error was not improving for five consecutive epochs. The batch size is 50 samples per iteration and a dropout layer with a small dropout probability (i.e., 0.1) that may act as a regularizer is added after the feature concatenation layer. Finally, we selected $\gamma = 2$ for the focusing parameter in the focal loss and weighted focal loss.

3.1 Gender Classification

Table 1 compares the performance of the four loss functions described for the PETA dataset. Although the gender distribution is nearly balanced, it can be seen that both weighted loss functions outperform their un-weighted counterparts. Specifically, WBCE performs 0.44% better in terms of the F1 score and 0.36% better in terms of the mAcc metric compared to BCE. Similarly, WBFL is by 1.8% better in terms of the F1 score and by 1.41% better in terms of the mAcc compared to BFL. Comparing the weighted loss functions, WBCE outperforms WBFL by 3.48% in the F1 score and by 3.16% in mAcc and subsequently, it is used to train the ResNet+AE model.

Table 1. Performance comparison of the four loss functions and the ResNet+AE model on the PETA dataset (in %).

	Prec	Rec	F1	mAcc	Acc
ResNet-BCE	88.80	86.07	87.42	88.57	88.81
ResNet-WBCE	**87.86**	**87.89**	**87.86**	**88.93**	**89.03**
ResNet-BFL	85.51	79.87	82.58	84.36	84.79
ResNet-WBFL	84.57	84.18	84.38	85.77	85.92
ResNet+AE	**91.67**	**89.79**	**90.71**	**91.53**	**91.70**

The proposed ResNet+AE model leverages the appearance-based attributes in the gender classification scheme, achieving 90.71% and 91.53% in the F1 score and mAcc, respectively, outperforming the single-ResNet architecture with any of the loss functions.

The gender distribution in the RAP v2 dataset is quite imbalanced given that the number of males is over twice the number of females. Table 2 compares the performance of the four loss functions for the RAP v2 dataset. WBCE performs 0.42% better in terms of the F1 score and 0.95% better in terms of the mAcc metric compared to BCE. BFL is by 0.6% better in terms of the F1 score compared to WBFL but WBFL is 0.25% better in terms of the mAcc compared to BFL. Nevertheless, WBCE outperforms WBFL by 2.87% in the F1 score and 2.47% in mAcc and this is the loss function of choice for the ResNet+AE model. The proposed ResNet+AE model performs comparably well achieving 91.72% and 94.12% in F1 score and mAcc respectively but does not outperform the single-ResNet architecture with the WBCE loss function.

The proposed ResNet+AE model demonstrates inferior performance, achieving 1.19% in the F1 score, which indicates that the performance is degraded. Therefore, the combined model cannot leverage the appearance-based attributes for the age classification, and the single-ResNet architecture with the WBCE being the best performing model.

Table 2. Performance comparison of the four loss functions and the ResNet+AE model on the RAP v2 dataset (in %).

	Prec	Rec	F1	mAcc	Acc
ResNet-BCE	93.18	91.81	92.49	94.38	95.35
ResNet-WBCE	91.00	**94.91**	**92.91**	**95.33**	**95.49**
ResNet-BFL	92.90	91.82	92.36	94.32	95.26
ResNet-WBFL	89.46	94.17	91.76	94.57	94.73
ResNet+AE	**91.16**	92.30	91.72	94.12	94.81

3.2   Age Classification

The age category distribution in the PETA dataset can be seen in Fig. 2(a). There are five age classes to be predicted, <16, $16 - 30$, $31 - 45$, $46 - 60$, and >60, with distributions of 0.9%, 49.77%, 32.92%, 10.24%, 6.17%, respectively. Hence, it is apparent that the age attribute suffers from a severe class imbalance.

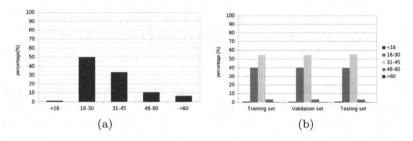

(a)   (b)

Fig. 2. The distribution of the age categories in (a) the PETA dataset and (b) the RAP v2 dataset.

Table 3 shows the performance of the four loss functions for the PETA dataset. Although the weighted loss functions balance each example according to the class it belongs to, giving more focus on the under-represented classes, they seem to improve none of the metrics. We consider that this behavior is caused by poor features since it is difficult for the ResNet to provide representative features given that there is no near-face information and sometimes the pedestrian is standing backward. Also, since the optimization method is performed in batches, it is not guaranteed that there are examples for each age group in each batch, hence the model is overwhelmed by the majority class and cannot ensure good discriminations among the five age categories. The categorical focal loss performs slightly better than the categorical cross-entropy by 0.66% in terms of the mF1 score and subsequently, it is used to train the ResNet+AE model.

The proposed ResNet+AE model outperforms the single ResNet architecture, achieving 75.84% in terms of the mF1 score. This means that there is some

Table 3. Performance comparison of the four loss functions and the ResNet+AE model on the PETA dataset (in %).

	mPrec	mRec	mF1	Acc
ResNet-CCE	85.55	66.76	73.19	77.29
ResNet-WCCE	67.37	70.53	68.72	70.76
ResNet-CFL	**84.01**	**68.03**	**73.85**	**76.89**
ResNet-WCFL	54.23	64.64	57.80	64.04
ResNet+AE	**80.06**	**72.75**	**75.84**	**79.61**

sort of interdependence among the appearance-based attributes, which helps the ResNet+AE model to yield a better age classification performance.

The age category distribution in the RAP v2 dataset can be seen in Fig. 2(b). There are five age groups to be predicted with distributions of 0.92%, 40.44%, 54.89%, 3.53%, and 0.22%, respectively. The distribution is heavily unbalanced with the second and third age categories to be more represented compared to the rest. Table 4 compares the performance of the four loss functions for the RAP v2 dataset. Similarly, with the PETA dataset, the weighted loss functions do not improve the performance compared to their un-weighted counterparts. CFL is the best performing loss function, which outperforms the CCE by 8.36% in the mF1 score, and it is used to consequently train the ResNet+AE model.

Table 4. Performance comparison of the four loss functions and the ResNet+AE model on the RAP v2 dataset (in %).

	mPrec	mRec	mF1	Acc
ResNet-CCE	41.73	29.97	31.45	65.71
ResNet-WCCE	26.27	49.92	24.51	39.36
ResNet-CFL	**48.46**	**36.82**	**39.81**	**64.82**
ResNet-WCFL	26.00	49.09	23.30	37.31
ResNet+AE	**41.57**	34.30	36.27	64.94

The proposed ResNet+AE model demonstrates inferior performance, achieving 36.27% in the mF1 score, which indicates that the performance is degraded. Therefore, the combined model cannot leverage the appearance-based attributes for the age classification, and the single-ResNet architecture with the CFL is the best performing model.

3.3   Multi-label Classification

The performance of the four different loss functions for the PETA dataset for the task of multi-label classification, where the model classifies both the gender and the age attributes is summarized in Table 5. Since the gender attribute is nearly balanced the heavy imbalance of the age attribute (Fig. 2(a)) overwhelms the distribution to be modeled. However, the performance is not degraded even though the model now has to predict both attributes simultaneously. The weighted loss functions manage to achieve better results compared to their un-weighted counterparts. More specifically, WBCE is 0.87% and 1.23% better in F1 score and mAcc respectively compared to the plain BCE. Similarly, WBFL performs better by 1.66% in the F1 score and by 1.14% in mAcc compared to plain BFL. The best among the four loss functions is the WBCE achieving 79.4% and 82.82% in F1 score and mAcc respectively and this loss function is used to consequently train the ResNet+AE model. The proposed ResNet+AE model outperforms the single-ResNet architecture, achieving 80.41% in the F1 score and 84.49% in mAcc.

Table 5. Performance comparison of the four loss functions and the ResNet+AE model on the PETA dataset (in %).

	Prec	Rec	F1	mAcc	Acc
ResNet-BCE	79.20	77.88	78.53	81.59	91.40
ResNet-WBCE	**79.22**	**79.58**	**79.40**	**82.82**	**91.09**
ResNet-BFL	76.90	75.95	76.42	80.64	90.47
ResNet-WBFL	77.64	78.52	78.08	81.78	90.37
ResNet+AE	**80.02**	**80.80**	**80.41**	**84.49**	**91.54**

Table 6 depicts the performance of the four different loss functions for the RAP v2 dataset when the model classifies both the gender and the age attributes. It can be seen that the weighted loss functions perform slightly better than the unweighted counterparts. Specifically, WBCE performs 0.26% better in terms of the F1 score and 4.3% better in terms of the mAcc compared to BCE, and WBFL performs 0.18% better in terms of the F1 score and 2.09% better in terms of the mAcc compared to BFL. Overall, in the single ResNet architecture, WBCE performs 1.51% better in terms of the F1 score, but WBFL performs 0.6% better in terms of the mAcc. We chose the WBFL as the best performing loss function, as mAcc is a label-based metric and is a more important metric in the multi-label classification case. Concerning the combined ResNet+AE model, although it is quite similar in performance compared to most of the single-ResNet architectures, it does not outperform the single-ResNet case with the WBFL loss function.

Table 6. Performance comparison of the four loss functions and the ResNet+AE model on the RAP v2 dataset (in %).

	Prec	Rec	F1	mAcc	Acc
ResNet-BCE	71.08	70.63	70.85	63.56	88.40
ResNet-WBCE	70.71	71.52	71.11	67.86	88.25
ResNet-BFL	69.31	69.53	69.42	66.37	87.97
ResNet-WBFL	**68.82**	**70.40**	**69.60**	**68.46**	**87.73**
ResNet+AE	67.63	68.30	67.96	67.76	87.29

4 Conclusion

In this paper, we studied the problem of gender and age classification from pedestrian images. The class imbalance which characterizes the datasets makes the task quite challenging. We focused on examining how four different loss functions perform under the class imbalance problem. We tested our model, which concatenates the features from the ResNet backbone and the features from an autoencoder, which is trained in parallel with appearance-based attributes. Taken into consideration the experimental results, the gender classification is an easier task, as the ResNet can extract representative features to make an accurate classification. The age classification is a more challenging problem since age categories are heavily imbalanced and with no near-face information. The multi-label classification is also a challenging task, as the age category imbalance overwhelms the distribution to be modeled. The experimental results showed that high classification accuracy may be obtained when the appearance-based attributes involve some sort of relationship.

Acknowledgments. This work has been co-funded by the European Union and Greek national funds through the Operational Program Competitiveness, Entrepreneurship and Innovation, under the call RESEARCH-CREATE-INNOVATE (project code: T1EDK-04517). The authors gratefully acknowledge the support of NVIDIA Corporation with the donation of the Titan Xp GPU used for this research. All statements of fact, opinion or conclusions contained herein are those of the authors and should not be construed as representing the official views or policies of the sponsors.

References

1. Bekele, E., Lawson, W.: The deeper, the better: Analysis of person attributes recognition. In: FG, pp. 1–8 (2019)
2. Chen, S., Zhang, C., Dong, M.: Deep age estimation: from classification to ranking. IEEE TM **20**(8), 2209–2222 (2017)
3. Deng, Y., Luo, P., Loy, C.C., Tang, X.: Pedestrian attribute recognition at far distance. In: ACM ICM, pp. 789–792 (2014)
4. Duan, M., Li, K., Yang, C., Li, K.: A hybrid deep learning CNN-ELM for age and gender classification. Neurocomputing **275**, 448–461 (2018)

5. Gonzalez-Sosa, E., Fierrez, J., Vera-Rodriguez, R., Alonso-Fernandez, F.: Facial soft biometrics for recognition in the wild: recent works, annotation, and cots evaluation. IEEE TIFS **13**(8), 2001–2014 (2018)
6. Huang, G.B., Zhu, Q.Y., Siew, C.K.: Extreme learning machine: theory and applications. Neurocomputing **70**(1), 489–501 (2006)
7. Juefei-Xu, F., Verma, E., Goel, P., Cherodian, A., Savvides, M.: Deepgender: occlusion and low resolution robust facial gender classification via progressively trained convolutional neural networks with attention. In: CVPRW, pp. 68–77 (2016)
8. Levi, G., Hassner, T.: Age and gender classification using convolutional neural networks. In: CVPRW, pp. 34–42 (2015)
9. Li, D., Zhang, Z., Chen, X., Huang, K.: A richly annotated pedestrian dataset for person retrieval in real surveillance scenarios. IEEE TIP **28**(4), 1575–1590 (2018)
10. Lin, T., Goyal, P., Girshick, R., He, K., Dollár, P.: Focal loss for dense object detection. In: ICCV, pp. 2999–3007 (2017)
11. Niu, Z., Zhou, M., Wang, L., Gao, X., Hua, G.: Ordinal regression with multiple output CNN for age estimation. In: CVPR, pp. 4920–4928 (2016)
12. Ranjan, R., Patel, V.M., Chellappa, R.: Hyperface: a deep multi-task learning framework for face detection, landmark localization, pose estimation, and gender recognition. TPAMI **41**(1), 121–135 (2017)
13. Rodríguez, P., Cucurull, G., Gonfaus, J.M., Roca, F.X., González, J.: Age and gender recognition in the wild with deep attention. Pattern Recogn. **72**, 563–571 (2017)
14. Russakovsky, O., et al.: ImageNet large scale visual recognition challenge. Int. J. Comput. Vision **115**(3), 211–252 (2015). https://doi.org/10.1007/s11263-015-0816-y
15. Sarafianos, N., Giannakopoulos, T., Nikou, C., Kakadiaris, I.A.: Curriculum learning for multi-task classification of visual attributes. In: ICCVW, pp. 2608–2615 (2017)
16. Sarafianos, N., Xu, X., Kakadiaris, I.A.: Deep imbalanced attribute classification using visual attention aggregation. In: ECCV, pp. 680–697 (2018)
17. Sarfraz, M.S., Schumann, A., Wang, Y., Stiefelhagen, R.: Deep view-sensitive pedestrian attribute inference in an end-to-end model. arXiv:1707.06089 (2017)
18. Smailis, C., Vrigkas, M., Kakadiaris, I.A.: Recaspia: recognizing carrying actions in single images using privileged information. In: ICIP, pp. 26–30 (2019)
19. Wang, J., Zhu, X., Gong, S., Li, W.: Attribute recognition by joint recurrent learning of context and correlation. In: ICCV, October 2017
20. Yi, D., Lei, Z., Li, S.Z.: Age estimation by multi-scale convolutional network. In: Asian Conference on Computer Vision, pp. 144–158 (2014)

Face Reenactment Based Facial Expression Recognition

Kamran Ali[(✉)] and Charles E. Hughes

Synthetic Reality Lab, CECS, University of Central Florida, Oviedo, USA
kamran@knights.ucf.edu, ceh@cs.ucf.edu

Abstract. Representations used for Facial Expression Recognition (FER) are usually contaminated with identity specific features. In this paper, we propose a novel Reenactment-based Expression-Representation Learning Generative Adversarial Network (REL-GAN) that employs the concept of face reenactment to disentangle facial expression features from identity information. In this method, the facial expression representation is learned by reconstructing an expression image employing an encoder-decoder based generator. More specifically, our method learns the disentangled expression representation by transferring the expression information from the source image to the identity of the target image. Experiments performed on widely used datasets (BU-3DFE, CK+, Oulu-CASIA, SEFW) show that the proposed technique produces comparable or better results than state-of-the-art methods.

Keywords: Facial expression recognition · Face reenactment · Disentangled representation learning · Image classification

1 Introduction

Facial expression recognition (FER) has many exciting applications in domains like human-machine interaction, intelligent tutoring system (ITS), interactive games, and intelligent transportation. As a consequence, FER has been widely studied by the computer vision and machine learning communities over the past several decades. Despite this extensive research, FER is still a difficult and challenging task. Most FER techniques developed so far do not consider inter-subject variations and differences in facial attributes of individuals present in data. Hence, the representation used for the classification of expressions contains identity-related information along with facial expression information, as observed in [1,2]. The main drawback of this entangled representation is that it negatively affects the generalization capability of FER techniques, which, as a result, degrades the performance of FER algorithms on unseen identities. We believe the key to overcoming the challenge of over-fitting of FER models to subjects involved in the training set lies in FER techniques to disentangle the expression features from the identity information.

© Springer Nature Switzerland AG 2020
G. Bebis et al. (Eds.): ISVC 2020, LNCS 12509, pp. 501–513, 2020.
https://doi.org/10.1007/978-3-030-64556-4_39

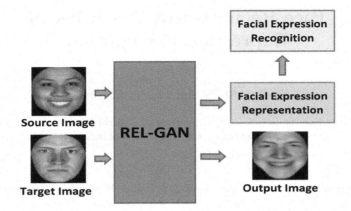

Fig. 1. REL-GAN takes a source image and target image as inputs and generates a synthetic image by transferring the expression of the source image to the identity of the target image. After training, REL-GAN is used to extract disentangled facial expression representation for FER.

Face reenactment is an emerging face synthesis task that has attracted the attention of the research community due to its applications in the virtual reality and entertainment domain, besides the challenging research problems that it offers. The main goal of face reenactment is to transfer the expression information from the source image to the identity of the target face. Therefore, an ideal face reenactment technique should be able to disentangle expression features from the identity information of the source image and transfer the disentangled expression features to the identity of the target image. In this paper, we employ a novel Reenactment-based Expression-Representation Learning Generative Adversarial Network (REL-GAN) that learns to disentangle expression features from the source image and synthesize an expression image by transferring the disentangled expression features to the identity of the target image. The overall framework of our proposed FER technique is shown in Fig. 1.

The architecture of REL-GAN is based on an encoder-decoder based generator G, that contains two encoders, an expression encoder G_{es} and an identity encoder G_{et}. These two encoders are then connected to a decoder G_{de}. The discriminator D of REL-GAN is designed to be a multi-task CNN. During training, the input to REL-GAN is a source image x_s, and a target image x_t, and the output of REL-GAN is a synthesized expression image $\bar{x}$. The goal of G_{es} is to map the source image x_s to an expression representation $f(e)$, while G_{et} is used to project the target image x_t to an identity embedding $f(i)$. The concatenation of the two embeddings,: $f(x) = f(e) + f(i)$, bridges the two encoders with a decoder G_{de}. The objective of decoder G_{de} is to synthesize an expression image $\bar{x}$ having the expression e of the source image and the identity i of the target image: $\bar{x} = G_{de}(f(x))$. The disentangled facial expression representation learned by the encoder G_{es} is mutually exclusive of identity information, which can be best used for FER. Thus, generator, G, is used for two purposes: 1. to disentangle facial expression features employing encoder G_{es}, 2. to reconstruct a facial expression image by transferring the expression information from the source image to the identity of the target image. The discriminator, D, of REL-GAN is used to classify not only between real and fake images but to also perform the classification of identities and facial expressions. The estimation of facial expressions and identities in the discriminator helps in improving the quality of generated images during training.

The main contributions of this paper are as follows:

- To the best of our knowledge, this is the first technique that employs the concept of face reenactment for the task of learning disentangled expression representation.
- We present a novel disentangled and discriminative facial expression representation learning technique for FER by employing concepts of adversarial learning and learning by reconstruction.
- Experimental results show that the proposed framework generalizes well to identities from various ethnic backgrounds and expression images captured both in lab-controlled and in-the-wild settings.

2   Related Work

The main goal of FER is to extract features that are discriminative and invariant to variations such as pose, illumination, and identity-related information. The feature extraction process can be divided into two main categories: human-engineered features and learned features. Before the deep learning era, most of FER techniques involved human-designed features using techniques such as Histograms of Oriented Gradients (HOG) [8], Scale Invariant Feature Transform (SIFT) features [9] and histograms of Local Phase Quantization (LPQ) [10].

The human-crafted features perform well in lab-controlled environment where the expressions are posed by the subjects with constant illumination and stable head pose. However, these features fail on spontaneous data with varying head position and illumination. Recently, deep CNN based methods [11–14,40] have been employed to increase the robustness of FER to real-world scenarios. However, the learned deep representations used for FER are often influenced by large variations in individual facial attributes such as ethnicity, gender, and age of subjects involved in training. The main drawback of this phenomenon is that it negatively affects the generalization capability of the model and, as a result, the FER accuracy is degraded on unseen subjects. Although significant progress has been made in improving the performance of FER, the challenge of mitigating the influence of inter-subject variations on FER is still an open area of research. Various techniques [15,16,20,39] have been proposed in the literature to increase the discriminative property of extracted features for FER by increasing the inter-class differences and reducing intra-class variations. Most recently, Identity-Aware CNN (IACNN) [17] was proposed to enhance FER performance by using an expression-sensitive contrastive loss and an identity-sensitive contrastive loss to reduce the effect of identity related information. However, the effectiveness of contrastive loss is negatively affected by large data expansion, which is caused due to the compilation of training data in the form of image pairs [2]. Similarly, in [7] and [2], the effect of identity-related information is mitigated by generating an expression image with a fixed identity. The main problem with these methods is that the performance of FER depends on the quality of the synthesized images because FER is performed employing the generated images. In [4], person-independent expression representations are learned by using residue learning. However, this technique, apart from being computationally costly, does not explicitly disentangle the expression features from the identity information, because the same intermediate representation is used to generate neutral images of same identities.

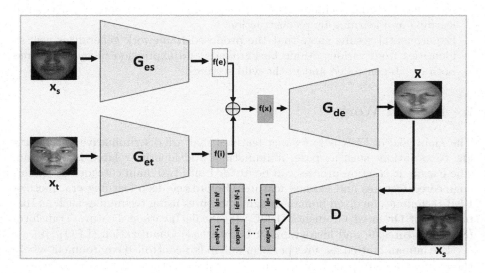

Fig. 2. Architecture of our REL-GAN

3 Proposed Method

The proposed FER technique consists of two stages: during the first stage of learning, a disentangled expression representation $f(e)$ is learned by employing face reenactment, and during the second stage of learning, the disentangled expression representation $f(e)$ is used for facial expression recognition. The overall architecture of REL-GAN is shown in Fig. 2. The generator G of REL-GAN is based on an encoder-decoder structure, while the discriminator D is a multi-task CNN [5]. Given a source image $x_s \in X$ and a target image $x_t \in X$, the goal of REL-GAN is to transfer the expression of x_s to the identity of x_t and

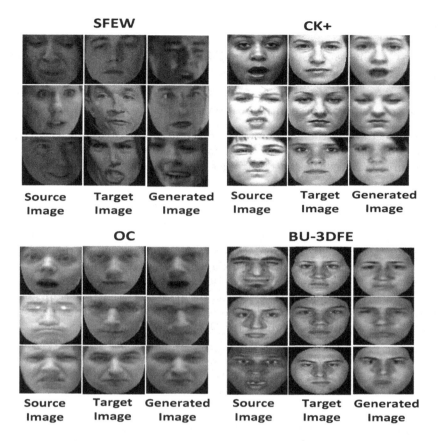

Fig. 3. REL-GAN extracts expression information from source images and transfers the disentangled expression information to the identity of target images.

generate an expression image $\bar{x}$ similar to the ground-truth image x_{t_g}. Specifically, an encoder $G_{es} : X \rightarrow E$ is used to encode the expression representation $f(e) \in E$ from x_s, and an encoder $G_{et} : X \rightarrow I$ is employed to encode the identity representation $f(i) \in I$ from x_t. A decoder $G_{de} : E \times I \rightarrow X$ is then used to map the expression and the identity latent embedding space back to the face space. The synthesized expression image $\bar{x}$ is generated by computing $\bar{x} = G_{de}(G_{es}(x_s), G_{et}(x_t))$. In order to efficiently transfer the expression of x_s to $\bar{x}$ while preserving the identity of x_t, the expression features of x_s should be captured in $f(e)$ in such a way that it does not contain the identity information of x_s. Thus, by explicitly inputting the extracted identity features $f(i)$ of x_t to G_{de}, we are able to disentangle the expression information of x_s from its identity features in $f(e)$. Figure 3 shows the result of transferring the extracted facial expression features from source images to the identity of the target images by employing our face reenactment technique. During the second stage of learning, encoder G_{es} is detached from REL-GAN after training, and all the filters of G_{es} are fixed. The disentangled expression representation $f(e)$ is extracted from the encoder G_{es} and becomes input into a Multilayer Perceptron (MLP) for facial expression recognition.

3.1   Expression Representation Learning

The architectures of the generator G and the discriminator D of REL-GAN is designed to fulfill two main objectives simultaneously: 1) disentangle and transfer a source facial expression to a target face; while 2) preserving the identity information of the target image.

Discriminator: The main objective of D is three-fold: 1. to classify between real and fake images, 2. to categorize facial expressions, and 3. to recognize the identities of expression images. Therefore, discriminator D is divided into two parts: $D = [D^e, D^i]$, where $D^e \in R^{N^e+1}$ corresponds to the part of D that is used for the classification of expressions, i.e N^e denotes the number of expressions, and an additional dimension is used to differentiate between real and fake images. Similarly, $D^i \in R^{N^i}$ is the part of D that is used to classify the identities of images, where N^i denotes the number of identities. The overall objective function of our discriminator D is given by the following equation:

$$\max_D \mathcal{L}_D(D, G) = E_{\substack{x_s,y_s \sim p_s(x_s,y_s) \\ x_t,y_t \sim p_t(x_t,y_t)}} [\log(D^e_{y^e_s}(x_s)) + \log(D^i_{y^i_t}(x_t))]$$

$$+ E_{\substack{x_s,y_s \sim p_s(x_s,y_s) \\ x_t,y_t \sim p_t(x_t,y_t)}} [\log(D^e_{N^e+1}(G(x_s, x_t)))] \qquad (1)$$

Given a real expression image x, the first part of the above equation corresponds to the objective function of D to classify the identity and expression of images. While the second part of the equation represents the objective of D to maximize the probability of a synthetic image $\bar{x}$ being classified as a fake. The expression and identity classification in the discriminator D helps in transferring expression information from a source image to a target face while preserving the identity of x_t. y^e denotes the expression label and y^i represents the identity labels in Eq. (1).

Generator: The generator G of REL-GAN aims to extract expression and identity features from source image x_s and target image x_t, respectively, and to synthesize an image $\bar{x}$ to fool D to classify it to the expression of x_s and the identity of x_t. Therefore, the generator G contains two encoders and a decoder: $G = (G_{es}, G_{et}, G_{de})$. The objective function of G is given by the following equation:

$$\max_G \mathcal{L}_G(D, G) = E_{\substack{x_s,y_s \sim p_s(x_s,y_s) \\ x_t,y_t \sim p_t(x_t,y_t)}} [\log(D^e_{y^e_s}(G(x_s, x_t)) + \log(D^i_{y^i_t}(G(x_s, x_t)))] \quad (2)$$

Pixel Loss: The goal of the generator G is to not only extract the disentangled expression features but also generate realistic-looking expression images. Therefore, to overcome the blurriness of generated images we employ a pixel-wise loss [32] in the raw-pixel space.

$$\mathcal{L}_{pixel} = L_1(G_{de}(G_{es}(x_s), G_{et}(x_t)), x_{t_g}). \tag{3}$$

The total REL-GAN loss is given by:

$$\mathcal{L}_{total} = \lambda_1 \mathcal{L}_{adv} + \lambda_2 \mathcal{L}_{pixel} + \lambda_3 \mathcal{L}_{D_e} + \lambda_4 \mathcal{L}_{D_i}. \tag{4}$$

Where $\mathcal{L}_{D_e}$ and $\mathcal{L}_{D_i}$ represents the expression and identity classification loss calculated by the discriminator D.

3.2 Facial Expression Recognition

After the first stage of training, the encoder G_{es} is detached from REL-GAN, and all the filters of G_{es} are kept fixed. To learn facial expressions, the disentangled expression representation $f(e)$ is used to train a simple MLP to classify facial expressions.

4 Experiments

The proposed REL-GAN based FER technique is evaluated on four publicly available facial expression databases: CK+ [18], Oulu-CASIA [19], BU-3DFE [28] and Static Facial Expression in the Wild (SFEW)[33].

4.1 Implementation Details

Face detection is performed by employing the technique proposed in [34]. The detected faces are then aligned using the face alignment method proposed by Hassner et al. [35]. Data augmentation is applied to avoid the over-fitting problem by increasing the number of training images. Therefore, five patches of size 96×96 are cropped-out from five different locations: the center and four corners of each image, and each cropped image are then rotated at four angles i.e $-6°$, $-3°$, $3°$, $6°$. Horizontal flipping is also applied on each rotated image.

REL-GAN is initially pre-trained using the BU-4DFE [22] dataset, which consists of 60,600 images from 101 identities. The architecture of both encoders is designed based on five downsampling blocks consisting of a 3×3 stride 1 convolution. The number of channels are 64, 128, 256, 512, 512 and a one 30-dimensional FC layer for expression feature vector $f(e)$, and a 50-dimensional identity representation $f(i)$, constitute G_{es} and G_{et}, respectively. The decoder G_{de} is built on five upsampling blocks containing a 3×3 stride 1 convolution. The number of channels are 512, 256, 128, 64, 32. The multi-task discriminator D network is designed in such a way that the initial four CNN blocks with 16, 32, 64, 128 channels and a 1024-dimensional FC layer are shared between D^e and

D^i. It is then divided into two branches, where, each branch has two additional FC layers with 512 and 256 channels. D^e then has an expression classification layer and D^i has an identity classification layer. The CNN baseline network used in this paper is the encoder G_{es} network with one additional FC layer for expression classification.

For the optimization of the hyper-parameters, we adopted the optimization strategies presented in [23] as part of our technique. Adam optimizer is used with a batch size of 64, learning rate of 0.0001 and momentum of 0.5. We empirically set $\lambda_1 = 0.7$, $\lambda_2 = 20$, $\lambda_3 = 50$ and $\lambda_4 = 30$. REL-GAN is trained for 300 epochs, and the MLP is trained for 50 epochs. Contrary to conventional GAN training strategies mentioned in [24], in later iterations of REL-GAN, when D reaches a near-optimal solution, G is updated more frequently than D, due to the supervised classification provided by the class labels.

Table 1. CK+: 10-fold Average Accuracy for seven expressions classification.

Method	Setting	Accuracy
HOG 3D [8]	Dynamic	91.44
3DCNN [14]	Dynamic	85.90
STM-Explet [25]	Dynamic	94.19
IACNN [17]	Static	95.37
DTAGN [26]	Static	97.25
DeRL [4]	Static	97.30
CNN(baseline)	Static	90.34
REL-GAN(Ours)	Static	**97.41**

4.2 Experimental Results

The **Extended Cohn-Kanade database CK+** [18] is a popular facial expression recognition database that contains 327 videos sequences from 118 subjects. Each of these sequences corresponds to one of seven expressions, i.e., anger, contempt, disgust, fear, happiness, sadness, and surprise, where each sequence starts from a neutral expression to a peak expression. To compile the training dataset, the last three frames of each sequence are extracted, which results in 981 images in total. To perform 10-fold cross validation, the dataset is divided into ten different sets with no overlapping identities.

The average accuracy of 10-fold cross-validation on the CK+ database is reported in Table 1. It can be seen that the proposed method produces a recognition accuracy of 97.41%, which is higher than the accuracy of previous FER methods. Our image-based technique outperforms the sequence-based methods, where the features for FER are extracted from videos or sequences of images.

Table 2. Oulu-CASIA: 10-fold Average Accuracy for six expressions classification.

Method	Setting	Accuracy
HOG 3D [8]	Dynamic	70.63
STM-Explet [25]	Dynamic	74.59
PPDN [27]	Static	84.59
DTAGN [26]	Static	81.46
DeRL [4]	Static	88.0
CNN(baseline)	Static	73.14
REL-GAN(Ours)	Static	**88.93**

The **Oulu-CASIA (OC) dataset** [19] used in this experiment corresponds to the section of the OC dataset that is compiled under strong illumination condition using the VIS camera. It contains 480 sequences from 80 subjects, and each sequence is labeled as one of the six basic expressions. The last three frames of each sequence are selected to create a training and testing dataset.

The average of the 10-fold person-independent cross-validation accuracy of the proposed method on Oulu-CASIA dataset, as shown in Table 2, demonstrates that the proposed method outperforms all state-of-the-art techniques with average accuracy of 88.93%. The accuracy obtained using the proposed method is much higher than the accuracy of video-based techniques.

Table 3. BU-3DFE database: Accuracy for six expressions classification.

Method	Setting	Accuracy
Wang et al. [29]	3D	61.79
Berretti et al. [30]	3D	77.54
Lopes [31]	Static	72.89
DeRL [4]	Static	**84.17**
CNN(baseline)	Static	72.74
REL-GAN(Ours)	Static	**83.46**

The **BU-3DFE database** [28] is a widely used FER database that contains static 3D face models and texture images from 100 subjects from various ethnic backgrounds with a variety of ages. For each subject, there are expression images corresponding to seven expressions (six basic expressions and a neutral expression) and these images are labeled with four different expression intensity levels. During this experiment, we only use texture images corresponding to the last two highest intensity expressions. We perform a 10-fold cross-validation by dividing the dataset into ten different sets in a person-independent manner.

The average of the 10-fold cross-validation on BU-3DFE dataset is shown in Table 3. The recognition accuracy obtained using the proposed REL-GAN-

Table 4. SFEW: The average accuracy on the validation set.

Method	Accuracy
AUDN [36]	26.14
STM-Explet [25]	31.73
Dhall et al. [33] (baseline of SFEW)	35.93
Mapped LBP [37]	41.92
FN2EN [38]	**48.19**
CNN(baseline)	29.75
REL-GAN(Ours)	**45.82**

based method is significantly higher than most of the state-of-the-art techniques. The highest accuracy is produced by the DeRL [4] method that involves the computationally costly residue learning process.

The **SFEW dataset** [33] is the most widely used benchmark for facial expression recognition in an unconstrained setting. The SFEW database contains 1,766 images, i.e. 958 for training, 436 for validation, and 372 for testing. All images are extracted from film clips, and each image has been labeled as one of the seven expression categories, i.e., anger, disgust, fear, neutral, happy, sad, and surprise. We validate our technique on the validation set of SFEW because the labels for the test set are held back by the challenge organizer.

In Table 4, we compare our result with techniques that use the training set of the SFEW dataset to train their models and do not use extra training data. The average accuracy obtained using our proposed method on the validation set of the SFEW dataset is higher than the accuracy of most of the state-of-the-art techniques. The highest accuracy, however, is obtained by the FN2EN [38] method. We hypothesize that it may be due to the reason that, during the first stage of training, the parameters of the convolutional layers of the FN2EN network are made close to the parameters of convolutional layers of the face-net (VGG-16) [41], which is trained on 2.6M face images. Our REL-GAN, on the other hand, is pre-trained on 60,600 images of the BU-4DFE [22] dataset. Table 4 shows that our proposed method produces promising recognition results not only in a lab-controlled setting but it can also be used to classify facial expressions in real-world scenarios.

5   Conclusions

In this paper, we present a novel FER architecture called REL-GAN that employs the concept of face reenactment to disentangle expression representation from identity features. More specifically, an encoder-decoder based generator is used in REL-GAN, in which the disentangled expression representation is learned by transferring the expression features from a source image to the identity of the target image. After training the REL-GAN architecture for face reenactment, the expression encoder is detached from the rest of the network and is used to extract a disentangled expression representation. A simple MLP is then trained using the disentangled expression features to perform facial expression recognition. The proposed method is evaluated on publicly available state-of-the-art databases, and the experimental results show that the accuracy of FER obtained by employing the proposed method is comparable or even better than the accuracy of state-of-the-art facial expression recognition techniques.

References

1. Yang, H., Zhang, Z., Yin, L.: Identity-adaptive facial expression recognition through expression regeneration using conditional generative adversarial networks. In: International Conference on Automatic Face and Gesture Recognition, pp. 294–301 (2018)
2. Cai, J., Meng, Z., Khan, A.S., Li, Z., O'Reilly, J., Tong, Y.: Identity-free facial expression recognition using conditional generative adversarial network. CoRR abs/1903.08051 (2019). https://arxiv.org/abs/1903.08051
3. Bai, M., Xie, W., Shen, L.: Disentangled feature based adversarial learning for facial expression recognition. In: IEEE International Conference on Image Processing, pp. 31–35 (2019)
4. Yang, H., Ciftci, U., Yin, L.: Facial expression recognition by de-expression residue learning. In: Proceedings of the IEEE Conference on Computer Vision and Pattern Recognition, pp. 2168–2177, April 2018
5. Tran, L., Yin, X., Liu, X.: Disentangled representation learning GAN for pose-invariant face recognition. In: Proceedings of the IEEE Conference on Computer Vision and Pattern Recognition, pp. 1415–1424 (2017)
6. Song, B.C., Lee, M.K., Choi, D.Y.: Facial expression recognition via relation-based conditional generative adversarial network. In: International Conference on Multimodal Interaction, pp. 35–39 (2019)
7. Ali, K., Isler, I., Hughes, C.E.: Facial expression recognition using human to animated-character expression translation. CoRR abs/1910.05595, https://arxiv.org/abs/1910.05595 (2019)
8. Klaser, A., Marszałek, M., Schmid, C.: A spatio-temporal descriptor based on 3d-gradients. In: Proceedings British Machine Vision Conference (2008)
9. Chu, W.S., Torre, F., Cohn, J.F.: Selective transfer machine for personalized facial expression analysis. IEEE Trans. Pattern Anal. Mach. Intell. **39**, 529–545 (2016)
10. Jiang, B., Valstar, M.F., Pantic, M.: Action unit detection using sparse appearance descriptors in space-time video volumes. In: International Conference on Automatic Face and Gesture Recognition, pp. 314–321 (2011)
11. Kim, B.K., Lee, H., Roh, J., Lee, S.Y.: Hierarchical committee of deep CNNs with exponentially-weighted decision fusion for static facial expression recognition. In: Proceedings of the International Conference on Multimodal Interaction, pp. 427–434 (2015)
12. Yu, Z., Zhang, C.: Image based static facial expression recognition with multiple deep network learning. In: Proceedings of the International Conference on Multimodal Interaction, pp. 435–442 (2015)
13. Ng, H.W., Nguyen, V.W., Vonikakis, V., Winkler, S.: Deep learning for emotion recognition on small datasets using transfer learning. In: Proceedings of the International Conference on Multimodal Interaction, pp. 443–449 (2015)

14. Liu, M., Li, S., Shan, S., Wang, R., Chen, X.: Deeply learning deformable facial action parts model for dynamic expression analysis. In: Asian Conference on Computer Vision, pp. 143–157 (2014)
15. Li, S., Deng, W., Du, J.P.: Reliable crowd sourcing and deep locality-preserving learning for expression recognition in the wild. In: Proceedings of the IEEE Conference on Computer Vision and Pattern Recognition, pp. 2852–2861 (2017)
16. Cai, J., Meng, Z., Khan, A.S., Li, Z., O'Reilly, J., Tong, Y.: Island loss for learning discriminative features in facial expression recognition. In: IEEE International Conference on Automatic Face and Gesture Recognition, pp. 302–309 (2018)
17. Meng, Z., Liu, P., Cai, J., Han, S., Tong Y.: Identity-aware convolutional neural network for facial expression recognition. In: IEEE International Conference on Automatic Face and Gesture Recognition, pp. 558–565 (2017)
18. Lucey, P, Cohn, J.F., Kanade, T., Saragih, J., Ambadar, Z., Matthews, I.: The extended cohn-kanade dataset (ck+): a complete dataset for action unit and emotion-specified expression. In: IEEE Computer Society Conference on Computer Vision and Pattern Recognition-Workshops, pp. 94–101 (2010)
19. Zhao, G., Huang, X., Taini, M., Li, S.Z., Pietikainen, M.: Facial expression recognition from near-infrared videos. Image Vis. Comput. **29**, 607–619 (2011)
20. Ali, K., Hughes, C.E.: Facial expression recognition using disentangled adversarial learning. CoRR abs/1909.13135 (2019). https://arxiv.org/abs/1909.13135
21. Zadeh, A., Lim, Y.C., Baltrusaitis, T., Morency, L.P.: Convolutional experts constrained local model for 3d facial landmark detection. In: Proceedings of the IEEE International Conference on Computer Vision, pp. 2519–2528 (2017)
22. Yin, L., Chen, X., Sun, Y., Worm, T., Reale, M.: A high-resolution 3d dynamic facial expression database. In: IEEE International Conference on Automatic Face and Gesture Recognition (2008)
23. Radford, A., Metz, L., Chintala, S.: Unsupervised representation learning with deep convolutional generative adversarial networks. CoRR abs/1511.06434 (2015). https://arxiv.org/abs/1511.06434
24. Goodfellow, I., et al.: Generative adversarial nets. In: Advances in neural information processing systems, pp. 2672–2680 (2014)
25. Liu, M., Shan, S., Wang, R., Chen, X.: Learning expressionlets on spatio-temporal manifold for dynamic facial expression recognition. In: Proceedings of the IEEE Conference on Computer Vision and Pattern Recognition, pp. 1749–1756 (2014)
26. Jung, H., Lee, S., Yim, J., Park, S., Kim, J.: Joint fine-tuning in deep neural networks for facial expression recognition. In: Proceedings of the IEEE international conference on computer vision, pp. 2983–2991 (2015)
27. Zhao, X., et al.: Peak-piloted deep network for facial expression recognition. In: European Conference on Computer Vision, pp. 425–442 (2016)
28. Yin, L., Wei, X., Sun, Y., Wang, J., Rosato, M.J.: A 3d facial expression database for facial behavior research. In: International Conference on Automatic Face and Gesture Recognition, pp. 211–216 (2006)
29. Wang, J., Yin, L., Wei, X., Sun, Y.: 3d facial expression recognition based on primitive surface feature distribution. In: IEEE Computer Vision and Pattern Recognition, pp. 1399–1406 (2006)
30. Berretti, S., Del Bimbo, A., Pala, P., Amor, B.B., Daoudi, M.: A set of selected sift features for 3d facial expression recognition. In: International Conference on Pattern Recognition, pp. 4125–4128 (2010)
31. Lopes, A.T., de Aguiar, E., De Souza, A.F., Oliveira-Santos, T.: Facial expression recognition with convolutional neural networks: coping with few data and the training sample order. Pattern Recogn. **61**, 610–628 (2017)

32. Song, L., Lu, Z., He, R., Sun, Z., Tan, T.: Geometry guided adversarial facial expression synthesis. In: Proceedings of the ACM International Conference on Multimedia, pp. 627–635 (2018)
33. Dhall, A., Murthy, O.R., Goecke, R., Joshi, J., Gedeon, T.: Video and image based emotion recognition challenges in the wild: Emotiw. In: Proceedings of the ACM on International Conference on Multimodal Interaction, pp. 423–426 (2015)
34. Zhang, K., Zhang, Z., Li, Z., Qiao, Y.: Joint face detection and alignment using multitask cascaded convolutional networks. IEEE Signal Process. Lett. **23**(10), 1499–1503 (2016)
35. Hassner, T., Harel, S., Paz, E., Enbar, R.: Effective face frontalization in unconstrained images. In: Proceedings of the IEEE Conference on Computer Vision and Pattern Recognition, pp. 4295–4304 (2015)
36. Liu, M., Li, S., Shan, S., Chen, X.: Au-aware deep networks for facial expression recognition. In: IEEE International Conference and Workshops on Automatic Face and Gesture Recognition, pp. 1–6 (2013)
37. Levi, G., Hassner, T.: Emotion recognition in the wild via convolutional neural networks and mapped binary patterns. In: Proceedings of the ACM on International Conference on Multimodal Interaction, pp. 503–510 (2015)
38. Ding, H, Zhou, S.K., Chellappa, R.: Facenet2expnet: regularizing a deep face recognition net for expression recognition. In: IEEE International Conference on Automatic Face and Gesture Recognition, pp. 118–126 (2017)
39. Halawa, M., Wollhaf, M., Vellasques, E., Sanz, U. S., Hellwich, O.: Learning Disentangled Expression Representations from Facial Images. CoRR abs/2008.07001 (2020). https://arxiv.org/abs/2008.07001
40. Alaghband, M., Yousefi, N., Garibay, I.: FePh: an annotated facial expression dataset for the RWTH-PHOENIX-Weather 2014 Dataset. CoRR abs/2003.08759 (2020). https://arxiv.org/abs/2003.08759
41. Parkhi, O.M., Vedaldi, A., Zisserman, A.: Deep face recognition. In: Proceedings British Machine Vision Conference (2015)

Motion and Tracking

Coarse-to-Fine Object Tracking Using Deep Features and Correlation Filters

Ahmed Zgaren[1], Wassim Bouachir[1(✉)], and Riadh Ksantini[2]

[1] Department of Science and Technology, TELUQ University, Montreal, Canada
{ahmed.zgaren,wassim.bouachir}@teluq.ca
[2] Department of Computer Science, University of Bahrain, Zallaq, Bahrain
rksantini@uob.edu.bh

Abstract. During the last years, deep learning trackers achieved stimulating results while bringing interesting ideas to solve the tracking problem. This progress is mainly due to the use of learned deep features obtained by training deep convolutional neural networks (CNNs) on large image databases. But since CNNs were originally developed for image classification, appearance modeling provided by their deep layers might be not enough discriminative for the tracking task. In fact, such features represent high-level information, that is more related to object category than to a specific instance of the object. Motivated by this observation, and by the fact that discriminative correlation filters (DCFs) may provide a complimentary low-level information, we present a novel tracking algorithm taking advantage of both approaches. We formulate the tracking task as a two-stage procedure. First, we exploit the generalization ability of deep features to coarsely estimate target translation, while ensuring invariance to appearance change. Then, we capitalize on the discriminative power of correlation filters to precisely localize the tracked object. Furthermore, we designed an update control mechanism to learn appearance change while avoiding model drift. We evaluated the proposed tracker on object tracking benchmarks. Experimental results show the robustness of our algorithm, which performs favorably against CNN and DCF-based trackers.

Keywords: Object tracking · CNN · Correlation filters

1 Introduction

The success of CNNs for visual object tracking (VOT) is mainly attributed to their rich feature hierarchy, and to the ability of convolutional layers to provide invariant feature representation against target appearance change. However, a major limitation relies in the fact that CNNs were developed following the principals of other visual classification tasks, where the goal is to predict a class label. They were thus designed without considering fundamental differences with the tracking task, that aims to locate a target object on an image sequence. Adopting such

© Springer Nature Switzerland AG 2020
G. Bebis et al. (Eds.): ISVC 2020, LNCS 12509, pp. 517–529, 2020.
https://doi.org/10.1007/978-3-030-64556-4_40

models for tracking may result in using general and redundant target representations, that are not enough discriminative for the tracking problem. For example, many trackers use feature representations from deep layers [3, 6, 12, 18, 27, 28]. These layers are naturally related to object category semantics and do not consider object specificities and intra-category variation. In the tracking task, object specific characteristics are important in order to determine its precise location on the image, and especially for distinguishing between the target and distractors (i.e. objects belonging to the same class and thus having similar appearance).

Some authors attempted to address this issue by combining feature representations provided by different CNN layers [10, 21, 22, 24, 26]. Such algorithms exploit multiple layers for feature extraction, based on the idea that different layers in a CNN model provide several detail levels in characterizing an object. Moreover, most of these methods incorporate adaptive correlation filters learned on multiple CNN layers, which is shown to improve tracking precision [21]. Our work proceeds along the same direction, in that it aims to investigate the optimal exploitation of deep features and correlation filters in order to improve tracking robustness. However, our approach differs from previous works by a new formulation of the VOT task, proposing a different way for combining CNNs and DCFs within the tracking framework. We formulate target search on a video frame as a two-stage procedure using deep features and DCFs sequentially. Since the last convolutional layers provide features that are related to object category semantics, we firstly exploit such representations to perform a coarse estimation of the target translation, while ensuring robustness against appearance change. Then, a precise localization is performed by applying a learned DCF filter and selecting the maximum correlation response within the coarse region. Unlike feature maps from deep layers, DCF filters are able to capture spatial details related to object specific characteristics, and thus provide low-level features that are important to determine a precise location.

In Fig. 1, we consider an example of a target face to emphasize the two feature levels that motivated our method. We can observe that CNN feature maps corresponding to deep convolutional layers encode the face appearance in a summarized fashion. This illustrates the generalization ability of such representations and their robustness to appearance change. But since these deep layers are naturally related to object category semantics, they do not guarantee precise localisation, nor robustness against distractors. On the contrary, the second row of Fig. 1 shows that DCF filters provide low-level visual information. This information is more related to object specific characteristics, which makes DCFs more appropriate for precise localisation of the target, and for handling tracking difficulties, such as the presence of distractors (e.g. tracking a face or a pedestrian in a crowded scene).

Once the new target position is predicted, we update the appearance model to learn appearance variations of the object. Handling appearance change is among the main challenges in VOT. Most DCF-based trackers (e.g. [9, 10]) are continuously updated on-the-fly, at a risk of contaminating the model by inappropriate updates. On the contrary, certain deep trackers use target features

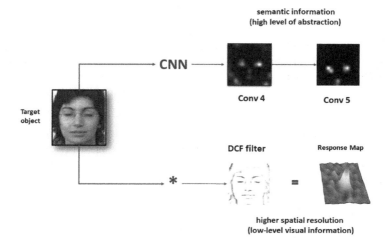

Fig. 1. illustration of our two feature extraction levels. Top: high-level semantic information can be extracted from deep convolutional layers (e.g. conv4 and conv5 from AlexNet). Bottom: DCF filters produce response maps corresponding to low-level spatial information.

extracted only from the first frame or the previous frame [1,13], which is known to speed-up tracking while reducing accuracy. We believe that a dynamic model that evolves during the tracking is important to handle appearance variations. However, we argue that excessive updates may contaminate the model due to an over-fitting to sudden variations. We therefore propose an update control mechanism to determine if the tracking status is appropriate for learning new feature representations. Such a mechanism makes it possible to optimize online appearance learning with respect to perturbation factors that may contaminate the model (e.g. occlusion).

To sum up, the main contributions of our work are as follows. First, we propose an effective coarse-to-fine approach to exploit deep features and correlation filters for object tracking. Second, to handle appearance change, we propose an update control mechanism, which allows learning new features during tracking, while avoiding model contamination. Third, we present extensive experiments on standard tracking benchmarks. The experimental work includes an ablation analysis to evaluate different design choices, as well as a comparative evaluation showing an improved performance compared to state-of-the-art trackers.

2   Related Work

2.1   CNN for Visual Tracking

Deep learning trackers typically use neural networks according to two main approaches:

1. As a feature extractor [4,5], by extracting the features produced by a single layer or multiple layers for appearance modeling. Target search is then performed using traditional methods.
2. For both feature extraction and target search, which is referred as end-to-end tracking [20,27]. In this case, target states are evaluated using the network output, that may have various forms such as probability maps and object classification scores.

An important limitation of many deep trackers is related to the fact that target localization mainly depends on features from the last convolutional layers. Since CNN models were initially developed for image classification, deep feature maps provide high-level information that is more related to an object class, than to a specific instance of an object. In our work, we argue that deep features are naturally more appropriate to coarsely estimate target translation during a preliminary prediction step of the tracking process.

2.2   Tracking with Discriminant Correlation Filters

The main idea of DCF tracking is to initially learn a filter from the target image region on the first frame. Then for each subsequent frame, the filter is used as a linear classifier to compute correlation over a search window, and discriminate between the target and the background. The new target position is predicted as the maximum value in the correlation output. Since the pioneering work of MOSSE [2], DCF trackers have been extensively studied as an efficient solution for the tracking problem. significant improvements have been then released on the DCF framework to address inherent limitations. For example, Henriques et al. [14,15] proposed to incorporate multiple channels and kernels to allow the non-linear classification of boundaries. Further, Daneljann et al. [9] proposed the Spatially Regularized Discriminative Correlation Filters (SRDCF). They introduced a spatial regularization component within the DCF tracking framework to handle the periodic assumption problems. The proposed regularization weights penalize the CF coefficients, to allow learning the filter on larger image regions. In addition, the DCF framework has been enhanced by, including scale estimation [7] and a long-term memory [23].

Despite major amelioration, DCF based trackers still suffer from high sensitivity to appearance change (e.g. object deformation, motion blur). This limitation is mainly due to their high spatial resolution, which limits their ability to generalize and learn semantic information on the target object. Another limitation relies to their continuous learning procedure, at the risk of contaminating the model by inappropriate update (e.g. occlusion). Our tracking framework takes advantage of the high spatial resolution of DCFs for precise localization of the target, while exploiting the high level of abstraction provided by deep CNN layers to ensure robustness to appearance change. Moreover, we handle the online learning problem by using a control mechanism to avoid inappropriate updates.

2.3   Combining CNNs and DCFs for Object Tracking

Existing CNN-based DCFs mainly focus on integrating convolutional features learned on deep network layers [5,8,10,21,24]. Ma et al. [21] propose a hierarchical ensemble method of independent DCF trackers to combine convolutional layers. Qi et al. [24] learn a correlation filter for each feature map, and use a modified Hedge algorithm to combine predictions. DeepSRDCF [8] investigates the use of features extracted from the first convolutional layer of a CNN to train a correlation filter for tracking. The C-COT [10] framework learns a convolutional operator in the continuous spatial domain using a pre-trained CNN, while ECO [5] proposes a factorized formulation to avoid the over-fitting problem observed with C-COT [10], and to reduce the number of learned filters.

In our work, we propose a different way to incorporate CNNs and DCFs within the tracking framework, in order to ensure the optimal exploitation of both models. We decompose target search into two stages to exploit the power of CNNs for high-level feature extraction, and the high accuracy of DCFs for precise target localization.

3   Proposed Method

We propose a coarse-to-fine tracking approach by combining CNNs with DCFs as two different, yet complementary, feature levels. In our framework, the correlation operation within the DCF acts similarly to a CNN convolutional layer. In fact, the learned correlation filter can be viewed as a final classification layer in the neural network. Thus, the tracker takes advantage of both models, while overcoming their limitations mutually. In this section, we decompose the tracking procedure into three steps: (1) coarse target search by using an incremental SVM fed with deep features, (2) fine target prediction as the maximum correlation response of a learned DCF within the coarse region, and (3) adaptation to appearance change through an update control mechanism. Figure 2 illustrates the main steps of our algorithm.

3.1   Convolutional Features for Coarse Search

We exploit deep convolutional layers of CNN to ensure representations that are robust to appearance variation and deformation. Our conception suggests to encode object information using a feature vector T that summarises the output of the K activation maps forming a convolutional layer. For dimensionality reduction, each activation map $\mathcal{M}_h$, $h \in \{1, 2, ..., K\}$ is up-sampled to produce a feature vector T as:

$$T(h) = \sum_{i=1}^{m} \sum_{j=1}^{n} \mathcal{M}_h(i,j)\lambda \,, \tag{1}$$

where $m \times n$ is the spatial resolution of the feature map, and λ is a regularization parameter.

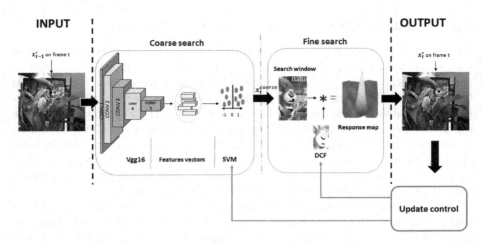

Fig. 2. The architecture of our coarse-to-fine tracker.

At the first frame, the feature vector T is extracted from target region using a pre-trained CNN. Since target information extracted from the first frame is initially insufficient for appearance modeling, we use data augmentation to generate additional learning examples through rotation, scale variation, and translation. The corresponding feature vectors are then used to feed a machine learning model used for identifying region proposals that are likely to be the target. During each tracking iteration, we evaluate several candidate regions in a search window centered around the last target location $\mathbf{x}_{t-1}^*$. Candidate regions are first generated by varying polar coordinates, with respect to the last target location center. Given the feature vector T_i of the ith candidate region, we compute the corresponding weight P_i ($P_i \in [-1, 1]$) using an incremental one-class SVM [17] learned from previous frames. P_i represents the likelihood of the candidate region of being the target, and is calculated using the SVM classification function:

$$P_i = \Delta_{W,b}(T_i). \tag{2}$$

Here, W and b denote the weight vector and the bias of the SVM, respectively.

The position $\mathbf{x}_t^{coarse}$ corresponding to the center of the coarse search region is finally estimated as the average weighted position over the best q candidate regions (based on their likelihoods), as follows:

$$\mathbf{x}_t^{coarse} = \frac{\sum_{i=1}^{q} P_i \, \mathbf{x}_i}{\sum_{i=1}^{q} P_i}, \tag{3}$$

where $\mathbf{x}_i$ is the center of the ith candidate region. The output of this step is considered as a coarse estimation of the target translation between two consecutive frames.

3.2   Fine Search

The second stage of our tracking procedure is based on DCF to find the maximum correlation output in a search region centered around $\mathbf{x}_t^{coarse}$. Since DCF trackers assume that the target undergoes small displacements between two consecutive frames, the search region at frame t is classically defined as a sub-window centered around the last predicted position. Instead, we define the correlation search region as the sub-window r_t of size $l \times z$, centered around $\mathbf{x}_t^{coarse}$. In this manner, we relax the small displacement assumption and rely on the coarse estimation of the target translation to determine the target search area.

The search sub-window r_t is extracted and augmented periodically. The filter f_{t-1} is then applied in a sliding window-like manner. The response map $Y_f(r_t)$ is constructed from the correlation scores at each position, as the inner product between the filter f_{t-1} and the shifted sub-image at that position. The correlation is computed in the Fourier domain, to produce the correlation output map $Y_f(r_t)$ using the convolution property of the FFT, that is:

$$Y_f(r_t) = F^{-1}\Big(F(f_{t-1}) \odot F(r_t) \Big), \tag{4}$$

where $\odot$ denotes point-wise multiplication, and F^{-1} the inverse FFT.

We note that the filter is applied at multiple resolutions to estimate target scale changes. Generally, the output response map approximately follows a Gaussian distribution, as CF-based trackers are trained with Gaussian shaped regression labels. The final position $\mathbf{x}_t^*$ of the target on frame t corresponds to the maximal correlation response calculated on all cyclic shifts of region r_t.

3.3   Model Update

During tracking, DCF-based trackers are typically updated on-the-fly at a risk of contaminating the model due to over-fitting to sudden changes or other inappropriate update situations such as occlusion. In order to optimize appearance modeling with respect to such perturbation factors, we use an update control mechanism to determine if the tracking status is appropriate for learning new feature representations. In particular, the feature vector T_t^* is extracted from the predicted target region (using Eq. 1), and a quality indicator I_t is calculated using the SVM score function:

$$I_t = \Delta_{W,b}(T_t^*). \tag{5}$$

Selective update is performed for each appearance model separately, if I_t exceeds the corresponding minimum quality threshold. That is to say, two minimum quality thresholds μ and γ are considered for the SVM and the DCF, respectively.

On the one hand, SVM adaptation is carried out by exploiting the incremental property of the model to incorporate the new observation, as stated in [17]. On the other hand, we update the filter according to a learning rate β as follows:

$$F(f_t) = \beta\, F(f_t) + (1 - \beta)\, F(f_{t-1}), \tag{6}$$

with f_t and f_{t-1} denoting the filter at frames t and $t-1$ respectively. The entire tracking process in summarized in algorithm 1.

Algorithm 1: Tracking

Result: Current position of the target $\mathbf{x}_t^*$
extract T from the first frame using Eq (1);
learn classifier $\Delta_{W,b}$;
learn filter f_0 from the first frame;
for *each subsequent frame t* **do**
    generate candidate regions around $\mathbf{x}_{t-1}^*$;
    for *each ith candidate region* **do**
        extract T_i using Eq (1);
        calculate P_i using Eq (2);
    end
    Compute $\mathbf{x}_t^{coarse}$ using Eq (3) ;
    Calculate correlation map using Eq (4);
    Select $\mathbf{x}_t^*$ as the maximum correlation response;
    calculate I_t using Eq (5);
    if $I_t \geq \mu$ **then**
        update $\Delta_{W,b}$;
    end
    if $I_t \geq \gamma$ **then**
        update f_t using Eq (6);
    end
end

---

4   Experiments

4.1   Implementation Details

For extracting deep features, we adopted the VGG16 network [25] trained on ImageNet [11]. More specifically, we used the output of the convolutional layer conv5-3, which produces $K = 512$ feature maps with a spatial size $m \times n$ equal to 14×14. The feature vector T is constructed by setting the regularization parameter λ to 0.1. For the iCOSVM [17], we set the internal training parameter ν to 0.1 and the update threshold μ to 0.4. Our implementation of the fine search step is based on SRDCF, where we use the same parameters in [9] for training the correlation filter. We set the search region $l \times z$ to four times the target size and the learning rate β to 0.025. We also fixed the update parameter γ to 0.0 (recall that $I_t \in [-1,1]$). The proposed Framework is implemented using Matlab on a PC with a Intel i7-8700 3.2 GHz CPU and a Nvidia GeForce GTX 1070 Ti GPU.

4.2   Evaluation Methodology

We performed a comprehensive evaluation of the proposed method on the standard benchmarks OTB100 [31] and OTB50 [30]. First, we present an ablation study to evaluate the importance of certain tracking mechanisms individually. We then compare our tracker to several state-of-the-art algorithms, including DCF-based trackers (SRDCF [9], DSST [7], KCF [14], CSK [15], and SAMF [19]), and CNN-based trackers (CNN-SVM [16], DLT [29], and SiamFC [1]). We follow the evaluation protocol presented in the benchmarks [31] and [30]. Tracking performance is evaluated based on (1) the bounding box overlap ratio, and (2) the center location error. The corresponding results are visualized by the success and precision plots, respectively. These plots are generated by calculating ratios of successful tracking iterations at several thresholds. The Area Under Curve (AUC) scores are used to rank the compared tracking methods in the success plot. In the precision plots, the final ranks depend on the tracking accuracy at a threshold of 20 pixels. Note that all the parameters of our method were fixed throughout the experiments. For the other compared methods, we used the parameter values defined by authors in the original papers.

4.3   Ablation Study

In this section, we perform an ablation analysis on OTB-100 to examine the contribution of individual components of our framework. We evaluate three variations of our tracker by comparison to the complete version of our algorithm. The four versions are denoted as follows.

– `complete-version`: The complete version of our tracker as described in algorithm 1.
– `no-fine-prediction`: We limit our appearance modeling to deep features. Target localisation is also limited to the coarse prediction step. In other words, we eliminate the fine prediction step and select the candidate region with the highest likelihood P_i as the final tracking status (see Eq. 2).
– `no-update`: We eliminate the update mechanism and limit the target appearance modeling to features from the first frame.
– `aggressive-update`: Both coarse and fine classifiers are automatically updated at each iteration, without evaluating tracking status (i.e. we do not use quality indicators and minimum quality thresholds).

Figure 3 shows precision and success plots on OTB100. It can be clearly observed that the complete implementation of our tracker outperforms all the other versions. The removal of the fine search component from our pipeline (`no-fine-prediction`) results in a drastic decrease for both precision and success measures. In fact, the convolutional features learned from deep CNN layers are not sufficient for precise localisation, as they do not capture spatial details of the object. Using DCF for subsequent fine prediction allows to considerably improve precision and success respectively by 22% and 18%.

Regarding the update procedure, Fig. 3 shows that the complete removal of the update mechanism (`no-update`) causes a decrease of about 18% in precision and 13% in success measures. Furthermore, we can see that the aggressive update strategy (`aggressive-update`) does not achieve optimal performance either.

These results confirm our initial assumption, stating that the proposed update control mechanism is efficient for handling appearance change, while avoiding model contamination.

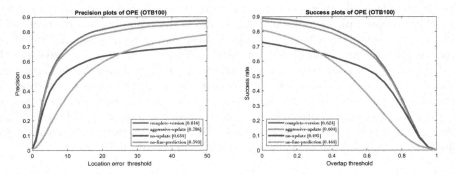

Fig. 3. Performance evaluation of different versions of our tracker.

4.4   Comparison with State-of-the Art Trackers

Quantitative Evaluation: We compared our algorithm to several state-of-the-art trackers on OTB100 and OTB50 datasets, which respectively consists of 100 and 50 fully annotated videos with various challenging attributes. Figure 4 shows the results under one-pass evaluation (OPE), using the distance precision rate and overlap success rate. The overall evaluation shows that our tacker achieved the best performance on both datasets. In particular, we outperformed the CNN-based tracker CNN-SVM [16] and the DCF-based tracker SRDCF [9]. Furthermore, the superiority of our algorithm with respect to DCF-based and CNN-based trackers demonstrates that the proposed coarse-to-fine combination of the two approaches allows to improve tracking.

Attribute-Based Evaluation: We evaluated the performance of our tracker in different challenging situations. Figure 5 shows that our tracker outperforms SRDCF [9], CNN-SVM [16], KCF [14], and DLT [29] on the majority of challenging situations. This evaluation underlines the ability of the proposed tracker to handle all tracking difficulties that generally require high-level semantic understanding of object appearance. In particular, our coarse appearance modeling is proved to be efficient in handling appearance variation caused by out-of-plane rotations, illumination variations, and deformations.

On the other hand, the advantage of using low-level features for fine prediction is illustrated in the background clutter (BC) curve. It is noteworthy that the BC attribute in the OTB is often manifested by the presence of other objects with similar appearance near the target (distractors). In this situation, the two best scores were achieved respectively by our method and SRDCF, as both of them share an important discriminative aspect (the DFC component), which performs favorably in presence of distractors. Our tracker also effectively deals

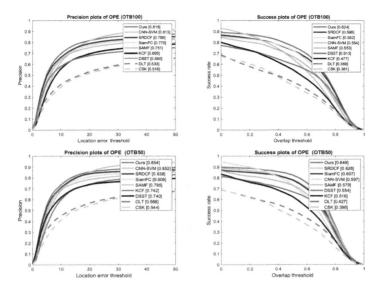

Fig. 4. Precision and success plots on OTB100 and OTB50 benchmarks using one-pass evaluation (OPE). The legend of precision plots shows the ranking of the compared trackers based on precision scores at a distance threshold of 20 pixels. The legend of success plots shows a ranking based on the area under-the-curve score.

with the out-of-view and the occlusion problems, where the target is partially or totally invisible during a period of time. Such situations lead to a decrease in the tracking quality indicator I_t (see Eq. 6), which prevents the model of being contaminated with features from the background.

5   Conclusion

We proposed an effective coarse-to-fine approach for integrating deep features and correlation filters within the tracking framework. First, we exploit the generalization ability of CNNs to coarsely predict target translation between subsequent frames. We then capitalize on the detailed feature representation and the discriminative power of DCFs to obtain a precise location of the target. Once the target is located, appearance model adaptation is carried out through an update control mechanism, which allows the tracker to learn appearance change while avoiding model drift. The performed experiments demonstrate the efficiency of our approach, indicating improved performances compared to both CNN and DCF-based trackers. Such results confirm that our approach for combining CNNs and DCFs represents a promising direction for developing more advanced and robust trackers.

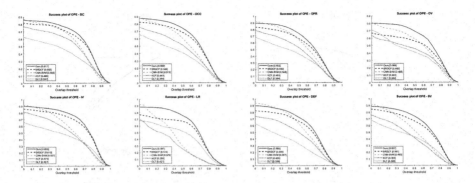

Fig. 5. The Success plots on OTB100 for eight attributes representing the challenging aspects in VOT: background clutter (BC), occlusion (OCC), out-of-plane rotation (OPR), out-of-view (OV), illumination variations (IV), low resolution (LR), deformation (DEF), scale variation (SV).

References

1. Bertinetto, L., Valmadre, J., Henriques, J.F., Vedaldi, A., Torr, P.H.S.: Fully-convolutional siamese networks for object tracking. In: Hua, G., Jégou, H. (eds.) ECCV 2016. LNCS, vol. 9914, pp. 850–865. Springer, Cham (2016). https://doi.org/10.1007/978-3-319-48881-3_56
2. Bolme, D.S., Beveridge, J.R., Draper, B.A., Lui, Y.M.: Visual object tracking using adaptive correlation filters. In: CVPR, pp. 2544–2550 (2010)
3. Chi, Z., Li, H., Lu, H., Yang, M.H.: Dual deep network for visual tracking. TIP **26**, 2005–2015 (2017)
4. Cui, Z., Xiao, S., Feng, J., Yan, S.: Recurrently target-attending tracking. In: CVPR, pp. 1449–1458 (2016)
5. Danelljan, M., Bhat, G., Khan, F.S., Felsberg, M.: Eco: Efficient convolution operators for tracking. In: CVPR, pp. 6931–6939 (2017)
6. Danelljan, M., Bhat, G., Khan, F.S., Felsberg, M.: Atom: accurate tracking by overlap maximization. In: CVPR, June 2019
7. Danelljan, M., Häger, G., Khan, F.S., Felsberg, M.: Accurate scale estimation for robust visual tracking. In: BMVC (2014)
8. Danelljan, M., Häger, G., Khan, F.S., Felsberg, M.: Convolutional features for correlation filter based visual tracking. In: ICCV Workshops, pp. 621–629 (2015)
9. Danelljan, M., Häger, G., Khan, F.S., Felsberg, M.: Learning spatially regularized correlation filters for visual tracking. In: ICCV, pp. 4310–4318 (2015)
10. Danelljan, M., Robinson, A., Shahbaz Khan, F., Felsberg, M.: Beyond correlation filters: learning continuous convolution operators for visual tracking. In: ECCV (2016)
11. Deng, J., Dong, W., Socher, R., Li, L.J., Li, K., Fei-Fei, L.: Imagenet: a large-scale hierarchical image database. In: CVPR, pp. 248–255 (2009)
12. Gao, J., Zhang, T., Xu, C.: Graph convolutional tracking. In: CVPR, pp. 4644–4654 (2019)
13. He, A., Luo, C., Tian, X., Zeng, W.: A twofold siamese network for real-time object tracking. In: CVPR, pp. 4834–4843 (2018)

14. Henriques, J.F., Caseiro, R., Martins, P., Batista, J.: High-speed tracking with kernelized correlation filters. TPAMI **37**, 583–596 (2015)
15. Henriques, J.F., Caseiro, R., Martins, P., Batista, J.P.: Exploiting the circulant structure of tracking-by-detection with kernels. In: ECCV (2012)
16. Hong, S., You, T., Kwak, S., Han, B.: Online tracking by learning discriminative saliency map with convolutional neural network. In: ICML (2015)
17. Kefi-Fatteh, T., Ksantini, R., Kaâniche, M.B., Bouhoula, A.: A novel incremental one-class support vector machine based on low variance direction. Pattern Recogn. **91**, 308–321 (2019)
18. Li, B., Wu, W., Wang, Q., Zhang, F., Xing, J., Yan, J.: Siamrpn++: evolution of siamese visual tracking with very deep networks. In: CVPR, pp. 4277–4286 (2019)
19. Li, Y., Zhu, J.: A scale adaptive kernel correlation filter tracker with feature integration. In: ECCV Workshops (2014)
20. Li, Z., Bilodeau, G.A., Bouachir, W.: Multi-branch siamese networks with online selection for object tracking. In: ISVC (2018)
21. Ma, C., Huang, J.B., Yang, X., Yang, M.H.: Hierarchical convolutional features for visual tracking. In: ICCV pp. 3074–3082 (2015)
22. Ma, C., Xu, Y., Ni, B., Yang, X.: When correlation filters meet convolutional neural networks for visual tracking. SPL **23**, 1454–1458 (2016)
23. Ma, C., Yang, X., Zhang, C., Yang, M.H.: Long-term correlation tracking. In: CVPR, pp. 5388–5396 (2015)
24. Qi, Y., et al.: Hedged deep tracking. In: CVPR, pp. 4303–4311 (2016)
25. Simonyan, K., Zisserman, A.: Very deep convolutional networks for large-scale image recognition. CoRR abs/1409.1556 (2015)
26. Touil, D.E., Terki, N., Medouakh, S.: Hierarchical convolutional features for visual tracking via two combined color spaces with SVM classifier. SIVP **13**(2), 359–368 (2019)
27. Wang, G., Luo, C., Sun, X., Xiong, Z., Zeng, W.: Tracking by instance detection: a meta-learning approach. In: CVPR, pp. 6288–6297 (2020)
28. Wang, G., Luo, C., Xiong, Z., Zeng, W.: SPM-tracker: series-parallel matching for real-time visual object tracking. In: CVPR, pp. 3638–3647 (2019)
29. Wang, N., Yeung, D.Y.: Learning a deep compact image representation for visual tracking. In: NIPS (2013)
30. Wu, Y., Lim, J., Yang, M.H.: Online object tracking: A benchmark. In: CVPR, pp. 2411–2418 (2013)
31. Wu, Y., Lim, J., Yang, M.H.: Object tracking benchmark. TPAMI **37**, 1834–1848 (2015)

Asynchronous Corner Tracking Algorithm Based on Lifetime of Events for DAVIS Cameras

Sherif A. S. Mohamed[1]([✉]), Jawad N. Yasin[1], Mohammad-Hashem Haghbayan[1], Antonio Miele[3], Jukka Heikkonen[1], Hannu Tenhunen[2], and Juha Plosila[1]

[1] University of Turku, 20500 Turku, Finland
samoha@utu.fi
[2] KTH Royal Institute of Technology, 11428 Stockholm, Sweden
[3] Politecnico di Milano, 20133 Milan, Italy

Abstract. Event cameras, i.e., the Dynamic and Active-pixel Vision Sensor (DAVIS) ones, capture the intensity changes in the scene and generates a stream of events in an asynchronous fashion. The output rate of such cameras can reach up to 10 million events per second in high dynamic environments. DAVIS cameras use novel vision sensors that mimic human eyes. Their attractive attributes, such as high output rate, High Dynamic Range (HDR), and high pixel bandwidth, make them an ideal solution for applications that require high-frequency tracking. Moreover, applications that operate in challenging lighting scenarios can exploit from the high HDR of event cameras, i.e., 140 dB compared to 60 dB of traditional cameras. In this paper, a novel asynchronous corner tracking method is proposed that uses both events and intensity images captured by a DAVIS camera. The Harris algorithm is used to extract features, i.e., frame-corners from keyframes, i.e., intensity images. Afterward, a matching algorithm is used to extract event-corners from the stream of events. Events are solely used to perform asynchronous tracking until the next keyframe is captured. Neighboring events, within a window size of 5×5 pixels around the event-corner, are used to calculate the velocity and direction of extracted event-corners by fitting the 2D planar using a randomized Hough transform algorithm. Experimental evaluation showed that our approach is able to update the location of the extracted corners up to 100 times during the blind time of traditional cameras, i.e., between two consecutive intensity images.

Keywords: Corner · Asynchronous tracking · Hough transform · Event cameras · Lifetime

1 Introduction

Simultaneous Localization And Mapping (SLAM) approaches use onboard sensors, such as Lidar, camera, and radar to observe the environment and estimate the position and the orientation of the robot [9,18,19]. For example, visual

Supported by the Academy of Finland under the project (314048).

SLAM methods use single or multiple cameras to obtain the pose by extracting and tracking a sufficient number of features from consecutive images. Over the past years, there are many methods have been presented to detect frame-corners (e.g., *Harris* [6]) and edges (e.g., *Canny* [4]).

Most of SLAM approaches in the literature obtain the pose of robots by progressing a sequence of intensity images captured by CMOS sensors, i.e., frame-based cameras. However, such cameras mostly suffer from some major hardware limitations. They generate grayscale or RGB images at a fixed rate, typically 60 Hz. Moreover, they produce unnecessary information when the camera is not moving and the scene is static, which increases the computational cost dramatically. On the other hand, when the camera and objects in the scene are highly dynamic they are affected by the motion blur phenomena, i.e., they generate insufficient information. In addition, a huge amount of information might be missed during the blind time, i.e., the time between two successive images, which might result in inaccurate pose estimates. In conclusion, the limitations of conventional cameras would degrade the tracking performance, resulting in inaccurate localization.

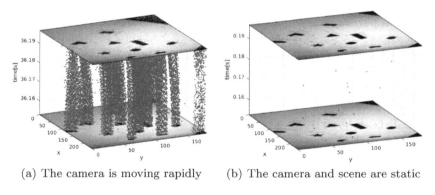

(a) The camera is moving rapidly   (b) The camera and scene are static

Fig. 1. Events (blue) triggered between two consecutive frame-images in two different scenarios. (Color figure online)

Newly emerged event cameras, such as DVS [7] and ATIS [13], overcome these problems through transmitting a stream of events by capturing the intensity changes instead of the "absolute" intensity. Events are triggered when the intensity of any pixel changes by a certain threshold. Thus, the number of triggered events depends on the texture of the environment and the motion of the camera and objects in the scene. rightness increases "1" or decreases "0". Figure 1 illustrates the output of the event camera in two different.

When the camera and the scene are static or the camera is moving slowly in a texture-less scene, event cameras only generate a few numbers of events and therefore only a small amount of resources would be enough to process those events (see Fig. 1(b)). Contrarily, when the scene is highly dynamic or the camera is moving rapidly, a large number of events (in order of millions) will be generated (see Fig. 1(a)). These powerful attributes make event cameras a great solution for applications that operates in high dynamic scenes and need to get their pose updated frequently, i.e., drones.

Given to the discussed necessity of robust and high-frequency corner detection algorithms, in this paper we present a novel algorithm that exploits the attractive attributes of event cameras and operates in an asynchronous fashion. Our algorithm uses both events and grayscale images captured by the DAVIS [3] cameras to extract and track corners. The proposed algorithm is composed of three main phases: observation, detection, and asynchronous tracking. A sufficient number of salient frame-corners are detected using Harris [6] from grayscale images. Afterward, a matching filter is applied to obtain event-corners by selecting the first event that occurs on the same pixel location of extracted frame-corners. A window size of 5×5 pixels around each event-corner is used to compute the lifetime of each event-corner. We use a randomized Hough transform to fit a local plane to the points in the 5×5 pixels matrix [17] and compute the lifetime and the direction of each event-corner. Lifetime indicates the time a event-corner will take to move from its current pixel to one of the eight neighboring pixels. Our algorithm is able to update the extracted corners up to 2.4 $\times 10^3$ times per second compared to 24 using only images.

The rest of the paper is organized as follows. Section 2 reviews related works In Sect. 3, the system architecture of the proposed work is presented. An experimental evaluation of the proposed approach is discussed in Sect. 4. Last section draws conclusion and presents future work.

2 Related Work

To unlock events' camera potential, novel methods are required to process the output, i.e., a stream of events. Methods in the literature can be categorized as indirect and direct.

Indirect methods pre-process the captured events to generate artificially synthesized frames, i.e., event-frames and then apply one of the state-of-the-art frame-based methods to extract and track frame-corners. In [2], the authors generate event-frames by accumulating events during a fixed time interval. In [14], the authors proposed another approach to generate event-frames by accumulating a fixed number of events, (e.g.., 2000 events) to form a frame. In [8], the authors presented a dynamic slicing method to generate event-frames based on the velocity of the event camera and the number of edges in the environment, i.e., *entropy*. The main disadvantage of using such techniques is that they omit the innate asynchronous nature of the event cameras.

Direct approaches, on the other hand, process the asynchronous stream of events directly. In [16], Vasco et al. proposed an algorithm to detect asynchronous corners using an adaptation of the original Harris score [6] on a spatiotemporal window, i.e., surface Active Events (SAE). The algorithm demands a lot of computational resources to compute the gradients of each incoming event.

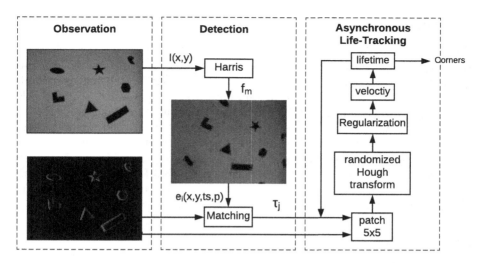

Fig. 2. Overview of the overall asynchronous corner detection and tracking algorithm.

In [10], the authors present an algorithm inspired by FAST [15] to detect event-corners, they call it eFAST. Corners are extracted on SAE by comparing the timestamp of the latest events, i.e., pixels on two circles. The radius of the inner and the outer circle is 3 and 4 pixels respectively. In [1], the authors used a similar technique (Arc) with an event filter to detect corner corners 4.5x faster than the eFAST. There are two main disadvantages of using such techniques mainly related to computational cost and accuracy. Since event cameras can generate millions of events per second and processing each incoming event to extract corners is computationally expensive. Thus, they are not feasible to run in real-time performance and especially on resource contained systems. On the other hand, some approaches rely on simple operations to perform real-time corner extraction. However, these methods produce inaccurate corners ($50 - 60\%$) compared to frame-based methods, such as Harris.

In conclusion, indirect methods omit one of the main characteristics of event-cameras, i.e., asynchronous. Direct methods, on the other hand, mistakenly detect more false event-corners and subsequently require a lot of computational resources to process all the incoming events.

3   Proposed Approach

The proposed approach, illustrated in Fig. 2, is composed of three main phases: observation, detection, and asynchronous tracking. Details of the various phases are discussed in the following subsections.

3.1   Observation

The sensor of DAVIS [3] cameras has an Active Pixel Sensor (APS) [5] and a Dynamic Vision Sensor (DVS) for each pixel, making them able to generate synchronized images and events at the same time. Generated images contain the absolute brightness of the scene and have a resolution of 240 × 180 pixels. Grayscale images are normally captured at a constant rate (equal to 24 Hz). In our approach, we use images as a *keyframe* to extract strong and robust corners. The other output of the DAVIS camera is events. Events represent the change of brightness of each pixel independently. Events are triggered asynchronously at a high rate (up to 1 MHz), which makes them ideal for tracking in a highly dynamic environment. Events contain simple information: the position of the pixel, the timestamp, and the polarity of the brightness changes [1, −1].

3.2   Detection

In the detection phase, we extract 2-dimensional interest points, i.e., corners from the scene, using Harris [6] algorithm. As illustrated in Fig. 3(a), a point in an image is considered as a corner when its local pixels have a significant change in all eight directions. Edges have significant changes in six direction but not along the edge direction Fig. 3(b). On the other hand, flat regions have no change in all directions Fig. 3(c). Thus, corners are important for location and object detection algorithm based in vision sensors, since they are invariant to motion changes, such as rotational and translation and illumination changes. Harris is considered one of the most robust corner detection algorithm in the literature.

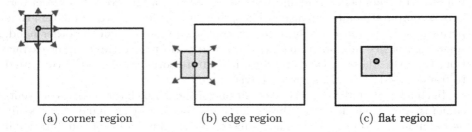

    (a) corner region   (b) edge region   (c) flat region

Fig. 3. A general presentation of three different regions in images: corners, edges, and flat regions.

Harris algorithm uses a score technique to extract strong corners from the capture images. A point is considered as a corner if its score is larger than a certain threshold. A window size of 3 × 3 pixels is used to calculate the S score of each pixel in the image, as follows

$$S = \lambda_1\lambda_2 - k(\lambda_1 + \lambda_2)^2 \tag{1}$$

where λ_1 and λ_2 are the eigenvalues of M, i.e.,

$$M = \sum w(x,y) \begin{bmatrix} I_x^2 & I_x I_y \\ I_x I_y & I_y^2 \end{bmatrix} \tag{2}$$

where $w(x,y)$ denotes the local window of each pixel. The horizontal and vertical gradients is denoted by I_x and I_y respectively. Point P is considered as a corner if its score S is large, in other words its λ_1 and λ_2 are large and $\lambda_1 \sim \lambda_2$. After we detect corners from grayscale images, we use a matching algorithm to extract event-corners.

Algorithm 1. Matching Unit

Input: frame-corners, events
Output: event-corners

1: Initialization
2: **if** e.position = corner.position **then**
3:     Select L_SAE
4:     Determine binary L_SAE
5:     Compute I_x and I_y
6:     Compute Score S
7:     **if** $S >$ threshold **then**
8:         Process event
9:     **else**
10:         Discard event
11:     **end if**
12: **else**
13:     Discard event
14: **end if**

The matching algorithm, as summarized in Algorithm 1, filters the incoming event and only processes the first corner-candidate that occurs on the same location of the extracted corners. Processed events, i.e., event-corners, are then fed to the next phase to track the event-corners in asynchronous fashion using neighbouring events. The inputs of the algorithm are the triggered events and the extracted frame-corners from Harris. If the incoming event is on the same location of a corner, a local surface active events (L_SAE) is extracted around the event. The L_SAE has a size of 7×7 pixels and contains the timestamp on neighboring events. As shown in Fig. 4, only the most recent N neighbours ($N = 12$) are included and labeled as "1" in binary L_SAE to compute the vertical and horizontal gradients. Those gradient are then used to compute the score of the incoming event. If the score is larger than the threshold, the incoming event is considered as event-corner and it's only updated when a new image, i.e., keyframe is captured.

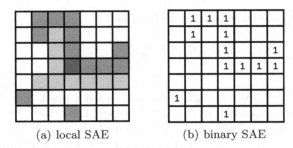

(a) local SAE   (b) binary SAE

Fig. 4. A presentation of local and binary SAE. Incoming event, i.e., corner-candidate, is in the center of the SAE in red. The most recent N neighbours are in green and are labeled as "1" in the binary SAE. Old neighbouring events are in gray and they are not included in the binary SAE.

3.3 Asynchronous Life-Tracking

In this section, we explain our asynchronous tracking algorithm which is based on the lifetime of events. The concept of lifetime refers to the time an event will take to move from the current pixel to one of the eight neighboring pixels. Since event cameras have a high temporal rate up to 8 million events per second, lifetime is feasible for event-based tracking. The summary of the asynchronous tracking algorithm is illustrated in Algorithm 2, in which we first extract a local L_SAE of size 5 × 5 pixels around each event-corner. The randomized Hough transform algorithm [17] is used to fit a local plane using the neighboring events in the L_SAE. The vector (a,b, and c) which is orthogonal onto the obtained plane is calculated. Then we compute the velocity of the event-corner in x- and y-directions v_x and v_y respectively, as follows:

$$v_x = c * (-a)/(a^2 + b^2) \tag{3}$$

$$v_y = c * (-b)/(a^2 + b^2) \tag{4}$$

The plane fitting algorithm is inspired by [11], in which we robustly compute candidate planes using three points, i.e., the event-corner and two additional neighboring events from L_SAE. The plane fitting algorithm is illustrated in Algorithm 3, where two neighboring are chosen randomly plus the event-corner to fit a local plane (Line 1). The algorithm calculated the Hough space parameters $H(\theta, \phi, \rho)$ and store in different spaces in cells C (Lines 3–4). For each vote, a cell counter C increments by one $C + 1$ (Lines 5–6) and the most voted cell is considered as the fitting plane. The Hough space is computed using two randomly picked points p_2,p_3 from the point set in L_SAE and the event-corner p_1, i.e.,

$$\rho = v \cdot p_1 = ((p_3 - p_1) \times (p_1 - p_2)) \cdot p_1 \tag{5}$$

$$p_x \cdot \cos \theta \cdot \sin \phi + p_y \cdot sin\phi \cdot \sin \theta + p_z \cdot \cos \phi = \rho \tag{6}$$

Algorithm 2. Asynchronous Life-Tracking

Input: $e_i = (x_i, y_i, t_i, pol_i)$ and $\tau = \{e_1, e_2, .., e_j\}$
Output: new location of events in τ

1: Extract SAE of size 5x5 for each event in τ
2: Fit a local plane for each SAE
3: Calculate a_j, b_j, and c_j
4: Calculate velocity $v_j(v_x, v_y)$
5: Calculate lifetime

---

where the distance to the centroid is denoted by ρ, ϕ is the angle between the vector v and the XY-plane in the z-direction and θ denotes the angle of v on the XY-plane.

Algorithm 3. Randomized Hough transform

Input: $\mathbf{P} = \{p_1, p_2, .., p_n\}$
Output: $\mathrm{H}(\theta, \phi, \rho)$

1: **while** points in $\mathbf{P} > 2$ **do**
2:     Select event-corner p_1 and two additional points p_2, p_3
3:     Calculate Hough space
4:     Store planes in cells
5:     Points vote for cells
6:     For each vote cell's Counter C = C + 1
7:     **if** C = threshold **then**
8:       Parameterize the detected plane
9:       Delete p_2 and p_3 from $\mathbf{P}$
10:      C = 0
11:    **else**
12:       Continue
13:    **end if**
14: **end while**

---

4 Experimental Evaluation

We evaluated the proposed approach on the publicly available datasets [12]. Subsets used in the experiment consists of slow and fast camera motions and low- and high-textured scenes to ensure comprehensive evaluation scheme. In general, DAVIS camera can generate up to 10 million events per second in textured and highly dynamic scenes. On other hand, in slow camera motion and texture-less scene, event camera triggers few events. As mentioned previously, DAVIS camera produce a sequence of intensity images along side a stream of asynchronous events. The subsets used in the experiment are recorded by a DAVIS240 camera which generates images with resolution of 240×180. We implemented our algorithm in C++, OpenCV and Eigen libraries. All experiments were carried out on an embedded system with an ARM-based processor, hosted on Jetson TX2 board and running at 2 GHz.

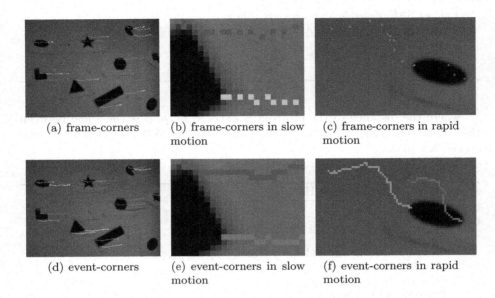

(a) frame-corners   (b) frame-corners in slow motion   (c) frame-corners in rapid motion

(d) event-corners   (e) event-corners in slow motion   (f) event-corners in rapid motion

Fig. 5. The qualitative result of proposed method compared with Harris method on intensity images.

The experimental results of the proposed asynchronous corner tracking algorithm are reported in Fig. 5. For this evaluation we used *shapes_6dof* dataset. The dataset includes various 2D geometric shapes mounted on a wall and recorded freely moving DAVIS-240 cameras with different speeds. We compared the proposed algorithm with normal Harris corner detection and at different speeds of the camera. In slow camera motions, frame-corner detection method, i.e., Harris performances considerably well as only break of 1 pixel appears in the detection, as shown in Fig. 5(b). However, when the speed of the camera, or some objects in the environment, is high, feature extraction and tracking based on intensity images cannot provide sufficient information about the environment. This can be shown in Fig. 5(c) where the increase in the speed of the camera imposes a break in detecting up to 4 pixels between two consecutive detections. In such an environment, an event-based camera and the proposed feature tracking technique can provide a seamless feature tracking for the algorithm, see Fig. 5(f).

Table 1 summarizes the execution time of different units in the proposed method. The intensity images have a resolution of 240 × 180, which leads to fast execution time for Harris algorithm, i.e., the average execution time is 1.8 ms. Execution time for Harris does not change significantly since the algorithm processes all pixels in the image and all captured images have the same size. On the other hand, event-based units, such as matching unit and lifetime calculation depends on the number of generated events that is based on the speed of the camera and the amount of information in the scene [8]. The execution time of both units is very low and especially the matching unit which has an average execution time of 3.6 ms. One of the main advantages of the proposed solution w.r.t. the state-of-the-art event-based approaches is the fact that it is able to provide high performance in all the scenarios; in particular, in case the camera moves very fast, up to 10 Millions events can be generated. This tremendous load causes an execution time of the classical matching unit equal to 36 s and of the lifetime calculation equal to 4900 s, thus not affordable in any real-time scenario. At the opposite, the proposed filtering solutions has an average execution time of 5.62 s. We extract a maximum of 50 corners per image using Harris algorithm from images. The DAVIS-240 camera captures a total number of 24 images per second. For each corner an average number of 10 events are checked to detect event-corners using the matching unit, which totals a number of 12×10^3 events are checked per second resulting a maximum execution time of 43.2 ms.

Table 1. The average execution time of units of the proposed method

Unit	Time (ms)
Harris per image	1.8
Matching per event	3.6×10^{-3}
Lifetime per event	0.49

5   Conclusion

Performing high-frequency corner detection and tracking based on traditional cameras is not feasible due to the limitations of such cameras, such as motions blur and blind time. In this paper, we exploit event-based cameras since they can cope well with rapid camera movements and highly dynamic scenes. We proposed an asynchronous tracking algorithm based on the lifetime of extracted event-corners. We first extract strong frame-corners from intensity images using Harris. Afterward, we match those corners with first generated events with the same pixel location. The tracking algorithm fits a local plane to the neighboring events of each extracted event-corner to compute the lifetime and velocity of each event-corner. A randomize Hough transform is used to fit a plane. Finally, we evaluated our proposed method by performing experiments on datasets with different speeds and compared the results with the extracted corner using only intensity images. In addition, the execution time of each unit of the proposed method is reported. The results show that our method has an average execution time of 5.62 s.

References

1. Alzugaray, I., Chli, M.: Asynchronous corner detection and tracking for event cameras in real time. IEEE Robot. Autom. Lett. **3**(4), 3177–3184 (2018). https://doi.org/10.1109/LRA.2018.2849882
2. Alzugaray, I., Chli, M.: Asynchronous corner detection and tracking for event cameras in real time. IEEE Robot. Autom. Lett. **3**(4), 3177–3184 (2018)
3. Brandli, C., Berner, R., Yang, M., Liu, S.C., Delbruck, T.: A 240 × 80 130 db 3μs latency global shutter spatiotemporal vision sensor. IEEE J. Solid-State Circ. **49**(10), 2333–2341 (2014)
4. Canny, J.: A computational approach to edge detection. IEEE Trans. Pattern Anal. Mach. Intell. PAMI **8**(6), 679–698 (1986)
5. Fossum, E.R.: Cmos image sensors: electronic camera-on-a-chip. IEEE Trans. Electron Dev. **44**(10), 1689–1698 (1997)
6. Harris, C., Stephens, M.: A combined corner and edge detector. In: Proceedings of the 4th Alvey Vision Conference, pp. 147–151 (1988)
7. Lichtsteiner, P., Posch, C., Delbrück, T.: A 128×128 120 db 15 μs latency asynchronous temporal contrast vision sensor. J. Solid-State Circ. **43**(2), 566–576 (2008)
8. Mohamed, S.A.S., Haghbayan, M.-H., Rabah, M., Heikkonen, J., Tenhunen, H., Plosila, J.: Towards dynamic monocular visual odometry based on an event camera and IMU sensor. In: Martins, A.L., Ferreira, J.C., Kocian, A. (eds.) INTSYS 2019. LNICST, vol. 310, pp. 249–263. Springer, Cham (2020). https://doi.org/10.1007/978-3-030-38822-5_17
9. Mohamed, S.A.S., Haghbayan, M., Westerlund, T., Heikkonen, J., Tenhunen, H., Plosila, J.: A survey on odometry for autonomous navigation systems. IEEE Access **7**, 97466–97486 (2019)
10. Mueggler, E., Bartolozzi, C., Scaramuzza, D.: Fast event-based corner detection. In: British Machine Vision Conference (BMVC) (2017)
11. Mueggler, E., Forster, C., Baumli, N., Gallego, G., Scaramuzza, D.: Lifetime estimation of events from dynamic vision sensors. In: Proceedings - IEEE International Conference on Robotics and Automation 2015 (05 2015)
12. Mueggler, E., Rebecq, H., Gallego, G., Delbrück, T., Scaramuzza, D.: The event-camera dataset and simulator: event-based data for pose estimation, visual odometry, and SLAM. I. J. Robot. Res. **36**(2), 142–149 (2017)
13. Posch, C., Serrano-Gotarredona, T., Linares-Barranco, B., Delbruck, T.: Retinomorphic event-based vision sensors: bioinspired cameras with spiking output. Proc. IEEE **102**(10), 1470–1484 (2014)
14. Rebecq, H., Horstschaefer, T., Gallego, G., Scaramuzza, D.: EVO: a geometric approach to event-based 6-DOF parallel tracking and mapping in real time. IEEE Robot. Autom. Lett. **2**(2), 593–600 (2017)
15. Rosten, E., Drummond, T.: Machine learning for high-speed corner detection. In: Leonardis, A., Bischof, H., Pinz, A. (eds.) ECCV 2006. LNCS, vol. 3951, pp. 430–443. Springer, Heidelberg (2006). https://doi.org/10.1007/11744023_34
16. Vasco, V., Glover, A., Bartolozzi, C.: Fast event-based harris corner detection exploiting the advantages of event-driven cameras. In: 2016 IEEE/RSJ International Conference on Intelligent Robots and Systems (IROS), pp. 4144–4149 (2016)
17. Xu, L., Oja, E.: Randomized hough transform (RHT): Basic mechanisms, algorithms, and computational complexities. CVGIP: Image Understand. **57**(2), 131–154 (1993)

18. Yasin, J.N., Mohamed, S.A.S., Haghbayan, M., Heikkonen, J., Tenhunen, H., Plosila, J.: Unmanned aerial vehicles (UAVS): Collision avoidance systems and approaches. IEEE Access **8**, 105139–105155 (2020)
19. Yasin, J.N., et al.: Energy-efficient formation morphing for collision avoidance in a swarm of drones. IEEE Access **8**, 170681–170695 (2020)

TAGCN: Topology-Aware Graph Convolutional Network for Trajectory Prediction

Arindam Biswas[1] and Brendan Tran Morris[2]($\boxtimes$) (iD)

[1] Indian Institute of Technology Kharagpur, Kharagpur 721302, West Bengal, India
`aribis369@iitkgp.ac.in`
[2] University of Nevada, Las Vegas, NV 89154, USA
`brendan.morris@unlv.edu`

Abstract. Predicting future trajectories of agents in a dynamic environment is essential for natural and safe decision making of autonomous agents. The trajectory of an agent in such an environment not only depends on the past motion of that agent but also depends on its interaction with other agents present in that environment. To capture the effect of other agents on trajectory prediction of an agent, we propose a three stream topology-aware graph convolutional network (TAGCN) for interaction message passing between the agents. In addition, temporal encoding of local- and global-level topological features are fused to better characterize dynamic interactions between participants over time. Results are competitive compared to previous best methods for trajectory prediction on ETH and UCY datasets and highlights the need for both local and global interaction structure.

Keywords: Trajectory prediction · Graph embedding · Graph convolutional network

1 Introduction

Trajectory prediction is an essential task needed for autonomous agents moving in an environment where other agents are present. The autonomous agents should traverse safely in the presence of other agents and avoid any collision. Trajectory prediction of other agents in a crowded environment provides the autonomous agents valuable information for safe and smooth path planning. The most vulnerable agents in such environments are pedestrians, so their trajectory prediction is quite important to ensure their safety. In this paper we focus our study on the prediction of pedestrian trajectories.

Predicting the future path of agents is a challenging task as it incorporates many complications. The path of an agent is not just determined by the agent's previous track but also on the presence of obstacles in the environment as well, interactions with other agents, and on the goal of the agent [1]. Some earlier works in trajectory prediction used hand-picked features like social forces [2]

© Springer Nature Switzerland AG 2020
G. Bebis et al. (Eds.): ISVC 2020, LNCS 12509, pp. 542–553, 2020.
https://doi.org/10.1007/978-3-030-64556-4_42

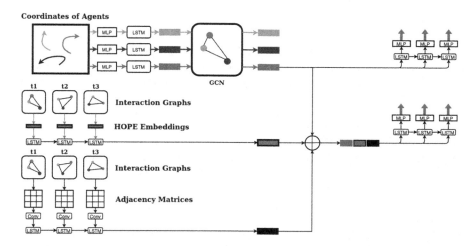

Fig. 1. Three stream TAGCN architecture. Stream1 (top) provides message passing between agents through a GCN for social interactions. Stream2 (middle) uses HOPE embedding to model local topology. Stream3 (bottom) encodes global topology. All streams are fused for trajectory prediction (Stream1 alone to reinforce training as an auxiliary task).

and energy potentials [3] to incorporate the interaction between the agents. Some prior work has also been done to incorporate the semantics of the environment in the model. Some recent methods use different types of maps like semantic segmentation maps [4] and rasterized maps [5] to get the semantics of the environment.

With the rise of deep learning based sequence encoders like Long-Short-Term-Memory (LSTM) networks [9] and Temporal Convolutional Network (TCN) [8], most works in this area use these networks for temporal encoding of the trajectories of agents. Much of the research has explored how to incorporate more context (e.g. social interactions with social pooling, graph convolutional network (GCN) message passing, scene structure with convolutional neural networks (CNNs), or semantic embedding) into the learning framework.

Some recent works also used multi-task learning for trajectory prediction, with trajectory prediction as the primary task. Jointly training a network for more than one task helps the model to learn more coherent knowledge from data and thus results in better predictions. Auxiliary tasks used in such models include agent behavior prediction [6], pose prediction [7], etc.

We propose a new topology-aware graph convolutional network (GCN) with LSTM decoder for pedestrian trajectory prediction which specifically considers not only the social influence of neighboring pedestrians but also their group evolution. The TAGCN framework, as shown in Fig. 1, utilizes three streams for 1) social interactions encoded by GCN, 2) dynamic local topology through HOPE [20] embeddings, and 3) global topology and structure evolution. Experimental results on standard pedestrian prediction datasets is competitive without the use of scene structure, attention, or stochastic prediction.

2   Related Research

To account for interactions among agents, many prior work have used social pooling [9], occupancy maps [10], attention mechanisms [11] and social tensors [12]. These methods do mot take into account the temporal nature of interaction among the agents (how interaction evolves over time). In very recent works [8, 13–15], interaction networks between agents are built to model the influence of surrounding agents. These interaction networks are used to model the spatial interactions among agents. These interaction networks are also dynamic in nature so that they can model the temporal interactions between agents effectively. Some methods use these interaction networks for encoding the dynamic interactions between agents while others use them to share information among agents. To have message passing between the agents in an interaction network, recent works use graph neural networks like Graph Convolutional Network (GCN) [19] or Graph Attention Network (GAT) [18]. Both these networks have been shown to encode the influence on the other agents effectively for trajectory prediction. These networks can handle varying number of agents unlike some methods discussed previously. Since both of these networks have similar performance, we elect to use GCN for message passing in our model.

Many recent works either use the messaging between agents or use temporal encoding of the interactions among agents. But none take advantage of both these techniques, as per our knowledge. In our work, we take advantage of both the messaging passing between agents in the interaction network and also fuse in temporal encoding of the dynamic interaction network. Most works use the entire interaction network for temporal encoding of interactions which provides a global context in the predictions. But there should be more information about the local context of an agent in the interaction network. To get local context we use graph embeddings (HOPE node embeddings [20]) which tend to preserve the structural properties of the interaction network. Temporal encoding of these graph embeddings provide a local context for the evolving topology around an agent. Thus our model uses message passing between the agents as well as local and global topological context of the dynamic interaction graph of the agents.

Trajectory prediction of pedestrians is complicated since one of many plausible tracks can be selected. To counter this, some methods generate multiple predictions of future trajectories using General Adversarial Network (GAN) [16] and Variational Autoencoders (VAE) [17]. Producing multi-modal trajectories increases the chances of getting the an accurate prediction. These methods tend to perform better than deterministic models which produce only a single forecasted trajectory. In our work we only explore the deterministic results of our model. Our deterministic model outperforms some stochastic models and gives competitive results.

3   Topology-Aware GCN Trajectory Prediction Method

Trajectory prediction is a complex task that requires not only the past trajectory as an observation but needs to take into account intentions of other neighboring agents in a scene and the *dynamic interactions* among the agents. Our framework is a seq-seq model which includes message passing using GCN and it also includes temporal encoding of node and graph embeddings of the dynamic interaction graph of the agents. The use of GCN brings in awareness about the future intentions of the neighboring agents while the use of temporal encoding of node and graph embeddings brings in awareness about the changing topology of the interaction network at local and global context respectively.

3.1   Problem Definition

We are given spatial coordinates of a set of N pedestrians which are represented by $X_t^i = (x_t^i, y_t^i)$ where the subscript denotes the t-th time frame and the superscript denotes the i-th pedestrian. We observe each of these pedestrians for T_{obs} ($t = 1 : Tobs$) time-steps and predict the coordinates of these pedestrians for the next T_{pred} ($t = Tobs + 1 : Tobs + Tpred$) time-steps all at once. Our objective is to produce future trajectories very close to the ground truth future trajectories of the pedestrians.

3.2   Overall Framework

The overview of the TAGCN framework for trajectory prediction can be seen in Fig. 1. The encoder part of our seq-seq model has three streams, each encodes a different type of information for trajectory prediction.

The first stream (Stream1) of the encoder network does temporal encoding of past coordinates $X_{t=1:Tobs}^i$ of the target followed by message passing using GCN between neighbor agents. Temporal encoding of these coordinates are done using LSTM network. The coordinates $X_{t=1:Tobs}^i$ are first passed through a fully connected layer to encode the two-dimension coordinates to higher dimension representations e_t^i. This encoding is passed to LSTM network to produce the temporal encoding of coordinates h_t^i.

$$e_t^i = MLP^H(X_t^i, W_{MLP}^H) \tag{1}$$
$$h_t^i = LSTM^H(e_t^i, (h_{en}^H(i), W_{LSTM}^H)). \tag{2}$$

Here W_{MLP}^H and W_{LSTM}^H are trainable weights of the MLP^H and $LSTM^H$ networks. All the agents share weights for temporal encoding of coordinates.

The temporal encoding of coordinates of all the agents are then passed to the GCN layer. The agents are considered as nodes in the interaction network and their respective temporal encoding h_t^i as features of these nodes. This graph along with its node features are passed to the GCN layer to produces new aggregated features H^i for each node.

$$H^i = GCN((h_t^i, A_g), W_{GCN}). \tag{3}$$

Here W_{GCN} are the trainable weights of the GCN layer and A_g is the weight matrix of the interaction graph which is designed to have more contribution from closer agents.

The second stream (Stream2) of the encoder network does temporal encoding of the local topological context (grouping) for agents. To achieve this, the interaction graph at each time-step is used to form node embeddings n_t^i of each node/agent. These node embeddings are formed using the High-Order-Proximity-Preserving-Embeddings (HOPE)[20] algorithm which takes the weight matrix A_t of the interaction graph. These sequence of node embeddings $n_{t=1:T_{obs}}^i$ are then passed into LSTM network to produce temporal encoding L^i of these embeddings.

$$L^i = LSTM^L(n_t^i, (h_{en}^L(i), W_{LSTM}^L)). \tag{4}$$

Here W_{LSTM}^L are trainable weights of the $LSTM^L$ network. The feature L^i signifies the local topological context.

The third stream (Stream3) of the encoder network does temporal encoding of the global topological context of the entire interaction network (group interactions). To achieve this we represent the interaction network as weight matrices A_t at each time step. The weight matrices are passed through a $Conv$ network. The $Conv$ network consist of 2-D convolution layers and average-pooling layer, followed by a flatten layer to get a representation m_t of the entire interaction network.

$$m_t = Conv(A_t, W_{conv}). \tag{5}$$

Here W_{conv} are trainable weights of the entire $Conv$ network and A_t is the weight matrice of the interaction graphs. The sequence of graph embeddings $m_{t=1:T_{obs}}$ is passed through a LSTM network to produce temporal encoding G.

$$G = LSTM^G(m_t, (h_{en}^G, W_{LSTM}^G)). \tag{6}$$

W_{LSTM}^G are trainable weights of the $LSTM^G$ network. The feature G signifies the global topological context.

Features from each of the three streams is concatenated and fed to the decoder part of the seq-seq model to produce future coordinates of the agent. The definition of weight matrix A_g used in the first stream is different from the A_t that used in the second and third stream. Their specific definitions are discussed in Sect. 3.3. Our model also has an auxiliary decoder based only on the first stream. This decoder was added to reinforce the learning of the network as an auxiliary task.

We use LSTM network as decoder in the seq-seq model. Here W_{MLP}^{DP} and W_{LSTM}^{DP} are trainable weights of the MLP^{DP} and $LSTM^{DP}$ networks of primary decoder while W_{MLP}^{DA} and W_{LSTM}^{DA} are trainable weights of the MLP^{DA} and $LSTM^{DA}$ networks of auxiliary decoder.

$$X_{pred}^i = MLP^{DP}(LSTM^{DP}(HLG_i, h_{dec}^{DP}(i), W_{LSTM}^{DP}), W_{MLP}^{DP}) \tag{7}$$

$$X_{pred,H}^i = MLP^{DA}(LSTM^{DA}(H_i, h_{dec}^{DA}(i), W_{LSTM}^{DA}), W_{MLP}^{DA}) \tag{8}$$

where $HLG_i = \text{concat}(H_i, L_i, G)$. The loss of the entire network is calculated by summing up the losses of the primary and the auxiliary streams with equal weight.

3.3   Agent Interaction Network

Information sharing among agents and knowledge of their dynamic interactions are beneficial for predicting future trajectories in crowded environments. We build interaction networks to facilitate information sharing among agents and to learn about the dynamic interactions among neighboring agents. These graphs are dynamic as they change at every time-step. Our interaction graphs have undirected edges which are defined by the criteria that the distance between two edges should be less than a neighborhood distance threshold D.

We define the graph weight matrix A_g ($R^{N \times N}$) for the first stream as

$$A_g = \{a_{i,j}\} = \begin{cases} 1/d\left(X^i, X^j\right) & d\left(X^i, X^j\right) < D \\ 0 & \text{otherwise} \end{cases}.\tag{9}$$

Here $d(.)$ is the Euclidean distance function and X^i, X^j are coordinates of i-th and j-th agent. The weight matrix has stronger message passing for closer agents and weaker for further agents.

The second and third stream use the temporal adjacency matrix A_t ($R^{N \times N}$) as

$$A_t = \{\alpha_{i,j}\} = \begin{cases} d\left(X^i, X^j\right) & d\left(X^i, X^j\right) < D \\ 0 & \text{otherwise} \end{cases}.\tag{10}$$

The resulting weight matrix is defined to learn the topological features of the interaction network - e.g. the manner in which neighborhood topology changes over time. This helps to differentiate between scenarios such as traveling in a group or agents approaching/passing one another

3.4   Graph Convolutional Networks

Message passing between the neighboring agents has been shown to improve trajectory prediction by providing information about the intent (future state) of neighboring agents. In our framework, the message passing/information sharing is accomplished by using a GCN to take in node features and modify them based on the neighborhood interaction graph. Let F^0 be the input node features and A is the weight matrix of the interaction graph. The output features of the graph convolution is given by:

$$F^l = \sigma\left(D^{-0.5}\hat{A}D^{-0.5}F^{l-1}W^l\right)\tag{11}$$

where $\hat{A} = A + I$, D is the diagonal degree matrix of the interaction network, W^l are the trainable weights of the graph convolution layer and σ is the activation function. F^{l-1} are the input node features and F^l are the output node features. The identity matrix is added to the weight matrix as it helps to incorporate shared features from other nodes with it's own features.

3.5   Graph Embeddings

Temporal encoding of local and global topological context is used to learn dynamic evolution of interactions between agent. For representing the local topological context of an agent in the interaction network, we use HOPE node embeddings [20]. This algorithm produces embeddings that preserve the high order proximities (local structure) of the network. This algorithm is based on matrix factorization of the node proximity matrix. The embedding are formed by minimizing the following objective function:

$$\min \|S_{Katz} - U_s \cdot U_t^T\|^2 \qquad \text{with} \qquad S_{Katz} = (I - \beta \cdot A)^{-1} \cdot \beta \cdot A. \quad (12)$$

Here S_{Katz} is the Katz Index which is a measure of high order proximity and β is a bias term. U_s and U_t are source and target embeddings.

For representing the global topological context we require whole-graph embeddings. Since techniques for whole graph embeddings are quite time consuming, we avoid their use and use the weight matrices A_t to represent whole interaction graphs. The weight matrices are further encoded using cheaper convolution layers and average pooling layers.

3.6   Implementation Details

The output size of the MLP layers is 16. The hidden state of all the LSTM units is of size 64. All the LSTM networks are single layer. We use two layers of GCN. We fix the size of node embedding to 40. We fix the value of parameter D of the interaction graph to be 10 m. We use Mean Square Error loss function with Adam optimizer. We use ReLu activations at all places. We trained our model for 200 epochs at a learning rate of 10^{-4}.

4   Experiment

We use ETH [20] and UCY [21] datasets for evaluating our model for trajectory prediction. ETH and UCY datasets have a total of five crowded scenes namely ETH, Hotel, Univ, Zara1 and Zara2 with a maximum of 51 pedestrians in a frame (Fig. 2). These datasets have a total of 1536 pedestrians (750 in ETH and 786 in UCY) performing complex interactions in real-world settings.

4.1   Evaluation Metrics

The models are evaluated following the leave-one-out policy [9,16], where the models are trained using all scenes except one (i.e four scenes) and tested on the remaining scene. The models observe 8 past time steps of a pedestrian and predict its trajectory for 12 future time steps. We calculate the individual scores for all scenes and their average for comparison amongst models.

Following the norms of previous works [9,23], we use standard metrics of Average Displacement Error (ADE) – mean L-2 distance error between predicted and real trajectory over all predicted time steps – and Final Displacement Error (FDE) – L-2 distance error between final predicted point and real trajectory – to evaluate the models.

(a) ETH   (b) Hotel   (c) Univ   (d) Zara

Fig. 2. Standard Pedestrian Prediction Datasets. (a) ETH has mostly vertical trajectories and lots of stopped pedestrians. (b) Hotel has mostly horizontal trajectories with scene obstacles and pedestrians waiting for the train on the top. (c) Univ is a dense campus walkway with significant grouping. (d) Zara has mostly horizontal trajectories.

4.2   Baselines

We compare the performance of our model with several deterministic and stochastic models. We list the models used for comparison below:

- LSTM – This model uses only a simple LSTM network for temporal encoding of trajectory without using any contextual information.
- Social-LSTM [9] – This model uses social pooling along with LSTM network to provide social context to the model.
- CNN [25] – This model uses a fast temporal CNN encoding of a trajectory without using any contextual information.
- MATF [12] – This model uses scene context as well as social context using tensor fusion of these information.
- CVAE [26] – This is a stochastic model that uses a VAE to generate multiple plausible trajectories using an LSTM-based seq-seq model for temporal encoding of trajectories.
- SGAN [16] – This is a stochastic model that uses GAN to generate multiple plausible trajectories. It also uses social pooling for social context and LSTM for temporal encoding of trajectories.
- SoPhie [24] – This is a stochastic model that GAN for multiple predictions, social pooling for social context and LSTM for temporal encoding. In addition to these it also uses scene attention mechanism to get scene context.
- SAGCN [14] – This model uses a TCN for temporal encoding of trajectories as well as relative distance between agents. It also uses GCN for information sharing among agents.
- STGAT [13] – This model uses LSTM for temporal encoding and uses a GAT for crowd interaction modeling.

Table 1. ADE/FDE result comparison in meters

Method	ETH	Hotel	Univ	Zara01	Zara02	Average
LSTM	1.09/2.41	0.86/1.91	0.57/1.21	0.61/1.31	0.41/0.88	0.70/1.52
Social-LSTM [9]	1.09/2.35	0.79/1.76	0.67/1.40	0.47/1.00	0.56/1.17	0.72/1.54
CNN [25]	1.04/2.07	0.59/1.17	0.57/1.21	0.43/0.90	0.34/0.75	0.59/1.22
MATF [12]	1.33/2.49	0.51/0.95	0.56/1.19	0.44/0.93	0.34/0.73	0.64/1.26
CVAE [26]	0.93/1.94	0.52/1.03	0.59/1.27	0.41/0.86	0.33/0.72	0.53/1.11
SGAN [16]	0.81/1.52	0.72/1.61	0.60/1.26	0.34/0.69	0.42/0.84	0.58/1.18
SoPhie [24]	**0.70/1.43**	0.76/1.67	0.54/1.24	0.30/0.63	0.38/0.78	0.54/1.15
SAGCN [14]	0.90/1.96	**0.41/0.83**	0.57/1.19	**0.41/0.89**	0.32/0.70	**0.52**/1.11
STGAT 1V-1 [13]	0.88/1.66	0.56/1.15	**0.52/1.13**	0.41/0.91	**0.31/0.68**	0.54/1.11
GCN	1.06/2.10	0.71/1.44	0.57/1.24	0.46/0.98	0.35/0.80	0.63/1.30
GCN+Global	0.88/1.61	0.60/1.16	0.55/1.26	0.43/0.92	0.32/0.72	0.56/1.13
GCN+Local	0.90/1.73	0.61/1.18	0.56/1.28	0.43/0.90	0.32/0.72	0.56/1.16
TAGCN	0.86/1.50	0.59/1.15	0.54/1.25	0.42/0.90	0.32/0.71	0.55/**1.10**

4.3 Quantitative Results

As we can see in Table 1, our TAGCN model has results competitive with recent methods. Our model has the best average FDE score and comparable ADE score to the top performing comparison methods. Even though our model is deterministic, it performs better/comparable with some of the stochastic models (e.g. SGAN, CVAE, and SoPhie).

We performed an ablation study to understand the contributions of the different streams of the TAGCN model. GCN represents only Stream1, Stream1 + Stream2 = GCN+Local, and Stream1 + Stream3 = GCN+Global. The use of the auxiliary interaction network streams increases prediction accuracy. Incorporating global topological features gives a slight advantage over incorporating local topological features. Using both global and local topological features together further enhances the performance of our model.

Examples predictions can be seen in Fig. 3. The historical trajectory is in red, prediction in blue, and ground truth in green. TAGCN is able to correctly predict future trajectories of agents who maintain their direction to some extent, as we can see in the three horizontal trajectories, and does a good job providing stable prediction for the stopped pedestrian (Fig. 3a). However, it produces distorted predictions when the agent more aggressively changes its direction as we can see in the vertical trajectory in Fig. 3b. Note that without image overlay it is difficult to guess the reason for this direction change which is a limitation of the current model. Future work will incorporate scene context to better reason on static objects that require avoidance.

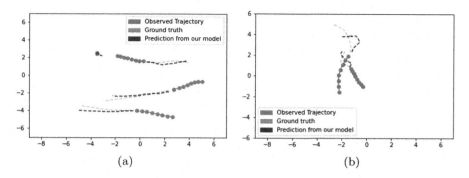

Fig. 3. Example predictions: observed trajectory (red), ground-truth (green), and TAGCN prediction (blue). (a) Strong prediction agreement for gradual maneuvers and stationary agents. (b) Poor prediction during more aggressive direction change. (Color figure online)

5   Concluding Remarks

In this work we present our model TAGCN which employs a LSTM based seq-seq model for human trajectory prediction. Our model uses GCN for information sharing amongst agents. It also uses node embeddings and graph embeddings to get local and global topological context of the evolving interactions among agents. Experimental results on the ETH and UCY datasets show our approach is quite competitive with recent pedestrian prediction networks. Further improvements could come from encoding scene context to handle agent-scene object in addition to agent-agent interactions.

References

1. Rudenko, A., Palmieri, L., Herman, M., Kitani, K.M., Gavrila, D.M., Arras, K.O.: Human motion trajectory prediction: a survey. arXiv preprint arXiv:1905.06113 (2019)
2. Helbing, D., Molnar, P.: Social force model for pedestrian dynamics.51, May 1998
3. Alahi, A., Ramanathan, V., Fei-Fei, L.: Socially-aware large-scale crowd forecasting. In: CVPR (2014)
4. Syed, A., Morris, B.T.: SSeg-LSTM: semantic scene segmentation for trajectory prediction. In: 2019 IEEE Intelligent Vehicles Symposium (IV), Paris, France, pp. 2504–2509 (2019). https://doi.org/10.1109/IVS.2019.8813801
5. Chou, F.-C., et al.: Predicting Motion of Vulnerable Road Users using High-Definition Maps and Efficient ConvNets (2019)
6. Chandra, R., et al.: Forecasting trajectory and behavior of road-agents using spectral clustering in graph-LSTMs (2019). ArXiv:1912.01118
7. Mangalam, K., Adeli, E., Lee, K.-H., Gaidon, A., Niebles, J.C.: Disentangling human dynamics for pedestrian locomotion forecasting with noisy supervision, pp. 2773–2782 (2020). https://doi.org/10.1109/WACV45572.2020.9093350

8. Wang, C., Cai, S., Tan, G.: GraphTCN: Spatio-Temporal Interaction Modeling for Human Trajectory Prediction. ArXiv, abs/2003.07167 (2020)
9. Alahi, A., Goel, K., Ramanathan, V., Robicquet, A., Li, F.-F., Savarese, S.: Social LSTM: human trajectory prediction in crowded spaces, pp. 961–971 (2016). https://doi.org/10.1109/CVPR.2016.110
10. Xue, H., Du, H., Reynolds, M.: SS-LSTM: a hierarchical lstm model for pedestrian trajectory prediction, pp. 1186–1194 (2018). https://doi.org/10.1109/WACV.2018.00135
11. Vemula, A., Muelling, K., Oh, J.: Social attention: modeling attention in human crowds. In ICRA pp. 1–7. IEEE (2018)
12. Zhao, T., et al.: Multi-agent tensor fusion for contextual trajectory prediction, pp. 12118–12126 (2019). https://doi.org/10.1109/CVPR.2019.01240
13. Yingfan, H., Bi, H., Li, Z., Mao, T., Wang, Z.: STGAT: modeling spatial-temporal interactions for human trajectory prediction (2019). https://doi.org/10.1109/ICCV.2019.00637
14. Sun, Y., He, T., Hu, J., Huang, H., Chen, B.: Socially-aware graph convolutional network for human trajectory prediction. In: 2019 IEEE 3rd Information Technology, Networking, Electronic and Automation Control Conference (ITNEC), Chengdu, China, pp. 325–333 (2019). https://doi.org/10.1109/ITNEC.2019.8729387
15. Kosaraju, V., Sadeghian, A., Martín-Martín, R., Reid, I.D., Rezatofighi, S.H., Savarese, S.: Social-BiGAT: Multimodal Trajectory Forecasting using Bicycle-GAN and Graph Attention Networks (2019). ArXiv, abs/1907.03395
16. Gupta, A., Johnson, J., Li, F.-F., Savarese, S., Alahi, A.: Social GAN: socially acceptable trajectories with generative adversarial networks, pp. 2255–2264 (2018). https://doi.org/10.1109/CVPR.2018.00240
17. Bhattacharyya, A., Schiele, B., Fritz, M.: Accurate and diverse sampling of sequences based on a "Best of Many" sample objective (2018). https://doi.org/10.1109/CVPR.2018.00885
18. Veličković, P., Cucurull, G., Casanova, A., Romero, A., Liò, P., Bengio, Y.: Graph Attention Networks. In: International Conference on Learning Representations (2018)
19. Jiang, B., Zhang, Z., Lin, D., Tang, J., Luo, B.: The IEEE Conference on Computer Vision and Pattern Recognition (CVPR), pp. 11313–11320 (2019)
20. Ou, M., Cui, P., Pei, J., Zhang, Z., Zhu, W.: Asymmetric transitivity preserving graph embedding, pp. 1105–1114 (2016). https://doi.org/10.1145/2939672.2939751
21. Pellegrini, S., Ess, A., Schindler, K., Van Gool., L.: You'll never walk alone: Modeling social behavior for multi-target tracking. In: 2009 IEEE 12th International Conference on Computer Vision, pp. 261–268. IEEE (2009)
22. Lerner, A., Chrysanthou, Y., Lischinski. D.: Crowds by example. In Computer Graphics Forum, vol. 26, pp. 655–664. Wiley Online Library (2007)
23. Lee, N., Choi, W., Vernaza, P., Choy, C.B., Torr, P.H.S., Chandraker, M.K. Desire: distant future prediction in dynamic scenes with interacting agents. In: 2017 IEEE Conference on Computer Vision and Pattern Recognition (CVPR), pp. 2165–2174 (2017)
24. Sadeghian, A., Kosaraju, V., Sadeghian, A., Hirose, N., Rezatofighi, H., Savarese, S.: SoPhie: an attentive GAN for predicting paths compliant to social and physical constraints. In: The IEEE Conference on Computer Vision and Pattern Recognition (CVPR), pp. 1349–1358 (2019)

25. Nikhil, N., Morris, B.T.: Convolutional neural network for trajectory prediction. In: Leal-Taixé, L., Roth, S. (eds.) ECCV 2018. LNCS, vol. 11131, pp. 186–196. Springer, Cham (2019). https://doi.org/10.1007/978-3-030-11015-4_16
26. Zhang, L., She, Q., Guo, P.: Stochastic trajectory prediction with social graph network. arXiv preprint arXiv:1907.10233 (2019)

3D Articulated Body Model Using Anthropometric Control Points and an Articulation Video

Chenxi Li$^{(\boxtimes)}$ and Fernand Cohen

Drexel University, Philadelphia, PA 19104, USA
{cl982,fsc22}@drexel.edu

Abstract. We introduce an efficient and practical integrated system for human body model personalization with articulation. We start with a 3D personalized model of the individual in a standard pose obtained using a 3D scanner or using body model reconstruction method based on canonical images of the individual. As the person moves, the model is updated to accommodate the new articulations captured in an articulation video. The personalized model is segmented into different parts using anthropometric control points on the boundary silhouette of the frontal projection of the 3D model. The control points are endpoints of the segments in 2D, and the segments are projections of corresponding regions of independently moving parts in 3D. These joint points can either be manually selected or predicted with a pre-trained point model such as active shape model (ASM) or using convolutional neural network (CNN). The evolution of the model through the articulation process is captured in a video clip with N frames. The update consists of finding a set of 3D transformations that are applied to the 3D model on its parts so that the projections of the 3D model 'match' those observed in the video sequence at corresponding frames. This is done by minimizing the error between the frontal projection body region points and the target points from the image for each independent moving part. Our articulation reconstructed method leads sub-resolution recovery errors.

Keywords: Articulation · Anthropometric points · Moving parts

1 Introduction

Articulated human joint model has been used in many areas including animation, pose capture and behavior analysis. A suitable and efficient articulation model allows for a realistic display of the 3D human's movement in virtual environments. Most of the articulated models build on skeleton joints that are used for estimating the body model's poses. Others focus on building the parametric model for both shape and pose reconstruction. The parameters of the body pose model could be predicted from images or estimated from body joints extracted from images. These methods always need a great number of examples to train on for accuracy.

In this paper, we introduce an efficient and practical integrated system for human body model personalization with articulation. We start with a 3D personalized model

© Springer Nature Switzerland AG 2020
G. Bebis et al. (Eds.): ISVC 2020, LNCS 12509, pp. 554–565, 2020.
https://doi.org/10.1007/978-3-030-64556-4_43

of the individual obtained using either a 3D scanner or reconstructed from canonical images of the individual. As the person moves, the model is updated to accommodate for the new articulations. This could be useful in applications such as the creation of a virtual fitting room, where a movie of the virtually reconstructed articulated 3D model is fitted with a garment for the individual to access how much s/he likes the garment and how it virtually fits.

The update consists of finding the set of 3D transformations that are needed to be applied to the 3D generalized model so that the projections of the 3D model 'match' those observed in the video sequence at corresponding frames. We use the contour(s) of the person's silhouette and minimize the error between the frontal projection contour and the target contour from the image. Since different parts on the individual can move independently, the body and consequently, the individual boundary's silhouette on the image plane are segmented into different regions, and the articulation for each part is separately estimated.

This paper is organized as follows, in Sect. 2, related works for articulated human model are introduced and compared with our current method. In Sect. 3, we discuss the process of partitioning the 3D model into independently moving parts using anthropometric control points on its boundary silhouette projected on a frontal view. In Sect. 4, the overall process for obtaining the articulated model is introduced and results and evaluations are shown. Conclusions are given in Sect. 5.

2 Related Work

Works focusing on modeling human body articulation aim at the analysis of human behavior, pose estimation, and motion capture. Attempts for estimating the pose of the human body from 2D images ranges from the use of a kinematic model [1, 2], a cardboard model [3], to a volumetric model [4, 5]. In this paper, we present a contour-based articulation model that tracks contour extracted segments in the image and builds 2D-3D correspondence pose for tracking the deformation due to articulation.

2.1 Contour-Based Pose Estimation Model

The work in [6] introduces a part-based contour model that captures the pose differences in two dimensions. This parametric model builds on shape completion and animation for people (SCAPE) [7] model. It learns body deformations by lumping together shape variation, view-point change, and rotating body parts. The model estimates the poses of individuals of different shapes and realizes individual segmentation from 2D images. Contour segments are generated using a correlation correspondence algorithm for surface mesh registration and partitioning [3, 4]. This lumping together results a simple model for pose estimation. It leads, however, to prediction inaccuracies. Like this contour people model, active shape model (ASM) also generates a point model for either boundary or connected joint estimation. ASM analyzes pose variations using sets with the same number of points and principle component analysis (PCA). [8] introduces a contour model based on ASM for pedestrian tracking, while the work in [9] trains the ASM based on joints of the human body skeleton to estimate the pose variation. These shape models need training examples from a variety of poses to get a complete point distribution model. In contrast, our reconstruction method focuses on the pose estimation for a specific individual using contours, needs no training example, and estimates the pose from 2D images using the estimated 3D shape model from the previous frame.

2.2 Volumetric Pose Estimation Model

Parametric models as SCAPE and skinned multi-person linear (SMPL) [5] model are also used for pose estimation. [4] estimates the joint position of individual from image and uses SMPL model to fit the connected joints. The position of joints is predicted with a pretrained CNN-based neural network, and the 3D pose of the individual is estimated using the fitted SMPL model. [10] also uses the CNN network to build the correspondence between 2D images and 3D body surface mesh, where the pose is estimated using the deformed 3D surface mesh derived from 2D image of the individual. [11] recovers the pose from 2D images by training an end-to-end neural network.

2.3 Novel Contributions

The paper makes the following contributions:

1. Unlike current methodologies of articulation recovery that mainly focus on predicting the pose using parametric models using a large set of training examples, our proposed articulation recovery method needs no training and recovers the articulation with errors below sub-resolution of the 3D point model.
2. Our method exploits the boundary of the projected silhouette and segments it into parts that correspond to 3D body region that move independently and hence are subjected to independent transformations.
3. The curve segments are obtained using a set of anthropometric control points that correspond to joint points or endpoints of the independently moving parts in 3D. Exploiting these anthropometric points makes the model universal to all human individuals.
4. The curve segments induce regions in 2D that, in turn, segment the 3D shape into data clusters of independent rigid moving parts in 3D.
5. Starting with an initial 3D model of the individual, the model is updated frame to frame in the video clip. The initial 3D model could assume any form. It could be a free form of scattered 3D data or in polygonal mesh form.
6. Our articulation model allows the shape prediction process to be cast as local transformation estimation on a 3D personalized model that is constantly updated with each articulation frame in a given video clip.

3 Segmenting the 3D Personalized Human Body Model Using Anthropometric Control Points on Its Frontal Projection Silhouette's Boundary

We introduce a human body articulation (pose) reconstruction method with a personalized 3D human body model (3D point model here) and images with different poses of the same person. The images we use in our experiments are consecutive frames in a video showing various poses. The 3D personalized model can be reconstructed using various methods such as: structure from motion with a series of images from different angles; elaborate optical measurement using 3D scanner; and depth camera. There are also reconstruction methods that build parametric models. An example is SCAPE [7] where the model is deformed for different individuals by adjusting the model parameters using images of individuals. In this paper, we start with a 3D model P of the individual in a given pose. This could have been obtained using a 3D scanner or using reconstruction based on canonical images of the individual and a generic model [12].

3.1 Anthropometric Control Points on the Frontal Projection, Curve Segments and Corresponding 3D Region Parts

Since different parts connected by joints on the individual can move independently, the 3D body of a human individual is divided into different parts (namely, head and neck, shoulders, forearms, arm, waist, hips, legs, and feet), with the articulation for each part a rotation in 3D space, which is tracked independently. Since the silhouette contour is used for tracking the local 3D movement of each of these parts, the silhouette's boundary is itself partitioned into those corresponding regions or segments (see Fig. 1). The endpoints of these segments are the anthropometric control points. The control points can also be points baring a geometric significance (e.g. inflection points, corner points, etc.). The personalized 3D mesh model P is in a standard pose (i.e. a stand with arms and legs open (see Fig. 1) corresponding to the starting pose in the articulation video. The personalized model P is segmented into different parts using anthropometric control points on the boundary silhouette of the frontal projection. These are endpoints of the segments shown in Fig. 1(a). The segments encapsulate regions in 2D, which are projection of corresponding regions or parts in 3D (see Fig. 1(b)). These joint points can either be manually selected or predicted with a pre-trained point model such as ASM

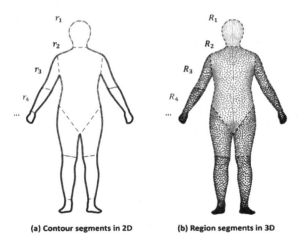

(a) Contour segments in 2D   (b) Region segments in 3D

Fig. 1. Frontal contour and body region segments

[13] or using convolutional neural network (CNN) [14, 15]. The evolution of the model P through the articulation process in the video clip (in its N Frames) is discussed in the next section.

4 Articulation and the Human Shape Model

In this section, we track the method to accommodate for changes in articulation by augmenting the virtual fitting process to allow for a sequence of articulations common to a model trying a garment. A generic movement articulation video is considered. This is provided by the user. The overall flow chart of the articulation reconstruction process is shown in Algorithm 1.

Algorithm 1: Articulation recovery process

Input: Articulation video clip and a personalized 3D point model P of an individual user.

Output: 3D personalized articulated point model with articulation.

1. Decompose the video clip into $Frames$ — a set of images with N consecutive articulations.
2. Project P on the frontal image plane, obtain the silhouette boundary, and segment the boundary into L different segments r_l corresponding to head and neck, shoulders, forearms, arms, hands, waist, hips, legs, and feet (details are given in section 4.1).
3. Partition 3D point model P into different regions R_l with its points being the back projected points encapsulated by segment r_l (details are given in section 3.1).
4. Find the $r'_{l,1}$ segment($l = 1, 2, .., L$) in $Frame$ 1 in the video clip corresponding to the r_l segment ($l = 1, 2, .., L$) (details are given in section 4.2);
5. Estimate the transformation $T_{l,1}$ that operates on R_l to yield the set $R'_{l,1}$ whose projection $\hat{r}_{l,1} = Proj\{T_{l,1}(R_{l,1})\}$ on the frontal image is as close as possible to the set $r'_{l,1}$ (details are given in section 4.3).
6. Update personalized 3D model $P \rightarrow P^{(1)}$, $R_l \rightarrow R_l^{(1)'}$, and $r_l \rightarrow r_l^{(1)'}$;
7. **For** $k = 2, ..., N$, **do**
   a) Find the $r_l^{(k)'}$ segment($l = 1, 2, .., L$) in $Frame$ k in the video clip corresponding to the $r_l^{(k-1)}$ segment ($l = 1, 2, .., L$);
   b) Estimate the transformation $T_{l,k}$ that operates on $R_l^{(k-1)}$ to yield the set $R_l^{(k)'}$, whose projection $\hat{r}_l^{(k)} = Proj\{T_{l,k}(R_l^{(k-1)})\}$ on the frontal image is as close as possible to the set $r_l^{(k)'}$, for $l = 1, 2, .., L$;
   c) Update $P^{(k-1)} \rightarrow P^{(k)}$, $R_l^{(k-1)'} \rightarrow R_l^{(k)'}$, and $r_l^{(k-1)} \rightarrow r_l^{(k)'}$;
   End for
8. Make a video out the sequence $P^{(1)}, P^{(2)}, ..., P^{(N)}$ depicting the moving articulation of the individual with a desired fitted garment.

4.1 Segmenting the Silhouette Contour into Different Regions

Since different parts connected by joints on the individual can move independently, the 3D body of a human individual is divided into different parts (namely, head and neck, shoulders, forearms, arm, waist hips, legs, and feet), with the articulation for each part a rotation in 3D space, which is tracked independently. Since the silhouette contour is used for tracking the local 3D movement of each of these parts, the silhouette's boundary is itself partitioned into those corresponding regions or segments (see Fig. 1). Note that for each considered articulation (in the video), each of the parts can either be standstill or moving independently of the others.

To be able to track these local movements from frame to frame, it is imperative that we can segment the individuals' silhouette in those image sequences, as well as the outline of their parts. There are many possible ways for doing that. We can perform binary class image segmentation interactively using the lazy snapping [16] method by marking out the foreground and background; or we can use end-to-end semantic segmentation using neural network to predict the mask for binary class segmentation [17]. For the sake of both automation and simplification of the system, we use one background image and a target image to perform the segmentation. The background image is the one without the individual, and target image is the one with the individual in it.

We firstly convert both the background and target images from the RGB color space into the CIELAB space. The lightness layer in the CIELAB space retains most of the luminance information. We then remove the luminance layer of the target and background images out by subtracting one from the other. This difference image is then passed through a Canny filter for edge detection. As we are just interested in the silhouette's boundary, we apply graph morphology to all the detected edges using a dilation of a 10-pixel line and connect the surrounding area of the graph. We then perform an erosion of a 10-pixel line and hence obtain the individual's silhouette segmented from the background. The overall process is shown in Fig. 2. The segmentation process yields a precise silhouette aside from in the head part because of the hair presence.

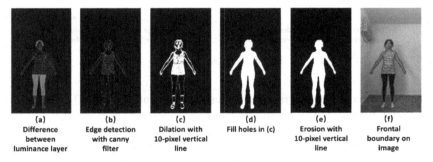

(a)	(b)	(c)	(d)	(e)	(f)
Difference	Edge detection	Dilation with	Fill holes in (c)	Erosion with	Frontal
between	with canny	10-pixel vertical		10-pixel vertical	boundary on
luminance layer	filter	line		line	image

Fig. 2. Individual segmentation from background.

With the silhouette obtained and its boundary delineated, the endpoints of its various segments are automatically obtained once the set of anthropometric set of control points on the boundary of the silhouette are declared.

4.2   Finding the Control Points and Segments on the Current Video Frame

We are given a 3D model of the individual in a given pose (articulation). This pose should closely be the pose of the starting pose in the articulation video sequence of the desired modeling video sequence. The first step is to find the equivalent control points residing on the silhouette contour of the first frame in the model articulation sequence that corresponds to those on the frontal projection of the personalized model. The contours of the personalized frontal projection and the first frame in the model articulation sequence are aligned after rotation and scaling to account for differences in focal length of the cameras used in the reconstruction and the video recording and for slight deviation in orientation.

The control points in the first frame in the model articulation sequence are the ones on its silhouette boundary that are the nearest neighbors to their corresponding ones on the boundary of the personalized frontal projection. The newly found control points determine the fourteen segments on the first frame of the video articulation sequence. The contour segments of the personalized 3D model's projection and the 2D first image frame in the video is shown in Fig. 3(b). Beginning from the second frame, the control points on frame k can be obtained with the silhouette boundary in this frame and the partitioned silhouette boundary with control points from its previous frame (frame $k-1$).

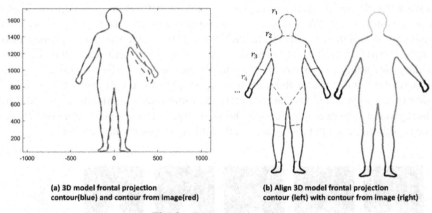

(a) 3D model frontal projection
contour(blue) and contour from image(red)

(b) Align 3D model frontal projection
contour (left) with contour from image (right)

Fig. 3. Contour registration

There are many ways to find the corresponding control points. The simplest and most straightforward method is to consider the endpoints that encapsulate a region in the $k-1$ frame, and search for their equivalent segments in frame k. For example, suppose we consider the upper left arm region (region r_l) in frame $k-1$ (shown in Fig. 4), which is encapsulated by the control points $r_{l,2}$, $r_{l,3}$, $r_{l,6}$, $r_{l,7}$ and which might have been articulated. Since we assume that the articulation of the arm in 3D is rigid, the transformation is a 3D rotation. This implies that in the image frames the transformational relation between the corresponding arm regions in frame $k-1$ and frame k is well approximated by an affine transformation. Suppose we pick the segments $(r'_{l,2}, r'_{l,3})$ and $(r'_{l,6}, r'_{l,7})$ in frame k and hypothesize that they are equivalent to the segments $(r_{l,2}, r_{l,3})$

and $(r_{l,6}, r_{l,7})$ from frame $k - 1$. Then under that assumption, we can estimate the affine transform t_l as follows

$$t_l = \arg \min \sum\nolimits_{i=2,3,6,7} \left\| \hat{r}_{l,i} - r_{l,i}^2 \right\| = \arg \min \sum\nolimits_{i=2,3,6,7} \left\| t_l(r'_{l,i}) - r_{l,i} \right\|^2 \quad (1)$$

where $(\hat{r}_{l,2}, \hat{r}_{l,3}, \hat{r}_{l,6}, \hat{r}_{l,7}) = t_l(r'_{l,2}, r'_{l,3}, r'_{l,6}, r'_{l,7})$. Associated with each choice $(r'_{l,2}, r'_{l,3}, r'_{l,6}, r'_{l,7})$, there will be a MMSE value $\sum_{i=2,3,6,7} \left\| t_l(r'_{l,i}) - r_{l,i} \right\|^2$. The minimum error yields the corresponding segments $r'_{l,2}, r'_{l,3}$ $r'_{l,6}$ and $r'_{l,7}$ along with the optimum affine transform t_l. This affine transform is applied to all points encapsulated in the region by the control points $r'_{l,2}, r'_{l,3}, r'_{l,6}, r'_{l,7}$ in region r'_l, and results into the set $r_l^{(k)'} = t_l \left(r_l^{(k-1)} \right)$. This set is used to estimate the 3D rotation, which results into an updated articulated region R_l.

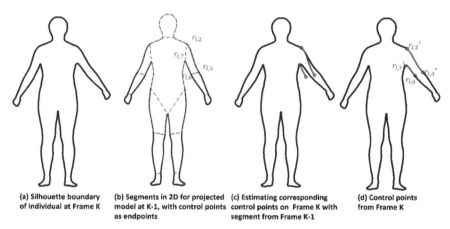

(a) Silhouette boundary of individual at Frame K

(b) Segments in 2D for projected model at K-1, with control points as endpoints

(c) Estimating corresponding control points on Frame K with segment from Frame K-1

(d) Control points from Frame K

Fig. 4. Finding the control points on the articulated image

We show in the next section how to update the 3D model once the control points in frame k are found.

4.3   Estimating the Local Articulations (Poses) and Updating the 3D Model

We are given the 3D model P_{k-1}, its frontal projection with its silhouette boundary, along with its control points as well its various segments, and that for frame k as described in Sect. 4.2. Suppose we want to find the articulation in 3D that occurred for region R_l that gave rise to segment l ($l = 1, 2, .., 14$) in the projected frontal space, i.e. we want to find the corresponding set R'_l that is an articulation of the set R_l and whose projection is the segment l in the observed k frame. Let T_l be the transformation between the two sets R_l and R'_l. Let $\hat{r}_l^{(k)}$ be the frontal projection of the set R_l under an arbitrary transformation T_l, i.e. $\hat{r}_l^{(k)} = Proj\{T_l(R_l)\}$ and let $r_l^{(k)'} = t_l \left(r_l^{(k-1)} \right)$. We estimate T_l by minimizing the

MSE in (2)

$$T_l = \arg\min \sum_{i=1}^{m} \left\| \hat{r}_{l,i}^{(k)} - r_{l,i}^{(k)'} \right\|^2 \tag{2}$$

where the index i denotes a point in the sets $\hat{r}_l^{(k)}$ and $r_l^{(k)'}$, respectively. We have only considered the transformation T_l to be a rotation in 3D space with its three parameters α, β, θ, being rotations around the x, y, and z axes, respectively. As there are 3 unknowns and only 2 variables, we need to impose an additional constraint to solve for the rotation. The constraint imposes that α should be greater than zero, which implies a "moving to the front of body" posture, which is a more frequent occurrence. Figure 5 compares the estimated articulation to the ground truth articulation. Figure 5(a) shows the 3D reconstruction of the whole body compared to the observed one with articulation, whereas Fig. 5(b) focuses on the reconstructed articulated parts (forearm and arm) compared to the observed one. In Fig. 5(c), the blue solid line represents the frontal projection $\hat{r}_l$ of the moving body region $R_{l,}$, while the black dashed line represents the observed segment r_l' after articulation in the frontal 2D image. The point to point average distance error for this articulated region (arm and forearm) in 3D is 5.06 mm compared to an average resolution of 17.82 mm of the original 3D body model. Hence the error is 0.28 of the resolution cell. This is further explained in the next section. This error is computed between each point on the reconstructed model (for the moving part) and its corresponding point on the ground-truth articulated 3D part.

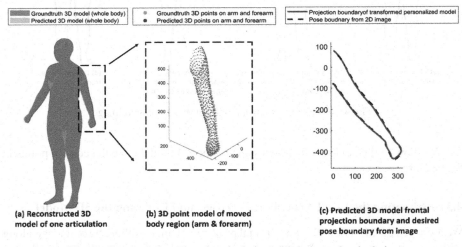

(a) Reconstructed 3D model of one articulation

(b) 3D point model of moved body region (arm & forearm)

(c) Predicted 3D model frontal projection boundary and desired pose boundary from image

Fig. 5. Compare ground truth articulation with estimated articulation

4.4 Evaluation

To test the accuracy of the articulation recovery, we compute the point error between points on the ground truth 3D personalized model subjected to a series of changing articulations and their corresponding ones on the reconstructed model after each frame averaged over N frames.

Different articulations are generated using the principle component shape (PCS) model introduced in [18] to generate different poses. The PCS model independently controls the movement of different articulated body regions in Fig. 1(b). Starting with a given 3D body point model in standard pose, by changing the variance (parameter) of one PCS model component, the corresponding part of 3D body point model changes accordingly whereas other parts stay still. We generate consecutive changing poses of the 3D body model with a set of gradually changing variances for only one component and take the frontal projection of each deformed 3D model as one frame. This set of frames are combined as a short video for the movement of one body region.

The ground truth 3D point model for each frame is the deformed body point set, generated by the PCS model for that frame, whereas the test 3D point model is the predicted body point model with the pose of body region estimated from this 2D frame (image). The error distance between each point on the moving region of test model and its corresponding point on the ground truth model is computed, as well as the average distance among all points in this region. We test on four movements of different body regions with each movement using a video of 50 frames for prediction. The final articulation recovery error for each body region is averaged over the 50 frames. The average recovery error is compared with the average distance over the 3D scattered point model, which constitutes the resolution cell. The 3D body point model used in our evaluation has resolution cell of 17.82 mm with standard deviation of 5.04 mm. The point-to-point distance errors for articulation recovery as well as their ratio over resolution cell of the point model is shown in Table 1.

Table 1. Point-to-point error over different body regions

Region names	Arm	Forearm	Leg (Thigh)	Leg (Shank)
Error (mm)	3.54	2.68	5.87	7.02
Ratio relative to the resolution cell	0.2	0.15	0.33	0.39

5 Conclusions

This work introduces an articulation recovery method that generates the 3D body point model of different poses starting with a 3D point model assume a free or polygonal mesh form and a video of consecutively changing poses. The proposed articulation/pose recovery method needs no training data or parametric models for pose prediction. The predicted articulations of the 3D body model are inferred from boundary deformation resulting from moving parts as manifested in the video frames. For each frame, the boundary of the possibly articulating part is extracted and the transformation for each part of body region in 3D is estimated by minimizing the distance error between projection points of the 3D model and corresponding points from this frame. Our articulation reconstructed method leads sub-resolution recovery errors. It also makes possible the simple creation of a garment fitting room where garments are virtually fitted to the individual allowing him/her to visualize virtually their fitting in different articulations.

References

1. Anguelov, D., Koller, D., Pang, H.-C., Srinivasan, P., Thrun, S.: Recovering articulated object models from 3D range data. arXiv preprint arXiv:1207.4129 (2012)
2. Anguelov, D., Srinivasan, P., Pang, H.-C., Koller, D., Thrun, S., Davis, J.: The correlated correspondence algorithm for unsupervised registration of nonrigid surfaces. In: Advances in neural information processing systems, pp. 33–40 (2005)
3. Ju, S.X., Black, M.J., Yacoob, Y.: Cardboard people: a parameterized model of articulated image motion. In: Proceedings of the Second International Conference on Automatic Face and Gesture Recognition, pp. 38–44. IEEE (1996)
4. Bogo, F., Kanazawa, A., Lassner, C., Gehler, P., Romero, J., Black, M.J.: Keep it SMPL: automatic estimation of 3D human pose and shape from a single image. In: Leibe, B., Matas, J., Sebe, N., Welling, M. (eds.) ECCV 2016. LNCS, vol. 9909, pp. 561–578. Springer, Cham (2016). https://doi.org/10.1007/978-3-319-46454-1_34
5. Loper, M., Mahmood, N., Romero, J., Pons-Moll, G., Black, M.J.: SMPL: a skinned multi-person linear model. ACM Trans. Graph. (TOG) 6(34), 1–16 (2015)
6. Freifeld, O., Weiss, A., Zuffi, S., Black, M.J.: Contour people: a parameterized model of 2D articulated human shape. In: 2010 IEEE Computer Society Conference on Computer Vision and Pattern Recognition, pp. 639–646. IEEE (2010)
7. Anguelov, D., et al.: SCAPE: shape completion and animation of people. In: ACM SIGGRAPH 2005, pp. 408–416 (2005)
8. Baumberg, A., Hogg, D.: Learning flexible models from image sequences. In: Eklundh, J.O. (ed.) ECCV 1994. LNCS, vol. 800, pp. 297–308. Springer, Heidelberg (1994). https://doi.org/10.1007/3-540-57956-7_34
9. Jang, C., Jung, K.: Human pose estimation using active shape models. Proc. World Acad. Sci. Eng. Technol. 46 (2008)
10. Alp Güler, R., Neverova, N., Kokkinos, I.: Densepose: dense human pose estimation in the wild. In: Proceedings of the IEEE Conference on Computer Vision and Pattern Recognition, pp. 7297–7306 (2018)
11. Kanazawa, A., Black, M.J., Jacobs, D.W., Malik, J.: End-to-end recovery of human shape and pose. In: Proceedings of the IEEE Conference on Computer Vision and Pattern Recognition, pp. 7122–7131 (2018)
12. Li, C., Cohen, F.: In-home application (App) for 3D virtual garment fitting dressing room. J. Multimedia Tools Appl. (2020, inpress). https://doi.org/10.1007/s11042-020-09989-x
13. Cootes, T.F., Taylor, C.J., Cooper, D.H., Graham, J.: Active shape models-their training and application. Comput. Vis. Image Underst. 1(61), 38–59 (1995)
14. Sun, Y., Wang, X., Tang, X.: Deep convolutional network cascade for facial point detection. In: Proceedings of the IEEE Conference on Computer Vision and Pattern Recognition, pp. 3476–3483 (2013)
15. He, Z., Kan, M., Zhang, J., Chen, X., Shan, S.: A fully end-to-end cascaded CNN for facial landmark detection. In: 2017 12th IEEE International Conference on Automatic Face & Gesture Recognition (FG 2017), pp. 200–207. IEEE (2017)
16. Li, Y., Sun, J., Tang, C.-K., Shum, H.-Y.: Lazy snapping. ACM Trans. Graph. (ToG) 3(23), 303–308 (2004)

17. Long, J., Shelhamer, E., Darrell, T.: Fully convolutional networks for semantic segmentation. In: Proceedings of the IEEE Conference on Computer Vision and Pattern Recognition, pp. 3431–3440 (2015)
18. Pishchulin, L., Wuhrer, S., Helten, T., Theobalt, C., Schiele, B.: Building statistical shape spaces for 3D human modeling. Pattern Recogn. **67**, 276–286 (2017)

Body Motion Analysis for Golf Swing Evaluation

Jen Jui Liu, Jacob Newman, and Dah-Jye Lee$^{(\boxtimes)}$

Brigham Young University, Provo, UT 84602, USA
djlee@byu.edu

Abstract. A golf swing requires full-body coordination and much practice to perform the complex motion precisely and consistently. The force from the golfer's full-body movement on the club and the trajectory of the swing are the main determinants of swing quality. In this research, we introduce a unique motion analysis method to evaluate the quality of golf swing. The primary goal is to evaluate how close the user's swing is to a reference ideal swing. We use 17 skeleton points to evaluate the resemblance and report a score ranging from 0 to 10. This evaluation result can be used as real-time feedback to improve player performance. Using this real-time feedback system repeatedly, the player will be able to train their muscle memory to improve their swing consistency. We created our dataset from a professional golf instructor including good and bad swings. Our result demonstrates that such a machine learning-based approach is feasible and has great potential to be adopted as a low-cost but efficient tool to improve swing quality and consistency.

Keywords: Computer vision · Deep learning · Sports analysis · Golf

1 Introduction

The game of golf is a very popular sport. It has an estimated 80 million players worldwide, and the total economic output by the golf industry is estimated to be \$191.9 billion in the United States alone [4]. In 2019, there were 2.5 million people in the United States who played golf for the first time on a golf course. [2] Because of the rise of new golf players who want to continuously improve their game, a machine learning based tool could be very helpful to assist players at all levels of experience.

The game of golf depends on a very precise swing, and a precise swing needs full-body coordination. Thus, a proficient golf swing can take years of practice and much instruction from coaches. For the players to improve their swing, they must make many incremental and very subtle adjustments to various aspects of the game, such as the mechanics of the swing, their stance, and how they hold the club. This has traditionally been done with either the assistance of an instructor who observes the player, or another type of instrumental analysis.

In recent years, research has produced good results in detecting key body, hand, and foot points on 2D images using deep neural networks [7]. However, most products that analyze golf swings and body motion use 3D information

© Springer Nature Switzerland AG 2020
G. Bebis et al. (Eds.): ISVC 2020, LNCS 12509, pp. 566–577, 2020.
https://doi.org/10.1007/978-3-030-64556-4_44

gathered from multiple cameras or other sensors. Thus, only using 2D images or videos to analyze body motion signifies progress in Computer Vision [5]. Quantifying the difference between data produced by an experienced golf player versus an inexperienced golf player is valuable. While the existing golf swing analysis programs are useful, they require special equipment and are time consuming to set up. It is also impractical for amateur golfers, who may not have the resources to obtain the equipment and programs. Feedback received from those expensive systems are far from the feedback from a professional instructor.

In practice, golf enthusiasts get feedback from professional golf instructors to provide instant feedback. Golf instructors could use the naked eye or a slow-motion video by mobile devices to analyze the golf swing. The instructor may view the golf swing in slow-motion videos frame by frame to analyze the golfer's biomechanics at sequencing key points of the body. We introduce an automatic body motion analysis method to reduce the instructor's workload and to assist the golf player. One of the challenges of such a method is to ensure the system provides consistent accuracy and performance. A reasonable architecture could reduce inference time and maintain the accuracy of each motion. Another challenge is data collection and labeling. Because of the uniqueness of this application, no suitable datasets are available for training and testing. A dataset on golf swing was generated specifically for our work.

2   Related Work

In recent years, golf swing analysis has been done using sensors [13,14], multiple cameras [16], and depth cameras [15]. Our research deals only with videos captured from a single camera, with deep learning techniques to determine the quality of a swing. This approach is unique because it attempts to mimic how most professional instructors provide their feedback.

2.1   Pose Estimation

Recently, deep learning has become an effective technique to be used in human pose estimation. Traditional computer vision techniques that use images from consecutive frames to trace the object path are becoming obsolete. Several works that use deep learning to obtain human pose data include AlphaPose [6], Open-Pose [7], DeepPose [8], and various DNN and CNN based models [9–11]. However, human pose estimation remains a challenging task. There continue to be some errors in localization, though state-of-the-art human body estimators have shown great performance [6].

2.2   Residual Network (ResNets)

With convolutional layer depth increasing dramatically, residual networks [12] became the state-of-the-art in 2015 for detection, classification, and localization tasks. ResNets use shortcut connections of residual blocks to skip the blocks of some convolutional layers, thereby enabling deep neural networks to perform well and more efficiently.

3   Golf Swing Evaluation

Estimating body motion in a 2D video is challenging because the key points of the skeleton structure change over time. Each key point moves differently from frame to frame, but evaluating static images would not provide information for the required time sequence analysis. When a golfer with great consistency uses the same swing techniques, the swing motion should be very similar. However, to analyze 2D video frame by frame in time domain is not a trivial task.

As golf swings are very fast, we speculate that the most important info last about 2/3, with 1/3 s immediately before the club makes contact with the ball and 1/3 s immediately after the club makes contact with the ball. For example, with a frame rate of 240 frames per second (fps), 80 of the relevant frames are immediately before the club makes contact with the ball, and 80 of the relevant frames are immediately after the club makes contact with the ball. Therefore, there will be a total of 161 frames of interest, 80 frames before contact, 1 frame during contact, and 80 frames after contact. We used a frame rate of 60 fps for data collection. This frame rate provided us with 41 frames of interest; 20 frames before contact, 1 frame during contact, and 20 frames after contact.

3.1   Video Collection

A professional golf instructor recorded the golf swing videos for our research. We collected a total of 134 video clips or 11614 images. They include 29 positive (good swing) samples recorded at 240 fps and 71 positive samples recorded at 60 fps. They also include 22 negative (bad swing) samples at 240 fps and 12 negative samples at 60 fps. To increase the size of our data set, the videos recorded at 240 fps were split into 5 sets of 60 fps to provide a total of 216 positive samples and 112 negative samples.

3.2   Annotation

With a frame rate of 60 fps, the precise moment when the club contacts the ball was rarely captured. Therefore, we chose the frame that is the closest to when contact occurred. A professional golf instructor performed the swings and labeled each one as a good swing or a bad swing.

3.3   Correction Filter

Because we are using 2D videos for our body motion estimation, body parts occlusion posts a critical challenge. The data we obtain from a video is a sequential estimation framework of information flow in the time domain without precise relative positions. We develop a unique framework to filter these false detection key points of body motion. During a golf swing, the left wrist and right wrist occasionally block one another when viewed from the front, which causes the left wrist or right wrist to be assigned a false localization.

3.4   Architecture

Our proposed architecture consists of six sections: 1) Obtaining the key points from the pose estimator, 2) putting the left and right wrist key points through a correction filter, 3) normalizing the data, 4) sequencing the key points of the golf swing into a 3 channel array, 5) inputting the 3 channel array into a ResNet for training, and 6) making a final prediction on the quality of the swing.

Key Points Detection. Using AlphaPose, we obtain the key body points for each frame in every 41 frame video clip. Figure 1 shows 16 sample frames of a swing and their key body points. There are 17 key points of interest in each frame, with the default keypoint order as follows: Nose, Left Eye, Right Eye, Left Ear, Right Ear, Left Shoulder, Right Shoulder, Left Elbow, Right Elbow, Left Wrist, Right Wrist, Left Hip, Right Hip, Left Knee, Right Knee, Left Ankle, and Right Ankle.

This produces a 41 × 17 × 2 matrix for a single video of 41 frames, 17 key body points per frame, and the x and y coordinates.

Fig. 1. Key points from pose estimator

Correction Filter. As mentioned previously, there are times when the left wrist gets occluded by the right wrist, or vice versa. Because of this, there are occasional spikes of noise when tracking the (x, y) coordinates of the wrists. To overcome this challenge, we've created a correction filter to eliminate the noise. Figure 2 shows the (x, y) coordinates of the right wrist, the left wrist, and the average coordinates of the left and right wrists before the filter is applied. Figure 3 shows the left and right wrist data after the filter is applied.

To eliminate the noise, we calculate a Detector value (Eq. 1), then compare it to a value equal to the average times a sensitivity factor (Eq. 2). A Detector value greater than the average value times the sensitivity factor signifies the presence of noise in the data. In this case, the noise will be replaced by a data point corresponding to a better representation of the real location of the wrist.

$$Detector = \sum_{t=-2}^{2} \frac{(X_t, Y_t)}{(Window\ size - 1)} \tag{1}$$

$$avg = \sum_{n=0}^{frame} \frac{(X_n, Y_n)}{(frame - 1)} \tag{2}$$

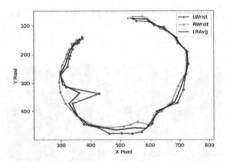

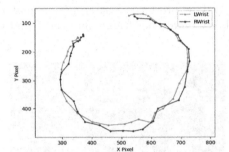

Fig. 2. Wrist location data before correction filter

Fig. 3. Wrist location data after correction filter

Data Normalization. When obtaining the video of a golf player's swing, the camera distance is not guaranteed. For example, one video may be closer to the golfer than others. We've addressed this issue by normalizing the video data. We find the minimum and maximum (x, y) coordinates of the golfer's wrists, and normalize the data points based on this bounding box.

Data Conversion. After the data has been normalized, we then convert them into a 3-channel array. One channel contains the average x coordinates of the wrists, one channel contains the average y coordinates of the wrists, and the last channel contains the average (x, y) coordinates of the wrists. Figure 4 shows an example of this conversion process. The output is a 3-channel 224 × 224 array.

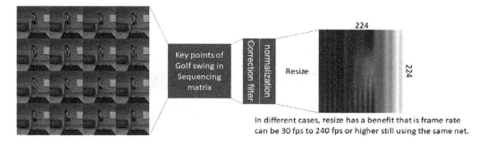

In different cases, resize has a benefit that is frame rate can be 30 fps to 240 fps or higher still using the same net.

Fig. 4. Converting a golf swing sequence into a 3 channel array

ResNet Training. We then use the resulting 3 channel arrays to train a ResNet architecture, as shown in Fig. 5 The output layer consists of 2 outputs which represent either a good (positive) swing or a bad (negative) swing. Figure 6 shows the flow of the prediction process.

Prediction. To determine the quality of the swing, a LogSoftMax is used on the output layer. This produces two values that correspond to either a good swing or a bad swing, and the one that is greater determines the quality of swing.

4 Experiments

As shown in Fig. 6, the LogSoftMax on the output layer will report two values that represent good and bad swings. If the good swing value is stronger than the bad swing value, the system will classify the test swing as a good swing, and vise versa. The histogram of these two output values of all positive predictions is shown in Fig. 7. There is a clear separation between good and bad swing values. The bad swing values (red) are clearly weaker than the good swing values (green), which indicates that the network is able to make correct positive predictions. Similarly, the histogram of these two values of all negative predictions is shown in Fig. 8. All bad swing values are stronger than the good swing values for negative predictions.

Figure 9 shows the histogram of good and bad swing values of all positive samples in our dataset. Our prediction result also shows a clear separation between the good and bad swing values with very minimal overlap. This overlap indicates the number of miss-classifications by our system.

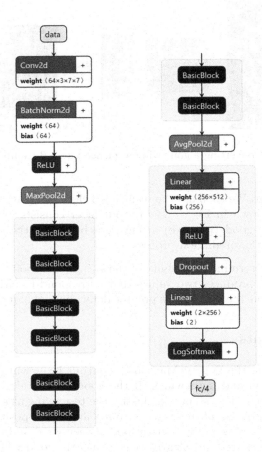

Fig. 5. Model Diagram

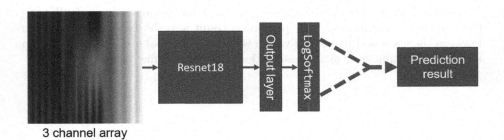

3 channel array

Fig. 6. Prediction of swing

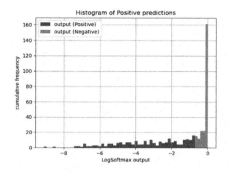

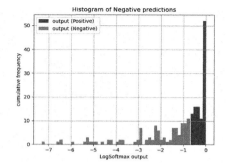

Fig. 7. Positive predictions   **Fig. 8.** Negative predictions

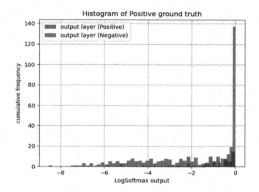

Fig. 9. Prediction of swing

As AlphaPose can process over 20 fps, and our ResNet can process over 30 fps, we obtained a processing time of just over two seconds for a single swing video.

We tested our architecture using 4-fold validation. We used 75% of our videos for training and 25% for testing. The average accuracy of our 4-fold validation was 87.65%, which was quite impressive for separating good from bad swings. It was noted that some samples were borderline swings. Since we only attempted to separate good from bad. A small number of miss-classifications was expected.

In the final system, a swing score representing the swing quality was also calculated. The swing score was calculated according to Eqs. 3–5 In Eq. 3, x is the absolute value of the good swing value as discussed in previous section. We then normalized this value to 0 10 using Eqs. 4 and 5.

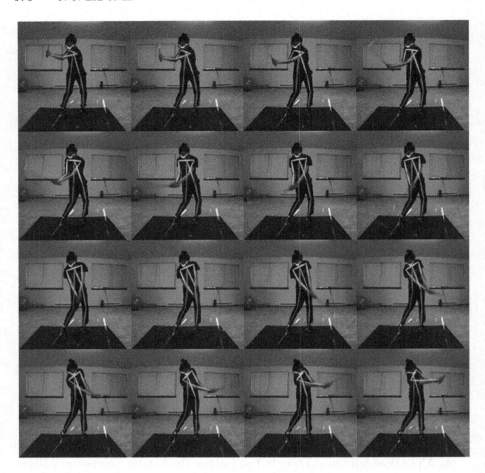

Fig. 10. Good swing with a score 10

Figure 10 shows 16 sample frames of a good swing, and Fig. 11 shows 16 sample frames of a poor swing.

$$x = |goodswingvalue| \tag{3}$$

$$\theta = \frac{x - min(x)}{median(x) - min(x)}\% \tag{4}$$

$$Score = \begin{cases} \theta/10 & \theta < 100\% \\ 10 & \theta > 100\% \end{cases} \tag{5}$$

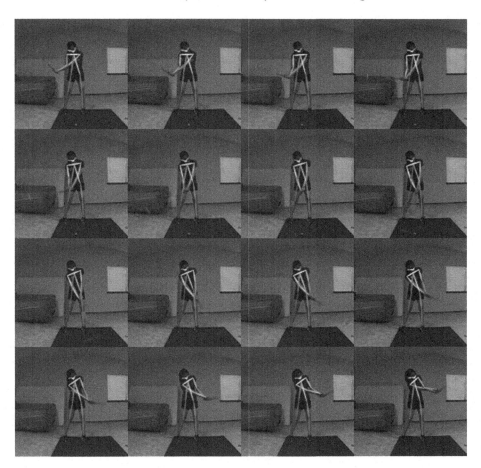

Fig. 11. Bad swing with a score 1

5   Conclusion

Artificial intelligence has become a preferred solution for many applications and the main focus of enhancing competitiveness for many sports. Golf instructors and motion analysis are very important for athletes. However, not everyone can have access to a professional instructor due to high cost or limited availability. In this research, we developed a method to automatically evaluate swing quality to help improve user's performance and consistency. We will continue to collect more video clips to increase the size of our dataset for experiments.

Our future work includes bypassing key point detection and using the video input directly for evaluation, analyzing the impact of frame timing variations, reporting more detail feedback for improvement, and integrating our algorithm with other motion sensors.

References

1. How amateur golfers deliver energy to the driver, Vol. 8, no. 1, 30 April 2020. https://www.golfsciencejournal.org/article/12640-how-amateur-golfers-deliver-energy-to-the-driver
2. Golf industry facts - national golf foundation. https://www.ngf.org/golf-industry-research/
3. McNally, W., Vats, K., Pinto, T., Dulhanty, C., McPhee, J., Wong, A.: GolfDB: a video database for golf swing sequencing. In: 2019 IEEE/CVF Conference on Computer Vision and Pattern Recognition Workshops (CVPRW), Long Beach, CA, USA, pp. 2553–2562 (2019). https://doi.org/10.1109/CVPRW.2019.00311
4. Golf 2020: 2016 golf economy report. Accessed 11 Feb 2019. https://golf2020.com/research/
5. Kamel, A., Sheng, B., Li, P., Kim, J., Feng, D.D.: Efficient body motion quantification and similarity evaluation using 3-d joints skeleton coordinates. IEEE Trans. Syst. Man Cybern. Syst., 1–15 (2019). https://ieeexplore-ieee-org.erl.lib.byu.edu/document/8727745
6. Fang, H.S., Xie, S., Tai, Y., Lu, C.: RMPE: Regional multi-person PoseEstimation. In: 2017 IEEE International Conference on Computer Vision (ICCV), Venice, pp. 2353–2362 (2017). https://ieeexplore.ieee.org/document/8237518. https://doi.org/10.1109/ICCV.2017.256
7. Cao, Z., Martinez, G.H., Simon, T., Wei, S., Sheikh, Y.A.: Open-pose: realtime multi-person 2D pose estimation using part affinity fields. IEEE Trans. Pattern Anal. Mach. Intell. (2017). https://doi.org/10.1109/TPAMI.2019.2929257.0. https://ieeexplore-ieee-org.erl.lib.byu.edu/document/8765346
8. Toshev, A., Szegedy, C.: Deeppose: human pose estimation via deepneural networks. In: IEEE Conference on Computer Vision and Pattern Recognition (CVPR) (2014). https://ieeexplore-ieee-org.erl.lib.byu.edu/document/6909610
9. Ouyang, W., Chu, X., Wang, X.: Multi-source deep learning for humanpose estimation. In: IEEE Conference on Computer Vision and Pattern Recognition (CVPR), June 2014. https://ieeexplore-ieee-org.erl.lib.byu.edu/document/6909696
10. Jain, A., Tompson, J., Andriluka, M., Taylor, G.W., Bregler, C.: Learning human pose estimation features with convolutional networks (2013). https://arxiv.org/abs/1312.7302
11. Tompson, J.J., Jain, A., LeCun, Y., Bregler, C.: Joint training of aconvolutional network and a graphical model for human pose estimation. In: Conference on Neural Information Processing Systems (NIPS), pp. 1799–1807 (2014). https://arxiv.org/abs/1406.2984
12. He, K., Zhang, X., Ren, S., Sun, J.: Deep residual learning for ImageRecognition. In: 2016 IEEE Conference on Computer Vision and Pattern Recognition (CVPR), Las Vegas, NV, pp. 770–778 (2016). https://doi.org/10.1109/CVPR.2016.90. https://arxiv.org/abs/1512.03385

13. Kim, Y.J., Kim, K.D., Kim, S.H., Lee, S., Lee, H.S.: Golf swing analysis system with a dual band and motion analysis algorithm. IEEE Trans. Consum. Electron. **63**(3), 309–317 (2017)
14. Kim, M., Park, S.: Golf swing segmentation from a single IMU using machine learning. Sensors **20**, 4466 (2020)
15. Ko, H., Marreiros, G.: Smart media and application. Concurr. Comput. Pract. Exp. (2019). https://doi.org/10.1002/cpe.5491
16. Severin, A.C., Barnes, S.G., Tackett, S.A., Barnes, C.L., Mannen, E.M.: The required number of trials for biomechanical analysis of a golf swing. Sports Biomech. (2019). https://doi.org/10.1080/14763141.2018.1554085

Computer Graphics

Simulation of High-Definition Pixel-Headlights

Mirko Waldner$^{(\boxtimes)}$ and Torsten Bertram

TU Dortmund University, Institute of Control Theory and Systems Engineering,
Dortmund, Germany
{Mirko.Waldner,Torsten.Bertram}@tu-dortmund.de

Abstract. This contribution presents a novel algorithm for real-time simulation of adaptive matrix- and pixel-headlights for motor vehicles. The simulation can generate the light distribution of a pair of pixel-headlamps with a resolution of more than one and a half million matrix-elements per light module in real-time. This performance is achieved by dividing the superposition process of the matrix-light-sources into an offline and an online part. The offline part creates a light database that is used by the online component to generate the illumination in memory access efficient way. For an ideal pixel-headlight the run-time of the approach is nearly constant by increasing the number of matrix-lights. This contribution evaluates the visual quality of the simulation. It also presents the changes in the run-time for different pixel-headlamp resolutions and solid angle discretizations.

Keywords: Matrix-headlights · Digital light · Real-time simulation

1 Introduction

The development of automotive adaptive matrix-headlights is driven by many technical objectives. Well-known design goals are the increase of driving safety and the creation of a better-looking, sales-promoting and more individual illumination in front of the ego vehicle. The illumination of the matrix-headlamp can be controlled with better selectivity and in smaller spatial areas to achieve the design goals. Lighting functions such as **G**lare-**F**ree **H**igh **B**eam (GFHB) [7] are getting increasingly advanced and adaptive, but system complexity is also increasing compared to headlamps decades ago [4,11].

The resolution of the matrix-headlamps increases with each new product generation, i.e. more individual light sources are integrated into a single light module. These small lights can be controlled individually and create the illumination in front of the headlamp by superposing their individual distributions. From the outside, it looks as if the light module consists of only one light source. The small light sources are arranged as a matrix and their illumination is called pixel in this article. A classic matrix headlight function is GFHB, which minimizes other road users' glare by dynamically switching off the pixels that would illuminate other road users.

© Springer Nature Switzerland AG 2020
G. Bebis et al. (Eds.): ISVC 2020, LNCS 12509, pp. 581–592, 2020.
https://doi.org/10.1007/978-3-030-64556-4_45

With increasing resolution matrix-headlamps are called pixel- or digital-headlamps in association with the illumination of a projector. The pixels get smaller and their edges sharper. There are many lighting technologies like Light-Emitting Diode (LED) [17], Liquid Crystal Display (LCD) [14] or Digital Micromirror Device (DMD) [2], which can produce a high-resolution light distribution. Combining a larger number of different technologies in a single headlamp and increasing in resolution makes the development of matrix/pixel headlamps more complex and challenging.

Fig. 1. Visualization of the light distribution of a pair of adaptive headlamps in false colors. A single headlamp consists of a forefront-module and a matrix-module with 84 lights (top left). It also has a pixel-light-module with 150 thousand pixels (down left). The complete illumination is the superposition of all modules (right).

A higher resolution increases the design possibilities, such as new light functions like symbol projection [8,13]. Figure 1 shows the illumination of a high-definition pixel-headlamp in false colors as an example of a possible future headlight. The headlamp consists of two major light modules. The one has 84 lights and realizes the classic GFHB, because the other driver is not illuminated. The selective non illumiation is visible as a dark tunnel around the car. The dark tunnel is visible on the virtual projection wall behind the car (Fig. 1 top left). The second light module consists of 150 thousand lights and creates a more advanced and selective GFHB. This module only reduces the intensity of the pixels, which interact with the windshield. The area above the vehicle is illuminated with high beam (Fig. 1 down left). This is possible, because the high-resolution module has more than 3 rows compared to the 84 matrix module. The low-resolution module cannot illuminate the area above without blinding the driver. The high-resolution module also simultaneously projects a symbol on the road in front of the ego-vehicle by deactivating its pixels.

The development of control software for high-resolution headlamps will become increasingly difficult as new problems arise. Possible problems are the dynamic adaptation of the projected symbol to the driver's or pedestrian's angle of vision or simply the control of more pixels at the same time. Overcoming these challenges requires virtual prototyping of the control algorithm in a night driving simulator. The simulator must visualize dynamic lighting functions in real-time for virtual test drives with high-resolution headlights. Not only the algorithm needs virtual prototyping, but the complete headlamp is also first designed with simulations and evaluated in virtual test drives. A better test drive simulation with matrix headlamps therefore improves the development process. It optimizes the product design and reduces the costs in development since design problems and optimization potentials can be identified earlier. A challenge in headlamp simulation is the visualization of high-resolution headlamps over ten thousand pixels in real-time, which is to be solved with this contribution.

2   Comparison with Known Headlight Simulations

Many driving simulators worldwide can simulate **A**daptive **F**ront **L**ighting **S**ystem (AFS) headlights in virtual night drives. The comparison of the presented approach and its performance with the publicly available state-of-the-art focuses on two simulators, which are Vrxperience [1] and LucidDrive [16]. According to the author, these software tools are the best known and most widely used in the industry for headlamp evaluation. Both simulators can simulate headlights in real-time in realistic night driving situations. They also offer visualization functions such as false colors or isolines for illumination levels.

The following numbers represent the performance data available on the company's website from June 2020. As both products are not open source, it is impossible to determine the performance of the pure headlight simulation independent of the rest of the virtual environment. The first simulation Vrxperience [1] is developed by Ansys and uses SCANeR [3] as the basis for world simulation. Its support "up to 500 pixels [per headlight] each side" [1]. The second simulation LucidDrive [16] from Synopsys can create "a beam pattern of ten thousand pixels or more, depending on your computer hardware" [16]. This simulation uses its own virtual environment.

The presented algorithm is compatible with the basic illumination model of Unity 3D [20]. The algorithm creates the pixel-headlight dynamically and transfers it into the illumination pipeline. In this engine, this contribution's approach can simulate the light distribution of a pair of headlights with over one million pixels per side. The simulation reaches over 60 fps in a night driving situation on a GTX 1050 Ti and i7-7700. By comparing only the pure pixel numbers, the computing power is better than the state-of-the-art.

3   Concept of the Algorithm and Related Work

A pair of headlamps creates its illumination in front of the ego vehicle as an additive superposition of the individual beam pattern of each headlamp. Matrix-headlamps work according to the same principle, as each pixel is generated by an individual light source. The classical approach to simulate headlights is Projective Texture Mapping [6,15]. In this approach, a point light source propagates a planar intensity distribution into the world. Real-time headlight simulations

[9,10] use measured light distributions as texture to model the beam pattern. This use of light distributions is only valid if the headlamp is measured outside the photometric limit distance so that it can be assumed to be a point light source.

Measured light distributions, e.g. with a goniophotometer, are typically stored in a spherical coordinate system. The coordinate system of the texture is two-dimensional Cartesian so that a coordinate transformation is required for error-free visualization. One approach for the conversion is to interpret the texture as a plane in front of the light source and to use a central (gnomonic) projection to map the spherical light distribution on the texture. Then the texture itself is projected into the world from the virtual light source [9,10] to simulate the illumination.

The algorithm presented focuses on the online creation of texture for matrix headlights. One design goal is the compatibility of existing engines [20]. The created texture is transferred into the existing illumination pipeline, which contains the described illumination model [19] with **P**hysically **b**ased **R**endering (PBR) as reflection model [5]. The focus of this contribution is therefore on the creation of the light texture.

The basic approach of the algorithm is visualizing the many matrix-lights by using one virtual point light. The same principle is used by [16] for the virtual representation of pixel-headlights. By using one virtual light as the source, the matrix lights are superposed by dynamically online generating and modifying the light texture. Similar to [15], the illumination of many real lights is created by one virtual light. This means for a texture $I \in \mathbb{R}^{n \times n}$ with $n \in \mathbb{N}$ discrete elements, that each element $I(u, v)$ is the superposition of all $m \in \mathbb{N}$ matrix-light sources with the distribution $I_{\mathrm{P},i} \in \mathbb{R}^{n \times n}$. The variables u and v are coordinates of the texture, which is square for simplification of the presented equations. The approach works for non square textures. To improve this contribution's readability, all light distributions in this paper are described as gray scale intensity distributions. The presented approach can also be used for colored lights by using three color channels and applying the algorithm separately to all three channels. This is important for the visualization of changes in headlight color due to chromatic aberration. The overlay for a texture element $I(u, v)$ can be formulated as

$$I(u, v) = \sum_{i=0}^{m-1} I_{\mathrm{P},i}(u, v) \ \forall \ 0 \le u < n \wedge 0 \le v < n. \tag{1}$$

To online control the headlight $I_{\mathrm{P},i}$ is the maximum intensity of the i-th light source. Online it is multiplied by the usage factor $p_{01,i} \in \Re$, which lies in the interval $[0, 1]$, to dynamically change the illumination of the i-th light source. By using $p_{01,i}$ (1) is

$$I(u, v) = \sum_{i=0}^{m-1} p_{01,i} \ I_{\mathrm{P},i}(u, v). \tag{2}$$

Fig. 2 shows a simple example of the weighted superposition of two pixels. In combination with Projective Texture Mapping high-resolution matrix headlights can be simulated dynamically by using (2).

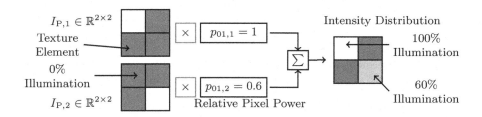

Fig. 2. Weighted superposition with (2) of two light distributions.

4   Creation of High-Definition Light Distributions

The concept explained in the previous section has two main problems, when it is used for simulating headlights with high-definition. The first problem is its memory consumption, because the complete light distribution of every matrix-light had to be loaded into memory to be online accessible. The second problem is the linearly increasing run-time of the algorithm as the number of pixels and the resolution of the texture increases. The linear scaling of (1) is caused by summing each pixel light $I_{P,i}$ on each texture element (u, v). The time for calculating one summation element of (1) is assumed to be constant, so an increasing m or n^2 increases the count of summations and with it directly the required run-time. This is especially worse for pixel-headlights, because when the number of pixels increases, the resolution of the texture will commonly increase too, as the illumination area of each light will get smaller.

The novel idea of this contribution is simply completely ignoring everything online that does not contribute to the lighting. As empirical experiences with [12] as the tool for creating the texture on the GPU has shown, memory access to $I_{P,i}$ will become the bottleneck for run-time improvements. The idea is to access only these $I_{P,i}$ online, which can illuminate a given direction and completely ignore the rest. The improved simulation process now consists of two parts, an offline (startup) and an online part. Figure 3 shows an overview of the main components of the new approach.

The offline part of the simulation loads the lighting data, for example measured intensity distributions form every matrix-light, and prepares them for the online part. At startup, the processed data set is transferred to the simulation hardware (the GPU as recommendation), which dynamically generates the illumination texture I. The simulation generates I by evaluating the control data $p_{01,i}$ of all relevant pixels.

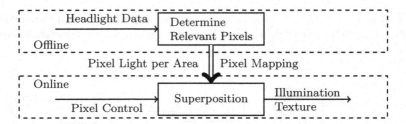

Fig. 3. Main components and signal flow of the headlight creation algorithm.

The online part only overlays the discrete texture element (u, v) of lights that illuminate the element with an intensity higher than the intensity threshold $I_{v,\text{Thr}} \in \mathbb{R}$. The first step in the offline part is to determine the pixels that actually illuminate a solid angle. The pixel mapping

$$\mathcal{P}_{\text{ID}} = \left\{ \begin{array}{ccc} \mathcal{P}_{\text{ID}}(0,0) & \cdots & \mathcal{P}_{\text{ID}}(0,n-1) \\ \vdots & & \vdots \\ \mathcal{P}_{\text{ID}}(n-1,0) & \cdots & \mathcal{P}_{\text{ID}}(n-1,n-1) \end{array} \right\} \tag{3}$$

is the database of illumination pixels for each of the n^2 elements of the texture. In this contribution, $\mathcal{P}_{\text{ID}}$ is interpreted as a three-dimensional set. The first two dimensions each contain n elements like I as a matrix structure and the third dimension is variable for each entry. Thus, an element of $\mathcal{P}_{\text{ID}}(u, v)$ is $\mathcal{P}_{\text{ID}}(u, v)(i) \in \mathbb{N}$, where the operation (u, v) gets a set similar to accessing a texture element and (i) returns a pixel index. The offline part creates an identifier set $\mathcal{P}_{\text{ID}}(u, v)$ for every element as a pixel mapping:

$$\mathcal{P}_{\text{ID}}(u, v) = \{i \in \mathbb{N} | 0 \leq i \leq m - 1 \wedge I_{v,\text{Thr}} < I_{\text{P},i}(u, v)\}. \tag{4}$$

Using the identifier set (2) is with a threshold $I_{v,\text{Thr}} = 0$ and using the mapping from (4) the summation is

$$I(u, v) = \sum_{i=0}^{|\mathcal{P}_{\text{ID}}(u,v)|-1} p_{01,\mathcal{P}_{\text{ID}}(u,v)(i)} \, I_{\text{P},\mathcal{P}_{\text{ID}}(u,v)(i)}(u, v). \tag{5}$$

The summation in Eq. (5) is not done over all m pixels of the spotlight, but only over $|\mathcal{P}_{\text{ID}}(u, v)|$, which actually illuminates the (u, v) segment. Without considering the memory access times it (5) has in the worst case the same run-time as Eq. 2), if both sum over all pixels.

The use of Eq. (5) has the advantage for the simulation of high-resolution pixel-headlights that its run-time is under two conditions theoretically constant if the resolution of the headlight increases. The size of the areas with the same number of light pixels is constant. This means, for example, that the entire texture area illuminated by two pixels remains constant. The second condition is that the maximum number of pixels that illuminate an element is also constant for the whole texture. Figure 4 shows an example where the two conditions are

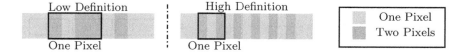

Fig. 4. Example of two light distributions with different number of pixels. The color represents the number of pixels that illuminate the area. In theory, the calculation time of the two illuminations is the same.

met. The maximum number of overlapping pixels is in both cases two and the areas do not change.

The algorithm's run-time is approximately the sum of the area content with a different number of luminous pixels, weighted by the number of luminous pixels. This means that the calculation time of illumination of an area doubles when the number of pixels per area doubles, because the number of summations in (5) doubles. An example of a constant run-time is a headlight in which the pixels' areas do not overlap, so that no matter what the resolution, only one pixel will illuminate an area. This can be an ideal projector or DMD headlamp. Increasing resolution with constant aperture angle will minimize pixel area, but the number of pixels per discrete texture element will theoretically remain constant. The run-time for calculating the illumination with (5) will remain the same in this case. The whole argumentation assumes that the size of the texture elements is infinitesimal, so that the edges of the illumination are always between the discrete grids. This and hardware access times are the reason why a constant run-time can only be achieved theoretically.

The use of (5) as an approach for headlamp simulation can not only improve the computing power. It also reduces the amount of memory required to store a light discharge of a matrix headlamp. The basic idea is to use the mapping of (4) to create a database $\mathcal{I}_{\mathrm{PA}}$. The set $\mathcal{I}_{\mathrm{PA}}$ stores only the illuminations per area above $I_{\mathrm{v,Thr}}$ and has the same set structure as $\mathcal{P}_{\mathrm{ID}}$

$$\mathcal{I}_{\mathrm{PA}}(u,v) = \{I_{\mathrm{P},i}(u,v)|0 \leq i \leq m-1 \wedge I_{\mathrm{v,Thr}} < I_{\mathrm{P},i}(u,v)\}. \qquad (6)$$

The pixel illumination $I_{\mathrm{P},i}$ must be processed in the same order to create $\mathcal{P}_{\mathrm{ID}}$ and $\mathcal{I}_{\mathrm{PA}}$. Figure 5 shows an example of the correct creation of the sets.

By using $\mathcal{P}_{\mathrm{ID}}$ and $\mathcal{I}_{\mathrm{PA}}$ as the new headlight database the summation (5) is

$$I(u,v) = \sum_{i=0}^{|\mathcal{I}_{\mathrm{PA}}(u,v)|-1} p_{01,\mathcal{P}_{\mathrm{ID}}(u,v)(i)} \, \mathcal{I}_{\mathrm{PA}}(u,v)(i). \qquad (7)$$

Using (7) it is not necessary to have all independent light distributions of every pixel available in memory. The combination of $\mathcal{P}_{\mathrm{ID}}$ and $\mathcal{I}_{\mathrm{PA}}$ is a compression format for light distributions of matrix-headlamps, where the under-threshold entries are removed. As the example in Fig. 5 shows, the memory consumption of the new format may be less than storing all light distributions individually. For an idealized memory space calculation, a headlight has m pixels and its

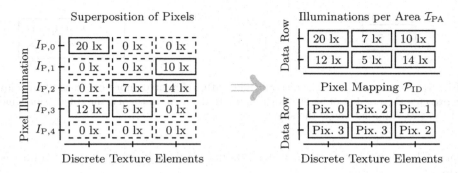

Fig. 5. Example for the preparation of headlamp data in the offline step. The algorithm divides the lighting data per pixel on the left side into the lighting per area and a pixel mapping.

data n^2 discrete texture elements. The maximum number of overlapping pixels is $n_{pix,max}$. The individual distributions require $m \, n^2$ space, but the new format only needs $2 \, n_{pix,max} \, n^2$ space. This means for the example in Fig. 5 is a reduction of $1 - \frac{2 \cdot 2 \cdot 3}{5 \cdot 3} = 1 - 0.8 = 20\%$.

The summation hardware can generate the overlayed light texture with (7) in parallel for each texture element. Computing time can be further reduced by processing only the summation (7) on elements with at least one pixel. For each element of the set

$$\{(u,v)|0 \le u \le n - 1 \wedge 0 \le v \le n - 1 \wedge 0 < |\mathcal{I}_{PA}(u,v)|\}, \tag{8}$$

the simulation creates one thread so that elements that are always dark will never be accessed online.

5   Evaluation

After the theoretical presentation of the simulation approach, this section shows the practical results. The implementation is carried out in Unity 2019.3 [20]. The algorithm is processed in an external dynamic library (DLL) in Cuda 10.1 C++ [12]. The multi-threaded DLL was created in the standard version configuration using Visual Studio 17 (v141) with Windows SDK 10.0.17763.0. The Windows 10 PC uses an i9-9980XE CPU and an RTX 2080 Ti-GPU.

5.1   Visual Quality of the Simulation

The visualization of the light distribution in a virtual scenario is realistic, since the visual impression of a virtual matrix-headlight and the real one is similar. This is difficult to prove in a written contribution, because only pictures taken with the camera can be displayed. The images do not have the same visual impression as the real one, because the dynamic range and the luminance are different.

Figure 6 tries to compare the simulation with reality. It shows the illumination of the same matrix headlight simulated from photometer data in the upper left and from the real device in the right. Both illuminate a projection surface. The headlamp has 84 pixels, which are ordered in 3 rows. To be able to compare reality and simulation better, the light distribution is digitized with the image processing approach in [21,22] and used as a virtual headlight in the same environment. This is shown in the part down left. The typical blue edges and yellow colors caused by chromatic aberration are visible in all cases in the same areas of illumination. The base color, gradients and sharpness are also similar.

Fig. 6. Comprehension of the visual quality of a simulated headlight (top left), digitized (down left) [21,22] with photographed (right).

5.2 Computing Performance

A headlamp with constant opening angles and varying resolution is used to evaluate the run-time changes of the simulation. The horizontal angle is $\pm 8°$ and the vertical $\pm 4°$, which is within the legal requirements [18] and represents a high-resolution pixel-headlight [4]. The edges of each pixel are sharp and they are no large overlapping areas. The ratio between columns and rows is always two to one and the pixels overlap with $\approx 25\%$. The texture is square and its virtual light has an opening angle of $\pm 8.1°$.

The five headlights have $45 \cdot 90 = 4.05 \cdot 10^3$, $125 \cdot 250 = 31.25 \cdot 10^3$, $390 \cdot 780 = 304.2 \cdot 10^3$, $670 \cdot 1340 = 897.8 \cdot 10^3$ and $870 \cdot 1740 = 1513.8 \cdot 10^3$ pixels. The resolutions should represent typical values of existing or future systems [2,4,14,17].

For the evaluation of the performance only the creation of the texture without 3D visualization is measured. The $p_{01,i}$ values are randomly selected and loaded to the GPU in each step. Before the measurement starts and ends, the GPU stream is synchronized [12] to ensure that all operations are complete. The superposition is performed 500 times. From the records, the minimum, maximum, mean, standard derivative σ_i (root of Bessel-corrected variance), median, and the 5% and 95% quantiles are calculated for each experiment. The Kolmogorov-Smirnov test on a sample rejects with a significance level of 5% the null hypothesis of a standard normal distribution for each presented experiment.

The first test runs sets the texture resolution to a constant $n^2 = 2048^2$. This means that each pixel will fully illuminate at least one texture element. Table 1 shows the results.

Table 1. Computing times over 500 steps in μs with constant texture resolution.

Pixels	$\mathbf{n^2}$	Min	Max	Mean	σ_i	Median	5% Quan	95% Quan
$4.05 \cdot 10^3$	2048^2	400.1	866.5	447	49.4	429.7	410.4	531.6
$31.25 \cdot 10^3$	2048^2	403.6	1074.1	460	80.1	432.9	411.5	556.1
$304.2 \cdot 10^3$	2048^2	457.0	782.2	491	37.1	480.3	465.1	579.3
$897.8 \cdot 10^3$	2048^2	420.2	875.3	472	57.5	454.9	433.1	561.9
$1513.8 \cdot 10^3$	2048^2	434.1	761.2	467	36.4	454.9	439.3	554.5

In the second runs of experiments, the texture resolution is adapted to the number of columns c_i of each headlamp with $n_i = 64 \lceil \lfloor 2.2c_i \rfloor / 64 \rceil$. This discretizes each pixel with the same quality. Table 2 shows the results.

Table 2. Computing times over 500 steps in μs with adaptive texture resolution.

Pixels	$\mathbf{n^2}$	Min	Max	Mean	σ_i	Median	5% Quan	95% Quan
$4.05 \cdot 10^3$	256^2	73.7	261.4	112	37.5	98.7	81.2	197.2
$31.25 \cdot 10^3$	576^2	104.4	265.0	145	33.3	135.1	115.4	224.7
$304.2 \cdot 10^3$	1728^2	372.6	706.4	408	35.9	397.8	381.5	493.1
$897.8 \cdot 10^3$	3008^2	820.6	1445.5	857	44.0	845.9	828.2	941.2
$1513.8 \cdot 10^3$	3840^2	1616.6	2719.1	1665	97.7	1646.3	1630.0	1744.7

For a better comparison of the results from Tables 1 and 2, relations between values are shown as a graph in the Fig. 7. The first value is the median of the set of run-times $\mathcal{T}_i$ per resolution as $\mathrm{median}(\mathcal{T}_i)/n_i^2$, which is normalized to $430\,\mu s/2048^2$. The second value is the median, which is normalized to $430\,\mu s$.

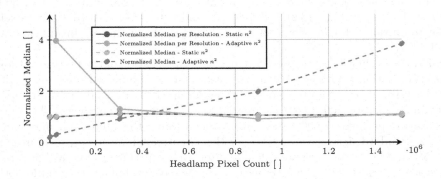

Fig. 7. Visualization of normalized values from the data form Tables 1 and 2.

The presented experiments confirm the presented theory of constant runtime by increasing headlamp resolution under special conditions. The headlamp structure with fixed procedural overlapping of the pixels was chosen to keep the weighted area sum constant for validation of the theory. Figure 7 shows small changes in the median of the run-time with increasing resolution. The experiments show an approximately linear scaling of the run-time with the number of texture elements. Assuming that the run-time is constant with different spotlight resolutions, the increase of the normalized median with adaptive n^2 is only caused by the increasing n^2. This is was may be expected, because more texture elements require proportionally more computational steps, unless they can be parallelized if the hardware has reserves. Finally, the experiments show a run-time offset for small n^2, because the normalized median per resolution with adaptive n^2 for $n = 256$ is ≈ 15 and converges to 1 with increasing n. A possible explanation is the generation of the processing threads on the GPU, which takes time.

6   Conclusion and Outlook

This contribution presented a novel simulation concept and algorithm that allows the dynamic light distribution of a high-resolution pixel headlamp to be visualized almost in real-time. To achieve this, the simulation consists of an offline part, which determines the allocation of pixels to the texture elements once when loading new headlights, and an online part, which determines the luminous intensity for all texture elements at runtime. The generation of a pixel headlight with $\approx 1.5 \cdot 10^6$ single matrix light sources requires online ≈ 0.5 ms on a GPU. This enables virtual prototyping and optimization of existing and future pixel headlights in virtual test drives. New lighting functions such as dynamic symbol projection can be evaluated with this approach in earlier stages of development. This increases safety for all road users and reduces the costs of product development.

This contribution focuses on an idealized DMD headlight as a demonstrator of computing power to determine the power for further systems. The next step would be evaluating other headlights with different structures. This may lead to a simulation algorithm where the structure of the headlamp is analyzed offline. The online processing then adapts its simulation strategy to the structure to achieve optimum performance in exceptional cases.

References

1. Ansys (ed.): Ansys Vrxperience Driving Simulator - Headlamp (2020). https://www.ansys.com/products/systems/ansys-vrxperience/vrxperience-capabilities#cap2. Accessed 13 June 2020
2. Automotive Lighting (ed.): Digital Light: Millions of Pixels on the Road (2018). https://rt.al.world/en/news/article/digital-light-millions-of-pixels-on-the-road/. Accessed 13 June 2020
3. AVSimulation (ed.): SCANeR - Headlights (2020). https://www.avsimulation.com/headlight/. Accessed 13 June 2020

4. Brunne, D., Kalze, F.J.: Outlook on high resolution pixel light. In: 12th International Symposium on Automotive Lightning-ISAL 2017, p. 243 (2017)
5. Burley, B.: Physically based shading at disney (2012). http://disney-animation. s3.amazonaws.com/uploads/production/publication_asset/48/asset/s2012_pbs_ disney_brdf_notes_v3.pdf
6. Everitt, C.: Projective texture mapping (2001). https://www.nvidia.com/en-us/ drivers/Projective-Texture-Mapping/
7. Hummels, B.: Blendfreies Fernlicht. Ph.D. thesis, Universität Karlsruhe(TH) (2009)
8. Kubitza, B., Wilks, C.: Digital light as support for the driver. ATZ worldwide **120**(4), 54–57 (2018)
9. Lecocq, P., Kelada, J., Kemeny, A.: Interactive headlight simulation. In: Proceedings of the DSC'99 Driving Simulation Conference, pp. 173–180 (1999)
10. Löwenau, J.P., Strobl, M.H.: Advanced Lighting Simulation (ALS) for the evaluation of the BMW System Adaptive Light Control (ALC). In: 2002 SAE International Body Engineering Conference and Automotive and Transportation Technology Conference (2002)
11. Moisel, J.: Requirements for future high resolution ADB modules. In: 11th International Symposium on Automotive Lighting - ISAL 2015, pp. 161–170 (2015)
12. Nickolls, J., Buck, I., Garland, M., Skadron, K.: Scalable parallel programming with CUDA. Queue **6**(2), 40–53 (2008). https://doi.org/10.1145/1365490.1365500. http://doi.acm.org/10.1145/1365490.1365500
13. Rosenauer, M., Muster, J., Forster, G.: Lighting solutions to increase acceptance of autonomous vehicles. ATZ Electron. Worldwide **15**(4), 54–57 (2020). https:// doi.org/10.1007/s38314-020-0177-3
14. Roslak, J., Wilks, C.: High-resolution LCD headlamps challenges for electronics architectures. ATZ Electron. Worldwide **12**(6), 46–51 (2017). https://doi.org/10. 1007/s38314-017-0082-6
15. Segal, M., Korobkin, C., van Widenfelt, R., Foran, J., Haeberli, P.: Fast shadows and lighting effects using texture mapping. SIGGRAPH Comput. Graph. **26**(2), 249–252 (1992)
16. Synopsys (ed.): LucidDrive: Night Driving Simulation (2020). https://www. synopsys.com/optical-solutions/lucidshape/luciddrive.html. Accessed 13 June 2020
17. Trommer, J., Feil, T., Wild, M.: LED modules for high-resolution matrix headlamps. ATZ Electron. Worldwide **14** (2019)
18. UNECE (ed.): UN Regulation No. 123 - Adaptive front-lighting systems (AFS) (2016). https://www.unece.org/?id=39147
19. Unity (ed.): Unity 3D Shader Sourcecode (2019). https://unity3d.com/de/get-unity/download/archive
20. Unity Technologies (ed.): Unity 3D 2019.3 (2020). https://unity3d.com/de
21. Waldner, M., Bertram, T.: Evaluation of the light distribution of a matrix-headlight with a hardware-in-the-loop-simulation. In: 13th International Symposium on Automotive Lighting - ISAL 2019 (2019)
22. Waldner, M., Krämer, M., Bertram, T.: Hardware-in-the-loop-simulation of the light distribution of automotive matrix-led-headlights. In: IEEE/ASME International Conference on Advanced Intelligent Mechatronics (AIM), vol. 2019 (2019)

ConcurrentHull: A Fast Parallel Computing Approach to the Convex Hull Problem

Sina Masnadi[✉] and Joseph J. LaViola Jr.

University of Central Florida, Orlando, FL, USA
{masnadi,jjl}@cs.ucf.edu

Abstract. The convex hull problem has practical applications in mesh generation, file searching, cluster analysis, collision detection, image processing, statistics, etc. In this paper, we present a novel pruning-based approach for finding the convex hull set for 2D and 3D datasets using parallel algorithms. This approach, which is a combination of pruning, divide and conquer, and parallel computing, is flexible to be employed in a distributed computing environment. We propose the algorithm for both CPU and GPU (CUDA) computation models. The results show that ConcurrentHull has a performance gain as the input data size increases. Providing an independently dividable approach, our algorithm has the benefit of handling huge datasets as opposed to other approaches presented in this paper which failed to manage the same datasets.

Keywords: Convex hull · Parallel algorithms · CUDA

1 Introduction

Computing the convex hull of a set of points is one of the substantial problems in computer graphics. The convex hull of a set of points P is the smallest convex polygon/polyhedron that contains the points and is denoted by $CH(P)$. Imagine using needle pins on a surface to represent the points, the convex hull can be visualized by wrapping a rubber band around these needles [4]. Given a set of n points in a plane, the convex hull of these points is the set of points which are located on the perimeter of the smallest area that contains all the points. The convex hull of a set of 3D points P is the smallest convex polyhedron containing all points of the set P.

The complexity of the algorithms are based on the total number of points (n) and the number of points that create the hull (h). Among these algorithms, the most popular ones are the "Graham scan" algorithm and the "divide-and-conquer" algorithm [9].

The $O(n \log n)$ complexity of Graham Scan algorithm is emanated from the radial sort of the points. The algorithm starts with one of the points that is sure to be in the convex set which is called P. For this purpose it will find the point with the lowest y-coordinate, if there exists more than one point with the minimum y-coordinate then it will find the one with the lowest x-coordinate. This can be done in $O(n)$ time. Then the rest of the nodes will be sorted by

© Springer Nature Switzerland AG 2020
G. Bebis et al. (Eds.): ISVC 2020, LNCS 12509, pp. 593–605, 2020.
https://doi.org/10.1007/978-3-030-64556-4_46

the angle they make with P and x-axis. The next step is figuring out if the next point is a right turn or a left turn regarding its preceding point and P. If it is a right turn (clockwise), then it means that p_2 is not a part of the convex hull and it will be swapped with p_3 and the algorithm will proceed to the next set of points. This process will end when it reaches the starting point P.

2   Related Work

The research on implementing parallel algorithms is scarce. In 1988, Miller et al. introduced a parallel solution for solving the convex hull problem which given a sorted set of points and a machine with $\theta(n)$ processors can solve it in $\theta(\log n)$ [8]. However the high amount of required processors reduces the practicality of this algorithm. Blelloch et al. introduced a new definition and analysis of the configuration dependence graph for the randomized incremental convex hull algorithm and showed it is inherently parallel with $O(log n)$ dependence depth [3].

The other approach is using GPU processing power for solving the problem. Jurkiewicz et al. introduced a CUDA algorithm which applies quick sort on the points and solve the problem in $O(k \log g)$. $g = \frac{n}{p}$ input size of the problem per SIMD-processor and $k = \frac{n}{U}$ input size of the problem per scalar processor [6]. GHull is a 3D CUDA-based convex hull algorithm that was proposed by Gao et al. which is up to 10x faster than the fastest CPU convex hull software, QuickHull [5]. CudaHull is another 3D convex hull algorithm which is based on the QuickHull approach [10].

Hybrid GPU-CPU is another approach to the convex hull problem Tang et al. presented a hybrid CPU-GPU algorithm to compute the convex hull of points in three or higher dimensional spaces [11]. The GPU is used to remove the points that do not lie on the boundary, then the CPU computes the convex hull for the remaining points.

Here we explain our approach for 2D and 3D convex hull and for each of them, we first describe the approach for CPU-based implementation and then the CUDA implementation approach. We will then discuss the benchmarking task and how our algorithm performed against other algorithms.

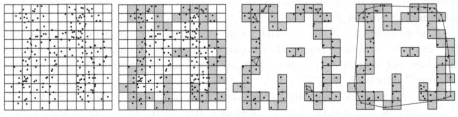

(a) Partitioning the input points   (b) Grey cells are valid partitions.   (c) Convex hull of valid partitions.   (d) Convex hull of finalized points.

Fig. 1. A demonstration of the 2D ConcurrentHull

3   ConcurrentHull

Our approach is based on highly parallel pruning of the interior points. The data is partitioned into an equal sized grid. The pruning is done by the crawlers. Each crawler can perform individually from other crawlers. A crawler starts from a partition in a given direction and tries to find the first valid partition and then it halts. We will discuss the implementation of the 2D and 3D ConcurrentHull algorithm for CPU and GPU.

4   2D Convex Hull

The following steps are a high-level presentation of how we are going to find the convex hull of 2D points:

- Loading the data and partitioning them using a grid.
- Pruning the partitions using *crawlers.*
- Finding convex hulls of remaining partitions and removing the points inside their convex hulls.
- Calculating the final convex hull using the remaining point.

Figure 1 shows a demonstration of 2D ConcurrentHull algorithm.

4.1   CPU 2D Convex Hull

Calculating the convex hull for a set of 2D points starts with loading the points and finding their extreme X and Y values. In the next step, the plane will be divided to a $k \times k$ grid. Each grid cell is called a *partition*. The partition which is located on i and j coordinates of the grid is represented by $\rho_{k \times i + j}$. A *valid partition* is a partition that we assume has at least one point in the convex hull, but there might be no point inside a valid partition that is a part of the final convex hull. In Fig. 1 the example set of points has been divided into a 12×12 grid.

In order to prune the partitions, we use crawlers. A *crawler* is a piece of code which crawls from a starting point towards a defined direction with a width of one partition. It checks if any partitions on its path have any points inside them. It will mark the first non-empty partition that it finds as valid partition and stops crawling. Three crawlers start from each partition of each side of the grid, one perpendicular, the other two in the direction of the grid diagonals (Fig. 2). The pruning is done using $12 \times (k - 2) + 4$ crawlers which run in parallel. Since each corner of the grid only has one diagonal crawler, we have $3 \times (k-2)$ crawlers for each side of the grid (excluding the corners) and 4 crawlers for the corners. Using crawlers we will find valid partitions and the rest of the partitions will be pruned. Figure 1b shows the sample pruned partitions, the white partitions will be removed. Algorithm 2 shows how a crawler works.

Convex hull for each partition is computed in parallel and the points inside the convex hull are removed. If a partition has less than four points, it will be

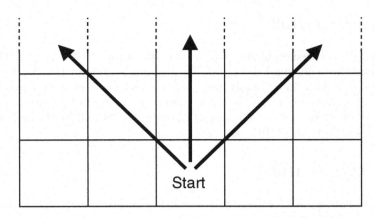

Fig. 2. The figure shows the directions for three 2D crawlers of a starting point. Each arrow represents one crawler's direction.

left untouched as a valid partition (note that at least three points are needed to compute a convex hull). Each partition's points is passed to a thread and each thread finds the $CH(\rho_v)$ using the *Quick Hull* algorithm. Points inside the convex hulls of the partitions can be removed as they are already surrounded by a convex hull inside the final convex hull. Figure 1c shows the calculated convex hull for the valid partitions. Yellow points will be removed from the set. The final convex hull will be computed using the remaining points.

The justification for using partitions and crawlers for pruning instead of using the Quick Hull algorithm in the first step is that the Quick Hull algorithm finds the points that lie inside the triangle [2] by comparing all of the points with the three lines that are created by the extreme points and although the operation is of $O(n)$, it is still a time-consuming task. On the other hand, to prune the points using partitions and crawlers, we only do one comparison in each crawler's step (partition.points.size()>0) which is faster and in the worst case is of $O(12k^2)$ in which k is a constant.

Lemma 1. *The final convex hull points are inside the valid partitions and none of the points from the final convex hull can be inside the pruned partitions.*

Proof. We prove this lemma by contradiction. Consider a set of 2D points P divided to $k \times k$ partitions. We denote $\bigcup_v CH(\rho_v)$ as CH'. If there exists a pruned point $p_p \in CH(P)$ and $P_p \notin CH'$. This means p_p is outside CH'. If it is outside the CH', crawlers have missed the partition (ρ_p). If there is a valid partition on the right of ρ_p, because we assumed p_p is outside the CH' there has been a crawler crawling from left to right that picked the partition on the right of ρ_p as a valid partition, but since crawlers stop when they find the first partition with at least one point inside, it should have stopped when it reached ρ_p and it is a contradiction to the crawler definition. The same case applies to the other directions around ρ_p.

Algorithm 1. Crawler2D

```
 1: procedure CRAWL
 2:     K ← side size
 3:     start_i ← start point x coordinate
 4:     start_j ← start point y coordinate
 5:     direction_i ← direction x coordinate
 6:     direction_j ← direction y coordinate
 7:     current_i ← start_i
 8:     current_j ← start_j
 9: loop:
10:     if size(partition(current_i, current_j)) > 0 then
11:         validPartitions.append(partition(current_i, current_j)
12:         return
13:     else
14:         current_i ← current_i + direction_i
15:         current_j ← current_j + direction_j
16:         if current_i < K &  current_j < K then
17:             goto loop.
```

For the points inside the partitions convex hulls, they cannot be outside the $CH(P)$ because if they are outside $CH(P)$ they should also be outside of the convex hull of a partition, which is a contradiction to the assumption.   □

4.2   GPU 2D Convex Hull

We apply the CPU approach for CUDA with some minor modifications. A CUDA kernel is responsible for partitioning the points. After copying the points data to the GPU memory, n threads assign the points to their partitions. Based on the thread ID, each thread picks one point and assign it to its appropriate partition using side size and extreme points values.

GPU crawlers use the same approach as the CPU crawlers. $12 \times k$ threads run the crawler kernel, each crawls in its direction and marks its appropriate valid partition.

To compute the convex hull on GPU, we modified CudaChain algorithm [7] to fit our needs. The points data in GPU memory are shared among CudaChain instances which helps algorithm to run faster without the need to make multiple copies of the data. After computing the convex hull of the partitions and removing the points inside them, the remaining points will be used to calculate the final convex hull.

5   3D Convex Hull

Applying the ConcurrentHull idea to 3D points can be done using the same steps as the 2D problem but with minor modifications to meet the 3D problem requirements. We will first describe the CPU algorithm and then the GPU one.

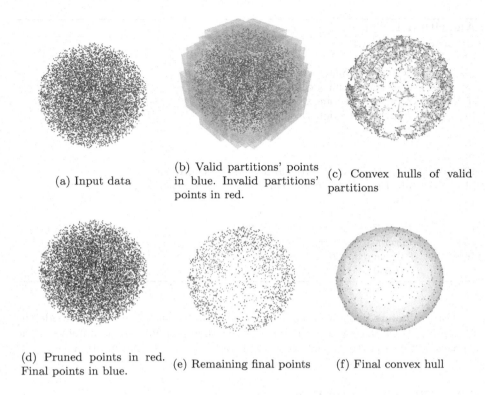

(a) Input data

(b) Valid partitions' points in blue. Invalid partitions' points in red.

(c) Convex hulls of valid partitions

(d) Pruned points in red. Final points in blue.

(e) Remaining final points

(f) Final convex hull

Fig. 3. ConcurrentHull 3D process demonstration.

5.1 CPU 3D Convex Hull

To apply the partitioning, we project a cubic 3D grid on the input data which is a set of 3D points. The grid bounding B is defined by the maximum of furthest points based on X, Y, and Z coordinates. Once we found B, the grid will have $k \times k \times k$ cells each of size $\frac{B}{k}$ and starts from (x_s, y_s, z_s) where $x_s = \min_{\forall p \in P} p.x$, $y_s = \min_{\forall p \in P} p.y$, and $z_s = \min_{\forall p \in P} p.z$.

Similar to 2D crawlers, 3D crawlers also have a starting partition and a direction to crawl. Each of the six sides of the cubic grid has k^2 partition which are the starting partitions of the crawlers. From each starting partition, nine crawlers will be initiated. The adjacent layer of the starting partition has nine partitions that are neighbors of the starting partition which define the directions from starting partitions center towards these partitions centers. In other words we define the direction using a vector $\boldsymbol{d} = (u, v, z)$, u,v and z are corresponding to X, Y, and Z directions. Depending on the side of the grid which the starting partition is located on, one of the elements of $\boldsymbol{d}$ is a fixed value (1 or -1) and the other 2 elements can be -1, 0, or 1, which means we have 3^2 different directions to cover. Figure 4 shows the directions for a sample starting partition which is

Algorithm 2. Crawler3D

```
 1: procedure CRAWL
 2:     K ← side size
 3:     start_i ← start point x coordinate
 4:     start_j ← start point y coordinate
 5:     start_k ← start point z coordinate
 6:     direction_i ← direction x coordinate
 7:     direction_j ← direction y coordinate
 8:     direction_k ← direction z coordinate
 9:     current_i ← start_i
10:     current_j ← start_j
11:     current_k ← start_k
12: loop:
13:     if size(partition(current_i, current_j, current_k)) > 0 then
14:         validPartitions.append(partition(current_i, current_j, current_k)
15:         return
16:     else
17:         current_i ← current_i + direction_i
18:         current_j ← current_j + direction_j
19:         current_k ← current_k + direction_k
20:         if current_i < K &  current_j < K &  current_k < K then
21:             goto loop.
```

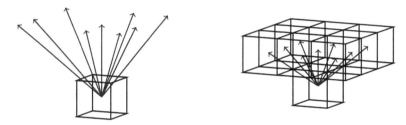

Fig. 4. 3D crawler directions for a sample starting point

located on the bottom of the grid. Overall, $54 \times k^2$ crawlers will be working on the grid to find the valid partitions.

After finding the partitions, 3D quick hull will be used to find the partitions' convex hulls and the same as the 2D algorithm, the points inside the convex hulls will be removed. Note that the partitions with less than four points will also be considered valid partitions. Using the remaining points, the final convex hull for the input problem will be calculated.

Lemma 2. *The final convex hull points are inside the valid partitions and none of the points from the final convex hull can be among the pruned points.*

Proof. The proof is the same as 2D proof.   □

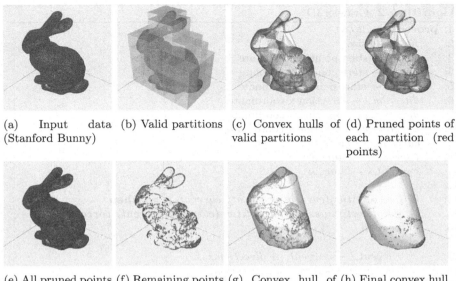

(a) Input data (Stanford Bunny) (b) Valid partitions (c) Convex hulls of valid partitions (d) Pruned points of each partition (red points)

(e) All pruned points (red points) (f) Remaining points (g) Convex hull of the remaining points (h) Final convex hull

Fig. 5. Finding the convex hull of the Stanford Bunny using ConcurrentHull

5.2 GPU 3D Convex Hull

To partition the input data on the GPU, CPU 3D convex hull partitioning logic is used with the same approach as the 2D partitioning kernel. Each thread is responsible for partitioning one point. Each crawler uses one thread to find its valid partition. The points data is shared among the threads. After finding the valid partitions, gHull [5] will be used to calculate the convex hull of the partitions. Figure 3 shows an example of the 3D algorithm process on a ball dataset and Fig. 5 shows the process for the Stanford bunny.

6   Benchmark

Both Synthetic data and real-world data were used to perform the benchmark tests. We performed the benchmarks for CPU 2D, CPU 3D, GPU 2D, and GPU 3D algorithms. The real-world benchmarks are performed for the 3D data as well as the synthetic data. Synthetic benchmarks are performed for the 2D algorithms. Further, the benchmarks for different values of k are plotted. The average values for the synthetic benchmarks are available in Table 1 and Fig. 7 shows plots of the average synthetic benchmarks. For each dataset or k value the benchmarks are performed three times and are averaged to minimize the errors in measurements.

(a) Cube with uni- (b) Ball with uni- (c) Sphere with (d) Gaussian distri-
form distribution   form distribution   thickness of 1%   bution

Fig. 6. Four different synthetic shapes used for 3D benchmark testings.

6.1 2D Benchmark

Synthetic. Four distribution of synthetic data were generated: Square with a thickness of 1%, Square uniform distribution, Circle with a thickness of 1%, Disk uniform distribution.

6.2 3D Benchmark

Synthetic. Four distribution of synthetic data were generated (Fig. 6): Cube with uniform distribution, Ball with uniform distribution, Sphere with thickness of 1%, Gaussian distribution.

Real-World. The data for the 3D real-world benchmarks were gathered from LiDAR scans of the Robotic 3D Scan Repository [1].

Table 1. Benchmark numeric results for synthetic data (time in seconds)

# Points	2D CPU			2D GPU			3D CPU			3D GPU		
	2D CPU	QHull	Speedup	2D GPU	CudaChain	Speedup	3D CPU	Qhull	Speedup	3D GPU	gHull	Speedup
10^5	0.00863	0.00713	0.83	0.90207	0.08673	0.1	0.17111	0.0192	0.11	0.41251	0.32855	0.8
10^6	0.01897	0.09982	5.26	0.95632	0.1122	0.12	0.62744	0.25563	0.41	0.56696	1.55492	2.74
10^7	0.06121	0.99196	16.21	1.21163	0.44502	0.37	2.93851	1.95294	0.66	1.19895	9.94595	8.3
10^8	0.31915	13.647	42.76	2.20155	3.38867	1.54	12.91387	26.94304	2.09	6.85567	OOM	
10^9	6.65961	OOM		12.03245	OOM		39.34611	OOM		11.99615	OOM	

(a) CPU 2D   (b) GPU 2D   (c) CPU 3D   (d) GPU 3D

Fig. 7. Average benchmark times (seconds) for different input sizes.

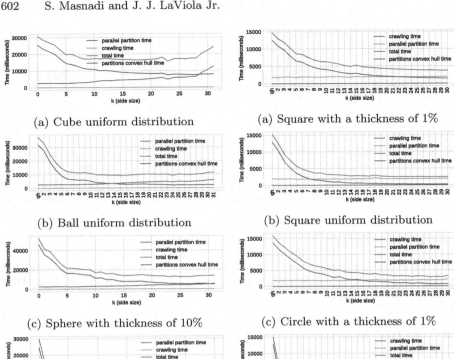

(a) Cube uniform distribution

(a) Square with a thickness of 1%

(b) Ball uniform distribution

(b) Square uniform distribution

(c) Sphere with thickness of 10%

(c) Circle with a thickness of 1%

(d) Gaussian distribution

(d) Disk uniform distribution

Fig. 8. Effect of k value for 10^8 3D points with different distributions using ConcurrentHull CPU 3D. The X axis shows side size for partitioning. qh stands for qhull times.

Fig. 9. Effect of k value for 10^8 2D points with different distributions using ConcurrentHull CPU 2D. The X axis shows side size for partitioning. qh stands for qhull times.

7   Results

We used a computer with a Core i7 (i7-8700K) CPU, 32GB of RAM, and a NVIDIA GTX 1080 Ti GPU with 11 GB GDDR5X memory to run the benchmarks.

For 2D and 3D comparisons, the input points are randomly distributed point sets generated on a square and a cube respectively. To evaluate the performance of ConcurrentHull for 2D and 3D CPU algorithms, inputs are benchmarked against Qhull. For GPU tests, 2D inputs are benchmarked against CudaChain, while 3D inputs are benchmarked against gHull. Convex hull execution time was used as the benchmark measure. Figure 7 shows the benchmark results.

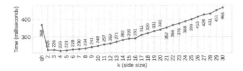

(a) Average times for thermobremen dataset.

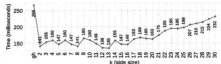

(a) Average times for thermobremen dataset.

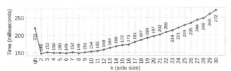

(b) Average times for andreasgart dataset.

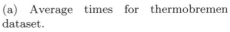

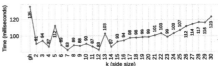

(b) Average times for andreasgart dataset.

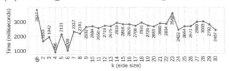

(c) Average times for zagreb dataset.

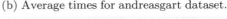

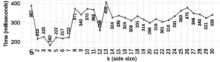

(c) Average times for zagreb dataset.

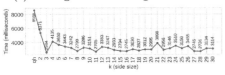

(d) Average times for wue city dataset.

(d) Average times for wue city dataset.

Fig. 10. Real world 3D data CPU algorithm. qh stands for qHull times.

Fig. 11. Real world 3D data GPU algorithm. gh stands for gHull times.

As the results show, on large inputs our approach performs much faster than other approaches, while for a small number of inputs, our approach does not show an improvement. This behavior is the result of partitioning overhead for a small number of points, whereas for a large number of points the overhead is negligible and the partitioning and pruning significantly improves the performance.

The other noteworthy outcome is that for huge input sizes ($>10^8$), all three other algorithms could not produce results due to memory management issues. Since our method first removes the unnecessary points, it can handle much larger input point sets.

The effect of changing the value of k is demonstrated in Figs. 8 and 9 for multiple distributions of 2D and 3D datasets. In the charts, k = 0 means using gHull directly. As results the suggest, increasing k will reduce the execution time up to a point (optimal k), after that the performance will deteriorate.

7.1   Limitations and Future work

One of the disadvantages of partitioning is that we do not know the optimum size for the grid (k). If we choose a small grid size, it can be ineffective because all of the points will end up in the valid partitions if we choose a large grid size we can end up with too many partitions which can compromise the performance. Partition pruning can underperform if invalid partitions are all empty or have a small number of points in them (Figs. 10 and 11).

For future work, we would like to investigate the application of partitioning and crawlers on the dynamic convex hull problem. Moreover, utilizing convex hull merging algorithms might help ConcurrentHull to achieve a better performance. In this case, instead of calculating the convex hull for the aggregated valid partitions pruned points, the already calculated convex hull of each partition can be merged with the others. Finding optimal k requires further investigation of the problem which is an opportunity for future work.

8   Conclusions

This paper introduces ConcurrentHull, a fast convex hull computation technique based on pruning. The results show that the ConcurrentHull algorithm can outperform other algorithms on large enough set of points. For instance, on an input of 10^8 2D points, our approach outperformed Qhull by a speedup of 42 times on synthetic data. This approach benefits from discarding of the points which certainly are not a part of the convex hull using a highly parallel algorithm. Further, the inherent attributes of crawlers help ConcurrentHull achieving a better memory management on large sets of points ($>10^8$).

References

1. Robotic 3D Scan Repository (2020). http://kos.informatik.uni-osnabrueck.de/3Dscans/
2. Barber, C.B., Dobkin, D.P., Huhdanpaa, H.: The quickhull algorithm for convex hulls. ACM Trans. Math. Softw. (TOMS) **22**(4), 469–483 (1996)
3. Blelloch, G.E., Gu, Y., Shun, J., Sun, Y.: Randomized incremental convex hull is highly parallel. In: Proceedings of the 32nd ACM Symposium on Parallelism in Algorithms and Architectures, pp. 103–115 (2020)
4. De Berg, M., Van Kreveld, M., Overmars, M., Schwarzkopf, O.C.: Computational geometry. Computational Geometry, pp. 1–17. Springer, Berlin (2000)
5. Gao, M., Cao, T.T., Nanjappa, A., Tan, T.S., Huang, Z.: gHull: a GPU algorithm for 3D convex hull. ACM Trans. Math. Softw. (TOMS) **40**(1), 1–19 (2013)
6. Jurkiewicz, T., Danilewski, P.: Efficient quicksort and 2D convex hull for CUDA, and MSIMD as a realistic model of massively parallel computations (2011)
7. Mei, G.: Cudachain: an alternative algorithm for finding 2D convex hulls on the GPU. SpringerPlus **5**(1), 696 (2016)
8. Miller, R., Stout, Q.F.: Efficient parallel convex hull algorithms. IEEE Trans. Comput. **37**(12), 1605–1618 (1988)

9. o'Rourke, J.: Computational Geometry in C. Cambridge University Press, Cambridge (1998)
10. Stein, A., Geva, E., El-Sana, J.: Cudahull: fast parallel 3D convex hull on the GPU. Comput. Graph. **36**(4), 265–271 (2012)
11. Tang, M., Zhao, J.Y., Tong, R.F., Manocha, D.: GPU accelerated convex hull computation. Comput. Graph. **36**(5), 498–506 (2012)

A Data-Driven Creativity Measure for 3D Shapes

Manfred Lau[1(✉)] and Luther Power[2]

[1] City University of Hong Kong, Hong Kong, China
manfred.lau@cityu.edu.hk
[2] Lancaster University, Lancaster, UK

Abstract. There has been much interest in generating 3D shapes that are perceived to be "creative" and previous works develop tools that can be used to create shapes that may be considered "creative". However, previous research either do not formally define what is a creative shape, or describe manually pre-defined methods or formulas to evaluate whether a shape is creative. In this paper, we develop a computational measure of 3D shape creativity by learning with raw data and without any pre-defined conception of creativity. We first collect various types of data on the human perception of 3D shape creativity. We then analyze the data to gain insights on what makes a shape creative, show results of our learned measure, and discuss some applications.

Keywords: Mesh models · Perception · Creativity

1 Introduction

The human perception of 3D shapes has been studied in various fields such as computing, psychology, and design. Creativity is a perceptual property that people in the past believe to be a spiritual process and "does not lend itself to scientific study" [14]. We believe that the creativity of 3D shapes is an interesting topic that has been underexplored despite existing research. In this paper, we develop a computational measure of shape creativity. As creativity is a subjective concept, we rely on humans to provide data on their perception of it and use this data to develop our measure of shape creativity. We are inspired by previous works using this data-driven concept to learn style similarity functions for clip art [7], fonts [11], and 3D models [9,10]. To the best of our knowledge, this data-driven concept has not been used to explore the concept of shape creativity.

There exist previous works that develop software tools for novice users to create 3D shapes that may be considered "creative". However, while these previous works focus on the software tools, we believe that the concept of how to compute the creativity of a 3D shape is still underexplored. For example, previous research sometimes do not formally define what is a creative shape [5] or

Manfred Lau acknowledges the Hong Kong Research Grants Council (General Research Fund numbers 11206319 and 11205420).

© Springer Nature Switzerland AG 2020
G. Bebis et al. (Eds.): ISVC 2020, LNCS 12509, pp. 606–614, 2020.
https://doi.org/10.1007/978-3-030-64556-4_47

allow the user to choose among alternatives to create new shapes [3,17]. While this is a good 3D modeling approach, there is no formal measure to say that the generated shapes are necessarily "creative". There are also previous works that use manually pre-defined features, procedures, and/or formulas to evaluate whether a shape is creative [13,19]. In contrast, we take a more general approach and start with no pre-defined notions of 3D shape creativity. We learn with raw data and allow the data itself to "define" a computational measure of shape creativity.

The contributions of this paper are:

– We develop a computational understanding of 3D shape creativity. In contrast to previous work, we have no manually pre-defined notions of creativity with our data-driven approach.
– We collect data on 3D shape creativity with various single-shape stimuli and two-shapes stimuli methods and compare them.
– We characterize what makes a shape creative by exploring whether some qualitative features and quantitative 3D shape descriptors are related to our computed creativity scores.
– We learn functions that predict creativity scores for 3D shapes.
– We discuss some applications of shape creativity.

2   Related Work

Tools for Designing Creative 3D Shapes. There exists various tools and methods that allow novice users to create and design shapes that may be considered creative.

The ExquiMo collaborative tool [13] is closely related to our work. Their tool allows different participants to design different parts of a 3D shape and it can produce unexpected and/or creative results. To measure creativity, they define specific criterias: novelty, surprise, and value. They perform a user study with shapes created with their tool and ask users about these criterias. In contrast, our key difference is in a data-driven shape creativity function with no pre-determined criterias.

"Fit and diverse" [19] is an evolution based method. A part of the evolving set of shapes is presented to the user and the user preferences define a fitness function. The fitness function is a multiple of two scores. An objective score is manually defined based on the shape geometry. A subjective score updates by: increasing in a fixed way whenever a user likes it, and during reproduction the new shapes get a linearly weighted combination of the parent shape scores. Hence the overall fitness function is manually defined. On the other hand, our creativity measure has no pre-determined criterias or formulas.

A creature grammar [8] is used to evolve 3D monsters. Although there is evolution and the user provides input, this process is also specific and pre-defined due to the rules of the grammar.

An exploratory modeling approach [17] generates 3D models and provides an exploratory space for the user to choose them. A suggestion based method [3] takes coarser shapes and suggests components that can be added to make the

Fig. 1. Data Collection Methods: (a) Single-shape stimuli with binary response. (b) Single-shape stimuli with Likert-scale response. (c) Two-shapes stimuli with ranked response.

shape more detailed. In both works, there is no definition of creativity, as they rely on the user to manually choose from some options.

Shape Analysis. There has been much work in this area [18] and in developing datasets of 3D shapes [1,4]. We develop a measure for shape creativity and our work is a start towards collecting a large dataset for this problem.

3   Collecting Data for Shape Creativity

The key idea to our data collection and also function is that we have no pre-defined notion of what shape creativity is, but we rely on the human provided data. We take the raw data (i.e. no features manually computed from raw data) to learn our function. As the data collection part is important, we investigate various methods and compare them. Figure 1 provides a summary of the three methods.

The first method is "Single-shape stimuli with binary response" and is the simplest. We take a single shape for each question and show it to human participants, and ask them to provide a simple response of true or false on whether they perceive the shape to be creative. We intentionally do not provide a definition of "creative" for the users. The reason is that many definitions tend to use other words (such as original, novel, surprise, unique, use of imagination, breaking with routine, or something different) to describe it, and these may confuse the participants or lead them to think of something else. The advantage of this method is that it is a simple question and most users are able to come up with a response, which is good for online data collection methods where the attention of the participants may not always be strong. The disadvantage is that it may not provide much information for the learning unless lots of data is collected. In addition, there may be shapes for which it is difficult to make a clear binary decision.

The second method is "Single-shape stimuli with Likert-scale response" and is slightly more advanced. We show participants a single shape in each question and ask them to provide a 5-scale Likert response on whether they perceive the shape to be creative. The advantage of this method is that users have more options to choose from which may be more accurate than the binary response. The disadvantage is that it can sometimes be difficult to choose between for example 4 or 5, and that the perception of what constitutes a 4 or 5 may depend on the individual.

The third method is "Two-shapes stimuli with ranked response" and is a bit more complex. We show participants two shapes in each question and ask them to choose the one that they perceive to be more creative. The advantage of this method is that it is simple as it is also a binary decision and it should be possible to come up with a response even if the differences in the two shapes are minor. The disadvantage is that there may also be not much information to learn from as there can be conflicts in the responses both for each pair of shapes and across multiple pairs of shapes.

Furthermore, we thought about having three or more shapes in each question, but it could confuse participants and should not provide much more information than the above regardless of the type of response. Overall, the three methods are all still quite simple, and we designed them this way such that we can collect good data.

3D Shapes. We take shapes from the ShapeNet dataset [1]. In this short paper, we have three shape categories: 44 lamps, 30 tables, and 45 chairs. To show a 3D shape on a 2D image, we create a *gif* image that repeatedly shows a rotating view of the shape for 3 s and a 0.5 s pause of a front view chosen manually.

Crowdsourced Questions. We collect data from many users with the Amazon Mechanical Turk crowdsourcing platform. As the user responses are subjective and there are no "right or wrong" answers, we do not filter out any responses after they have been given. In the instructions, we specify that: "If you randomly choose your answers, your responses will not be taken, and you will not be paid".

For each method above, we generate 30 to 40 questions randomly for each set of questions. At the end of a set of questions, we include a text box where the participants can optionally provide "a few words describing why you gave the responses that you did". There were a total of 180 participants. We did not collect data about their demographics background, as this was not our concern. The participants took between 1 and 11 min per question and were paid $0.20 per question. For each method, we collected 6000 samples of data, where each question can be answered by multiple participants and be counted as different samples.

Checking for Data Consistency. We wish to check that the collected data is consistent. We describe our process for the first method above. For the other methods, the idea and results are similar. The main idea is to take each question, collect some user responses, sample a subset many times, and check whether the subsets have similar distributions of responses. For this process, we collect additional data for a set of 30 questions and for 100 users. For each question, we randomly subsample 50 of the responses for 20 times, and each time we note the number of "true" responses out of the 50. We then check that these 20 values come from the same distribution by performing a one-sample Kolmogorov-Smirnov test. We find that the p-value is larger than 0.05, which provides evidence that the 20 subsamples are similar. We repeat this for all 30 questions and find the same result. The above process simulates if we were to collect the data at for example a different time, then it would still lead to the same distribution of data.

4   Learning a 3D Shape Creativity Measure

The purpose of the learning is to show that the concept of shape creativity can be learned and to compare among the data collection methods. Since the functions or neural networks themselves are not the key contribution of this paper, we will describe only in words at a high-level their key aspects. We take the collected data and learn functions separately for each method. Each function takes as input a 3D shape (or some representation of it). For the output, using the data from the first method leads to a creativity score between 0 and 1 (real number) for the whole shape. For the second method, the output is a discretized score corresponding to the five Likert scales. For the third method, the output is also a real number. These learned functions are our human perceptual shape creativity measures.

Our functions are multi-layer neural networks. For the third data collection method, as we have pairwise data (for the pairs of shapes), we also incorporate learning-to-rank [2]. For this case, the learned function also predicts a score for each shape. We have data augmentation by creating 10 training samples per sample of data by randomly generating the multiple images or views for each shape. For the multi-layer neural network, the 3D shape input is represented as multi-view rendered images [15], and we have 6 views to represent each shape. For each view, we have a shared convolutional neural network that computes a feature vector. We then concatenate the features from the multiple views, and have fully-connected layers to predict a creativity score in the last layer (i.e. a real number corresponding to the first and third data collection methods and one of five discretized categories for the second method).

For evaluation, we compute the accuracy of each of the three learned functions using its corresponding collected data by performing 10-fold cross-validation. Note that even for the shape pairs data, the learned function can predict a score for each shape of each pair and then we can predict the shape with the higher score to be more creative. For the first data collection method, we convert the predicted real number output to 0 or 1 (false or true) such that it can be compared with the data. The percentages of accurately predicted samples for the three data collection methods are 69.2%, 67.1%, and 74.5% respectively. Hence their prediction abilities are similar, with the third method of the pairwise data being slightly better.

5   Results and Analysis

Most and Least Creative Shapes.   As the third data collection method is best (see above), we use its learned creativity function to find the most and least creative 5 shapes for each shape category (Figs. 2 and 3). We attempt to describe the major patterns in these results, even though the descriptions can be subjective and we encourage the reader to observe the shapes for themselves. For the lamps in Fig. 2, the least creative shapes consist of simple parts while the most creative shapes have some special patterns. In Fig. 3, the least creative

Fig. 2. Lamps ranked by our data-driven creativity measure, from the least creative 5 on the left to the most creative 5 on the right.

Fig. 3. Tables and chairs ranked by our data-driven creativity measure, from the least creative 5 (left) to the most creative 5 (right).

tables are regular while the most creative tables have more interesting patterns and table legs. For the chairs, the most creative ones are special or different in some way.

Participant Descriptions of Their Shape Selections. Based on the participants' own descriptions (in optional text box) of why they gave their responses, we try to understand more into the characteristics of what makes a shape "creative". 124 participants gave descriptions. 57 participants said they selected responses based on shapes that are *simple, planar, or regular*. 42 users said that the shapes are *aesthetic*. 38 users mentioned they thought that the shapes are *detailed or intricate*.

Correlation with Qualitative Features. Based on the participant descriptions, we collect additional data to check whether each of three major features that they mention are quantitatively related to creativity. For each feature and each shape, we ask users to provide a 1–5 scale Likert score (e.g. 5 for strongly agree that a shape is aesthetic). We use the Amazon Mechanical Turk platform and collected data for 15 participants. Table 1 shows the correlations between the scores for each feature and the learned creativity scores (for the third data collection method) for the shapes in each category. The correlations confirm the informal participant descriptions above. The correlation for "aesthetic" is positive, so more aesthetic shapes are more creative. The correlations for both "simple" and "planar" are negative, so more simple or more planar shapes are less creative. Note that the correlations are not consistently strong which means that creativity cannot be represented or be predicted well by any one of them.

Table 1. Pearson correlation coefficients between three qualitative features and shape creativity scores. For the largest five values, the corresponding p-values are less than 0.05 which means those correlations are significant.

Correlations between	Creativity		
	Lamps	Tables	Chairs
Aesthetic	0.653	0.512	0.435
Simple	−0.303	−0.527	−0.236
Planar	−0.274	−0.445	−0.160

Prediction with Quantitative 3D Shape Descriptors. To gain more understanding of shape creativity in a quantitative way, we test whether some 3D shape descriptors can be used to predict creativity (only using the data from the third data collection method). We learn a function that takes as input the 3D shape descriptors and compute as output a creativity score for the shape. The 3D shape descriptors are: D2 shape distribution [12], Gaussian and Mean curvatures [16], and shape diameter function [6]. Each descriptor is represented by a histogram and we concatenate them into a single vector. The function is a multi-layer neural network and we use the procedure as in Sect. 4 with learning-to-rank and 10-fold cross-validation. The percentage of samples predicted correctly is 37.5%. The results are as expected and show that the concept of shape creativity is more complex than these geometric descriptors.

6   Applications

We discuss the possible uses of 3D shape creativity in some creativity-based shape applications.

Creativity-Guided Visualization. Our computed creativity scores can be useful for clustering the shapes and for better visualization of them. For example, for the three shape categories in Figs. 2 and 3, it is visually quite clear that the shapes on the left side can be clustered separately from those on the right side. For the right side of the chairs that are "highly creative", it would otherwise be difficult to place them together this way, since for example traditional shape descriptors such as D2 distribution or curvature may group them differently. For example, the egg-shaped and hand-shaped chairs are special due to their content rather than shape geometry.

Creativity-Guided Shape Search. The concept of creativity can be useful for shape search. For example, if we search with one of the lamps on the right side of Fig. 2 as the query shape, it may return the other more creative lamps on the right and not the simpler lamps on the left. Again, the content of the shapes rather than geometry and specifically the lamp details help here.

7   Discussion

We have started to develop a computational understanding of the creativity of 3D shapes in this work. We hope that our work can inspire future work in this interesting topic.

One limitation is that we have a small number of shape categories. Future work can explore more shape categories and a larger number of shapes for this problem. We also only consider just a few qualitative features and a few shape descriptors in the analysis section, and exploring a more extensive set of these can further help our understanding of shape creativity.

Currently, we handle the collected data from the three methods separately to learn their corresponding functions. While this still works well in showing that the concept of shape creativity can be learned, future work can perform the learning with perhaps multiple loss terms, with a term corresponding to each of the three data collection methods. Then it may be possible to have one overall function to handle all types of data which can be more general.

References

1. Chang, A.X., et al.: ShapeNet: an information-rich 3D model repository. CoRR (2015)
2. Chapelle, O., Keerthi, S.: Efficient algorithms for ranking with SVMs. Inf. Retrieval J. **13**(3), 201–215 (2010)
3. Chaudhuri, S., Koltun, V.: Data-driven suggestions for creativity support in 3D modeling. ACM Trans. Graph. **29**(6), 1–10 (2010)
4. Chen, X., Golovinskiy, A., Funkhouser, T.: A benchmark for 3D mesh segmentation. ACM Trans. Graph. **28**(3), 1–12 (2009)
5. Cohen-Or, D., Zhang, H.: From inspired modeling to creative modeling. Vis. Comput. **32**(1), 7–14 (2016)
6. Gal, R., Shamir, A., Cohen-Or, D.: Pose-oblivious shape signature. IEEE TVCG **13**(2), 261–271 (2007)
7. Garces, E., Agarwala, A., Gutierrez, D., Hertzmann, A.: A similarity measure for illustration style. ACM Trans. Graph. **33**(4), 1–9 (2014)
8. Guo, X., Lin, J., Xu, K., Jin, X.: Creature grammar for creative modeling of 3D monsters. Graph. Models **76**(5), 376–389 (2014)
9. Liu, T., Hertzmann, A., Li, W., Funkhouser, T.: Style compatibility for 3D furniture models. ACM Trans. Graph. **34**(4), 1–9 (2015)
10. Lun, Z., Kalogerakis, E., Sheffer, A.: Elements of style: learning perceptual shape style similarity. ACM Trans. Graph. **34**(4), 1–14 (2015)
11. O'Donovan, P., Libeks, J., Agarwala, A., Hertzmann, A.: Exploratory font selection using crowdsourced attributes. ACM Trans. Graph. **33**(4), 1–9 (2014)
12. Osada, R., Funkhouser, T., Chazelle, B., Dobkin, D.: Matching 3D models with shape distributions. In: SMI, pp. 154–166 (2001)
13. Ranaweera, W., Chilana, P., Cohen-Or, D., Zhang, H.: ExquiMo: an exquisite corpse tool for collaborative 3D shape design. J. Comput. Sci. Technol. **32**(6), 1138–1149 (2017)
14. Sternberg, R.: Handbook of Creativity. Cambridge University Press, Cambridge (1999)

15. Su, H., Maji, S., Kalogerakis, E., Learned-Miller, E.: Multi-view convolutional neural networks for 3D shape recognition. In: ICCV (2015)
16. Surazhsky, T., Magid, E., Soldea, O., Elber, G., Rivlin, E.: A comparison of gaussian and mean curvatures estimation methods on triangular meshes. In: ICRA (2003)
17. Talton, J.O., Gibson, D., Yang, L., Hanrahan, P., Koltun, V.: Exploratory modeling with collaborative design spaces. ACM Trans. Graph. **28**(5), 1–10 (2009)
18. Xu, K., Kim, V.G., Huang, Q., Kalogerakis, E.: Data-driven shape analysis and processing. Comput. Graph. Forum **36**(1), 101–132 (2017)
19. Xu, K., Zhang, H., Cohen-Or, D., Chen, B.: Fit and diverse: set evolution for inspiring 3D shape galleries. ACM Trans. Graph. **31**(4), 1–10 (2012)

Virtual Reality

Walking in a Crowd Full of Virtual Characters: Effects of Virtual Character Appearance on Human Movement Behavior

Michael G. Nelson, Angshuman Mazumdar, Saad Jamal, Yingjie Chen, and Christos Mousas[✉]

Purdue University, West Lafayette, IN, USA
{nelso430,amazumda,jamal4,victorchen,cmousas}@purdue.edu

Abstract. This paper describes a study on the effects that a virtual crowd composed of virtual characters with different appearance has on human movement behavior in a virtual environment. The study examines five virtual crowd conditions that include the following virtual characters: neutral, realistic, cartoon, zombies, and fantasy. Participants were instructed to cross a virtual crosswalk and each time, one of the examined crowd conditions shown. The movement behavior of participants was captured and objectively analyzed based on four measurements (speed, deviation, distance traveled, and interpersonal distance). It was found that the appearance of the virtual characters significantly affected the movement behavior of participants. Participants walked slower when exposed to a virtual crowd composed of cartoon characters and faster when exposed to fantasy characters. Moreover, participants deviated more when exposed to a crowd composed of fantasy characters compared to cartoon and zombie characters. Finally, the interpersonal distance between participants and fantasy characters was significantly greater compared to human and zombie characters. Our findings, limitations and future directions are discussed in the paper.

Keywords: Virtual crowd · Human-crowd interaction · Character appearance · Human movement behavior · Virtual reality

1 Introduction

In our modern age, navigating crowds are an unavoidable aspect of participating in society. In order to travel any significant distance, it is nearly impossible to not end up as part of one. They are found on our sidewalks, in shopping centers, and any place that humans congregate. It naturally follows then that they will be found in our virtual societies as well. From films and games to interactive simulations crowd forms and provides a sense of realism for these virtual spaces. Although there is significant research on the analysis, modeling, and simulation of crowds and crowd dynamics [25, 32] as well as a number of published papers have examined interactions with virtual characters or groups of virtual characters, only a limited number of studies have examined the way

© Springer Nature Switzerland AG 2020
G. Bebis et al. (Eds.): ISVC 2020, LNCS 12509, pp. 617–629, 2020.
https://doi.org/10.1007/978-3-030-64556-4_48

that humans walk along with virtual crowd populations surrounding them [4,16, 18,24]. However, there are no conclusive results as to whether a moving virtual crowd population affects the movement behavior of humans or as to how it would have such an effect [4,24]. In turn, understanding how humans perceive and interact with these simulations of society may prove to be vital for effectively guiding humans through them.

This paper explores human movement behavior in immersive virtual crowds and tries to answer whether and how the appearance of virtual characters that belong to a virtual crowd affected the movement of participants that have been simply instructed to cross a virtual crosswalk (see Fig. 1). Based on the appearance of the virtual characters, five crowd conditions namely neutral, realistic,

Fig. 1. A participant walking in the motion capture studio and moving toward the opposite sidewalk in the virtual metropolitan city.

cartoon, zombies, and fantasy were examined. Participants were placed into a virtual metropolitan city and were instructed to cross a virtual crosswalk while surrounded by a virtual crowd population that was moving toward the same direction. During the walking task, the movement behavior of participants was captured and four measurements (speed, deviation, distance traveled, and interpersonal distance) were extracted. Considering that researchers determined that as the characters started deviating more towards non-human-like characteristics, the eeriness factor—i.e. the inhuman and otherworldly characteristics of the character—increased with them [3], this paper tries to understand the impact that a crowd has upon a human movement behavior, when the composition changes from neutral to pleasant and aversive appearance of the virtual characters.

The structure of this paper is organized as follows. In Sect. 2 related work is discussed. Section 3 covers the methodology of the experimental study. Section 4 presents the results. A discussion of the results is drawn in Sect. 5. Finally, Sect. 6 covers the conclusions are future research directions.

2   Related Work

Numerous studies have been conducted in the past concerning interaction with virtual characters. It has been found that when humans interact with characters inside a virtual environment, the exhibited interaction behavior was similar to that of a situation in real life [26,28] even if humans are aware that the interaction was taking place with virtual characters and not with real humans [9]. Apart from studies concerning interactions with a single character at a time [15,22,26], studies concerning interaction in either small groups of characters or virtual crowds have also been a point of interest to the research community [17,18].

There has also been work on how humans interact differently with different virtual characters. de Borst et al. [3] explores emotional elicitation, recognition, and familiarity of virtual characters ranging from human-like to non-human-like. They show that human-like characteristics create a better sense of familiarity and less eeriness. They also show that non-human characteristics were also more familiar and approachable. Pan et al. [27] explored how participants mimic a virtual character. They found that where participants had to follow a character, their error rate was incredibly low in comparison to where they had to follow a ball. Hamilton et al. [11] focused on how participants mimicked virtual characters. They found that participants tended to replicate character's actions by measuring the elevations of their hands in comparison to the virtual character, which heavily correlated. Latoschik et al. [19] explored the approachability of humans and mannequins characters. They found that humans were far more approachable and less eerie than their mannequin counterparts.

There has been much research done on crowd interactions and walking simulations within virtual environments. A study [24] concerning human movement has focussed on the density aspect of the crowd. The results that were obtained, showed indications that the participant's movements changed as the density of the crowd as well as the speed increased. Another aspect of crowd simulation is to understand the flow of the crowd. There is a huge implication of how a crowd moves with respect to the participant. Studies showed that crowd movement and outflow was significantly better when the elements in the crowd merged into each other in or under a T-junction, instead of approaching each other from the opposite direction [29].

The flocking behavior participants exhibit while walking with virtual crowds was explored by Moussaïd et al. [23]. They found that patterns occur while moving, which could be attributed to the participants following their closest characters while avoiding collisions with others. Bruneau et al. [4] explored interactions in regards to crowd sizes in virtual environments. They found that participants tend to go around small crowds and participants tend to go through larger crowds. Kyriakou et al. [18] explored collision avoidance in virtual crowds and how that relates to realism. They found that, when participants visualized collision avoidance in crowds, they believed the environment to be more realistic.

In Ahn et al. [1] participants were put in two situations, one where they had a goal to accomplish and one where they did not. They showed that in situations where they had goals to accomplish, participants tend to focus less on the minor imperfections of the crowd, hence those crowds seem more realistic. Ennis et al. [7] explored the realism of synthetic crowds, they showed that participants perceive the realism of a synthetic crowd when the synthetic crowd's positions were based on the positions within a real crowd. Finally, Dickinson et al. [6] showed how crowd densities affect participants' ability to complete a goal. They found that crowds with larger densities hindered the participant's movement more.

In terms of movement analysis, Cirio et al. [5] compared participant interactions within a virtual environment and a real environment using a goal-centric study. They found that the shape of the trajectories the participants took, their velocity and angular velocity showed similar trends between virtual environments and real life. Sohre et al. [30] explored the role of collision avoidance between virtual character and the participants on overall comfort and perceptual experience in an immersive virtual environment. They found that when collision avoidance was used participants took more direct paths, with less jittering or backtracking, and found the resulting simulated motion to be less intimidating, more realistic, and more comfortable. Finally, Bailenson et al. [2] explored interpersonal distance for characters in a virtual environment. They showed that when characters approached a participant from the front versus when they approach them from their side, participants tend to be more apprehensive. Moreover, they showed that participants are more comfortable when characters approach from their peripheral rather than directly in front of them.

Our research leverages elements from these fields and ponders how virtual crowd interactions are influenced by character appearances. There has not been much research done in this field, therefore, our study tries to extend current knowledge and contributes toward this direction.

3   Materials and Methods

Details on the materials and methods of this study are provided in the following subsections.

3.1   Participants

In total, 18 participants, aged 19 to 40 ($M = 24.89$, $SD = 6.58$) took part in our study. Participants were graduate students and faculty of our department recruited by email and class announcements. All students had some experience of being in a virtual environment prior to this study. No participant complained of motion sickness. All participants were volunteers and there was no type of compensation involved.

3.2   Experimental Conditions

The study utilized five experimental conditions (see Fig. 2) to investigate the effects of a virtual crowd composed of characters with a different appearance on human movement behavior. A within-group study design was implemented to ensure direct comparisons across the experimental conditions. Apart from the virtual character, all other aspects of the virtual environment were identical. The experimental conditions were the following:

- **Neutral Crowd (NC):** This crowd condition includes virtual mannequin characters. The characters are faceless and colored in various colors.
- **Human Crowd (HC):** The characters in the crowd are realistic human appearing characters.
- **Cartoon Crowd (CC):** The characters in the crowd are cartoon styled human appearing characters.

- **Zombie Crowd (ZC):** The characters in the crowd are realistic skeletal and clothed zombies.
- **Fantasy Crowd (FC):** The characters in the crowd are realistic fantasy humans.

Fig. 2. The five different virtual crowd conditions based on the characters' appearance that were used in this study in which participants were asked to walk with and cross a virtual crosswalk. Top (from left to right): neutral crowd (NC), human crowd (HC), and cartoon crowd (CC). Bottom (from left to right): zombie crowd (ZC) and fantasy crowd (FC).

3.3   Setup and Virtual Reality Application

The research was performed at the departmental motion capture studio. The dimensions of the studio were eight meters long and eight meters wide, with a ceiling height of four meters. The HTC Vive Pro head-mounted display device was used for projecting the virtual reality content and the MSI VR One backpack computer (Intel Core i7, NVIDIA GeForce GTX1070, 16 GB RAM) was used to run the application. A user wearing the mentioned devices when walking within our motion capture studio space is shown in Fig. 1.

The application used for this study was developed in the Unity3D game engine version 2019.1.4. A virtual metropolitan city was designed in Autodesk 3ds Max and then imported to the Unity3D game engine to be used for the study. The virtual environment (crosswalk) used for this experiment is illustrated in Fig. 3. The participant is placed on the sidewalk at a crosswalk in the virtual metropolitan city. Virtual pedestrians (virtual crowd) were pre-scripted to cross the road and reach the opposing sidewalk. The virtual characters for each of the conditions were either designed in Adobe Fuse or taken from various Unity Asset Store assets and the motion sequences were retargeted using the Adobe Mixamo. Note that all virtual characters had roughly the same height and shoulder width. Each character was initialized to surround the participant and was scripted to reach a target position on the opposite sidewalk. After reaching the assigned target position, each character was scripted to move to another location in the virtual environment to help alleviate congestion on the sidewalk. The crowd density, speed, and trajectories were automatically generated by randomly placing the virtual characters in positions that created consistent average movement speed and with a low density. This was achieved using the Unity3D NavMesh system and directing NavMesh Agents towards to their assigned position.

Fig. 3. The virtual crosswalk in the metropolitan city (left) populated with a virtual crowd composed by fantasy virtual characters (right).

Each virtual character that belongs to that crowd was implemented to not violate the close phase of the personal space (76 cm) of any other character, according to the proxemics model [10,12]. Moreover, we set the crowd's speed to not exceed 1.2 m/s. This choice was based on the U.S. Manual of Uniform Traffic Control Devices [8], which defines that the normal walking speed of humans has been estimated to be 1.2 m/s. We also considered the crowd model of Still [31], and more specifically the low-density crowd that places one pedestrian per square meter; therefore, participants exposed within a virtual crowd that gave the ability to move freely. These three parameters were constant across conditions, and we consider them as key aspects that helped us standardize the experimental conditions. We decided not to represent the participants with a self-avatar. One previous study found that representing participants with virtual avatars during a walking task might affect their movement within a virtual environment [21]. This was important to consider since the omission of an avatar to represent participants helped in extracting movement behavior that was not influenced by parameters other than those examined, such as a virtual body that does not match the participant's own body in size and appearance.

3.4   Measurements

The objective measures are a combination of factors that have been identified by our review of the previous literature [13,14,20]. Each of the measures is taken in a series of one hundred in set intervals along the path walked by the participants. The examined measurements were as follows:

– **Speed:** The average speed of the participants' walking motion from the start to the goal position. The speed was measured in meters/second.

– **Distance Traveled:** The total distance traveled when crossing the road. This was measured in meters.
– **Deviation:** The average deviation (absolute value) between the global trajectory of the virtual crowd and the trajectory of the participant. The average deviation was measured in meters.
– **Interpersonal Distance:** The average distance of the closet four characters directly in front of the participant. The chosen four characters were the same for the participants and the simulated characters and did not change during the walking task. Note that for each trial, different nearby were chosen. This was measured in meters.

3.5 Procedure

Once the participants arrived at the motion capture studio of our department, the research team provided information to them about the project, and they were asked to read the provided consent form, which was approved by the Institutional Review Board of Anonymous University, and sign it in case they agree to participate in the study. Upon agreement, the participants were asked to complete a demographic questionnaire. In the next step, the researcher helped the participants with the backpack computer and the head-mounted display. Once everything was set, the participants were asked to take a short walk within a virtual replica of the motion capture studio to ensure they were comfortable enough when wearing all the devices.

After becoming comfortable and familiar with the virtual reality equipment, the researchers asked the participants to remove the headset and move toward a marked location in the real environment and face the opposite direction. Once participants landed on the marked position and before the experiment started, the researcher informed them that once the application started, they would be placed into a virtual metropolitan city and the task they would have to perform was to cross the road. The participants were informed that once the traffic light would turn green they should start walking. Participants were told they could have breaks between the trials of the conditions if needed and that they had full permission to leave at any time.

All participants were informed that they would cross the virtual crosswalk to reach the opposing sidewalk 20 times (5 conditions × 4 trials). They were also told they would be informed when the experiment had ended. Once the participant finished each trial, they were asked to remove the head-mounted display and move back to the marked location on the other side of the room. This process is repeated for all repetitions. Participants were informed by the research team once the experiment was completed. The balance for first-order carry-over effects across the conditions was handled using Latin squares. The total duration of the experiment lasted on average 30 min.

4   Results

This section presents the results obtained from the main study. One-way repeated measure analysis of variance (ANOVA) was used to analyze the obtained data using the five experimental conditions as independent variables and the motion measurements as dependent variables. The individual differences were assessed using a post hoc Bonferroni corrected estimates were used if the ANOVA was significant. Boxplots of the results are presented in Fig. 4.

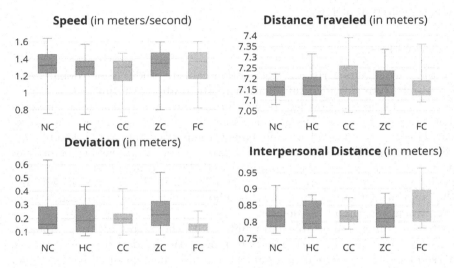

Fig. 4. Boxplots of the obtained results for each measurement. NC: neutral crowd, HC: human crowd, CC: cartoon crowd, ZC: zombie crowd, and FC: fantasy crowd.

The effect of crowd characters on the participants' movement behavior was compared using four objective measurements (speed, deviation, distance traveled, and interpersonal distance) across the five experimental conditions (NC, HC, CC, ZC, and FC). No significant differences were found for the **distance traveled** measurement [$\Lambda = .249$, $F(4, 14) = 1.160$, $p = .370$, $\eta_p^2 = .249$].

Significant results were found in participants' walking **speed** in the virtual environment [$\Lambda = .456$, $F(4, 14) = 4.019$, $p < .05$, $\eta_p^2 = .535$] across the five experimental conditions. Pairwise comparisons indicated that the mean speed for the CC condition was significantly lower than the FC condition at the $p < .005$ level. No other difference was found across the examined condition.

The **deviation** of participants was also significant across the five experimental conditions [$\Lambda = .466$, $F(4, 14) = 4.018$, $p < .05$, $\eta_p^2 = .534$]. Pairwise comparison indicated that the mean deviation for the FC condition was significantly lower than that for the CC condition at the $p < .05$ level, and the ZC condition at the $p < .05$ level. No other difference was found across the examined condition.

Finally, in relation to the average **interpersonal distance**, significant results were found across the five experimental conditions [$\Lambda = .440$, $F(4, 14) = 4.456$, $p < .05$, $\eta_p^2 = .560$]. Pairwise comparison indicated that the mean interpersonal distance during the FC condition was significantly higher than that for the HC condition at the $p < .005$ level, and the ZC condition at the $p < .05$ level. No other differences across conditions were found.

5   Discussion

The study was conducted to understand the effects of virtual characters' appearances that belong to a moving virtual crowd on human movement behavior. The participants were immersed in a virtual metropolitan city surrounded by a virtual crowd population that was moving towards the opposite sidewalk and they were instructed to walk toward that direction. No additional instructions on moving in the virtual environment were given to participants. The collected data was analyzed to determine whether the participants' movement behavior affected by the virtual crowd and more specifically, by the appearance of the virtual characters that composed the examined crowd condition.

We found that the speed, deviation, and interpersonal distance variables were altered when participants walked in the different crowd conditions. Participants' speed was significantly lower when exposed to a virtual crowd composed of cartoon characters compared to a virtual crowd composed of fantasy characters. We also found that participants' deviation during the crowd condition composed of fantasy virtual characters was significantly lower than that for the crowd composed of cartoon and zombie characters. Finally, participants' interpersonal distance to the four closest characters in the forward direction was significantly higher during the fantasy crowd condition compared to human and zombie crowd conditions.

Because the cartoon characters could be considered to be cuter and more approachable than the zombie or fantasy characters [22], this might have made our participants to walk slower. This may be because participants felt more at ease with the simpler character designs. By similar metrics, an explanation for the difference in interpersonal distance is that the participants felt more natural being closer to the human-like characters and might have been wary of the zombie and fantasy characters, so they kept their distance.

The deviation in speed could be attributed to the fantasy characters sharing similar physical proportions and body structure to real humans, which could be interpreted by a participant as being included in a crowd that more closely mirrors a typical crowd of humans, albeit in unusual attire. This, in turn, may have caused the participants to become more cautious while moving with the cartoon characters, due to them being constantly aware of the disproportionated body features, and accidentally moving into the personal space of (or in this case, colliding with) the virtual cartoon characters. Similar interpretations can be made when comparing the cartoon and zombie crowds, with the fantasy crowd in regard to the deviation of the participant.

Fantasy characters had the most interpersonal distance in comparison to zombies and humans. An explanation could be that, even though the interpersonal distance was higher, participants easily recognized it as the most comfortable distance they should keep from the characters. Interpersonal distance with the other characters could be more sporadic, which leads to it being less as an average. This also explains why the deviation was less and the speed was more with fantasy characters.

Even though participants' behaviors may imply that they were more comfortable moving with the fantasy characters, in comparison to the zombies and cartoon characters, the results show they kept the most distance between themselves and the fantasy characters. This could indicate that the ability to identify characters as humans could be the root cause of the differences here. The cartoon characters have slightly different proportions and the zombies are unmistakably not human while the fantasy characters are human with non-standard attire.

Unfortunately, we were not able to see any significant differences in the distance traveled of the participants' path. The total distance was included to confirm whether or not the global deviation was significant, the various characters were not triggering avoidance mechanisms in the participants where its statistical significance was found. While anecdotally there were a few instances of participants moving out of the way in both zombie and fantasy characters, no statistical significance was found. This could be for a number of reasons, but we find the most likely case to be the objective of walking to the other side of the road to be more enticing that the characters surrounding it.

A few limitations should be noted in this study. The lack of including a questionnaire that includes the participants' presence, embodiment, and trust would have been helpful additional information for analysis but would have taken too long to implement. The extent of a participant's immersion may have assisted in understanding their movement patterns. Additionally, the characters walked at a consistent speed which may have had an effect on the participants' perception of realism. There may also be a potential issue with the proportions of the cartoon characters used. While all models had roughly the same heights and shoulder widths, there are some minor variations in the head size and limb proportions of a few cartoon characters. The methods used to calculate the interpersonal distances will not be affected by these minor variations but the participant's perception of proximity to the characters may have been affected. This could potentially lead to the participants to change either their trajectory or movement speed slightly.

6   Conclusions and Future Works

While this study has a limited scope on the role of characters on human locomotion behaviors in virtual reality crowds, we believe this may provide useful insights for future researchers on similar lines of inquiry. According to our results, the appearance of virtual characters that belong to a virtual crowd could be a factor to alter the movement behavior of participants. We found that different types of avatars will affect the distance they keep in a crowd, their overall speed, and the deviation from the global crowd trajectory. We believe that researchers and developers of virtual reality games and applications can utilize our results to better predict the implications of designs that include virtual reality crowds.

There are numerous avenues in which to investigate virtual crowds and the effects they have on participants that extend beyond changes in appearance. One such way is to change various locomotive aspects of the crowd including the direction to be towards the participant, curving the angle of the path that the crowd should follow, or setting the crowd to a pattern like Perlin noise or flocking behavior. It would also be possible to extend these studies to other crowd population interactions (walking alone or in groups, stopping at storefronts, talking, waiting, etc.) and understand the way the participants interact with such behaviors and understand the virtual crowd in general.

References

1. Ahn, J., Wang, N., Thalmann, D., Boulic, R.: Within-crowd immersive evaluation of collision avoidance behaviors. In: ACM SIGGRAPH International Conference on Virtual-Reality Continuum and its Applications in Industry, pp. 231–238 (2012)
2. Bailenson, J.N., Blascovich, J., Beall, A.C., Loomis, J.M.: Interpersonal distance in immersive virtual environments. Pers. Soc. Psychol. Bull. **29**(7), 819–833 (2003)
3. de Borst, A.W., de Gelder, B.: Is it the real deal? perception of virtual characters versus humans: an affective cognitive neuroscience perspective. Front. Psychol. **6**, 576 (2015)
4. Bruneau, J., Olivier, A.H., Pettre, J.: Going through, going around: a study on individual avoidance of groups. IEEE Trans. Vis. Comput. Graph. **21**(4), 520–528 (2015)
5. Cirio, G., Olivier, A.H., Marchal, M., Pettre, J.: Kinematic evaluation of virtual walking trajectories. IEEE Trans. Vis. Comput. Graph. **19**(4), 671–680 (2013)
6. Dickinson, P., Gerling, K., Hicks, K., Murray, J., Shearer, J., Greenwood, J.: Virtual reality crowd simulation: effects of agent density on user experience and behaviour. Virtual Reality **23**(1), 19–32 (2018). https://doi.org/10.1007/s10055-018-0365-0
7. Ennis, C., Peters, C., O'Sullivan, C.: Perceptual effects of scene context and viewpoint for virtual pedestrian crowds. ACM Trans. Appl. Percept. **8**(2), 10 (2011)
8. Federal Highway Administration: U.S. manual on uniform traffic control, revisions 1 and 2 incorporated edition. Washington, D.C.: U.S. Department of Transportation Federal Highway Administration (2003)
9. Freeman, D., et al.: Can virtual reality be used to investigate persecutory ideation? J. Nerv. Mental Dis. **191**(8), 509–514 (2003)
10. Hall, E.T.: The Hidden Dimension, vol. 609. Doubleday, Garden City, NY (1966)
11. Hamilton, A., Pan, X.S., Forbes, P., Hale, J.: Using virtual characters to study human social cognition. In: Traum, D., Swartout, W., Khooshabeh, P., Kopp, S., Scherer, S., Leuski, A. (eds.) IVA 2016. LNCS (LNAI), vol. 10011, pp. 494–499. Springer, Cham (2016). https://doi.org/10.1007/978-3-319-47665-0_62
12. Hickson, M., Stacks, D.W., Moore, N.J.: Nonverbal Communication: Studies and Applications. Roxbury Publication (2004)

13. Koilias, A., Mousas, C., Anagnostopoulos, C.N.: I feel a moving crowd surrounds me: exploring tactile feedback during immersive walking in a virtual crowd. Comput. Animation Virtual Worlds **31**(4–5), e1963 (2020)
14. Koilias, A., Nelson, M., Gubbi, S., Mousas, C., Anagnostopoulos, C.N.: Evaluating human movement coordination during immersive walking in a virtual crowd. Behav. Sci. **10**(9), 130 (2020)
15. Koilias, A., Mousas, C., Anagnostopoulos, C.N.: The effects of motion artifacts on self-avatar agency. In: Informatics, vol. 6, p. 18 (2019)
16. Koilias, A., Nelson, M.G., Anagnostopoulos, C.N., Mousas, C.: Immersive walking in a virtual crowd: the effects of the density, speed, and direction of a virtual crowd on human movement behavior. Comput. Animation Virtual Worlds, e1928 (2020)
17. Krogmeier, C., Mousas, C., Whittinghill, D.: Human-virtual character interaction: toward understanding the influence of haptic feedback. Comput. Animation Virtual Worlds **30**(3–4), e1883 (2019)
18. Kyriakou, M., Pan, X., Chrysanthou, Y.: Interaction with virtual crowd in immersive and semi-immersive virtual reality systems. Comput. Animation Virtual Worlds **28**(5), e1729 (2017)
19. Latoschik, M.E., Roth, D., Gall, D., Achenbach, J., Waltemate, T., Botsch, M.: The effect of avatar realism in immersive social virtual realities. In: ACM Symposium on Virtual Reality Software and Technology, p. 39 (2017)
20. Mousas, C., Kao, D., Koilias, A., Rekabdar, B.: Real and virtual environment mismatching induces arousal and alters movement behavior. In: IEEE Conference on Virtual Reality and 3D User Interfaces, pp. 626–635. IEEE (2020)
21. Mousas, C., Koilias, A., Anastasiou, D., Rekabdar, B., Anagnostopoulos, C.N.: Effects of self-avatar and gaze on avoidance movement behavior. In: IEEE Conference on Virtual Reality and 3D User Interfaces, pp. 26–734 (2019)
22. Mousas, C., Anastasiou, D., Spantidi, O.: The effects of appearance and motion of virtual characters on emotional reactivity. Comput. Hum. Behav. **86**, 99–108 (2018)
23. Moussaïd, M., Schinazi, V.R., Kapadia, M., Thrash, T.: Virtual sensing and virtual reality: how new technologies can boost research on crowd dynamics. Front. Robot. AI **5**, 82 (2018)
24. Nelson, M., Koilias, A., Gubbi, S., Mousas, C.: Within a virtual crowd: exploring human movement behavior during immersive virtual crowd interaction. In: International Conference on Virtual-Reality Continuum and its Applications in Industry, p. 3 (2019)
25. O'Connor, S., Liarokapis, F., Jayne, C.: Perceived realism of crowd behaviour with social forces. In: International Conference on Information Visualisation, pp. 494–499 (2015)
26. Pan, X., Gillies, M., Barker, C., Clark, D.M., Slater, M.: Socially anxious and confident men interact with a forward virtual woman: an experimental study. PLoS ONE **7**(4), e32931 (2012)
27. Pan, X., Hamilton, A.F.D.C.: Automatic imitation in a rich social context with virtual characters. Front. Psychol. **6**, 790 (2015)
28. Pertaub, D.P., Slater, M., Barker, C.: An experiment on public speaking anxiety in response to three different types of virtual audience. Presence: Teleoperators Virtual Environ. **11**(1), 68–78 (2002)
29. Shiwakoti, N., Shi, X., Ye, Z., Wang, W.: Empirical study on pedestrian crowd behaviour in right angled junction. In: 37th Australasian Transport Research Forum, vol. 1 (2015)

30. Sohre, N., Mackin, C., Interrante, V., Guy, S.J.: Evaluating collision avoidance effects on discomfort in virtual environments. In: IEEE Virtual Humans and Crowds for Immersive Environments, pp. 1–5 (2017)
31. Still, G.K.: Introduction to Crowd Science. CRC Press, United States (2014)
32. Zhao, M., Cai, W., Turner, S.J.: Clust: simulating realistic crowd behaviour by mining pattern from crowd videos. Comput. Graph. Forum **37**(1), 184–201 (2018)

Improving Chinese Reading Comprehensions of Dyslexic Children via VR Reading
A Step Towards Tackling Dyslexia with Top-Down Teaching

Billy C. Y. Fu[✉], Zackary P. T. Sin, Peter H. F. Ng, and Alice Cheng-Lai

The Hong Kong Polytechnic University, Hong Kong, China
`chiuyung.fu@connect.polyu.hk`

Abstract. Dyslexia cause neurological limitations upon its patients such that they have poor phonological awareness and orthographical skills. This in turn limit the patients' abilities to derive meaning from words which are keys to effective reading. To aid dyslexics in their comprehensions, a top-down approach to reading is proposed. In the meanwhile, a graphical model is also proposed as a tool to help researchers pinpoint neurological processes. It cleanly shows that the top-down approach could bypass dyslexic patients' neurological limitations. It is also hypothesized that by aiding their understanding of articles and words, it is also possible for patients to improve their phonological awareness and orthographical skills. Our implementation to the research goals is VR reading, which uses multimedia feedback to give cues to dyslexic students on the meaning of words and articles. VR reading consists of aiding images, voice-overs, videos and a background theme dome that gives encapsulated cues on the meanings of the article and its words that are detached from the article itself. This is an important design decision as we want dyslexic students to rely more on multimedia feedback in deriving the meaning. We also show a preliminary evaluation which is a step towards testifying the aforementioned hypotheses with VR reading. It involves primary school children to read a Chinese article and be evaluated afterwards. The result seems to indicate that VR reading is useful in aiding students in their reading comprehension and additionally, has potential to improve their phonological awareness and orthographical skills.

Keywords: Dyslexia · Top-down teaching · VR educational application · Neurological processes as graphical models · Reading comprehension · Chinese language

1 Introduction

In a traditional education setting on language reading, a teacher teaches the meaning of words to students. It is hoped that the students can become more proficient to a language by linking words and their mental representations themselves. Although this method may work for the majority of students, students with dyslexia are known to have difficulties learning language in such a way. The problem lies in the fact that dyslexia cause neurological limitations to its patients such that they have problems in phonological

© Springer Nature Switzerland AG 2020
G. Bebis et al. (Eds.): ISVC 2020, LNCS 12509, pp. 630–641, 2020.
https://doi.org/10.1007/978-3-030-64556-4_49

awareness and orthographical skills [1]. In our view, the traditional teaching method could be described as a bottom-up approach in which high-level understanding comes from words as units. Dyslexic patients have problems using words and derive upward to their meaning. Therefore, we proposed top-down approach. The key objective of the top-down approach to teaching is to help dyslexic students to understand an article and its words by avoiding their neurological limitations. Since a top-down approach will require a student to firstly understand the meanings of words and articles, and from there pair it back down to the actual words, an obvious question is how a particular meaning could be conveyed to the student as the word itself is already representing a meaning. Our proposal to this seemingly contradictory problem is to introduce non-textual modals. By providing multimedia input to the student, the student would be able to guess what is the meaning we are referring to at the moment. For example, if we want to infer to a frog, we could show a picture of a frog. Or, if we want to infer to jumping, we could show a short video with a jumping person.

To validate our hypothesis that a top-down approach to teaching reading would facilitate improvements on dyslexic students' reading comprehensions along with their orthographical skills and phonological awareness, we also propose VR reading. A VR-based implementation is chosen because it is thought that this could help detach students from a traditional reading environment (where dyslexic students are weak at) while have an advantage in immersing students to the multimedia input (which dyslexic students have little problem processing). VR reading implements the top-down approach to teaching reading with several multimedia inputs, including pictures, voice-overs, videos and a background dome.

To evaluate VR reading, we have chosen a Chinese reading curriculum. The reason that motivates us to choose Chinese reading is that given Chinese is the last major written language that follows a logographic system, it is permissible to assume that it is one of the most unique languages in the world. If VR reading is applicable to Chinese, it could be argued that it could also be applicable to other languages. A variant of the graphical model for Chinese reading is also proposed as an example to show that it could be applied to other languages. In the latter part of this study, we will show that dyslexic students who have used VR reading shown a marked improvement in comprehension. In addition, we also find evidence that implies VR reading could improves the students' orthographical skills and phonological awareness which are the key limitations that prevent dyslexic students from learning reading in a traditional bottom-up setting.

To conclude, the contributions of this study are as follows.

1. Proposing a top-down approach to teaching that could help avoid the neurological limitations of dyslexic students.
2. A top-down teaching application, VR reading, that involves multimedia input. Results show that VR reading has a marked improvement on dyslexic students' comprehension and that it could also improve their orthographical skills and phonological awareness.

2 Literature Review

As summarized by Lyon [1], Dyslexia is a type of learning disabilities that is neurobiological in its origin. It impairs its patients' phonological awareness and orthographical skills which are important to effective reading. Dyslexics are characterized by their inaccurate and/or non-fluent word recognition. In Hong Kong, the local prevalence rate is up to 10% for dyslexia in the HK Test for Specific Learning Difficulties [2]. Studies showed that their dyslexic symptoms include difficulties in phonological awareness, orthographical awareness, morphological awareness and rapid automatized naming [3, 4]. These symptoms cause significant weaknesses in reading and writing. Many researchers have proved that there is no correlation between their learning motivation and dyslexic symptoms. Most of the dyslexic children have normal intelligence quotient (IQ) level or even above average level, their academic achievement in language-based subject, including, general studies and science, results poor performance in ordinary school setting. This situation of Dyslexic children is started from the primary grade to the secondary school grade. They are used to be described by negative labels in school, families and social-circle.

The situation is worse in the Chinese education system. Chinese is a difficult language for Dyslexic children. Unlike English is phonogram (letter-sound corresponding language), Chinese is logogram (character-syllable language). One English word is a combination of phonemes. You can get English vocabulary's pronunciation by grouping its characters or phonemes. However, Chinese word is a combination of shape, pronunciation, and its meaning. Individual word has its own pronunciation [5]. For Chinese Dyslexic Children, even they can recognize a word, but they cannot pronounce the word, or get its meaning, i.e., They lost the connection between shape and pronunciation, also between shape and meaning. There is some research that identify this problem.

Attree [6] has proved that adolescents with dyslexia may exhibit superior visuospatial strengths on certain pseudo real-life tests of spatial ability. Attree [6], Kalyvioti [7], Passig [8], and Berninger [9] have also found that VR technologies could help dyslexia. However, there is a framework to explain. In this paper, we will propose a connection model that based on the VR approach to build the connection among Chinese word's shape, pronunciation, i.e., Dyslexic children could have a better understanding of the written contexts.

3 Methodology

The goal of top-down teaching is to utilize improve dyslexics' reading comprehensions along with their phonological awareness and orthographic skills via multimedia input.

VR reading involves two major components, the adventure book and background theme dome (Fig. 1). The key idea of these two components is to provide an encapsulated environment that students could immersive into. Both components could provide contextual information to the students regarding the meaning of the article and its words via multimedia input. Thus, they are the key to top-down teaching in VR reading. In addition, we develop our model with consideration to Burdea's 3 I's of VR [11]. In Burdea's model, VR should be combined by immersion, interaction, and imagination. In our model the theme dome provides immersion while the adventure book provide interaction.

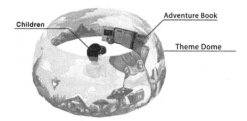

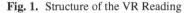

Fig. 1. Structure of the VR Reading

Fig. 2. The functionalities of VR reading. Readers can click to play the clip with Acrobat Reader.

Adventure Book. The adventure book (Fig. 2) is the learning material and its main purpose is to provide multimedia feedback for words. It contains four pages, including (from right to left) tools page, article page, word bank page, and dictionary page. For the order, we arrange the pages by relation. The article page is near the center of book. The tools page put at the right of article page as most of the children are right-handed. Children can highlight the word on article page, then the highlighted word will be shown on word bank page. So, the word bank page put at the left of article page. The dictionary page put at the left of word bank page because children can interact with the keywords or highlighted words to get the definition and multimedia cues on dictionary page. The multimedia feedback includes images, voice-overs and videos.

Also, we design the adventure book by peripheral vision. Peripheral vision contains a sets of vision area differentiated by the field of view (FOV). Human eyes have about 90 degrees of FOV. But for mobile VR headset, normally has about 100 degrees of FOV.

Refer to Fig. 3 and Fig. 4, they illustrate how the peripheral vision applied to the adventure book design. Within the central and paracentral vision (<16 degrees FOV), it should be the most clear and concentrated part in vision. Normally, two to three words make a complete meaning vocabulary in primary three level. Therefore, there should be around two to three words in central and paracentral vision. In the near-peripheral vision (<60 degrees FOV), it provides adequate colour perception. Human can recognize things within near-peripheral vision. Therefore, whole page of Adventure Book should be within the near-peripheral vision, when children look at the center of page. Outside the near-peripheral vision, human can recognize the shape, but not clear details. Therefore, half of the adjacent page can be seen. Children can recognize the changes or tools next to them.

Background Theme Doom. The theme dome is a skybox surrounded the children and the interactive objects. When designing the theme dome, we would like to draw user's attention to the adventure book. The theme dome also acts as a part of memory cues to recall the article content and give hints on its meaning. There are four considerations to design the theme dome.

First, the theme dome has been separated into two parts, empty space and the working space. Figure 4 has shown the structure of separated parts. For the empty space, it is combined by the sky and the ground. The empty space has less color changes, use light

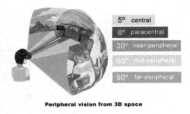
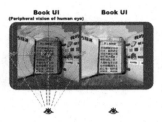

Fig. 3. Peripheral vision applied to VR reading   **Fig. 4.** Peripheral vision applied to adventure book

color, and no interesting point. That makes the children mainly focus on the working space.

Second, the working space is designed with two-layer space. One is a near space, another one is a far space. The two-layer design is used to increase the scene of space. With a space appearing large, children can feel more comfortable.

Third, the far objects and near objects in the working space are in far-near-far-near pattern. The pattern is used to guide the children sight from a far object to a near object. Refer to Fig. 5, there is a line linking every far object and near object. At the end of line is the adventure book. The pattern is used to guide children sight back to the adventure book (learning materials).

Fig. 5. Structure of the theme dome in panorama

Fourth, the objects on theme dome are the keywords from the adventure book's word bank. There are frog, well, river, snake, and others on the theme dome. Only concrete keywords will be shown on the theme dome. The abstract keywords will not be shown. Children will easily understand and recognize the key elements from the theme dome if there is only concrete keywords on the theme dome.

Attention Design. Dyslexic children have difficulty in understanding the meaning of individual Chinese words (both shape and pronunciation). Therefore, they are unable to engage the written contexts and lead to low motivation to read and to write. Spending time on reading and writing cause significant difficulties to Dyslexic children, i.e., it is hard for them to maintain interest and positive attitude to accomplish all this information.

Meanwhile, high percentage (40%) of dyslexic children suffer difficulties in attention [12]. The characteristic of their shorter attention time span reduces their reading abilities than normal children. Using VR and immersive environment is a reasonable approach to trigger the attention problem. However, it remains difficulty to draw the attention of the dyslexic children in immersive environment

When we design the visual space of application. Attention is one of our main consideration. Dyslexic children have short attention time on reading. Comfort visual elements can extent the reading time in VR Reading. An attention design can keep dyslexic children focus on the learning materials. In this paper, we will propose a design method to guide the sight to the learning materials effectively. Also, the design method to memorize the learning materials efficiently by an immersive approach.

Gaze and Control. For the control system, a gaze-based system is chosen in the application. In current VR interaction method on mobile devices, there are mainly two methods. One is using a free moving, space-tracking controller, another one is a center gaze interaction. There are two considerations. First, the target user are dyslexic children. They are lack of attention when reading texts. If a free moving controller point is shown on the screen, it will easily distract them. Second, control the peripheral vision. Gaze is at the center of vision. It helps to control the design of pages on Adventure Book. Dyslexic children are required to look at the gaze to interact with keywords. Therefore, the center gaze interaction is chosen as the control system.

4   Evaluation

To evaluate whether VR reading (and to a further extent top-down teaching) could improve dyslexic students' reading comprehensions along with their phonological awareness and orthographic skills, we recruited four school children (N = 4, one female) tasked with reading a Chinese article (Fig. 6). All four students have confirmed diagnoses of dyslexia and are from the same primary school (primary 3) in Hong Kong.

Fig. 6. Participant using VR reading

To capture the change in participants' reading abilities, the experiment spreads across 2 months with 4 rounds (Table 1). Each round includes a VR Reading testing and a traditional paper reading testing. Experiments were done for every two weeks. To minimize day-of-the-week effect and order effect, the order of VR Reading and traditional paper reading were switched for every round of experiment.

Table 1. Experiment schedule

	Tuesday	Thursday
1st Round (Week 1)	Paper Reading	VR Reading
2nd Round (Week 3)	VR Reading	Paper Reading
3rd Round (Week 5)	Paper Reading	VR Reading
4th Round (Week 7)	VR Reading	Paper Reading

The VR devices given to the children are Samsung S8 + with Samsung Gear VR. Comparing with other mobile Devices, Samsung Gear VR has a controller, which provide easy interaction between children and application. Samsung S8 + provides a 2960 × 1440 resolution (theoretically 1480 × 1440 per eye) with 529ppi. That means children can read the words clearly, without jagged edge.

4.1 An Experiment's Round

In the experiment, the participants are required to read the article once via VR Reading or paper (depends on the above timetable) for 15 min. When they were reading the article, they can use the tools in VR Reading, or dictionary and stationery if they read on paper. After reading the article, participants are required to do the 10-min test (on paper). When they did the test, the article on paper was given as reference.

To compare the performance of participants' performance, there are two marks have been calculated to evaluate. First, scoring rate is used to value the performance against total marks. The scoring rate is indicated the degree of participants' understanding of the Chinese article.

$$Scoring\ Rate = \frac{s_p}{S_q} \tag{1}$$

where s_p is the score obtained by a participant and S_q is the total marks of the test paper's questions. Second, correct rate is used to evaluate the performance, not efficiency, when answering questions. That is, this metric evaluate the accuracy a student have when answering a question such that unanswered questions are not taken into consideration

$$Correct\ Rate = \frac{s_p}{s_c} \tag{2}$$

where s_c is the total mark of questions that the participant has attempted to answer. In the following, there will be 4 comparisons, and 3 observations to review the top-down model and the concept elements by VR Reading.

4.2   Article Comprehension

The performance of overall article's comprehension (α_r) is reflected by the ordering (third part) of the test paper. Figure 7 is the ordering's average scoring rate of participants. X-axis is the number of rounds. Y-axis is the scoring rate. From the 1st time of experiment, the scoring rate after using VR Reading (50%) is lower than traditional paper reading (56%) by 6%. At the last time of experiment, the scoring rate after using VR Reading (88%) is higher than traditional paper reading (31%) by 57%. In average, the scoring rate after using VR Reading (58%) is higher than traditional paper reading (45%) by 13%.

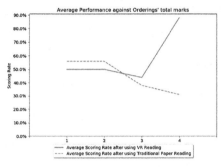

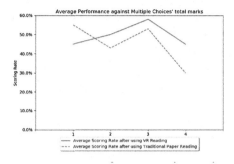

Fig. 7. Average performance against total marks of ordering questions

Fig. 8. Average performance against total marks of multiple choices questions

As the participant answered all the question each time, the correct rate is exactly same as the scoring rate. From the scoring rate, we can conclude that the participants have better understanding of the overall article's meaning after using VR Reading. This reflect that the multimedia input (α_m) may have a positive effect on the participants' article comprehension (α_r).

4.3   Sentence Comprehension

The performance of sentence comprehension is reflected by the multiple choices (second part) of the test paper. Figure 8 is the multiple choices' average scoring rate of participants. X-axis is the number of rounds. Y-axis is the scoring rate. From the 1st time of experiment, the scoring rate after using VR Reading (45%) is lower than traditional paper reading (55%) by 10%. Then, the scoring rate after using VR Reading is higher than after using traditional reading from the second round of experiment. At the last time of experiment, the scoring rate after using VR Reading (45%) is higher than traditional paper reading (30%) by 57%. In average, the scoring rate after using VR Reading (49%) is higher than traditional paper reading (45%) by 4%.

As the participant answered all the question each time, the correct rate is exactly same as the scoring rate. From the scoring rate, we can conclude that the participants have slightly better understanding of the sentences after using VR Reading. Participants perform better in the sentences-based questions after using VR Reading. The good performance in overall article's meaning may help to keep the performance of article's details.

4.4 Overall Reading Comprehension

Figure 9 is the average scoring rate of participants. X-axis is the number of rounds. Y-axis is the scoring rate. From the 1st time of experiment, the scoring rate after using VR Reading (41%) is lower than traditional paper reading (48%) by 7%. Then, the difference is narrowing in the 2nd time of experiment. At the last time of experiment, the scoring rate after using VR Reading (43%) is higher than traditional paper reading (24%) by 19%. In average, the scoring rate after using VR Reading (44%) is higher than traditional paper reading (40%) by 4%.

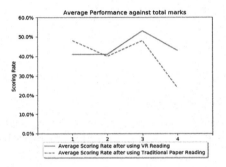

Fig. 9. Average performance against total marks

We can observe that the scoring rate after using VR Reading is not significantly increased in the experiment. The participants were not kept improving their knowledge. But, we can also observe that the scoring rate after traditional paper reading was decreasing in the experiment. We can conclude that the VR Reading can consolidate the knowledge of Chinese article.

Figure 10 is average correct rate of participants in each round of experiment. X-axis is the number of rounds. Y-axis is the correct rate. We can observe that the correct rate after traditional paper reading is decreasing (from 58% to 23%) in the whole experiment. The average correct rate after traditional paper reading is 44%. i.e. the efficiency is decreasing when doing traditional paper reading. For VR Reading, the correct rate is increased in overall (From 46% to 49%). The average correct rate after using VR Reading is 48%. i.e. the efficiency is increased after using VR Reading.

The decreasing correct rate after using traditional paper reading is reflected that dyslexic children cannot remember the article content only by texts. Also, they cannot keep attention on the article when only texts provided. The correct rate after using VR Reading shows that dyslexic children has better understanding and longer memory of article than traditional paper reading. If the experiment can be run a long period with more rounds, we believe that the performance will be increasing by rounds. The performance

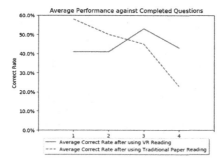

Fig. 10. Average Performance against completed questions

against total marks can proof that VR Reading could keep the degree of understanding of Chinese article.

4.5 Motivation

During the experiment, we had observed that there are some behavior differences between working on the test paper after using VR Reading and after traditional paper reading. From Fig. 11, participants spent more time in one question after using VR Reading than after traditional paper reading. In average, participants spent 0.97 min (around 58 s) in one question after using VR Reading, while 0.92 min (around 52 s) after traditional paper reading.

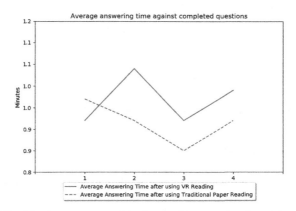

Fig. 11. Average answering time against completed questions

Participants had higher focusing on answering a question. They would focus on a single question for a long time and try their best to answer the question. When they answered fill-in blanks question, we observed that they can focus on one question and try to answer it after they used VR Reading.

In the case of traditional paper reading, or in normal situation, they have low motivation on doing test paper. As dyslexia, they have huge difficulties on reading and writing. So, they give up easily and tend to surf whole test paper.

In Hong Kong, additional time is the existing method to help dyslexic students in examinations. One example is additional exam time. The method provides extra 10 or 15 min for an original 1-h examination. However, in current situation, adding time did not help much because they cannot focus on the exam paper, and this is longer their torture time. If the VR Reading help improving their focusing, then the additional exam time will be useful.

4.6 Word Focus

We found that the participants have difficulties in answering adjectives or adverbs. They performed better in answering nouns. We believed that this is related to their behavior during using VR Reading.

As written before, in VR Reading that participants could choose vocabularies from the article, and build their own word bank for further study, like check dictionary, watch related immersive videos.

In 4 rounds of experiment, we observed that the participants were watching immersive videos in most of the time. The participants love watching immersive videos instead of reading texts. Therefore, the immersive videos can an element to connect the word and meaning (i.e. concept of word).

However, we also observed that the participants were focusing on concrete words and noun. For examples, snake, sun, fire, and frog. They were seldomly searching for abstract word, like beautiful, strong, and quiet.

The reason behind is the participants would like to watch immersive videos of the vocabulary that its concept or idea is they understood or clear in mind. Also, the understood vocabularies are most likely some objective, real things. i.e. concrete word.

However, as the experiment only allows short time (15 min) on using the VR Reading. And the participants tend to repeat the same their interested immersive videos again and again. We did not know whether they would watch immersive videos of abstract word if there was longer time in the experiment. We need further study in this issue.

5 Conclusion and Future Work

In this paper, we proposed using graphical models to visualize and conceptualize the neurological processes of learning to read. With the graphical models, we cleanly show that the bottom-up approach may be not optimal to dyslexic students due to their poor phonological awareness and orthographical skills blocking the information flow upward. With this in mind, we propose top-down teaching as an alternative. The key to top-down teaching is the multimedia input which gives cue on the meaning of words and articles. Not only does this design help with their reading comprehension, it allows dyslexics to be able to pair meaning back down to a word. Thus, this expected result implies that their phonological awareness and orthographical skills may improve as well. To test these hypotheses, we implemented VR reading which involves an adventure book and a background theme dome, providing multimedia feedback in multiple location. We performed a small-scale study requiring a group of dyslexic school children to complete a Chinese article reading to test VR reading. Chinese is chosen as it is considered as an unique language that if VR reading is applicable, it may imply that other languages could be applicable as well. The result shows that the children has an improved understanding of Chinese article. It also implies that their orthographical skills have improved.

There are several limitations in our current study. For example, although it could be expected there is an improvement over phonological awareness since orthographical skills indeed has an improvement, we did not have a method to capture this change as we used a paper-based evaluation upon the students. In addition, there are many environment variables that we could test, for example, would VR reading have different impact on students with different school year? For the design of VR reading, what multimedia input (i.e. images, voice-overs and videos) could provide the most impact on the students' improvements is also an interesting question. In our next study, we hope to be able to answer these broad range of questions.

References

1. Lyon, R.G., Shaywitz, S.E., Shaywitz, B.A.: A definition of dyslexia. Ann. Dyslexia **53**(1), 1–14 (2003)
2. Ho, C.S.: The Hong Kong Test of Specific Learning Difficulties in Reading and Writing for Junior Secondary School Students-Second Edition (HKT-JS-II). Hong Kong Specific Learning Difficulties Research Team, Hong Kong (2012)
3. Luan, H., Ho, C.S.: The Role of Morphological Awareness among Mandarin-speaking and Cantonese-speaking Children (Thesis). The University of Hong Kong, Hong Kong (2005)
4. Ho, C.S., Chan, D., Lee, S., Tsang, S., Luan, V.: Cognitive profiling and preliminary subtyping in Chinese developmental dyslexia. Cognition **91**(1), 43–75 (2004)
5. Guan, S.: A Comparison of Sino-American Thinking Patterns and the Function of Chinese Characters in the Difference In Chinese Perspectives in Rhetoric and Communication, pp. 25–43. Ablex Publishing Corporation, Stamford (2000)
6. Attree, E., Turner, M., Corwell, N.: A virtual reality test identifies the visuospatial strength of adolescents with Dyslexia. CyberPsychol. Behav. **12**(2), 163–168 (2009)
7. Kalyvioti, K., Mikropoulos, T.: A virtual reality test for the dentification of memory strengths of dyslexic students in higher education. J. Univ. Comput. Sci. **19**(18), 2698–2721 (2013)
8. Passig, D., Eden, S., Rosenbaum, V.: The impact of virtual reality on parents' awareness of cognitive perceptions of a dyslectic child. Educ. Inf. Technol. **13**(4), 329–344 (2008)
9. Berninger, V., et al.: Tier 3 specialized writing instruction for students with dyslexia. Read. Writ. **21**(1–2), 95–129 (2007)
10. Leong, C.K.: Paradigmatic Analysis of Chinese Word Reading: Research Findings and Classroom Practices. in Cross-Language Studies of Learning to Read and Spell, pp. 379–417. Kluwer Academic Publishers, Dordrecht/ Boston/ London (1997)
11. Burdea, G., Coiffet, P.: Virtual Reality Technology. John Wiley & Sons Inc., New Jersey (2003)
12. Dahle, A., Knivsberg, A.: Internalizing, externalizing and attention problems in dyslexia. Scandinavian J. Disability Res. **16**(2), 179–193 (2013)

Improving User Experience in Augmented Reality Mirrors with 3D Displays

Gun A. Lee[1]([✉]) [iD], Hye Sun Park[2], Seungwon Kim[1], and Mark Billinghurst[1]

[1] University of South Australia, Adelaide, Australia
gun.lee@unisa.edu.au
[2] Electronics and Telecommunications Research Institute, Daejeon, Republic of Korea

Abstract. Optical-reflection type Augmented Reality (AR) mirror displays use half-silvered mirrors attached in front of a digital display to show virtual objects overlaid into the physical world reflected in the mirror. Prior works mostly displayed 2D images on the surface of the mirror hence suffered from visual depth mismatch between the optical reflection of the 3D physical space and the virtual image. In this paper, we propose to use 3D visualisation to overcome this problem and improve the user experience by providing better depth perception for watching and interacting with the content displayed on an AR mirror. As a proof-of-concept, we developed two prototype optical-reflection type 3D AR mirror displays, one using a multi-view autostereoscopic 3D display and another using a head tracked stereoscopic 3D display that supports hand gesture interaction. A preliminary user study showed that the participants were able to perform selection tasks faster and with less error under 3D visualisation, and felt the 3D visualisation required less mental effort, was more comfortable to watch and interact with compared to the traditional 2D visualisation. The results also indicated the participants felt the virtual image was closer to their body, supporting the visual perception model of 3D AR mirror we postulated.

Keywords: Augmented mirror · 3D visualisation · Depth mismatch

1 Introduction

Mirrors are physical displays that show our real world in reflection. With advancement of digital technology, we not only can show what is in the real-world scene, but also alter the reality reflected in the mirror. Prior research explored various visualisation and interaction techniques for Augmented Reality (AR) displays referred to as augmented mirrors or AR mirrors [13]. AR mirrors have been actively investigated in both research and industry for their application in retail, training, and entertainment applications [1, 6, 9, 12].

There are two common types of AR mirror displays: video-reflection and optical-reflection. Video-reflection type AR mirrors use a video camera to show the captured image of the real-world environment to mimic a mirror in a virtual way. In comparison, optical-reflection type AR mirrors combines a half-silvered mirror with a digital display, blending the optical reflection of the real-world space with the digital image.

© Springer Nature Switzerland AG 2020
G. Bebis et al. (Eds.): ISVC 2020, LNCS 12509, pp. 642–653, 2020.
https://doi.org/10.1007/978-3-030-64556-4_50

Although it provides a more realistic image of the real world, optical-reflective AR mirrors are less common as they suffer from mismatch in the perceived depth of the images between the optical reflection of the real-world environment and the digital objects. This mismatch is more obvious when trying to show virtual images appear near to the user's body. Our research investigates applying 3D display and visualisation techniques to optical reflection-based AR mirror displays to resolve the problem of depth mismatch, hence improving the user experience.

2 Related Work

The concept of AR mirrors has been actively explored in both industry and research. A typical application of AR mirrors has been in fashion retail shops for advertisement and promotion of fashion products [6]. These systems typically use video or depth cameras to capture the user standing in front of the AR mirror display and overlay a virtual image of clothing or fashion accessories onto the captured video or image. Researchers have also investigated technologies for AR mirrors. For example, Ehara and Saito [3] developed a computer vision based cloth tracking method for visualising a virtual t-shirt design overlaid onto a marker t-shirt worn by the user. Mottura et al. [11] demonstrated using AR mirrors to try on shoes using a foot-worn tracker, while Eisert et al. [4] developed a computer vision technique to track user's feet and visualise virtual shoes overlaid onto them. AR mirrors have also been applied to sports and motion training applications. For example, Ng et al. [12] developed an AR mirror for training playing musical instruments using a motion capture system, while Marquardt et al. [10] and Anderson et al. [1] explored using the Kinect[1] motion sensor for training body motions, such as dancing.

Optical-reflection type AR mirrors are not as common as the video-based AR display setups used in examples above. Fujinami et al. [5] used a half-silvered mirror backed with a display for presenting 2D information (e.g. weather, schedule, etc.). Chu et al. [2] used a similar setup with added camera for recording and replaying photos of the user wearing jewelry. These examples used an AR mirror merely as a 2D display without precise registration between the mirror reflected real-world space and the virtual image shown on the display. Exploring how to relate the virtual information space to the physical space, Ushida et al. [14] used an optical-reflection type AR mirror for recording and replaying a video of the physical environment. Li and Fu [9] added interactivity using a Kinect depth sensor, enabling users to interact with virtual objects projected on the mirror, such as playing virtual drums with physical drumsticks.

To the best of our knowledge, none of the prior examples of optical-reflection type AR mirror displays used 3D display to overcome the visual depth mismatch between the optical reflection of 3D physical space and the 2D image displayed on the mirror surface. Due to such limitation, users not only had to stand at a certain position to see correct alignment of virtual objects in optical reflection of the physical world, but also had to actively change focus between physical and virtual objects even when they were aligned with each other. This may typically lead to users experiencing discomfort in both

---

[1] https://developer.microsoft.com/en-us/windows/kinect.

watching the display and also interacting with it. In our research we use 3D displays in optical-reflection type AR mirrors to overcome this problem and improve the user experience. While Plasencia et al. [15] did investigate novel displays combining optical half-silvered mirrors and 3D displays, their focus was on exhibition cabinet style display where the physical objects were placed behind the optical half-silvered mirror. Our work focuses on investigating the concept of AR mirrors that augments the physical world in front of the display and explore how 3D displays can be useful for improving user experience with AR mirrors.

3   3D Augmented Mirror – Concept

3.1   Visual Perception

With a typical 3D display, 3D objects are rendered with negative parallax to be shown popping out of the display, causing the user to perceive the object in the display is close to himself. The amount of negative parallax that can be achieved in a 3D display is limited by the display size. The closer the object needed to be displayed to the user's eyes, the wider parallax that is required, and hence the display must be larger to cover a wider field of view in the user's perspective. On the other hand, showing objects to appear pushed into behind the display surface is relatively less restricted, as the positive parallax has a limited range depending on the user's inter-pupillary distance (a.k.a. stereo baseline), which is less affected by the screen size.

The image of the physical environment reflected in the mirror shows the real-world space inverted in depth direction. Due to this, AR mirror displays have a unique configuration of how depth of objects could be perceived mentally by the users. While typical 3D displays need to show 3D objects with negative parallax to make them appear closer to the user, an optical-reflection type AR mirror displays reflect the image of the user and his/her real-world surroundings into the space behind the mirror. The user's body image reflected in the mirror is shown to the user with positive parallax, appearing as if it is behind the mirror surface.

This gives an interesting configuration in optical-reflection type 3D AR mirror display, where virtual objects could be visualised with positive parallax to appear near the user's body. We hypothesise that the users would perceive the virtual objects that are visualised close to the optical reflection of their body as if they are placed near the user's actual body in the physical space. Figure 1 illustrates this concept showing the virtual object perceived by the user is mentally reflected as if it's close to her physical body, although the computer rendered virtual object is actually visualised near the optical reflection of the user's body that appears behind the mirror display surface.

3.2   Gesture Interaction

Gesture interaction is one of the main interaction techniques used in AR mirror displays. Among various gestures, hovering is widely accepted by the users as a gesture for selection in AR mirror displays [8]. This approach works well in video-reflection type AR mirrors as the image of the user's hand is shown at the same display surface as the

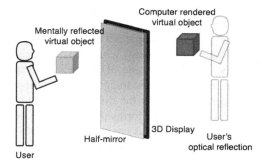

Fig. 1. Perceptual model of 3D AR mirror display.

virtual UI elements (e.g. button). However, when interacting with an optical-reflection type 2D AR mirror display, users easily encounter a problem of disparity in depth between the reflection of user's hand and the virtual object displayed on the display surface (see left of Fig. 2). To overcome this problem, we propose using a multi-view autostereoscopic 3D display in combination with half-silvered mirror, so that the virtual UI elements could be visualised at the correct depth where the optical reflection of the user is shown in the mirror (see right of Fig. 2).

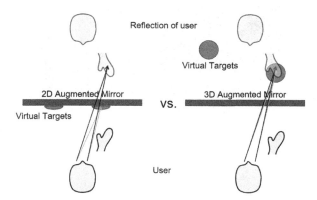

Fig. 2. Gesture interaction with 2D vs. 3D AR mirrors.

4 Prototype System Implementation

As a proof-of-concept, we implemented two prototype systems. The first prototype used a glasses-free multi-view autostereoscopic 3D display, while the second prototype used a shutter glasses based stereoscopic 3D display with integrated head tracking and gesture interaction.

4.1 Multi-view Autostereoscopic 3D AR Mirror

We integrated a multi-view autostereoscopic 3D display (Exceptional 3D 28-inch 4 K resolution 8-view slanted lenticular display) with a custom built half-silvered mirror to build our first prototype. To visualise the 3D scene, the system renders a special format image that combines multiple view images into a multi-view autostereoscopic image matching the lenticular pattern on the display. The 3D scene is first rendered with a multiple virtual camera array that forms the multi-view perspective of the final autostereoscopic view. The virtual cameras are set to render into texture buffers which are then processed by a custom shader that composites the individual view image textures into a multi-view image by combining the texture array at sub-pixel level.

We used the Unity 3D v2017.x game engine on a Windows 10 PC to develop the prototype software, setting up a scene that implements the multi-view 3D rendering process described above. The scene included a C# script that automatically creates an array of virtual cameras, arranging them properly for multi-view 3D rendering. Each virtual camera is then set to render-to-texture mode with the assigned texture buffers that are provided as an input to a Cg based custom shader module that combines the textures into a multi-view autostereoscopic image displayed onto the screen. Figure 3 shows a simple multi-view 3D scene with animated red virtual spheres visualised on our prototype hardware setup using an autostereoscopic 3D display.

Fig. 3. A prototype autostereoscopic 3D AR mirror display showing animated virtual spheres.

4.2 Head Tracked Stereoscopic 3D AR Mirror

Autostereoscopic 3D displays have the benefit of not requiring users to wear glasses, hence are useful as a proof-of-concept demonstration of optical-reflection type 3D AR mirrors. However, they also have limitations with the viewing volume requiring users to view the display from a specific position relative to the display. This could be potentially solved in the future as the 3D display technology advances, yet at the current stage it hinders further experimenting user interactions with 3D AR mirrors.

To work around this problem and further investigate gesture interaction with optical-reflection type 3D AR mirror displays, we developed a second prototype system using a 3D stereoscopic display with shutter glasses. As a 3D display, we used a 55-inch 3D TV (Sony 55X9300D) and a pair of LCD shutter glasses (TDG-BT500A). Figure 4 shows the prototype hardware setup.

Fig. 4. 3D AR Mirror using a 3D TV with shutter glasses and a motion tracking senor.

In AR mirror displays, it is important to visualise 3D objects registered to the physical environment reflected in the mirror so that the users would recognize the augmented virtual objects in 3D space and interact with them using motion gestures. In order to display 3D objects correctly registered to the physical 3D space, head-tracked off-axis stereo projection is necessary in addition to the correct calibration of the tracking sensor and display coordinate systems. For tracking the user's head relative to the display, we used the Microsoft Kinect motion sensor (v1) which can track the user's body motion. The motion tracking function was integrated with a custom plug-in for Unity using Microsoft Kinect SDK v1.7.

The position of the virtual camera relative to the display is calculated based on the head tracking results and calibration of the coordinate systems. In our implementation, this calibration is based on physical measurements of the position of the Kinect sensor and the accelerometer readings from the sensor indicating its orientation. Based on the relationship between the coordinate frames of the Kinect sensor and the display, we can calculate the user's eye positions relative to the display center which defines the position of the virtual cameras. The user's eye position is calculated based on the head position and a relative offset of each eyes from the head based on physical measurement including inter-pupillary distance. Based on the positions of both left and right eyes relative to the tracking sensor coordinate frame, we can calculate the user's eye positions relative to the screen coordinate frame. In order to render the 3D image in correct perspective, we applied an off-axis projection matrix to a virtual camera. We calculated the parameters based on the head tracking results, calibration of the coordinate systems as described above, and physical dimensions of the 3D display.

Figure 5 shows images of the 3D stereoscopic visualisation in our second prototype AR mirror display. A set of buttons are visualised around the user, anchored to the user's chest so that as the user moves around the space, the buttons also follow. The user can select a button by placing his or her hand on the button and holding in place for 1.5s to confirm the selection. To provide visual feedback to the user, the button gets slightly bigger when the user places his or her hand on it, and then the button gradually scales down over the time as the user keeps his or her hand in place to confirm selection. The system also provides audio feedback when the user's hand is placed on a button, and also when the selection gets confirmed. Users can use either left or right hands for selecting the buttons.

Fig. 5. Button selection on the 3D AR mirror display.

To further demonstrate the potential of using gesture interaction with 3D AR mirror displays, we also implemented a sample application of a virtual character following the user's hand (see Fig. 6). The user can freely move around the space in front of the 3D AR mirror as the virtual butterfly follows the user's hand in the mirror reflected 3D space. We envision such virtual characters could be used as UI agents for engaging and guiding user interaction [7].

Fig. 6. A virtual butterfly following the user's hand.

5   User Study

5.1   Study Design

To evaluate our prototype system, we conducted a preliminary user study to show that using 3D displays with AR mirrors could improve user's performance and experience through reducing mental effort and discomfort. We recruited eight participants (age: 26–46, 2 female) to try our head tracked stereoscopic 3D AR mirror prototype. None of the participants had tried the system before. Participants were asked to select a randomly highlighted button as shown in Fig. 5. They performed the task under both 2D and 3D visualisation to compare the two conditions. The only difference between the conditions were either using stereoscopic visualisation or not. Both conditions included head tracking based off-axis projection, and the participants were to wear the LCD stereoscopic shutter glasses in both conditions, even though it did not have any stereoscopic effect, in order to control the variability due to wearing the 3D glasses (e.g. discomfort or image brightness). For interaction, users were asked to use hand gestures with their comfortable hand. To avoid the bias of requiring the participants to match their hand position in depth only in 3D visualisation condition, the system was modified to recognise selection gestures in 2D projection space in both conditions. Participants were merely asked to place their hand in the mirror on the button to select, without being told that the gestures are recognised in 2D projection space.

The order of the conditions was counter balanced to prevent ordering bias. Six buttons were visualised around the user and one of them was randomly highlighted in red at a time for selection task. Participants were asked to stand at a fixed location (1.2 m away from the screen) while performing the experimental task. Before the experimental trials, participants practiced selecting the buttons until they felt confident performing the task. During this practice in the 2D condition, an adjustment was made to the visualisation based on the participant's choice of either left or right eye as a dominant eye for 2D projection or the middle point in-between the two eyes, whichever the participants felt the most comfortable. The participants had to select 18 targets (6 button × 3 times in random order) which took about 2 min to complete in each condition.

As objective measures, task completion time and positional error were measured through system log data. For subjective feedback, participants answered a questionnaire measuring their perceived level of mental effort [16], visual and interaction discomfort, perception of the task space in mirror display, and preference. For statistical analysis of the quantitative results we used paired t-tests (two-tailed) for parametric data, or Wilcoxon Signed Rank tests (two-tailed) for non-parametric results. The alpha level of the inferential statistics was set at 0.05 in all the tests unless described otherwise.

5.2 Task Performance

Task completion time measured with the log file showed a significant difference between the conditions ($t(7) = 3.85$, $p = .006$). Figure 7 shows that the participants took significantly less time to complete the button selection task under the 3D visualisation condition ($M = 106.7s$, $SD = 13.19$) compared to the 2D visualisation condition ($M = 131.8$, $SD = 18.43$). We also measured the positional error between user's hand and the button through analyzing the log file. The results showed that there is a significant difference ($t(7) = 6.69$, $p < .001$) between the two conditions. As shown in the right of Fig. 7, the 3D visualisation condition showed less error ($M = 0.09$ meters, $SD = 0.003$) compared to the condition with 2D visualisation ($M = 0.12$, $SD = 0.009$). This indicates that the participants were able to match the hand position to the target with less error in 3D condition.

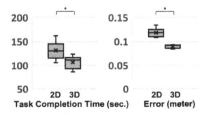

Fig. 7. Results of task completion time and positional error (*: $p < .01$).

5.3 Subjective Measures

Rating results on the Subjective Mental Effort Question (0: Not at all hard to do ~ 150: Tremendously hard to do) [16] indicated the participants felt the task was easier in 3D condition. Figure 8 shows that the 3D condition required less mental effort to the participants for performing the task, with the ratings falling in the range of 'not very hard to do' ($Md = 10$, $IQR = [4.5–12.5]$), compared to the 2D condition being considered as at a level labeled as 'a bit hard or fairly hard to do' ($Md = 32.5$, $IQR = [10–40]$). The difference between the conditions were found statistically significant (Wilcoxon Signed Rank test: $Z = -2.371, p = .018$).

Fig. 8. Results of Subjective Mental Effort questionnaire (*: $p < .05$).

Participants were also asked if they felt uncomfortable watching the display (visual discomfort) or interacting with the interface (interaction discomfort), rating on an 11-point rating scale (0: Not at all ~ 10: Severely). Wilcoxon Signed Rank tests showed participants felt the 2D visualisation was significantly more uncomfortable compared to 3D visualisation (see Fig. 9) for both watching ($Z = -2.214$, $p = .027$; 2D: $Md = 3$, $IQR = [1.5–5]$; 3D: $Md = 1$, $IQR = [0.5–2]$) and interacting ($Z = -2.527$, $p = .012$; 2D: $Md = 5$, $IQR = [3.5–6.5]$; 3D: $Md = 1.5$, $IQR = [0–2.5]$).

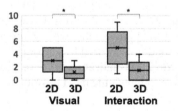

Fig. 9. Results of discomfort rating (0: Not at all – 10: Severely; *: $p < .05$).

Figure 10 summarizes the rating (1: Strongly Disagree ~ 7: Strongly Agree) results on how participants spatially perceived the interaction space. The results show that participants "*felt like the buttons were near to my body*" significantly more ($Z = -2.263$, $p = .024$) in the 3D condition ($Md = 6$, $IQR = [5.5–7]$) compared to the 2D condition ($Md = 4$, $IQR = [3.5–5]$). In comparison, participant rated slightly less on "*felt like pointing at a distance*" in the 3D condition ($Md = 2.5$, $IQR = [2–4]$) than in the 2D condition ($Md = 3.5$, $IQR = [3–4.5]$), yet the difference was not statistically significant ($Z = -1.382, p = .167$). Participants reported that they "*felt could place my hand where the button is*" in the space significantly more ($Z = -.242, p = .025$) under the 3D condition ($Md = 6, IQR = [5.5-6.5]$) than in the 2D condition ($Md = 3.5, IQR = [2.5-5.5]$).

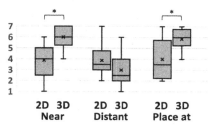

Fig. 10. Results of spatial perception rating (1: strongly disagree ~ 7: strongly agree; Near: *felt like the buttons were near to my body*; Distant: *felt like pointing at a distance*; Place at: *felt could place my hand where the button is*; *: $p < .05$).

When asked to rate their preference between the two conditions (from-3: *strongly prefer 2D* to 3: *strongly prefer 3D*), most participants preferred the 3D condition ($Md = 3, IQR = [2-3]$), while only one participant slightly preferred the 2D (rating -1). When asked to describe the reason for preferring the 3D over 2D, half of the participants replied it was easier to perform the task. Some also mentioned the 3D visualisation felt more natural and intuitive. One said that the graphical objects looked better aligned with what is shown in the mirror. The participant who preferred 2D explained that it was easier to perform the task as he did not need to exactly match the position in 3D space (note that the participant did not had to exactly match the 3D position).

5.4 Qualitative Feedback

Qualitative feedback indicated that participants felt viewing and interacting with the buttons with 3D visualisation was easier as they felt buttons are closer to their body. One user said, "I felt like the buttons were right in front of me," regarding the 3D visualisation. Another said, "It felt like the button is closer and bigger. Therefore, it is easier to press," confirming that the 3D visualisation made the virtual objects appear closer to the user's body. Another participant said, "I felt like the buttons were right in front of me and I reach my hands out to touch them." The images of the buttons were actually further inside the display surface as they were visualised in the mirror space, yet it appeared users were perceiving it as closer to them relative to the reflection of their body in the mirror. The buttons in 2D and 3D visualisations had the same size in visual angles, yet participants reported the button felt larger in 3D visualisation.

Most of the participants felt the task was harder under 2D visualisation. One described it as, "It wasn't as obvious where to put my hand," while another mentioned, "It was difficult to find the correct alignment of the hand behind the target." Aligning the 2D image of a button on the screen with a 3D position of the user's hand was clearly a problem in 2D visualisation. One of the user's said, "I felt like I need to offset my hands to align with the buttons which locate in front of the mirror."

5.5 Discussion

Although the number of participants was low in our preliminary study, the results were still able to draw statistically significant results. The results indicated the 3D visualisation in AR mirror helped the participants to perform the target selection task compared to the conventional 2D AR mirror. While the error may not indicate the user performance as they were not required to match the 3D position, the results of participants still having significantly less positional error indicates that the participants tended to perceive the target being in space where they can match the position of their hand to. The 3D condition also appeared to be requiring less mental effort and being more comfortable to use. Interestingly, participants reported that they felt the target virtual objects (i.e. buttons) were closer to their body in the 3D condition, while in fact the imagery was displayed further away from the physical body of the user with positive parallax (i.e. the virtual objects were visualised further into screen). This indicates the users perceive the virtual object's spatial relationship to their body based on the reflection of themselves shown in the mirror as we proposed. Participants' qualitative feedback also supported this concept as they described the virtual objects felt being closer or even right in front of them.

While the study was able to provide initial evidence and validation of the proposed concept, the study was limited with small number of participants and involving simple task. Further experiments with larger population and more complex real-world task would be needed as a future work.

6 Conclusion

We applied 3D display to optical-reflection type AR mirror displays to provide correct depth perception. As a proof-of-concept, we developed two prototype systems, one with a multi-view autostereoscopic 3D monitor, and another with a head-tracked stereoscopic 3D TV with shutter glasses. We also integrated a motion tracking sensor with the second prototype to enable gesture interaction. A preliminary user study showed that the participants were able to perform selection tasks faster and with less error with 3D visualisation. The results also showed that the participants felt 3D visualisation more comfortable to watch and interact with compared to 2D visualisation, hence performing the task with the 3D visualisation was easier and more preferable. The results of spatial perception supported our proposed concept of 3D AR mirror in terms of user's perceived spatial relationship between the virtual objects and the user's body. For future work, we plan to further develop the system with larger multi-view autostereoscopic 3D displays, as well as conduct more user evaluation based on various applications.

Acknowledgement. This work was supported by Institute for Information & communications Technology Promotion (IITP) grant funded by the Korea government (MSIT) (No.2017-0-01849, Development of Core Technology for Real-Time Image Composition in Unstructured In-outdoor Environment).

References

1. Anderson, F., Grossman, T., Matejka, J., Fitzmaurice, G.: YouMove: enhancing movement training with an augmented reality mirror. In: *Proceedings of the 26th annual ACM symposium. on User interface software and technology.* pp. 311–320. ACM, New York, NY, USA (2013)
2. Chu, M., Dalal, B., Walendowski, A., Begole, B.: Countertop responsive mirror: supporting physical retail shopping for sellers, buyers and companions. In: *Proceedings of the SIGCHI Conference on Human Factors in Computing Systems*, pp. 2533–2542. (2010)
3. Ehara, J., Saito, H.: Texture overlay for virtual clothing based on PCA of silhouettes. In: *Proceedings of the 5th IEEE and ACM International Symposium on Mixed and Augmented Reality*, pp. 139–142 (2006)
4. Eisert, P., Fechteler, P., Rurainsky, J.: 3-D tracking of shoes for virtual mirror applications. In: *IEEE Conf. on Computer Vision and Pattern Recognition 2008*, pp. 1–6 (2008)
5. Fujinami, K., Kawsar, F., Nakajima, T.: AwareMirror: a personalized display using a mirror. In: *Pervasive*, pp. 315–332 (2005)
6. Kinect for Windows Retail Clothing Scenario Video. https://www.youtube.com/watch?v=Mr71jrkzWq8 Accessed 2 Oct 2020
7. Lee, G., Rudhru, O., Park, H., Kim, H., Billinghurst, M.: User interface agents for guiding interaction with augmented virtual mirrors. In: *Proceedings of the 27th International Conference on Artificial Reality and Telexistence and 22nd Eurographics Symposium on Virtual Environments (ICAT-EGVE 2017)*, pp. 109–116 (2017)
8. Lee, G. A., Wong, J., Park, H., Choi, J., Park, C., Billinghurst, M.: User Defined Gestures for Augmented Virtual Mirrors: A Guessability Study. In: *Proceedings of the 33rd Annual ACM Conference Extended Abstracts on Human Factors in Computing Systems (CHI EA 2015)*, pp. 959–964. ACM, New York, NY, USA (2015)
9. Li, W.H.A., Fu, H.: Augmented reflection of reality. In: *ACM SIGGRAPH 2012 Emerging Technologies*, Article No. 3, pp. 1 (2012)
10. Marquardt, Z., Beira, J., Em, N., Paiva, I., Kox, S.: Super Mirror: a kinect interface for ballet dancers. In: *CHI'12 Extended Abstracts on Human Factors in Computing Systems*, pp. 1619–1624 (2012)
11. Mottura, S., Greci, L., Travaini, E., Viganò, G., Sacco, M.: MagicMirror & FootGlove: a new system for the customized shoe try-on. *The future of product development*, pp. 441–450 (2007)
12. Ng, K.C., Weyde, T., Larkin, O., Neubarth, K., Koerselman, T., Ong, B.: 3d augmented mirror: a multimodal interface for string instrument learning and teaching with gesture support. In: *Proceedings of the 9th international conf. on Multimodal interfaces*, pp. 339–345 (2007)
13. Portalés, C., Gimeno, J., Casas, S., Olanda, R., Martínez, F.G.: Interacting with augmented reality mirrors. In: *Handbook of Research on Human-Computer Interfaces, Developments, and Applications*, pp. 216–244. IGI Global (2016)
14. Ushida, K., Tanaka, Y., Naemura, T., Harashima, H.: I-Mirror: an interaction/information environment based on a mirror metaphor aiming to install into our life space. In: *Proceedings of the 12th International Conference on Artificial Reality and Telexistence (ICAT 2002)*, pp. 113–118 (2002)
15. Plasencia, D. M., Berthaut, F., Karnik, A., Subramanian S.: Through the combining glass. In: *Proceedings of the 27th annual ACM symposium on User interface software and technology (UIST 2014)*, pp. 341–350. ACM, New York, NY, USA (2014)
16. Zijlstra, F.: *Efficiency in work behaviour: A design approach for modern tools* (1993)

Passenger Anxiety About Virtual Driver Awareness During a Trip with a Virtual Autonomous Vehicle

Alexandros Koilias[1], Christos Mousas[2(✉)], Banafsheh Rekabdar[3],
and Christos-Nikolaos Anagnostopoulos[1]

[1] University of the Aegean, Mytilene, Greece
{ctd17008,canag}@aegean.gr
[2] Purdue University, West Lafayette, IN, USA
cmousas@purdue.edu
[3] Southern Illinois University, Carbondale, IL, USA
brekabdar@cs.siu.edu

Abstract. A virtual reality study concerning participants' anxiety levels when immersed in a virtual reality interaction with an autonomous vehicle was conducted. Five conditions were tested. The examined conditions are based on awareness of the virtual character (driver). During the external awareness conditions the virtual character either focuses on the road traffic or does not. During the internal awareness conditions the virtual character either pays attention to the car or not. For the fifth condition, the virtual character is completely unaware; since a head-mounted display (HMD) was placed on his face. Results, implications, and limitations are discussed.

Keywords: Virtual reality · Virtual driver awareness · Autonomous vehicle · Cognitive anxiety · Somatic anxiety · Car passenger

1 Introduction

An autonomous vehicle, which is also known as a self-driving car, is capable of sensing the environment and the nearby obstacles in order to navigate itself without the need of a driver (i.e., human input) [33]. Autonomous vehicles enable hands-off-wheel and foot-off-pedal operation [2], and there is no need for the driver to fully focus on the internal operations of the car or on the external road traffic. Autonomous vehicles are becoming increasingly popular [32] and according to Calvert et al. [3], the production of autonomous vehicles will start to increase significantly from 2020. To make this happen, car manufacturing companies are trying to incorporate intelligent technologies to the cars to allow them to more precisely navigate autonomously without causing any issues to other cars, pedestrians, and of course the passengers [22]. To achieve this, a variety of techniques and hardware are combined [14].

Even if car manufacturing companies try to improve the reliability of the autonomous vehicle, many drivers and passengers remain skeptical about this new technology [15]. The car manufacturing companies need to gain consumer

G. Bebis et al. (Eds.): ISVC 2020, LNCS 12509, pp. 654–665, 2020.
https://doi.org/10.1007/978-3-030-64556-4_51

trust [35]. Therefore, it is imperative that both the transportation organizations and the car manufacturing companies understand the way car users (both drivers and passengers) interact with such cars. Measurements of anxiety and comfort levels along with passenger trust when the car is involved in difficult situations (e.g., a possible collision with another car) should be explored. In addition, the development of rules regarding driving behavior/habits of the autonomous vehicle should be refined in such a way that the behavior assigned to the car can accommodate the behavior of the passenger. Thus, considering that a human might become anxious when seated in an autonomous vehicle, a virtual reality (VR) study was conducted to explore this assumption by testing five conditions (see Fig. 1).

Fig. 1. The five conditions developed for this study concerning internal and external awareness of the driver.

2   Related Work

Research on interaction with autonomous vehicles is usually performed in simulators [20,23]. In such cases, VR technology is used to immerse participants into virtual environments and driving conditions that seem real. A number of studies have been conducted in the past with a variety of purposes such as the usability evaluation [28] of driving simulators, the physiological responses of participants when immersed in car simulators [7], and the differences between real and virtual driving experiences [25].

Concerning the interaction with autonomous vehicles in VR, the current research is mainly focused on the training process of the driver [31], the take-over control [10,11,30], the evaluation of driver reaction in critical situations [12], and the design of interfaces [5] that would allow the driver or pedestrians to more precisely interact with such cars [27]. It should be noted that most of the current research aims to evaluate the behavior of the drivers [23] and their cognition [16] during the take-over control process from car to driver.

Besides the plethora of studies aiming at trying to understand the way drivers interact with the autonomous vehicles, only limited research on the passengers of such cars has been conducted, despite the fact that such a study could provide important insight [21]. The internal environment of a car can be modified in such a way that the passenger can effectively support the driver [24]. Entertainment and multimedia systems can be developed to entertain the passengers without disturbing the driver. Finally, given the growth of autonomous vehicles, soon all people accommodated in the car will be considered passengers. Therefore, any information regarding the passengers and the way they interact with the car is useful in making autonomous vehicles more comfortable for everyone.

In most cases, studies that are concerned with car passengers usually focus on the way that the passenger can be an assistant to the driver [4]. On the other hand, design decisions can be made when conducting studies with passengers. Specifically, Wilfinger et al. [36] found that when designing UIs for the rear seat, it is important to focus on passenger experience. When car designers start taking into consideration passenger experience, they can then deploy the appropriate interface solutions. Meschtscherjakov et al. [24] conducted five research activities that explore the experience of passengers and argues that improving user experience in cars can best be done if all occupants are taken into account, including passengers. Finally, the ride comfort of passengers was investigated by Elbanhawi et al. [8].

As far as we are aware of, studies that examine the behavior of passengers when seated at the co-pilot seat in an autonomous vehicle have not been conducted yet. Therefore, the current study aims to understand how the behavior of VR car passengers' alternates when observing different behaviors of the driver.

3   Methodology and Implementation

3.1   Participants

All of the participants are students (both undergraduate and graduate) recruited by e-mail, in-class announcements, and posters placed in the department and the student center. All participants received a €5 voucher. In total, 82 people came to the lab in which the study was conducted but only 75 were able to fully complete the study ($M = 22.98$, $SD = 3.19$). Five of the participants that did not follow though the study expressed that they did not expect it would take so long. The other two participants expressed that they did not feel any difference in the conditions, and that they preferred to terminate the study early.

3.2   Conditions of the Study

Five conditions were developed for this study (see Fig. 1). The *Internal-External Awareness* (*IEA*) condition denotes the full awareness of the virtual character. The virtual character's hands hold the steering wheel and the virtual character's gaze is focused on the road traffic, which suggests that the virtual character pays attention to the internal and external parameters that influence the way the autonomous vehicle behaves, and the virtual character is ready to react if necessary, even if it is not the one driving the autonomous vehicle. The reason for placing the virtual character's hands on the steering wheel is based on Tesla's instructions that drivers should never take their hands off the steering wheel, even in autopilot mode [6].

The second and third condition denote partial awareness of the virtual character. In *Internal-No External Awareness (INEA)* condition, the virtual character is internally aware of the car i.e., the virtual character holds the steering wheel with his hands, but his gaze is not focused on the road; instead it is focused on the buildings and the pedestrians. In *No Internal-External Awareness (NIEA)* condition, the virtual character is externally aware since his gaze focuses on the road traffic. However, the virtual character taps his legs with his hands to the rhythm of a background radio song, which makes him unaware of the internal behavior of the car. Based on the second and third condition, it can be said that since the virtual character is not fully aware of the car and the road traffic, it might take longer to gain control of the car if an emergency arises; therefore, participants might feel more anxious.

In the *No Internal-No External Awareness (NINEA)* condition, the virtual character was designed to be both internally and externally unaware of the car and road traffic. In this condition, the gaze of the virtual character focuses again on the buildings and the pedestrians and the hands tap his legs following the rhythm of the background song. In the *Completely Unaware (CU)* condition, which is the last one developed for this study, the virtual character is also fully unaware. In this condition, the hands of the virtual character tap his legs, and the virtual character wears an HMD to entertain himself. It should be noted that there are cases of autonomous vehicle manufacturers providing modern entertainment systems and HMDs to entertain passengers and drivers during travel [9]. Though the fifth condition seems extreme, it is a potential reality in the near future. Based on the fourth and fifth conditions, it can be said that since the virtual character is not aware of the car or the road traffic, the virtual character might not be able to gain control of the car in an emergency; therefore, participants are likely to have the highest levels of anxiety.

We considered adding one more condition in which no virtual character is in the car, but we realized that the absence of a driver might provide different findings from the ones we were trying to investigate in this study, i.e., the anxiety of participants based on virtual character awareness. Therefore, we are planning to perform an additional study that will investigate the behavior of participants when they are seated as passengers in an autonomous vehicle with no virtual character seated next to them.

3.3 Study

The participants came in our lab and the research team informed them that they would be seated as passengers in a VR autonomous vehicle. They were also informed that they would be exposed to five conditions and that each condition would last four minutes. After the car reached its final position in the virtual environment the condition that was being examined would change, and the system would be ready to proceed with the next stage of the study.

Participants were told that they would have short breaks between the conditions. During the breaks, they would be asked to take off the HMD and respond to a number of questions in a computer-based questionnaire. It was mentioned that the research team would be there to assist them and control (start and stop) the VR application; however, unless a need arose, there would be no further communication throughout the study. The research team would inform the participants when the study was complete and would inform them they were free to leave and terminate the study at any time.

The order of the five conditions (see Sect. 3.2) was randomized for each participant. Before the beginning of the study participants were asked to provide written consent. This study was granted approval by the IRB of the Anonymous University. Figure 2 illustrates the study setup.

Fig. 2. A participant observing the VR scenario in the lab space in which the study was conducted.

3.4 Questionnaires

Two questionnaires were used in this study. The first asks questions related to their presence and is based on the SUS [29] questionnaire. The questionnaire on presence was used only once for each participant at the end of the first condition to which they were exposed. This part of the study had a between-group design with $N = 15$ participants in each group (condition of the study). The altered version [18] of the Anxiety Modality Questionnaire [34] was also used in this study. In both questionnaires, a seven-point Likert scale was used to capture the participants' responses. The Anxiety Modality Questionnaire initially was proposed with a five-point scale; however, a seven-point scale was used to make both questionnaires have the same anchors and avoid unwanted participant confusion.

3.5   Application and Equipment

The application was developed in Unity3D game engine. For the VR part of it, the Oculus Rift HMD and its associated SDK was used. Five scenes in Unity3D were developed, one for each condition. The virtual environment in which the driving simulation takes place was designed in Autodesk 3ds Max. All characters (pedestrians, driver, and self-avatar) used in this study were designed using Adobe's Fuse software.

The virtual character placed in the driver seat was assigned a simple idle animation and the FinalIK was used to make the hands of the virtual character move according to the rotation of the steering wheel. The hands of the virtual character were attached to the steering wheel only during the first and second conditions. For the gaze of the virtual character, the LookAt functionality of Unity3D was used to make the virtual character's head always focus on the buildings and pedestrians. To make the virtual character look realistic, the target positions were switched between the buildings and pedestrians, and the head of the driver was animated using the spherical linear interpolation (Slerp) function.

The rest of the animations used for the study were captured using a motion capture system. For the hand tapping animation of the driver character, a simple motion was captured in our motion capture lab and looped throughout the VR scenario. The hand tap animation was captured while the background song was playing. Synchronization between the song and hand tapping motion was performed afterwards manually. Thus, during the VR scenario the hand tapping motion was following the rhythm of the song. The pedestrians in the virtual environment were assigned a simple walking motion and a path finding method to make them move to different target positions. Additional pedestrians were assigned to reach the opposite sidewalk when traffic indicators forced the autonomous vehicle to stop. Finally, the virtual car was also pre-scripted to stop at a road crossing sign to allow pedestrians cross the road. Figure 3 shows the first-person view the participants had of the scene.

4   Results

For the questionnaire on presence, a between-group analysis of variance (ANOVA) was used because each participant was asked to respond to it once. It should be noted that an equal number of participants ($N = 15$) answered this questionnaire for each condition of the study. For the anxiety modality questionnaire one-way repeated-measures ANOVA was used. The post-hoc comparisons were performed using Bonferroni corrected estimates. The obtained results are shown in Fig. 4.

4.1   Presence

The effect of the participants' presence on the developed conditions of virtual character's awareness were examined. Based on the obtained results, we found

Fig. 3. First-person view of the VR scenario with an autonomous vehicle, during the *NINEA* condition. Car stopped to allow pedestrians to cross the road.

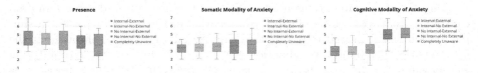

Fig. 4. The results on presence and anxiety (both somatic and cognitive) obtained from this study.

that there was not a significant effect across the five conditions of the study $[F(4, 70) = 0.92, p = 0.45]$. This means that for each of the five developed conditions, participants felt the same level of presence. Considering the mean values that participants assigned to presence, it can be said that this finding indicates that the developed scenario and VR application captivated the participants and made them feel part of the VR experience.

4.2 Anxiety

No significant effects were found regarding somatic anxiety $[\Lambda = 0.89, F(4, 71) = 2.07, p = 0.09, \eta_p^2 = 0.11]$. These were not the expected results; therefore, they need to be discussed. However, significant results were found when examining the cognitive anxiety $[\Lambda = 0.12, F(4, 71) = 127.39, p < 0.01, \eta_p^2 = 0.88]$. Post-hoc comparisons indicated that the *IEA* ($M = 2.98, SD = 0.73$), *INEA* ($M = 3.06, SD = 0.75$), and the *NIEA* ($M = 3.31, SD = 0.95$) were significantly lower than the *NINEA* ($M = 4.98, SD = 0.81$), and *CU* ($M = 5.08, SD = 1.84$) conditions. We partially expected these results. More specifically, we expected differences between the *IEA* and the partial awareness conditions in which the virtual character is not aware of the road traffic or the behavior of the car (*INEA* and *NIEA*). We also expected to find differences between the *NINEA* and *CU* conditions since in the latter condition, the virtual character is fully blind, does not know what might cause an unexpected event, and needs to perform an additional action with his hands to remove the HMD before taking the control of the car. Based on the cognitive anxiety, it can be said that the developed stimuli altered the behavior of participants, which means that participants are sensitive to the awareness of a virtual character when in a VR autonomous vehicle.

5   Discussion

Concerning participants' presence, the results from the analysis indicated that there is no difference in the five developed conditions. This result indicates that all participants felt that they were part of the VR scenario. Additionally, this result indicates that the way that the virtual character reacted did not influence their sense of being part of the virtual environment. The initial assumption was that when the virtual character is fully unaware of the road traffic and the behavior of the car, the participants might feel less present since this is an imaginary experience that contradicts prior knowledge of the way that a virtual character interacts with a car.

Based on the results that concern the somatic anxiety of participants, it can be said that regardless of the awareness of the virtual character, participant anxiety did not change at all, and it remained low. This result indicates that neither the VR technology used nor the developed stimulus had any influence on the somatic anxiety of participants. Specifically, the study was conducted by using a commodity VR headset and during the study participants sat in a desk chair, so no tactile feedback was given to them. The participants were aware of the way they experience the VR stimulus, so their somatic modality of anxiety did not respond as expected. A possible interpretation is that participants were not somatically present, which might have been a result of the low-cost VR setup that was used in this study.

Regarding the developed stimulus, it can be said that a rational/neutral driving condition was used. It seems that this behavior assigned to the autonomous vehicle, did not cause the participants any anxiety, so their responses were not influenced across the five conditions of the study. In case the stimulus was responsible for not causing any change in the participant's somatic anxiety, it can be said that this finding is in line with previous studies that examine the effects of neutral (in terms of speed) stimulus on user behavior [1]. However, to validate this assumption we would like to capture the physiological responses of participants in future studies.

The results concerns the cognitive part of participants' anxiety shown that participants' anxiety affected according to the observed awareness of the virtual character. Specifically, lower levels of anxiety were captured for the *IEA* and the partial awareness conditions (*INEA* and *NIEA*) compared to the condition (*NINEA* and *CU*) in which the virtual character is unaware of both the road traffic and the behavior of the car. It is worth mentioning that our study was limited by our focus on the behavior of the virtual character rather than the behavior of the car itself. In the current study, we made an implicit assumption that passengers would be more anxious about the virtual characters' behavior than the car's behavior. However, in Level-5 autonomous vehicles, one major issue is to make the virtual characters, passengers, and pedestrians confident in the behavior of the car.

Additionally, the driver was a virtual character with whom there was no interaction at all. According to discussions we had with a number of participants after the study, since there was no actual interaction with the virtual character, they felt that the virtual character was not highly realistic. Participants indicated that they were able to perceive occasional movements—as assigned by motion sequences—in the upper body of the virtual character. However, participants suggested that a virtual character who initiated a conversation by asking simple questions might enhance the realism of the developed VR scenarios.

In this study, the participant was seated as a passenger in an autonomous vehicle that moves in a virtual world. It is common that such VR scenarios can produce motion sickness to the participants [13]. This study did not consider thoroughly exploring the motion sickness of participants. Therefore, considering that severe motion sickness can possibly influence the study results, providing Simulator Sickness Questionnaire (SSQ) [17] may also help us understand what symptoms the subjects felt in the studies as well as how the obtained results altered by the motion sickness of participants.

6   Conclusions and Future Work

As the popularity of autonomous vehicles daily increases, the need to understand the way that passengers interact with them does also. To do so, user studies that place participants as passengers and ask them to interact with autonomous vehicles should be conducted. However, conducting such studies involves challenges that can be found in public roads and might compromise the safety of the participants. To avoid these issues, one possible solution is the use of expensive simulators. However, these simulators can be found only in a limited number of research centers and labs. Therefore, a possible alternative solution is the use of modern VR technologies that are cheaper than driving simulators and allow researchers to immerse participants in more sophisticated VR scenarios.

Understanding how passengers' behavior changes in different self-driving conditions is important to developing frameworks and regulations concerning the comfort of passengers [19]. However, there is a need to further investigate the behavior of passengers in autonomous vehicles, and many possible studies can be conducted to understand passenger behavior. For this reason, we plan to conduct additional studies. Among them we would like to examine participant anxiety based on different driving habits [18] instead of only developing a single neutral/rational driving habit that was assigned to the autonomous vehicle. Another interesting investigation is related to the sitting position of the passenger inside the car. In the current study, the participants were placed as passengers in the front seat. Investigating the behavioral changes of passengers that are placed in the back seat of the car would be also interesting and we plan to do so in the near future. Moreover, investigating the emotional reactivity [26] of passengers is another direction we are willing to explore.

In conclusion, the use of VR seems necessary for cases in which the real situation either would be too dangerous or not feasibly testable, given the current state of technology and legislation. However, more studies are needed to further understand the use of low-cost VR setups for conducting such studies. Finding the minimal feedback necessary to enhance the somatic and cognitive presence of participants, as well as to capture the anxiety or even mental disorders of the participants while experiencing VR scenarios, is essential for the use of VR as an efficient tool for understanding human behavior.

References

1. Bornstein, R.F., Leone, D.R., Galley, D.J.: The generalizability of subliminal mere exposure effects: Influence of stimuli perceived without awareness on social behavior. J. Pers. Soc. Psychol. **53**(6), 1070 (1987)
2. Burns, L.D.: Sustainable mobility: a vision of our transport future. Nature **497**(7448), 181 (2013)
3. Calvert, S., Schakel, W., van Lint, J.: Will automated vehicles negatively impact traffic flow? J. Adv. Transp. **2017** (2017)
4. Chan, M., Nyazika, S., Singhal, A.: Effects of a front-seat passenger on driver attention: an electrophysiological approach. Transp. Res. F: Traffic Psychol. Behav. **43**, 67–79 (2016)
5. Dalipi, A.F., Liu, D., Guo, X., Chen, Y., Mousas, C.: Vr-pavib: the virtual reality pedestrian-autonomous vehicle interaction benchmark. In: 12th International Conference on Automotive User Interfaces and Interactive Vehicular Applications, pp. 38–41 (2020)
6. DeBord, M.: If you have a tesla and use autopilot, please keep your hands on the steering wheel. Business Insider
7. Deniaud, C., Honnet, V., Jeanne, B., Mestre, D.: An investigation into physiological responses in driving simulators: an objective measurement of presence. In: Science and Information Conference (SAI), pp. 739–748. IEEE (2015)
8. Elbanhawi, M., Simic, M., Jazar, R.: In the passenger seat: investigating ride comfort measures in autonomous cars. IEEE Intell. Transp. Syst. Mag. **7**(3), 4–17 (2015)
9. Engadget: renault's concept ev drove me at 80mph while i wore a vr headset. https://www.engadget.com/2017/12/13/renault-symbioz-concept-ev-vr-impressions/
10. Funkhouser, K., Drews, F.: Reaction times when switching from autonomous to manual driving control: a pilot investigation. In: Proceedings of the Human Factors and Ergonomics Society Annual Meeting. SAGE Publications Sage CA: Los Angeles, CA, pp. 1854–1858 (2016)
11. Gold, C., Damböck, D., Lorenz, L., Bengler, K.: "take over!" how long does it take to get the driver back into the loop? In: Proceedings of the Human Factors and Ergonomics Society Annual Meeting. SAGE Publications Sage CA: Los Angeles, CA, pp. 1938–1942 (2013)

12. Gold, C., Körber, M., Lechner, D., Bengler, K.: Taking over control from highly automated vehicles in complex traffic situations: the role of traffic density. Hum. Factors **58**(4), 642–652 (2016)
13. Griffin, M.J., Newman, M.M.: Visual field effects on motion sickness in cars. Aviat. Space Environ. Med. **75**(9), 739–748 (2004)
14. Häne, C., Sattler, T., Pollefeys, M.: Obstacle detection for self-driving cars using only monocular cameras and wheel odometry. In: Intelligent Robots and Systems (IROS), 2015 IEEE/RSJ International Conference on, pp. 5101–5108. IEEE (2015)
15. Howard, D., Dai, D.: Public perceptions of self-driving cars: the case of berkeley, california. In: Transportation Research Board 93rd Annual Meeting. **14**, 4502 (2014)
16. Johns, M., Sibi, S., Ju, W.: Effect of cognitive load in autonomous vehicles on driver performance during transfer of control. In: Adjunct Proceedings of the 6th International Conference on Automotive User Interfaces and Interactive Vehicular Applications, pp. 1–4. ACM (2014)
17. Kennedy, R.S., Lane, N.E., Berbaum, K.S., Lilienthal, M.G.: Simulator sickness questionnaire: an enhanced method for quantifying simulator sickness. Int. J. Aviat. Psychol. **3**(3), 203–220 (1993)
18. Koilias, A., Mousas, C., Rekabdar, B.: Virtual reality car passenger anxiety on driving habits. In: EuroVR International Conference on Virtual Reality and Augmented Reality (2019)
19. Koilias, A., Mousas, C., Rekabdar, B., Anaqnostopoulos, C.N.: Passenger anxiety when seated in a virtual reality self-driving car. In: IEEE Virtual Reality and 3D User Interfaces, pp. 1024–1025. IEEE (2019)
20. Koo, J., Kwac, J., Ju, W., Steinert, M., Leifer, L., Nass, C.: Why did my car just do that? explaining semi-autonomous driving actions to improve driver understanding, trust, and performance. Int. J. Interact. Des. Manuf. (IJIDeM) **9**(4), 269–275 (2015)
21. Kun, A.L., et al.: Human-machine interaction for vehicles: review and outlook. Found. Trends® Hum. Comput. Inter. **11**(4), 201–293 (2018)
22. Levinson, J., et al.: Towards fully autonomous driving: systems and algorithms. In: Intelligent Vehicles Symposium (IV), 2011 IEEE, pp. 163–168. IEEE (2011)
23. Merat, N., Jamson, A.H., Lai, F.C., Daly, M., Carsten, O.M.: Transition to manual: driver behaviour when resuming control from a highly automated vehicle. Transp. Res. F: Traffic Psychol. Behav. **27**, 274–282 (2014)
24. Meschtscherjakov, A., Perterer, N., Trösterer, S., Krischkowsky, A., Tscheligi, M.: The neglected passenger—how collaboration in the car fosters driving experience and safety. In: Meixner, G., Müller, C. (eds.) Automotive User Interfaces. HIS, pp. 187–213. Springer, Cham (2017). https://doi.org/10.1007/978-3-319-49448-7_7
25. Milleville-Pennel, I., Charron, C.: Driving for real or on a fixed-base simulator: is it so different? an explorative study. Presence: Teleoperators Virtual Environ. **24**(1), 74–91 (2015)
26. Mousas, C., Anastasiou, D., Spantidi, O.: The effects of appearance and motion of virtual characters on emotional reactivity. Comput. Hum. Behav. **86**, 99–108 (2018)
27. Sadigh, D., Driggs-Campbell, K., Bajcsy, R., Sastry, S.S., Seshia, S.: User interface design and verification for semi-autonomous driving. In: Proceedings of the 3rd International Conference on High Confidence Networked Systems, pp. 63–64. ACM (2014)
28. Schultheis, M.T., Rebimbas, J., Mourant, R., Millis, S.R.: Examining the usability of a virtual reality driving simulator. Assistive Technol. **19**(1), 1–10 (2007)

29. Slater, M., Usoh, M., Steed, A.: Depth of presence in virtual environments. Presence: Teleoperators & Virtual Environ. **3**(2), 130–144 (1994)
30. Sportillo, D., Paljic, A., Boukhris, M., Fuchs, P., Ojeda, L., Roussarie, V.: An immersive virtual reality system for semi-autonomous driving simulation: a comparison between realistic and 6-dof controller-based interaction. In: Proceedings of the 9th International Conference on Computer and Automation Engineering, pp. 6–10. ACM (2017)
31. Sportillo, D., Paljic, A., Ojeda, L.: Get ready for automated driving using virtual reality. Accid. Anal. Prev. **118**, 102–113 (2018)
32. Thrun, S.: Toward robotic cars. Commun. ACM **53**(4), 99–106 (2010)
33. Urmson, C., et al.: Autonomous driving in urban environments: boss and the urban challenge. J. Field Robot. **25**(8), 425–466 (2008)
34. Van Gerwen, L.J., Spinhoven, P., Van Dyck, R., Diekstra, R.F.: Construction and psychometric characteristics of two self-report questionnaires for the assessment of fear of flying. Psychol. Assess. **11**(2), 146 (1999)
35. Wagner, M., Koopman, P.: A philosophy for developing trust in self-driving cars. In: Meyer, G., Beiker, S. (eds.) Road Vehicle Automation 2. LNM, pp. 163–171. Springer, Cham (2015). https://doi.org/10.1007/978-3-319-19078-5_14
36. Wilfinger, D., Meschtscherjakov, A., Murer, M., Osswald, S., Tscheligi, M.: Are we there yet? a probing study to inform design for the rear seat of family cars. In: Campos, P., Graham, N., Jorge, J., Nunes, N., Palanque, P., Winckler, M. (eds.) INTERACT 2011. LNCS, vol. 6947, pp. 657–674. Springer, Heidelberg (2011). https://doi.org/10.1007/978-3-642-23771-3_48

Investigating the Effects of Display Fidelity of Popular Head-Mounted Displays on Spatial Updating and Learning in Virtual Reality

Bryson Rudolph[1], Geoff Musick[1], Leah Wiitablake[1], Kelly B. Lazar[1],
Catherine Mobley[1], D. Matthew Boyer[1], Stephen Moysey[2],
Andrew Robb[1], and Sabarish V. Babu[1]

[1] Clemson University, Clemson, SC 29631, USA
{brysonr,gmusick,lwiitab,klazar,camoble,dmboyer,arobb,sbabu}@clemson.edu
[2] East Carolina University, East 5th Street, Greenville, NC 27858, USA
moyseys18@ecu.edu

Abstract. Often users in VR are required to make mental models, develop spatial awareness, and gain survey knowledge of the environment that they are exploring while learning the content of the simulation. In a between-subjects empirical evaluation, we examined the effect of the display fidelity of popular commercial head-mounted display systems based on display properties such as screen resolution, field of view, and screen size in three conditions, namely low, medium, and high fidelity. Our dependent variables were spatial updating (assessing survey knowledge by measuring the perceived orientation to landmarks previously visited when unseen) and content learning (measured via a pre and post cognitive questionnaire created by domain experts based on Blooms taxonomy of learning). In a VR simulation for geology education, participants explored a terrain, modeled after a segment of the Grand Canyon, collecting and testing rock samples. These landmarks were explored along a winding path through a realistic geological terrain, modeled based on Lidar and photogrammetry data. As the pathway through the Grand Canyon is distinctly sloping and varied, the task of pointing to the perceived location of landmarks in this environment provided rich insights into participants' survey knowledge and content learning, and how such knowledge differed between the display conditions.

Keywords: Spatial updating · Display fidelity · Educational VR.

1 Introduction

Educational VR simulations have been shown to enhance basic knowledge and understanding in fields such as history, science, and engineering, as well as enhance evaluation and creation via 3D interaction with the learning content [5]. Furthermore, these simulations have also been shown to enhance the motor skills

© Springer Nature Switzerland AG 2020
G. Bebis et al. (Eds.): ISVC 2020, LNCS 12509, pp. 666–679, 2020.
https://doi.org/10.1007/978-3-030-64556-4_52

associated with the task, in essence building muscle memory, potentially due to simulated hands-on interaction, first person perspective, and immersive viewing [2]. In simulated real-world activities, VR has also been shown to enhance students' efficacy and effectiveness in performing the task, as immersion and interaction have been shown to enhance attention to the material and executive functioning [4,17].

In contemporary settings, users have a wide variety of immersive head mounted displays (HMDs) to view learning content. On one hand, there has been an explosion of low cost, easily accessible headsets such as GearVR [9] and Google Cardboard [10] that allows users to leverage their smartphones as the display. Although smartphone VR viewing these days can enable stereoscopic viewing at relatively high resolutions, it may suffer from lower frame rates with complex scenes, lower field of view, and a lack of head position tracking to provide motion parallax. These low fidelity devices are ubiquitous and most learners possess smartphone devices [14]. On the other hand, there have been some recent developments of ultra high resolution (4K pixels per eye) and larger field of view experiences (greater than 150° total horizontal field of view). These high fidelity HMDs, such as the Pimax 8K [18] and StarVR [7], aim to provide close to or near the human visual horizontal field of view. However, the cost of these high fidelity HMDs can be twice as much as other popular commercial models and require advanced graphics cards as well as high end processors to render the scene. These high-end HMDs may not be cost effective for students and may not be as accessible as the low fidelity smartphone based HMD devices. In the middle of the display fidelity spectrum are mid-to-high fidelity HMDs, such as the Oculus Rift [8] and HTC Vive Pro, which may provide an intermediate fidelity of viewing (approximated 110° horizontal field of view) and approximately half the pixel resolution per eye (approximately 2K pixels per eye) to that of the high display fidelity HMDs. Therefore, it is critical in contemporary VR applications to evaluate how the display fidelity of commodity HMDs affects user perception and performance in learners.

A constant in any VR experience is travel in an immersive virtual space, such as those found in numerous VR applications, from factory simulations, field explorations, to educational experiences. When exploring unfamiliar simulated spaces, there is a need to continuously create and update a mental picture or model of the virtual environment [13,27]. As users visually perceive landmarks and features along their path, they update an internal mental representation or model of their surroundings in order to better perform tasks and understand their environment better over time. This process is also a contributing factor in survey knowledge acquisition of the scene explored, and allows users to understand the spatial relationships of objects relative to their present location [12]. This action of updating the mental model of one's surroundings is referred to as spatial updating and is of great importance for the success of many education and training applications in VR [19].

Despite the importance of spatial updating in VR, the effects of display fidelity aspects of visual quality (i.e. screen resolution, field of view, screen size, clarity, and contrast) in commercial contemporary HMDs on spatial updating performance and learning have not been extensively studied. It is important for VR developers, educators, and consumers alike to understand the cost-benefit trade-offs of display fidelity of commercial HMDs on spatial awareness and content learning in educational VR simulations. Our study investigates this need in the literature by empirically evaluating three display fidelity classes of commercial HMD VR systems on a linear continuum from low, mid, to high fidelity and comparing and contrasting their effects on spatial updating and content learning in a geology education simulation.

2   Related Works

The ability for our brain to automatically or continuously create a model of its surroundings during self-motion instead of afterwards through reflection is often referred to as "automatic spatial updating" or "spatial updating" [21]. Though of great importance to the survival of animals, spatial updating in virtual reality is essential for effective training in both educational and entertainment-related tasks.

2.1   Virtual Spatial Updating

Although internal cues were previously thought to be necessary for spatial updating, Riecke et al. [21] showed that visual feedback can be sufficient for perception of self motion. These findings have great implications for virtual reality. As spatial updating is so important in VR, research often focuses on methods to optimize spatial updating performance in VR. Ruddle et al. [22] worked with large-scale virtual environments to determine the optimal travel and rotation metaphors for spatial updating. Their findings indicate that translational body-based information is more important than rotational body-based information for large scaled environments. Riecke et al. [20] compared navigation and search task performance for three conditions, as follows: a) walking, b) physical rotations with a joystick for translations, and c) joystick for both translations and rotations. They found that walking performed the best, but also suggested that methods for experiencing natural rotation in the scene would assist in spatial updating [20]. Weißker et al. [26] investigated the effects of steering compared to teleportation on spatial updating performance. Their findings indicate that steering as a transportation metaphor significantly outperforms teleportation, but at the cost of increased simulator sickness. Cherep et al. [6] similarly researched the effect of travel metaphors on spatial updating. They found that teleportation with head rotation consistently outperformed teleportation without head rotation with regards to spatial updating performance.

2.2   Measuring Spatial Updating

Pointing tasks have become one of the most common methods for evaluating a participant's spatial updating performance [13,15,26]. In these tasks, participants often perform some navigational task that involves both translation and rotation. Periodically, or at the end of the navigation, participants are asked to recall by pointing where they perceive the start or some other landmark that they observed en route. This task often, but not always, takes the form of a triangle completion task where participants move along two legs of a path before pointing to where they perceive the path origin to be [13].

2.3   User Studies on Display Fidelity

In recent years, VR hardware has provided consumers with a variety of improvements in VR, including in the realms of field of view (FoV), resolution, and comfort. As the difference between price points of varying equipment are drastically different, consumers need to know the importance of differing aspects of varying headsets based on their priorities or needs. For example, Young et al.'s research [28] compares two cost-differentiated virtual reality systems. Their work focused on perception and action tasks using the more affordable Oculus Rift versus the much more expensive Nvis SX60. Interestingly, they found that the low-cost system outperformed the high-cost system for perception and action tasks, though at the cost of increased simulator sickness.

The type of trade-offs investigated here and in previous work in contemporary HMD viewing is of great importance to consumers, researchers, and developers alike. Up until now, very little work has been performed in investigating the role of display fidelity of popular commercial head-mounted displays on the differential benefits of spatial updating and content learning in educational VR. Furthermore, as the experiment apparatus in this research utilized a geology education VR simulation that we created with a varied and expansive terrain, the research presented in this paper not only documents spatial updating performance in 2D, but also reports data on spatial updating performance in 3D analyzed using circular statistics in the simulated large scale terrain.

3   Experiment Design

3.1   Research Question

The aim of this study is to investigate the following question: **how does display fidelity of contemporary HMDs differentially affect spatial updating and content learning?** Our hypotheses are as follows:

- H1: *Spatial updating performance will be superior in higher fidelity head mounted displays as compared to lower fidelity displays.*
- H2: *Content learning performance will be superior in higher fidelity head mounted displays as compared to lower fidelity displays.*

For this study, the independent variable, display fidelity, will take the form of three varying-fidelity HMD displays: *High Fidelity* (*Hi-Fi* utilizing the Pimax 8K HMD), *Medium Fidelity* (*Mi-Fi* utilizing the HTC Vive Pro), and *Low Fidelity* (*Lo-Fi* utilizing a Gear-VR-like inexpensive plastic head mount with a Samsung Galaxy S9 for viewing). The specifications of these conditions are described in detail in the "Conditions" section.

3.2 Experiment Simulation

Grand Canyon Model: Participants navigated through a model of a section of the Grand Canyon. This model was created using height map data of the actual Grand Canyon near a point of interest called "Hopi Point." This modeling ensured a realistic and accurate representation of the relative topography of the "Hopi Point" area of the Grand Canyon. Part of the texturing of the model included a clear path that participants were instructed to stay on during the whole experiment that also had invisible boundaries preventing them from straying too far. The path was purposely designed so that the spatial updating tests would not be trivial. In other words, the path was not linear in any fashion, but rather had at least one curve between each rock that was tested (see "Rock Tests" below). Furthermore, each rock that needed to be tested had some unique feature in the immediate surrounding environment designed to make that rock memorable and distinct from the others.

Navigation: Movement through the space was implemented using a continuous travel metaphor. Previous studies [26] indicate that spatial updating performance is better using continuous travel rather than teleportation, though at the cost of an increased risk for cybersickness. Participants simply had to press and hold down the designated button on their controller to make their virtual self move forward in the direction that they were facing based on head orientation. For the Lo-Fi condition (Smartphone VR HMD), this was a single button on a Bluetooth controller. For the Mi-Fi and Hi-Fi conditions (Vive Pro and Pimax 8K HMDs, respectively), this was the trigger on the Vive controller. To ensure that participants tested every rock, the user was frozen in place when they came within interaction range of each rock. Participants were allowed to move again once that rock test was completed.

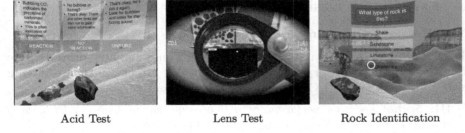

   Acid Test   Lens Test   Rock Identification

Fig. 1. Participants performed multiple geology tests to identify rocks in the environment.

Rock Tests: Participants interacted with nine rocks in the form of 3D models that they came across along their path. The rock tests involved two geological field experiments used to identify the rock. Both experiments had to be completed, though in any order, before the user could identify the rock. One test was the acid test (Fig. 1a) where users determined whether or not the sample reacted with hydrochloric acid, a common indication of a limestone sample. This selection was made based on whether or not visual bubbles and audible fizzing occurred. The other test involved a grain size test (Fig. 1b) where participants looked at the rock under a magnifying hand lens to observe the grain size. After selections were made pertaining to the grain size and acid reactivity of the sample, participants identified the rock (Fig. 1c) using multiple choices with the help of audio hints. The choices included shale, conglomerate, sandstone, or limestone samples. Performing both tests and correctly identifying the rock were necessary for the participant to move on. Requiring participants to test rocks provided an opportunity to improve their geology learning. However, these rock tests also served as a natural distraction task. Distractions in spatial updating tasks can be used as a way to prevent participants from using excessive techniques to improve their spatial updating performance [26]. An example of this would be participants counting steps or time between samples to create a robust mental model of the environment. Furthermore, rock tests served as a way for participants to become familiar with each waypoint by interaction and remembering each rock by name.

Spatial Updating Task: During the course of participants' travel through the Grand Canyon, they were required to complete three spatial updating pointing tasks. These tasks all functioned in an identical fashion. After the participant completed the third rock test in each rock group, they continued on the path until they triggered the spatial updating test. The environment surrounding the participant faded out to gray, and a small stationary square appeared at eye-level. This square served as a reference point; in other words, it provided a reminder to the participant about the direction they were facing when the test began. This reference point was helpful for users to re-calibrate their direction between pointing tasks so that error was not accumulated between pointing tasks. The participant was then prompted to select the location of a certain rock that they had previously tested (or, during some tests, the location of the path origin). A 2D image of this rock and its immediate surrounding environment was shown, along with the rock's name and number indicating the order in which that rock was encountered (i.e., 1–9). Participants were instructed to rotate their head/pointing direction to where they perceived the indicated waypoint to be. When their head was in the orientation they perceived to be correct, they pressed a designated button on the controller to log their head orientation; then, the participant was either presented with another waypoint for another pointing task, or the spatial updating task was ended and the environment faded back in. The reference point square was always visible during these tests, so at any point the participant could turn their head and find the square if re-calibration was desired. In total, 14 pointing tasks were recorded for each participant.

3.3   Participants

Thirty participants, 10 females and 20 males aged 19 to 51, were recruited by use of flyers and word-of-mouth. Ten participants were used for each of the three viewing fidelity conditions, Lo-Fi, Mi-Fi, and Hi-Fi. With three conditions across one-way comparisons as well as 14 measurement repetitions per person, assuming a small to medium effect size of f = 0.40 and a correlation of 0.5 between measurements, alpha threshold of p = 0.05 and a power of 0.72, we determined a total sample size of 30 (10 per group). All participants were tested to ensure that they did not have any prior domain knowledge in geology and geosciences. Our experiment was conducted using protocols that were approved by the University's Institutional Review Board.

3.4   Conditions

There were three main conditions, *Lo-Fi*, *Mi-Fi*, and *Hi-Fi*. Though 6 degrees of freedom (DoF) tracking is often used with headsets like the HTC Vive Pro or Pimax8K, both of the Mi-Fi and Hi-Fi conditions were limited to 3 DoF (three rotational) in order to match that of the Smartphone condition. The Mi-Fi and Hi-Fi conditions used headsets connected to a desktop with an Intel Core i7-8700 processor and an NVIDIA GeForce RTX 2080 graphics card and were tracked by two HTC Vive base stations. Furthermore, in these two conditions, participants used a single HTC Vive controller for input. The Smartphone condition was characterized by the use of a Samsung Galaxy S9 inserted into a plastic head-mounted display case. Participants in this condition utilized a Bluetooth shutter remote for input. We tried to constrain aspects of the rendering such as scene complexity, level of detail, and refresh rate to be consistent across the viewing fidelity conditions. Please see Table 1 for technical viewing specifications of the condition.

Table 1. Table showing the specs for the three display fidelity conditions in the experiment.

Condition	*Lo-Fi*	*Mi-Fi*	*Hi-Fi*
Hardware	Samsung S9	HTC Vive Pro	Pimax 8K
Total Resolution	2960 × 1440	2880 × 1600	7680 × 2160
Per Eye Resolution	1480 × 1440	1440 × 1600	3840 × 2160
Field of View	80° × 40°	100° × 50°	160° × 60°
Pixels per Inch	570	615	800
Mean Frame Rate	65 Hz	90 Hz	80 Hz

3.5   Methodology and Measurements

Prior to the simulation, participants each took a demographics survey and then the Guilford-Zimmerman Spatial Ability test in order to test that participants across the conditions had similar spatial abilities. During the VR experience, participants completed a total of 14 pointing tasks. For each pointing task, user error was recorded in 3D based on the direction that they perceived the way-points as compared to their actual direction. Participants also completed a pre and post geology cognition questionnaire in order to assess the learning effects of VR-simulation-based education in the three conditions. The pre and post cognition questionnaire consisted of 15 questions that span the geoscience of the rocks in the Grand Canyon that participants learned via 3D interaction in the VR education simulation. These questionnaires were designed by geologists who are involved in the project and contributed to the design and implementation of the simulation. After the post experiment cognition questionnaire, participants also provided their responses in an object recall list and object placement map, as well as sketching the path that they took in another top-down map of the simulation terrain.

4   Results

4.1   Data Preprocessing

A pre-processing step was necessary since the simple difference between the participants' perceived angle and landmark angle would not be sufficient due to angle wrapping. For example, let's consider a participant's judgements of $5°$ from the north axis, as compared to an angle of $355°$ for the perceived landmark direction (with respect to the north axis). If we simply subtract the two, we compute a difference of $350°$; however, in reality, the difference is only $10°$. To overcome this difficulty, angles can be "wrapped" by adding or subtracting 360, or by employing circular statistics [1, 25]. This is a very popular technique in classical perception research on spatial updating and other similar measures that involve a circular quantitative response. We have also analyzed the mean relative error in pointing direction in an absolute angle from the ground truth or actual direction of each landmark as $0°$. The analysis of the mean relative error in perceived landmark direction in an absolute angle between the different conditions may reveal any systematic difference in spatial updating by display type overall. The participants' score on the cognition questionnaire was converted to a percentage and was prepared for subsequent data analysis. The two key circular statistics used to ascertain absolute spatial updating performance in our data analysis were: α, the average estimated angle for a particular landmark, and h, the homing coefficient that measures how well the participants' perceived directions "home in" on the actual landmark direction with respect to 3D pointing error. The h value includes information about the accuracy of the perceived direction to the landmark. Please see Turvey et al. [25] for a more detailed explanation of circular statistics. The Grand Canyon terrain that we used as an experiment testbed also has elevation and it would be relevant to examine the participants' spatial updating performance in 3D as a result. The latter analyses also sheds light on how spatial updating in most large scale virtual environments in which terrain elevation is also a factor affects the spatial knowledge acquisition performance of spatial updating.

On all the quantitative spatial updating and learning assessment objective variables, parametric ANOVA analyses were conducted on the data after carefully verifying that the underlying assumptions were met - namely the data in the samples were normally distributed and error variance between samples were equivalent. We ensured that Box's test was not significant. Levene's test was conducted to verify homogeneity of variance, and Mauchly's test of sphericity was conducted to ensure that the error variance in groups of samples were equivalent. Pairwise post-hoc tests between levels of the between-subjects condition variables were conducted using Tukey's HSD analysis.

4.2 Spatial Ability Between Conditions

Before comparing the participants' performance between conditions, it is important to examine the influence of any confounding variables. One relevant confounding variable is the participants' innate spatial ability. We collected the participants' spatial ability scores using the GZ test [11]. Analyzing the GZ scores between the conditions via a Kruskal-Wallis H test revealed that there were no significant differences in the GZ scores between the conditions. Overall, when we analyzed the spatial ability variables by gender, we did not find any significant differences by gender in our data set.

4.3 Circular Statistics

Average Estimated Angle to Perceived Location of Landmarks (α.) The α scores in 3D were compared via a one-way independent samples ANOVA analysis. The ANOVA analysis revealed a significant effect of condition, $F(2, 27) = 3.86$, $p = 0.034$ (See Fig. 2 left). Post-hoc pairwise comparisons using Tukey's HSD analysis revealed that participants' average estimated angle to the perceived location of landmarks they examined were significantly lower in the Hi-Fi condition (M = 43.15, SD = 16.09) than the Lo-Fi condition (M = 69.16, SD = 24.24) $p = 0.028$. The popular Mi-Fi condition α scores were in the middle (M = 52.10, SD = 22.58).

Ability of the Participants' Perceived Direction to "Home In" on Landmark Direction. The homing coefficient h scores in 3D were compared via a one-way independent samples ANOVA analysis. The ANOVA analysis revealed a significant effect of condition, $F(2, 27) = 3.58$, $p = 0.042$ (See Fig. 2 right). Post-hoc pairwise comparisons using Tukey's HSD analysis revealed that participants' average estimated angle to the perceived location of landmarks they examined were significantly higher in the Hi-Fi (M = 0.62, SD = 0.22) condition than the Lo-Fi condition (M = 0.27, SD = 0.32) $p = 0.036$. The popular Mi-Fi condition h scores were in the middle (M = 0.50, SD = 0.31).

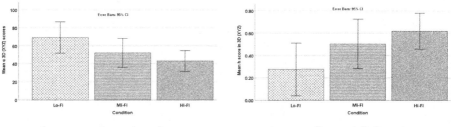

Average estimated angle α Average "home in" direction

Fig. 2. The average estimated angle α to perceived location of landmarks (left), and the average ability to "home in" on landmark direction (right) in 3D by condition.

4.4   Absolute Angular Error

Absolute 3D Angular Error in Perceived Direction to Landmark Orientation. To place the results in simpler terms, we also calculated the mean absolute value of the 3D angular offsets between the pointing direction and landmark orientation in 3D. We explored the mean absolute angular errors in perceived direction to landmarks by the closest landmarks that they saw, namely the last landmark they saw or 2 landmarks prior or 3 landmarks prior or pointing to the origin, in order to examine if participants perceived the landmark direction more accurately when it was the most recent landmark that they examined. We analyzed the 3D angular error in perceived location in a 3 (between-subjects conditions) x 4 (within-subjects previous landmark visit order) mixed model ANOVA analysis. The ANOVA analysis revealed a significant main effect of condition $F(2, 108) = 7.70$, $p = 0.001$, part. $\eta^2 = 0.13$ (Fig. 3 left). The order of previous landmarks visited or the interaction term were not significant. Post-hoc pairwise comparisons using Tukey's HSD analysis revealed that 3D angular errors were significantly higher in the Lo-Fi condition (M = 68.47, SD = 31.38) as compared to the Mi-Fi condition (M = 52.98, SD = 27.48) $p = 0.035$, and the Hi-Fi viewing condition (M = 44.47, SD = 22.42) $p = 0.001$.

4.5   Cognition Questionnaire

The participants' pre and post VR simulation geology cognition scores as a percentage were subjected to a 3(condition) $\times$ 2(session) mixed model ANOVA analysis, after verifying the assumptions of the parametric test. The ANOVA analysis revealed a significant main effect of session $F(1, 29) = 49.1$, $p = 0.001$, part. $\eta^2 = 0.65$, and a significant session by condition interaction $F(2, 29) = 3.94$, $p = 0.03$, part. $\eta^2 = 0.23$ right. Post-hoc pairwise comparisons using the Bonferroni method revealed that post-test scores (M = 58.90%, SD = 20.55) were significantly higher than the pre-test scores (M = 28.70%, SD = 12.07) in the Mi-Fi condition $p = 0.001$. Post-hoc pairwise comparisons also revealed that post-test scores (M = 64.50%, SD =1 8.18) were significantly higher than the pre-test scores (M = 35.6%, SD = 19.72) in the Hi-Fi condition $p = 0.001$.

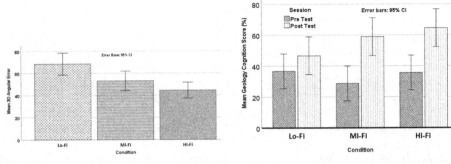

Mean 3D angular error   Mean pre and post cognition Scores

Fig. 3. The mean 3D angular error in perceived direction to target by condition (left), and graph showing mean cognition scores as a percentage in the pre and post test session by condition (right).

4.6   Other Variables

Non-parametric statistical analysis on the object recall, object order recall, and path recall scores did not reveal any significant differences by condition. Non-parametric statistical analysis was also conducted separately on the four dimensions of the I-Group presence questionnaire (perceived presence, spatial presence, immersion and realism) [16]. There were no statistically significant differences by condition on these variables. Similarly, non-parametric statistical analysis was also conducted on the system usability scores, gathered via the IBM system usability survey (IBM SUS) [3]. There were no statistically significant differences by condition.

5   Discussion

Our first hypothesis stated that spatial updating performance would be superior in higher display fidelity HMDs as compared to lower fidelity displays. From our spatial updating data analysis, we found highly significant differences to support this hypothesis. Circular statistical values for α, pointing error, were significantly lower for the high-fidelity condition than they were for the low-fidelity viewing condition. Furthermore, h values, homing scores or the ability to home in on a perceived landmark direction, were significantly higher for the high-fidelity viewing condition than they were for the low-fidelity condition. These significant α and h differences held true for pointing values. Though the mid-fidelity condition, with the popular contemporary HMD hardware, scored in the middle for both α and h, there was interestingly no significant differences between the mid-fidelity and the high-fidelity viewing condition, or between the mid-fidelity and the low-fidelity display conditions.

In addition to examining at circular statistics for hypothesis 1, we examined the spatial updating data through the lens of absolute angular error. Similar to the circular statistics data, the high-fidelity display condition contained significantly less pointing error than the low-fidelity display condition. Interestingly, when comparing absolute angular error for the mid-fidelity condition, the mid-fidelity display condition contains significantly more error than the high-fidelity display condition and significantly less error than the low-fidelity display condition.

We also examined the effects of display fidelity on content learning in the geological sciences, as participants had to learn the geology of the rocks they encountered via 3D interactions in the virtual world. In examining how the display fidelity differentially affected learning, we formulated hypothesis 2, which predicted that participants would learn the content more effectively in the high-fidelity display as compared to the low-fidelity display condition. We found that participants learned the task significantly higher in the post-test session, as compared to the pre-test session in both the high-fidelity and mid-fidelity display condition, but not in the low-fidelity condition. Our result indicates that content learning is equivalently effective in popular commercial mid-fidelity as well as high-fidelity viewing HMDs, but not in popular low-fidelity HMD devices.

One of the limitations of our work that we aim to explore in further research is that this study opens up several open questions that are ripe for investigation. The results of our study now opens up further questions such as how FoV and screen resolution of contemporary commodity HMDs can individually affect content learning and spatial updating. Although past research has shown that physically large displays can enhance spatial performance [23, 24], as contemporary HMDs evolve in terms of display quality, it becomes crucial to thoroughly evaluate the effects of the innovative display components on user performance and behavior.

6 Conclusion and Future Work

Our data supports the notion that high-fidelity contemporary HMDs allow users to have better spatial updating and content learning than popular lower fidelity displays. This finding should interest developers of VR educational and training applications that take place in expansive and potentially complex virtual environments. Developing an application for a lower or mid-fidelity display will, based on our research, not provide the same experience in terms of spatial updating or survey knowledge acquisition and content learning. Furthermore, consumers of these types of applications could use our findings to justify the need to purchase a popular commercial higher-fidelity device in order to have spatially richer and educationally meaningful experiences. This recommendation also holds true for those in industry applications that use HMDs for training exercises in which spatial knowledge acquisition might be essential. We recommend current visual display hardware designers to continue to invest in advancements in HMDs, since there is evidence that higher-fidelity HMDs are able to provide experiences that lower to mid-fidelity ones cannot. Future work will focus on how factors such as screen size, resolution and field of view specifically in popular contemporary

HMDs contribute to the differences we found on spatial updating and learning performance. We also plan to empirically evaluate how display fidelity affects other measures such as affordances and perception-action coordination.

Acknowledgements. This contribution is based upon work supported by National Science Foundation under Grant no. 1911445. The authors also gratefully acknowledge the participants of the study for their time.

References

1. Batschelet, E.: Second-order statistical analysis of directions. In: Schmidt-Koenig, K., Keeton, W.T. (eds.) Animal Migration, Navigation, and Homing. Proceedings in Life Sciences. Springer, Berlin, Heidelberg (1978) https://doi.org/10.1007/978-3-662-11147-5_1
2. Bhargava, A., Bertrand, J.W., Gramopadhye, A.K., Madathil, K.C., Babu, S.V.: Evaluating multiple levels of an interaction fidelity continuum on performance and learning in near-field training simulations. IEEE Trans. Visual Comput. Graphics **24**(4), 1418–1427 (2018)
3. Brooke, J., et al.: Sus-a quick and dirty usability scale. Usability Eva. Ind. **189**(194), 4–7 (1996)
4. Chan, J.C., Leung, H., Tang, J.K., Komura, T.: A virtual reality dance training system using motion capture technology. IEEE Trans. Learn. Technol. **4**(2), 187–195 (2011)
5. Chen, Y.T., Hsu, C.H., Chung, C.H., Wang, Y.S., Babu, S.V.: Ivrnote: design, creation and evaluation of an interactive note-taking interface for study and reflection in vr learning environments. In: 2019 IEEE Conference on Virtual Reality and 3D User Interfaces (VR). pp. 172–180. IEEE (2019)
6. Cherep, L.A., et al.: Spatial cognitive implications of teleporting through virtual environments. PsyArXiv (2019)
7. Corp, S.: Starvr one (2020), https://www.starvr.com/product/
8. Facebook Technologies, L.: Oculus rift (2020) https://www.oculus.com/rift-s/
9. GearVR, S.: Samsung gearvr with controller powered by oculus (2020), https://www.samsung.com/global/galaxy/gear-vr/
10. Google: Google cardboard (2020), https://arvr.google.com/cardboard/
11. Guilford, J.P., Zimmerman, W.S.: The guilford-zimmerman aptitude survey. J. Appl. Psychol. **32**(1), 24 (1948)
12. He, Q., McNamara, T.P., Bodenheimer, B., Klippel, A.: Acquisition and transfer of spatial knowledge during wayfinding. J. Exp. Psychol. Learn. Mem. Cogn. **45**(8), 1364 (2019)
13. Klatzky, R.L., Loomis, J.M., Beall, A.C., Chance, S.S., Golledge, R.G.: Spatial updating of self-position and orientation during real, imagined, and virtual locomotion. Psychol. Sci. **9**(4), 293–298 (1998)
14. Matar Boumosleh, J., Jaalouk, D.: Depression, anxiety, and smartphone addiction in university students-a cross sectional study. PLoS ONE **12**(8), e0182239 (2017)
15. Napieralski, P.E., Altenhoff, B.M., Bertrand, J.W., Long, L.O., Babu, S.V., Pagano, C.C., Davis, T.A.: An evaluation of immersive viewing on spatial knowledge acquisition in spherical panoramic environments. Virt. Real. **18**(3), 189–201 (2014). https://doi.org/10.1007/s10055-014-0245-1

16. Panahi-Shahri, M.: Reliability and validity of igroup presence questionnaire (ipq). Int. J. Behav. Sci. **3**(1), 27–34 (2009)
17. Parmar, D., et al.: A comparative evaluation of viewing metaphors on psychophysical skills education in an interactive virtual environment. Virt. Real. **20**(3), 141–157 (2016). https://doi.org/10.1007/s10055-016-0287-7
18. Pimax: Pimax vision 8k x (2020), https://www.pimax.com/products/vision-8k-x?variant=31554031550507
19. Richardson, A.E., Montello, D.R., Hegarty, M.: Spatial knowledge acquisition from maps and from navigation in real and virtual environments. Memory Cogn. **27**(4), 741–750 (1999)
20. Riecke, B.E., Bodenheimer, B., McNamara, T.P., Williams, B., Peng, P., Feuereissen, D.: Do we need to walk for effective virtual reality navigation? physical rotations alone may suffice. In: Hölscher, C., Shipley, T.F., Olivetti Belardinelli, M., Bateman, J.A., Newcombe, N.S. (eds.) Spatial Cognition 2010. LNCS (LNAI), vol. 6222, pp. 234–247. Springer, Heidelberg (2010). https://doi.org/10.1007/978-3-642-14749-4_21
21. Riecke, B.E., Cunningham, D.W., Bülthoff, H.H.: Spatial updating in virtual reality: the sufficiency of visual information. Psychol. Res. **71**(3), 298–313 (2007)
22. Ruddle, R.A., Volkova, E., Bülthoff, H.H.: Walking improves your cognitive map in environments that are large-scale and large in extent. ACM Trans. Comput-Hum. Int. (TOCHI) **18**(2), 10 (2011)
23. Tan, D.S., Gergle, D., Scupelli, P., Pausch, R.: With similar visual angles, larger displays improve spatial performance. In: Proceedings of the SIGCHI Conference on Human Factors in Computing Systems. pp. 217–224 (2003)
24. Tan, D.S., Gergle, D., Scupelli, P., Pausch, R.: Physically large displays improve performance on spatial tasks. ACM Trans. Comput.-Hum. Int. (TOCHI) **13**(1), 71–99 (2006)
25. Turvey, M., Burton, G., Pagano, C.C., Solomon, H.Y., Runeson, S.: Role of the inertia tensor in perceiving object orientation by dynamic touch. J. Exp. Psychol. Hum. Percept. Perform. **18**(3), 714 (1992)
26. Weißker, T., Kunert, A., Fröhlich, B., Kulik, A.: Spatial updating and simulator sickness during steering and jumping in immersive virtual environments. In: 2018 IEEE Conference on Virtual Reality and 3d User Interfaces (VR). pp. 97–104. IEEE (2018)
27. Wraga, M., Creem, S.H., Proffitt, D.R.: The influence of spatial reference frames on imagined object-and viewer rotations. Acta Psychol. **102**(2–3), 247–264 (1999)
28. Young, M.K., Gaylor, G.B., Andrus, S.M., Bodenheimer, B.: A comparison of two cost-differentiated virtual reality systems for perception and action tasks. In: Proceedings of the ACM Symposium on Applied Perception. pp. 83–90. ACM (2014)

ST: Computer Vision Advances in Geo-Spatial Applications and Remote Sensing

Natural Disaster Building Damage Assessment Using a Two-Encoder U-Net

William Ermlick[1], Nick Newman[1], Devayani Pawar[1], Tyler Richardett[1],
Christian Conroy[2], James Baldo[1], Rajesh Aggarwal[1], and Marc Bosch[2(✉)]

[1] Department of Statistics, George Mason University, Fairfax, VA 22030, USA
[2] Accenture Federal Services, Arlington, VA 22203, USA
marc.bosch.ruiz@accenturefederal.com

Abstract. When a natural disaster occurs, damaged regions rely on
timely damage assessments to receive relief. Currently, this is a slow and
laborious process, during which emergency response groups conduct on-
the-ground evaluations to form fiscal estimates. This project attempts
to expedite relief efforts by applying novel computer vision algorithms
to satellite images to quickly and accurately estimate physical and fiscal damage caused by natural disasters. This paper investigates a modified U-Net architecture to jointly localize buildings, classify damage, and
establish change detection. In particular, a second encoder is added to
the U-Net architecture to simultaneously process pre- and post-event
imagery, with both encoders sharing weights. In this way, the decoder is
trained to both locate buildings and classify damage estimates by formulating it as a single semantic segmentation problem – producing damage
estimates in one pass without needing to re-visit pixels (*i.e.* detection
+ classification tasks). Finally, a downstream task is added that provides a pixel-based financial model capable of outputting financial costs
according to the United States National Grid (USNG) coordinate system
through an interactive web application.

Keywords: Natural disaster · U-Net · United states national grid ·
Damage assessment · Mask R-CNN · Remote sensing

1 Introduction

Natural disasters are costly and time-sensitive events that have the potential to
wreak havoc on an entire region. Currently, the Federal Emergency Management
Agency (FEMA) and other agencies conduct assessments to determine the extent
of damage in a region following a natural disaster, but these are often slow,
unsafe, and laborious processes. The regions are dependent upon the assessments,
and the funding that follows, in order to rebuild lost infrastructure.

Automated processing of space-borne imagery offers the possibility to accelerate damage assessment. Government agencies presently manually search and
annotate these images for damage or obstructions, and make limited use of automatic forms of analysis. Due to the scale of most disasters, manually searching

© Springer Nature Switzerland AG 2020
G. Bebis et al. (Eds.): ISVC 2020, LNCS 12509, pp. 683–695, 2020.
https://doi.org/10.1007/978-3-030-64556-4_53

and annotating these images for damage or obstructions is a tenuous process for analysts that can benefit from improved automation. We propose a framework that leverages computer vision (CV) and analytics to estimate building damage cost using earth observation data. We posit a problem of detection (building detection) and classification (damage level). However, we are interested in computational efficiency as a cost control measure as many of these algorithms must process large images, and likely run in cloud environments using public funds. Thus, we propose to address the detection and classification problem in one (end-to-end) pass by formulating it as a semantic segmentation problem where the network learns both location, spatial extent, and certain semantics. In our case we are interested on combining the semantics of building/no-building with damage type (*e.g.* no damage, minor damage, etc.). In addition, we need to distinguish damage caused by a natural disaster vs. already existing damage.

U-Nets [8] have shown success in many image analysis tasks. They are the *de facto* semantic segmentation architecture in remote sensing. We have modified the standard U-Net architecture to simultaneously process two images to localize buildings and estimate damage in one pass. This dual image processing allows the network to extract features that encode changes pertinent to damage. After this step, fiscal costs of the damage are estimated using a pixel-based financial model. The ability to rapidly project and damage estimates using different coordinate systems is critical to summarize damage assessment results (*e.g.* United States National Grid coordinate system, county level, zip code, etc.). In particular, the U.S. National Grid is utilized by government agencies to visualize and describe different information streams during and after disaster response. Integration of the output from CV automated assessment techniques into this coordinate system speeds up the analysis process and aids in providing fast, accurate, safely obtained, damage summaries. As part of this work, we introduce a novel web application that uses satellite imagery to estimate and summarize the fiscal damage to a region impacted by a natural disaster as shown in Fig. 1. This tool can efficiently reduce the fiscal evaluation processes required by government agencies, and in turn, accelerate the relief of affected regions.

2   Related Work

Several studies have used tiled, pre- and post-disaster satellite images to remotely assess the degree of damage sustained by physical structures during and after such events [2–4,20]. Fujita et al. trained Convolutional Neural Networks (CNNs) from scratch to localize buildings and classify whether they had survived or were washed away by the 2011 Tōhoku tsunami [2]. Xu et al. compared the performance of four AlexNet architectures in detecting whether buildings suffered any level of damage [3], following one of three major earthquakes. This study originally sought to classify post-disaster buildings based on the severity of damage observed, but the authors abandoned this approach due to noisy assessments in their dataset. Doshi et al. [4] applied a framework for change detection over larger, gridded regions, using CNNs, to quantify the impact of one flooding and

Fig. 1. Pixel-based financial damage assessment application.

one fire event. Their work covered roads and buildings but left the extension of other natural or man-made structures for future exploration.

Conversely, other studies explore the merits of only using post-disaster satellite images for remote damage detection [6] as high-quality, pre-disaster satellite images will not always be available for every region impacted by a significant natural disaster. Finally, Ji *et al.* [6] used a SqueezeNet architecture [7] on post-disaster satellite images to detect whether physical structures had collapsed following the 2010 Haiti earthquake. In contrast to this related work, our study takes the model outputs one step further—applying spatiotemporal property value estimates to produce region-by-region, dollar-value damage estimations according to the United States National Grid (USNG).

3 Damage Assessment Using Satellite Images and Computer Vision

3.1 Web Application Pipeline

Processing begins by ingesting satellite images of an area before and after a natural disaster has occurred. These images are then fed into a damage segmentation model to return a pixel level damage estimate. Financial costs are then estimated according to the damage estimate, aggregated according to USNG coordinates, and displayed via an interactive visualization. Figure 2 includes the before/after input images, the damage estimate pixel prediction output and the final interactive USNG cost visualization.

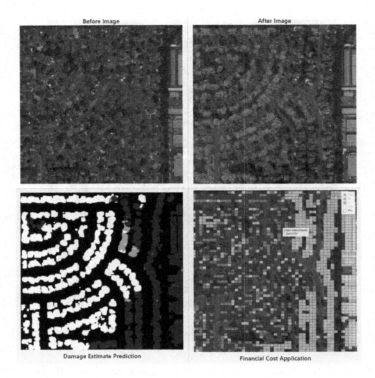

Fig. 2. Application workflow

3.2 U-Net Architecture

As the goal of this endeavor was to develop an interactive application for damage assessment, minimizing the prediction time during model inference was emphasized. Creating separate models for building localization and classification would have significantly increased the time from input to output, and thus, compute cost. This led to the creation a single model to simultaneously perform localization and classification.

Due to its success in the domain of image segmentation, a U-Net architecture was decided on for this project [8]. Normally, the standard U-Net architecture takes an image as input and returns that same image segmented into regions based on the class semantics specified during the network initialization. With this structure, only one image can be processed at a time, which would have required the use of two U-Nets - one to generate masks for the buildings and another to generate damage predictions. To remedy this issue, we created a U-Net architecture with an additional encoder branch, allowing for dual image input. This not only streamlined the inference process, but enhanced the training process as well. Through this method, the network was able to learn the difference between the pre- and post-disaster images, and therefore more effectively classified the level of damage. EfficientNet is used as the backbone for the U-Net.

The input for the network consisted of pre- and post-disaster image tensors of shape (1024, 1024, 3). During the encoder stage, the images were simultaneously processed by the network, each image convolving through separate layers, but sharing the same kernel weights. At each step of the decoder stage, the layers were concatenated with the difference between the outputs of the pre- and post-disaster image encoder layers. The output of the model was a tensor of shape (1024, 1024, 5), with each channel in the final dimension representing one of the distinct classes (five total classes). For joint building and damage detection, we considered five classes: No Damage, Minor Damage, Major Damage, and Destroyed plus one class for a background. The indices of the maximum values across this axis were returned to receive the predicted class for each pixel of the image. This resulted in a tensor of shape (1024, 1024) where each pixel is a distinct class. A visual representation of the network is shown in Fig. 3.

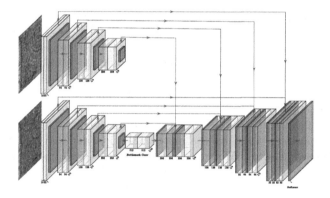

Fig. 3. U-Net architecture used for damage assessment.

3.3   U-Net Training

One of the main challenges in damage assessment is the unbalanced training data - the number of instances in certain classes of interest is very large (*e.g.* no damage or not-a-building) and others can be rare (*e.g.* completely destroyed or major damage). Our training set images contained a significant amount of class imbalance [1]. To address this we took a few different measures during training.

The loss functions consisted of a combination of generalized Dice loss [11] and cross entropy with class weights. Using weights with cross entropy allowed us to place a greater penalty on the misclassification of certain classes to encourage the network to focus on under represented classes. The drawback to weighted cross entropy is that it tends to be overly sensitive to any change in class weights. Combining this function with Dice loss allowed a smoother convergence, while still focusing on correctly predicting the under represented classes. Originally, predictive performance on minor and major damage was poor; therefore, any image containing pixels in either of these classes was oversampled to assist in learning. By implementing these changes, the model was able to significantly improve its ability to delineate between the Minor and Major Damage classes. These results are further shown in Table 1.

4   Financial Modeling Process

4.1   United States National Grid Mapping

The United States National Grid (USNG) is a hierarchical grid system adopted in 2009 as the standard for disaster response operational maps provided by several government agencies [12]. These grids are defined at various levels of precision, the smallest grids being one square meter in area and the largest covering six degrees latitude by eight degrees longitude. The grid lines follow latitude and longitude lines and essentially provide a 15 character reference system over-top of the Universal Transverse Mercator (UTM) coordinate system. The USNG is for all intents and purposes a subset of the Military Grid Reference System (MGRS), the USNG being defined over the United States and the MGRS the entire world. While shape-files of the USNG exist [13], importable python libraries which allow for fast plotting of grid polygon coordinates are not readily available. The *mgrs* library is the nearest python package [14] that is made use of in this effort. This library allows fast conversion of lat/lon coordinates into the MGRS coordinate grid reference system down to one meter precision and, inversely, returns the lat/lon of the southwest corner of a particular MGRS grid. Polygon lat/lon coordinates of each grid coordinate is not provided within the function, as the C library on which it is built, GeoTrans, does not provide this functionality [15]. Utilizing the *mgrs* library and knowledge of the MGRS/USNG coordinate system, a function was developed to determine polygon coordinates of USNG grids to a high degree of precision.

The approach for obtaining grid polygon coordinates was as follows: (1) the southwestern coordinate of a particular grid was found using *mgrs*, (2) using the regular repetition of grid main group and easting/northing values, the grids directly north, northeast, and east of the grid of interest were identified, (3) once these adjacent grids were known, *mgrs* was utilized to determine the lat/lons of the southwest corner of each of these grids, thereby obtaining the lat/lon positions of the four corners of the particular grid of interest. This approach was applied at all levels of precision within the USNG system with minor variations.

Edge cases exist for the present approach, some of which proved difficult to resolve perfectly. Easily managed cases consisted of changes at precision levels below ten kilometers at the edge of main group grid boundaries. These take the form of an easting or northing value ending in nine (e.g., "9", or "9999"). These cases were resolved by moving to the appropriate adjacent main group and zeroing out the affected easting or northing value. More difficult edge cases existed within the changing of Grid Zone Designation (GZD) zones, as these changes alter the main group letter progression pattern. These issues were resolved by using an approximation for longitudinal cross-over values as these GZD zone changes occur along regular longitudinal lines. While not perfectly accurate for all levels of precision, this assumption was sufficient for fast visualization purposes.

4.2   Projecting Computer Vision Outputs to the U.S. National Grid

Once building polygons were found using the U-Net based approach described earlier, the *mgrs* module was applied to the centroid of each and the lat/lons polygons of each USNG grid were obtained using the plotting function for all precision levels as described earlier. The latitude and longitude values of the USNG polygons were then converted to image pixel coordinates. This was done using the resolution of the uploaded images and the inputted image lat/lon values to determine a change in latitude/longitude per pixel and then scaling and translating each point in the USNG polygons. Linear interpolation was done to connect the USNG polygon corners within the image coordinates. However, this method was not always sufficient. The damage model tended to connect nearby buildings into a single, large building. This resulted in centroids which represented groups of buildings and an inaccurate listing of the USNG grids present in the image. To combat this, the obtained polygons were further subdivided into smaller polygons along their largest dimensions until the width of any polygon was less than a ten meter real world distance. This ensured that when taking the centroids of each polygon all of the ten meter precision level USNG grids within the image are identified. An image of the subdivided polygons is shown in Fig. 4.

4.3   Financial Model

To estimate the expected cost associated with predicted damage levels, a simple financial model was developing using a pixel area based approach based on building square footage. Real-estate companies like Zillow provide price per square footage costs for each zip-code. We used the 2018 Zillow Home Value Index (ZHVI) [16] as a proxy value. The centroids of each building were used to tag an appropriate zipcode for each building using data and an API provided by the United States Census Bureau [17]. This was done through a series of conversions from lat/lons to GeoIDs to county tract, and then finally to zip-code. With square footage costs in place for each building, various models were attempted. The final model is shown in Eq. 1.

$$buildingcost = \frac{\$\big/sqft}{zipcode} * sqft * 2 * damagefactor \qquad (1)$$

The identified ZHVI cost per square-foot is multiplied by the square footage of the footprint of the building and by a damage factor which is based upon the damage classes within the competition, *i.e.* No damage (0), minor damage (0.5), major damage (0.8), destroyed (1). The square footage of the building

Fig. 4. Subdivided Polygons

footprint is multiplied by two to account for multiple stories. The particular values of the damage factors and number of stories were obtained by roughly validating the estimates against county property damage costs obtained from the National Oceanic and Atmospheric Administration (NOAA) [18]. We used a few counties that had been impacted by natural disasters to establish comparison between our imagery and the NOAA data. The model provided here was tuned to best correspond with the property damage estimate data, providing estimates accurate to at least the same order of magnitude. Figure 5 shows the overall pixel-based financial model using the computer vision resulting artifacts.

5   Damage Assessment Results

5.1   U-Net Performance and Comparison with Mask R-CNN

We evaluated the proposed U-Net architecture using subsets of the xBD dataset. The xBD dataset contains images across 19 natural disasters consisting of events such as volcanic eruptions, fires, floods, hurricanes, etc. The dataset also introduces a Joint Damage Scale, which is an attempt to create consistency by having a unified damage scale across natural disasters [1]. The dataset is conveniently provided with pre-split train, holdout, and test image sets. We combined the holdout and test sets into a unified test set to provide greater confidence in our performance. Rather than having a specifically hold-out validation set, we opted

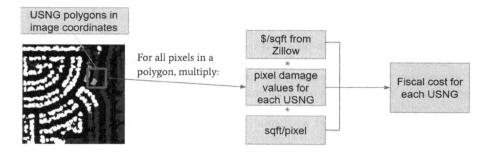

Fig. 5. Pixel based financial model

to use a random subset of the training set for validation after every epoch. While the results were not as consistent as having a singular validation set, it helped to alleviate any sort of bias in the results due to the heavy class imbalance present in the training set.

Minimal pre-processing was needed for the dataset. Each pre- and post-disaster image pair was associated with a JSON file containing a list of polygons representing the locations of the buildings within the images. Each of these polygons was also linked to a label containing the post-disaster damage level. We used these polygon coordinates to create image masks for each set of images. The resulting masks were of shape (1024, 1024, 5), with the final dimension consisting of binary numbers, representing of the presence of a particular class in the relative pixel. Table 1 shows the overall performance achieved with the proposed U-Net compared to an earlier version without the described training optimizations and to the xBD baseline that included a two-step (building localization and damage classification) approach. Final F1 scores were calculated using a 70/30 weighting between macro localization and classification scores, respectively.

Table 1. Proposed method performance for damage assessment

Metric	Our model	Our model without training opt.	xBD Baseline
F1 - Score	**0.616**	0.448	0.265
F1 - Localization	**0.808**	0.751	N/A
F1 - No Damage	**0.813**	0.688	0.663
F1 - Minor Damage	**0.365**	0.165	0.144
F1 - Major Damage	**0.476**	0.27	0.009
F1 - Destroyed	0.701	**0.704**	0.466

In parallel, we also investigated Mask R-CNN [9] as an alternative to U-Net in order to understand the value and efficacy of the proposed U-Net framework. Mask-RCNN solves multi-bounding box problems and semantic segmentation independently, which efficiently solves the task of instance segmentation. It is a simple model that combines two extremely powerful existing models together - Faster R-CNN and semantic segmentation. As in the case of U-Net we were interested on establishing a one-pass end-to-end flow where pre-/post-event images are simultaneously processed. To do so, we combined both images to get 6-channel input image for damage detection. Experimentation with semantic segmentation in place of instance segmentation was also conducted. We used pre-trained weights initially trained on the same model for detecting buildings. Overall, Mask R-CNN struggled with small footprint buildings and found to not be as effective as U-Net. Figure 6 shows a visual comparison between the proposed approach and Mask R-CNN – colored portions indicate building locations, with red indicating the building was destroyed. Overall, we observed a substantial qualitative performance gain using the U-Net model over Mask R-CNN. We did not pursue obtaining comparable numeric performance metrics between the models due to high training costs and objectively better qualitative performance differences.

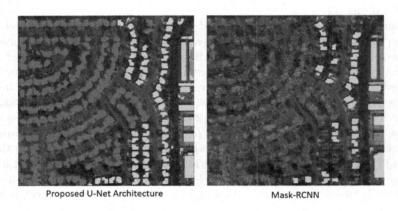

Proposed U-Net Architecture   Mask-RCNN

Fig. 6. Comparison between the proposed 2-encoder U-Net architecture and Mask-RCNN for building damage assessment.

5.2   Large-Scale Visualization

To demonstrate the USNG mapping and financial model on a larger geographic region as compared to the single image application in Fig. 1, a large-scale visualization was produced utilizing the xBD training data[1]. First, building centroids were run through the *mgrs* module to identify the list of USNGs represented by the data for a particular disaster. Polygons for each USNG were then obtained using the developed mapping function. The financial cost for each building was calculated using the financial formula described above and these values summed

---

[1]   A partial visualization is publicly hosted at https://ermlickw.github.io/.

for each USNG at each level of precision. A color coding scheme was provided to quickly visualize costs associated with each grid, with darker colors indicating greater cost. The xBD images were also placed within the visualization in their correct geographic positions, with blank spaces indicating no image data. An interactive toolbar was provided to select and/or hide each level of precision. A Bokeh visualization of the resulting calculations is provided in Fig. 7.

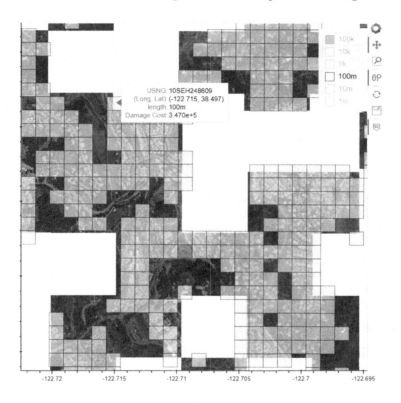

Fig. 7. Bokeh xBD usng visualization

5.3 Performance

Computation speed and estimation accuracy were a principal concerns in the application design. The application was hosted on Amazon Web Services (AWS) on a single core, dual threaded t3a.small instance. Damage assessment was performed with frozen weights in approximately 5 s per image. The financial modeling and rendering process was performed in approximately 20 s. Implementation on four core machines has seen total processing times around 10 s with the use of multiprocessing. The estimations appear to be roughly representative of damage estimates at the 10 m level of precision and above. While computing at the one meter level of precision is theoretically possible, issues with ground sampling distance of the images being greater than a single meter render the results inaccurate and an unreasonable computational time is required.

6   Conclusions

This paper sets out the design and implementation of a proof-of-concept natural disaster geospatial damage assessment application. Various modeling techniques were explored to automatically locate and classify building damage from satellite images by detecting changes between pre- and post-disaster imagery. We presented a modified U-Net architecture that allows one-pass end-to-end image analysis. In addition, we described some of the training methodologies established to handle training data imbalance for the problem of damage assessment. A pixel based financial model and a mapping function for the United States National grid was proposed. These aspects were integrated together into an application which allows fast identification and visualization of damage costs associated with a region to expedite and inform relief efforts. The financial analysis model is based on several assumptions which help simplify the model as economic loss data has heavy variance with respect to the region and type of disaster. Additional considerations such as transportation, obstructions, and demolition costs, raw material price fluctuations, building types (e.g., residential vs. industrial), and the like are all factors that may be included in the financial model and is left as future work. Being able to identify materials using other image modalities like SWIR or incorporate other semantic features into our proposed framework are other avenues for improvement.

References

1. Gupta, R., et al.: xBD: A dataset for assessing building damage from satellite imagery. arXiv:1911.09296 [cs.CV] (2019)
2. Fujita, A., Sakurada, K., Imaizumi, T., Ito, R., Hikosaka, S., Nakamura, R.: Damage detection from aerial images via convolutional neural networks. In: 2017 Fifteenth IAPR International Conference on Machine Vision Applications (MVA), pp. 5–8, Nagoya, Japan, IEEE (2017)
3. Xu, J., Lu, W., Li, Z., Khaitan, P., Zaytseva, V.: Building damage detection in satellite imagery using convolutional neural networks. arXiv:1910.06444 [cs.CV] (2019)
4. Doshi, J., Basu, S., Pang, G.: From satellite imagery to disaster insights. arXiv:1812.07033 [cs.CV] (2018)
5. Krizhevsky, A., Sutskever, I., Hinton, G.E.: Imagenet classification with deep convolutional neural networks. Commun. ACM **60**(6), 84–90 (2017)
6. Ji, M., Liu, L., Buchroithner, M.: Identifying collapsed buildings using post-earthquake satellite imagery and convolutional neural networks: a case study of the 2010 haiti earthquake. Remote Sens. **10**(11), 1689 (2018)
7. Iandola, F.N., Han, S., Moskewicz, M.W., Ashraf, K., Dally, W.J., Keutzer, K.: SqueezeNet: AlexNet-level accuracy with 50x fewer parameters and <0.5MB model size. arXiv:1602.07360 [cs.CV] (2016)

8. Ronneberger, O., Fisher, P., Brox, T.: U-Net: Convolutional networks for biomedical image segmentation. arXiv:1505.04597 [cs.CV] (2015)
9. He, K., Gkioxari, G., Dollar, P., Girshick, R.: Mask R-CNN: Facebook AI Research (FAIR) arXiv:1703.06870 [cs.CV] (2018)
10. Waleed, A.: Mask R-CNN for object detection and instance segmentation on Keras and TensorFlow https://github.com/matterport/MaskRCNN
11. Sudre, C.H., et al.: Generalised dice overlap as a deep learning loss function for highly unbalanced segmentations. In: Cardoso, M.J., et al. (eds.) DLMIA/ML-CDS -2017. LNCS, vol. 10553, pp. 240–248. Springer, Cham (2017). https://doi.org/10. 1007/978-3-319-67558-9_28
12. Clinton County Ohio, United States National Grid. http://www. clintoncountyohgis.org/Maps/MapsIndex/Pages/MapsU/...united_states_ national_grid.html (2020)
13. Federal Geographic Data Committee, United States National Grid. https://www. fgdc.gov/usng (2020)
14. Howard Butlet, mgrs. https://pypi.org/project/mgrs/ (2011)
15. National Geospatial-Inteligence Agency, MSP Geotrans Assistance. https://earth-info.nga.mil/GandG/update/index.php?action=home (2020)
16. Zillow Research, Zillow Home Value Index. https://www.zillow.com/research/ data/ (2018)
17. United States Census Bureau, Geography Program. https://www.census.gov/ programs-surveys/geography.html (2020)
18. National Ocean and Atomsphereic Administration, Billion-Dollar Weather and Climate Disasters: Events. https://www.ncdc.noaa.gov/billions/events (2020)
19. AI for Humanitarian Assistance and Disaster Relief, xView2unet. https://github. com/canktech/xview2unet (2020)
20. Ortiz, B., et al.: Improving Community Resiliency and Emergency Response with Artificial Intelligence. In: ISCRAM (2020)

Understanding Flooding Detection Using Overhead Imagery - Lessons Learned

Abdullah Said[1], Omar Shaat[1], Po-Hsuan Su[1], Philip Bogden[2], Robert Kraig[1], and Marc Bosch[2]($\boxtimes$)

[1] Department of Statistics, George Mason University, Fairfax, VA 22030, USA
[2] Accenture Federal Services, Arlington, VA 22203, USA
`marc.bosch.ruiz@accenturefederal.com`

Abstract. Floods are one of the most devastating and costly natural disasters, posing a significant threat to human life and property, and necessitating systematic and timely response to flood risks. While most floods cannot be prevented, they can be detected, and a quick response can greatly reduce the consequences. Recent advancements in artificial intelligence, computing power, and earth observation data availability has enabled researchers to use computer vision and satellite/aerial imagery to help assess ground conditions and decision-makers' prioritization of response efforts. This paper investigates different algorithmic design decisions to determine best flood line detection performance. We also investigated the value of adding non-imagery proxy data used for flood prediction into a computer vision pipeline, which includes the combination of Height Above Nearest Drainage (HAND)-based inundation map data and aerial imagery to train a semantic segmentation convolutional neural network. In our experiments, we trained several U-Net shaped fully convolutional neural networks using aerial imagery of hurricane Harvey retrieved from the National Oceanic and Atmospheric Administration (NOAA) repositories, and rasterized HAND map data retrieved from The Texas Advanced Computing Center (TACC). The paper contributes by showcasing the results of combining both a hydrologic and computer vision method for flood detection.

Keywords: Natural disaster · Flooding detection · U-Net · HAND · Remote sensing

1 Introduction

According to the Centre for Research on the Epidemiology of Disasters (CRED), 280 floods occurred globally from 2008–2018, making flooding the most common natural disaster by far, and one of the most devastating [7]. As a result of climate change and increasing global surface temperatures, the possibility of more floods, droughts, and increased intensity of storms has increased. More powerful storms are likely to develop as a result of an increase in the amount of water vapor being evaporated in the atmosphere. Climate change is increasing the amount of heat in the atmosphere, resulting in warmer ocean surface temperatures which

G. Bebis et al. (Eds.): ISVC 2020, LNCS 12509, pp. 696–706, 2020.
https://doi.org/10.1007/978-3-030-64556-4_54

can eventually lead to increased wind speeds in tropical storms. Also, as a result of excessive rainfall, rising sea levels expose higher locations not usually subjected to the power of the sea and to the erosive forces of waves and currents. Natural disasters' impact on people and property can be highly variable from year-to-year. Although it is a relatively unexplored topic within computer vision, recently there has been several scholarly activities exploring the application of computer vision (along with wireless sensor data technology) to help equip flood management authorities with flood response and management solutions [1–4]. The state-of-the-art computer vision flood detection models from overhead use convolutional neural networks (CNNs) to learn to extract flooded areas [1,4]. Other work include use of other sensors like Synthetic Aperture Radar (SAR) combined with neural networks [3]. Authors stressed how auxiliary data could potentially lead to more representation, and therefore more accurate results.

In this paper, we have studied how different algorithmic design decisions impact performance of flood line detection models. For example, one of the bottlenecks in many computer vision frameworks which rely on supervised learning is the acquisition of annotated data that can be used as training data. In this work we investigate the effect of using available annotations from publicly available sources (e.g. OpenStreetMaps) compared to the added cost of custom data annotation. In addition, we have investigated the added value to additional sources of data complementary to imagery and the effect of training a network from scratch versus a network which is pre-trained on completely unrelated tasks with ground-based imagery. This paper offers a new perspective on the problem of flood detection using image analysis augmented with orthogonal data that encodes the height above nearest drainage point. Our intent is to investigate the effect of adding a terrain model to complement the imagery. Our research revolving around flood detection focused on two domains. (1) information regarding terrain properties such as digital elevation models (DEMs), floodplains, digital terrain maps, or other hydrologic modelling data sources; (2) the second domain consisting of high-altitude aerial imagery. Our proposed solution is to build a scalable U-Net based architecture that combines image data and terrain-related information. We focused our experiments in the U.S. States of Texas and North Carolina post Hurricane Harvey and Florence respectively.

2   Computer Vision Model

We approach the problem of flood line detection as a semantic segmentation problem. As such, we selected U-Net architecture as our base neural network [5]. U-Net was originally proposed for biomedical segmentation, but it quickly gained attention in other domains of image analysis. We selected an EfficientNet B2 encoder backbone due to its recent success [6]. Since in our domain label scarcity is a prevalent issue we needed an architecture that can leverage strong use of data augmentations. Ronneberger *et al.* proposed the U-Net architecture as a network that can use data more efficiently, while addressing shortcomings of predecessor architectures regarding localization. U-Net consists of a symmetric encoder-decoder structure, which enables precise localization and assignment of a class label to each pixel in the image. Unlike many other visual tasks, the U-Net's architecture is more organized, works with very few images, produces more accurate segmentations, and can take less than a second to process a 512 × 512 image on a consumer grade GPU [5]. In addition, we used Lovasz-Softmax loss, which is tailored to our accuracy metric and has shown better performance than the traditional cross-entropy loss [13].

3 Integration of Terrain-Based Models with U-Nets

Terrain-based approaches for inundation mapping have proven to produce accurate maps from a known streamflow and carefully created data layers. One of these data sources is the Height Above Nearest Drainage (HAND) technique. HAND is a terrain model that normalizes input national elevation datasets (NED) according to the local relative elevations/heights found along a drainage network. It encodes information regarding elevation data, discharge-height relationships, and streamflow inputs. In this work, we were interested on studying the impact of combining HAND data with imagery for inland flood detection. HAND data is represented as a rasterized grid map of a particular location, containing the vertical distance between a specific location (grid-cell), and its nearest stream reach. The calculation of the HAND map requires several data inputs from the USGS National Elevation Dataset (NED) and USGS National Hydrography Dataset (NHD). The NHD represents the water drainage network of the United States with features such as rivers, streams, canals, lakes, ponds, coastline, dams, and stream gages. As a part of the standardized approach to river classification, a particular length of a stream, river, or arm of the sea extending up into the land, and either located between two tributaries or between a tributary and the start (source) or end (sink, delta) is defined as a "reach". Moreover, the contributing sub-catchment pertains to the area that contributes only and directly to this river reach. The upstream watershed is related to the entire upstream area that is hydrologically connected to this reach. Figure 1 shows an illustration of how reach and catchment relate. In the NHD, reaches are represented by a polyline, and assigned a unique common identifier (COMID). To proceed with calculating the "nearest drainage" portion of HAND, the contributing sub-catchment for each reach is rasterized to match the spatial resolution of the DEM in use [8–10]. Therefore, HAND is a series of raster calculations:

- Rasterization of contributing catchment to a defined outlet given the supporting DEM.
- Reclassification of raster to match the ID of outlet.
- Identification of in-stream and out-stream cells using flow line vectors.
- Conversion from flow to stage given a rating curve.
- Creation of reclassification table relating reach ID and stage.
- Reclassification of catchment mask into a water level mask to create HAND raster.

– Subtraction of HAND raster from the water-level raster yielding a water-level above-surface raster. Negative values are set to 0.

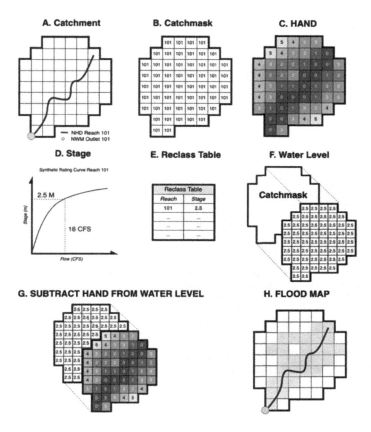

Fig. 1. The HAND methodological workflow.

Once we obtained HAND data for a specific region (guided by the imagery geolocation), we proceeded to combine HAND data and imagery, which involves augmenting the images by stacking an extra "channel" to the input tensor, which included the RGB channels and the HAND output values contained within the HAND images. As for our algorithm and architecture, we used a U-Net architecture, as mentioned earlier, and experimented using different encoders. The EfficientNet B-2 backbone proved to be the best suited for our needs since it has a scaling method that uniformly scales all dimensions of depth/width/resolution using a simple yet highly effective compound coefficient, which benefits fusion of different inputs. Moreover, we applied a series of pre-processing data augmentations and transformations including image rotations, brightness/contrast adjustments, and normalization applied per separate to RGB and HAND channels. Figure 3 shows the scheme followed to merge RGB and HAND data.

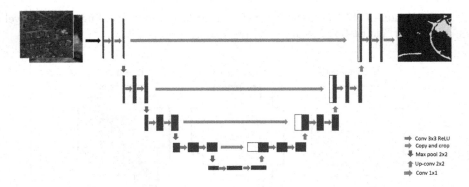

Fig. 2. U-Net architecture used combining HAND and RGB data.

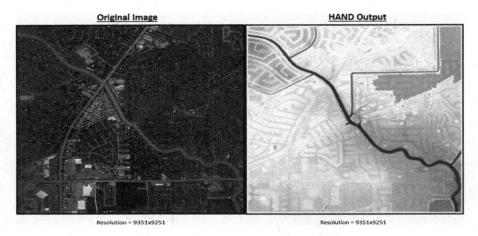

Fig. 3. Examples of aligned imagery and HAND data.

4   Results

4.1   Datasets

As mentioned earlier, aerial imagery was obtained from NOAA NGS Coastal Image Services. In addition, we leveraged OpenStreetMap (OSM) labels to generate an initial training set - we were interested in reducing cost of training set production. We used the geolocation information from the images to extract OpenStreetMap annotated features as polygons and create image masks that served as training data. OSM is an editable open source project maintained by volunteers and distributed under the Open Data Commons Open Database License. OSM offers a breadth of high quality and high-precision features of our planet. Using their publicly available API we were able to create label points using their data, and define polygons around water bodies in our aerial images [14]. Figure 4 shows an example of an aligned image and OSM (water sources) mask. In order to identity if the regions were flooded due to hurricane Harvey, OSM was applied to label the natural water areas in the NOAA images. We were able to find the corresponding features using the Longitude and Latitude information embedded within the images. Moreover, the natural water areas shown in OSM were retrieved as polygons filled with integer values, where 1 labels the presence of water and 0 labels areas where there is no water present.

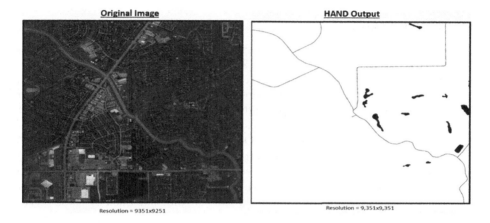

Fig. 4. Examples of aligned imagery and OSM labels of water sources.

Data conditioning - NOAA aerial images consisted of 4 bands and had a 9,351 × 9,351 resolution, while the HAND model output varied based on the area it covered. The HAND image covering the Harvey affected area had a 61,439 × 67,714 resolution. On the other hand, OSM labels generation was flexible based on the coordinates specified while querying the API. Moreover, our goal was to have 1,000 × 1,000 input tensors passed into our neural network, and ended up using 1,024 × 1,024 tensors after padding and tiling. The HAND output was originally saved as a GeoTiff image file, loading in as an array of float values with geo referenced information. However, the HAND images had a different coordinate system than that of which the NOAA imagery had. In order to start tiling both the HAND mosaics and the NOAA images, we had to first generate projections of the HAND images for the same covering regions as NOAA imagery. Therefore, the HAND images were converted to the WGS 84 coordinates system to match the NOAA imagery, and were then projected to match the NOAA images' Latitudes and Longitudes, and further upscale the resolution after projection to match the NOAA tiling images' resolutions. After we had consistent 9,351 × 9,351 resolution HAND model output/images, NOAA images, and OSM labels, we started tiling the images down to 1,024 × 1,024. To ensure that all tiles' resolution was equal, the algorithm added padding where necessary.

In the final stages, we wanted to make sure that the model generalized well on other types of water/floods, and that it was not overfitting to the type of water and floods contained within the Texas/Harvey area. Therefore, we retrieved NOAA imagery for Hurricane Florence which occurred in the Carolinas and conducted the same data preparation procedures and tested the model's performance.

4.2 Experiments

Our analysis considered the following design variables: (1) data supplementation with an orthogonal feature (HAND), (2) annotation method (manual vs. pre-existing crowdsourced labels), and (3) training set used (flooded vs. non-flooded conditions). Because the imagery obtained during flood conditions had no OSM labels available, we were not able to conduct an exhaustive exploration of the last two design variables independently. Instead, we trained water-detection models in three different ways: (a) using OSM annotation on a dataset of 13,294 non-disaster images, (b) training with a much smaller dataset of 123 manually-annotated images from Hurricane Harvey, and (c) a combination of these two procedures, wherein the model trained from experiment (a) was subsequently fine-tuned to fit the manually-annotated Harvey imagery. Each of these methods was implemented both with and without HAND inclusion, for a total of six different segmentation models.

All six models were initialized with ImageNet weights, and all layers were fully trainable. All six datasets incorporated augmentation using the image transformations described previously. We validated each experiment using 41 Harvey images. In each case, a final model was chosen to maximize validation-set IOU at the end of an epoch.

Table 1 shows performance comparison for all three experiments on a separate holdout set of 41 Harvey images. We observe that inclusion of manually annotated flooded imagery is essential for model success, as our models trained on OSM-annotated non-flood images scored very poorly on Intersection-over-Union (IOU). We assume this is contributed to inconsistency in OSM-annotation since there are some bodies of water that share similar properties to flooded water in terms of color. The examples of inconsistency we observed were that ponds may be completely untagged, bridges over water being tagged as water, and the width of rivers and streams being thinly represented. A comparison of results of experiments (b) and (c) indicates that training on OSM-annotated non-disaster imagery could actually hurt performance; our model performed better when training started from ImageNet weights directly than it did when the extra step of modifying ImageNet weights to fit the OSM non-disaster imagery was inserted. This too suggests that poor OSM label quality was compromising our task results.

Comparing the performance of adding HAND data as an input did not seem to bring overall performance improvement and in instances it seemed to worsen

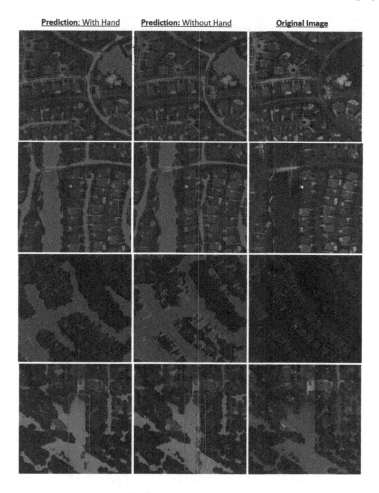

Fig. 5. Examples where RGB+HAND outperformed RGB-only model.

the outputs. We believe that urban activity caused by temporal discrepancy between HAND data production and imagery acquisition introduced noise into the network that negatively impacted its performance, as it can be seen in Fig. 6. Nevertheless, we observed that adding HAND data seemed to help resolve cases of wet pavement vs. actual flooding and other areas where there was a noticeable improvement. Figure 5 shows different scene examples where RGB+HAND outperformed RGB-only cases. There is a task ahead of manually cleaning HAND data to filter out confusion. All in all, we believe that HAND is a good supplementary data source to improve flood line detection. However, perhaps it can be better used as a post-processing guide in a framework like conditional random fields where HAND consistency can guide flood line refinement, or extend a second encoder that independently extracts features from HAND and a single decoder combines features from both sides (RGB and HAND) as opposed to the simple stacking of inputs. Lessons learned. These activities will be the focus of our future research endeavors.

Table 1. Test set performance on Intersection-Over-Union (IOU) metric.

Training procedure	IOU, Image only	IOU, Image + HAND
(a) OSM-labeled non-flood imagery only	0.36	0.34
(b) Manually-labeled flood imagery only	**0.80**	**0.80**
(c) OSM non-flood followed by manual flood	0.76	0.76

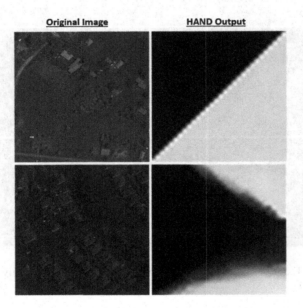

Fig. 6. Examples of mismatches between HAND and imagery.

Another increasingly important factor for Human Assistance and Disaster Relief (HADR) type applications is the development cost. Many of these capabilities are developed with public funds, so being able to find a good compromise between cost and performance is critical. For the first experiment using the non-flooded labeled imagery from OSM, we trained using a total of 13,294 images at a 1,024 × 1,024 resolution, which took about a day and a half to train a 25 epochs model. However, the second and third experiments used a total of 123 manually annotated flooded imagery and corresponding HANDs at the same resolution, and took only 2–3 h to train 25 epochs while resulting in significantly improved performance when compared to the first experiment. The primary cost for this increase in performance was the labor cost associated with manually annotating flooded imagery and preparing a good quality dataset for the model. However, if we are to assess the marginal cost associated with these experiments, despite manual annotation's cost, it could very much compensate the additional cost that would have been incurred if a larger model was ran using automatically labeled images from a resource such as OSM. In our experiments, we observed that targeted annotation efforts are important, thus, cost aware methodologies to monitor data annotation exercises [12] are critical, resulting in long term cost savings during model development.

5 Conclusions

In this work we investigated several design decisions during algorithmic development for the problem of flood line detection. We evaluated the trade-offs between leveraging open source annotations, targeted annotations, the importance of the pretrained backbone, as well as the value of adding terrain models. We studied the addition of HAND data to complement the analysis of overhead imagery. These results showed that terrain based modeling is useful but requires close examination and filtering. Temporal inconsistencies between urban development and available terrain information will have a negative impact to the model and simple architectures strategies are not enough to overcome this. We also showed the importance and impact that small and targeted annotation efforts can have in overhead image analysis, and can lead to cost savings. We hope that work in the area of human assistance and disaster relief continues and can help local and federal organization and government officials protect lives and property through tackling unprecedented floods (e.g. Where should resources be deployed?).

References

1. Gebrehiwot, A., Hashemi-Beni, L., Thompson, G., Kordjamshidi, P., Langan, T.E.: Deep convolutional neural network for flood extent mapping using unmanned aerial vehicles data. Sensor **19**, 1485–1488 (2019)
2. Sarker, C., Mejias, L., Maire, F., Woodley, A.: Flood mapping with convolutional neural networks using spatio-contextual pixel information. Remote Sens. **11**, 2331 (2019)
3. Kang, W., Xiang, Y., Wang, F., Wan, L.: Flood detection in Gaofen-3 SAR images via fully convolutional networks. Sensors **18**(9), 2915 (2018)
4. Ortiz, B., et al.: Improving community resiliency and emergency response with artificial intelligence. ISCRAM. arXiv:2005.14212 (2020)
5. Ronneberger, O., Fisher, P., Brox, T.: U-Net: convolutional networks for biomedical image segmentation. arXiv:1505.04597 [cs.CV], May 2015
6. Tan, M., Le, Q.V.: EfficientNet: rethinking model scaling for convolutional neural networks. arXiv:1905.1194, November 2019
7. CRED. Natural Disasters 2018. Brussels: CRED (2019)

8. Nobre, A.D., et al.: Height above the nearest drainage - a hydrologically relevant new terrain model. J. Hydrol. **404**(1), 13–29 (2011)
9. Zheng, J.: Height Above Nearest Drainage in Houston, report University of Texas at Austin (2016)
10. Ouellet, C., Lehner, B., Sayre, R., Thieme, M.: A multidisciplinary framework to derive global river reach classifications at high spatial resolution. Environ. Res. Lett. **14**(2), 024003 (2019)
11. Johnson, M., Munasinghe, D., Eyelade, D., Cohen, S.: An integrated evaluation of the national water model - height above nearest drainage flood mapping methodology. Nat. Hazards Earth Syst. Sci. **19**, 2405–2420 (2019)
12. Nassar, J., Pavon, V., Bosch, M., McCulloh, I.: Assessing data quality of annotations with Krippendorff alpha for applications in computer vision. In: AAAI Fall Symposium (2019)
13. Berman, M., Triki, A.R., Blaschko, M.B.: The lovasz-softmax loss: a tractable surrogate for the optimization of the intersection-over-union measure in neural networks. arXiv:1705.08790 [cs], April 2018
14. OpenStreetMap - https://www.openstreetmap.org/

Hyperspectral Image Classification via Pyramid Graph Reasoning

Tinghuai Wang[1]($\boxtimes$) (iD), Guangming Wang[1], Kuan Eeik Tan[1], and Donghui Tan[2]

[1] Huawei Helsinki Research Center, Helsinki, Finland
tinghuaiwang@huawei.com
[2] Huawei Technologies, Shenzhen, China

Abstract. Convolutional neural networks (CNN) have made significant advances in hyperspectral image (HSI) classification. However, standard convolutional kernel neglects the intrinsic connections between data points, resulting in poor region delineation and small spurious predictions. Furthermore, HSIs have a unique continuous distribution along the high dimensional spectrum domain - much remains to be addressed in characterizing the spectral contexts considering the prohibitively high dimensionality and improving reasoning capability in light of the limited amount of labelled data. This paper presents a novel architecture which explicitly addresses these two issues. Specifically, we design an architecture to encode the multiple spectral contextual information in the form of spectral pyramid of multiple embedding spaces. In each spectral embedding space, we propose graph attention mechanism to explicitly perform interpretable reasoning in the spatial domain based on the connection in spectral feature space. Experiments on three HSI datasets demonstrate that the proposed architecture can significantly improve the classification accuracy compared with the existing methods.

1 Introduction

The rapid development of hyperspectral sensors enables the observation of hundreds of continuous bands throughout the electromagnetic spectrum with high spectral resolution. The rich spectral signatures of hyperspectral images (HSIs) facilitate the study of the chemical properties of scene materials remotely. Hyperspectral image classification has consequently been playing an increasingly important role in various fields, such as mining, agriculture, environmental monitoring, and land-cover mapping.

Early methods largely relied on hand-crafted features empirically designed for HSI data which have limited discriminative power. Inspired by the success of deep neural networks (DNN) in natural image classification, deep learning based methods have been proposed for hyperspectral image classification which have significantly boosted the performance thanks to the strong representation capability. The first DNN approach was proposed by Chen *et al.* [5], which utilized stacked autoencoders to learn high-level features. Recurrent Neural Network (RNN) based architecture was proposed by Mou *et al.* [16]. More powerful

G. Bebis et al. (Eds.): ISVC 2020, LNCS 12509, pp. 707–718, 2020.
https://doi.org/10.1007/978-3-030-64556-4_55

end-to-end Convolutional Neural Network (CNN) [4,8,10,12,18] based architectures have advanced the state-of-the-art recently. Lee *et al.* [12] explored local contextual interactions by jointly exploiting local spatio-spectral relationships of neighboring individual pixel vectors. Song *et al.* [18] introduced residual learning [9] to build very deep network for extracting more discriminative features for HSI classification.

Despite of the remarkable performance by the CNN-based methods, they suffer from several drawbacks. Specifically, standard convolutional kernels work in regular receptive fields for feature response, whose weights are fixed given their position within the small convolution window. Such position-determined weights lead to the isotropy of the kernel with respect to the feature attributes of neighboring locations. This limitation of the standard convolutional kernel neglects the intrinsic or extrinsic structural connections between data points, resulting in poor region delineation and small spurious predictions. To address this problem, graph convolutional network (GCN) based approach S^2GCN has been proposed by Qin *et al.* [17] which operated on a graph constructed on the local data points and is able to aggregate and transform feature information from the neighbors of every graph node given their relative spatial distance [21–23,25]. However, there are several limitations of this approach. Firstly, the graph is constructed based on the rigid pixel lattice which inherently limited the scope of interaction between data points. Secondly, the relation between nodes only accounts for their spatial distance neglecting their correlation in the feature space. Furthermore, S^2GCN only conducts reasoning at a single feature space which is potentially limited to the capacity of the early feature extraction block of the network. Thirdly, S^2GCN is a graph-based semi-supervised approach which predicts unlabeled data with the presence of labeled data which potentially harms its accuracy on dataset without any available labels.

To explicitly address the above issues, we presents a novel architecture to encode the multiple spectral contextual information in a hierarchical manner, forming multiple spectral embedding spaces. In multiple spectral embedding spaces, we propose graph attention mechanism to explicitly perform context based reasoning in the spatial domain based on the connection in spectral feature space. Our graphs are dynamically constructed based on the intrinsic structure of the data, *i.e.,* nodes of a same neighborhood are assigned with different importance, enabling thorough interaction between comprising data points while increasing the model capacity. After the graph reasoning, an attention based aggregation reminiscent of *multi-head attention* [19] with focus on specific spectral channels given the contextual scopes is applied on the spectral feature pyramid rather than a simply *averaging* in GAT [20]. This is based on the observation that features from different contextual level carry different degrees of discriminative power for classification. Extracting the key discriminative features from each contextual level and enforcing this information during the aggregation can effectively improve the classification accuracy.

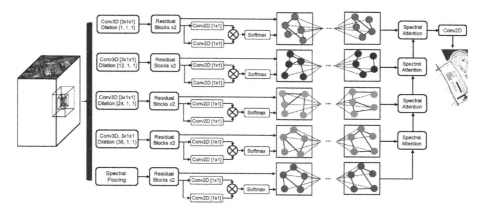

Fig. 1. Illustration of the our spectral pyramid graph attention network (SPGAT).

2   Method

We propose a novel end-to-end graph attention architecture for spectral feature learning and reasoning of HSIs, which consists of mainly two blocks, *i.e.*, spectral feature pyramid learning and graph attention based reasoning, as illustrated in Fig. 1.

2.1   Spectral Pyramid Learning

We propose to utilize *atrous* convolution to probe the HSI signal along the spectral dimension at multiple sampling rates for capturing varying spectral contextual information, forming a spectral pyramid. It brings us mainly two advantages: (1) multiple spectral contextual information is captured without introducing large convolutional kernel or fully connected layer which significantly reduces the number of trainable model parameters and computational complexity (2) large effective fields-of-views is achieved without resorting to resampling features which in turn causes downsampled feature map.

As illustrated in Fig. 2, we adopt 3D convolutions of kernel size $3 \times 1 \times 1$ and dilation rates $\{(1,1,1),(12,1,1),(24,1,1),(36,1,1)\}$ respectively. With the spatial kernel size 1×1, the 3D convolution is equivalent to 1D convolution over the spectral vector at each pixel location. The output $y[s,i,j]$ of the *atrous* convolution at signal location (s,i,j) with a filter $w[k]$ of length K is defined as

$$y(s,i,j) = \sum_{k=1}^{K} x[s+r \cdot k,i,j]w[k] \tag{1}$$

where r indicates the stride with which we sample the input signal, and $r = 1$ corresponds to the standard convolution.

A spectral pooling layer is also proposed to gather the global spectral context. Specifically, the spectral pooling layer consists of [AdaptiveAvgPool3d +

Conv3d[1 × 1 × 1] + BatchNorm3d + ReLU], inspired by [3] in the spatial domain. As illustrated in Fig. 1, the *atrous* spectral pyramid comprises 5 streams, *i.e.*, feature maps from 4 Conv3D with different dilation rates and spectral level features from spectral pooling. The spectral pyramid thus captures spectral contextual information at multiple scales while maintaining a very low computational complexity.

Residual blocks [9] are applied on each feature stream to further aggregate local spatial and spectral contexts and transform feature embeddings. Specifically, two bottleneck modules with filter size (64, 128) respectively and expansion factor of 4 are applied per feature stream.

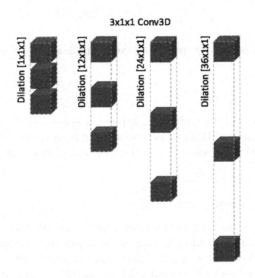

Fig. 2. Illustration of *atrous* convolutional kernels along the spectral dimension.

2.2   Graph Attention Based Reasoning

Consider a graph $\mathcal{G}(\mathcal{V}, \mathcal{E})$ constructed from a set of node features $\mathbf{h} = \{h_1, h_2, \ldots, h_N\} \in \mathbb{R}^d$, where N is the number of nodes and d is the number of features in each node. The graph attention layer generates as its output a new set of node features $\mathbf{h}' = \{h_1', h_2', \ldots, h_N'\} \in \mathbb{R}^{d'}$, $h_i' \in \mathbb{R}^{d'}$. Two 1-D convolutionary layers, $\theta(\cdot)$ and $\phi(\cdot)$ are applied on the input feature map respectively in order to initially transform the input features into two sets of higher-level features while obtaining sufficient expressive power. Unlike the relatively fixed neighboring relation in pixel lattice, the graph attention layer should be able to dynamically adjust to varying graph structures.

Specifically, a data-dependent graph which learn a unique graph for each input feature map is formed by determining the connection as well as its strength between two nodes,

$$\alpha_{i,j} = a(\theta(h_i), \phi(h_j)) \tag{2}$$

where $a(\cdot)$ is an attention mechanism to compute the attention weight of node j to node i.

Here, we utilize the dot product followed by a linear transformation ψ, a LeakyReLU nonlinearity and a *softmax* operation to measure the normalized attention between two nodes in an embedding space,

$$\alpha_{i,j} = \frac{e^{\text{LeakyReLU}(\mathbf{W}_\psi h_i^T \mathbf{W}_\theta^{\mathbf{T}} \mathbf{W}_\phi h_j)}}{\sum_{j=1}^{N} e^{\text{LeakyReLU}(\mathbf{W}_\psi h_i^T \mathbf{W}_\theta^{\mathbf{T}} \mathbf{W}_\phi h_j)}}, \tag{3}$$

where $\mathbf{W}_\theta$, $\mathbf{W}_\phi$ and $\mathbf{W}_\psi$ are the trainable parameters of embedding functions $\theta(\cdot)$, $\phi(\cdot)$ and ψ respectively. To make the attention weights comparable across nodes, they are normalized by *softmax* operation. As opposed to GAT [20], which computes the attention weights based on the concatenation of a pair of features, we compute the feature differences which is more efficient and explicit to characterize the correlation between features.

Finally, the normalized attention weights are used to perform a weighted combination all nodes to obtain a new set of features,

$$h_i^{'} = \text{LeakyReLU}(\sum_{j=1}^{N} \alpha_{i,j} \mathbf{W}_\xi h_j), \tag{4}$$

where $\mathbf{W}_\xi$ indicates the weights of a 1-D convolutionary layer $\xi(\cdot)$ before applying a LeakyReLU nonlinearity.

After obtaining a new set of feature streams from the multiple graph attention layers, we propose an attention based aggregation with focus on specific spectral channels given the contextual scopes, rather than a simply *averaging* in GAT [20]. As illustrated in Fig. 3, spectral attention module takes the feature maps from neighboring contextual levels as input and computes spectral level attention coefficients to guide the upper level feature to focus on certain spectral channels. This is based on the observation that features from different contextual level carry different degrees of discriminative power for classification. Extracting the key discriminative features from each contextual level and enforcing this information during the aggregation can effectively encode the contextual information at multiple scales.

3 Experimental Results

In this section, we conduct extensive experiments on three publicly available hyperspectral image datasets[1], and present results using four metrics including per-class accuracy, overall accuracy (OA), average accuracy (AA), and Kappa coefficient. The network architecture of our proposed SPGAT is identical for

---

[1] http://www.ehu.eus/ccwintco/index.php/Hyperspectral_Remote_Sensing_Scenes.

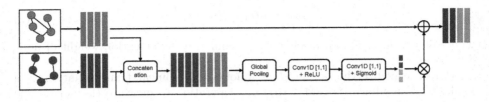

Fig. 3. Illustration of spectral attention module.

all the datasets. Specifically, two graph attention layers per contextual level are used, with graphs constructed on 7 × 7 image patches. Learning rate of 0.001 and Adam optimizer are adopted. We follow [27] for selecting the disjoint training and testing sets. The number of training epochs is set to 500. All the reported accuracies are calculated based on the average of ten training sessions to obtain stable results.

3.1 Datasets

The University of Pavia dataset captured the University of Pavia with the ROSIS sensor in 2001. It consists of 610 × 340 pixels with a spatial resolution of 1.3 m × 1.3 m and has 103 spectral channels in the wavelength range from 0.43 μm to 0.86 μm after removing noisy bands. This dataset includes 9 land-cover classes as listed in Table 1. The false color image and ground-truth map are shown in Fig. 4.

The Indian Pines dataset was collected by Airborne Visible/Infrared Imaging Spectrometer sensor which consists of 145 × 145 pixels with a spatial resolution of 20 m × 20 m and has 220 spectral channels covering the range from 0.4 μm to 2.5 μm. Figure 5 exhibits the false color image and ground-truth map of the Indian Pines dataset. This dataset includes 16 land-cover classes as listed in Table 2.

The Kennedy Space Center dataset which was taken by AVIRIS sensor over Florida with a spectral coverage ranging from 0.4 μm to 2.5 μm, contains 224 bands and 614 × 512 pixels with a spatial resolution of 18 m. This dataset comprises 13 land-cover classes as listed in Table 3, and Fig. 6 exhibits the false color image and ground-truth map.

3.2 Classification Results

We quantitatively and qualitatively evaluate our proposed method and compare with various recent deep learning based methods to demonstrate its effectiveness.

The University of Pavia Dataset. Table 1 presents the quantitative results obtained by different methods on the University of Pavia dataset, where the highest value in each row is highlighted in bold. Our proposed SPGAT outperforms the competing methods on 7 out of 9 categories and exhibits the best overall results, *i.e.*, OA, AA and Kappa. In general, all methods except SSLSTMs [27] and SPGAT fail to capture larger context, which consequentially produce inferior results. SSLSTMs applies LSTM to learn both spatial and spectral features, however it fails to characterize the large scale spectral contexts due to the limitation of LSTM models on high dimension feature. On the contrary, our SPGAT encodes the spectral contexts in a hierarchical manner and utilizes graph attention models to explicitly perform multi-scale inference in the spatial domain based on the connection in spectral feature space.

Figure 4 shows a visual comparison of SPGAT and SSLSTMs on the University of Pavia dataset. We can observe that SSLSTMs suffers from misclassifications even in large regions of the same category, due to the lack of inference in the spatial space as well as the failure to encode the most discriminative spectral features. We can see that our SPGAT is able to produce both accurate and coherent predictions.

The Indian Pines Dataset. Table 2 presents the quantitative results obtained by different methods on the Indian Pines dataset. In addition to tradition methods, we also compare with methods based on graph neural networks, *i.e.*, GCN [11] and S^2GCN [17], to demonstrate the effectiveness of our method. Overall, our method surpasses all the compared methods, with a significant margin of 5.11% comparing to the best competing method S^2GCN. GCN and S^2GCN both construct their graphs based the pixel lattice, whereas S^2GCN encodes the spatial distance between adjacent nodes in graph which enables it to capture the local intrinsic structure in HSI data. However, SPGAT has the advantages over the compared GNN based methods as follows: (a) SPGAT constructs data-driven graph rather than a rigid spatial structure (b) SPGAT assigns adjacency matrix with both connectivities and strengths between nodes which fully characterize their correlation in spectral feature space (c) SPGAT features the multiple spectral contextual graph based inference which enables robustness and accuracy in generalizing to HSI data captured by various sensors.

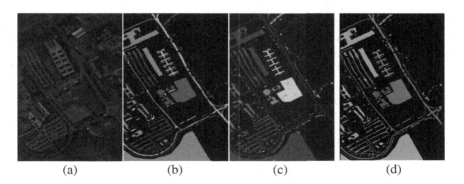

(a)   (b)   (c)   (d)

Fig. 4. The university of Pavia dataset: (a) False color image (b) Groundtruth map (c) Prediction of SSLSTMs [27] (d) Prediction of the proposed SPGAT

Table 1. Per-class accuracy, OA, AA (%), and Kappa coefficient achieved by different methods on the University of Pavia dataset.

Class	R-PCA CNN [14]	PPF-CNN [13]	CD-CNN [12]	SS-CNN [15]	3D-CNN [4]	SSLSTMs [27]	SPGAT
1	92.43	97.42	94.60	97.40	96.72	96.83	**98.60**
2	94.84	95.76	96.00	**99.40**	96.31	98.74	96.11
3	90.89	94.05	95.50	**98.84**	97.15	96.57	97.83
4	93.99	97.52	95.90	99.16	96.16	98.43	**99.23**
5	**100.0**	100.0	100.0	100.0	99.81	99.94	100.0
6	92.86	99.13	94.10	98.70	94.87	99.43	100.0
7	93.89	98.96	96.19	100.0	97.44	99.31	100.0
8	91.18	93.62	88.80	94.57	98.23	97.98	**99.92**
9	99.33	99.60	99.5	99.87	98.04	99.39	100.0
OA	93.87	96.48	96.73	98.41	96.55	98.48	**98.92**
AA	94.38	97.03	95.77	98.22	97.19	98.51	**99.07**
Kappa	–	–	–	–	95.30	97.56	**97.86**

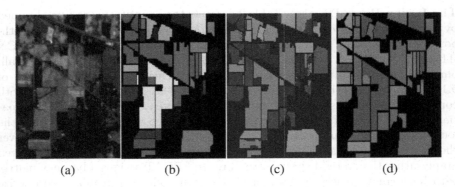

(a)   (b)   (c)   (d)

Fig. 5. Indian Pines dataset: (a) False color image (b) Groundtruth map (c) Prediction of LBMSELM [1] (d) Prediction of the proposed SPGAT.

The Kennedy Space Center Dataset. Table 3 presents the quantitative results obtained by different methods on the Kennedy Space Center dataset. Similar to the results on the University of Pavia dataset, SPGAT produces the best OA accuracy among all compared methods, and SSLSTMs achieves the second best. It is worth-noting that two other graph based approaches, *i.e.*, GCN [11] and ELP-RGF [6] also show promising results compared with traditional methods, which demonstrates the advantage of conducting graph reasoning.

3.3   Ablation Study

In this section, we conduct ablation study on the University of Pavia dataset to investigate the effectiveness of various novel parts of our proposed architecture. To show the importance of generating multiple spectral contextual feature, we remove the branches where the dilation rate is larger than 1, keeping the branch

Table 2. Per-class accuracy, OA, AA (%), and Kappa coefficient achieved by different methods on the Indian Pines dataset

Class	LapSVM [26]	S^{2}SL [7]	SSGEL [2]	GCN [11]	S^{2}GCN [17]	LBMSELM [1]	SPGAT
1	91.81	84.96	**100.0**	20.03	**100.0**	98.03	96.22
2	72.89	70.45	84.72	60.92	92.22	89.97	**99.27**
3	63.45	65.21	84.70	45.99	84.97	65.73	**94.42**
4	86.78	85.90	83.02	37.29	91.11	82.82	**98.43**
5	77.40	87.81	84.05	89.08	**100.0**	81.89	95.86
6	96.39	96.30	90.28	84.83	99.18	98.20	**99.95**
7	**100.0**	91.24	**100.0**	**100.0**	98.2	100.0	95.78
8	97.25	98.51	100.0	51.76	97.53	99.69	**100.0**
9	**100.0**	95.55	26.30	61.01	**100.0**	100.0	96.80
10	73.44	83.91	76.68	65.90	97.41	74.49	**98.15**
11	61.67	69.23	86.34	51.57	83.95	92.38	**98.29**
12	66.55	83.47	66.10	77.04	91.35	81.86	**98.79**
13	98.41	99.05	99.03	70.91	100.0	**100.0**	99.88
14	89.05	93.81	**99.79**	66.87	99.01	93.80	99.76
15	80.92	67.94	76.46	63.38	87.19	76.10	**88.19**
16	99.55	85.81	**100.0**	62.22	94.85	94.94	98.93
OA	75.71	79.85	86.53	66.87	91.64	87.47	**96.75**
AA	84.72	84.61	83.41	63.38	94.92	89.37	**97.42**
Kappa	72.62	77.25	84.72	62.22	90.41	85.61	**96.30**

Table 3. Per-class accuracy, OA, AA (%), and Kappa coefficient achieved by different methods on the Kennedy Space Center dataset.

Class	LapSVM [26]	SSLP-SVM [24]	GCN [11]	ELP-RGF [6]	SSLSTMs [27]	SPGAT
1	87.17	87.19	86.91	**100.0**	99.56	97.86
2	95.63	77.38	83.29	**99.75**	90.41	95.86
3	70.90	85.87	87.57	93.06	**100.0**	99.72
4	83.97	51.97	24.86	75.49	**99.56**	91.24
5	79.08	41.13	63.36	55.95	**93.79**	89.62
6	89.62	36.43	61.01	95.64	**95.15**	92.53
7	96.34	72.06	91.20	98.79	**100.0**	94.06
8	93.34	76.47	78.20	99.10	88.40	**98.65**
9	98.12	89.52	85.39	97.21	99.57	**99.89**
10	92.90	75.53	84.28	84.79	**100.0**	99.87
11	94.92	84.47	94.68	99.95	99.47	**99.95**
12	94.22	68.16	82.14	94.21	98.90	**99.31**
13	99.08	99.15	98.99	**100.0**	99.88	100.0
OA	91.25	75.52	83.60	93.21	97.89	**98.15**
AA	90.41	72.72	78.60	91.84	**97.28**	96.81
Kappa	90.25	72.88	81.70	92.45	97.65	**97.84**

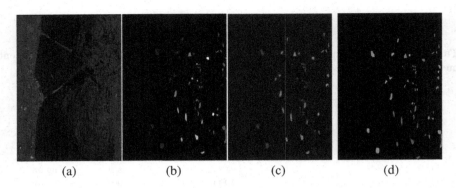

| (a) | (b) | (c) | (d) |

Fig. 6. Kennedy Space Center dataset: (a) False color image (b) Groundtruth map (c) Prediction of SSLSTMs [27] (d) Prediction of the proposed SPGAT

with dilation rate of 1 (SPGAT-1). In order to demonstrate the effectiveness of attention graph layer, we compare with the baseline model replacing GAT with GCN [11] layers (SPGCN). Finally we show that the spectral attention block aggregates features preserving the discriminative information across multiple spectral contextual level compared with averaging (SPGAT-Avg). As summarized in Table 4, introducing multiple spectral contextual embedding spaces enables an OA gain of 3.67%, whilst replacing graph attention layer with GCN leads to OA drop of 2.55%. We also observe that the spectral attention block also boosts the performance by 0.31%.

Table 4. OA achieved by different baselines on the University of Pavia dataset.

	SPGAT-1	SPGCN	SPGAT-Avg	SPGAT
OA	95.25	96.37	98.61	98.92

4   Conclusions

In this paper, we proposed a novel architecture for hyperspectral image classification. We demonstrated that using *Atrous* convolution to probe the HSI signal along the spectral dimension at multiple sampling rates could efficiently and effectively encode varying spectral contextual information. We further proposed graph attention based reasoning in each spectral embedding space which produced significantly boosted classification accuracy compared with existing methods.

References

1. Cao, F., Yang, Z., Ren, J., Chen, W., Han, G., Shen, Y.: Local block multilayer sparse extreme learning machine for effective feature extraction and classification of hyperspectral images. IEEE Trans. Geosci. Remote Sens. **57**(8), 5580–5594 (2019)
2. Cao, J., Wang, B.: Embedding learning on spectral-spatial graph for semisupervised hyperspectral image classification. IEEE Geosci. Remote Sens. Lett. **14**(10), 1805–1809 (2017)
3. Chen, L.C., Zhu, Y., Papandreou, G., Schroff, F., Adam, H.: Encoder-decoder with atrous separable convolution for semantic image segmentation. arXiv preprint arXiv:1802.02611 (2018)
4. Chen, Y., Jiang, H., Li, C., Jia, X., Ghamisi, P.: Deep feature extraction and classification of hyperspectral images based on convolutional neural networks. IEEE Trans. Geosci. Remote Sens. **54**(10), 6232–6251 (2016)
5. Chen, Y., Lin, Z., Zhao, X., Wang, G., Gu, Y.: Deep learning-based classification of hyperspectral data. IEEE J. Selected Topics Appl. Earth Observ. Remote Sens. **7**(6), 2094–2107 (2014)
6. Cui, B., Xie, X., Hao, S., Cui, J., Lu, Y.: Semi-supervised classification of hyperspectral images based on extended label propagation and rolling guidance filtering. Remote Sens. **10**(4), 515 (2018)
7. Dópido, I., Li, J., Marpu, P.R., Plaza, A., Dias, J.M.B., Benediktsson, J.A.: Semisupervised self-learning for hyperspectral image classification. IEEE Trans. Geosci. Remote Sens. **51**(7), 4032–4044 (2013)
8. Hamida, A.B., Benoit, A., Lambert, P., Amar, C.B.: 3-d deep learning approach for remote sensing image classification. IEEE Trans. Geosci. Remote Sens. **56**(8), 4420–4434 (2018)
9. He, K., Zhang, X., Ren, S., Sun, J.: Deep residual learning for image recognition. In: Proceedings of the IEEE Conference on Computer Vision and Pattern Recognition, pp. 770–778 (2016)
10. Hu, X., Wang, X., Zhong, Y., Zhao, J., Luo, C., Wei, L.: SPNet: a spectral patching network for end-to-end hyperspectral image classification. In: IGARSS 2019–2019 IEEE International Geoscience and Remote Sensing Symposium, pp. 963–966. IEEE (2019)
11. Kipf, T.N., Welling, M.: Semi-supervised classification with graph convolutional networks. In: Proceedings of International Conference on Learning Representations (2017)
12. Lee, H., Kwon, H.: Going deeper with contextual CNN for hyperspectral image classification. IEEE Trans. Image Process. **26**(10), 4843–4855 (2017)
13. Li, W., Wu, G., Zhang, F., Du, Q.: Hyperspectral image classification using deep pixel-pair features. IEEE Trans. Geosci. Remote Sens. **55**(2), 844–853 (2016)
14. Makantasis, K., Karantzalos, K., Doulamis, A., Doulamis, N.: Deep supervised learning for hyperspectral data classification through convolutional neural networks. In: 2015 IEEE International Geoscience and Remote Sensing Symposium (IGARSS), pp. 4959–4962. IEEE (2015)
15. Mei, S., Ji, J., Hou, J., Li, X., Du, Q.: Learning sensor-specific spatial-spectral features of hyperspectral images via convolutional neural networks. IEEE Trans. Geosci. Remote Sens. **55**(8), 4520–4533 (2017)
16. Mou, L., Ghamisi, P., Zhu, X.X.: Deep recurrent neural networks for hyperspectral image classification. IEEE Trans. Geosci. Remote Sens. **55**(7), 3639–3655 (2017)

17. Qin, A., Shang, Z., Tian, J., Wang, Y., Zhang, T., Tang, Y.Y.: Spectral-spatial graph convolutional networks for semisupervised hyperspectral image classification. IEEE Geosci. Remote Sens. Lett. **16**(2), 241–245 (2019)
18. Song, W., Li, S., Fang, L., Lu, T.: Hyperspectral image classification with deep feature fusion network. IEEE Trans. Geosci. Remote Sens. **56**(6), 3173–3184 (2018)
19. Vaswani, A., et al.: Attention is all you need. In: Advances in Neural Information Processing Systems, pp. 5998–6008 (2017)
20. Velickovic, P., Cucurull, G., Casanova, A., Romero, A., Liò, P., Bengio, Y.: Graph attention networks. In: Proceedings of International Conference on Learning Representations (2018)
21. Wang, H., Raiko, T., Lensu, L., Wang, T., Karhunen, J.: Semi-supervised domain adaptation for weakly labeled semantic video object segmentation. In: Lai, S.-H., Lepetit, V., Nishino, K., Sato, Y. (eds.) ACCV 2016. LNCS, vol. 10111, pp. 163–179. Springer, Cham (2017). https://doi.org/10.1007/978-3-319-54181-5_11
22. Wang, H., Wang, T.: Primary object discovery and segmentation in videos via graph-based transductive inference. Comput. Vis. Image Underst. **143**, 159–172 (2016)
23. Wang, H., Wang, T., Chen, K., Kämäräinen, J.K.: Cross-granularity graph inference for semantic video object segmentation. In: IJCAI, pp. 4544–4550 (2017)
24. Wang, L., Hao, S., Wang, Q., Wang, Y.: Semi-supervised classification for hyperspectral imagery based on spatial-spectral label propagation. ISPRS J. Photogram. Remote Sens. **97**, 123–137 (2014)
25. Wang, T., Wang, H.: Graph transduction learning of object proposals for video object segmentation. In: Cremers, D., Reid, I., Saito, H., Yang, M.-H. (eds.) ACCV 2014. LNCS, vol. 9006, pp. 553–568. Springer, Cham (2015). https://doi.org/10.1007/978-3-319-16817-3_36
26. Yang, L., Yang, S., Jin, P., Zhang, R.: Semi-supervised hyperspectral image classification using spatio-spectral Laplacian support vector machine. IEEE Geosci. Remote Sens. Lett. **11**(3), 651–655 (2013)
27. Zhou, F., Hang, R., Liu, Q., Yuan, X.: Hyperspectral image classification using spectral-spatial LSTMs. Neurocomputing **328**, 39–47 (2019)

Semi-supervised Fine-Tuning for Deep Learning Models in Remote Sensing Applications

Eftychios Protopapadakis[(✉)], Anastasios Doulamis, Nikolaos Doulamis, and Evangelos Maltezos

National Technical University of Athens, Heroon Politechniou 9, Zografou Campus, 15780 Athens, Greece
eftprot@mail.ntua.gr

Abstract. A combinatory approach of two well-known fields: deep learning and semi supervised learning is presented, to tackle the land cover identification problem. The proposed methodology demonstrates the impact on the performance of deep learning models when SSL approaches are used as performance functions during training. The generated soft labels, by SSL approaches, over the encoded inputs, provided by stacked encoders, allow the utilization of the entire data set during the fine-tuning step, for any deep classifier. Obtained results, at pixel level segmentation tasks over orthoimages, suggest that SSL enhanced loss functions can be beneficial in models' performance.

Keywords: Semi-supervised learning · Deep learning · Building detection · Remote sensing · Semantic segmentation

1 Introduction

Land cover classification is a widely studied field since the appearance of the first satellite images. The technological advance made detection/ classification of man-made structures from satellite images possible [1]. The automatic identification of buildings in urban areas, using remote sensing data, can be beneficial in many applications including cadastre, urban and rural planning, urban change detection, mapping, geographic information systems, monitoring, housing value and navigation.

Building detection from 2D images is feasible using a variety of methods, e.g., through a group of pixels sharing common properties or as an object described by specific features or geometric properties [2]. Convolutional Neural Networks (CNNs) have been considered extremely beneficial for semantic segmentation tasks in multiple remote sensing applications [3] – [5]. Stacked autoencoders or similar deep neural network (DNN) are also used [6], and provide accurate results. A DNN can be trained in a two-step process: a) *training per layer* and b) *fine tuning of the entire network*. Training per layer is an unsupervised process, exploiting all available data, labeled or not. Yet, the fine-tuning approach is limited only to available labelled data instances.

Since labeled data are sparce, someone could understand the impact of using both labeled and unlabeled data simultaneously. Semi supervised learning (SSL) is the

© Springer Nature Switzerland AG 2020
G. Bebis et al. (Eds.): ISVC 2020, LNCS 12509, pp. 719–730, 2020.
https://doi.org/10.1007/978-3-030-64556-4_56

machine learning field that can be used for such cases [7]. SSL provides a variety of tools that allow the usage of unlabeled data in conjunction with a small amount of labeled data. These tools are mainly regularizers; i.e. functionals, defined by the user and the SSL assumption(s).

In this study, we implement fine-tuning over a DNN, by coupling information provided by the labeled instances (i.e. actual labels) with information provided by the unlabeled instances (i.e. soft labels). The latter can be estimated using state of the art SSL techniques over the mapped values, provided by the encoder. The proposed DNN is a stacked encoder, as in [8], followed by a SoftMax classification layer. This approach offers multiple advantages, analyzed in the following sections.

2 Related Work

Depending on the data source, building extraction techniques can be classified into three groups: i) the ones that use radiometric information (airborne or satellite imagery data) [9, 10], ii) the ones that exploit height information (LIDAR) [11] and iii) those that combine both of data sources [12]. The most common problems of using only image information for building detection are: i) the presence of shadows, and ii) the fact that urban objects usually present similar pixel values (e.g., building rooftops vs. roads, or vegetation vs. vegetation on building rooftops). The exclusive use of 3D data, e.g. LIDAR Digital Surface Models (LIDAR/DSMs), provides low position accuracy estimations and suffers from local under-sampling, reducing the detection accuracy in areas of small buildings [13]. DSM alone makes it difficult to distinguish objects of similar height and morphological characteristics.

A combination of LIDAR/DSM with image information sources, e.g., combining LIDAR data with orthoimages, is applied to improve the building detection accuracy [5]. However, the limitations of using information from multi-modal sources (e.g., LIDAR and imagery data) are the additional cost of acquisition and processing and the co-registration related issues. Building detection techniques are bounded, in terms of performance, by the available data. Typically, a vast amount of labeled data is required for training and validation. Towards that direction two approaches gained interest past years: a) SSL and b) tensor-based learning. The former [14] employ graph-based approaches, as in [15] that are not scalable and co-trained or are prone to errors induced by wrong predictions between the models [16]. The latter tensor case is not useful if the amount of data exceeds a threshold [17]. In this paper, we concentrate on SSL learnings to improve classification performance in building detection when the number of available data is limited.

To tackle the challenges for accuracy and economy in building detection, the present study focuses on data that are extracted from one sensor, i.e., from camera devices (aerial images combined with the corresponding Dense Image Matching- DIM point clouds [18]). These data are fed to a semi-supervised deep network scheme. The main contribution lies in the incorporation of all available data, labeled or unlabeled, during all steps of the training process, layer-wise training and fine-tunning. This is achieved by employing different SSL approaches. These techniques modify existing loss functions during the fine-tuning phase. Generated DNN outperforms SotA approaches by using less than 20% of the already limited annotated data and many unlabeled instances. All the employed SSL approaches operate on the non-linear transformation of the input data, imposed by the autoencoders. As such, dimensionality related problems are partially handled [8]. The SSL techniques require no modifications, e.g. custom layers. As such, produced (trained) DNN can be easily utilized by third party applications.

3 Proposed Methodology

In this section, we describe the proposed deep SSL approaches for the detection of buildings from color infrared orthoimages. It is a four-step process, involving the creation of a SAE, utilization of the encoder to map all the available data onto a reduced feature space, SSL techniques for the estimation of soft-labels (unlabeled data) and a fine tuning process of the DNN classifier using all data.

Let as denote as $\mathcal{X} \in \mathbb{R}^d$ the space of input values (i.e. features originating from available data) and $\mathcal{Y} \in \mathbb{R}^m$, the space of output values. The space of input values, $X = \{x_1, \ldots, x_n\}$, is divided in two sub sets $X_L = \{x_1, \ldots, x_l\}$ and $X_U = \{x_{l+1}, \ldots, x_n\}$, namely labeled and unlabeled data, respectively. We also have $Y_L \subset Y$ available outputs, where $Y_L = \{y_i\}_{i=1}^{l}$.

Phase 1 starts with establishing a stacked autoencoder using all available data, X. Then, as a second step we maintain the encoder, $\mathcal{E} : \mathcal{X} \rightarrow \mathcal{X}^{(r)}$, and use it to map all data to a reduced feature space, $\mathcal{X}^{(r)} \in \mathbb{R}^o$, $o \ll d$. Consequently, we now have a new set $X^{(r)} = \mathcal{E}(X)$

The third step involves application of SSL techniques for the generation of label estimations (soft labels) for the unlabeled instances. Mapped data $X^{(r)}$, both labeled and unlabeled, are fed to three different SS label prediction schemes. The final step involves the creation of a DNN classifier using the existing encoder, an additional hidden layer, and a fine-tuning process. The fine-tuning utilizes all data, since we have the actual labels for a few and soft labels for the rest.

In our case, we used crowdsourced annotations to create the label data set. The main advantage is that the system can be easily adjusted to the user's need. In particular, the provided user-specific annotations were limited to less than 5% of the available data.

3.1 SSL Based Performance Functions

Assume a loss function $\mathcal{E}(\cdot)$, e.g., MAE or MSE. Then for a given network topology the loss over the labeled data is set as:

$$\mathcal{E}\left(\widehat{Y}^{(l)} - Y^{(l)}\right) = \mathcal{E}\left(\begin{bmatrix} \hat{y}_1 \\ \vdots \\ \hat{y}_l \end{bmatrix} - \begin{bmatrix} y_1 \\ \vdots \\ y_l \end{bmatrix}\right) \tag{1}$$

where $\hat{y}_i$, $i = 1, \ldots, l$ is the networks output for input x_i, and y_i is the actual target corresponding value. That is, y_i are the annotations (targets) for labeled data. Our approach utilizes and the unlabeled instances by extending Eq. (1) to Eq. (2),

$$\mathcal{E}\left(\widehat{Y}^{(n)} - Y^{(n)}\right) = \mathcal{E}\left(\begin{bmatrix} \hat{y}_1 \\ \vdots \\ \hat{y}_l \\ \hat{y}_{l+1} \\ \vdots \\ \hat{y}_n \end{bmatrix} - \begin{bmatrix} y_1 \\ \vdots \\ y_l \\ \tilde{y}_{l+1} \\ \vdots \\ \tilde{y}_n \end{bmatrix}\right) \tag{2}$$

where $\hat{y}_i$, $i = 1, \ldots, l$ and $\hat{y}_k$, $k = l + 1, \ldots, n$ are the estimated soft target values, i.e. $\hat{y}_i, \hat{y}_k \in \mathbb{R}^c$, where c denotes the number of available classes, over the remaining unlabeled data. In this setup, target value $\tilde{y}_k$ is an estimation for the unlabeled instance x_k, provided by any SSL technique, described in next section.

At this point we should note that utilization of estimations, as actual targets, is extremely risky; back-propagation adjust the weights so that the outputs match the targets. If targets' values are incorrect the DNN will perform poorly. Three different approaches are considered regarding the exploitation of unlabeled data instances during the fine-tuning step of the DNN: i) graph-based [19], ii) performance gain maximization [20] and iii) probabilistic framework [21].

3.2   Anchor Graph

Anchor graph estimates a labeling prediction function $f : \mathbb{R}^m \rightarrow \mathbb{R}$, by employing the following SSL framework [19]:

$$\min_{A=[a_1,\ldots,a_c]} Q(A) = \frac{1}{2}\|ZA - Y\|_F^2 + \frac{\gamma}{2}\text{trace}\left(A^T\widehat{L}A\right) \tag{3}$$

where Z is a sample-adaptive weights matrix, $\widehat{L} = Z^T L Z$ is a memory-wise and computationally tractable alternative of the Laplacian matrix L. The matrix $A = [a_1, \ldots, a_c] \in \mathbb{R}^{p \times c}$ is the soft label matrix for the representative samples, in which each column vector accounts for a class. Recall that c denotes the number of classes. The matrix $Y = [y_1, \ldots, y_c] \in \mathbb{R}^{n \times c}$ is a class indicator matrix on ambiguously labeled samples with $Y_{ij} = 1$ if the label l_i of sample i is equal to j and $Y_{ij} = 0$ otherwise.

The Laplacian matrix L, is calculated as $L = D - W$, where $D \in \mathbb{R}^{n \times n}$ is a diagonal degree matrix and W is approximated as $W = Z\Lambda^{-1}Z^T$. Matrix $\Lambda \in \mathbb{R}^{p \times p}$ is defined as: $\Lambda = \sum_{i=1}^{n} Z_{ik}$. The solution of the Eq. (3) has the form of:

$A^* = \left(Z^T Z + \gamma\widehat{L}\right)Z^T Y$. Each sample label is, then, given by:

$$\hat{l}_i = \arg \max_{j \in \{1,\ldots,c\}} \frac{Z_i a_j}{\lambda_j} \tag{4}$$

where $Z_i \in \mathbb{R}^{1 \times p}$ denotes the i-th row of Z, and factor $\lambda_j = 1^T Z\alpha_j$ balances skewed class distributions.

3.3 Maximal Performance Gain

Assume a set of b semi-supervised regressors (SSRs) applied over the same unlabeled data set X_U. The outcome would be b predictions, i.e. $\{f_1, \ldots, f_b\}$, where $f_i = \{f(x_{l+1}), \ldots, f(x_{l+u})\}, i = 1, \ldots, b$. Let as, also, denote as f_0 the predictions over X_U, of a traditional supervised approach, and $\alpha = [a_o, \ldots, a_b]$, $a_i \geq 0$, the weights of the individual regressors, which are not known a priori, at this point certain assumptions have to be made.

At first, we state that a is from a convex linear set $\mathcal{M} = \{a | A^T a \leq b, a \geq 0\}$, where A and b are task-dependent coefficients. Without further knowledge to determine the weights of individual regressors, one aim to optimize the worst-case performance gain:

$$\max_{f} \min_{a \in \mathcal{M}} \sum_{i=0}^{b} a_i \left(\|f_0 - f_i\|^2 - \|f - f_i\|^2 \right) \tag{5}$$

The equation above is concave to f and convex to a and thus it is recognized as saddle-point convex-concave optimization [22]. As described in recent work [20] Eq. (5) can be formulated as a geometric projection problem, handling that way the computational load.

3.4 Information Maximization Principle

The Information Maximization Principle (IMP) is a probabilistic classifier is trained in an unsupervised manner, so that a given information measure between data and cluster assignments is maximized. The proposed squared-loss mutual information regularization (SMIR) model [21] is convex (under mild conditions) and results in globally optimal solution.

Let $\mathcal{X} \subseteq \mathbb{R}^d$ and $\mathcal{Y} = \{1, \ldots, c\}$, where $d, c \in Z^+$. Any pair $(x, y) \in \mathcal{X} \times \mathcal{Y}$ has an underlying $p(x|y)$ and $p(x) > 0$. If we can estimate $p(y|x)$, any $x \in \mathcal{X}$ can be mapped to a $\hat{y}$ as: $\hat{y} = \arg \max_{y \in \mathcal{Y}} p(y|x)$. The described SMIR approach approximates the class-posterior probability $p(y|x)$. The SMIR optimization problem is formulated as:

$$\min_{a_1, \ldots, a_c \in \mathbb{R}^n} \Delta(p, q) - \gamma \widehat{SMI} + \lambda \sum_{y} \frac{1}{2} \|\alpha_y\|_2^2 \tag{6}$$

where $\gamma, \lambda > 0$ are regularization parameters, $= \{a_1, \ldots, a_c\}$ are model parameters, $K \in \mathbb{R}^{n \times n}$ is the kernel matrix, and D is a degree matrix. Assuming a uniform class-prior probability $p(y) = 1/c$, and an estimation for the class posterior probability $p(y|x)$, denoted as $q(y|x; a)$, $\widehat{SMI}$ can be written as:

$$\widehat{SMI} = \frac{c}{2n} tr \left(A^T D^{-\frac{1}{2}} K D^{-\frac{1}{2}} A \right) - \frac{1}{2} \tag{7}$$

In this convex formulation, there are three objectives: (i) minimize $\Delta(p, q)$, (ii) maximize $\widehat{SMI}$ and (iii) regularize α.

4 Experimental Setup

Pixel level building detection is a traditional multiclass classification approach. The problem at hand entail to the creation of a robust classifier, capable to understand the difference of an area depicting a building from anything else, e.g. roads and vegetation. This can be achieved by incorporating meaningful information as input values and create a model capable of handling complex patterns.

Study areas namely Area 1, Area 2 and Area 3, situated in Vaihingen city in Germany, were used for training and evaluation purposes (Fig. 1). The Area 1 mainly consists of historic buildings with notably complex building structure but also has sporadically some, often high, vegetation. The Area 2 mainly has high residential buildings with horizontal multiple planes surrounded by long arrays or groups of dense high trees. The Area 3 is a purely residential area with small detached houses that consist of sloped surfaces but there also exists a relatively low vegetation.

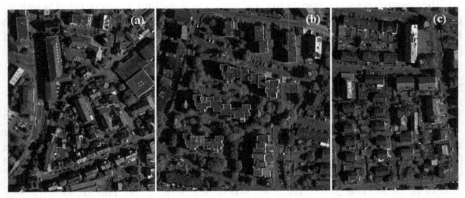

Fig. 1. Illustrating the manually annotated regions in each of the three investigated areas. Polygons in color correspond to annotations, obtained using crowdsourcing.

A Multi-Dimensional Feature Vector (MDFV) was created to feed the classifiers, as in [5]. The MDFV includes image information from the color-infrared (CIR) aerial images, the DIM point clouds and the vegetation index. Additional to infrared intensities, 3D information was also considered. The cloth simulation [23] and the closest point method are applied to estimate a normalized height DIM/DSM, denoted as nDSM.

The selected parameters of the cloth simulation algorithm for all the test sites were (i) steep slope and slope processing for the scene, (ii) cloth resolution $= 1.5$, (iii) max iterations $= 500$ and (iv) classification threshold $= 0.5$. This approach addresses issues related with the cost of acquisition and processing and co-registration aspects arising when data from multi-modal sources are fused together such as LIDAR/DSM and image information. Lastly, the vegetation index for every pixel p_{ij} is considered and estimated through the near infrared NIR band, as: $NDVI = (NIR - R)/(NIR + R)$, where R and NIR refer to the red and near infrared image band.

4.1 Setting up the DNN Topology

A deep neural network classifier has been implemented. Figure 2 illustrates the proposed approach. The first two encoder layer parameters, were initially set using the autoencoder approach; i.e., an unsupervised training approach, where inputs and outputs are the same [8]. Parameters for the hidden and output layers were randomly initialized. Then, a fine-tuning training step, using backpropagation algorithm, is applied to the entire network. Fine-tuning training process involved six different performance functions: standard approaches, i.e. MSE and MAE and four custom ones. The four custom performance functions are:

1. "Manifold" approach, based on the anchor graph SSL technique.
2. "SMIR" approach, based on the maximal performance Gain SSL technique.
3. "SAFER" approach, based on the squared-loss mutual information SSL technique.
4. "Weighted average" approach, based on a harmonic mean of the previous three methods and "MSE" and "MAE" errors.

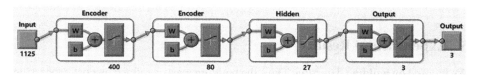

Fig. 2. Proposed DNN topology for detecting buildings over multiple channel orthoimages.

The initial image is separated into overlapping blogs of size $15 \times 15 \times 5$. The DNN classifier utilizes these 1,125 values and decides the corresponding class for the pixel at the center of the patch. The first two hidden layers are encoders, trained in an unsupervised way. They serve as non-linear mappers reducing the dimensionality of the feature space from 1,125 to 400 and then to 80. Then a hidden layer of 27 neurons perform a final mapping, allowing for the classification in one of the three pre-defined classes. Figure 2 illustrates the proposed DNN topology.

4.2 Amount of Data Required

This work aims to demonstrate the usability of SSL techniques when limited data are available. Towards that direction, a crowdsourcing approach was considered. We ask the users to draw few polygons over the images. The only limitation was that users had to create at least one polygon, for each of the following three categories: Buildings (1), Vegetation (2) and Ground (3). The final areas are shown in Fig. 1. At this point, we need to clarify that less than 5% of the pixels are annotated.

Then, from available data within the polygons, we collect less than half of them, and use them to train/validate the classifiers. Concerning the vegetation class, trees with medium and high height are considered as "good" indicative samples. The ground class contains the bare-earth, roads, and low vegetation (grass, low shrubs, etc.). The class buildings contain all the man-made building structures. To improve the classification process, shadowed areas of each class are also included. In addition, the training sample polygons are spatially created to improve representativity of each class and consider the spatial coherency of the content (Table 1).

Table 1. Data distribution utilized for the training process and testing process.

	Area 1			Area 2			Area 3		
Available annotated data (pixels)	21428 instances in 1125 dimensional space.			19775 instances in 1125 dimensional space.			22452 instances in 1125 dimensional space.		
	Class	Count	Percentage	Class	Count	Percentage	Class	Count	Percentage
Initial instances (pixel level) distribution	1	13730	64.08%	1	9271	46.88%	1	9205	41.00%
	2	3971	18.53%	2	4969	25.13%	2	6003	26.74%
	3	3727	17.39%	3	5535	27.99%	3	7244	32.26%
	Class	Count	Percent	Class	Count	Percent	Class	Count	Percent
Labeled data distribution (used for training)	1	2197	64.05%	1	1484	46.87%	1	1473	40.98%
	2	636	18.54%	2	796	25.14%	2	961	26.74%
	3	597	17.41%	3	886	27.98%	3	1160	32.28%
	Class	Count	Percentage	Class	Count	Percentage	Class	Count	Percentage
Unlabeled data distribution (used for training)	1	8787	64.08%	1	5933	46.88%	1	5891	41.00%
	2	2541	18.53%	2	3180	25.13%	2	3842	26.74%
	3	2385	17.39%	3	3542	27.99%	3	4636	32.26%
	Class	Count	Percentage	Class	Count	Percentage	Class	Count	Percentage
Unseen (test) data (used for evaluation)	1	2746	64.08%	1	1854	46.89%	1	1841	41.01%
	2	794	18.53%	2	993	25.11%	2	1200	26.73%
	3	745	17.39%	3	1107	28.00%	3	1448	32.26%

5 Experimental Results

We focused on building detection. Thus, the building mask is refined by post-processing. The goal of the post processing is to remove noisy regions such as isolated pixels or tiny blobs of pixels and retains local coherency of the data. Initially a majority voting technique with a radius of 21 pixels is implemented. Also, an erosion filter of a 7×7 window is applied.

The majority voting filter categorizes the potential building block with respect to the outputs of the neighboring output data. This filter addresses the spatial coherency that a building has. Since the orthoimages generated based on DSMs, the building boundaries are blurred due to mismatches during the application DIM algorithm. This affects the building results dilating their boundaries. Thus, the erosion filter was applied to "absorb" possible excessive interpolations on the boundaries of the buildings by reducing their dilated size.

Two alternative approaches were considered for the evaluation of the models' performance: i) over the polygons-bounded areas and ii) over the original annotations provided with the dataset. The former case involves the test data, as described in IV.A This is a typical multiclass classification approach. The latter case entails to a binary classification problem: buildings and non-buildings. Figure 3 demonstrates the former case. There are minor changes in the detection performance. Pixel annotation similarity exceeds 85% for all images. However, significant changes in annotations are observed over single objects typically vegetation. Generally, when the object spans less than 10×10 pixels, detection capabilities decline. This could be partially explained since most of the block pixels, i.e. $(15 \times 15) - (10 \times 10) = 125$ pixels, describe something different. The best DNN model, in this case, was trained using a weighted average as a performance function.

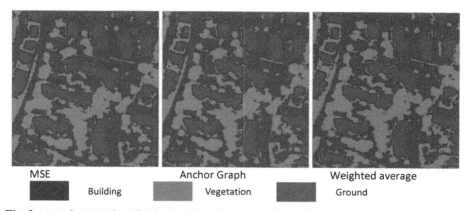

| MSE | Anchor Graph | Weighted average |

Building ▮   **Vegetation** ▮   **Ground** ▮

Fig. 3. Area 2 annotations for the DNN classifier, using three different performance functions for fine-tuning.

5.1 Building Detection

Table 2 demonstrates the ranking scores among the proposed approaches. The highest F1 scores are achieved when the weighted average approach is adopted, for areas 1 and 2. Area 3 best score was achieved using SAFER. The same is observed for the Critical Success Index (CSI), which is another metric, more descriptive regarding a specific class description. There are also no clear outcomes regarding the second-best technique; Area 1 - MAE (89.9%), Areas 2 -SAFER (92.6%), Area 3 Manifold (90.4%).

Table 2. Performance comparison for the proposed methodologies in building detection. Index in parenthesis corresponds to ranking score.

Area	Performance Function	Rec (%)	Pr (%)	CSI (%)	F1
Area 1	MSE	95.4 (2)	84.9 (3)	81.5 (3)	89.8 (3)
	MAE	94.9 (4)	85.4 (2)	81.6 (2)	89.9 (2)
	ManifScore	95.0 (3)	84.3 (4)	80.8 (4)	89.3 (4)
	SMIRScore	95.9 (1)	83.1 (6)	80.3 (5)	89.0 (5)
	SAFERScore	93.2 (6)	84.3 (4)	79.4 (6)	88.5 (6)
	WeiAveTwo	94.3 (5)	87.1 (1)	82.7 (1)	90.6 (1)
Area 2	MSE	92.8 (1)	91.8 (6)	85.7 (3)	92.3 (3)
	MAE	85.3 (6)	95.5 (1)	82.0 (6)	90.1 (6)
	ManifScore	88.6 (5)	95.1 (2)	84.7 (5)	91.7 (5)
	SMIRScore	90.3 (4)	94.1 (4)	85.4 (4)	92.2 (4)
	SAFERScore	91.6 (2)	93.7 (5)	86.3 (2)	92.6 (2)
	WeiAveTwo	91.2 (3)	94.6 (3)	86.7 (1)	92.9 (1)
Area 3	MSE	86.0 (6)	94.9 (1)	82.2 (4)	90.2 (4)
	MAE	91.3 (1)	86.9 (6)	80.3 (6)	89.0 (6)
	ManifScore	87.7 (5)	93.3 (2)	82.5 (2)	90.4 (2)
	SMIRScore	87.8 (4)	92.7 (3)	82.1 (5)	90.2 (4)
	SAFERScore	88.7 (3)	92.6 (4)	82.9 (1)	90.6 (1)
	WeiAveTwo	89.6 (2)	91.1 (5)	82.4 (3)	90.3 (3)

In this case, DNN classification capabilities become apparent. Segmentation for building blocks is extremely accurate considering the limited training sample. Misclassification involved inner yards, kiosk size buildings (e.g. bus stations), and the edges of the buildings. An increase of the training samples could mitigate such effects.

Table 3 demonstrates the advantages of our approach against other techniques, using Critical Success Index (CSI) scores. If LiDAR is not available (i.e. the common case scenario), our approach is at par or even better compared to other techniques, despite the limited data used.

Table 3. Comparative results against other techniques

Technique	Data type	CSI
[5]	Orthoimages + DIM/DSM	82.7
DNN (MSE)	Orthoimages + DIM/DSM	83.2
DNN (MAE)	Orthoimages + DIM/DSM	81.3
DNN (Manif)	Orthoimages + DIM/DSM	82.7
DNN (SMIR)	Orthoimages + DIM/DSM	82.6
DNN (SAFER)	Orthoimages + DIM/DSM	82.8
DNN (WeiAve)	Orthoimages + DIM/DSM	83.9
[24]	LIDAR (as point cloud) + images	83.5

Figure 4 illustrates the best building detection outcomes for the proposed approaches. Yellow color corresponds to pixels showing a building and model classified them as building (True Positive). Red color indicates pixels that model classified as buildings, but the actual label was either vegetation or ground (False Positive). Finally, blue color indicates areas that were buildings, but model failed recognizing them (False Negative).

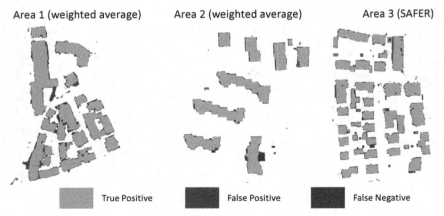

Fig. 4. Illustrating best building detection results per area. Left: Area 1 (weighted average), center: Area 2 (weighted average), right: Area 3 (SAFER).

6 Conclusions

Semi-supervised inspired performance functions have been utilized to fine-tune DNN for the detection of buildings over orthoimages. Results indicate that using crowdsourcing and limited train data instances, i.e. selected polygons span less than 5% of the total images area, suffice for the creation of robust detectors. The approach is based on stacked autoencoders capabilities of non-linear dimensionality reduction. That way the information of $15 \times 15 \times 5$ is summarized to 80-values feature space. The reduced dimensionality allows the implementation of SSL approaches in a way that unlabeled data can be beneficial to the model's training process. The DNN is a stacked network using the encoding layers of the stacked autoencoders. The fine-tuning performance function is designed from scratch, so that the information provided from the unlabeled data is also considered. At the end, the generated network can be easily used to any kind of new data.

Acknowledgments. Financial support has been provided by the Innovation and Networks Executive Agency (INEA) under the powers delegated by the European Commission through the Horizon 2020 program "PANOPTIS–Development of a decision support system for increasing the resilience of transportation infrastructure based on combined use of terrestrial and airborne sensors and advanced modelling tools", Grant Agreement number 769129.

References

1. Makantasis, K., Karantzalos, K., Doulamis, A., Loupos, K.: Deep learning-based man-made object detection from hyperspectral data. In: Bebis, G., et al. (eds.) ISVC 2015. LNCS, vol. 9474, pp. 717–727. Springer, Cham (2015). https://doi.org/10.1007/978-3-319-27857-5_64
2. Konstantinidis, D., Stathaki, T., Argyriou, V., Grammalidis, N.: Building detection using enhanced HOG–LBP features and region refinement processes. IEEE J. Sel. Topics Appl. Earth Obs. Remote Sens. **10**(3), 888–905 (2017). https://doi.org/10.1109/JSTARS.2016.260 2439
3. Chen, K., et al.: Residual shuffling convolutional neural networks for deep semantic image segmentation using multi-modal data. ISPRS Ann. Photogrammetry, Remote Sens. Spat. Inf. Sci. **4**(2) (2018)
4. Schenkel, F., Middelmann, W.: Domain adaptation for semantic segmentation using convolutional neural networks. In: IGARSS 2019 – 2019 IEEE International Geoscience and Remote Sensing Symposium, pp. 728–731, July 2019. https://doi.org/10.1109/igarss.2019.8899796
5. Maltezos, E., Protopapadakis, E., Doulamis, N., Doulamis, A., Ioannidis, C.: Understanding historical cityscapes from aerial imagery through machine learning. In: Ioannides, M., et al. (eds.) EuroMed 2018. LNCS, vol. 11196, pp. 200–211. Springer, Cham (2018). https://doi. org/10.1007/978-3-030-01762-0_17
6. Liang, P., Shi, W., Zhang, X.: Remote sensing image classification based on stacked denoising autoencoder. Remote Sens. **10**(1), 16 (2018)
7. Doulamis, N., Doulamis, A.: Semi-supervised deep learning for object tracking and classification. In: 2014 IEEE International Conference on Image Processing (ICIP), pp. 848–852 (2014)
8. Protopapadakis, E., Voulodimos, A., Doulamis, A., Doulamis, N., Dres, D., Bimpas, M.: Stacked autoencoders for outlier detection in over-the-horizon radar signals. Comput. Intell. Neurosci. **2017** (2017)

9. Ham, S., Oh, Y., Choi, K., Lee, I.: Semantic segmentation and unregistered building detection from Uav images using a deconvolutional network. Int. Arch. Photogrammetry, Remote Sens. Spat. Inf. Sci. **42**, 2 (2018)

10. Liu, Xiaolong., Deng, Zhidong, Yang, Yuhan: Recent progress in semantic image segmentation. Artif. Intell. Rev. **52**(2), 1089–1106 (2018). https://doi.org/10.1007/s10462-018-9641-3

11. Kashani, A.G., Olsen, M.J., Parrish, C.E., Wilson, N.: A review of LiDAR radiometric processing: from ad hoc intensity correction to rigorous radiometric calibration. Sensors **15**(11), 28099–28128 (2015)

12. Nahhas, F.H., Shafri, H.Z., Sameen, M.I., Pradhan, B., Mansor, S.: Deep learning approach for building detection using lidar–orthophoto fusion. J. Sens. **2018** (2018)

13. Maltezos, E., Doulamis, A., Doulamis, N., Ioannidis, C.: Building extraction from LiDAR data applying deep convolutional neural networks. IEEE Geosci. Remote Sens. Lett. **16**(1), 155–159 (2018)

14. Protopapadakis, E., Voulodimos, A., Doulamis, A.: On the impact of labeled sample selection in semisupervised learning for complex visual recognition tasks. Complexity (2018). https://doi.org/10.1155/2018/6531203

15. Chaudhuri, B., Demir, B., Chaudhuri, S., Bruzzone, L.: Multilabel remote sensing image retrieval using a semisupervised graph-theoretic method. IEEE Trans. Geosci. Remote Sens. **56**(2), 1144–1158 (2017)

16. Han, W., Feng, R., Wang, L., Cheng, Y.: A semi-supervised generative framework with deep learning features for high-resolution remote sensing image scene classification. ISPRS J. Photogrammetry Remote Sens. **145**, 23–43 (2018)

17. Makantasis, K., Doulamis, A.D., Doulamis, N.D., Nikitakis, A.: Tensor-based classification models for hyperspectral data analysis. IEEE Trans. Geosci. Remote Sens. **56**(12), 6884–6898 (2018)

18. Remondino, F., Spera, M.G., Nocerino, E., Menna, F., Nex, F.: State of the art in high density image matching. Photogrammetric Rec. **29**(146), 144–166 (2014)

19. Liu, W., He, J., Chang, S.-F.: Large graph construction for scalable semi-supervised learning. In: Proceedings of the 27th International Conference on Machine Learning (ICML-10), pp. 679–686 (2010). http://machinelearning.wustl.edu/mlpapers/paper_files/icml2010_LiuHC10.pdf. Accessed 24 Jan 2014

20. Li, Y.-F., Zha, H.-W., Zhou, Z.-H.: Learning safe prediction for semi-supervised regression. In: AAAI, vol. 2017, pp. 2217–2223 (2017)

21. Niu, G., Jitkrittum, W., Dai, B., Hachiya, H., Sugiyama, M.: Squared-loss mutual information regularization: a novel information-theoretic approach to semi-supervised learning. In: International Conference on Machine Learning, pp. 10–18 (2013)

22. Nesterov, Y.: Introductory Lectures on Convex Optimization: A Basic Course, vol. 87. Springer Science & Business Media (2013)

23. Zhang, W., et al.: An easy-to-use airborne LiDAR data filtering method based on cloth simulation. Remote Sens. **8**(6), 501 (2016). https://doi.org/10.3390/rs8060501

24. Gerke, M., Xiao, J.: Fusion of airborne laserscanning point clouds and images for supervised and unsupervised scene classification. ISPRS J. Photogrammetry Remote Sens. **87**, 78–92 (2014). https://doi.org/10.1016/j.isprsjprs.2013.10.011

Scene Classification of Remote Sensing Images Based on ConvNet Features and Multi-grained Forest

Ronald Tombe, Serestina Viriri$^{(\boxtimes)}$, and Jean Vincent Fonou Dombeu

School of Mathematics, Statistics and Computer Science,
University of KwaZulu-Natal, Durban, South Africa
viriris@ukzn.ac.za

Abstract. Scene interpretation of remote sensing images entails effective spatial feature information extraction and application of an appropriate pattern recognition algorithm for feature learning. In literature, state-of-the-art results are attained in remote sensing using pre-trained convolutional neural networks (convNets or CNNs) for transfer learning in deep feature extraction and then applying classifiers to learn the features for scene classification. This work proposes a method that utilizes VGG-16 model for feature extraction and the multi-grain forest for feature learning and classification with ensemble classifiers majority voting. The Effectiveness of the proposed method is evaluated with ucmerced and WHU-Siri public datasets. Improved classification results are attained with the proposed method as compared to methods in the literature.

Keywords: Scene classification · Ensemble learning · Pretrained convolutional neural network · Transfer learning · Multi-grain forest

1 Introduction

Scene-analysis has been attracting a lot of interest by remote sensing due to the availability of remote sensing images from globe observation gadgets including aerial systems, satellites, and unmanned aerial vehicles. Scene classification aims to utilize computer vision techniques to interpret the semantics of remote sensing images and to consequently categorize them accurately to their respective classes. The development of deep convolutional neural networks has enhanced the classification accuracies significantly compared to conventional ones which are based on hand-engineered features.

There are different strategies of utilizing the convNets for the scene classification of remote sensing images. Nogueira et al. [1] examines various strategies of exploiting CNNs for the scene classification of remote sensing images and they sum up their finding into three: 1) fine-tuning of CNNs, 2) Fully-training and 3) applying CNNs to extract features. They establish that pre-trained CNNs give

© Springer Nature Switzerland AG 2020
G. Bebis et al. (Eds.): ISVC 2020, LNCS 12509, pp. 731–740, 2020.
https://doi.org/10.1007/978-3-030-64556-4_57

the best results when they apply as feature extractors. The power of pre-trained CNNs for feature extraction is investigated in transfer learning [2].

The support vector machine [3] and softmax function [4] are common machine learning techniques for pattern recognition problems. Recently, Zhou et al. [5] developed a multi-grain forest than can utilize multiple classifiers on different forests for feature learning. Some literature [5,6] have shown that ensemble learning [7] attain superior performance compared to individual classifiers.

In this work, the logical process for scene interpretation is summed up into two major steps: 1.) feature engineering and extraction with ConvNets, and 2.) feature classification based on multi-grain forest. The rest of this work is organized as follows, Sect. 2 presents literature works that are related to this work. Section 3 discusses the framework and details of the proposed method, while Sect. 4 gives the experimentation details which include a description of the properties of the datasets used and experiment setups. In Sect. 5 reports experiment findings, analyzes, and discusses the results. Finally, Sect. 6 concludes this paper.

2   Related Work

The remote sensing field lacks enough labeled images to train CNNs from scratch due to the huge cost implications of the image labeling process. Utilizing CNNs for remote sensing images scene classification at small-medium levels with labeled scene images has been extensively researched on; [1] examines various strategies of exploiting CNNs for the scene classification of remote sensing images and they sum up their finding into three: 1) fine-tuning of CNNs, 2) Fully-training and 3) applying CNNs to extract features. They establish that pre-trained CNNs give the best results when they apply as feature extractors. The power of pre-trained CNNs for feature extraction is investigated in transfer learning [2]. In their work [8], they use the bag of visual words to encode the extracted features in the last convolution layer.

Several research works utilize various features from CNNs layers for remote sensing images scene classification. The adaptive deep pyramid matching [9] extracts image features of different scales, then optimally fuses them. The deep salient feature-based transfer network [10] extracts scene patches with *visual-attention* strategy and then feds them to a pre-trained CNN model for extraction of deep salient features. The fusion of deep features [11] from different fully connected layers is accomplished by discriminant correlation analysis of features. In the aforementioned works, the classification stage is carried out either by the softmax or support vector machine. [6] proposes a framework that applies the XGBoost [12] classifiers for classification of feature maps which are extracted from the last convolutional layer of the pre-trained VGG16 model. In [13], they develop a low dimensional CNN which extracts non-linearly separable feature maps with a multi-layer perceptron convolution layer. Then, a global-average-pooling layer applies to compute spatial-averages of these feature maps to produce the comparable feature maps for every class.

The multi-grained forest (gcForest) classifier [5] utilizes a cascading structure, Fig. 1, whereby each level obtains feature-information in a cascaded manner through processing its previous level, and then the results are outputs to the following level. Every level represents an ensemble of classifiers (decision tree forests). The classifier hyper-parameter is the number of trees in every forest. Each forest generates a prediction on the distribution of classes via frequency counts of the different training classes at the leaf nodes where the involved sample falls, then an average for all the trees in the same forest is performed.

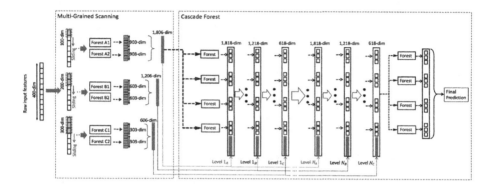

Fig. 1. Feature learning with multi-grained cascading forest [5]

3   Proposed Method

Scene classification of remote sensing images entails two major steps: 1) Extraction of features and 2) Feature learning with pattern recognition algorithm for feature classification. The proposed method comprises of two main parts.

3.1   Feature Extraction with CNNs

ConvNets are effective on spatial feature extraction from images [14,15]. In this work, VGG16 [16] a pre-trained convNet apply for feature extraction. The VGG16 consists of 13 convolutional-layers and 5 pooling-layers divided into 5 sections, and 3 fully-connected layers. This research work applies feature maps rather than the fully-connected-layer features as this reduces the network parameters with over 80% [6].

Assume $conv_l(Image_i) = FeatureMaps_i$, where $FeatureMaps_i \in^{l \times w \times d}$ are output feature maps of size $(l \times w \times d)$ obtained from the layer lth by $conv_l$ of pretrained CNNs.

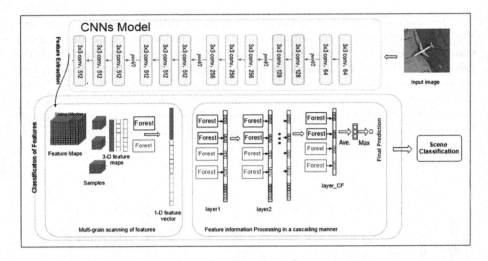

Fig. 2. Scene classification with gcForest

3.2   Multi-grain Forest Feature Learning and Classification

The proposed method has two main phases as depicted in Fig. 2 and they are described as follows:

1. Multi-grain Forest Scanning of Features. This phase applies sliding windows to scan for features in a manner that preserves their spatial relationships. At this stage, the multi-grain forest scans and transform the 3-D feature maps into a 1-D feature vector(FV) representation.

For an input $FeatureMaps_i$ that characterizes the input image $Image_i$, the sliding window (SLW) with dimensions $(l_s \times w_s)$ slides on the $FeatureMaps_i$ with s strides to generate NSample feature samples that are of size SLW.

If the number of forests used is F, in the multi-grainForest, and $sample_k$, $k \in [1, NSampe]$; every forest f_p, where $p \in [1, F]$ generates the class outputs that correspond to probability vectors (PV). $f_p(sample_d) = PV_k^p$, where $|PV_k^p| = C$.

All class probabilities, $C = |PV_k^p|$ generated with F forests, and NSample samples are concatenated to form a final feature vector(FV) output of the multi-grain features scans.

$$|FV| = NSample \times F \times C \tag{1}$$

2. Feature Processing with Multi-grain Cascade Forest. The multi-grained forest provides a means to process the extracted feature vectors layer-by-layer, and the final layer performs the scene label prediction using a majority vote. Every level (layer) of the multi-grain forest has decision trees dT.

Consider the cascade forest layer L_q, $q \in [1, Q]$, where q^{th} is cascade layer while Q is the number of layers in the multi-grain Forest. Every layer comprise of Z forest classifiers, F_z^q, $z \in [1, Z]$. The features FV_q outputs by the L_q^{th} are inputs to the following layer $q + 1$. For each tree $(T_z^q)_{fvt}$, $fvt \in [1, dT]$, the forest classier z in this layer f_z^q obtains the $\sqrt{d}$ features vector tree (fvt) that are selected randomly [5] from the previous layer $(q - 1)_{fvt}$ with class probability $(C_z^q)_{fvt}$ outputs. Each forest in every generates a class distribution (CD) vector by computing the average class probabilities which are estimated by their total trees:

$$CD_z^q = average_{fvt}^{dT}\{(C_z^q)_{fvt}\} \tag{2}$$

Then, aggregation of the different CD_z^q generated with Forests F is performed using the original feature vector input. This gives the final layer output; the final layer gets all the class probabilities vectors and averages them (3), and by the majority-voting (4), a prediction of scene class $\hat{j}$ is performed.

$$CD^q = average_{z=1}^{NForests}(CD_z^q) \tag{3}$$

$$\hat{j} = argmax CD^q(j), for j \in [1, C] \tag{4}$$

4   Experimentation

To evaluate the performance of the proposed scene classification of remote sensing images method, ucmerced [17] and WHU-SIRI Dataset [18] datasets publicly available are used. Properties of the datasets are as described:

4.1   UCMerced Dataset

UCMerced dataset [17] consist of 21 classes (Fig. 3) and each class contain 100 images with three color channels. Each image dimension is 256×256 pixels and they have a spatial resolution of 1-ft. The classes are highly overlapped e.g. (agricultural and forest are differ by vegetation cover; dense residence and medium residence differ by the number of units), this diverse image content pattern is a challenge for effective feature representations. Further, the images of ucmerced dataset have many common low-level features with multipurpose visible images hence they are suitable candidates for fine-tuning with pre-trained convolutional neural networks.

WHU-SIRI Dataset. WHU-SIRI Dataset [18] comprises of 12 classes (Fig. 4) with a total of 2400 aerial images with three color channels. Each class contains 200 image samples with a size of 200×200 pixels and 2 m of spatial resolution. WHUR-SIRI images are in different scales, orientations under differing lighting conditions. These dataset properties are diverse and challenging thus requiring effective feature learning techniques for accurate scene analysis and interpretation.

Fig. 3. Sample images of UCMerced Dataset [17]

Fig. 4. Sample images of WHU-SIRI Dataset [18]

4.2 Experiment Setup

To evaluate the performance of the proposed method for the scene classification of remote sensing, the VGG-16 pre-trained convNet model is applied for spatial image feature extraction. The training, validation, and testing ratios are set to 70%:20%:10% on the ucmerced and 60%:30%:10% on WHU-SIRI datasets respectively. Then, the multi-grained forest is used for feature learning. We also report results of feature extraction with VGG-16 and classification with softmax function.

5   Results Analysis and Discussion

Table 1 compares the classification accuracy of the proposed method with others in the literature on ucmerced dataset and gives an overall accuracy [20] in classification performance evaluation. It can be observed that the proposed method gives improved results as compared to other methods in the literature. This can be attributed to the fact that VGG-16 extracts high-level features that are better

Table 1. Accuracy classification performances on ucmerced dataset

Methods	Accuracy (%)
Adaptive deep pyramid matching [9]	94.75
caffeNet [19]	95.02
GoogLeNet [19]	94.31
VGG-16	95.21
The proposed method	96.85

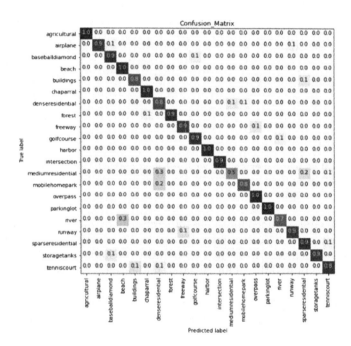

Fig. 5. VGG-16 as feature extractor with softmax classier Confusion matrix with test images on ucmerced dataset

Table 2. Accuracy classification performances on whu-siri Dataset

Methods	Accuracy (%)
Structural Satellite Image Indexing [18]	81.67 80
VGG-16	92.4
Proposed method	94.85

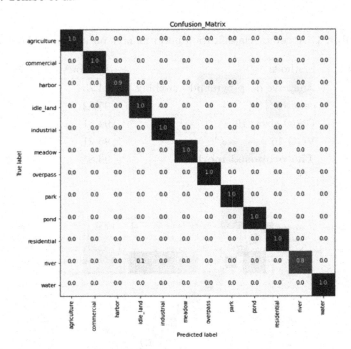

Fig. 6. VGG-16 as feature extractor with softmax classier Confusion matrix with test images on whu-siri dataset

learned by the multi-grained forest ensemble classifiers (in this case random forests and completely random forests [21]). The ensemble classifiers make average class predictions and then vote using their probability predictions to determine the class with the highest probability. Our research findings are consistent with [1] which confirms that convNet model attains the best results when used as a feature extractor. In addition to the overall accuracy given in Table 1, a corresponding confusion matrix is computed for VGG-16 as a feature extractor VGG-16 and softmax as a classifier and is given in Fig. 5 to indicates the accuracy performance analysis on ucmerced dataset. From the confusion matrix, it can be observed that dense residential and medium residential are semantically and visually similar (Fig. 3), thus they are difficult to distinguish hence a lower true positive predictive value of 0.5 and false-positive prediction of 0.3. There is also some confusion between the river and beach classes since the semantics are closely similar in some cases.

The evaluation performance of the proposed method with whu-siri dataset indicated in Table 2 achieves a significant improvement of approximately 14% as compared to the conventional feature extraction method [18]. This is consistent with the fact that deep features extracted with convNets abstract the spatial feature information better resulting in superior scene classification accuracy of remote sensing images. The confusion matrix in Fig. 6 indicates a confusion matrix with VGG-16 as a feature extractor and softmax as a classifier.

6   Conclusion

Convolutional neural networks are a popular computer vision strategy in extracting spatial feature information of remote sensing images. This work utilizes a pretrained VGG16 model in feature extraction and then applies a multi-grained forest for feature learning and classification. The experimental results with ucmerced and WHU-SIRI datasets demonstrate an improved accuracy on scene classification of remote sensing images. This indicates that convNet features with ensemble voting classifiers achieve better scene classification performance. In the future work will evaluate the performance of the proposed method with other computer vision tasks.

References

1. Nogueira, K., Penatti, O.A., Dos Santos, J.A.: Towards better exploiting convolutional neural networks for remote sensing scene classification. Pattern Recogn. **61**, 539–556 (2017)
2. Hu, F., Xia, G.S., Hu, J., Zhang, L.: Transferring deep convolutional neural networks for the scene classification of high-resolution remote sensing imagery. Remote Sens. **7**(11), 14680–14707 (2015)
3. Cortes, C., Vapnik, V.: Support-vector networks. Mach. Learn. **20**(3), 273–297 (1995). https://doi.org/10.1007/BF00994018
4. Bishop, C.M.: Pattern Recognition and Machine Learning. Springer, New York (2006)
5. Zhou, Z.H., Feng, J.: Deep forest. arXiv preprint arXiv:1702.08835 (2017)
6. Jiang, S., Zhao, H., Wu, W., Tan, Q.: A novel framework for remote sensing image scene classification. Int. Arch. Photogram. Remote Sens. Spatial Inf. Sci. **42**(3), 657–663 (2018)
7. Zhou, Z.H.: Ensemble Methods: Foundations and Algorithms. CRC Press, Boca Raton (2012)
8. Cheng, G., Li, Z., Yao, X., Guo, L., Wei, Z.: Remote sensing image scene classification using bag of convolutional features. IEEE Geosci. Remote Sens. Lett. **14**(10), 1735–1739 (2017)
9. Liu, Q., Hang, R., Song, H., Zhu, F., Plaza, J., Plaza, A.: Adaptive deep pyramid matching for remote sensing scene classification. arXiv preprint arXiv:1611.03589 (2016)
10. Gong, X., Xie, Z., Liu, Y., Shi, X., Zheng, Z.: Deep salient feature based anti-noise transfer network for scene classification of remote sensing imagery. Remote Sens. **10**(3), 410 (2018)
11. Chaib, S., Liu, H., Gu, Y., Yao, H.: Deep feature fusion for VHR remote sensing scene classification. IEEE Trans. Geosci. Remote Sens. **55**(8), 4775–4784 (2017)
12. Chen, T., Guestrin, C.: Xgboost: a scalable tree boosting system. In: Proceedings of the 22nd ACM SIGKDD International Conference on Knowledge Discovery and Data Mining, pp. 785–794, August 2016
13. Zhou, W., Newsam, S., Li, C., Shao, Z.: Learning low dimensional convolutional neural networks for high-resolution remote sensing image retrieval. Remote Sens. **9**(5), 489 (2017)

14. Bazi, Y., Al Rahhal, M.M., Alhichri, H., Alajlan, N.: Simple yet effective fine-tuning of deep CNNs using an auxiliary classification loss for remote sensing scene classification. Remote Sens. **11**(24), 2908 (2019)
15. Krizhevsky, A., Sutskever, I., Hinton, G.E.: Imagenet classification with deep convolutional neural networks. In: Advances in Neural Information Processing Systems, pp. 1097–1105 (2012)
16. Simonyan, K., Zisserman, A.: Very deep convolutional networks for large-scale image recognition. arXiv preprint arXiv:1409.1556 (2014)
17. Yang, Y., Newsam, S.: Bag-of-visual-words and spatial extensions for land-use classification. In: Proceedings of the 18th SIGSPATIAL International Conference on Advances in Geographic Information Systems, pp. 270–279, November 2010
18. Xia, G.S., Yang, W., Delon, J., Gousseau, Y., Sun, H., Maître, H.: Structural high-resolution satellite image indexing, July 2010
19. Xia, G.S., et al.: AID: A benchmark data set for performance evaluation of aerial scene classification. IEEE Trans. Geosci. Remote Sens. **55**(7), 3965–3981 (2017)
20. Cheng, G., Han, J., Lu, X.: Remote sensing image scene classification: benchmark and state of the art. Proc. IEEE **105**(10), 1865–1883 (2017)
21. Breiman, L.: Random forests. Mach. Learn. **45**(1), 5–32 (2001). https://doi.org/10.1023/a:1010933404324

Author Index

Printed in the United States
By Bookmasters